ALL ■ IN ■ ONE

CompTIA

Security+™

EXAM GUIDE

(Exam SY0-601)

ALL ■ IN ■ ONE

CompTIA Security+™

EXAM GUIDE

Sixth Edition (Exam SY0-601)

Dr. Wm. Arthur Conklin
Dr. Gregory White
Chuck Cothren
Roger L. Davis
Dwayne Williams

McGraw Hill

New York Chicago San Francisco
Athens London Madrid Mexico City
Milan New Delhi Singapore Sydney Toronto

McGraw Hill books are available at special quantity discounts to use as premiums and sales promotions, or for use in corporate training programs. To contact a representative, please visit the Contact Us pages at www.mhprofessional.com.

CompTIA Security+™ All-in-One Exam Guide, Sixth Edition (Exam SY0-601)

4 5 6 7 8 9 LCR 26 25 24

ISBN 978-1-260-46400-9
MHID 1-260-46400-8

Sponsoring Editor
Tim Green

Editorial Supervisor
Janet Walden

Project Editor
Rachel Fogelberg

Acquisitions Coordinator
Emily Walters

Technical Editor
Chris Crayton

Copy Editor
Bart Reed

Proofreader
Paul Tyler

Indexer
Ted Laux

Production Supervisor
Thomas Somers

Composition
KnowledgeWorks Global Ltd.

Illustration
KnowledgeWorks Global Ltd.

Art Director, Cover
Jeff Weeks

This book is dedicated to the many information security professionals who quietly work to ensure the safety of our nation's critical infrastructures. We want to recognize the thousands of dedicated individuals who strive to protect our national assets but who seldom receive praise and often are only noticed when an incident occurs. To you, we say thank you for a job well done!

ABOUT THE AUTHORS

Dr. Wm. Arthur Conklin, CompTIA Security+, CISSP, GICSP, GRID, GCIP, GCFA, GCIA, GCDA, CSSLP, CRISC, is a professor and director at the Center for Information Security Research and Education in the College of Technology at the University of Houston. He holds two terminal degrees—a PhD in business administration (specializing in information security) from the University of Texas at San Antonio (UTSA) and an electrical engineer degree (specializing in space systems engineering) from the Naval Postgraduate School in Monterey, California. He is a fellow of ISSA and $(CS)^2AI$ as well as a senior member of ASQ, IEEE, and ACM. His research interests include the use of systems theory to explore information security, specifically in cyber-physical systems. He has a strong interest in cybersecurity education and is involved with the NSA/DHS Centers of Academic Excellence in Cyber Defense (CAE CD) and the NIST National Initiative for Cybersecurity Education (NICE) Cybersecurity Workforce Framework (NICE Framework). He has coauthored six security books and numerous academic articles associated with information security. He is co-chair of the steering committee for the DHS-sponsored Industrial Control Systems Joint Working Group (ICSJWG) efforts associated with workforce development and cybersecurity aspects of industrial control systems. He has an extensive background in secure coding and has been co-chair of the DHS/DoD Software Assurance Forum Working Group for workforce education, training, and development.

Dr. Gregory White has been involved in computer and network security since 1986. He spent 19 years on active duty with the United States Air Force and 11 years in the Air Force Reserves in a variety of computer and security positions. He obtained his PhD in computer science from Texas A&M University in 1995. His dissertation topic was in the area of computer network intrusion detection, and he continues to conduct research in this area today. He is currently the director for the Center for Infrastructure Assurance and Security (CIAS) and is a professor of computer science at the University of Texas at San Antonio (UTSA). Dr. White has written and presented numerous articles and conference papers on security. He is also the coauthor of six textbooks on computer and network security and has written chapters for two other security books. Dr. White continues to be active in security research. His current research initiatives include efforts in community incident response, intrusion detection, and secure information sharing.

Chuck Cothren, CISSP, is Manager of Development Operations at Ionic Security, applying over 20 years of information security experience in consulting, research, and enterprise environments. He has assisted clients in a variety of industries, including healthcare, banking, information technology, retail, and manufacturing. He advises clients on topics such as security architecture, penetration testing, training, consultant management, data loss prevention, and encryption. He is coauthor of the books *Voice and Data Security* and *Principles of Computer Security.*

Roger L. Davis, CISSP, CISM, CISA, is a Senior Customer Success Account Manager for Microsoft supporting enterprise-level companies. He has served as president of the Utah chapter of the Information Systems Security Association (ISSA) and various board positions for the Utah chapter of the Information Systems Audit and Control Association (ISACA). He is a retired Air Force lieutenant colonel with 40 years of military and information systems/security experience. Mr. Davis served on the faculty of Brigham Young University and the Air Force Institute of Technology. He coauthored McGraw-Hill's *Principles of Computer Security* and *Voice and Data Security*. He holds a master's degree in computer science from George Washington University, a bachelor's degree in computer science from Brigham Young University, and performed post-graduate studies in electrical engineering and computer science at the University of Colorado.

Dwayne Williams, CISSP, CASP, is Associate Director, Technology and Research, for the Center for Infrastructure Assurance and Security (CIAS) at the University of Texas at San Antonio and is Director of the National Collegiate Cyber Defense Competition. Mr. Williams has over 24 years of experience in information systems and network security. His experience includes six years of commissioned military service as a Communications-Computer Information Systems Officer in the United States Air Force, specializing in network security, corporate information protection, intrusion detection systems, incident response, and VPN technology. Prior to joining the CIAS, he served as Director of Consulting for SecureLogix Corporation, where he directed and provided security assessment and integration services to Fortune 100, government, public utility, oil and gas, financial, and technology clients. Mr. Williams graduated in 1993 from Baylor University with a Bachelor of Arts in computer science. Mr. Williams is a coauthor of *Voice and Data Security* and *Principles of Computer Security*.

About the Technical Editor

Chris Crayton, MCSE, is an author, technical consultant, and trainer. He has worked as a computer technology and networking instructor, information security director, network administrator, network engineer, and PC specialist. Chris has authored several print and online books on PC repair, CompTIA A+, CompTIA Security+, and Microsoft Windows. He has also served as technical editor and content contributor on numerous technical titles for several of the leading publishing companies. He holds numerous industry certifications, has been recognized with many professional teaching awards, and has served as a state-level SkillsUSA competition judge.

CONTENTS AT A GLANCE

CONTENTS

Part IV Operations and Incident Response

PREFACE

Cybersecurity has moved from the confines of academia to mainstream America. From the ransomware attacks to data disclosures such as Equifax and U.S. Office of Personnel Management that were heavily covered in the media and broadcast into the average American's home, information security has become a common topic. In boardrooms, the topic has arrived with the technical attacks against intellectual property and the risk exposure from cybersecurity incidents. It has become increasingly obvious to everybody that something needs to be done in order to secure not only our nation's critical infrastructure but also the businesses we deal with on a daily basis. These issues have brought to light the serious shortage of cybersecurity professionals. The question is, "Where do we begin?" What can the average information technology professional do to secure the systems that he or she is hired to maintain?

The answer to these questions is complex, but certain aspects can guide our actions. First, no one knows what the next big threat will be. APTs, ransomware, data disclosures—these were all known threats long before they became the major threat *du jour*. What is next? No one knows, so we can't buy a magic box to fix it. Yet. But we do know that we will do it with the people we have, at their current level of training, when it arrives. The one investment we know will be good is in our people, through education and training, because that will be what we bring to the next incident, problem, challenge, or, collectively, our national defense in the realm of cybersecurity. One could say security today begins and ends with our people, and trained people will result in better outcomes.

So, where do you, the IT professional seeking more knowledge on security, start your studies? The IT world is overflowing with certifications that can be obtained by those attempting to learn more about their chosen profession. The security sector is no different, and the CompTIA Security+ exam offers a basic level of certification for security. CompTIA Security+ is an ideal starting point for one interested in a career in security. In the pages of this exam guide, you will find not only material that can help you prepare for taking the CompTIA Security+ examination but also the basic information you will need in order to understand the issues involved in securing your computer systems and networks today. In no way is this exam guide the final source for learning all about protecting your organization's systems, but it serves as a point from which to launch your security studies and career.

One thing is certainly true about this field of study—it never gets boring. It constantly changes as technology itself advances. Something else you will find as you progress in your security studies is that no matter how much technology advances and no matter how many new security devices are developed, at the most basic level, the human element is still the weak link in the security chain. If you are looking for an exciting area to delve into, then you have certainly chosen wisely. Security offers a challenging blend of technology and people issues. We, the authors of this exam guide, wish you luck as you embark on an exciting and challenging career path.

—Wm. Arthur Conklin, Ph.D.
—Gregory B. White, Ph.D.

ACKNOWLEDGMENTS

We, the authors of *CompTIA Security+ All-in-One Exam Guide, Sixth Edition*, have many individuals who we need to acknowledge—individuals without whom this effort would not have been successful.

The list needs to start with those folks at McGraw Hill who worked tirelessly with the project's multiple authors and led us successfully through the minefield that is a book schedule and who took our rough chapters and drawings and turned them into a final, professional product we can be proud of. We thank the good people from the Acquisitions team, Tim Green and Emily Walters. Tim made these journeys possible, and we are forever indebted for his trust and patience. From the Editorial Services team, we thank Janet Walden, and from the Production team, Thomas Somers. We also thank the technical editor, Chris Crayton; the project editor, Rachel Fogelberg; the copy editor, Bart Reed; the proofreader, Paul Tyler; and the indexer, Ted Laux, for all their attention to detail that made this a finer work after they finished with it.

We also need to acknowledge our current employers who, to our great delight, have seen fit to pay us to work in a career field that we all find exciting and rewarding. There is never a dull moment in security because it is constantly changing.

We would like to thank Art Conklin for again herding the cats on this one.

Finally, we would each like to individually thank those people who—on a personal basis—have provided the core support for us. Without these special people in our lives, none of us could have put this work together.

—The Author Team

To my wife Susan: your love and support are crucial to works such as this. Thank you.

—Art Conklin

I would like to thank my wife, Charlan, for the tremendous support she has always given me.

—Gregory B. White

Josie, Macon, and Jet: thank you for the love, support, and laughs.

—Chuck Cothren

Geena, all I am is because of you. Thanks for being my greatest support. As always, love to my powerful children and wonderful grandkids!

—Roger L. Davis

To my wife and best friend Leah for her love, energy, and support—thank you for always being there. To my kids—this is what Daddy was typing on the computer!

—Dwayne Williams

INTRODUCTION

Computer security has become paramount as the number of security incidents steadily climbs. Many corporations now spend significant portions of their budget on security hardware, software, services, and personnel. They are spending this money not because it increases sales or enhances the product they provide but because of the possible consequences should they not take protective actions.

Why Focus on Security?

Security is not something that we want to have to pay for; it would be nice if we didn't have to worry about protecting our data from disclosure, modification, or destruction from unauthorized individuals, but that is not the environment we find ourselves in today. Instead, we have seen the cost of recovering from security incidents steadily rise along with the number of incidents themselves. Cyberattacks and information disclosures are occurring so often that one almost ignores them on the news. But with the theft of over 145 million consumers' credit data from Equifax, with the subsequent resignation of the CSO and CEO, and hearings in Congress over the role of legislative oversight with respect to critical records, a new sense of purpose with regard to securing data may be at hand. The days of paper reports and corporate "lip service" may be waning, and the time to meet the new challenges of even more sophisticated attackers has arrived. This will not be the last data breach, nor will attackers stop attacking our systems, so our only path forward is to have qualified professionals defending our systems.

A Growing Need for Security Specialists

In order to protect our computer systems and networks, we need a significant number of new security professionals trained in the many aspects of computer and network security. This is not an easy task, as the systems connected to the Internet become increasingly complex with software whose lines of code number in the millions. Understanding why this is such a difficult problem to solve is not hard if you consider just how many errors might be present in a piece of software that is several million lines long. When you add the factor of how fast software is being developed—from necessity, as the market is constantly changing—understanding how errors occur is easy.

Not every "bug" in the software will result in a security hole, but it doesn't take many to have a drastic effect on the Internet community. We can't just blame the vendors for this situation, because they are reacting to the demands of government and industry. Many vendors are fairly adept at developing patches for flaws found in their software, and patches are constantly being issued to protect systems from bugs that may introduce security problems. This introduces a whole new problem for managers and administrators—patch management. How important this has become is easily illustrated by how many of the most recent security events have occurred as a result of a security bug that was discovered months prior to the security incident, and for which a patch has been available but the community has not correctly installed it, thus making the incident possible. The reasons for these failures are many, but in the end the solution is a matter of trained professionals at multiple levels in an organization working together to resolve these problems.

But the issue of trained people does not stop with security professionals. Every user, from the board room to the mail room, plays a role in the cybersecurity posture of a firm. Training the non-security professional in the enterprise to use the proper level of care when interacting with systems will not make the problem go away either, but it will substantially strengthen the posture of the enterprise. Understanding the needed training and making it a reality is another task on the security professional's to-do list.

Because of the need for an increasing number of security professionals who are trained to some minimum level of understanding, certifications such as the CompTIA Security+ have been developed. Prospective employers want to know that the individual they are considering hiring knows what to do in terms of security. The prospective employee, in turn, wants to have a way to demonstrate his or her level of understanding, which can enhance the candidate's chances of being hired. The community as a whole simply wants more trained security professionals.

The goal of taking the CompTIA Security+ exam is to prove that you've mastered the worldwide standards for foundation-level security practitioners. The exam gives you a perfect opportunity to validate your knowledge and understanding of the computer security field, and it is an appropriate mechanism for many different individuals, including network and system administrators, analysts, programmers, web designers, application developers, and database specialists, to show proof of professional achievement in security. According to CompTIA, the exam is aimed at individuals who have

- A minimum of two years of experience in IT administration with a focus on security
- Day-to-day technical information security experience
- Broad knowledge of security concerns and implementation, including the topics that are found in the specific CompTIA Security+ domains

The exam objectives were developed with input and assistance from industry and government agencies. The CompTIA Security+ exam is designed to cover a wide range of security topics—subjects a security practitioner would be expected to know. The test includes information from five knowledge domains:

Domain	Percent of Exam
1.0 Threats, Attacks, and Vulnerabilities	24%
2.0 Architecture and Design	21%
3.0 Implementation	25%
4.0 Operations and Incident Response	16%
5.0 Governance, Risk, and Compliance	14%

The exam consists of a series of questions, each designed to have a single best answer or response. The other available choices are designed to provide options that an individual might choose if he or she had an incomplete knowledge or understanding of the security topic represented by the question. The exam will have both multiple-choice and performance-based questions. Performance-based questions present the candidate with a task or a problem in a simulated IT environment. The candidate is given an opportunity to demonstrate his or her ability in performing skills. The exam questions are based on the "CompTIA Security+ Certification Exam Objectives: SY0-601" document obtainable from the CompTIA website at https://certification.comptia.org/certifications/security.

CompTIA recommends that individuals who want to take the CompTIA Security+ exam have the CompTIA Network+ certification and two years of IT administration experience with an emphasis on security. Originally administered only in English, the exam is now offered in testing centers around the world in English, Japanese, Portuguese, and Simplified Chinese. Consult the CompTIA website at www.comptia.org to determine a test center location near you.

The exam consists of a maximum of 90 questions to be completed in 90 minutes. A minimum passing score is considered 750 out of a possible 900 points. Results are available immediately after you complete the exam. An individual who fails to pass the exam the first time will be required to pay the exam fee again to retake the exam, but no mandatory waiting period is required before retaking it the second time. If the individual again fails the exam, a minimum waiting period of 30 days is required for each subsequent retake. For more information on retaking exams, consult CompTIA's retake policy, which can be found on its website.

Preparing Yourself for the CompTIA Security+ Exam

CompTIA Security+ All-in-One Exam Guide, Sixth Edition, is designed to help prepare you to take CompTIA Security+ certification exam SY0-601.

How This Book Is Organized

The book is divided into sections and chapters to correspond with the objectives of the exam itself. Some of the chapters are more technical than others—reflecting the nature of the security environment, where you will be forced to deal with not only technical details but also other issues such as security policies and procedures as well as training and education. Although many individuals involved in computer and network security have advanced degrees in math, computer science, information systems, or computer or electrical engineering, you do not need this technical background to address security effectively in your organization. You do not need to develop your own cryptographic algorithm, for example; you simply need to be able to understand how cryptography is used, along with its strengths and weaknesses. As you progress in your studies, you will learn that many security problems are caused by the human element. The best technology in the world still ends up being placed in an environment where humans have the opportunity to foul things up—and all too often do.

As you can see from the table of contents, the overall structure of the book is designed to mirror the objectives of the CompTIA Security+ exam. The majority of the chapters are designed to match the objectives order as posted by CompTIA. This structure was used to make it easier to search specific content based on the objective. When studying certain topics, you may be required to go to several places in the book to fully cover a topic that has multiple objectives.

In addition, there are two appendixes in this book. Appendix A provides an additional in-depth explanation of the OSI Model and Internet protocols, should this information be new to you, and Appendix B explains how best to use the online materials included with the book.

Located just before the Index, you will find a useful Glossary of security terminology, including many related acronyms and their meanings. We hope that you use the Glossary frequently and find it to be a useful study aid as you work your way through the various topics in this exam guide.

Special Features of the All-in-One Series

To make these exam guides more useful and a pleasure to read, the *All-in-One* series has been designed to include several features.

Objective Map

The objective map that follows this introduction has been constructed to allow you to cross-reference the official exam objectives with the objectives as they are presented and covered in this book. References have been provided for each objective exactly as CompTIA presents it, along with a chapter reference.

Icons

To alert you to an important bit of advice, a shortcut, or a pitfall, you'll occasionally see Notes, Tips, Cautions, and Exam Tips peppered throughout the text.

NOTE Notes offer nuggets of especially helpful stuff, background explanations, and information, and they define terms occasionally.

TIP Tips provide suggestions and nuances to help you learn to finesse your job. Take a tip from us and read the Tips carefully.

CAUTION When you see a Caution, pay special attention. Cautions appear when you have to make a crucial choice or when you are about to undertake something that may have ramifications you might not immediately anticipate. Read them now so you don't have regrets later.

EXAM TIP Exam Tips give you special advice or may provide information specifically related to preparing for the exam itself.

End-of-Chapter Reviews and Questions

An important part of this book comes at the end of each chapter, where you will find a brief review of the high points along with a series of questions followed by the answers to those questions. Each question is in multiple-choice format. The answers provided also include a small discussion explaining why the correct answer actually is the correct answer.

The questions are provided as a study aid to you, the reader and prospective CompTIA Security+ exam taker. We obviously can't guarantee that if you answer all of our questions correctly you will absolutely pass the certification exam. Instead, what we can guarantee is that the questions will provide you with an idea about how ready you are for the exam.

Security+ Proposed Hardware and Software List

CompTIA provides this sample list of hardware and software in its Exam Objectives description to assist candidates as they prepare for the Security+ exam. Because the material includes elements that require hands-on competency, it is useful to build a lab and practice hands-on skills as part of the study process. The bulleted lists below each topic are sample lists and are not exhaustive.

Hardware

- Laptop with Internet access
- Separate wireless network access card (NIC)
- Wireless access point (WAP)
- Firewall
- Unified threat monitor (UTM)
- Mobile device
- Server/cloud server
- IoT devices

Software

- Virtualization software
- Penetration testing OS/distributions (for example, Kali Linux, Parrot OS)
- Security information and event management (SIEM)
- Wireshark
- Metasploit
- Tcpdump

Other

- Access to a cloud service provider

The Online TotalTester

CompTIA Security+ All-in-One Exam Guide, Sixth Edition, also provides you with a test engine containing even more practice exam questions and their answers to help you prepare for the certification exam. Read more about the companion online TotalTester practice exam software and how to register for and access your exams in Appendix B.

Onward and Upward

At this point, we hope you are now excited about the topic of security, even if you weren't in the first place. We wish you luck in your endeavors and welcome you to the exciting field of computer and network security.

Objective Map: Exam SY0-601

Official Exam Domains and Objectives	All-in-One Coverage Chapter
1.0 Threats, Attacks, and Vulnerabilities	
1.1 Compare and contrast different types of social engineering techniques.	1
1.2 Given a scenario, analyze potential indicators to determine the type of attack.	2
1.3 Given a scenario, analyze potential indicators associated with application attacks.	3
1.4 Given a scenario, analyze potential indicators associated with network attacks.	4
1.5 Explain different threat actors, vectors, and intelligence sources.	5
1.6 Explain the security concerns associated with various types of vulnerabilities.	6
1.7 Summarize the techniques used in security assessments.	7
1.8 Explain the techniques used in penetration testing.	8
2.0 Architecture and Design	
2.1 Explain the importance of security concepts in an enterprise environment.	9
2.2 Summarize virtualization and cloud computing concepts.	10
2.3 Summarize secure application development, deployment, and automation concepts.	11
2.4 Summarize authentication and authorization design concepts.	12
2.5 Given a scenario, implement cybersecurity resilience.	13
2.6 Explain the security implications of embedded and specialized systems.	14

Official Exam Domains and Objectives	All-in-One Coverage Chapter
2.7 Explain the importance of physical security controls.	15
2.8 Summarize the basics of cryptographic concepts.	16
3.0 Implementation	
3.1 Given a scenario, implement secure protocols.	17
3.2 Given a scenario, implement host or application security solutions.	18
3.3 Given a scenario, implement secure network designs.	19
3.4 Given a scenario, install and configure wireless security settings.	20
3.5 Given a scenario, implement secure mobile solutions.	21
3.6 Given a scenario, apply cybersecurity solutions to the cloud.	22
3.7 Given a scenario, implement identity and account management controls.	23
3.8 Given a scenario, implement authentication and authorization solutions.	24
3.9 Given a scenario, implement public key infrastructure.	25
4.0 Operations and Incident Response	
4.1 Given a scenario, use the appropriate tool to assess organizational security.	26
4.2 Summarize the importance of policies, processes, and procedures for incident response.	27
4.3 Given an incident, utilize appropriate data sources to support an investigation.	28
4.4 Given an incident, apply mitigation techniques or controls to secure an environment.	29
4.5 Explain the key aspects of digital forensics.	30
5.0 Governance, Risk, and Compliance	
5.1 Compare and contrast various types of controls.	31
5.2 Explain the importance of applicable regulations, standards, or frameworks that impact organizational security posture.	32
5.3 Explain the importance of policies to organizational security.	33
5.4 Summarize risk management processes and concepts.	34
5.5 Explain privacy and sensitive data concepts in relation to security.	35

PART I

Threats, Attacks, and Vulnerabilities

CHAPTER 1

Social Engineering Techniques

In this chapter, you will

- Examine the types of attacks associated with social engineering
- Compare and contrast the different social engineering techniques

Social engineering is a method of using people as part of an attack process. Social engineering is just a step in the overall attack process, but it is an effective way of starting an attack on a system. There are various forms of technical attacks against the computer components of a system, but in each case, there is a starting point by which the attack is presented to the system. In this chapter, we examine the various types of social engineering techniques that can be employed to begin the attack cycle.

Certification Objective This chapter covers CompTIA Security+ exam objective 1.1: Compare and contrast different types of social engineering techniques.

Social Engineering Methods

Social engineering is an attack against a user, and typically involves some form of social interaction. The weakness that is being exploited in the attack is not necessarily one of technical knowledge or even security awareness. Social engineering at its heart involves manipulating the very social nature of interpersonal relationships. It, in essence, preys on several characteristics we tend to desire. The willingness to help, for instance, is a characteristic one would like to see in a team environment. We want employees who help each other, and we tend to reward those who are helpful and punish those who are not.

If our work culture is built around collaboration and teamwork, then how can this be exploited? It is not simple, but it can be accomplished through a series of subtle ruses. One is built around the concept of developing a sense of familiarity—making it seem as if you belong to the group. For example, by injecting yourself into a conversation or encounter, armed with the right words and the correct information, you can make it seem as if you belong. Through careful name dropping and aligning your story with current events and expectations, you can just slip in unnoticed. Another example is by arriving at a door at the same time as a person with an ID card, carrying something in both your hands, you probably can get them to open and hold the door for you. An even more successful technique is to have a conversation on the way to the door over something that makes you fit in. People want to help, and this tactic encourages the person to help you.

A second method involves creating a hostile situation. People tend to want to avoid hostility, so if you are engaged in a heated argument with someone as you enter the group you wish to join—making sure not only that you are losing the argument, but that it also seems totally unfair—you instantly can build a connection to anyone who has been similarly mistreated. Play on sympathy, their desire for compassion, and use the situation to bypass the connection opportunity.

A good social engineer understands how to use body language to influence others—how to smile at the right time, how to mirror movements, how to influence others not through words but through body language cues. Eye contact can signal interest to others. Gestures and posture can be used to gain the attention of those watching. Gaining someone's attention can lead to interactions that can be further exploited. When someone has the key information you need for a project, a proposal, or any other important thing, trading a quid pro quo is an unspoken ritual. And if you do this with someone who has malicious intent, then remember the saying, "Beware of Greeks bearing gifts."

NOTE Much of social engineering will play to known stereotypical behavior. Detailing this material is not meant to justify the behaviors, for they are in fact wrong. But it is important to watch for them, for these are the tools used by social engineers—crying babies, flirting, hiding in plain sight (the janitor, plant waterer, pizza delivery person). We are all blinded by biases and conditioning, and social engineers know and exploit these weaknesses. And if called out on their behavior, they will even go with that and protest too much or agree too much—whatever it takes to win a person over. Don't be that person—either the one using stereotypes or the one falling prey to them.

The best defense against social engineering attacks is a comprehensive training and awareness program that includes social engineering, but this does not mean that employees should be trained to be stubborn and unhelpful. Rather, training should emphasize the value of being helpful and working as a team but doing so in an environment where trust is verified and is a ritual without social stigma. No one will get past Transportation Security Administration (TSA) employees with social engineering techniques when checking in at an airport, because they dispassionately enforce and follow set procedures, but they frequently do so with kindness, politeness, and helpfulness while also ensuring that the screening procedures are always completed.

EXAM TIP For the exam, be familiar with all of the various social engineering attacks and the associated effectiveness of each attack.

Tools

The tools in a social engineer's toolbox are based on a knowledge of psychology and don't necessarily require a sophisticated knowledge of software or hardware. The social engineer will employ strategies aimed at exploiting people's own biases and beliefs in a manner to momentarily deny them the service of good judgment and the use of standard procedures. Employing social engineering tools is second nature to a social engineer, and with skill they can switch these tools in and out in any particular circumstance, just as a plumber uses various hand tools and a system administrator uses OS commands to achieve complex tasks. When watching any of these professionals work, we may marvel at how they wield their tools, and the same is true for social engineers—except their tools are more subtle, and the targets are people and trust. The "techniques" that are commonly employed in many social engineering attacks are described next.

Phishing

Phishing (pronounced "fishing") is a type of social engineering in which an attacker attempts to obtain sensitive information from users by masquerading as a trusted entity in an e-mail or instant message sent to a large group of often random users. The attacker attempts to obtain information such as usernames, passwords, credit card numbers, and details about the users' bank accounts. The message that is sent often encourages the user to go to a website that appears to be for a reputable entity such as PayPal or eBay, both of which have frequently been used in phishing attempts. The website the user actually visits is not owned by the reputable organization, however, and asks the user to supply information that can be used in a later attack. Often the message sent to the user states that the user's account has been compromised and requests, for security purposes, the user to enter their account information to verify the details.

In another very common example of phishing, the attacker sends a bulk e-mail, supposedly from a bank, telling the recipients that a security breach has occurred and instructing them to click a link to verify that their account has not been tampered with. If the individual actually clicks the link, they are taken to a site that appears to be owned by the bank but is actually controlled by the attacker. When they supply their account and password for "verification" purposes, the individual is actually giving it to the attacker.

EXAM TIP Phishing is now the most common form of social engineering attack related to computer security. The target could be a computer system and access to the information found on it (as is the case when the phishing attempt asks for a user ID and password), or it could be personal information, generally financial, about an individual (in the case of phishing attempts that ask for an individual's banking information).

Smishing

Smishing is an attack using Short Message Service (SMS) on victims' cell phones. It is a version of phishing via SMS. It begins with an SMS message directing a user to a URL that can serve up a variety of attack vectors, including forms of malware. This attack works primarily due to the use of urgency and intimidation in the message, which might use a warning such as "You are subscribed to XYZ service, which will begin regular billings of $2 a month. Click here to unsubscribe before billing takes place." When the user clicks the URL, the next phase of the attack can begin.

Vishing

Vishing is a variation of phishing that uses voice communication technology to obtain the information the attacker is seeking. Vishing takes advantage of the trust that some people place in the telephone network. Users are unaware that attackers can spoof (simulate) calls from legitimate entities using Voice over IP (VoIP) technology. Voice messaging can also be compromised and used in these attempts. This tactic is used to establish a form of trust that is then exploited by the attacker over the phone. Generally, the attacker is hoping to obtain credit card numbers or other information that can be used in identity theft. The user may receive an e-mail asking them to call a number that is answered by a potentially compromised voice message system. Users may also receive a recorded message that appears to come from a legitimate entity. In both cases, the user will be encouraged to respond quickly and provide the sensitive information so that access to their account is not blocked. If a user ever receives a message that claims to be from a reputable entity and asks for sensitive information, the user should not provide it but instead should use the Internet or examine a legitimate account statement to find a phone number that can be used to contact the entity. The user can then verify that the message received was legitimate and report the vishing attempt.

NOTE A great video showing the use of several social engineering tools can be found at https://www.youtube.com/watch?v=lc7scxvKQOo ("This is how hackers hack you using simple social engineering"). This video demonstrates the use of vishing to steal someone's cell phone credentials.

EXAM TIP Phishing, smishing, vishing—these are attacks against users' cognitive state. Using the principles for effectiveness, discussed later in the chapter, one can craft a message that makes falling victim to these attacks more likely. The attack is a combination of technical elements and psychological pressure, and together they cause the user to take the bait and click the link.

Spam

Spam, as just about everybody knows, is bulk unsolicited e-mail. Though not generally considered by many as a social engineering issue, or even a security issue for that matter, spam can still be a security concern. It can be legitimate in the sense that it has been sent by a company advertising a product or service, but it can also be malicious and could include an attachment that contains malicious software designed to harm your system, or a link to a malicious website that may attempt to obtain personal information from you. As spam is unsolicited, one should always consider the source before clicking any links or directly responding. Because spam can result in users clicking links, it should be regarded as a form of altering human behavior or social engineering.

Spam over Instant Messaging (SPIM)

Though not as well known, a variation on spam is *SPIM,* which is basically spam delivered via an instant messaging application. The purpose of hostile SPIM is the same as that of spam—getting an unsuspecting user to click malicious content or links, thus initiating the attack.

Spear Phishing

Spear phishing is a term created to refer to a phishing attack that targets a specific person or group of people with something in common. Because the attack targets a specific group, such as senior executives, the ratio of successful attacks (that is, the number of responses received) to the total number of e-mails or messages sent usually increases because a targeted attack will seem more plausible than a message sent to users randomly.

Dumpster Diving

The process of going through a target's trash in hopes of finding valuable information that might be used in a penetration attempt is known in the security community as *dumpster diving*. One common place to find information, if the attacker is in the vicinity of the target, is in the target's trash. The attacker might find little bits of information that could be useful for an attack. The tactic is not, however, unique to the computer community; it has been used for many years by others, such as identity thieves, private investigators, and law enforcement personnel, to obtain information about an individual or organization. If the attacker is very lucky, and the target's security procedures are very poor, they may actually find user IDs and passwords.

An attacker may gather a variety of information that can be useful in a social engineering attack. In most locations, trash is no longer considered private property after it has been discarded (and even where dumpster diving is illegal, little enforcement occurs). An organization should have policies about discarding materials. Sensitive information should be shredded and the organization should consider securing the trash receptacle so that individuals can't forage through it. People should also consider shredding personal or sensitive information that they wish to discard in their own trash. A reasonable quality shredder is inexpensive and well worth the price when compared with the potential loss that could occur as a result of identity theft.

Shoulder Surfing

Shoulder surfing does not necessarily involve direct contact with the target; instead, the attacker directly observes the individual entering sensitive information on a form, keypad, or keyboard. The attacker may simply look over the shoulder of the user at work, for example, or may set up a camera or use binoculars to view the user entering sensitive data. The attacker can attempt to obtain information such as a personal identification number (PIN) at an automated teller machine (ATM), an access control entry code at a secure gate or door, or a calling card or credit card number. Many locations now use a privacy screen or filter to surround a keypad so that it is difficult to observe somebody as they enter information. More sophisticated systems can actually scramble the location of the numbers so that the top row at one time includes the numbers 1, 2, and 3 and the next time includes 4, 8, and 0. While this makes it a bit slower for the user to enter information, it thwarts an attacker's attempt to observe what numbers are pressed and then enter the same button pattern since the location of the numbers constantly changes.

Pharming

Pharming consists of misdirecting users to fake websites made to look official. Using phishing, attackers target individuals, one by one, by sending out e-mails. To become a victim, the recipient must take an action (for example, respond by providing personal information). In pharming, the user will be directed to the fake website as a result of activity such as DNS poisoning (an attack that changes URLs in a server's domain name table) or modification of local host files (which are used to convert URLs to the appropriate IP address). Once at the fake site, the user might supply personal information, believing that they are connected to the legitimate site.

Tailgating

Tailgating (or piggybacking) is the simple tactic of following closely behind a person who has just used their own access card or PIN to gain physical access to a room or building. People are often in a hurry and will frequently not follow good physical security practices and procedures. Attackers know this and may attempt to exploit this characteristic in human behavior. An attacker can thus gain access to the facility without having to know the access code or having to acquire an access card. It is similar to shoulder surfing in that it relies on the attacker taking advantage of an authorized user who is not following security procedures. Frequently the attacker may even start a conversation with the target before reaching the door so that the user may be more comfortable with allowing the individual in without challenging them. In this sense, piggybacking is related to social engineering attacks.

Both the piggybacking and shoulder surfing attack techniques rely on the poor security practices of an authorized user in order to be successful. Thus, both techniques can be easily countered by training employees to use simple procedures to ensure nobody follows them too closely or is in a position to observe their actions. A more sophisticated countermeasure to piggybacking involves the use of a *mantrap*, which utilizes two doors to gain access to the facility. The second door does not open until the first one is closed, and the doors are closely spaced so that an enclosure is formed that only allows one individual through at a time.

Eliciting Information

Calls to or from help desk and tech support units can be used to *elicit information*. A skilled social engineer can use a wide range of psychological techniques to convince people, whose main job is to help others, to perform tasks resulting in security compromises. Posing as an employee, an attacker can get a password reset, information about some system, or other useful information. The call can go the other direction as well, where the social engineer is posing as the help desk or tech support person. Then, by calling employees, the attacker can get information on system status and other interesting elements that they can use later.

Whaling

High-value targets are referred to as whales. A *whaling* attack is thus one where the target is a high-value person, such as a CEO or CFO. Whaling attacks are not performed by attacking multiple targets and hoping for a reply, but rather are custom built to increase the odds of success. Spear phishing is a common method used against whales, as the communication is designed to appear to be ordinary business for the target, being crafted to appear nonsuspicious. Whales can be deceived in the same manner as any other person; the difference is that the target group is limited, so an attacker cannot rely upon random returns from a wide population of targets.

Prepending

Prepending is defined as the act of adding something else to the beginning of an item. When used in a social engineering context, prepending is the act of supplying information that another will act upon, frequently before they ask for it, in an attempt to legitimize the actual request, which comes later. Using the psychological constructs of authority, an attacker can use prepending by stating that they were sent by the target's boss, or another authority figure, as a means to justify why the target should perform a specific action—typically one that, in the absence of the prepending, would not be normal.

Identity Fraud

Identity fraud is the use of fake credentials to achieve an end. This can be high risk, pretending to be an official representative of a government agency or a regulator, or lower risk, showing up as the person who waters the plants. One could pretend to be a delivery agent, show up with a box—or better yet, a server—and attempt direct delivery to the server room. This works best when the victim is expecting the person, as in the case of a broken server under a repair warranty. Identity fraud can be done online as well, using known information about the person you are impersonating (see the "Impersonation" section later in the chapter), and deceiving the victim you are attacking. Defense against identity fraud is the same as most other social engineering attacks: use strong policies and procedures without exceptions. For example, all packages must be dropped at the security desk, all visitors who need access must be escorted, with no exceptions, and so on. Also, there should be no exceptions on disclosure policies, like resetting passwords or giving a party access. Doing everything by the rules works—just look at TSA security, where there is no way to sneak past their line. The accuracy and effectiveness of their screening may be called into question, but getting around it is not. This is key for stopping most social engineering attacks.

Invoice Scams

Invoice scams use a fake invoice in an attempt to get a company to pay for things it has not ordered. The premise is simple: send a fake invoice and then get paid. In practice, since most companies have fairly strong accounting controls, the scam involves getting someone outside of the accounting group to initiate the process, lending a sense of legitimacy. This all seems like it wouldn't work, yet cybercriminals collect literally billions of dollars using this method. Common items used in the scams are office products such as toner and typical office supplies, cleaning products, organizational memberships, and a wide range of corporate services. Sometimes, to add urgency, a final notice is included, threatening to report the organization to a collection agency, thus making a person hesitate before just throwing the bill away.

Credential Harvesting

Credential harvesting involves the collection of credential information, such as user IDs, passwords, and so on, enabling an attacker a series of access passes to the system. A common form of credential harvesting starts with a phishing e-mail that convinces a user to click a link and, in response, brings up a replica of their bank's web page. Users typically do not check the security settings of their browser connection, and when they enter their user ID and password, their credentials are harvested and stored for later use by the criminal.

The objective of a credential harvest is just to obtain credentials. Once the criminal has tricked you into providing your credentials, they will either redirect you to the correct website or provide an error and a new connection to the correct website for you to try again. They want to mask the fact that they stole your credentials. This attack method has been highly successful, and it is now standard practice for financial firms to follow a normal user ID and password with a second-factor, out-of-band inquiry to prevent subsequent use of harvested credentials. While this adds a layer of complexity and inconvenience to the user, it has become an accepted practice and is necessary to prevent harvested credential reuse.

NOTE Many of the attacks are designed to get a user's credentials. Any credential you can share is a risk, and to combat this risk, organizations have adopted two-factor authentication. The second factor is a different method of identifying the user and is typically unique and only valid for a limited time. An example is when you log in to your bank website, you get a text message with a code to authorize your entry. The use of this code significantly complicates the problem for an attacker if they get your credentials.

Reconnaissance

Reconnaissance is a military term used to describe the actions of surveying a battlefield to gain information prior to hostilities. In the field of cybersecurity, the concept is the same: an adversary will examine the systems they intend to attack, using a wide range of methods. Some of these methods are outside the purview of the victim: Google searches, public record searches, and so on. But other aspects are involved in directly manipulating people to gain information. Surveying a company's org charts, calling and asking for people's contact information and building a personnel directory, asking questions about hardware and software via surveys, and reading press releases can all be used to obtain information that goes into a description of the system that will be under attack. Although most reconnaissance is accepted as inevitable, some of it is helped via press releases telling the world who your security partners are, what products you are employing, and so on. Each of these items of information will be used later as part of the attack process. Known weaknesses against specific products can be employed and are easier to find if the attacker knows what products the company is using. Performing solid reconnaissance before attacking provides the attacker with key informational elements later when these items are needed.

Hoax

At first glance, it might seem that a hoax related to security would be considered a nuisance and not a real security issue. This might be the case for some hoaxes, especially those of the urban legend type, but the reality of the situation is that a *hoax* can be very damaging if it causes users to take some sort of action that weakens security. One real hoax, for example, described a new, highly destructive piece of malicious software. It instructed users to check for the existence of a certain file and to delete it if the file was found. In reality, the file mentioned was an important file used by the operating system, and deleting it caused problems the next time the system was booted. The damage caused by users modifying security settings can be serious. As with other forms of social engineering, training and awareness are the best and first line of defense for both users and administrators. Users should be trained to be suspicious of unusual e-mails and stories and should know who to contact in the organization to verify their validity if they are received. A hoax often also advises the user to send it to their friends so that they know about the issue as well—and by doing so, the user helps spread the hoax. Users need to be suspicious of any e-mail telling them to "spread the word."

Impersonation

Impersonation is a common social engineering technique and can be employed in many ways. It can occur in person, over a phone, or online. In the case of an impersonation attack, the attacker assumes a role that is recognized by the person being attacked, and in assuming that role, the attacker uses the potential victim's biases against their better judgment to follow procedures. Impersonation can occur in a variety of ways—from third parties, to help desk operators, to vendors, or even online sources.

Third-Party Authorization

Using previously obtained information about a project, deadlines, bosses, and so on, the attacker (1) arrives with something the victim is quasi-expecting or would see as normal, (2) uses the guise of a project in trouble or some other situation where the attacker will be viewed as helpful or as someone not to upset, and (3) name-drops the contact "Mr. Big," who happens to be out of the office and unreachable at the moment, thus avoiding the reference check. Also, the attacker seldom asks for anything that seems unreasonable or is unlikely to be shared based on the circumstances. These actions can create the appearance of a third-party authorization, when in fact there is none.

Contractors/Outside Parties

It is common in many organizations to have outside contractors clean the building, water the plants, and perform other routine chores. In many of these situations, without proper safeguards, an attacker can simply put on clothing that matches a contractor's uniform, show up to do the job at a slightly different time than it's usually done, and, if challenged, play on the sympathy of the workers by saying they are filling in for *X* or covering for *Y*. The attacker then roams the halls unnoticed because they blend in, all the while photographing desks and papers and looking for information.

Online Attacks

Impersonation can be employed in online attacks as well. In these cases, technology plays an intermediary role in the communication chain. Some older forms, such as pop-up windows, tend to be less effective today because users are wary of them. Yet phishing attempts via e-mail and social media scams abound.

Defenses

In all of the cases of impersonation, the best defense is simple—have processes in place that require employees to ask to see a person's ID before engaging with them if the employees do not personally know them. That includes challenging people such as delivery drivers and contract workers. Don't let people in through the door, piggybacking, without checking their ID. If this is standard process, then no one becomes offended, and if someone fakes offense, it becomes even more suspicious. Training and awareness do work, as proven by trends such as the diminished effectiveness of pop-up windows. But the key to this defense is to conduct training on a regular basis and to tailor it to what is currently being experienced, rather than a generic recitation of best practices.

EXAM TIP A training and awareness program is still the best defense against social engineering attacks.

Watering Hole Attack

The most commonly recognized attack vectors are those that are direct to a target. Because of the attacks' direct nature, defenses are crafted to detect and defend against them. But what if the user "asked" for the attack by visiting a website? Just as a hunter waits near a watering hole for animals to come drink, attackers can plant malware at sites where users are likely to frequent. First identified by the security firm RSA, a *watering hole attack* involves the infecting of a target website with malware. In some of the cases detected, the infection was constrained to a specific geographical area. These are not simple attacks, yet they can be very effective at delivering malware to specific groups of end users. Watering hole attacks are complex to achieve and appear to be backed by nation-states and other high-resource attackers. In light of the stakes, the typical attack vector will be a zero-day attack to further avoid detection.

Typosquatting

Typosquatting is an attack form that involves capitalizing upon common typographical errors. If a user mistypes a URL, then the result should be a 404 error, or "resource not found." But if an attacker has registered the mistyped URL, then the user would land on the attacker's page. This attack pattern is also referred to as *URL hijacking*, *fake URL*, or *brandjacking* if the objective is to deceive based on branding.

There are several reasons that an attacker will pursue this avenue of attack. The most obvious is one of a phishing attack. The fake site collects credentials, passing them on to the real site, and then steps out of the conversation to avoid detection once the credentials are obtained. It can also be used to plant drive-by malware on the victim machine. It can move the packets through an affiliate network, earning click-through revenue based on the typos. There are numerous other forms of attacks that can be perpetrated using a fake URL as a starting point.

Pretexting

Pretexting is a form of social engineering in which the attacker uses a narrative (the pretext) to influence the victim into giving up some item of information. An example would be calling up, posing as a fellow student from college, or a fellow admin to a senior executive. The pretext does not have to be true; it only needs to be believable and relevant in convincing the victim to give help. Pretexting uses deception and false motives to manipulate the victim. The main goal of the attacker is to gain the target's trust and exploit it. A pretext attack can occur in person, by email, over the phone, or virtually any other form of communication.

Influence Campaigns

Influence campaigns involve the use of collected information and selective publication of material to key individuals in an attempt to alter perceptions and change people's minds on a topic. One can engage in an influence campaign against a single person, but the effect is limited. Influence campaigns are even more powerful when used in conjunction with social media to spread influence through influencer propagation. Influencers are people who have large followings of people who read what they post, and in many cases act in accordance or agreement. This results in an amplifying mechanism, where single pieces of disinformation can be rapidly spread and build a following across the Internet. The effects are strong enough that nation-states have used these techniques as a form of conflict, termed *hybrid warfare,* where the information is used to sway people toward a position favored by those spreading it. What makes this effective is the psychological effects of groups, experiencing the bandwagon effect, where when one leads, many follow, typically without critically examining the premise they are then following. In previous wars, this was called *propaganda,* and today, with rapid communication worldwide via social media platforms, these methods are even more effective at moving mass beliefs of groups of populations.

Principles (Reasons for Effectiveness)

Social engineering is very successful for two general reasons. The first is the basic desire of most people to be helpful. When somebody asks a question for which we know the answer, our normal response is not to be suspicious but rather to answer the question. The problem with this is that seemingly innocuous information can be used either directly in an attack or indirectly to build a bigger picture that an attacker can use to create an aura of authenticity during an attack—the more information an individual has about an organization, the easier it will be to convince others that they are part of the organization and have a right to even more sensitive information.

The second reason that social engineering is successful is that individuals normally seek to avoid confrontation and trouble. If the attacker attempts to intimidate the target, threatening to call the target's supervisor because of a lack of help, the target may give in and provide the information to avoid confrontation. The following sections will look at the concepts of authority, intimidation, consensus, scarcity, familiarity, trust, and urgency as applied to their use in furthering a successful social engineering attack.

NOTE The effectiveness of social engineering attacks is part technical and part psychological. For an attack to trick most users, psychological hooks are used to make attacks more effective in getting a user to perform a desired action. Understanding the psychological component of these attacks is important.

Authority

The use of *authority* in social situations can lead to an environment where one party feels at risk in challenging another over an issue. If an attacker can convince a target that they have authority in a particular situation, they can entice the target to act in a particular manner or else face adverse consequences. In short, if you act like a boss when requesting something, people are less likely to withhold it.

The best defense against this and many social engineering attacks is a strong set of policies that has no exceptions. Much like security lines in the airport, when it comes to the point of screening, everyone gets screened, even flight crews, so there is no method of bypassing this critical step.

Intimidation

Intimidation can be either subtle, through perceived power, or more direct, through the use of communications that build an expectation of superiority. The use of one's title, or fancy credentials, like being a "lead assessor for the standard," creates an air of authority around one's persona.

Consensus

Consensus is a group-wide decision. It frequently comes not from a champion, but rather through rounds of group negotiation. These rounds can be manipulated to achieve desired outcomes. The social engineer simply motivates others to achieve their desired outcome.

Scarcity

If something is in short supply and is valued, then arriving with what is needed can bring rewards—and acceptance. "Only *X* widgets left at this price" is an example of this technique. Even if something is not scarce, implied scarcity, or implied future change in availability, can create a perception of scarcity. By giving the impression of *scarcity* (or short supply) of a desirable product, an attacker can motivate a target to make a decision quickly without deliberation.

Familiarity

People do things for people they like or feel connected to. Building this sense of *familiarity* and appeal can lead to misplaced trust. The social engineer can focus the conversation on familiar items, not the differences. Again, leading with persuasion that one has been there before and done something, even if they haven't, will lead to the desired "familiar" feeling in the target.

Trust

Trust is defined as having an understanding of how something will act under specific conditions. Social engineers can shape the perceptions of a target to where they will apply judgments to the trust equation and come to false conclusions. The whole objective of social engineering is not to force people to do things they would not do but rather to give them a pathway that leads them to feel they are doing the correct thing in the moment.

Urgency

Time can be manipulated to drive a sense of *urgency* and prompt shortcuts that can lead to opportunities for interjection into processes. Limited-time offers should always be viewed as suspect. Perception is the key. Giving the target a reason to believe that they can take advantage of a timely situation, whether or not it is real, achieves the outcome of them acting in a desired manner.

EXAM TIP The key in all social engineering attacks is that you are manipulating a person and their actions by manipulating their perception of a situation. A social engineer preys on people's beliefs, biases, and stereotypes—to the victim's detriment. This is hacking the human side of a system.

Defenses

While many of these social engineering attacks may make you want to roll your eyes and think they never work, the fact is they do, and billions are lost every year to these methods. Whether it is a direct scam or the first stages of a much larger attack, the elements presented in this chapter are used all the time by hackers and criminals. Fortunately, effective defenses against these social engineering attacks are easier to establish than those needed for many of the more technical attacks. Stopping social engineering begins with policies and procedures that eliminate the pathways used by these attacks. Visitor access, rules before assisting a customer, verifying requests as legitimate before sharing certain sensitive elements—these are all doable items. Once you have layered policies and procedures to avoid these issues, or their outcomes, the critical element is employee training. Maintaining vigilance on the part of employee actions is the challenge, and frequent reminders, retraining, and notification of violations can go a long way toward achieving the desired defense. Lastly, have multiple layers of defenses, including approvals and related safeguards so that a single mistake from an employee will not give away the keys to the kingdom. Also, a healthy dose of knowledge, through sharing the large cases started by social engineering techniques in the form of public awareness campaigns, will keep employees engaged in actively defending against social engineering.

NOTE Many high-profile "hacking" cases began with social engineering:

- Target data breach, 2013: phishing e-mail
- Sony, 2014: phishing
- Democratic National Committee e-mail leak, 2016: spear phishing
- Ukraine electric grid attack, 2018: phishing

Chapter Review

This chapter examined various tools and techniques employed in social engineering. The use of deception to get users to respond to messages via different channels of communication include phishing, smishing, vishing, spear phishing, spam, SPIM, and whaling. The chapter also covers physical methods like tailgating, dumpster diving, and shoulder surfing. Other techniques such as watering holes, credential harvesting, typosquatting, and influence campaigns are also covered. The chapter closes with an examination of some of the psychological traits that make users susceptible to social engineering as well as the techniques to defend against social engineering.

Questions

To help you prepare further for the CompTIA Security+ exam, and to test your level of preparedness, answer the following questions and then check your answers against the correct answers at the end of the chapter.

1. While waiting in the lobby of your building for a guest, you notice a man in a red shirt standing close to a locked door with a large box in his hands. He waits for someone else to come along and open the locked door and then proceeds to follow her inside. What type of social engineering attack have you just witnessed?
   - **A.** Impersonation
   - **B.** Phishing
   - **C.** Boxing
   - **D.** Tailgating
2. A colleague asks you for advice on why he can't log in to his Gmail account. Looking at his browser, you see he has typed www.gmal.com in the address bar. The screen looks very similar to the Gmail login screen. Your colleague has just fallen victim to what type of attack?
   - **A.** Jamming
   - **B.** Rainbow table
   - **C.** Whale phishing
   - **D.** Typosquatting

3. A user in your organization contacts you to see if there's any update to the "account compromise" that happened last week. When you ask him to explain what he means, and the user tells you he received a phone call earlier in the week from your department and was asked to verify his user ID and password. The user says he gave the caller his user ID and password. This user has fallen victim to what specific type of attack?
   - **A.** Spear phishing
   - **B.** Vishing
   - **C.** Phishing
   - **D.** Replication
4. Coming into your office, you overhear a conversation between two security guards. One guard is telling the other she caught several people digging through the trash behind the building early this morning. The security guard says the people claimed to be looking for aluminum cans, but only had a bag of papers—no cans. What type of attack has this security guard witnessed?
   - **A.** Spear phishing
   - **B.** Pharming
   - **C.** Dumpster diving
   - **D.** Rolling refuse
5. Which of the following are specifically used to spread influence, alter perceptions, and sway people toward a position favored by those spreading it?
   - **A.** Identity fraud, invoice scams, credential harvesting
   - **B.** Hoaxes, eliciting information, urgency
   - **C.** Influence campaigns, social media, hybrid warfare
   - **D.** Authority, intimidation, consensus
6. Which of the following is a type of social engineering attack in which an attacker attempts to obtain sensitive information from a user by masquerading as a trusted entity in an e-mail?
   - **A.** Phishing
   - **B.** Pharming
   - **C.** Spam
   - **D.** Vishing
7. Which of the following is/are psychological tools used by social engineers to create false trust with a target?
   - **A.** Impersonation
   - **B.** Urgency or scarcity

C. Authority

D. All of the above

8. Once an organization's security policies have been established, what is the single most effective method of countering potential social engineering attacks?

A. An active security awareness program

B. A separate physical access control mechanism for each department in the organization

C. Frequent testing of both the organization's physical security procedures and employee telephone practices

D. Implementing access control cards and the wearing of security identification badges

9. You notice a new custodian in the office, working much earlier than normal, emptying trash cans, and moving slowly past people working. You ask him where the normal guy is, and in very broken English he says, "Out sick," indicating a cough. What is happening?

A. Watering hole attack

B. Impersonation

C. Prepending

D. Identity fraud

10. Your boss thanks you for pictures you sent from the recent company picnic. You ask him what he is talking about, and he says he got an e-mail from you with pictures from the picnic. Knowing you have not sent him that e-mail, what type of attack do you suspect is happening?

A. Phishing

B. Spear phishing

C. Reconnaissance

D. Impersonation

Answers

1. **D.** Tailgating (or piggybacking) is the simple tactic of following closely behind a person who has just used their own access card, key, or PIN to gain physical access to a room or building. The large box clearly impedes the person in the red shirt's ability to open the door, so they let someone else do it for them and follow them in.

2. **D.** Typosquatting capitalizes on common typing errors, such as gmal instead of gmail. The attacker registers a domain very similar to the real domain and attempts to collect credentials or other sensitive information from unsuspecting users.

3. **B.** Vishing is a social engineering attack that uses voice communication technology to obtain the information the attacker is seeking. Most often the attacker will call a victim and pretend to be someone else in an attempt to extract information from the victim.
4. **C.** Dumpster diving is the process of going through a target's trash in the hopes of finding valuable information such as user lists, directories, organization charts, network maps, passwords, and so on.
5. **C.** Influence campaigns are used to alter perceptions and change people's minds on a topic. They are even more powerful when used in conjunction with social media to spread influence through influencer propagation. Nation-states often use hybrid warfare to sway people toward a position favored by those spreading it.
6. **A.** This is the definition of a phishing attack, as introduced in the chapter. The key elements of the question are e-mail and the unsolicited nature of its sending (spam).
7. **D.** Social engineers use a wide range of psychological tricks to fool users into trusting them, including faking authority, impersonation, creating a sense of scarcity or urgency, and claiming familiarity.
8. **A.** Because any employee may be the target of a social engineering attack, the best thing you can do to protect your organization from these attacks is to implement an active security awareness program to ensure that all employees are cognizant of the threat and what they can do to address it.
9. **B.** This is a likely impersonation attack, using the cover of the janitor. Because of the unusual circumstances, it would be wise to report to a manager for investigation.
10. **B.** This is spear phishing, which is a targeted phishing attack against a specific person.

CHAPTER 2

Type of Attack Indicators

In this chapter, you will

- Compare and contrast different types of attacks
- Learn to analyze potential indicators to determine the type of attack

Attacks can be made against virtually any layer or level of software, from network protocols to applications. When an attacker finds a vulnerability in a system, they exploit the weakness to attack the system. The effect of an attack depends on the attacker's intent and can result in a wide range of effects, from minor to severe. An attack on a system might not be visible on that system because the attack is actually occurring on a different system, and the data the attacker will manipulate on the second system is obtained by attacking the first system. Attacks can be against the user, as in social engineering, or against the application, the network, or the cryptographic elements being employed in a system. This chapter compares and contrasts these types of attacks.

Although hacking and viruses receive the most attention in the news, they are not the only methods used to attack computer systems and networks. This chapter addresses many different ways computers and networks are attacked on a daily basis. Each type of attack threatens at least one of the three security requirements: confidentiality, integrity, and availability (the CIA of security).

From a high-level standpoint, attacks on computer systems and networks can be grouped into two broad categories: attacks on specific software (such as an application or the operating system) and attacks on a specific protocol or service. Attacks on a specific application or operating system are generally possible because of an oversight in the code (and possibly in the testing of that code) or because of a flaw, or bug, in the code (again indicating a lack of thorough testing). Attacks on specific protocols or services are attempts either to take advantage of a specific feature of the protocol or service or to use it in a manner for which it was not intended. This chapter discusses various forms of attacks of which security professionals need to be aware.

Certification Objective This chapter covers CompTIA Security+ exam objective 1.2: Given a scenario, analyze potential indicators to determine the type of attack.

Malware

Malware refers to software that has been designed for some nefarious purpose. Such software can be designed to cause damage to a system, such as by deleting all files, or it can be designed to create a backdoor into the system to grant access to unauthorized individuals. Generally the installation of malware is done so that it is not obvious to the authorized users. Several different types of malicious software can be used, such as viruses, trojan horses, logic bombs, spyware, and worms, and they differ in the ways they are installed and their purposes.

Ransomware

Ransomware is a form of malware that performs some action and extracts a ransom from the user. Ransomware typically encrypts files on a system and then leaves them unusable either permanently, acting as a denial of service, or temporarily until a ransom is paid, thus the name. Ransomware is typically a worm, completely automated, and when targeted as a means of denial of service, the only repair mechanism is to rebuild the system. This can be time consuming and/or impractical in some cases, making this attack mechanism equivalent to the physical destruction of assets.

A current ransomware threat, first appearing in 2013, is CryptoLocker. CryptoLocker is a trojan horse that encrypts certain files using RSA public key encryption. When the user attempts to get these files, they are provided with a message instructing them how to purchase the decryption key. Because the system is using 2048-bit RSA encryption, brute force decryption is out of the realm of recovery options. The system is highly automated, and users have a short time window in which to get the private key. Failure to get the key will result in the loss of the data. In 2017, a ransomware worm called NotPetya spread across the globe, hitting only a few firms, but where it hit, it destroyed everything. The reason was, although it looked like and operated like ransomware, there was no decryption key. Earlier in 2017, a strain of ransomware called WannaCry hit many companies, including the UK National Health Service (NHS). This ransomware created havoc by exploiting the EternalBlue vulnerability in Microsoft Windows systems that was exposed by the group known as Shadow Brokers. WannaCry was stopped by a hacker turned white hat, Marcus Hutchins, who found a vulnerability in the WannaCry worm and was able to disable it globally.

EXAM TIP Ransomware is a form of malware that locks the user out of their files or even the entire device until an online ransom payment is made to restore access.

Trojans

A trojan horse, or simply *trojan,* is a piece of software that appears to do one thing (and may, in fact, actually do that thing) but hides some other functionality. The analogy to the famous story of antiquity is very accurate. In the original case, the object appeared to be a large wooden horse, and in fact it was. At the same time, it hid something much more sinister and dangerous to the occupants of the city of Troy. As long as the horse was left outside the city walls, it could cause no damage to the inhabitants. However, it had to be taken in by the inhabitants of Troy, and it was inside that the hidden purpose was activated. A computer trojan works in much the same way. Unlike a virus, which reproduces by attaching itself to other files or programs, a trojan is a standalone program that must be copied and installed by the user—it must be "brought inside" the system by an authorized user. The challenge for the attacker is enticing the user to copy and run the program. This generally means that the program must be disguised as something that the user would want to run—a special utility or game, for example. Once it has been copied and is inside the system, the trojan will perform its hidden purpose with the user often still unaware of its true nature.

A good example of a trojan is Back Orifice (BO), originally created in 1999 and now offered in several versions. BO can be attached to a number of types of programs. Once it is attached, and once an infected file is run, BO will create a way for unauthorized individuals to take over the system remotely, as if they were sitting at the console. BO is designed to work with Windows-based systems. Many trojans communicate to the outside through a port that the trojan opens, and this is one of the ways trojans can be detected.

EXAM TIP Ensure you understand the differences between viruses, worms, trojans, and various other types of threats for the exam.

Worms

It was once easy to distinguish between a worm and a virus. Recently, with the introduction of new breeds of sophisticated malicious code, the distinction has blurred. *Worms* are pieces of code that attempt to penetrate networks and computer systems. Once a penetration occurs, the worm will create a new copy of itself on the penetrated system. Reproduction of a worm thus does not rely on the attachment of the virus to another piece of code or to a file, which is the definition of a virus.

Viruses were generally thought of as a system-based problem, and worms were network-based. If the malicious code is sent throughout a network, it may subsequently be called a worm. The important distinction, however, is whether the code has to attach itself to something else (a virus) or if it can "survive" on its own (a worm).

Some examples of worms that have had high profiles include the Sobig worm of 2003, the SQL Slammer worm of 2003, the 2001 attacks of Code Red and Nimda, and the 2005 Zotob worm that took down CNN Live. Nimda was particularly impressive in that it used five different methods to spread: via e-mail, via open network shares, from browsing infected websites, using the directory traversal vulnerability of Microsoft IIS 4.0/5.0, and most impressively through the use of backdoors left by Code Red II and sadmind worms. Recently, worms have become a tool of choice for ransomware attacks, as they can spread from system to system without operator intervention. The NotPetya worm of 2017 caused an estimated $10 billion in damage.

EXAM TIP Worms act like a virus but also have the ability to travel without human action. They do not need help to spread.

Potentially Unwanted Programs

Potentially unwanted program (PUP) is a designation used by security companies and antivirus vendors to identify programs that may have adverse effects on a computer's security or privacy. Frequently these involve adware or spyware components and are used for revenue generation purposes.

NOTE Potentially unwanted programs are a form of malware. The name is one the industry chose because the makers of PUPs claim you read and agreed to their terms as part of a download agreement. It is easy to miss these details when installing programs, and then you have unwanted apps. PUPs can exhibit some very undesired characteristics, such as the following:

- Slowing down your computer
- Displaying a ton of annoying ads
- Adding toolbars that steal space on the browser
- Collecting private information

A common source of PUPs is third-party download sites for downloading apps—even legitimate apps can be bundled by third-party distributers. The use of an anti-malware solution should catch and enable PUPs to be stopped before installation.

Fileless Viruses

Most antivirus/anti-malware solutions find malware through monitoring the filesystem for writes and then filter the writes for known signatures. When a piece of malware operates only in memory, never touching the filesystem, it is much harder to detect. This type of attack is called a *fileless virus,* or memory-based attack.

EXAM TIP Remember that unlike a traditional virus, which attaches itself to a file, a fileless virus lives in memory and will continue to run until the device is powered down.

Command and Control

Command-and-control servers are used by hackers to control malware that has been launched against targets. Malware infections are seldom a single file on a single machine when an attack occurs in an enterprise. Multiple malware elements, on multiple systems, under various IDs, all working to provide a means for hackers to re-enter a system, are commonly found in enterprises. These malware elements also work to exfiltrate stolen data.

Bots

A *bot* is a functioning piece of software that performs some task, under the control of another program. A series of bots is controlled across the network in a group, and the entire assembly is called a *botnet* (combining the terms *bot* and *network*). Some botnets are legal and perform desired actions in a distributed fashion. Illegal botnets work in the same fashion, with bots distributed and controlled from a central set of command-and-control servers. Bots can do a wide array of things—from proliferating spam to committing fraud, installing spyware, and more.

Botnets continue to advance malware threats. Some of the latest botnets are designed to mine bitcoins, using distributed processing power for gain. One of the more famous botnets is Zeus, a botnet that performs keystroke logging and is used primarily for the purpose of stealing banking information. Zeus has been linked to the delivery of CryptoLocker ransomware. Another famous botnet is Conficker, which has infected millions of machines worldwide. The Conficker botnet is one of the most studied pieces of malware, with a joint industry–government working group convened to battle it.

Crypto-malware

The first thought when one sees the term *crypto-malware* is to think of ransomware. But that would be wrong. Crypto-malware is the name the security industry has given to malware that uses a system's resources to mine cryptocurrency. This is really just a theft-of-services attack where an attacker is using the CPU cycles of someone else's computer to do the crypto mining.

Logic Bombs

Logic bombs, unlike viruses and trojans, are a type of malicious software that is deliberately installed, generally by an authorized user. A *logic bomb* is a piece of code that sits dormant for a period of time until some event or date invokes its malicious payload. An example of a logic bomb might be a program that is set to load and run automatically, and that periodically checks an organization's payroll or personnel database for a specific employee. If the employee is not found, the malicious payload executes, deleting vital corporate files.

If the event is a specific date or time, the program will often be referred to as a *time bomb*. In one famous example, a disgruntled employee left a time bomb in place just prior to being fired from his job. Two weeks later, thousands of client records were deleted. Police were eventually able to track the malicious code to the disgruntled ex-employee, who was prosecuted for his actions. He had hoped that the two weeks that had passed since his dismissal would have caused investigators to assume he could not have been the individual who had caused the deletion of the records.

Logic bombs are difficult to detect because they are often installed by authorized users and, in particular, have been installed by administrators who are also often responsible for security. This demonstrates the need for a separation of duties and a periodic review of all programs and services that are running on a system. It also illustrates the need to maintain an active backup program so that if your organization loses critical files to this sort of malicious code, it loses only transactions that occurred since the most recent backup, resulting in no permanent loss of data.

Spyware

Spyware is software that "spies" on users, recording and reporting on their activities. Typically installed without the user's knowledge, spyware can perform a wide range of activities. It can record keystrokes (commonly called *keylogging*) when the user logs on to specific websites. It can monitor how a user applies a specific piece of software, such as to monitor attempts to cheat at games. Many uses of spyware seem innocuous at first, but the unauthorized monitoring of a system can be abused very easily. In other cases, the spyware is specifically designed to steal information. Many states have passed legislation banning the unapproved installation of software, but spyware can circumvent this issue through complex and confusing end-user license agreements.

Keyloggers

As the name suggests, a *keylogger* is a piece of software that logs all of the keystrokes that a user enters. Keyloggers in their own respect are not necessarily evil, for you could consider Microsoft Word to be a keylogger. What makes a keylogger a malicious piece of software is when its operation is (1) unknown to the user, and (2) not under the user's control. Keyloggers have been marketed for a variety of uses—from surveillance over your children's activity, or the activity of a spouse, to maintaining records of what has been done on a machine. Malicious keyloggers have several specific characteristics: they are frequently hidden from the user's view, even when looking at Task Manager, and they are used against the end user's interests. Hackers use keyloggers to obtain passwords and other sensitive pieces of information, enabling them to use these secrets to act as the user without the user's consent. Keylogger functionality has even been found in legitimate programs, where keystrokes are recorded for "legitimate" purposes and then are stored in a fashion that enables unauthorized users to steal the data.

Remote-Access Trojans (RATs)

A *remote-access trojan (RAT)* is a toolkit designed to provide the capability of covert surveillance and/or the capability to gain unauthorized access to a target system. RATs often mimic the behavior of keyloggers and packet sniffers using the automated collection of keystrokes, usernames, passwords, screenshots, browser history, e-mails, chat logs, and more, but they also do so with a design of intelligence. RATs can also employ malware to infect a system with code that can be used to facilitate the exploitation of a target. Rather than just collect the information, RATs present it to an attacker in a form to facilitate the capability to gain unauthorized access to the target machine. This frequently involves the use of specially configured communication protocols that are set up upon initial infection of the target computer. This backdoor into the target machine can allow an attacker unfettered access, including the ability to monitor user behavior, change computer settings, browse and copy files, access connected systems, and more. RATs are commonly employed by the more skilled threat actors, although there are RATs that are easy enough for even beginners to employ.

A RAT should be considered another form of malware, but rather than just being a program, it has an operator behind it, guiding it to do even more persistent damage. RATs can be delivered via phishing e-mails, watering holes, or any of a myriad of other malware infection vectors. RATs typically involve the creation of hidden file structures on a system and are vulnerable to detection by modern anti-malware programs. There are several major families of RATs, but an exhaustive list would be long and ever increasing. When facing a more skilled adversary, it is not uncommon to find RAT packages that have been modified for specific use, such as the program used in the Ukraine electric grid attack in 2015.

Rootkit

Rootkits are a form of malware that is specifically designed to modify the operation of the operating system in some fashion to facilitate nonstandard functionality. The history of rootkits goes back to the beginning of the UNIX operating system, where rootkits were sets of modified administrative tools. Originally designed to allow a program to take greater control over an operating system's functions when it fails or becomes unresponsive, the technique has evolved and is used in a variety of ways. One high-profile case occurred at Sony BMG Corporation, when rootkit technology was used to provide copy protection technology on some of the company's CDs. Two major issues led to this being a complete debacle for Sony: First, the software modified systems without the users' approval. Second, the software opened a security hole on Windows-based systems, creating an exploitable vulnerability at the rootkit level. This led the Sony case to be labeled as *malware,* which is the most common use of rootkits.

A rootkit can do many things—in fact, it can do virtually anything that the operating system does. Rootkits modify the operating system kernel and supporting functions, changing the nature of the system's operation. Rootkits are designed to avoid, either by subversion or evasion, the security functions of the operating system to avoid detection. Rootkits act as a form of malware that can change thread priorities to boost an application's performance, perform keylogging, act as a sniffer, hide other files from other applications, or create backdoors in the authentication system. The use of rootkit functionality to hide other processes and files enables an attacker to use a portion of a computer without the user or other applications knowing what is happening. This hides exploit code from antivirus and anti-spyware programs, acting as a cloak of invisibility.

Rootkits can load before the operating system loads, acting as a virtualization layer, as in SubVirt and Blue Pill. Rootkits can exist in firmware, and these have been demonstrated in both video cards and expansion cards. Rootkits can exist as loadable library modules, effectively changing portions of the operating system outside the kernel. Further information on specific rootkits in the wild can be found at www.antirootkit.com.

EXAM TIP Five types of rootkits exist: firmware, virtual, kernel, library, and application level.

Once a rootkit is detected, it needs to be removed and cleaned up. Because of rootkits' invasive nature, and the fact that many aspects of rootkits are not easily detectable, most system administrators don't even attempt to clean up or remove a rootkit. It is far easier to use a previously captured clean system image and reimage the machine than to attempt to determine the depth and breadth of the damage and attempt to fix individual files.

Backdoors

Backdoors were originally (and sometimes still are) nothing more than methods used by software developers to ensure that they can gain access to an application, even if something were to happen in the future to prevent normal access methods. An example would be a hard-coded password that could be used to gain access to the program in the event that administrators forgot their own system password. The obvious problem with this sort of backdoor (also sometimes referred to as a *trapdoor*) is that, since it is hard-coded, it cannot be removed. Should an attacker learn of the backdoor, all systems running that software would be vulnerable to attack.

The term *backdoor* is also, and more commonly, used to refer to programs that attackers install after gaining unauthorized access to a system to ensure that they can continue to have unrestricted access to the system, even if their initial access method is discovered and blocked. Backdoors can also be installed by authorized individuals inadvertently if they run software that contains a trojan horse (introduced earlier). Common backdoors include NetBus and Back Orifice. Both of these, if running on your system, can allow an attacker remote access to your system—access that allows them to perform any function on your system. A variation on the backdoor is the rootkit, discussed in a previous section, which is established not to gain root access but rather to ensure continued root access.

EXAM TIP The Security+ exam objectives include analyzing potential indicators to determine the type of attack, including keyloggers, spyware, bots, RATs, logic bombs, backdoors, and more. To prepare for the exam, you should understand the differences between the many malware attacks discussed in this chapter.

Password Attacks

The most common form of authentication is the user ID and password combination. While it is not inherently a poor mechanism for authentication, the combination can be attacked in several ways. All too often, these attacks yield favorable results for the attacker, not as a result of a weakness in the scheme, but usually due to the user not following good password procedures.

Spraying

Password *spraying* is an attack that uses a limited number of commonly used passwords and applies them to a large number of accounts. Traditional brute-force attacks attempt to gain unauthorized access to a single account by guessing the password. Spraying is the reverse of this, using a limited number of passwords and trying them against all the accounts. This is a useful attack when you don't care which account you get and is fairly successful when given a large set of accounts. Defending against this is important in organizations, because if one account is breached, it is the foothold needed to gain entry.

Dictionary

Another method of determining passwords is to use a password-cracking program that uses a list of dictionary words to try to guess the password, hence the name *dictionary* attack. The words can be used by themselves, or two or more smaller words can be combined to form a single possible password. A number of commercial and public-domain password-cracking programs employ a variety of methods to crack passwords, including using variations on the user ID.

These programs often permit the attacker to create various rules that tell the program how to combine words to form new possible passwords. Users commonly substitute certain numbers for specific letters. If the user wants to use the word *secret* for a password, for example, the letter *e* could be replaced with the number *3*, yielding *s3cr3t*. This password will not be found in the dictionary, so a pure dictionary attack would not crack it, but the password is still easy for the user to remember. If a rule were created that tried all words in the dictionary and then tried the same words substituting the number *3* for the letter *e*, however, the password would be cracked.

Rules can also be defined so that the password-cracking program will substitute special characters for other characters or combine words. The ability of the attacker to crack passwords is directly related to the method the user employs to create the password in the first place, as well as the dictionary and rules used.

A dictionary attack involves the use of a lookup table to try and find an answer. With that in mind, repeated use of passwords, coupled with data breaches, provides a set of passwords to try. This is why unique passwords for security-sensitive sites are so important, because a data breach at one firm could cost you all of your accounts, because the attacker's job becomes as simple as looking them up.

Brute Force

If the user has selected a password that is not found in a dictionary, even if various numbers or special characters are substituted for letters, the only way the password can be cracked is for an attacker to attempt a *brute force* attack, in which the password-cracking program attempts all possible password combinations.

The length of the password and the size of the set of possible characters in the password will greatly affect the time a brute force attack will take. A few years ago, this method of attack was very time consuming, since it took considerable time to generate all possible combinations. With the increase in computer speed, however, generating password combinations is much faster, making it more feasible to launch brute force attacks against certain computer systems and networks.

A brute force attack on a password can take place at two levels: it can attack a system, where the attacker is attempting to guess the password at a login prompt, or it can attack the list of password hashes contained in a password file. The first attack can be made more difficult if the account locks after a few failed login attempts. The second attack can be thwarted if the password file is securely maintained so that others cannot obtain a copy of it.

Offline

Offline, brute force attacks can be employed to perform hash comparisons against a stolen password file. This has the challenge of stealing the password file, but if accomplished, it is possible to use high-performance GPU-based parallel machines to try passwords at very high rates and against multiple accounts at the same time.

Online

When the brute force attack occurs in real time against a system, it is frequently being done to attack a single account with multiple examples of passwords. Success or failure is determined by the system under attack, and the attacker either gets in or doesn't. *Online* brute force attacks tend to be very noisy and easy to see by network security monitoring, and they are also limited by system response time and bandwidth.

Rainbow Tables

Rainbow tables are precomputed tables or hash values associated with passwords. Using rainbow tables can change the search for a password from a computational problem to a lookup problem. This can tremendously reduce the level of work needed to crack a given password. The best defense against rainbow tables is *salted hashes*, as the addition of a salt value increases the complexity of the problem by making the precomputing process not replicable between systems. A *salt* is merely a random set of characters designed to increase the length of the item being hashed, effectively making rainbow tables too big to compute.

EXAM TIP A *salt* is a random set of characters designed to increase the length of the item being hashed. It is an effective defense against rainbow table attacks.

Plaintext/Unencrypted

Passwords that are stored are subject to retrieval. Any time a system can send you a copy of your password, there is a security issue. Plaintext password attacks are those taken against these specific issues. Lest anyone think that this is only a problem from rogue systems or programs, even mainstream systems can fall prey to this trap. Microsoft allows administrators to push out passwords for local accounts via group policy preferences. To protect the passwords, they are encrypted using Advanced Encryption Standard (AES). For reasons of compatibility with other systems, Microsoft published the AES key—see the problem.

In Microsoft Windows systems, Mimikatz is a security tool that can extract Kerberos tickets from memory, and it also possesses the ability to extract plaintext passwords from process dumps of the LSASS process. This means that by using the security tools ProcDump and Mimikatz, one can harvest plaintext passwords from a system.

EXAM TIP Be sure you are familiar with the various attacks, including spraying, dictionary, brute force, rainbow tables, and plaintext/unencrypted. Understand how they are different and how to recognize each attack.

Physical Attacks

Most of the attacks listed in the chapter to this point are logical attacks in that they are attacking the system from a computer logic perspective. Chapter 1, "Social Engineering Techniques," dealt with social engineering attacks—attacks designed to get users to perform actions that lead into a vulnerability being exposed. Another class of attacks, physical attacks, occur when a physical element such as a flash drive is left for someone to use. The act of using these "normal" physical devices initiates an attack sequence.

Malicious Universal Serial Bus (USB) Cable

Most users view a USB cable as just a wire, but in fact a USB cable can have embedded electronics in it. "Poisoned" cables have been found with electronics that can deliver malware to machines. This has been found in both normal USB cables and in lightning cables for Apple devices. Demo cables have even been made with embedded Wi-Fi devices, enabling attacks against a Wi-Fi network from the cable itself.

Malicious Flash Drives

Malicious USB storage devices have been around for a long time. They have been used to dupe users into picking them up, plugging them into their machine, and accessing an attractive folder such as "HR data" or "Sensitive pictures." Clicking these folders is the mistake because they deliver to the machine. USB dropping is a well-known means of attack, where the attacker leaves tainted USB devices for people to pick up and use. And once they plug them into the network, the attack is automated. A recent study done on a college campus showed 98 percent of the dropped devices were picked up, and over 45 percent were later used and phoned home their data.

For user convenience, operating systems adopted an Auto Run or Auto Play feature on USB devices, enabling content to run when the device was plugged in. As this is an obvious security issue, the ability to automatically execute the autorun.inf file on a USB was disabled post–Windows XP. You can re-enable this setting in Windows 10, through Settings | Devices | AutoPlay, although this is not recommended. In enterprises, this setting can be controlled via group policies that restrict users from changing it.

Card Cloning

Should someone get physical possession of your credit card, it is possible to copy the information on the magnetic strip, enabling the person to later make a clone of your card. Smart cards made this more difficult, as the chip itself cannot be cloned. But in the case of a credit card having a damaged chip, many systems resort back to the magnetic strip information, making the cloning attack still a potentially effective scam.

Another type of card that can be cloned is the contactless ID card. These cards are used by transit systems, access systems, and even passports. The NFC (near field communications) chip can be read, information copied, and a clone implemented. Rather than implementing the device on an actual card, the current systems use a small electronic device to replicate the functionality. When data is stored on the card, as has been done in many transit systems, cloning a card can be like collecting the unused fares. These attacks have been shown to be effective in several major cities against several different card systems.

Skimming

Skimming devices are physical devices built to intercept a credit card. These devices are placed on credit card readers to skim the data from the card while passing it on to the legitimate reader. Skimmers can collect all the information from a magnetic strip on the card as well as the PIN being entered, enabling a clone to be manufactured. Although smart card–based credit cards are difficult if not impossible to clone, in the US, blocking the smart card features will trip most systems to a downgraded method of just using the magnetic strip data, thus bypassing the security features associated with the smart chip part of the card.

NOTE Credit card skimmers can be found at gas stations and convenience stores. The overlay, shown here, can be discovered by handling the machine in a manner to dislodge it. For example, minor tugging on the physical interface will typically reveal the skimmer.

Adversarial Artificial Intelligence (AI)

Artificial intelligence (AI) is the use of complex models to simulate functions of the brain—in essence, a means to impart analytical abilities to the things we use, from robot vacuum cleaners to smartphone apps, to digital assistants. AI brings power to computer solutions because AI models can analyze more combinations of inputs than a human, and do so faster and with more accuracy. AI-enabled systems are used in anti-malware products to find new threats based on analytical analysis of programmatic behaviors. Can AI also be used to evade defenses? The answer is yes, and this is known as *adversarial AI*. Just as defenders can write AI-enabled tools, attackers can use AI to enable their attacks, such as phishing, to avoid machine detection.

Tainted Training Data for Machine Learning (ML)

Machine learning (ML) is one of the techniques used in AI. ML works by using a training data set to calibrate the detection model to enable detection on sample data. One of the weaknesses of ML is this training set dependency. The ability of the model to detect is a function of the efficacy of the training data set. A good training data set can build a solid detection model. A deficient training set of data can build a model with holes in it—holes that allow conditions to go undetected. Tainting the training data is one of the attack vectors that attackers can use against ML systems. Over time, as conditions change, an ML algorithm needs retraining or updating to make it effective against differing inputs. Each of these updates represents an opportunity to taint the input data set. Also, if you train the algorithm against normal network traffic, marking it as good when in fact there is an adversary already in that training data set, you effectively blind the algorithm to the attack by having already labeled it as good.

Security of Machine Learning Algorithms

Understanding the details of a machine learning algorithm once it is trained is crucial to the security of the algorithm. Should an attacker be able to reproduce the exact same set of parameters, they would be able to create attack data sets that could slip past the ML algorithm. Maintaining security around the parameters of an ML algorithm is essential to maintaining its effectiveness.

Supply-Chain Attacks

Everything has a supply chain. Supply chains are the network of suppliers that provide the materials for something to be built. In the case of a computer, the supply chain provides the parts. In the case of a program, the programmers are one part, but the libraries they use are another. The parts that are used—be they physical like a hard drive or logical like a library module—can be tainted, either by accident or on purpose. However, the result is the same: the final product can have vulnerabilities. Knowing this, attackers have learned to attack supply chains and let the normal build process instantiate the attack vector. Manufacturers have shipped PCs with preinstalled malware, courtesy of a hard drive manufacturer, which itself became infected by one of its vendors. The Target data breach case was initiated by an attack on a heating, ventilation, and air conditioning (HVAC) company that was a supplier to Target, and when they connected to Target's network, the final objectives were achieved. This means that the true attack surface is not just within your firm or your product, but ultimately a function of everyone and everything in your supply chain.

Cloud-Based vs. On-Premises Attacks

Attacks against data can happen whether the system is in house (on-premises) or in the cloud (cloud based). Using cloud computing to improve security only works if you choose a cloud vendor with a security solution as part of the package. While big-name vendors such as Oracle, Microsoft, Google, and Amazon have resources and security knowledge, not all vendors have the same level of protection. Moving computing or storage to the cloud, in itself, does not change the security equation. Cloud computing is merely using someone else's resources, and you get what you pay for, as in all contracts. Whether you are doing security in house against in-house systems or against cloud-based systems, the objectives and methods are the same. You must define the security you desire and the methods of attaining it, and then follow through, either by doing the work or contracting it. Just sticking something into the cloud does nothing to address security.

Cryptographic Attacks

Attacks against the cryptographic system are referred to as *cryptographic attacks*. These attacks are designed to take advantage of two specific weaknesses. First, users widely view cryptography as "magic," or otherwise incomprehensible stuff, leading them to trust the results without valid reasons. Second, although understood by computer scientists, algorithmic weaknesses that can be exploited are frequently overlooked by developers.

Birthday

The *birthday* attack is a special type of brute force attack that gets its name from something known as the birthday paradox, which states that in a group of at least 23 people, the chance that two individuals will have the same birthday is greater than 50 percent. Mathematically, we can use the equation $1.25k^{1/2}$ (with k equaling the size of the set of possible values), and in the birthday paradox, k would be equal to 365 (the number of possible birthdays). This same phenomenon applies to passwords, with k (the number of passwords) being quite a bit larger than 50, but still a manageable number for computers and today's storage capacities.

Collision

A *collision* attack is where two different inputs yield the same output of a hash function. Through the manipulation of data, subtle changes are made that are not visible to the user yet create different versions of a digital file. With the creation of many different versions and the use of the birthday attack to find a collision between any two of the many versions, an attacker has a chance to create a file with changed visible content but identical hashes.

Downgrade

As part of a Transport Layer Security/Secure Sockets Layer (TLS/SSL) setup, a specification of the cipher suite can be employed. This is done to enable the highest form of encryption that both server and browser can support. In a *downgrade* attack, the attacker takes advantage of a commonly employed principle to support backward compatibility, to downgrade the security to a lower or nonexistent state.

EXAM TIP The Security+ exam objective for attacks (1.2) is, "Given a scenario, analyze potential indicators to determine the type of attack." This means that you need to be able to differentiate attacks based on a set of given symptoms and indications. Learning how these attacks are performed, what they look like, and how to recognize specific attacks is essential for the exam.

Chapter Review

This chapter examined the attack methods used by hackers. Seven major categories of attack were covered: malware, password attacks, physical attacks, adversarial artificial intelligence, supply-chain attacks, cloud-based vs. on-premises attacks, and cryptographic attacks. Each of these sections details several specific attacks.

The malware section examined ransomware, trojans, worms, potentially unwanted programs (PUPs), fileless virus attacks, command and control, bots, crypto-malware, logic bombs, spyware, keyloggers, remote-access trojans (RAT), rootkits, and backdoors. The password attack section covered password-spraying attacks, dictionary and brute force attacks, offline and online attacks, rainbow tables, and attacks against plaintext/unencrypted passwords.

The section on physical attacks examined attacks using physical manipulation, including malicious USB cables, malicious USB devices, card cloning, and skimming attacks. The section on the adversarial use of artificial intelligence covered the concept of tainting a machine learning system through contaminating the training data. This section also covered the importance of security for machine learning algorithms and parameters.

The chapter concluded with sections on supply-chain attacks and cloud-based vs. on-premise attacks. The last section covered cryptographic attacks, including birthday attacks, collision attacks, and downgrade attacks. What is important to remember is that this material is designed to assist you in understanding CompTIA Security+ exam objective 1.2: Given a scenario, analyze potential indicators to determine the type of attack. You need to be prepared to differentiate between the types of attacks.

Questions

To help you prepare further for the CompTIA Security+ exam, and to test your level of preparedness, answer the following questions and then check your answers against the correct answers at the end of the chapter.

1. A disgruntled administrator is fired for negligence at your organization. Thirty days later, your organization's internal file server and backup server crash at exactly the same time. Examining the servers, you determine that critical operating system files were deleted from both systems. If the disgruntled administrator was responsible for administering those servers during her employment, this is most likely an example of what kind of malware?
   - **A.** Crypto-malware
   - **B.** Trojan
   - **C.** Worm
   - **D.** Logic bomb

2. A colleague has been urging you to download a new animated screensaver he has been using for several weeks. While he is showing you the program, the cursor on his screen moves on its own and a command prompt window opens and quickly closes. You can't tell what if anything was displayed in that command prompt window. Your colleague says, "It's been doing that for a while, but it's no big deal." Based on what you've seen, you suspect the animated screensaver is really what type of malware?

   A. A worm

   B. A trojan

   C. Ransomware

   D. Spyware

3. Several desktops in your organization are displaying a red screen with the message "Your files have been encrypted. Pay 1 bitcoin to recover them." These desktops have most likely been affected by what type of malware?

   A. Spyware

   B. Spraying

   C. Ransomware

   D. Crypto-malware

4. While port-scanning your network for unauthorized systems, you notice one of your file servers has TCP port 31337 open. When you connect to the port with the security tool netcat, you see a prompt that reads, "Enter password for access:". Your server may be infected with what type of malware?

   A. PUP

   B. Fileless virus

   C. Backdoor

   D. Man in the middle attack

5. While port-scanning your network for unauthorized systems, you notice one of your file servers has TCP port 61337 open. When you use Wireshark and examine the packets, you see encrypted traffic, in single packets, going back and forth every five minutes. The external connection is a server outside of your organization. What is this connection?

   A. Command and control

   B. Backdoor

   C. External backup location

   D. Remote login

6. A user in your organization is having issues with her laptop. Every time she opens a web browser, she sees different pop-up ads every few minutes. It doesn't seem to matter which websites are being visited—the pop-ups still appear. What type of attack does this sound like?

A. A potentially unwanted program (PUP)
B. Ransomware
C. Worm
D. Virus

7. Users at your organization are complaining about slow systems. Examining several of them, you see that CPU utilization is extremely high and a process called "btmine" is running on each of the affected systems. You also notice each of the affected systems is communicating with an IP address outside your country on UDP port 43232. If you disconnect the network connections on the affected systems, the CPU utilization drops significantly. Based on what you've observed, you suspect these systems are infected with what type of malware?
   A. Rainbow tables
   B. Crypto-malware
   C. Dictionary
   D. Hybrid attack

8. A piece of malware is infecting the desktops in your organization. Every hour, more systems are infected. The infections are happening in different departments and in cases where the users don't share any files, programs, or even e-mails. What type of malware can cause this type of infection?
   A. Virus
   B. Trojan
   C. RAT
   D. Worm

9. Which of the following are characteristics of remote-access trojans?
   A. They can be deployed through malware such as worms.
   B. They allow attacks to connect to the system remotely.
   C. They give attackers the ability to modify files and change settings.
   D. All of the above.

10. To test your systems against weak passwords, you as an admin (with proper permissions) test all the accounts using the top 100 commonly used passwords. What is this test an example of?
   A. Dictionary
   B. Password spraying
   C. Rainbow tables
   D. Online

Answers

1. **D.** Because both servers crashed at exactly the same time, this is most likely a logic bomb. A *logic bomb* is a piece of code that sits dormant for a period of time until some event or date invokes its malicious payload—in this case, 30 days after the disgruntled employee was fired.
2. **B.** The animated screensaver is most likely a trojan. The software appears to do one thing, but contains hidden, additional functionality. Your colleague brought the trojan "inside the walls" when he downloaded and installed the software on his desktop.
3. **C.** This is quite clearly ransomware. The malware has encrypted files on the affected systems and is demanding payment for recovery of the files.
4. **C.** This prompt most likely belongs to a backdoor—an alternate way of accessing the system. The TCP service is listening for incoming connections and prompts for a password when connections are established. Providing the correct password would grant command-line access to the system.
5. **A.** Periodic traffic that looks like a heartbeat on high ports to an unknown server outside the network is suspicious, and this is what many command-and-control signals look like.
6. **A.** This behavior is often seen in a potentially unwanted program—a type of application that has been bundled with others and is performing tasks that are undesired.
7. **B.** These systems are most likely infected with crypto-malware and are now part of a botnet that's mining cryptocurrency. The systems are running an unknown/unauthorized process, communicating with an external IP address, and using significant resources. These are all classic signs of crypto-malware.
8. **D.** This is most likely a worm attack. Attacks that move across the network, seemingly without user intervention, are commonly worms.
9. **D.** All of these are characteristics of remote-access trojans (RATs). RATs are often deployed through other malware, allow remote access to the affected system, and give the attacker the ability to manipulate and modify the affected system.
10. **B.** Using preset passwords against all accounts is an example of password spraying.

CHAPTER 3

Application Attack Indicators

In this chapter, you will

- Explore various attack patterns
- Connect attack indicators to a specific form of attack

This chapter examines the types of attacks and their attributes, with the objective of demonstrating how one can connect the dots between a series of potential attack indicators and a specific type of application attack.

Certification Objective This chapter covers CompTIA Security+ exam objective 1.3: Given a scenario, analyze potential indicators associated with application attacks.

Privilege Escalation

A cyberattack is a multistep process. Most attacks begin at a privilege level associated with an ordinary user. From this level, the attacker exploits vulnerabilities that enable them to achieve root- or admin-level access. This step in the attack chain is called *privilege escalation* and is essential for many attack efforts.

There are a couple of ways to achieve privilege escalation. One way is to use existing privileges to perform an action that steals a better set of credentials. You can obtain "better" credentials by using sniffers to grab credentials or by getting the Windows Security Account Manager (SAM) or the Linux/Unix etc/passwd file. Another method is by exploiting vulnerabilities or weaknesses in processes that are running with escalated privileges. Injecting malicious code into these processes can also achieve escalated privilege.

EXAM TIP Blocking privilege escalation is an important defensive step in a system. This is the rationale behind Microsoft's recent reduction in processes and services that run in elevated mode. This greatly reduces the attack surface available to an attacker to perform this essential task.

Cross-Site Scripting

Cross-site scripting (XSS) is one of the most common web attack methodologies. The cause of the vulnerability is weak user input validation. If input is not validated properly, an attacker can include a script in their input and have it rendered as part of the web process. There are several different types of XSS attacks, which are distinguished by the effect of the script:

- **Non-persistent XSS attack** The injected script is not persisted or stored but rather is immediately executed and passed back via the web server.
- **Persistent XSS attack** The script is permanently stored on the web server or some back-end storage. This allows the script to be used against others who log in to the system.
- **DOM-based XSS attack** The script is executed in the browser via the Document Object Model (DOM) process as opposed to the web server.

Cross-site scripting attacks can result in a wide range of consequences, and in some cases, the list can be anything that a clever scripter can devise. Here are some common uses that have been seen in the wild:

- Theft of authentication information from a web application
- Session hijacking
- Deploying hostile content
- Changing user settings, including future users
- Impersonating a user
- Phishing or stealing sensitive information

Controls to defend against XSS attacks include the use of anti-XSS libraries to strip scripts from the input sequences. Various other ways to mitigate XSS attacks include limiting the types of uploads, screening the size of uploads, and whitelisting inputs. However, attempting to remove scripts from inputs can be a tricky task. Well-designed anti-XSS input library functions have proven to be the best defense. Cross-site scripting vulnerabilities are easily tested for and should be a part of the test plan for every application. Testing a variety of encoded and unencoded inputs for scripting vulnerability is an essential test element.

EXAM TIP Input validation is helpful at preventing XSS attacks.

NOTE Input validation, also commonly known as *data validation*, is the structured and proper testing of any input that is supplied by an application or user. Input validation prevents improperly formed (malformed) data from entering a system.

Injection Attacks

User input without input validation results in an opportunity for an attacker to craft input to create specific events that occur when the input is parsed and used by an application. Structured Query Language (SQL) injection attacks involve the manipulation of input, resulting in a SQL statement that is different from the statement the designer intended. Extensible Markup Language (XML) injection attacks and Lightweight Directory Access Protocol (LDAP) injection attacks are performed in the same fashion. Because SQL, XML, and LDAP are used to store data, this can give an attacker access to data against business rules. Command injection attacks can occur when input is used in a fashion that allows command-line manipulation. This can give an attacker command-line access at the privilege level of the application.

Structured Query Language (SQL)

A SQL injection attack is a form of code injection aimed at any SQL-based database, regardless of vendor. An example of this type of attack is where the function takes the user-provided inputs for username and password and substitutes them in a **where** clause of a SQL statement with the express purpose of changing the **where** clause into one that gives a false answer to the query.

For example, assume the desired SQL statement is as follows:

```
select count(*) from users_table where username = 'JDoe' and
password = 'newpass'
```

The values JDoe and newpass are provided by the user and are simply inserted into the string sequence. Though seemingly safe functionally, this can be easily corrupted by using the sequence

```
' or 1=1 –
```

which changes the **where** clause to one that returns all records, as shown here:

```
select count(*) from users_table where username = 'JDoe' and
password = '' or 1=1 –'
```

The addition of the **or** clause, with an always true statement and the beginning of a comment line to block the trailing single quote, alters the SQL statement to one in which the **where** clause is rendered inoperable. If the **where** clause is altered to return all records, this can result in a data breach.

Stored procedures are precompiled methods implemented within a database engine. Stored procedures act as a secure coding mechanism because they isolate user input from the actual SQL statements being executed. This is the primary defense mechanism against SQL injection attacks—in other words, separation of user input from the SQL statements. User-supplied input data is essential in interactive applications that use databases; these types of applications allow the user to define the specificity of search, match, and so on. But what cannot happen is to allow a user to write the actual SQL code that is executed—too many things could go wrong, and it provides the user with too much power to be allowed wield it directly. Therefore, eliminating SQL injection attacks by "fixing" input has never worked.

All major database engines support stored procedures. Stored procedures have a performance advantage over other forms of data access. The downside is that stored procedures are written in another language, SQL, and typically need a database programmer to implement the more complex ones.

> **Testing for SQL Injection Vulnerability**
> Two main steps are associated with testing for SQL injection vulnerability. The first step is to confirm that the system is at all vulnerable. This can be done using various inputs to test whether an input variable can be used to manipulate the SQL command. The following are common test vectors used:
>
> ‘ or 1=1—
> “ or 1=1—
> or 1=1—
> ‘ or ‘a’=’a
> “ or “a”=”a
> ‘) or (‘a’=’a
>
> Note that the use of single or double quotes is SQL implementation dependent because there are syntactic differences between the major database engines.
> The second step is to use the error message information to attempt to perform an actual exploit against the database.

EXAM TIP Stored procedures are the gold standard for preventing SQL injection attacks and are specifically mentioned in the Security+ objectives.

Dynamic-Link Library (DLL)

A *dynamic-link library (DLL)* is a piece of code that can add functionality to a program through the inclusion of library routines linked at runtime. *DLL injection* is the process of adding to a program, at runtime, a DLL that has a specific function vulnerability that can be capitalized upon by the attacker. A good example of this is Microsoft Office, a suite of programs that use DLLs loaded at runtime. Adding an “evil” DLL in the correct directory, or via a registry key, can result in additional functionality being incurred.

Lightweight Directory Access Protocol (LDAP)

LDAP-based systems are also subject to injection attacks. When an application constructs an LDAP request based on user input, a failure to validate the input can lead to a bad LDAP request. Just as SQL injection can be used to execute arbitrary commands in a database, LDAP injection can do the same in a directory system. Something as simple as a wildcard character (*) in a search box can return results that would normally be beyond the scope of a query. Proper input validation is important before a request is passed to an LDAP engine.

Extensible Markup Language (XML)

XML can be tampered with via injection as well. XML injections can be used to manipulate an XML-based system. Because XML is nearly ubiquitous in the web application world, this form of attack has a wide range of targets. XML that is maliciously altered can affect changes in configurations, changes in data streams, changes in outputs—all from the injection.

EXAM TIP For the exam, you should understand injection-type attacks and how they manipulate the systems they are injecting, including SQL, DLL, LDAP, and XML.

Pointer/Object Dereference

Some computer languages use a construct referred to as a *pointer,* a construct that refers to the memory location that holds the variable, as opposed to a variable, where the value is stored directly in the memory location. To get the value at the memory location denoted by a pointer variable, one must dereference the pointer. The act of dereferencing a pointer now changes the meaning of the object to the contents of the memory location, not the memory location as identified by the pointer. Pointers can be very powerful and allow fast operations across a wide range of structures. However, they can also be dangerous, as mistakes in their use can lead to unexpected consequences. When a programmer uses user input in concert with pointers, for example, this lets the user pick a place in an array and use a pointer to reference the value. Mistakes in the input validation can lead to errors in the pointer dereference, which may or may not trigger an error, as the location will contain data and it will be returned. Because the pointer is connected to an object, CompTIA Security+ refers to this topic as *pointer/object dereference,* as dereferencing the pointer causes a dereference to the object.

Directory Traversal

A *directory traversal* attack is when an attacker uses special inputs to circumvent the directory tree structure of the filesystem. Adding encoded symbols for "../.." in an unvalidated input box can result in the parser resolving the encoding to the traversal code, bypassing many detection elements, and passing the input to the filesystem. The program then executes the commands in a different location than designed. When combined with a command injection, the input can result in the execution of code in an unauthorized manner. Classified as input validation errors, these can be difficult to detect without doing code walkthroughs and specifically looking for them. This illustrates the usefulness of the CWE Top 25 Most Dangerous Software Errors checklist during code reviews because it alerts developers to this issue during development.

Directory traversals can be masked by using the encoding of input streams. If the security check is done before the string is decoded by the system parser, then recognition of the attack form may be impaired. There are many ways to represent a particular input form, the simplest of which is the canonical form (see Chapter 11 for an example: "A Rose Is a Rose Is a r%6fse"). Parsers are used to render the canonical form for the operating system (OS), but these embedded parsers may act after input validation, making it more difficult to detect certain attacks from just matching a string.

Buffer Overflow

If there's one item that could be labeled as the "most wanted" in coding security, it would be the *buffer overflow*. The CERT/CC at Carnegie Mellon University estimates that nearly half of all exploits of computer programs stem historically from some form of buffer overflow. Finding a vaccine to buffer overflows would stamp out half of these security-related incidents by type, and probably 90 percent by volume. The Morris finger worm in 1988 was an exploit of an overflow, as were more recent big-name events such as Code Red and Slammer. The generic classification of buffer overflows includes many variants, such as static buffer overruns, indexing errors, format string bugs, Unicode and ANSI buffer size mismatches, and heap overruns.

The concept behind these vulnerabilities is relatively simple. The input buffer that is used to hold program input is overwritten with data that is larger than the buffer can hold. The root cause of this vulnerability is a mixture of two things: poor programming practice and programming language weaknesses. For example, what would happen if a program that asks for a seven- to ten-character phone number instead receives a string of 150 characters? Many programs will provide some error checking to ensure that this will not cause a problem. Some programs, however, cannot handle this error, and the extra characters continue to fill memory, overwriting other portions of the program. This can result in a number of problems, including causing the program to abort or the system to crash. Under certain circumstances, the program can execute a command supplied by the attacker. Buffer overflows typically inherit the level of privilege enjoyed by the program being exploited. This is why programs that use root-level access are so dangerous when exploited with a buffer overflow, as the code that will execute does so at root-level access.

Programming languages such as C were designed for space and performance constraints. Many functions in C, like **gets()**, are unsafe in that they will permit unsafe operations, such as unbounded string manipulation into fixed buffer locations. The C language also permits direct memory access via pointers, a functionality that provides a lot of programming power but carries with it the burden of proper safeguards being provided by the programmer.

EXAM TIP Buffer overflows can occur in any code, and code that runs with privilege has an even greater risk profile. In 2014, a buffer overflow in the OpenSSL library, called Heartbleed, left hundreds of thousands of systems vulnerable and exposed critical data for millions of users worldwide.

Buffer overflows are input validation attacks, designed to take advantage of input routines that do not validate the length of inputs. Surprisingly simple to resolve, all that is required is the validation of all input lengths prior to writing to memory. This can be done in a variety of manners, including the use of safe library functions for inputs. This is one of the vulnerabilities that has been shown to be solvable, and in fact the prevalence is declining substantially among major security-conscious software firms.

Race Condition

A *race condition* is an error condition that occurs when the output of a function is dependent on the sequence or timing of the inputs. It becomes a bug when the inputs do not happen in the order the programmer intended. The term *race condition* relates to the idea of multiple inputs racing each other to influence the output first. Race conditions can occur in multithreaded or distributed programs when the sequence or timing of processes or threads is important for the program to operate properly. A classic race condition is when one thread depends on a value (A) from another function that is actively being changed by a separate process. The first process cannot complete its work until the second process changes the value of A. If the second function is waiting for the first function to finish, a lock is created by the two processes and their interdependence. These conditions can be difficult to predict and find. Multiple unsynchronized threads, sometimes across multiple systems, create complex logic loops for seemingly simple atomic functions. Understanding and managing record locks is an essential element in a modern, diverse object programming environment.

Race conditions are defined by race windows, a period of opportunity when concurrent threads can compete in attempting to alter the same object. The first step to avoid race conditions is to identify the race windows. Then, once the windows are identified, the system can be designed so that they are not called concurrently, a process known as *mutual exclusion*. The impact of a race condition is usually the failure of a system in the form of a crash. Race conditions can be combated with reference counters, kernel locks, and thread synchronization. Reference counters are structures in the kernel that detail whether or not a resource is actively being used at the current moment. Locking the kernel was an early method, but it causes performance issues. Thread synchronization prevents threads from accessing the shared data at the same time.

Another timing issue is the infinite loop. When program logic becomes complex—for instance, date processing for leap years—care should be taken to ensure that all conditions are covered and that errors and other loop-breaking mechanisms do not allow the program to enter a state where the loop controls will fail. Failure to manage this exact property resulted in Microsoft Zune devices failing when they were turned on in a new year following a leap year. The control logic entered a sequence where a loop would not be satisfied, resulting in the device crashing by entering an infinite loop and becoming nonresponsive.

EXAM TIP Race conditions can be used for privilege elevation and denial-of-service attacks. Programmers can use reference counters, kernel locks, and thread synchronization to prevent race conditions.

Time of Check/Time of Use

In today's multithreaded, concurrent operating model, it is possible for different systems to attempt to interact with the same object at the same time. It is also possible for events to occur out of sequence based on timing differences between different threads of a program. Sequence and timing issues such as race conditions and infinite loops influence both the design and implementation of data activities. Understanding how and where these conditions can occur is important to members of the development team. In technical terms, what develops is known as a race condition, or from the attack point of view, the system is vulnerable to a time of check/time of use (TOC/TOU) attack.

EXAM TIP A time of check/time of use attack is one that takes advantage of a separation between the time a program checks a value and when it uses the value, allowing an unauthorized manipulation that can affect the outcome of a process.

Improper Error Handling

Every application will encounter errors and exceptions, and these need to be handled in a secure manner. One attack methodology includes forcing errors to move an application from normal operation to exception handling. During an exception, it is common practice to record/report the condition, typically in a log file, including supporting information such as the data that resulted in the error. This information can be invaluable in diagnosing the cause of the error condition. The challenge is in where this information is captured. The best method is to capture it in a log file, where it can be secured by an access control list (ACL). The worst method is to echo the information to the user. Echoing error condition details to users can provide valuable information to attackers when they cause errors on purpose.

Improper error handling can lead to a wide range of disclosures. Errors associated with SQL statements can disclose data structures and data elements. Remote procedure call (RPC) errors can give up sensitive information such as filenames, paths, and server names. Programmatic errors can disclose line numbers that an exception occurred on, the method that was invoked, and information such as stack elements. Attackers can use the information they gather from errors to further their attack on a system, as the information typically gives them details about the composition and inner workings of the system that they can exploit.

Improper Input Handling

Improper input handling is the true number-one cause of software vulnerabilities. Improper input handling or input validation is the root cause behind most overflows, injection attacks, and canonical structure errors. Users have the ability to manipulate input, so it is up to the developer to handle the input appropriately to prevent malicious entries from having an effect. Buffer overflows (discussed earlier in the chapter) have long been recognized as a class of improper input handling. Newer input handling attacks include canonicalization attacks and arithmetic attacks. Probably the most effective defensive mechanism you can employ is input validation. Considering all inputs to be hostile until properly validated can mitigate many attacks based on common vulnerabilities. This is a challenge, as the validation efforts need to occur after all parsers have completed manipulating input streams, a common function in web-based applications using Unicode and other international character sets.

Input validation is especially well suited for the following vulnerabilities: buffer overflow, reliance on untrusted inputs in a security decision, cross-site scripting (XSS), cross-site request forgery (XSRF), path traversal, and incorrect calculation of buffer size. Input validation may seem suitable for various injection attacks, but given the complexity of the input and the ramifications from legal but improper input streams, this method falls short for most injection attacks. What can work is a form of recognition and whitelisting approach, where the input is validated and then parsed into a standard structure that is then executed. This restricts the attack surface to not only legal inputs but also expected inputs.

The impact of improper input handling can be catastrophic, allowing an attacker to either gain a foothold on a system or increase their level of privilege. Because this type of error is dependent upon the process being attacked, the results can vary but almost always lead to attackers advancing their kill chain.

EXAM TIP Input validation is especially well suited for the following vulnerabilities: buffer overflow, reliance on untrusted inputs in a security decision, cross-site scripting (XSS), cross-site request forgery (XSRF), path traversal, and incorrect calculation of buffer size. When taking the Security+ exam, look for questions that address a large number of related problems with a common potential cause.

Replay Attacks

Replay attacks work against applications by attempting to re-create the conditions that existed the first time the sequence of events occurred. If an attacker can record a series of packets and then replay them, what was valid before may well be valid again. An example of this would be repeating the previous set of transactions, like getting paid twice or successfully passing a security check at a login event. There is a wide range of defenses against replay attacks, and as such this type of attack should not be an issue. However, developers who do not follow best practices can create implementations that lack replay protections, enabling this attack path to persist.

Session Replay

When a user connects to a system via the web, the connection forms a "session" in the respect that the various elements that are transmitted back and forth form a conversation between the client and the server. A *session replay* event is the re-creation of this interaction after it has occurred. This can be a good or a bad thing, depending on the circumstances. If the session is a transaction between the user and a bank, the ability to replay (that is, re-create) the session after the fact would be a bad thing. So for transactional systems, replay prevention is important and needs to be built into the system. For other web interactions, replay can provide information as to what is or isn't working on a web-based client/server interaction basis.

For replay to work, there needs to be instrumentation because most of the content and transactions are stateless by themselves, in that they don't have the information of where the user came from or where they went. Replay can be managed from either the client side or the server side, each having advantages and disadvantages. The server side can be captured based on history of requests, but won't show the mouse movements and such of client-only activity. On client side, tags allow you to capture details of pages. But like all client-side solutions, any data coming from a client is subject to blocking and manipulation.

Integer Overflow

An *integer overflow* is a programming error condition that occurs when a program attempts to store a numeric value, which is an integer, in a variable that is too small to hold it. The results vary by language and numeric type. In some cases, the value saturates the variable, assuming the maximum value for the defined type and no more. In other cases, especially with signed integers, it can roll over into a negative value because the most significant bit is usually reserved for the sign of the number. This can create significant logic errors in a program.

Integer overflows are easily tested for, and static code analyzers can point out where they are likely to occur. Given this, there is no excuse for having these errors end up in production code.

Request Forgery

Request forgery is a class of attack where a user performs a state-changing action on behalf of another user, typically without their knowledge. It is like having someone else add information to your web responses. These attacks utilize the behavioral characteristics of web-based protocols and browsers, and they occur because of client-side issues but they can be seen on both the server side and the client side.

Server-Side Request Forgery

Server-side request forgery is when an attacker sends requests to the server-side application to make HTTP requests to an arbitrary domain of the attacker's choosing. These attacks exploit the trust relationship between the server and the target, forcing the vulnerable application to perform unauthorized actions. The typical trust relationships exploited are those that exist in relation to the server itself, or in relation to other back-end systems within the same organization. Common attacks include having the server attack itself or attack another server in the organization.

Cross-Site Request Forgery

Cross-site request forgery (XSRF) attacks utilize unintended behaviors that are proper in defined use but are performed under circumstances outside the authorized use. This is an example of a "confused deputy" problem, a class of problems where one entity mistakenly performs an action on behalf of another. An XSRF attack relies upon several conditions to be effective. It is performed against sites that have an authenticated user and exploits the site's trust in a previous authentication event. Then, by tricking a user's browser into sending an HTTP request to the target site, the trust is exploited. Assume your bank allows you to log in and perform financial transactions but does not validate the authentication for each subsequent transaction. If a user is logged in and has not closed their browser, then an action in another browser tab could send a hidden request to the bank, resulting in a transaction that appears to be authorized but in fact was not done by the user.

EXAM TIP There are two different types of request forgeries: server-side request forgery and cross-site request forgery. Given a scenario, be sure you can distinguish them based on a description of what has happened.

Many different mitigation techniques can be employed, from limiting authentication times, to cookie expiration, to managing specific elements of a web page (for example, header checking). The strongest method is the use of random XSRF tokens in form submissions. Subsequent requests cannot work because a token was not set in advance. Testing for XSRF takes a bit more planning than for other injection-type attacks, but this, too, can be accomplished as part of the design process.

Application Programming Interface (API) Attacks

The "normal" method of interacting with a web service is via a series of commands that are executed on the server, with the results sent back to the application—the browser. However, with the rise of smartphones, tablets, and other mobile devices came the application. An application (or app) typically interfaces with the service via an application programming interface (API). As with all entry points, APIs are subject to attack and abuse. An *application programming interface attack* is one where an attacker specifically attacks the API and the service behind it by manipulating inputs. APIs for web services require at a minimum the same level of security concern as a standard web interface, but in some cases, they may require an enhanced level. The reasoning behind enhanced levels is simple: APIs are used to feed data to an application, so some of the processing is done in the application. This means that the interface is more of a raw feed into the server, with less work, and less checking, done on the server. API interfaces that are not monitored or moderated on the server side can result in data breaches and data disclosures, among other security risks.

Resource Exhaustion

All systems are defined as a process that creates specific outputs as a result of a defined set of inputs. The internals of the system use a variety of resources to achieve the transition of input states to output states. *Resource exhaustion* is the state where a system does not have all of the resources it needs to continue to function. Two common resources are capacity and memory, which are interdependent in some scenarios but completely separate in others. Capacity is defined by a system having the necessary amount of communication bandwidth, processing bandwidth, and memory to manage intermediate states. When one of these resources becomes exhausted, failure can ensue. For instance, if a system has more TCP SYN requests than it can handle, it fails to complete handshakes and enable additional connections. If a program runs out of memory, it will fail to operate correctly. This is an example of a resource exhaustion attack, where the attack's aim is to deplete resources.

EXAM TIP Like race conditions, resource exhaustion vulnerabilities tend to result in a system crash. These attacks can result in less damage, but from the aspect of an attacker advancing persistence as a strategy, it's necessary to change system functions as part of an overall attack strategy. However, in some cases, the outages can stop essential services, including customer-facing systems.

Memory Leak

Memory management encompasses the actions used to control and coordinate computer memory, assigning memory to variables, and reclaiming it when no longer being used. Errors in memory management can result in a *memory leak*, which can grow over time, consuming more and more resources. A garbage collection routine is used to clean up memory that has been allocated in a program but is no longer needed. In the C programming language and in C++, where there is no automatic garbage collector, the programmer must allocate and free memory explicitly. One of the advantages of newer programming languages such as Java, C#, Python, and Ruby is that they provide automatic memory management with garbage collection. This may not be as efficient as specifically coding in C, but it is significantly less error prone.

Secure Sockets Layer (SSL) Stripping

Secure sockets layer (SSL) stripping is a man in the middle attack against all SSL and early versions of TLS connections. The attack is performed anywhere a man in the middle attack can happen, which makes wireless hotspots a prime location. The attack works by intercepting the initial connection request for HTTPS, redirecting it to an HTTP site, and then mediating in the middle. The reason the attack works is because the beginning of an SSL or TLS (v1.0 or v1.1) handshake is vulnerable to attack. The main defense is technical: only use TLS 1.2 or 1.3, as these versions have protections against the specific attack method.

Driver Manipulation

Drivers are pieces of software that sit between the operating system and a peripheral device. In one respect, drivers are a part of the OS, as an extension. In another respect, drivers are code that is not part of the OS and are developed by firms other than the OS developer. *Driver manipulation* is an attack on a system by changing drivers, thus changing the behavior of the system. Drivers may not be as protected as other parts of the core system, yet they join it when invoked. This has led to drivers being signed and significantly tightening up the environment of drivers and ancillary programs.

Shimming

Shimming is a process of putting a layer of code between the driver and the OS. Shimming allows flexibility and portability by enabling changes between different versions of an OS without modifying the original driver code. Shimming also represents a means by which malicious code can change a driver's behavior without changing the driver itself.

Refactoring

Refactoring is the process of restructuring existing computer code without changing its external behavior. Refactoring is done to improve nonfunctional attributes of the software, such as improving code readability and/or reducing complexity. Refactoring can uncover design flaws that lead to exploitable vulnerabilities, allowing these to be closed without changing the external behavior of the code. Refactoring is a means by which an attacker can add functionality to a driver yet maintain its desired functionality. Although this goes against the original principle of refactoring—improving code efficiency—it speaks to the ingenuity of attackers.

EXAM TIP For the exam, remember that shimming is a process of putting a layer of code between the driver and the OS and that refactoring is the process of restructuring existing computer code without changing its external behavior.

Pass the Hash

Pass the hash is a hacking technique where the attacker captures the hash used to authenticate a process. They can then use this hash by injecting it into a process in place of the password. This is a highly technical attack that targets the Windows authentication process by injecting a copy of the password hash directly into the system. The attacker does not need to know the password, but instead can use a captured hash and inject it directly, which when correctly verified will grant the attacker access. As this is a very technically specific hack, tools have been developed to facilitate its operation.

Chapter Review

This chapter presented material associated with application attacks. The chapter opened with a discussion of privilege escalation and cross-site scripting and then followed with injection attacks, including SQL, DLL, LDAP, and XML variants. The next topics covered were pointer/object dereferencing and directory traversals. Buffer overflows, race conditions, and improper error handling followed, and then the chapter addressed improper input handling. The attack methods of replay attacks, integer overflows, and request forgeries were also covered. Under request forgeries, server-side and cross-site variants were covered.

Attacks on API interfaces, resource exhaustion, and memory leaks were covered. In addition, the man in the middle method of SSL stripping as well as driver manipulation through shimming and refactoring were covered. The chapter closed with a discussion of the pass-the-hash attack.

Questions

To help you prepare further for the CompTIA Security+ exam, and to test your level of preparedness, answer the following questions and then check your answers against the correct answers at the end of the chapter.

1. When an attacker captures network traffic and retransmits it at a later time, what type of attack are they attempting?
   - **A.** Denial-of-service attack
   - **B.** Replay attack
   - **C.** Bluejacking attack
   - **D.** Man in the middle attack
2. What type of attack involves an attacker putting a layer of code between an original device driver and the operating system?
   - **A.** Refactoring
   - **B.** Trojan horse
   - **C.** Shimming
   - **D.** Pass the hash
3. You're reviewing a custom web application and accidentally type a number in a text field. The application returns an error message containing variable names, filenames, and the full path of the application. This is an example of which of the following?
   - **A.** Resource exhaustion
   - **B.** Improper error handling

C. Generic error message

D. Common misconfiguration

4. You're working with a group testing a new application. You've noticed that when three or more of you click Submit on a specific form at the same time, the application crashes every time. This is most likely an example of which of the following?

   A. A race condition

   B. A nondeterministic error

   C. An undocumented feature

   D. A DLL injection

5. An externally facing web server in your organization keeps crashing. Looking at the server after a reboot, you notice CPU usage is pegged and memory usage is rapidly climbing. The traffic logs show a massive amount of incoming HTTP and HTTPS requests to the server. Which type of attack is this web server experiencing?

   A. Input validation

   B. Distributed error handling

   C. Resource exhaustion

   D. Race condition

6. Your organization is considering using a new ticket identifier with your current help desk system. The new identifier would be a 16-digit integer created by combining the date, time, and operator ID. Unfortunately, when you've tried using the new identifier in the "ticket number" field on your current system, the application crashes every time. The old method of using a five-digit integer works just fine. This is most likely an example of which of the following?

   A. Common misconfiguration

   B. Zero-day vulnerability

   C. Memory leak

   D. Integer overflow

7. While examining a laptop infected with malware, you notice the malware loads on startup and also loads a file called netutilities.dll each time Microsoft Word is opened. This is an example of which of the following?

   A. Race condition

   B. DLL injection

   C. System infection

   D. Memory overflow

8. A web application you are reviewing has an input field for username and indicates the username should be between 6 and 12 characters. You've discovered that if you input a username that's 150 characters or more in length, the application crashes. What is this is an example of?
    A. Memory leak
    B. Buffer overflow
    C. Directory traversal
    D. Integer overflow
9. Your organization is having issues with a custom web application. The application seems to run fine for a while but starts to lock up or crash after seven to ten days of continuous use. Examining the server, you notice that memory usage seems to climb every day until the server runs out of memory. The application is most likely suffering from which of the following?
    A. Memory leak
    B. Overflow leak
    C. Zero-day exploit
    D. Pointer dereference
10. Your database server is returning a large dataset to an online user, saturating the network. The normal return of records would be a couple at most. This is an example of what form of attack?
    A. Memory leak
    B. LDAP injection
    C. Man in the middle
    D. SQL injection

Answers

1. **B.** A *replay attack* occurs when the attacker captures a portion of the communication between two parties and retransmits it at a later time. For example, an attacker might replay a series of commands and codes used in a financial transaction to cause the transaction to be conducted multiple times. Generally, replay attacks are associated with attempts to circumvent authentication mechanisms, such as the capturing and reuse of a certificate or ticket.
2. **C.** *Shimming* is the process of putting a layer of code between the device driver and the operating system.
3. **B.** When an application fails to properly trap an error and generates error messages containing potentially sensitive information, this is known as *improper error handling*.

4. **A.** This is most likely an example of a race condition. A *race condition* is an error condition that occurs when the output of a function is dependent on the sequence or timing of the inputs. In this case, the application crashes when multiple inputs are submitted at the same time because the application is not receiving the inputs or handling the inputs in the expected order.
5. **C.** *Resource exhaustion* is the state where a system does not have all of the resources it needs to continue to function. In this case, the server does not have the memory or CPU capacity to handle the massive volume of incoming HTTP/HTTPS requests.
6. **D.** An *integer overflow* is a programming error condition that occurs when a program attempts to store a numeric value, an integer, in a variable that is too small to hold it. In this case, the 16-digit integer is too large for the field, which is working just fine with the five-digit integer.
7. **B.** This is an example of *DLL injection,* which is the process of adding to a program, at runtime, a DLL that has a specific function vulnerability that can be capitalized upon by an attacker.
8. **B.** This is a fairly classic example of a *buffer overflow*. The input routine does not validate the provided input to ensure a maximum of 12 characters is received and processed. In this case, the application tries to store all 150 (or more) characters of the username, resulting in areas of memory being overwritten and causing the application to crash.
9. **A.** *Memory leaks* are programming errors caused when a computer program does not properly handle memory resources. Over time, while a program runs, if it does not clean up memory resources as they are no longer needed, chunks of dead memory can become scattered across the program's footprint in memory. If a program executes for a long time, these dead memory areas can grow in size and consume resources, causing the system to crash.
10. **D.** Excessive records being returned from a SQL query is a sign of *SQL injection.*

CHAPTER 4

Network Attack Indicators

In this chapter, you will

- Learn about various network attacks
- Analyze potential indicators associated with network attacks

This chapter explores the indicators associated with network attacks. These indicators can provide information as to what the attack is, what is happening, and what measures are needed to defend against it.

Certification Objective This chapter covers CompTIA Security+ exam objective 1.4: Given a scenario, analyze potential indicators associated with network attacks.

Wireless

Wireless is a common networking technology that has a substantial number of standards and processes to connect users to networks via a radio signal, thus freeing machines from wires. As in all software systems, wireless networking is a target for hackers. This is partly because of the simple fact that wireless removes the physical barrier.

Evil Twin

The *evil twin* attack is an attack against the wireless protocol via substitute hardware. This attack uses an access point (AP) owned by an attacker that usually has been enhanced with higher-power and higher-gain antennas to look like a better connection to the users and computers attaching to it. By getting users to connect through the "evil" access point, attackers can more easily analyze traffic and perform man in the middle–type attacks. For simple denial of service (DoS), an attacker could use interference to jam the wireless signal, not allowing any computer to connect to the access point successfully.

Rogue Access Point

By setting up a *rogue access point,* an attacker can attempt to get clients to connect to it as if it were authorized and then simply authenticate to the real AP—a simple way to have access to the network and the client's credentials. Rogue APs can act as a man in the middle and easily steal users' credentials. Enterprises with wireless APs should routinely scan for and remove rogue APs, as users have difficulty avoiding them.

EXAM TIP A rogue AP is an AP that is usually placed on an internal network either by accident or for nefarious reasons. It is not administered by the network owner or administrator. An evil twin is an AP that appears to be legitimate but isn't and is often used to eavesdrop on wireless communications.

Bluesnarfing

Bluesnarfing is similar to bluejacking (discussed next) in that it uses the same contact transmission protocol. The difference is that instead of sending an unsolicited message to the victim's phone, the attacker copies off the victim's information, which can include e-mails, contact lists, calendars, and anything else that exists on that device. More recent phones with media capabilities can be snarfed for private photos and videos. Bluesnarfing used to require a laptop with a Bluetooth adapter, making it relatively easy to identify a possible attacker, but bluesnarfing applications are now available for mobile devices. Bloover, a combination of Bluetooth and Hoover, is one such application that runs as a Java applet. The majority of Bluetooth phones need to be discoverable for the bluesnarf attack to work, and the phones do not necessarily need to be paired. In theory, an attacker can also brute force the device's unique 48-bit name. A program called RedFang attempts to perform this brute force attack by sending all possible names and seeing what gets a response. This approach was addressed in Bluetooth 1.2 with an anonymity mode.

EXAM TIP The Security+ exam objective is to analyze network-based attacks, and in the case of bluejacking and bluesnarfing, these are both attacks against Bluetooth. They differ in that bluejacking is the sending of unauthorized data via Bluetooth, whereas bluesnarfing is the unauthorized taking of data over a Bluetooth channel. Understanding this difference is important.

Bluejacking

Bluejacking is a term used for the sending of unauthorized messages to another Bluetooth device. This involves sending a message as a phonebook contact:

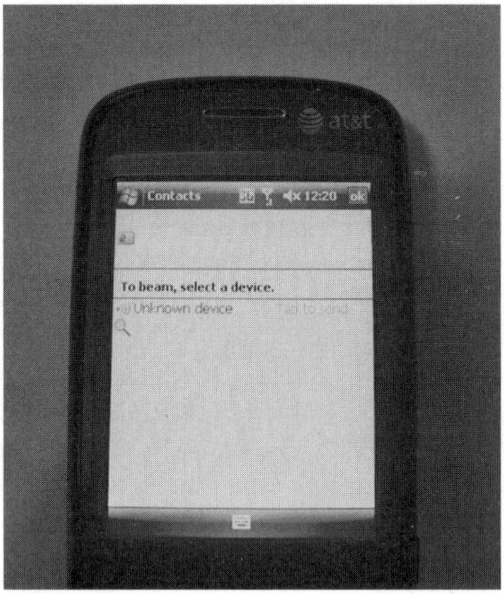

The attacker then sends the message to the possible recipient via Bluetooth. Originally, this involved sending text messages, but more recent phones can send images or audio as well. A popular variant of this is the transmission of "shock" images, featuring disturbing or crude photos. As Bluetooth is a short-range protocol, the attack and victim must be within roughly 10 yards of each other. The victim's phone must also have Bluetooth enabled and must be in discoverable mode. On some early phones, this was the default configuration, and while it makes connecting external devices easier, it also allows attacks against the phone. If Bluetooth is turned off, or if the device is set to nondiscoverable, bluejacking can be avoided.

Disassociation

Disassociation attacks against a wireless system are attacks designed to disassociate a host from the wireless access point and from the wireless network. Disassociation attacks stem from the de-authentication frame that is in the IEEE 802.11 (Wi-Fi) standard. The de-authentication frame is designed as a tool to remove unauthorized stations from a Wi-Fi access point, but because of the design of the protocol, these frames can be implemented by virtually anyone. An attacker only needs to have the MAC address of the intended victim, which enables them to send a spoofed message to the access point, specifically spoofing the MAC address of the victim machine. This results in the disconnection of the victim machine, making this attack a form of denial of service.

Disassociation attacks are not typically used alone but rather in concert with another attack objective. For instance, if you disassociate a connection and then sniff the reconnect, you can steal passwords. After a machine is disassociated, the user attempting to reestablish a WPA/WPA2/WPA3 session will need to repeat the four-way handshake.

This gives the hacker a chance to sniff this event, the first step in gathering needed information for a brute force or dictionary-based WPA password-cracking attack. Forcing users to reconnect creates a chance to mount a man in the middle attack against content provided during a connection. This has been used by the Wifiphisher tool to collect passwords.

NOTE Wifiphisher is a security tool often used by the red team in penetration testing that mounts automated phishing attacks against Wi-Fi networks in order to obtain credentials or infect victims with malware.

Jamming

Jamming is a form of denial of service that specifically targets the radio spectrum aspect of wireless. Just as other DoS attacks can manipulate things behind the scenes, so can jamming on a wireless AP, enabling actions such as attaching to a rogue AP.

Radio Frequency Identification (RFID)

Radio frequency identification (RFID) tags are used in a wide range of use cases. From tracking devices to keys, the unique serialization of these remotely sensible devices has made them useful in a wide range of applications. RFID tags come in several different forms and can be classified as either active or passive. Active tags have a power source, while passive tags utilize the RF energy transmitted to them for power. RFID tags are used as a means of identification, and they have an advantage over barcodes in that they do not have to be visible, just within radio wave range (a few centimeters up to 200 meters, depending on tag type). RFID tags are used in a range of security situations, including contactless identification systems such as smart cards.

RFID tags have multiple security concerns. First and foremost, because they are connected via RF energy, physical security is a challenge. Security is an important issue for RFID tag systems because they form a means of identification, and there is a need for authentication and confidentiality of the data transfers. Several standards are associated with securing the RFID data flow, including ISO/IEC 18000 and ISO/IEC 29167 for cryptography methods to support confidentiality, untraceability, tag and reader authentication, and over-the-air privacy, whereas ISO/IEC 20248 specifies a digital signature data structure for use in RFID systems.

Several different attack types can be performed against RFID systems:

- Against the RFID devices themselves (the chips and readers)
- Against the communication channel between the device and the reader
- Against the reader and back-end system

The last type is more of a standard IT/IS attack, depending on the interfaces used (web, database, and so on) and is not covered any further. Attacks against the communication channel are relatively easy because the radio frequencies are known and devices exist to interface with tags. The two main attacks are replay and eavesdropping. In a replay attack, the RFID information is recorded and then replayed later. In the case of an RFID-based access badge, it could be read in a restaurant from a distance and then replayed at the appropriate entry point to gain entry. In the case of eavesdropping, the data can be collected, monitoring the movement of tags for whatever purpose needed by an unauthorized party. Both of these attacks are easily defeated using the ISO/IEC security standards previously listed.

If eavesdropping is possible, then what about man in the middle attacks? These are certainly possible, as they would be a combination of a sniffing (eavesdropping) action followed by a replay (spoofing) attack. This leads to the question as to whether an RFID can be cloned. The answer is yes, if the RFID information is not protected via a cryptographic component.

RFID theft, or skimming, has been a security topic in the news. It is possible for thieves to use small devices that will scan your card, exploiting the contactless technology to take information from it, which can then be used to make copycat cards or other ways of accessing money. It is unknown exactly how common this practice is, but it's thought to be on the rise as contactless technology becomes more common and the devices using this technology become cheaper.

NOTE Many wallets on the market now offer some sort of RFID protection. This varies from wallet to wallet, but in general they work by blocking the frequency used to access the data, thus securing your card.

Near Field Communication (NFC)

Near field communication (NFC) is a set of wireless technologies that enables smartphones and other devices to establish radio communication over a short distance, typically 10 cm (3.9 in) or less. This technology did not see much use until recently when it started being employed to move data between cell phones and in mobile payment systems. Now that NFC has become the mainstream method of making payments via mobile phones, it is becoming ubiquitous, and in many cases is connected directly to financial information. Therefore, the importance of understanding and protecting this communication channel is paramount.

EXAM TIP It is important to know that RFID is a process by which a credit card or phone communicates with a reader using radio waves and that NFC is a high-frequency subset of RFID and acts over a much shorter distance.

Initialization Vector (IV)

The *initialization vector (IV)* is used in wireless systems as the randomization element at the beginning of a connection. Attacks against it are aimed at determining the IV, thus finding the repeating key sequence.

The IV is the primary reason for the weaknesses in Wired Equivalent Privacy (WEP). The IV is sent in the plaintext part of the message, and because the total keyspace is approximately 16 million keys, the same key will be reused. Once the key has been repeated, an attacker has two ciphertexts encrypted with the same key stream. This allows the attacker to examine the ciphertext and retrieve the key. This attack can be improved by examining only packets that have weak IVs, reducing the number of packets needed to crack the key. When only weak IV packets are examined, the number of required captured packets is reduced to around four or five million, which can take only a few hours to capture on a fairly busy AP. For a point of reference, this means that equipment with an advertised WEP key of 128 bits can be cracked in less than a day, whereas to crack a normal 128-bit key would take roughly 2,000,000,000,000,000,000 years on a computer able to attempt one trillion keys a second. In other words, the weak IV means the true level of security is nowhere near 128 bits. AirSnort is a modified sniffing program that takes advantage of this weakness to retrieve the WEP keys. The biggest weakness of WEP is that the IV problem exists regardless of key length because the IV always remains at 24 bits.

On-path Attack

A *man in the middle (MITM)* attack, as the name implies, generally occurs when an attacker is able to place himself in the middle of two other hosts that are communicating. Ideally (from the attacker's perspective), this is done by ensuring that all communication going to or from the target host is routed through the attacker's host (which can be accomplished if the attacker can compromise the router for the target host). The attacker can then observe all traffic before relaying it and can actually modify or block traffic. To the target host, it appears that communication is occurring normally, since all expected replies are received. Figure 4-1 illustrates this type of attack.

There are numerous methods of instantiating a man in the middle attack. One of the common methods is via *session hijacking*, which can occur when information such as a cookie is stolen, allowing the attacker to impersonate the legitimate session. This attack can be a result of a cross-site scripting attack, which tricks a user into executing code resulting in cookie theft. The amount of information that can be obtained in a man in

Figure 4-1
A man in the middle attack

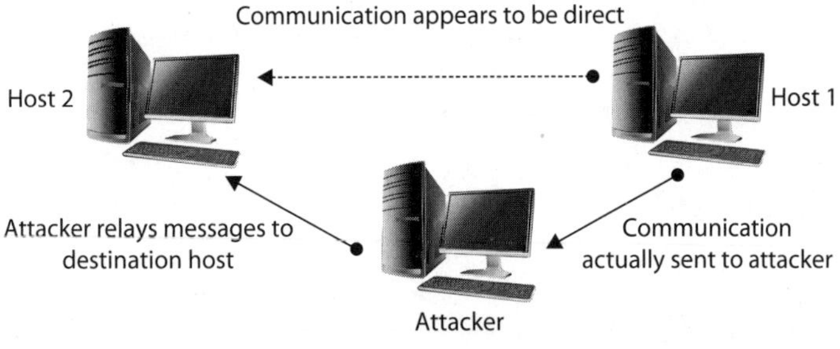

the middle attack will be limited if the communication is encrypted. Even in this case, however, sensitive information can still be obtained, since knowing what communication is being conducted, and between which individuals, may in fact provide information that is valuable in certain circumstances.

The *man in the browser (MITB)* attack is a variant of a man in the middle attack. In an MITB attack, the first element is a malware attack that places a trojan element that can act as a proxy on the target machine. This malware changes browser behavior through browser helper objects or extensions. When a user connects to their bank, for instance, the malware recognizes the target (a financial transaction) and injects itself in the stream of the conversation. When the user approves a transfer of $150 to pay a utility bill, for example, the malware intercepts the user's keystrokes and modifies them to perform a different transaction. A famous example of an MITB attack was the financial malware Zeus, which targeted financial transactions on users' machines, manipulating and changing them after the users had entered password credentials.

EXAM TIP MITM and MITB are similar, yet different. Be able to differentiate between the two based on the details of the question.

Layer 2 Attacks

Layer 2 of a network is where local addressing decisions are made. Switches operate at layer 2, or media access control (MAC) addresses. There are many ways of tampering with this level of addressing, and Security+ identifies three of significance: Address Resolution Protocol (ARP) poisoning, media access control (MAC) flooding, and MAC cloning.

EXAM TIP Understanding the way layer 2 works helps you to understand how it is abused. Attacks at the layer 2 level just use the system differently than intended, but still in a proper way. Therefore, learning how layer 2 works enables you to see how the attacks work.

Address Resolution Protocol (ARP) Poisoning

In moving packets between machines, a device sometimes needs to know where to send a packet using the MAC or layer 2 address. Address Resolution Protocol (ARP) handles this problem through four basic message types:

- **ARP request** "Who has this IP address?"
- **ARP reply** "I have that IP address; my MAC address is…"
- **Reverse ARP request (RARP)** "Who has this MAC address?"
- **RARP reply** "I have that MAC address; my IP address is…"

These messages are used in conjunction with a device's ARP table, where a form of short-term memory associated with these data elements resides. The commands are used as a simple form of lookup. When a machine sends an ARP request to the network, the reply is received and entered into all devices that hear the reply. This facilitates efficient address lookups, but also makes the system subject to attack.

When the ARP table gets a reply, it automatically trusts the reply and updates the table. Some operating systems will even accept ARP reply data if they never heard the original request. There is no mechanism to verify the veracity of the data received. An attacker can send messages, corrupt the ARP table, and cause packets to be misrouted. This form of attack is called *ARP poisoning* and results in malicious address redirection. This can allow a mechanism whereby an attacker can inject himself into the middle of a conversation between two devices—a man in the middle attack.

Media Access Control (MAC) Flooding

Addressing at the layer 2 interface is done by media access control (MAC) addresses and switches and hubs. Hubs send all packets to everyone, but switches look up the address in a stored table and send to only that address. *MAC flooding* is an attack where an attacker floods the table with addresses, making the switch unable to find the correct address for a packet. The switch responds by sending the packet to all addresses, in essence acting as a hub. The switch also asks for the correct device to give it its address, thus setting the switch up for ARP poisoning, as described in the previous section.

MAC Cloning

MAC cloning is the act of changing a MAC address to bypass security checks based on the MAC address. This can work when the return packets are being routed by IP address and can be properly linked to the correct MAC address. Not all MAC cloning is an attack; small firewall routers commonly have a MAC clone function by which the device can clone a MAC address to make it seem transparent to other devices such as the cable modem connection.

Domain Name System (DNS)

The Domain Name System (DNS) is the phone book for addressing. When you need to know where to send a packet that is not local to your network, DNS provides the correct address to get the packet to its destination. This makes DNS one of the primary targets of attackers, because if you corrupt DNS, you can control where all the packets go. Several technical attacks and one operational attack on this level of addressing are covered in this objective.

Domain Hijacking

Domain hijacking is the act of changing the registration of a domain name without the permission of its original registrant. Technically a crime, this act can have devastating consequences because the DNS system will spread the false domain location far and wide automatically. The original owner can request it to be corrected, but this can take time.

DNS Poisoning

The Domain Name System (DNS) is used to convert a name into an IP address. There is not a single DNS system but rather a hierarchy of DNS servers—from root servers on the backbone of the Internet, to copies at your ISP, your home router, and your local machine, each in the form of a DNS cache. To examine a DNS query for a specific address, you can use the **nslookup** command. Figure 4-2 shows a series of DNS queries executed on a Windows machine. In the first request, the DNS server was from an ISP, while in the second request, the DNS server was from a virtual private network (VPN) connection. Between the two requests, the network connections were changed, resulting in different DNS lookups. The changing of where DNS is resolved can be a *DNS poisoning* attack. The challenge in detecting these attacks is knowing what the authoritative DNS entry should be and then detecting when it changes in an unauthorized fashion. Using a VPN can change a DNS source, and this may be desired, but unauthorized changes can be attacks.

At times, **nslookup** will return a nonauthoritative answer, as shown in Figure 4-3. This typically means the result is from a cache as opposed to a server that has an authoritative answer (that is, an answer known to be current).

There are other commands you can use to examine and manipulate the DNS cache on a system. In Windows, the **ipconfig /displaydns** command will show the current

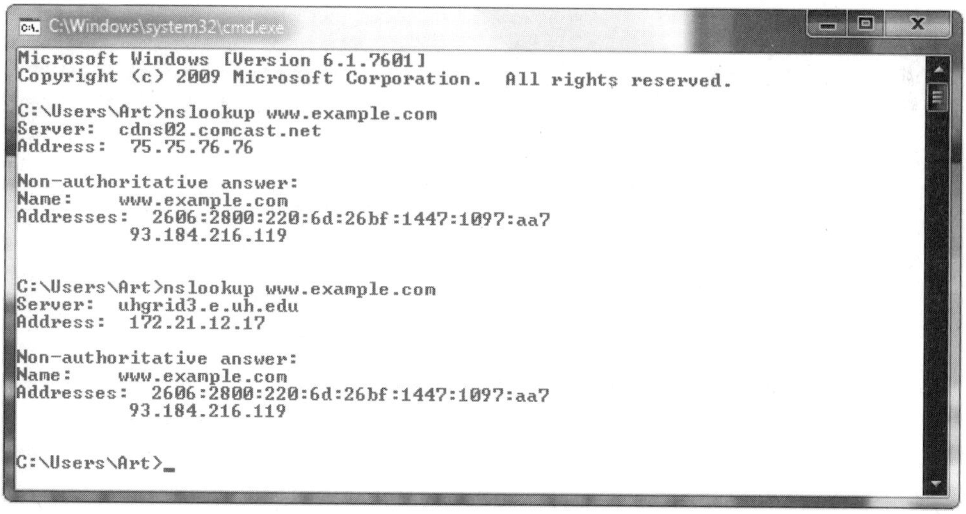

Figure 4-2 nslookup of a DNS query

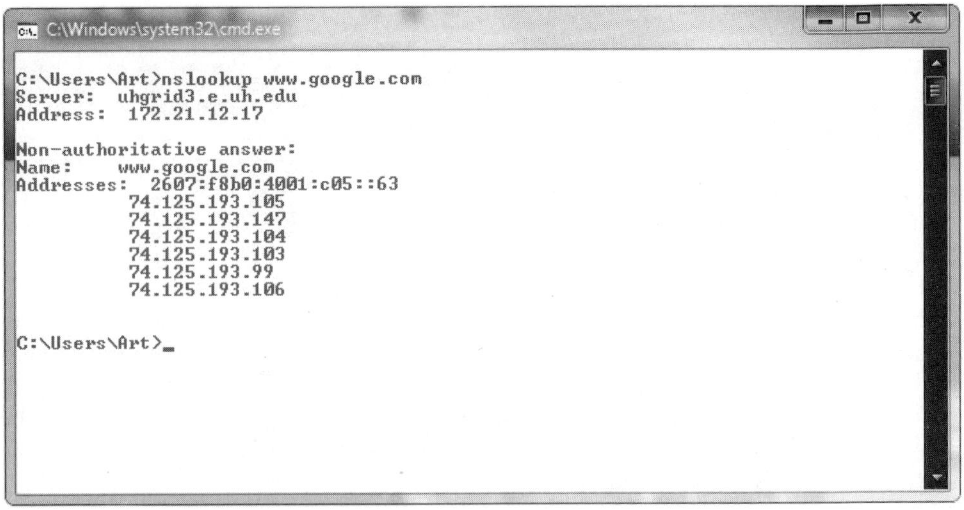

Figure 4-3 Cache response to a DNS query

DNS cache on a machine. Figure 4-4 shows a small DNS cache. This cache was recently emptied using the **ipconfig /flushdns** command to make it fit on the screen.

Looking at DNS as a complete system shows that there are hierarchical levels from the top (root server) down to the cache in an individual machine. DNS poisoning can

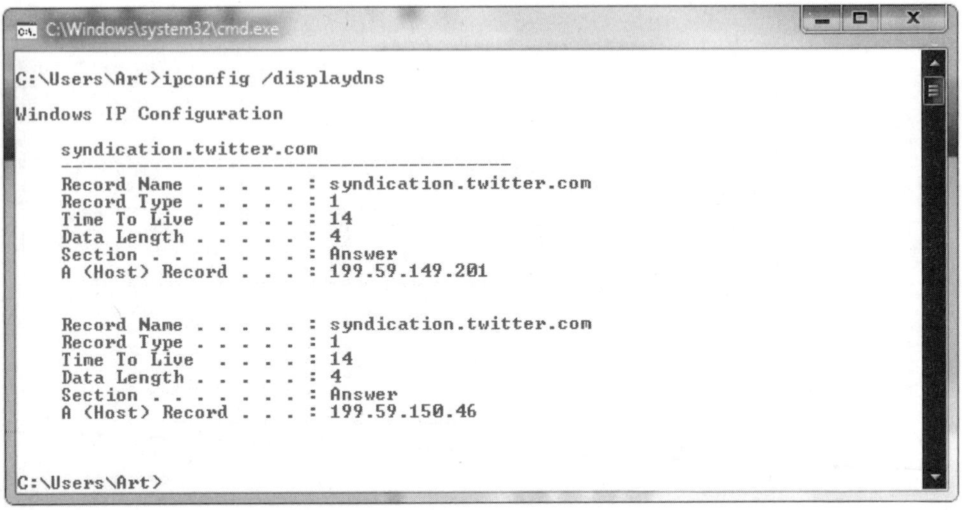

Figure 4-4 Cache response to a DNS table query

occur at any of these levels, with the effect of the poisoning growing wider the higher up it occurs. In 2010, a DNS poisoning event resulted in the "Great Firewall of China" censoring Internet traffic in the United States until caches were resolved.

DNS poisoning is a variant of a larger attack class referred to as *DNS spoofing*. In DNS spoofing, an attacker changes a DNS record through any of a multitude of means. There are many ways to perform DNS spoofing, a few of which include compromising a DNS server, the use of the Kaminsky attack, and the use of a false network node advertising a false DNS address. An attacker can even use DNS cache poisoning to result in DNS spoofing. By poisoning an upstream DNS cache, all of the downstream users will get spoofed DNS records.

Because of the importance of integrity on DNS requests and responses, a project has begun to secure the DNS infrastructure using digital signing of DNS records. This project, initiated by the US government and called Domain Name System Security Extensions (DNSSEC), works by digitally signing records. This is done by adding records to DNS, a key, and a signature attesting to the validity of the key. With this information, requestors can be assured that the information they receive is correct. It will take a substantial amount of time (years) for this new system to propagate through the entire DNS infrastructure, but in the end, the system will have much greater assurance.

Universal Resource Locator (URL) Redirection

Universal resource locator (URL) is the method of describing where you want a browser to go, and it is the main interface to the DNS process that converts it to a machine-readable address. So, how can you tamper with this? Social engineers use psychology and cognitive science to trick users into doing things. For example, a slight difference in the name displayed in an e-mail or a link can be missed by your brain. If the attacker has registered this different site in DNS and cloned the site you think you are going to, when you click without carefully reading, you end up on a different site that looks just like the one you are wanting to go to. Why the issue? Well, this is a man in the middle attack where all of your traffic is being read and redirected—passwords and all. So how does one defend against it? Many security vendors and e-mail vendors have built in support that looks for the differences and alerts a user before going to a site that might be an issue.

Domain Reputation

Your IP address is an address, much like the one for your house, and like all addresses it can have a reputation. Do you live in a good neighborhood, or a bad one? Does your house have activity that makes neighbors nervous enough to call the police or other issues? IP addresses have reputations as well, and if you do not protect your address, its reputation may suffer. Security companies track where spam comes from, and if your IP address becomes associated with spam, botnets, or other bad behaviors, your *domain reputation* will suffer. Also, many interconnected services will literally stop working if your score gets low enough. So, just like your credit score, you have to take certain positive actions to maintain your IP reputation score. If you violate rules against a Google API, or an Amazon Web Services (AWS) API, or another Internet-based service, don't be surprised when that service is no longer available for your use.

How do you prevent this from happening? Begin with making certain others are not piggybacking on your address. Open mail relays can lead to spamming. Bots can abuse APIs. The attackers that use these channels don't care about your domain reputation; when it goes too low, they move to another victim. Maintaining a secure system is how you keep this from happening.

EXAM TIP Methods of changing the addresses of messages enable many attacks, and how they are changed is key. The ultimate effects of all the addressing attacks are similar, but how they happen will be an element of the question. Look for DNS poisoning, domain hijacking, URL redirection, and reputation attacks to be differentiated by tiny details in the description of the question.

Distributed Denial-of-Service (DDoS)

In a denial-of-service (DoS) attack, the attacker attempts to deny authorized users access either to specific information or to the computer system or network itself. This can be accomplished by crashing the system—taking it offline—or by sending so many requests that the machine is overwhelmed. A DoS attack employing multiple attacking systems is known as a *distributed denial-of-service (DDoS) attack.* The goal of a DDoS attack is also to deny the use of or access to a specific service or system. DDoS attacks were made famous in 2000 with the highly publicized attacks on eBay, CNN, Amazon, and Yahoo!

Creating a DDoS network is no simple task. The attack agents are not willing agents—they are systems that have been compromised and on which the DDoS attack software has been installed. To compromise these agents, the attacker has to have gained unauthorized access to the system or tricked authorized users to run a program that installed the attack software. The creation of the attack network may in fact be a multistep process in which the attacker first compromises a few systems that are then used as handlers or masters, which in turn compromise other systems. Once the network has been created, the agents (zombies) wait for an attack message that will include data on the specific target before launching the attack. One important aspect of a DDoS attack is that with just a few messages to the agents, the attacker can have a flood of messages sent against the targeted system. Figure 4-5 illustrates a DDoS network with agents and handlers.

This is how the Mirai botnet created a DDoS against a well-known security researcher in September of 2016, and later the DNS service Dyn in October. The Mirai botnet used the millions of simple IoT (Internet of Things) devices that lacked basic security to do the amplification.

A defensive approach involves changing the time-out option for TCP connections so that attacks such as the SYN flooding attack are more difficult to perform, because unused connections are dropped more quickly.

For DDoS attacks, much has been written about distributing your own workload across several systems so that any attack against your system would have to target several hosts to be completely successful. While this is true, if large enough DDoS networks are created (with tens of thousands of zombies, for example), any network, no matter how

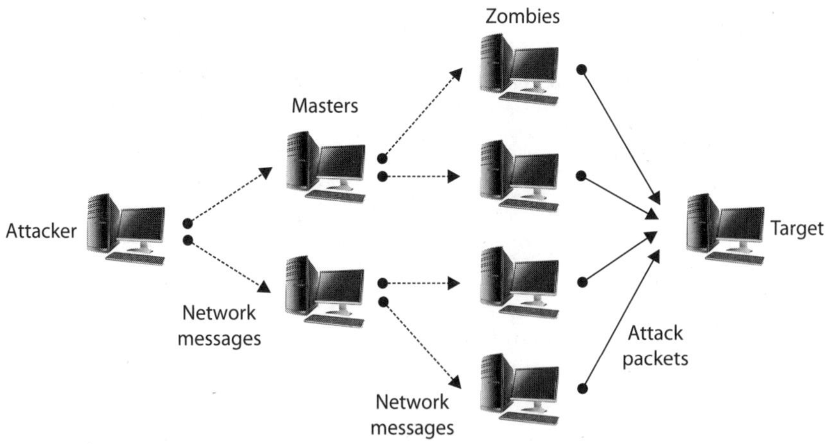

Figure 4-5 DDoS attacks

much the load is distributed, can be successfully attacked. Such an approach also involves additional costs to your organization to establish this distributed environment. Addressing the problem in this manner is actually an attempt to mitigate the effect of the attack, rather than preventing or stopping an attack.

To prevent a DDoS attack, you must be able either to intercept or block the attack messages or to keep the DDoS network from being established in the first place. Tools have been developed that will scan your systems, searching for sleeping zombies waiting for an attack signal. Many of the current antivirus/anti-malware security suite tools will detect known zombie-type infections. The problem with this type of prevention approach, however, is that it is not something you can do to prevent an attack on your network—it is something you can do to keep your network from being used to attack other networks or systems. You have to rely on the community of network administrators to test their own systems to prevent attacks on yours.

Network

In a DDoS attack, service is denied by overwhelming the target with traffic from many different systems. A network of attack agents (sometimes called zombies) is created by the attacker, and upon receiving the attack command from the attacker, the attack agents commence sending a specific type of traffic against the target. If the attack network is large enough, even ordinary web traffic can quickly overwhelm the largest of sites, such as the 400Gbps CloudFlare attack in early 2014. Since 2016, a newer reflection technique using Connectionless Lightweight Directory Access Protocol (CLDAP) has upped the volume further, with a 1.35Tbps attack against GitHub, a 1.7Tbps attack mitigated by Abor in 2018, and a 2.3Tbps attack mitigated by Amazon Web Services (AWS) in 2020.

The purpose of a DDoS/DoS attack is to prevent access to the target system, and blocking network connections will do this. One method, a SYN flooding attack, can be

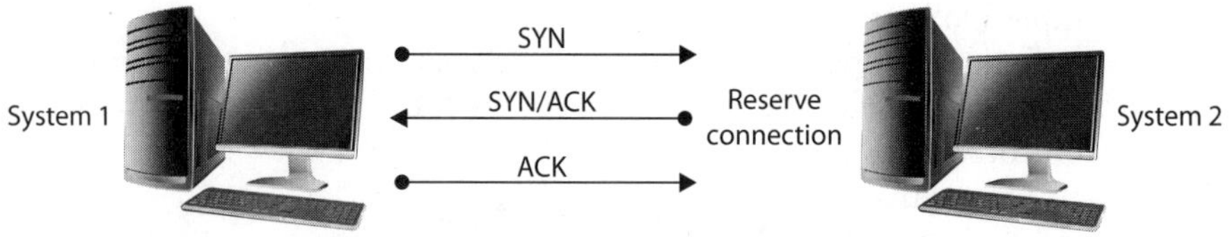

Figure 4-6 The TCP three-way handshake

used to prevent service to a system temporarily in order to take advantage of a trusted relationship that exists between that system and another. SYN flooding is an example of a DoS attack that takes advantage of the way TCP/IP networks were designed to function, and it can be used to illustrate the basic principles of any DoS attack. SYN flooding uses the TCP three-way handshake that establishes a connection between two systems. Under normal circumstances, the first system sends a SYN packet to the system with which it wants to communicate. The second system responds with a SYN/ACK if it is able to accept the request. When the initial system receives the SYN/ACK from the second system, it responds with an ACK packet, and communication can then proceed. This process is shown in Figure 4-6.

In a SYN flooding attack, the attacker sends fake communication requests to the targeted system. Each of these requests will be answered by the target system, which then waits for the third part of the handshake. Since the requests are fake (a nonexistent IP address is used in the requests, so the target system is responding to a system that doesn't exist), the target will wait for responses that never come, as shown in Figure 4-7. The target system will drop these connections after a specific time-out period, but if the attacker sends requests faster than the time-out period eliminates them, the system will quickly be filled with requests. The number of connections a system can support is finite, so when more requests come in than can be processed, the system will soon be reserving all its connections for fake requests. At this point, any further requests are simply dropped (ignored), and legitimate users who want to connect to the target system will not be able to do so, because use of the system has been denied to them.

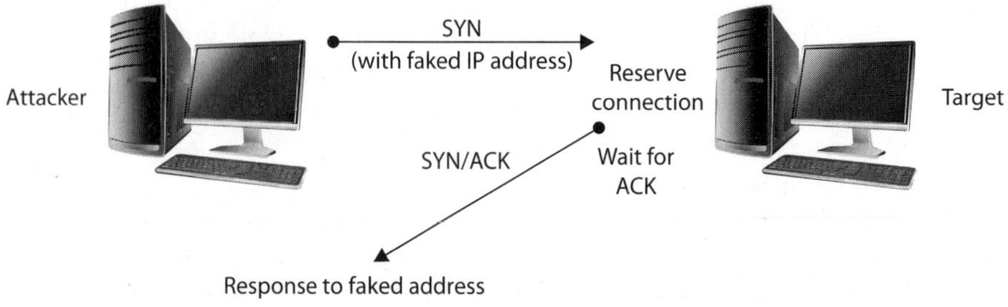

Figure 4-7 A SYN flooding DoS attack

Another simple DoS attack is the infamous ping of death (POD), and it illustrates the other type of attack—one targeted at a specific application or operating system, as opposed to SYN flooding, which targets a protocol. In the POD attack, the attacker sends an Internet Control Message Protocol (ICMP) ping packet equal to, or exceeding, 64 KB (which is to say, greater than 64 × 1024 = 65,536 bytes). This type of packet should not occur naturally (there is no reason for a ping packet to be larger than 64 KB). Certain systems are not able to handle this size of packet, and the system will hang or crash.

As previously mentioned, a newer form of reflection attack uses the Connectionless Lightweight Directory Access Protocol (CLDAP). In this attack, the attacker asks for all the information on all accounts in the Active Directory, pointing the information to the victim machine. Because the attack is spoofed to appear to be coming from a legitimate requestor, the data is sent to the victim machine. This type of attack is clearly preventable, as the UDP port 389 request will have a source IP from inside the network, yet it will come from outside the network. Blocking this port on the inbound firewalls will block this attack.

Application

Applications are subject to DDoS as well, because like all systems, they take user inputs, process the data, and create user outputs. This activity takes resources, and the objective of an application-level DDoS attack is to consume all the resources or to put the system into a failed state. One of the most common targets of an application layer attack is HTTP. Because of the nature of the protocol and because requesters to the application are typically outside of the local network, the packets are not spoofed, and detection of attack packets versus legitimate packets is challenging. Advanced next-generation web application firewalls have some resiliency built in to detect this type of attack, but in severe cases, the issue of DoS is just moved to the firewall.

These types of attacks also work against API interfaces as well. The underlying principles behind the attack come from the disparity between the level of resources it takes to attack versus the level of resources it takes to mitigate this action. Because the resource being attacked is typically processing power, this is not a bandwidth type of attack. To examine this, let's look at the resources for logging in to an online account, such as Gmail. When an attacker sends a request to log in to the account, the amount of data and resources the attacker's computer must process are minimal. The work on the server is disproportionate to this, as it has to check the login credentials, open a session, load any relevant user data from a database, and then send back a response containing the requested web page. This disparity between attacker work and victim workloads is what leads to making this attack successful.

Operational Technology (OT)

Operational technology (OT) is the name given to networks of industrial devices in cyber-physical systems. These devices use computers to control physical processes—from traffic lights, to refineries, to manufacturing plants, and more. There are literally thousands of different industrial processes under computer control. One big differentiator between

OT and IT systems is the protocols. OT systems have OT-specific protocols that are used to perform the communications of equipment control. One of the system characteristics of these processes is the reliance on properly timed signals. These systems do not perform correctly when communications are interrupted, so DoS attacks of any kind, including DDoS, can result in significant problems. For these reasons, and more, OT systems are not directly connected to the Internet and have significant barriers preventing outside packets from getting into these networks.

EXAM TIP Denial-of-service attacks are used as part of a toolset of attacks. These attacks can be temporary against a service such as DNS or other parts of an infrastructure. They are not just "stop everything" events. They can be used as part of an attack strategy, so understand how they interact with the various parts of your enterprise: networks, applications, and systems.

Malicious Code and Script Execution

There are many reasons to use scripts and automation in systems: they promote speed, accuracy, reproducibility, and portability as well as offer a ton of other advantages. Many of these reasons are why attackers use them as well. *Malicious code* and *script execution* are real threats in today's environment. Attackers have a wide range of technologies to choose from when automating their attacks—PowerShell, Python, Bash, macros, and even Visual Basic for Applications are some of the vectors that need to be defended against.

PowerShell

PowerShell is a built-in command-line tool suite that has a rich set of Microsoft Windows commands. PowerShell is completely integrated with the Windows environment, allowing administrators to program virtually any function that can be done in the OS. This is why attackers love PowerShell—it is there, enabled, powerful, and not monitored by most security systems. A wide range of toolsets built to leverage the power of PowerShell can be used to attack a system. A very commonly used tool is PowerSploit, which includes routines such as Invoke-Mimikatz.

Python

Python is a widely used programming language/scripting language. Python is an effective scripting tool that is easy to learn, widely supported, and good at automating tasks and data analysis. This makes it very useful for cybersecurity teams and attackers alike. Hackers use Python for the same reasons, and across GitHub are numerous libraries of Python-driven attack toolsets and utilities.

Bash

Bash (aka Bourne Again Shell) is an interpreter that processes shell commands on Linux systems. Bash takes commands in plaintext format and calls OS services to perform the specified tasks. This enables complete automation of a Linux environment and is therefore valuable to system administrators and attackers alike. One of the strengths of Linux is the ease of programming complex scripts to automate significant system changes and data manipulation. Hackers use Bash to search through systems and perform tasks on Linux systems.

EXAM TIP Differentiating between PowerShell, Python, and Bash use is primarily along operating system lines. PowerShell is used for Windows, Bash is used for Linux, and Python can be used for both.

Macros

Macros are recorded sets of instructions, typically presented to an application to automate their function. The term *macro* is used for scripting applications. Virtually every desktop has PDF functionality or Microsoft Office functionality, and the use of macros in these products enables a great deal of functionality. However, with this functionality comes risk in the form of unwanted macros calling the system and performing system activities. For this reason, restricting macros in these and other applications is an important part of managing the cybersecurity of a workstation.

Visual Basic for Applications (VBA)

Visual Basic for Applications (VBA) is an older technology from Microsoft that was used to automate many internal processes in applications. This is an older form of macro that has significant programming capability but has mostly fallen out of favor. However, it is still valid on a lot of platforms and, as such, is still a vector for attackers. You should therefore protect systems from attack by disabling macros or VBA from running in applications unless you are sure that the source of the document containing the code can be trusted.

EXAM TIP Macros and VBA have their place in enterprises, as this is how applications are automated. However, they should be restricted to trusted sources only.

Chapter Review

In this chapter, you learned about potential indicators associated with network attacks. The chapter begins with wireless attacks, including evil twin, rogue access points, bluesnarfing and bluejacking, disassociation, jamming, RFID, NFC, and IV attacks. Then man in the middle and man in the browser are discussed. The next sections look at network addressing attacks, with layer 2 attacks of ARP poisoning, MAC flooding, and MAC cloning. DNS attacks follow, including domain hijacking, DNS poisoning, URL redirection, and domain reputation attacks.

Denial-of-service attacks are examined with respect to three different types of service: network, applications, and OT systems. The chapter closes with an examination of malicious code and script execution from PowerShell, Python, Bash, macros, and Visual Basic for Applications.

Questions

To help you prepare further for the CompTIA Security+ exam, and to test your level of preparedness, answer the following questions and then check your answers against the correct answers at the end of the chapter.

1. A user reports "odd" certificate warnings on her web browser this morning whenever she visits Google. Looking at her browser, you see these certificate warnings. Looking at the network traffic, you notice that all HTTP and HTTPS requests from that system are being routed to the same IP regardless of destination. Which of the following attack types are you seeing in this case?
   - **A.** Evil twin
   - **B.** Man in the middle
   - **C.** Disassociation
   - **D.** MAC cloning
2. Users are reporting that the wireless network on one side of the building is broken. They can connect but can't seem to get to the Internet. While investigating, you notice all of the affected users are connecting to an access point you don't recognize. These users have fallen victim to what type of attack?
   - **A.** Rogue AP
   - **B.** WPS
   - **C.** Bluejacking
   - **D.** Disassociation
3. You're sitting at the airport when your friend gets a message on her phone. In the text is a picture of a duck with the word "Pwnd" as the caption. Your friend doesn't know who sent the message. Your friend is a victim of what type of attack?
   - **A.** Snarfing
   - **B.** Bluejacking
   - **C.** Quacking
   - **D.** Collision
4. All of the wireless users on the third floor of your building are reporting issues with the network. Every 15 minutes, their devices disconnect from the network. Within a minute or so they are able to reconnect. What type of attack is most likely underway in this situation?
   - **A.** Evil twin
   - **B.** Jamming
   - **C.** Domain hijacking
   - **D.** Disassociation

5. Your e-commerce site is crashing under an extremely high traffic volume. Looking at the traffic logs, you see tens of thousands of requests for the same URL coming from hundreds of different IP addresses around the world. What type of attack are you facing?
   - **A.** Domain hijacking
   - **B.** DDoS
   - **C.** DNS poisoning
   - **D.** URL redirection
6. A user wants to know if the network is down because she is unable to connect to anything. While troubleshooting, you notice the MAC address for her default gateway setting doesn't match the MAC address of your organization's router. What type of attack has been used against this user?
   - **A.** MAC cloning
   - **B.** ARP poisoning
   - **C.** Disassociation
   - **D.** Rogue access point
7. You have a helpdesk ticket for a system that is acting strangely. Looking at the system remotely, you see the following in the browser cache: www.micros0ft.com/office. What type of attack are you seeing?
   - **A.** PowerShell
   - **B.** Domain hijacking
   - **C.** URL redirection
   - **D.** Disassociation
8. You are seeing a bunch of PDFs flood people's inboxes with titles such as "New Tax Rates for 2021." What attack vector is most likely in use?
   - **A.** Python
   - **B.** Macro
   - **C.** Man in the middle
   - **D.** DDoS
9. When you update your browser, you get a warning about a plugin not being compatible with the new version. You do not recognize the plugin, and you aren't sure what it does. Why is it important to understand plugins? What attack vector can be involved in plugins?
   - **A.** Man in the middle attack
   - **B.** Domain hijacking attack
   - **C.** Man in the browser attack
   - **D.** URL redirection attack

10. Your network scan is showing a large number of address changes to the MAC tables and lots of ARP and RARP messages. What is happening?
    A. MAC flooding attack
    B. Disassociation attack
    C. Jamming attack
    D. DNS poisoning

Answers

1. **B.** This is most likely some type of man in the middle attack. This attack method is usually done by routing all of the victim's traffic to the attacker's host, where the attacker can view it, modify it, or block it. The attacker inserts himself into the middle of his victim's network communications.
2. **A.** This is a rogue AP attack. Attackers set up their own access points in an attempt to get wireless devices to connect to the rogue APs instead of the authorized access points.
3. **B.** This is most likely a bluejacking attack. If a victim's phone has Bluetooth enabled and is in discoverable mode, it may be possible for an attacker to send unwanted texts, images, or audio to the victim's phone.
4. **D.** Disassociation attacks against a wireless system are attacks designed to disassociate a host from the wireless access point and from the wireless network. If the attacker has a list of MAC addresses for the wireless devices, they can spoof de-authentication frames, causing the wireless devices to disconnect from the network.
5. **B.** This is a DDoS attack. DDoS (or distributed denial-of-service) attacks attempt to overwhelm their targets with traffic from many different sources. Botnets are quite commonly used to launch DDoS attacks.
6. **B.** ARP poisoning is an attack that involves sending spoofed ARP or RARP replies to a victim in an attempt to alter the ARP table on the victim's system. If successful, an ARP poisoning attack will replace one of more MAC addresses in the victim's ARP table with the MAC address the attacker supplies in their spoofed responses.
7. **C.** This is a URL redirection, as the name Microsoft has a zero in place of the *o* character.
8. **B.** PDFs have macro capability and can execute a variety of code bases if allowed.
9. **C.** Man in the browser attacks are frequently carried out via browser extensions or plugins.
10. **A.** This is a MAC flooding attack—an attempt to overflow the MAC tables in the switches.

CHAPTER 5

Threat Actors, Vectors, and Intelligence Sources

In this chapter, you will

- Explore the different types of threat actors and their attributes
- Examine different threat vectors and be able to differentiate them
- Explain the different threat intelligence sources and associated research sources

Threats are actions that can result in risk to a system. A threat actor is the source of the threat on the system. Vectors are the methods that threat actors use to attack a vulnerability in a system in order to achieve their objective. Threat intelligence is knowledge based on evidence that allows you to prevent or mitigate cyber threats.

Certification Objective This chapter covers CompTIA Security+ exam objective 1.5: Explain different threat actors, vectors, and intelligence sources.

Actors and Threats

The act of deliberately accessing computer systems and networks without authorization is generally referred to as *hacking,* with individuals who conduct this activity being referred to as *hackers.* The term *hacking* also applies to the act of exceeding one's authority in a system. This would include authorized users who attempt to gain access to files they aren't permitted to access or who attempt to obtain permissions they have not been granted. While the act of breaking into computer systems and networks has been glorified in the media and movies, the physical act does not live up to the Hollywood hype. Intruders are, if nothing else, extremely patient, since the process of gaining access to a system takes persistence and dogged determination. The attacker will conduct many pre-attack activities in order to obtain the information needed to determine which attack will most likely be successful. Typically, by the time an attack is launched, the attacker will have gathered enough information to be very confident that the attack will succeed.

Generally, attacks by an individual or even a small group of attackers fall into the *unstructured threat* category. Attacks at this level generally are conducted over short periods of time (lasting at most a few months), do not involve a large number of individuals, have little financial backing, and are accomplished by insiders or outsiders who do not

Figure 5-1 Distribution of attacker skill levels

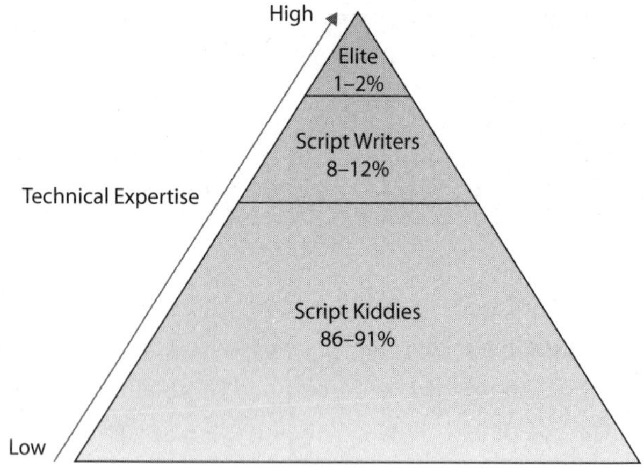

seek collusion with insiders. Intruders, or those who are attempting to conduct an intrusion, definitely come in many different varieties and have varying degrees of sophistication (see Figure 5-1).

NOTE Figure 5-1 will be referenced throughout this chapter as we discuss different hacker skill levels.

EXAM TIP Be prepared for questions that require you to identify differences between the types of threat actors, including those listed in sections later in this chapter.

Advanced Persistent Threats (APTs)

A major advance in cyberattacks is the development of *advanced persistent threats (APTs)*. An APT attack is characterized by using toolkits to achieve a presence on a target network and then, instead of just moving to steal information, focusing on the long game by maintaining a persistent presence on the target network. The tactics, tools, and procedures of APTs are focused on maintaining administrative access to the target network and avoiding detection. Then, over the long haul, the attacker can remove intellectual property and more from the organization, typically undetected.

Operation Night Dragon was the name given to an intellectual property attack executed against oil, gas, and petrochemical companies in the United States in 2006. Using a set of global servers, attackers from China raided global energy companies for proprietary and highly confidential information such as bidding data for leases. The attack shed new light on what constitutes critical data and associated risks. Further, as demonstrated by the Stuxnet attacks against Iranian uranium plants, the cyberattacks in Estonia, and the attacks on electricity distribution in Ukraine, the risk of nation-state attacks is real. There have been numerous accusations of intellectual property theft being sponsored by, and in some cases even performed by, nation-state actors. In a world where information dominates government, business, and economies, the collection of information is the key to success, and with large rewards, the list of characters willing to spend significant resources is high.

Insider Threats

It is generally acknowledged by security professionals that *insiders* are more dangerous in many respects than outside intruders. The reason for this is simple: insiders have the access and knowledge necessary to cause immediate damage to an organization. Most security is designed to protect against outside intruders and thus lies at the boundary between the organization and the rest of the world. Insiders may actually already have all the access they need to perpetrate criminal activity such as fraud. In addition to unprecedented access, insiders also frequently have knowledge of the security systems in place and are better able to avoid detection. Attacks by insiders are often the result of employees who have become disgruntled with their organization and are looking for ways to disrupt operations. It is also possible that an "attack" by an insider may be an accident and not intended as an attack at all. An example of this might be an employee who deletes a critical file without understanding its critical nature.

EXAM TIP One of the hardest threats that security professionals will have to address is that of the insider. Since employees already have access to the organization and its assets, additional mechanisms need to be in place to detect attacks by insiders and to lessen the ability of these attacks to succeed.

Employees are not the only insiders who organizations need to be concerned about. Often, numerous other individuals have physical access to company facilities. Custodial crews frequently have unescorted access throughout the facility, often when nobody else is around. Other individuals, such as contractors or partners, may have not only physical access to the organization's facilities but also access to computer systems and networks. A contractor involved in U.S. intelligence computing, Edward Snowden, was charged with espionage in 2013 after he released a wide range of data illustrating the technical capabilities of U.S. intelligence surveillance systems. He was the ultimate insider, with his name becoming synonymous with the insider threat issue.

NOTE One of the ways to protect against a skilled hacker is to prevent any individual from performing critical duties alone. The method of doing this is through separation of duties, a policy whereby critical functions require more than one person to affect the changes.

State Actors

At the top end of the spectrum shown in Figure 5-1 are those highly technical individuals, often referred to as *elite hackers,* who not only have the ability to write scripts that exploit vulnerabilities but also are capable of discovering new vulnerabilities. This group is the smallest of the lot, however, and is responsible for, at most, only 1 to 2 percent of intrusive activity. Many of these elite hackers are employed by major cybersecurity firms in an effort to combat criminal activity. Others are employed by nation-states and other international organizations, to train and run large groups of skilled hackers to conduct nation-state attacks against a wide range of adversaries. In the United States, government rules and regulations prevent government workers from attacking companies for reasons of economic warfare. Not all countries live by this principle, and many have organized hacking efforts designed to gather information from international companies, stealing intellectual property for the express purpose of advancing their own country's national companies.

EXAM TIP State actors are employed by governments to compromise or gain access to the intelligence data of targeted governments. They are typically well funded and often carry out APT attacks.

As nations have increasingly become dependent on computer systems and networks, the possibility that the essential elements of society might be targeted by organizations or other nations determined to adversely affect them has become a reality. Many nations today have developed to some extent the capability to conduct *information warfare*. There are several definitions for information warfare, but a simple one is that it is warfare conducted against the information and information-processing equipment used by an adversary. In practice, this is a much more complicated subject, because information not only may be the target of an adversary, but also may be used as a weapon. Whatever definition you use, information warfare falls into the *highly structured threat* category. This type of threat is characterized by a much longer period of preparation (years is not uncommon), tremendous financial backing, and a large and organized group of attackers. The threat may include attempts not only to subvert insiders but also to plant individuals inside of a potential target in advance of a planned attack.

An interesting aspect of information warfare is the list of possible targets available. We have grown accustomed to the idea that, during war, military forces will target opposing military forces but will generally attempt to destroy as little civilian infrastructure as possible. In information warfare, military forces are certainly still a key target, but much has been written about other targets, such as the various infrastructures that a nation relies on for its daily existence. Water, electricity, oil and gas refineries and distribution, banking and finance, telecommunications all fall into the category of critical infrastructures for a nation. Critical infrastructures are those whose loss would have severe repercussions on the nation. With countries relying so heavily on these infrastructures, it is inevitable that they will be viewed as valid targets during conflict. Given how dependent these infrastructures are on computer systems and networks, it is also inevitable that these same computer systems and networks will be targeted for a cyberattack in an information war.

Hacktivists

As shown in Figure 5-1, at the next level below elite hackers are those people who are capable of writing scripts to exploit known vulnerabilities. These individuals are much more technically competent than script kiddies (the bottom end of the spectrum) and account for an estimated 8 to 12 percent of malicious Internet activity. When hackers work together for a collectivist effort, typically on behalf of some cause, they are referred to as *hacktivists*. Hacktivist groups may include script kiddies, but in general script kiddies do not have the skills to participate in a meaningful manner in advancing a hacktivist cause, although they may be enlisted as ground troops to add volume to an attack.

Script Kiddies

At the low end of the spectrum, technically speaking, are what are generally referred to as *script kiddies*—individuals who do not have the technical expertise to develop scripts or discover new vulnerabilities in software, but who have just enough understanding of computer systems to be able to download and run scripts that others have developed. These individuals generally are not interested in attacking specific targets but instead simply want to find any organization that may not have patched a newly discovered vulnerability for which the script kiddie has located a script to exploit. It is hard to estimate how many of the individuals performing activities such as probing networks or scanning individual systems are part of this group, but it is undoubtedly the fastest growing group, and the vast majority of the "unfriendly" activity occurring on the Internet is probably carried out by these individuals.

Criminal Syndicates

As businesses became increasingly reliant upon computer systems and networks, and as the amount of financial transactions conducted via the Internet increased, it was inevitable that *organized crime* would eventually turn to the electronic world as a new target to exploit. One of the major changes over the past decade in cybersecurity has been the ability for hackers to monetize their efforts. Part of this is due to the rise in cryptocurrency, such as bitcoin, but an entire marketplace on the dark web exists for stolen identities, financial data, and intellectual property that, in terms of dollars, is larger than the international drug trade. This has led to a whole new class of organized crime figure, cybersecurity criminals, who can lurk in the shadows of anonymity and create malware and perform attacks, all with an eye on making money.

Criminal activity on the Internet at its most basic is no different from criminal activity in the physical world. Fraud, extortion, theft, embezzlement, and forgery all take place in the electronic environment.

One difference between criminal groups and the "average" hacker is the level of organization that criminal elements employ in their attack. Criminal groups typically have more money to spend on accomplishing the criminal activity and are willing to spend extra time accomplishing the task, provided the level of reward at the conclusion is great enough. With the tremendous amount of money that is exchanged via the Internet on a daily basis, the level of reward for a successful attack is high enough to interest criminal elements. Attacks by criminal organizations usually fall into the *structured threat* category, which is characterized by a greater amount of planning, a longer period of time to conduct the activity, more financial backing to accomplish it, and possibly corruption of, or collusion with, insiders.

Hackers

Hackers is a loaded term, as it is used by many for different purposes. The original use of the term related to individuals who spent time trying to figure out how something worked so that they could control it in ways it wasn't designed. This sometimes meant subverting controls, leading to unauthorized uses. Today, this group still exists. But many also use the term to describe anyone who improperly uses computers, including criminals. This has led to the descriptors authorized, unauthorized, and semi-authorized.

Authorized

Authorized individualswho use their computer "hacking" skills for good purposes have the common name "white hat" hackers. They can be security consultants chasing vulnerabilities or performing penetration tests, as well as many other security activities. The difference between a white hat and someone breaking the law is that the white hat hacker is using the same tools and techniques as the threat actors, but is doing so with permission so that a firm can learn its weaknesses and fix them.

Unauthorized

Black hat hackers are the opposite of white hats. Rather than use their skills for good, they use their skills for illegal and criminal activities. Individuals and groups that act in an unauthorized manner are violating laws and causing risk to systems. There are many different motivations behind black hat hackers, but in the end, they are performing activities that are illegal.

Semi-authorized

Gray hat hackers live with one foot in each world. They may use their skills for good at their job as a white hat hacker, but then at other times they use the same skills illegally acting as a black hat hacker. This group of semi-authorized hackers works in both the legally sanctioned world of security and the illegal realm of criminal activity.

EXAM TIP Know that white hat/authorized hackers are experts who protect systems, black hat/unauthorized hackers are criminals who hack devices and apps to steal data, and gray hat/semi-authourized hackers often violate ethics and laws, but do not always have the same malicious intent as black hat hackers.

NOTE Why the terms *black hat* and *white hat*? These are a throwback reference to old cowboy movies, where the good guy wore a white hat and the villain wore a black hat.

Shadow IT

Shadow IT is a name given to the parts of an organization that perform their own IT functions. These groups rise up out of a desire to "get things done" when central IT does not respond in what the unit considers to be a reasonable time frame. While this vigilante IT effort might seem helpful, because it is outside the control of the central IT function, the IT systems created are not in the same realm of protection. If you set up a wireless access point so you can move about your office untethered by a network cable, the question becomes, who keeps this network connection safe from outside threats? If a hard drive fails on a shadow IT part of the infrastructure, was it backed up correctly? How will data be recovered? Generally speaking, shadow IT is a symptom of a less that perfectly functioning central IT process and can lead to increased risk. Shadow IT can become a significant risk as its infrastructure provides inside users with increased access and connections.

Competitors

Competitors can be a threat to a business on the field of battle: sales, markdowns, rival products—it is a battle for customers every day. But this is just business—legal and normal. But competitors have been known to attack other firms' IT processes. The methods vary from simple false product reviews to more serious elements such as the actual hacking of systems. There have been several recorded cases of criminal activity on the part of one firm against another. This includes stealing intellectual property or customer lists as well as other activities such as denial-of-service attacks.

Attributes of Actors

Threat actors can be divided into groups based on abilities. There are other ways to differentiate the threat actors: by location (internal or external), level of sophistication, level of resources, and intent. These attributes are described next.

Internal/External

Internal threat actors have one significant advantage over external actors: they have access to the system. Although the access may be limited to the user level, it still provides the threat actor the ability to pursue their attack. External actors have an additional step to take: the establishment of access to the target system.

Level of Sophistication/Capability

As shown earlier in Figure 5-1, attacker skill or sophistication can be divided into a few categories. However, within a group of threat actors, the skill level of the individual members of the group may well be mixed, with a few highly skilled individuals acting to move larger numbers of less skilled participants. The greater the skill level, the more an individual will be expected to lead and design the attacks. When it comes to the sophistication level of the attack itself, one notable trend is that as the skill level goes up, so too does the use of minimal methods. Although zero-day attacks are widely covered in the news, true zero-day vulnerabilities are rarely used; they are reserved for the few cases where there are no other options, because once these they vulnerabilities are exploited, they will be patched. Even with highly sophisticated and resourced nation-state teams employing APT methods, a surprising number of attacks are old attacks, exploit old vulnerabilities, and use simple methods that take advantage of "low-hanging fruit." This is not to say that newer, more advanced methods are not used, but rather there is an economy of mechanism in the attacks themselves, using just what is needed at each step. There is also a lot of data missing in this scenario, as we do not know of the methods that have been used successfully if the threat actor remains undetected.

Resources/Funding

As mentioned earlier, criminal organizations and nation-states have larger budgets, bigger teams, and the ability to pursue campaigns for longer periods of time. Cybersecurity is challenging for attackers as well as defenders, and there are expenses associated with maintaining teams and tools used by threat actors against a system. APTs, with their penchant for long-term attacks, some lasting for years, require significant resources to engage in this type of activity, so there is a need for long-term resources that only major organizations or governments can manage over time.

Intent/Motivation

The intent or motivation behind an attack can be simple or multifold in nature. A script kiddie is just trying to make a technique work. A more skilled threat actor is usually pursuing a specific objective, such as trying to make a point as a hacktivist. At the top of the intent pyramid is the APT threat actor, whose intent or motivation is at least threefold: First is the drive to maintain continual access. Second is the drive to remain undetected. In most APTs that are discovered, the length of intrusion is greater than a year and in many cases determining the original date of infection is not possible, as it is limited by the length of logs. Third is the goal of stealing something of value on the network. APTs do not go to all the trouble of maintaining access and remaining invisible just to crash a system or force a rebuild.

EXAM TIP The Security+ exam will describe threat actors in terms of attributes: resources, level of sophistication, location, and motivation. Be sure to understand how these differences matter with respect to the types of attacks.

Vectors

Threats are perpetuated by threat actors, and they use various vectors to exploit vulnerabilities in a system, giving them unauthorized access. *Vectors* is the term for the various methods that an attacker can use to get in—whether it is direct access via wireless or e-mail channels, social media, supply chain, an external data source such as removable media, or the cloud. The bottom line is, if there is a way to move data into your system, this can be a potential vector for attackers to use, so you must take appropriate safeguards.

EXAM TIP Be prepared for questions that require you to identify differences between the types of threat vectors.

Direct Access

Direct access is just that: the attacker has direct access to the system. This can be an insider attack, or perhaps outsiders are given the ability to interact directly with the systems, such as web servers. Direct access is why we need to use the principle of least privilege, only giving the necessary permissions and blocking all others. In the case of an outsider being granted permission to use a system (say, to create pages on the site), it is imperative that all outside input is treated as dangerous until proven otherwise.

Wireless

Wireless networks bring much in the way of networking simplicity. But with this ease of connecting machines comes a whole host of security issues. For details on the issues of overall wireless security, see Chapter 20. With respect to attack vectors, *wireless* access brings a host of new opportunities. No longer does the attacker have to have direct physical access to the network—a wireless signal can bring it to the attacker, who may only have to sit in the parking lot to perform their attack.

E-mail

E-mail is one of the preferred vectors for social engineering attacks. Sending an e-mail that includes links or attachments is a manner of interacting with a user. If a convincing message is included, users may click on the links or open the attachment, and the vector has done its job—delivering the payload.

Supply Chain

A *supply chain* vector involves using a company's supply chain as an unwitting agent in the attack. There are numerous forms of attacks that can be delivered in this fashion, and several are covered in Chapters 1 and 33. The concept is relatively simple: an attacker finds a means by which they can get their attack code into the supply chain for a product or an update—for example, attacking a vendor and leaving the code on a program used to test storage hardware, thus leaving the bad code on new storage device, or attacking the update mechanism by poisoning one of the update files that is distributed via the web. Firms tend to trust their vendors and may skip security checks such as validating downloads with hashes. This is an area where Microsoft has excelled: its update process has numerous security checks, making it virtually impossible to poison one of the company's updates.

In December 2020, a popular centralized management software package, Solar Winds Orion, was discovered to have been breached by a nation-state actor. This breach into the product chain went unnoticed for nine months, spreading across the top corporations and government agencies. The list of breached firms will not be known until sometime in 2021, but the biggest names in tech, Microsoft, Cisco, FireEye, and major

US government agencies, have already begun dealing with the damage. The attack, using the supply chain of a commonly used tool suite, was sophisticated and remarkably advanced, remaining in the shadows for months. Supply chain attacks are a real threat and one that can't be stopped just by policy and contracts.

Social Media

Social media can be a vector for social engineering attacks because it connects an attacker directly to a user, and many of the security checks seen with corporate e-mail and other communication channels are not present. By sending a shortened URL, the attacker can often get people to click on it, and then with crafty redirection, bad things can happen prior to the desired GIF showing up, and the user is never the wiser of the payload that was delivered. Social media–based social engineering attacks are covered in Chapter 1.

Removable Media

Removable media, typically in the form of USB memory sticks, represents a clear threat vector. This type of storage is small, ubiquitous, and takes no skill to attach to a PC. How this becomes a threat is driven by social engineering. An attacker takes a USB storage device and puts the attacking module on it so that it can be executed. Then, the trick is to get someone to interact with the file. Placing the USB device in a location prone to discovery leads to an attack referred to as a "USB drop attack" (see Chapter 2). As with all behavioral attacks, user education is needed (in this case, users should be taught not to touch "abandoned" USB drives). They should view USB storage devices as "dog poop" and avoid picking them up and using them. You can also employ USB blockers and disable AutoPlay (which may be enabled by default) for USB and removable media. These system-level protections may make a lot of sense in specific machines such as kiosks or those machines exposed to the public.

Cloud

The *cloud* is another attack vector. If you are connected to the cloud, it will be for business purposes, and therefore you will have some form of trust in it. But if you view the cloud, and especially cloud storage, as just someone else's computer, you can see the vector. If your cloud agreement does not include antivirus protections on files, then it is really no different from any other Internet-connected source.

Threat Intelligence Sources

Cybersecurity is a game of resource management. No firm has the resources to protect everything against all threats, and even attempting to do so would add complexity that would open up other threat avenues. One of the important decisions to be made is where to apply one's resources in the complex landscape of cybersecurity defense. Threat intelligence is the gathering of information from a variety of sources, including nonpublic sources, to allow an entity to properly focus its defenses against the most likely threat actors. *Threat intelligence sources* are the places where one can get this information, and there is a wide range of them—from open source, to proprietary, to specialized sources. These are covered in the following sessions.

EXAM TIP Be prepared for questions that require you to identify the differences between the types of threat intelligence sources.

Open Source Intelligence (OSINT)

Open source intelligence, sometimes called *open source threat intelligence*, refers to intelligence data collected from public sources. There is a wide range of public sources of information concerning current cybersecurity activity. From news articles, to blogs, to government reports, there seems to be a never-ending stream of news concerning what is happening, to whom, and how. The challenge is in collating the information into a usable format, which is a need that open source intelligence feeds fill.

There are a wide range of open source feeds, and each can add value, but the important question for each feed is where its information comes from, how vetted the information is, and how up to date the collection is. Here is a list of several sources and basic answers to these questions:

- **Department of Homeland Security (DHS)** Automated Indicator Sharing is a collection of information such as malicious e-mail addresses, IP addresses, and other bad material reported by private companies to the DHS via its Automated Indicator Sharing (AIS) portal. This list is curated, and depends on firms contributing to it to keep it up to date and comprehensive.
- **Federal Bureau of Investigation (FBI)** InfraGard Portal is a vetted access collection of security information reported to the FBI. It tends to focus on critical infrastructure and can have significant time lags, as the FBI holds information involved in investigations.
- **SANS** Internet Storm Center (ISC) is a distributed sensor network that processes over 20 million intrusion detection log entries per day and generates alerts concerning security threats.
- **VirusTotal** Now operated by Google, VirusTotal uses feeds from a myriad of antivirus scanners to maintain a signature database of malware and related information.
- **Cisco** The Talos Intelligence team produces a feed of information for Cisco customers (a free version is also available). The breadth of Cisco's collection and the depth of its research team makes this an important feed for new and emerging dangers.

Closed/Proprietary

The threat intelligence marketplace is filled with security firms offering threat intelligence products. One of their primary offerings is access to their *closed* or *proprietary* threat intelligence database. In evaluating these offerings, one of the key factors is the number and diversity of data feeds. What is the source of their data and what characteristics do they have with respect to the data in their database? Most firms will offer an automatable file format feed from their data structures to provide information to security tools from their data. Common formats include CSV, XML, JSON, and STIX. STIX (the Structured Threat Information Expression format) is specifically covered later in this chapter. Other important factors include things such as how often the data is updated and what industries are the focus of the data. The industry question is important because, although at one level all IT systems face the same sea of vulnerabilities, threat actors have patterns and they tend to operate by industry, making industry exposures different from one to the next.

Vulnerability Databases

Vulnerabilities are the weaknesses in software that allow an attacker a means of entry. You need to know what is vulnerable and either patch the vulnerability or provide a defensive solution to prevent the vulnerability from being exposed to an attacker. Knowing what vulnerabilities exist in software is a challenge. Because there are so many pieces of software and so many vulnerabilities, this is a data problem that needs a database to catalog and maintain. And there are *vulnerability databases*—and not one but several. For example, the National Vulnerability Database (NVD) hosted at nvd.nist.gov is a repository of vulnerabilities and related information such as security checklist references, security-related software flaws, misconfigurations, product names, and impact metrics.

There have been other attempts at creating vulnerability databases, including the long-running Open Source Vulnerability Database (OSVDB), which ran from 2004 until 2016, when it became a subscription model. Most of the vulnerability databases marketed by security firms are modified from the NVD. One major exception is the Metasploit vulnerability database, which is a curated repository of vetted exploits to vulnerabilities that are used in the Metasploit framework.

Public/Private Information Sharing Centers

In the realm of *public/private information sharing centers* are Information Sharing and Analysis Centers (ISACs) and Information Sharing and Analysis Organizations (ISAOs). ISAOs vary greatly in capability but essentially include any organization, whether an industry sector or geographic region, that is sharing cyber-related information for the purpose of enhancing their members' cybersecurity posture. ISACs are a special category of ISAO consisting of privately run, but government approved, industry-based cybersecurity. ISACs may be considered fusion centers where real-time information can be shared between members. ISAOs and ISACs work on a very simple premise: share what is happening to you, and together learn what is happening in your industry. The sharing is anonymized, the analysis is performed by highly skilled workers in a security operations center, and the resulting information is fed back to members as close to real time as possible. Highly skilled analysts are expensive, and this mechanism shares the costs across all of the member institutions.

A U.S. government program, InfraGard, is run by the FBI and also acts as a means of sharing, although timeliness and level of analysis are nowhere near that of an ISAC, but the price is right (free).

Dark Web

The *dark web* is a subset of the worldwide content on the Internet that has its access restricted via specific obfuscation methods. Dark web sites are sites that require Tor—a free, open source software that enables anonymous communication. Because the dark web exists only in the realm of onion routing, dark web sites end with .onion, as opposed to .com, .net, and so on. When a browser is on the dark web, because of the onion routing protocol, the access is anonymous. This has made the dark web a haven for criminal activity, and one can find a lot of illegal items there—from stolen information to illicit substances.

NOTE There is an area of the Internet called the deep web, which is the part of the Internet that is not indexed by search engines. One example of the deep web is material that requires you to log in to an account before it is exposed. Yes, the deep web is readily accessible to a browser, but only with specific information, such as a login to get there. This is different from the dark web. So, while some may use the terms interchangeably, there is a difference between the deep web and dark web.

Indicators of Compromise

Indicators of compromise (IoCs) are just as the name suggests: indications that a system has been compromised by unauthorized activity. When a threat actor makes changes to a system, either by direct action, malware, or other exploit, forensic artifacts are left behind in the system. IoCs act as breadcrumbs for investigators, providing little clues that can help identify the presence of an attack on a system. The challenge is in looking for, collecting, and analyzing these bits of information and then determining what they mean for a given system. This is one of the primary tasks for an incident responder: gathering and processing these disparate pieces of data and creating a meaningful picture of the current state of a system.

Fortunately, there are toolsets to aid the investigator in this task. Tools such as YARA can take a set of signatures (also called IoCs) and then scan a system for them, determining whether or not a specific threshold is met indicating a particular infection. Although the specific list will vary based on the system and the specific threat that one is looking for, a common set of IoCs that firms should monitor include the following:

- Unusual outbound network traffic
- Anomalies in privileged user account activity
- Geographical irregularities in network traffic
- Account login red flags
- Increases in database read volumes
- HTML response sizes
- Large numbers of requests for the same file

- Mismatched port-application traffic, including encrypted traffic on plain ports
- Suspicious registry or system file changes
- Unusual DNS requests
- Unexpected patching of systems
- Mobile device profile changes
- Bundles of data in the wrong place
- Web traffic with nonhuman behavior
- Signs of DDoS activity, even if temporary

No single compromise will exhibit everything on this list, but monitoring these items will tend to catch most compromises, because at some point in the compromise lifecycle, every compromise will exhibit one or more of the preceding behaviors. Then, once a compromise is detected, the responder can zero in on the information and fully document the nature and scope of the problem.

EXAM TIP Be aware that typical indicators of compromise may include virus signatures, domain names or URLs of botnet servers, and MD5 hashes of malware.

Automated Indicator Sharing (AIS)

Created by the U.S. Department of Homeland Security, *Automated Indicator Sharing (AIS)* is an automated, bidirectional cyber-threat indicator method that's used for reporting. A key element of AIS is that it operates at machine speed, permitting near-real-time reporting and response. Firms must sign up to join this effort, and once they agree to anonymized information sharing, their connection is established. The goal of the AIS program is to commoditize collection of threat intelligence information to enable everyone access to feeds of cyber threats. The AIS system uses the Structured Threat Information Expression (STIX) and Trusted Automated Exchange of Intelligence Information (TAXII) specifications to enable machine-to-machine communication at machine speed. Participants in AIS must be able to produce and consume these protocols.

Structured Threat Information Expression (STIX) / Trusted Automated Exchange of Intelligence Information (TAXII)

To communicate cyber-threat information at machine speed, the U.S. Department of Homeland Security initiated the STIX/TAXII (Structured Threat Information Expression / Trusted Automated Exchange of Intelligence Information) program in 2012. Now governed by the international consensus body OASIS, both STIX and TAXII provide a set of community-driven standards that enable the automated exchange of information associated with cyber threats, network defense, and threat analysis. STIX is a standardized, machine-readable (yet also human-readable) structured language to represent cyber-threat information. TAXII defines a set of services and message exchanges that enable the automated sharing of actionable cyber-threat information across organizational, product line, and service boundaries. TAXII represents the transport method, and STIX represents the message.

EXAM TIP Remember that STIX represents the cyber-threat information (threat intelligence) while TAXII defines how the information is exchanged. You can think of TAXII as "how you get there."

Predictive Analysis

Predictive analysis is the use of threat intelligence information to anticipate the next move of a threat. Typically this is done by curating large quantities of data from multiple sources and sifting through this sea of data to find the key pieces of information that are necessary to put together a hypothesis about what threats are potentially up to and determine how to find them in your enterprise. As each industry has different threat actors, and each set of threat actors tends to use specific methods, this effort works best when tailored to the specifics of an industry. It can also be useful in examining new threats that emerge because of some specific factor, such as negative press surrounding your firm, making it a target for a variety of hacktivists.

Threat Maps

Threat maps are geographical representations of attacks showing where packets are coming from and going to, as shown in Figure 5-2. These gain a lot of media attention and are nice to look at, but one must approach them with caution. Attribution is difficult, and just because an attack comes from an IP in a certain city does not mean the attack actually originated from there. The machine that is attacking you may well be a victim, with the attacker working from somewhere else to make investigations across borders more difficult and expensive.

File/Code Repositories

One of the major areas of growth in software development over the past decade has been *file/code repositories*. Repositories such as GitHub act as locations where people can work together on projects and develop software. These repositories can play two distinct roles in threat intelligence. First, they can offer a source of information to adversaries about how software is built, giving them a chance to examine the source code for vulnerabilities. If your organization uses code from a repository and you make it known to the world (typically because one of your employees is a contributor), then you are providing adversaries information about your infrastructure that could be used against you. Second, you can use the same sources to examine the capabilities of some of the tools your adversaries will use against you. Therefore, code repositories are neither good nor bad with respect to threat intelligence; rather, they are a source for both sides of the equation.

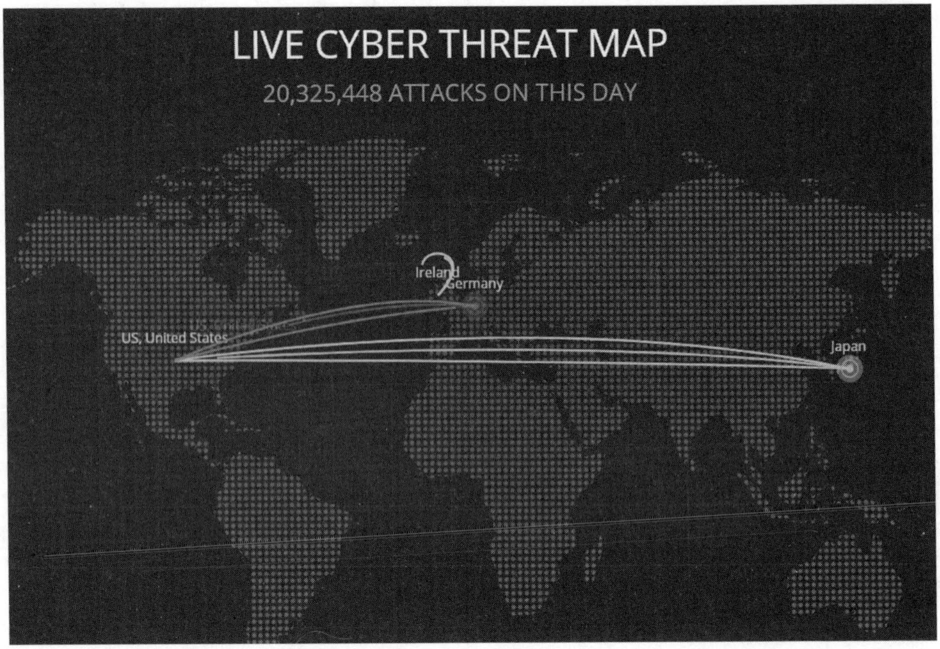

Figure 5-2 Threat map example

NOTE When you develop software in house, maintaining a repository of where all the modules came from, including versions, is important for tracing issues. This is called a software bill of material (software BOM) and is important when you learn of vulnerabilities in code you are reusing.

Research Sources

When someone wants to research a topic, one of the challenges is finding sources of information that are vetted for veracity. Threat intelligence is no different. There are a wide range of sources, from vendors to local industry groups, from vulnerability feeds to threat feeds, from conferences to academic journals to requests for comment (RFCs) entries. These and more will be reviewed in this section, but note that each has strengths and weaknesses, which can be critical, so a good mix of sources is important to employ.

EXAM TIP Be prepared for questions that require you to identify differences between the types of threat research sources.

Vendor Websites

Every vendor wants to be a valued partner in your security problem and share in your budget. To get there, they have marketing teams that develop nice-looking websites. These *vendor websites* appear to be teeming with information—information designed to make you want to partner with them. But remember, this is just marketing—you need to find out what their sources are, how they are curated, and what standards they use. This is not saying that the material is bad, just that the old axiom *caveat emptor* applies.

Vulnerability Feeds

As mentioned in the previous section, the quality of vulnerability feeds can vary greatly from one source to another. To ensure you have good sources, it is important to vet your feeds for a variety of issues, including what the source of the data is and what specific characteristics are presented as part of the feed. Additionally, multiple feeds are almost mandatory for coverage, but that also means you need to compare the items between the feeds because two sets of feeds with a single common source (say, the NVD) do not actually provide more value. Using multiple feeds, with different sources and characteristics, consolidated to a single database is the path to better coverage.

Conferences

Academics perform research, and when the research has a timeliness component, then waiting for a journal article (covered in the next section) is a problem. The solution to this problem is publishing the material and presenting it at a conference. This has two advantages: First, the timelines for conference submissions are much shorter than journals. Second, the presentation of the material at the conference is a good way to get multiple points of view in the form of feedback in a quicker fashion. The downside is that until this feedback is considered and vetted, most conference papers have little serious peer review, so they need to be treated with an open eye toward accuracy and applicability.

Another source is industry conferences, which provide the chance for people from various companies to come together to share information on a series of related topics. Sometimes sponsored by governments or industry trade groups, the main advantage of attending these conferences is not the sessions, because the content is frequently available elsewhere afterwards, but rather the in-person networking. Three major security conferences are held each year: the RSA conference in San Francisco and the Black Hat USA and DEF CON conferences in Las Vegas. Although each has a slightly different audience, they all number in the tens of thousands of attendees. The primary reason professionals attend these shows is to network with other professionals and to learn new and useful methods they can apply after the event.

Academic Journals

A major element of academics is performing novel research—research that has been peer reviewed and is published in *academic journals*. However, academic journals have two issues: timeliness and applicability. Publishing a paper in an academic journal can take from a year to 18 months at the minimum—*after the work is done*. This delay is due to peer reviews and editing. In many cases, this means that academic research in journals is outdated by the time it is printed. What's more, academics are seldom experts in the application of the technologies they research. They look at things as theoretical problems and ignore many of the applied aspects. An academic would examine things like defense in depth to secure a system addressing XYZ vulnerability, based on a theory, and not something that can be done in a practical sense. Academics deconstruct an issue to its base components to find an answer, but whether that answer is applicable in real life is a totally different issue.

Requests for Comment (RFCs)

Requests for comment (RFCs) are the sets of standards used to define how the Internet and the protocols involved in the World Wide Web are established and managed. They are free and openly available, and unlike some constantly evolving items like wikis, they are fixed in time when written. Changes to these documents are formal and noted, and if an Internet standard requires updating, a new RFC is drafted and approved. These are useful as source documents because they list the details by which the protocols operate, including methods not widely used but available.

Local Industry Groups

Local industry groups are a valuable resource from a couple perspectives. First, they are a good source of practical information concerning threats, threat actors, and what can be done to defend networks. Second, they are a solid networking source of information that enables one to get answers to questions that have been vetted by others in similar positions. Much of cybersecurity revolves around sharing of information between trusted parties, and joining and being active in local industry groups is a good way to build these trusted relationships. The time to build these relationships is before you need them, not when you need an answer or help.

Social Media

Social media is ubiquitous these days, with a variety of different platforms targeting different market segments. At the end of the day, each of these platforms is designed so that users can share ideas with like-minded people. For example, Facebook or Instagram might not be the best place to have meaningful discussions concerning threat intelligence, but communicating with contacts on a business-oriented site like LinkedIn might be more appropriate. As with all sources, the key is in vetting the sources of information. Therefore, if your trusted colleagues have chosen one of the social media platforms and hang out there, then that is where you will probably find your answers. However, as with many sources of information, remember *caveat emptor* still applies.

Threat Feeds

Threat feeds are very much like vulnerability feeds when you are evaluating them for utility as a research source. Understanding where the information comes from, how it has been vetted, and how it applies to your industry are all important elements. Likewise, the need exists for multiple, non-overlapping feeds, as there is no single source that covers all needs.

Adversary Tactics, Techniques, and Procedures (TTPs)

The acronym *TTP* is used to describe how threat agents organize and orchestrate their efforts. Like any other organization, hackers evolve to use repeatable methods that are effective. These methods can be cataloged and understood as attack patterns, enabling defenses to have countering plays developed in advance. TTPs, or the patterns used by adversaries, are a key element of a threat intelligence program. Different sources of information associated with TTPs exist, and what is important is to find a solid source based on understandable sources that fit your industry.

Chapter Review

This chapter covered five main topics; actors and threats, attributes of actors, vectors, threat intelligence sources, and research sources. Under actors and threats, the topics of APTs, insider threats, and nation-state actors were covered first, followed by hacktivists, script kiddies, criminal syndicates, and hackers (including white hat, black hat, and gray hat hackers). The section finished with a discussion of shadow IT and competitors. The section on the attributes of threat actors covered internal versus external threats, level of sophistication/capability, resources/funding, and intent/motivation.

The chapter then moved on to the topic of vectors, or pathways for attacks. This section included the topics of direct access, wireless, e-mail, and supply chain methods of entry. The section concluded with social media, removable media, and cloud vectors.

The chapter finished with sections covering threat intelligence sources and research sources. The section on threat intelligence sources opened with the topic of open source intelligence and closed/proprietary sources, followed by a discussion of vulnerability databases, public/private information-sharing centers, and the dark web as sources. The methods of indicators of compromise, Automated Indicator Sharing, and Structured Threat Information Expression/Trusted Automated Exchange of Intelligence Information were also presented. The threat intelligence sources section closed with predictive analysis, threat maps, and file/code repositories as sources. The final section of the chapter was an examination of research sources. These included vendor websites, vulnerability feeds, conferences, academic journals, and requests for comment. The last elements presented were local industry groups, social media, threat feeds, and adversaries' tactics, techniques, and procedures.

Questions

To help you prepare further for the CompTIA Security+ exam, and to test your level of preparedness, answer the following questions and then check your answers against the correct answers at the end of the chapter.

1. Your senior financial people have been attacked with a piece of malware targeting financial records. Based on talking to one of the executives, you now know this is a spear phishing attack. Which of the following is the most likely vector used?
   A. Cloud
   B. Wireless
   C. Direct access
   D. Removeable media
2. You are new to your job, new to the industry, and new to the city. Which of the following sources would be the best to connect with your peers on threat intelligence information?
   A. Vendors
   B. Social media
   C. Local industry groups
   D. Vulnerability or threat feeds
3. Your company has had bad press concerning its support (or lack of support) for a local social issue. Which type of hacker would be the most likely threat to attack or deface your website with respect to this issue?
   A. State actor
   B. Hacktivist
   C. Black hat
   D. Competitor
4. Proper use of separation of duties with respect to privileged users on your systems is a defense against which type of hacker?
   A. Nation-state actor
   B. Insider
   C. Criminal syndicate
   D. All of the above
5. You have read about a new threat against software that is vulnerable to hacking. The vulnerability is in a Python library, and your firm uses Python for the development of many in-house projects. Where is the best source of information with respect to this threat?
   A. File/code repositories
   B. Vulnerability databases

- **C.** Open source intelligence
- **D.** Indicators of compromise

6. Your threat intelligence vendor is sending out urgent messages concerning a new form of memory-resident malware. What is the likely item they are sharing with you?

- **A.** Vulnerability database
- **B.** Indicator of compromise
- **C.** Dark web
- **D.** Trusted Automated Exchange of Intelligence Information (TAXII)

7. You use a "golden disk" to provision new machines from your vendors. As part of the incident response, you have discovered that the source of the malware you are seeing comes from this golden disk. This is an example of what vector?

- **A.** Insider
- **B.** Direct access
- **C.** Removeable media
- **D.** Supply chain

8. Understanding how an attacker operates so that you can develop a defensive posture is done through the use of which of the following?

- **A.** Predictive analysis
- **B.** TTPs
- **C.** Threat maps
- **D.** Automated Indicator Sharing

9. Which of the following items do you as a defender have control over with respect to using threat intelligence to defend your systems?

- **A.** Vectors
- **B.** Actors
- **C.** Threat intelligence sources
- **D.** Attributes of actors

10. You want to get specific information on a specific threat that you have read about in your online newsfeed on your phone. Which of the following is the best source for detailed information?

- **A.** Vulnerability database
- **B.** Open source intelligence
- **C.** Dark web
- **D.** Predictive analysis

Answers

1. **D.** Removeable media is commonly linked to social engineering attacks such as spear phishing.
2. **C.** Networking between peers is a useful attribute of local industry groups.
3. **B.** Hacktivists are hackers that are pursuing a mission associated with a cause.
4. **D.** Separation of duties is designed to provide defenses against malicious insiders. But nation-state actors and criminal organizations have the resources and abilities to hack accounts and gain insider access. There are no external accounts, so once a well-resourced hacker is in, they will have permissions associated with an insider.
5. **A.** File/code repositories is the correct answer because the code you are concerned about was developed in-house; hence, it will not show up in commercial databases or other sources.
6. **B.** An indicator of compromise (IoC) provides the details associated with how one can find active malware on a system.
7. **D.** This is a supply chain vector. Although the work was done in-house, the supply chain stretches from each part to functioning system, and you added the final software to create the functioning system, so your own team is part of the supply chain.
8. **B.** Adversary tactics, techniques, and procedures (TTPs) provide details on how an adversary operates.
9. **A.** Vectors is the correct answer because this is the only item you have any direct control over. The other items are real issues, just not ones you have any measure of direct control over.
10. **B.** Open source intelligence is the best answer. Because you are looking for threat information, this eliminates vulnerability information as an answer. The dark web may or may not have information, and you would have to find it, and predictive analysis needs the information you seek in order to function.

CHAPTER 6

Vulnerabilities

In this chapter, you will

- Learn about various security concerns associated with vulnerabilities
- Learn about a range of system vulnerabilities

Enterprise systems are composed of many different parts, with multiple technologies and numerous elements that can be less than perfect. Virtually anything designed and built will have weaknesses and vulnerabilities. Understanding where these weaknesses and vulnerabilities exist, and how to manage the security of the enterprise in spite of them, is a critically important element of a security program. This chapter examines the types and effects of various vulnerabilities in an enterprise.

Certification Objective This chapter covers CompTIA Security+ exam objective 1.6: Explain the security concerns associated with various types of vulnerabilities.

Cloud-based vs. On-premises Vulnerabilities

Cloud computing has been described by pundits as computing on someone else's computer, and to a degree there is truth in that statement. As vulnerabilities exist in all systems, then regardless of whether a system is *on premises* or *cloud based,* it will always have potential vulnerabilities. With on-premises vulnerabilities, the enterprise has unfettered access to the infrastructure elements, making the discovery and remediation of vulnerabilities a problem defined by scope and resources. With the cloud, the economies of scale and standardized environments give cloud providers an advantage in the scope and resource side of the equation. What is lacking in vulnerability management from the enterprise point of view is visibility into the infrastructure element itself, as this is under the purview of the cloud provider.

EXAM TIP Data can be stored locally on premises or remotely in the cloud. It is important to remember that no matter where data is stored, there will always be potential vulnerabilities that exist.

Zero Day

Zero day is a term used to define vulnerabilities that are newly discovered and not yet addressed by a patch. Most vulnerabilities exist in an unknown state until discovered by a researcher or developer. If a researcher or developer discovers a vulnerability but does not share the information, then this vulnerability can be exploited without the vendor's ability to fix it, because for all practical knowledge, the issue is unknown except to the person who found it. From the time of discovery until a fix or patch is made available, the vulnerability goes by the name "zero day," indicating that it has not been addressed yet. The most frightening thing about a zero-day threat is the unknown factor—its capability and effect on risk are unknown because it is unknown. Although there are no patches for zero-day vulnerabilities, you can use compensating controls to mitigate the risk. Security controls are covered in depth in Chapter 31, "Security Controls."

EXAM TIP Zero-day threats have become a common topic in the news and are a likely target for exam questions. Keep in mind that defenses exist, such as compensating controls, which are controls that mitigate the risk indirectly; for example, a compensating control may block the path to the vulnerability rather than directly address the vulnerability.

Weak Configurations

Most systems have significant configuration options that administrators can adjust to enable or disable functionality based on usage. When a system suffers from misconfiguration or *weak configuration,* it may not achieve all of the desired performance or security objectives. Configuring a database server to build a complete replica of all actions as a backup system can result in a system that is bogged down and not capable of proper responses when usage is high. Similarly, old options, such as support for legacy protocols, can lead to vulnerabilities. Misconfiguration can result from omissions as well, such as when the administrator does not change default credentials, which is equivalent to having no credentials at all, thus leaving the system vulnerable. This form of vulnerability provides a means for an attacker to gain entry or advance their level of privilege, and because this can happen on components with a wide span of control, such as routers and switches, in some cases an attacker can effectively gain total ownership of an enterprise.

Open Permissions

Permissions is the term used to describe the range of activities permitted on an object by an actor in a system. Having properly configured permissions is one of the defenses that can be employed in the enterprise. Managing permissions can be tedious, and as the size of the enterprise grows, the scale of permissions requires automation to manage. When permissions are not properly set, the condition of *open permissions* exists. The risk associated with an open permission is context dependent, as for some items, unauthorized access leads to little or no risk, whereas in other systems it can be catastrophic. The vulnerability of open permissions is equivalent to no access control for an item, and this needs to be monitored in accordance with the relative risk of the element in the enterprise.

Unsecure Root Accounts

Unsecure root accounts are like leaving master keys to the enterprise outside on the curb. Root accounts have access to everything and the ability to do virtually any activity on a network. All root accounts should be monitored, and all accesses should be verified as correct. One method of protecting high-value accounts such as root accounts is through access control vaults, where credentials are checked out before use. This prevents unauthorized activity using these accounts.

EXAM TIP Strong configurations include secure root (Linux) and Administrator (Windows) accounts. Without securing these accounts, anything they are connected to, including processes and services, is exposed to vulnerabilities.

Errors

Errors are the condition where something has gone wrong. Every system will experience errors, and the key to managing this condition is in establishing error trapping and responses. How a system handles errors is everything, because unhandled errors are eventually handled at some level, and the higher up through a system an error goes, the less likely it will be handled correctly. One of the biggest weaknesses exploited by attackers is improper input validations. Whether against a program input, an API, or any other interface, inserting bad information that causes an error and forces a program into a non-normal operating state can result in an exploitable vulnerability. Trapping and handling errors can reduce the possibility of an error becoming exploitable.

Errors should be trapped by the program and appropriate log files generated. For example, web server logs include common error logs, customized logs, and W3C logs. W3C logs are web server logs that focus on recording specific web-related events. The Windows System log records operating system error messages. Windows can be configured to log records of success and failure of login attempts and other audited events. The Windows Application log records events related to local system applications.

Weak Encryption

Cryptographic errors come from several common causes. One typical mistake is choosing to develop your own cryptographic algorithm. Development of a secure cryptographic algorithm is far from an easy task, and even when it's attempted by experts, weaknesses can be discovered that make the algorithm unusable. Cryptographic algorithms become trusted only after years of scrutiny and repelling attacks, so any new algorithms would take years to join the trusted set. If you instead decide to rely on secret algorithms, be warned that secret or proprietary algorithms have never provided the desired level of protection. A similar mistake to attempting to develop your own cryptographic algorithm is attempting to write your own implementation of a known cryptographic algorithm. Errors in coding implementations are common and lead to weak implementations of secure algorithms that are vulnerable to bypass. Do not fall prey to creating a weak implementation; instead, use a proven, vetted cryptographic library.

The second major cause of cryptographic weakness, or *weak encryption,* is the employment of deprecated or weak cryptographic algorithms. Weak cipher suites are those that at one time were considered secure but are no longer considered secure. As the ability to use ever faster hardware has enabled attackers to defeat some cryptographic methods, the older, weaker methods have been replaced by newer, stronger ones. Failure to use the newer, stronger methods can result in weakness. A common example of this is SSL; all versions of SSL are now considered deprecated and should not be used. Everyone should switch their systems to TLS-based solutions.

The impact of cryptographic failures is fairly easy to understand: whatever protection that was provided is no longer there, even if it is essential for the security of the system.

Unsecure Protocols

Another important weak configuration to guard against in the enterprise is *unsecure protocols*. One of the most common protocols used, HTTP, is by its own nature unsecure. Adding TLS to HTTP, using HTTPS, is a simple configuration change that should be enforced everywhere. But what about all the other protocol stacks that come prebuilt in OSs and are just waiting to become a vulnerability, such as FTP, Telnet, and SNMP? Improperly secured communication protocols and services and unsecure credentials increase the risk of unauthorized access to the enterprise Network infrastructure devices can include routers, switches, access points, gateways, proxies, and firewalls. When infrastructure systems are deployed, these devices remain online for years, and many of them are rarely rebooted, patched, or upgraded.

Default Settings

Default settings can be a security risk unless they were created with security in mind. Older operating systems used to have everything enabled by default. Old versions of some systems had hidden administrator accounts, and Microsoft's SQL Server used to have a blank system administrator password by default. Today, most vendors have cleaned these issues up, setting default values with security in mind. But when you instantiate something in your enterprise, it is then yours. Therefore, you should make the settings what you need and only what you need, and you should create these settings as the default configuration baseline. This way, the settings and their security implications are understood. Not taking these steps leaves too many unknowns within an enterprise.

Open Ports and Services

For a service to respond to a request, its port must be open for communication. Having *open ports* is like having doors in a building. Even a bank vault has a door. Having excess *open services* only leads to pathways into your systems that must be protected. Disabling unnecessary services, closing ports, and using firewalls to prevent communications except on approved channels creates a barrier to entry by unauthorized users. Many services run with elevated privileges by default, and malware takes advantage of this. Security professionals should make every effort to audit services and disable any that aren't required.

EXAM TIP Weak configurations greatly increase the likelihood of successful attacks and infiltration. Make every effort to remove unnecessary apps, disable any unnecessary services, change default account usernames and passwords, and close or secure unnecessary ports.

Third-Party Risks

The enterprise computing environment is full of third parties, and their risks become enterprise risks. Common *third-party risks* that are often overlooked are issues of vendor management, system integration, and lack of vendor support. These are all related in the fact that when you chose a vendor as part of your enterprise solution, it made sense. But over time, enterprises change, vendors change, capabilities and needs change, and what was once a good fit might not be at a future point in time. Keeping systems optimized is not a simple task, and many times later conditions will result in different decisions with regard to third parties and their risks.

Supply chains seldom stop with the next hop, and in technology those chains can be long and complex. With these supply chains comes risk from elements such as outsourced code development, maintenance of systems, and, in the world of cloud systems, data storage on another party's computer.

With respect to third-party software running in the enterprise, it is important to have an inventory of what the software is, by version, and where it is used. This assists the security team in monitoring sources for vulnerabilities through sources like the Common Vulnerabilities and Exposures database. This list will also help in determining risk levels as software reaches its end of life or end of service life.

Additional policy-related issues associated with third-party risk management are covered in detail later in Chapter 33, "Organizational Policies."

EXAM TIP Remember that supply chain concerns and lack of vendor support are concerns directly related to third-party risks and management.

Vendor Management

A vendor or supplier is a firm that has a business relationship with the enterprise. In most cases, this relationship in the enterprise is one of many customers. While the voice of the customer is important, the voice of a single customer is almost never heard. The challenge of *vendor management* is one of determining one's own needs and then finding the vendors that offer the best value proposition against those needs. This is more than just selecting and buying a product for most components in an enterprise; issues of support, system lifetime, and maintenance all play a role in the long-term value of a vendor and their products. Mapping the needs and managing the multidimensional problem of determining the best fit and then maintaining that relationship over time is essential in the ever-changing enterprise environment.

System Integration

Enterprises are composed of many different components that all work together to process the information that flows through the enterprise. Different components serve different functions, but in the end, they have to work together. *System integration* is the connecting of these components, each representing a portion of the system into a complete functioning unit. System integration is an area where vulnerabilities can exist, as the pieces can have gaps in their integration or capabilities that do not manifest per the desired specification. System integration is coupled with configuration management because the configurations of the individual pieces can affect how the system as a whole functions. Any deviations from design specifications represent an opportunity for risk.

Lack of Vendor Support

Lack of vendor support can become an issue at several different levels. The most obvious scenario is when the original manufacturer of the item, be it hardware or software, no longer offers support. When an item reaches its end of life (EOL) from the original manufacturer's standpoint, this signifies the finality of its life under almost all circumstances. After the manufacturer stops supporting an item, options to keep it up to date with patches and fixes seldom exist. At this point, an organization that continues to use the product assumes all of the risk associated with issues uncovered after the product has entered EOL status, and the options to address these risks are limited to compensating controls.

EXAM TIP Do not be confused! *End of life (EOL)* is the term used to denote that something has reached the end of its "useful life." *End of service life (EOSL)* or *end of support* is when the manufacturer quits selling an item. In most cases, the manufacturer no longer provides maintenance services or updates.

Another scenario in which lack of vendor support arises is when the system in question is implemented by a third-party vendor and that vendor either no longer supports the configuration or is no longer in business. The underlying technology may still be supported by the original manufacturers, but the lack of support for the middleware provided by the third-party implementer raises questions as to whether the underlying products can be updated or patched. This places the testing burden on the end user, and in many cases the end user does not have the knowledge or skills necessary to conduct thorough regression testing.

EXAM TIP A system can have vulnerabilities related to its age. Whether the system is composed of old parts, as in an embedded system, or has become an end-of-life legacy system, the lack of vendor support can result in the owner's inability to address many newly discovered issues.

Supply Chain

Supply chain risk is caused by vulnerabilities that lie within the supply chain. Whether these vulnerabilities are in the actual supply chain itself or a product coming from a third party, the results are the same—a level of increased risk. As we saw in 2020 as a result of the pandemic, global supply chains can be interrupted by external events that then go on to cause issues for firms that depend on the supply chain functioning efficiently. Delays of product launches, updates, and milestones can all occur when parts, components, or software elements are not delivered on time.

EXAM TIP A supply chain attack typically occurs at the weakest security link in the supply chain, and this is common during the manufacturing process or even in the product delivery phase.

Outsourced Code Development

Code can be one of the greatest sources of vulnerabilities and risk in an enterprise. Code is embedded in so many aspects of the enterprise—from the equipment to the business processes, from the applications that make things run to the infrastructure it all runs on. Code is the glue that holds it all together. However, when code is buried in the processes, and that code was developed by a third party, often using third-party code fragments, the chain of risk becomes long and difficult to manage. The risk isn't just in the fact that the code is outsourced, but actually in the fact that the visibility and control over these risks becomes harder to manage with every step away from the source.

Creating code that is both maintainable and secure is not a simple task. It is important to have conditions in contracts requiring appropriate development measures be in place for third-party code, including the rights to inspect and verify security functionality. Items such as backdoors, either placed intentionally or left from a testing process, typically require access to the source code to find and remove. Ensuring third-party developers have appropriately secure coding practices and having their code reviewed by independent testers and placed in escrow for safekeeping are considered best practices.

Data Storage

Data storage is an important aspect of every enterprise, and it is typically distributed throughout the enterprise in different capacities and configurations. If all data was in a single location, then data storage management, including backup and recovery functions, would be easy to manage. As data storage is distributed across the enterprise into multiple enclaves with differing requirements and criticalities, the management of data storage becomes more difficult. Ensuring the correct access controls and security protections, such as backups, is important for all data stores, and when gaps in these controls emerge, this creates vulnerabilities. If attackers can manipulate data stores, then they can affect enterprise operations. To ensure all data is protected from becoming a vulnerability to the system, having a standardized data storage policy and checklist is good practice in the enterprise. Elements can be varied based on criticality of the data store, but following a standard procedure will reduce the chances of gaps existing from oversight or errors.

Improper or Weak Patch Management

All systems need patches periodically as errors and vulnerabilities are discovered and vendors issue software fixes to these vulnerabilities. One of the important takeaways from patching is that once a supplier patches their software, hackers can reverse engineer the vulnerability from the patch. Therefore, once the patch is released, attackers learn where to attack. To manage the risk associated with patch management vulnerabilities, it is important to establish a strong patch management program that covers all systems and all software. The literature of security failures is full of examples where the missing of a system or two was all it took for an attacker to get into the system. Having an *improper or weak patch management* system is an open invitation to having vulnerabilities exploited. This makes patch management one of the essential security controls and one where there should be no excuses as to why it was not implemented.

To minimize the risks associated with applying patches to production systems, it is recommended that the enterprise change control process be used. Because patches can be time sensitive, it is important to have defined periods of time when patches must be installed as well as an automated means of determining what patches are needed, where they are needed, and status of the current patch level by target location.

Firmware

Firmware is just another form of software with one noted distinction: it is stored in hardware to be present when the system boots up. However, it is still software, with all the baggage of software—bugs, vulnerabilities, patch requirements, updates, and so on. With firmware being part of the system itself, always present, it is frequently missed when considering how to keep software up to date. This goes for manufacturers as well. If you are looking at a system that has firmware, reasonable questions to ask as part of your research before selection include: How is the firmware updated? How often? And how are updates distributed? The lifecycle, vulnerabilities, and maintenance issues associated with firmware mirror those of software. Patching firmware is an often-neglected issue, and this can lead to vulnerabilities, especially given the typical lifetime of some equipment.

EXAM TIP Updates and patching are used to ensure software and firmware are up to date and secure. Manufacturers of hardware often provide updates for firmware, and it is the organization's responsibility to ensure firmware updates are applied.

Operating System (OS)

Operating system (OS) patch management was a chore years ago, with patches coming haphazardly over time, each requiring manual intervention. Today, major operating systems can patch themselves, and with a little automation, the tracking and management of patches is easy. There are only a couple of steps to get this right. First, have a patch management policy, and make it patch everything and track all patches. Second, follow up on that policy. There are excuses about not being able to patch for a wide range of reasons, but a properly executed patch management strategy overcomes all of those risks.

Worried about a patch breaking a crucial system? If it is a crucial system, you have more than one, right? Patch one system, test to see if it still works, and then patch the rest.

The list of enterprises that missed a patch that then became the pathway for an attacker is long. Attackers have it easy when it comes to testing whether you have patched—they try to exploit the known vulnerability, and if it works, they know you haven't patched and they have gained access.

Applications

Applications are the programs that comprise the functional aspect of the enterprise. From server-based elements such as web servers and database servers, to desktop applications like Microsoft Office, applications are the tools that handle the data and add value to the system. Applications, like all software, require updating and patching to fix vulnerabilities and bugs. The challenge with application patching across an enterprise is in the tracking of all of the applications used, including even small, seemingly meaningless programs that are installed on desktops. Not only does the enterprise have to keep track of all the applications it has, but it has to determine which ones have updates and when. Some major software vendors make this process easy, but the myriad of additional vendors make the task of knowing what needs updating, when and where, a real challenge. There are applications designed to manage this aspect, and it is highly recommended that enterprises use patch-tracking software that can identify when patches are available and install them.

EXAM TIP Part of a security professional's responsibilities is to keep up with current Common Vulnerabilities and Exposures (CVEs) and update or patch systems to keep the enterprise environment secure. This applies to firmware, operating systems, applications, virtual machines, and devices.

Legacy Platforms

Legacy platforms is the term used to describe systems that are no longer being marketed or supported. They are also considered old, which in IT terms can be as little as a few years. Legacy systems represent an interesting vulnerability because, by being in the legacy category, they are no longer supported, so if new problems are discovered, the only fix is a compensating control. Having systems that can't be patched is a risk, but like all risks, it must be measured and weighed against the costs of change. In a properly architected secure environment, the risk of legacy vulnerabilities is partially covered by the compensating controls that make executing those vulnerabilities extremely hard if not impossible.

Impacts

Impacts are the resulting effects of a risk that is realized. Impacts are the items that an organization is attempting to avoid with a security incident. Impacts can be categorized in several different groups, and these are described in the sections that follow. Risk management implications of impacts are covered in detail in Chapter 34, "Risk Management." For details on risk and impact, the material in that chapter works together with the following items.

Data Loss

Data loss is when an organization actually loses information. Files can be deleted, overwritten, or even misplaced. Ransomware is the most dangerous form of data loss because it is driven by outside forces and its very nature is to make the data unavailable to the enterprise until a ransom is paid. Hardware failure is another source of data loss. The primary defense for data loss is a solid backup program that can restore lost data.

Data Breaches

Data breaches are the release of data to unauthorized parties. Attackers that infiltrate a system are frequently looking to steal information such as personally identifiable information (PII), financial data, corporate data with value on the open market, and intellectual property. Having a data breach can be a legal issue, a financial issue, a reputation issue, or any combination of these issues, depending on the type and scope of the breach. Strong access controls, encryption of data at rest, and data loss prevention (DLP) elements can lessen the impact. Encryption is the strongest control because a breach of encrypted data without the key isn't actually a breach.

Data Exfiltration

Data is a unique asset in many ways. One of the more relevant ways it is unique is in the fact that it can be copied, and then stolen, without affecting the original data. Stealing data becomes an exercise in data exfiltration or taking the copy out of the enterprise. Just as when a thief steals anything, the true theft only occurs when they escape with the item. *Data exfiltration* is the exporting of stolen data from an enterprise. Data exfiltration impact is related to the data being stolen. If it is intellectual property, then the impact can be directly to the bottom line. Loss of intellectual property can result in loss of future sales.

The loss of customer data can have impacts to reputation as well as direct financial impacts via regulatory penalties. Major data breaches have cost companies hundreds of millions of dollars in penalties, fines, and court settlements.

Identity Theft

Identity theft is a crime where someone uses information on another party to impersonate them. This is a secondary impact once data is exfiltrated. The loss of data can come from commercial systems and even home systems, and the results are the same: people can lose money, property, and time cleaning up an identity theft claim. The impact of data exfiltration that includes personally identifiable information (PII) can be significant in terms of regulatory costs. Recent major breaches have had substantial regulatory fines and legal costs associated with the loss of PII. The most expensive type of record to lose was customer PII records, which were involved in around 80 percent of breaches in the Verizon breach report. This is not just a big company financial issue. With the average cost of each lost record being roughly $150, it makes even small breaches of 1000 records a potential problem for smaller businesses.

Financial

At the end of the day, risk is measured in *financial* terms, and the impact from vulnerabilities can be expressed in financial terms as well. While it is sometimes difficult to directly trace each issue to a financial figure, there have been numerous examples where the results are easy to connect to the financials. A German steel mill was destroyed by attackers, Sony lost a movie release to North Korean hackers, Equifax paid out nearly $2 billion in response to its 2017 breach—these are all costs that are easily attributed to the direct impact of a cyber attack.

Here's a list of items that can contribute to the financial costs of a cyber attack:

- Costs associated with investigating and fixing enterprise systems
- Lost orders/revenue due to system downtime
- Fines for regulatory noncompliance on privacy laws
- Attorney fees from lawsuits
- Ransom payments made for ransomware
- Losses due to stolen intellectual property
- Share price decline and market capitalization loss

Most of the financial numbers seen in the press are skewed by the large settlements of big companies with big losses, but the effect on small to medium-sized enterprises is even more dramatic. An average cybersecurity loss can cost a small to medium-sized business $400,000. For many businesses, that number is large enough to destroy them.

Reputation

Reputation impact as a result of a cyber attack comes in two main forms: loss of customer confidence and, in cases where skilled workforce is involved, a competitive field loss of key employees. If your customer base has questions about your ability to fulfill orders and manage their information, or just has a general loss of confidence in company management, then your customers may go to a competitor. This is true of businesses that have consumer-based customers as well as businesses with corporate-based customers.

Companies that have highly skilled workforce members who are in short supply also have to be concerned with their reputation in the eyes of their employees. After all, who wants to work for a company that embarrasses them due to news stories about management failures that result in cybersecurity losses? Every tech worker wants Google or Apple on their resume, but no one in cybersecurity wants to talk about working for a firm like Equifax, where mismanagement of IT resources caused one of the costliest breaches in history. Having workers quit because they don't trust their company and finding replacements for highly skilled personnel when the company is in a reputational crisis is not a position management ever wants to find itself in.

Availability Loss

The CIA triad is confidentiality, integrity, and availability. Availability is defined as resources being available for authorized users when they are supposed to be available. When the impact of a cyber attack affects infrastructure elements, either by system damage, data loss, or loss of systems during recovery efforts, the effect is one that results in the loss of system capability. If this loss in capability is high enough, the system will stop processing records. For some firms, this is survivable for relatively short periods of time. For others, the downtime translates directly into lost revenue, and in some cases costs associated with service level agreements (SLAs) being broken. The loss of availability on the part of any system will have an impact on the enterprise; otherwise, why have the system? Determining the actual scale of an availability loss is simple in some transactional systems and more complicated in others, but at the end of the day, a firm invests business resources into its IT systems to facilitate business operations, not interrupt them.

EXAM TIP Unchecked vulnerabilities due to weak configurations, third-party risks, improper/weak patch management, and legacy platforms can result in major impacts, including data loss, breaches, exfiltration, and identity theft, as well as financial, reputational, and availability loss.

Chapter Review

In this chapter, you became acquainted with security concerns associated with various types of vulnerabilities. The chapter opened with a discussion of cloud-based vs. on-premises vulnerabilities and zero-day vulnerabilities. The first major section covered weak configurations. In this section, the topics of open permissions, unsecured root accounts, errors, weak encryption, unsecure protocols, default settings, and open ports and services were covered.

The next major section was on third-party risks. In this section, the subtopics of vender management, system integration, lack of vendor support, supply chain, outsourced code development, and data storage were covered. Next was a discussion of improper or weak patch management. In this section, firmware, operating systems, and applications were covered. The next section covered legacy systems.

The chapter closed with a discussion on the impacts of a vulnerability that has been exploited. In this section, data loss, data breaches, data exfiltration, identity theft, and financial, reputational, and availability loss were covered.

Questions

To help you prepare further for the CompTIA Security+ exam, and to test your level of preparedness, answer the following questions and then check your answers against the correct answers at the end of the chapter.

1. Direct third-party risks include which of the following? (Choose all that apply.)
   - **A.** System integration
   - **B.** Supply chain
   - **C.** Financial management
   - **D.** Vendor management
2. Common sources of vulnerability issues for systems include which of the following? (Choose all that apply.)
   - **A.** Weak patch management
   - **B.** Data loss
   - **C.** Identity theft
   - **D.** Weak configurations
3. Weak configurations can include which of the following? (Choose all that apply.)
   - **A.** Open ports
   - **B.** Lack of vendor support
   - **C.** Firmware
   - **D.** Use of unsecure protocols
4. A patch management process should include which of the following? (Choose all that apply.)
   - **A.** Automated management of software assets
   - **B.** Automated verification of current patch levels
   - **C.** A specified period by which systems should be patched
   - **D.** Connection of the patch management process to the change control process
5. Financial risks associated with vulnerabilities can include which of the following? (Choose all that apply.)
   - **A.** Regulatory fines and penalties
   - **B.** Business reputation loss
   - **C.** Loss of revenue due to downtime
   - **D.** Loss of data

6. What type of threat exploits system and application vulnerabilities that are unknown to software developers and even anti-malware manufacturers?
   - **A.** An on-premises attack
   - **B.** A zero-day attack
   - **C.** A cloud-based attack
   - **D.** A legacy platform attack
7. As a security professional, what should you do to address weak configurations that pose security risks to your organization? (Choose all that apply.)
   - **A.** Change default usernames and passwords.
   - **B.** Remove unnecessary apps.
   - **C.** Disable unnecessary services.
   - **D.** Open all ports so that everything can be scanned.
8. Which statement is false regarding cryptographic practices and weak encryption?
   - **A.** Developing your own cryptographic algorithm is considered an insecure practice.
   - **B.** Cryptographic algorithms become trusted only after years of scrutiny and repelling attacks.
   - **C.** The ability to use ever-faster hardware has enabled attackers to defeat some cryptographic methods.
   - **D.** Because TLS is deprecated, SSL should be used instead.
9. Who assumes the risk associated with a system or product after it has entered EOL status?
   - **A.** The original manufacturer
   - **B.** The vendor
   - **C.** The organization
   - **D.** The supply chain manager
10. Which of the following best describes the exporting of stolen data from an enterprise?
    - **A.** Data loss
    - **B.** Data breach
    - **C.** Data exfiltration
    - **D.** Identity theft

Answers

1. **A, B, and D.** System integration, supply chain, and vendor management are sources of third-party risk. Financial management is related to impacts, not mainly third-party risks.
2. **A and D.** Improper or weak patch management and weak configurations are defined as common sources for vulnerabilities.
3. **A and D.** Having open ports and using unsecure protocols can both provide openings for attackers to get into a system. Lack of vendor support is a third-party risk, and firmware has a fixed configuration.
4. **A, B, C, and D.** A good patch management process should include automated management of software assets, automated verification of current patch levels, a specified period by which systems should be patched, and connection of the patch management process to the change control process.
5. **A and C.** Regulatory fines and penalties as well as lost income because of downtime are direct financial impacts of cybersecurity problems. Business reputation may lead to a loss of customers, but this is not a direct connection. Loss of data may or may not have a financial impact depending upon the data and its connection to revenue.
6. **B.** A zero-day attack exploits system and application vulnerabilities that are unknown to others except the person who found it. The other answer options are not attack types. Vulnerabilities can exist on premises or be cloud based, and legacy platforms is the term used to describe systems that are no longer being marketed or supported.
7. **A, B, and C.** Every effort should be made to remove unnecessary apps, disable any unnecessary services, and change default account usernames and passwords. Opening all ports is a recipe for disaster. Unnecessary or unused ports should be closed or secured.
8. **D.** All versions of SSL are now considered deprecated and should not be used. Everyone should switch their systems to TLS-based solutions. All other statements are true.
9. **C.** An organization that continues to use a system or product assumes all of the risk associated with issues uncovered after the product has entered end-of-life (EOL) status. The manufacturer is in fact most often the vendor, and from their standpoint, the product reaches EOL when they stop supporting it. The supply chain manager is a distractor answer choice.
10. **C.** Data exfiltration is the exporting of stolen data from an enterprise. Data loss is when an organization actually loses information. Data breaches are the release of data to unauthorized parties. Identity theft is a crime where someone uses information on another party to impersonate them.

CHAPTER 7

Security Assessments

In this chapter, you will

- Learn about threat hunting
- Examine the details of vulnerability scans
- Explore syslog/SIEM/SOAR technologies

Assessment is the examination of something against a standard, to see how it stacks up. In security, the primary standard should be your set of security policies—and they should align with any external requirements. So how do you examine your systems to see if things are really working in the manner you desire? This chapter will explore several aspects of doing assessments. One of the major methods of performing security assessments is through the use of penetration tests, and these tests are covered in Chapter 8, "Penetration Testing."

Certification Objective This chapter covers CompTIA Security+ exam objective 1.7: Summarize the techniques used in security assessments.

Threat Hunting

Threat hunting is the practice of proactively searching for cyber threats that are inside a network, yet remain undetected. Cyber threat hunting uses tools, techniques, and procedures (TTPs) to uncover unauthorized actors in your network that have not been detected by your defenses. Most defensive elements are outward facing and are on or near the network perimeter, as this is where you are most likely to catch an unauthorized user. But if the attacker can get past that line of defense, they can hide in a network for months, if not years. During this time they can quietly collect data, look for confidential material, or obtain login credentials as they move laterally across the environment. Attackers can use system resources to continue their presence, a technique known as "living off the land."

Threat hunting uses tools and techniques to specifically detect this type of user—tools such as tactical threat intelligence data sources and threat feeds that characterize the activities of hackers, as well as tools such as indicators of attack (IOAs) and indicators of compromise (IOCs). Indicators of attack comprise a series of actions an attacker must accomplish to perform an attack. This includes activities such as creating an account, connecting out to a command-and-control server, and moving data off a network in an encrypted stream. These are actions taken by a threat actor as part of their work process to compromise a system. Looking for these activities constitutes part of threat hunting. Indicators of compromise are artifacts left behind by the activities of an attacker. Specific strings in memory from malware, forensic artifacts such as link files, and fake executables—these are all indicators of malicious activity, but also activity that is in the past. Threat hunters use these clues to focus on where an attacker has been, what they have done, and where they are likely to go next as the attacker follows their version of the Cyber Kill Chain.

Intelligence Fusion

Threat intelligence is the knowledge behind a threat's capabilities, infrastructure, motives, goals, and resources. Threat *intelligence fusion* enables a defender to identify and contextualize the threats they face in the environment, using the information from threat intelligence in the Diamond Model of Intrusion Analysis, as illustrated in Chapter 27, "Incident Response Policies, Processes, and Procedures." Once you understand your adversary, you can take decisive action to better protect your organization.

EXAM TIP Intelligence fusion is a process involving collecting and analyzing threat feeds from both internal and external sources on a large scale.

Threat Feeds

Threat feeds are sources of information concerning adversaries. Threat feeds can come from internal and external sources. By leveraging threat data from your own network based on incident response data (that is, log files, alerts, and incident response findings), it is possible to find other locations of the same threat in your environment. External sources of threat information come from various outside entities, and as a result they may or may not align with your particular environment. External feeds take more curating to adapt the information into a form that is useful in your own enterprise, but automated exchange methods, such as Structured Threat Information eXpression (STIX), assist in the movement of this critical information between firms. Ultimately, it's up to your security team with their specific knowledge of your organization's environment and threat landscape to determine external feed relevance.

Advisories and Bulletins

Advisories and bulletins are published sets of information from partners, such as security vendors, industry groups, the government, information-sharing groups, and other sources of "trusted" information. These are external sources of threat feeds and need to be processed by security personnel to determine their applicability and how to use them to improve defenses for the enterprise.

Maneuver

Maneuver refers to the ability to move within a network, a tactic commonly used by advanced adversaries as they move toward their objectives. Threat hunting can counter an attacker maneuvering via a couple mechanisms. First, the threat hunter can watch for traffic at chokepoints (that is, points where the unauthorized entity must pass). Second, the threat hunter can analyze the company's own network infrastructure, through the eyes of an attacker, and provide insight into how the network can be connected to provide better defenses against lateral movement, both in terms of connections and logging. These efforts make undetected maneuvering a much greater challenge for an attacker, and because much of the defense can be done passively with regard to what the attacker sees, it is even more effective.

EXAM TIP Maneuvering is also a defensive tactic used by security professionals to disrupt or prevent an attacker from moving laterally as part of the attack chain.

Vulnerability Scans

Vulnerability scanning is the process of examining services on computer systems for known vulnerabilities in software. This is basically a simple process of determining the specific version of a software program and then looking up the known vulnerabilities. The Common Vulnerabilities and Exposures database can be used as a repository; it has recorded over 145,000 specific vulnerabilities. This makes the task more than just a manual one; numerous software programs can be used to perform this function.

False Positives

Any system that uses a measurement of some attribute to detect some other condition can be subject to errors. When a measurement is used as part of a decision process, external factors can introduce errors. In turn, these errors can influence a measurement to a condition that creates an error in the final number. When a measurement is used in a decision process, the possibility of errors and their influence must be part of the decision process. For example, when a restaurant cooks a steak to a medium temperature, the easiest way to determine if the steak is cooked correctly would be to cut it open and look. But this can't be done in the kitchen, so other measures are used, such as time, temperature, and so on. When the customer cuts into the steak is the moment of truth, because then the actual condition is revealed.

EXAM TIP False positives and false negatives depend on the results of the test and the true outcome. If you test for something, get a positive indication, but the indication is wrong, that is a false positive. If you test for something, do not get an indication, but the results should have been true, this is a false negative.

Two types of errors are involved: false positive and false negative. The choice of the terms *positive* and *negative* relate to the result of the test. If you are using Nmap as a tool to test an operating system, it will report the operating system as a specific type (say, Windows 10). If this result is incorrect, then this is a *false positive* error if you were counting on the result to be true.

EXAM TIP This is a highly tested item. A false positive occurs when expected or normal behavior is wrongly identified as malicious. The detection of a failed login followed by a successful login being labeled as malicious, when the activity was caused by a user making a mistake after recently changing their password, is an example of a false positive.

False Negatives

False negative results are the opposite of false positive results. If you test something and it comes back negative, but it was in fact positive, then the result is a false negative. For example, if you scan ports to find any open ones and you miss a port that is open because the scanner could not detect it being open, and you do not run a test because of this false result, you are suffering from a false negative error.

EXAM TIP When an intrusion detection system (IDS) does not generate an alert from a malware attack, this is a false negative.

Log Reviews

A properly configured log system can provide tremendous insight into what has happened on a computer system. The key is in proper configuration so that you capture the events you want without adding extraneous data. That being said, a log system is a potential treasure trove of useful information to someone attacking a system. It will have information on systems, account names, what has worked for access, and what hasn't. *Log reviews* can provide information as to security incidents, policy violations (or attempted policy violations), and other abnormal conditions that require further analysis.

Credentialed vs. Non-Credentialed

Vulnerability scans can be performed with and without credentials. Performing a scan without credentials can provide some information as to the state of a service and whether or not it might be vulnerable. This is the view of a true outsider on the network. It can be done quickly, in an automated fashion, across large segments of a network. However, without credentials, it is not possible to see the detail that a login provides. *Credentialed vulnerability scans* can look deeper into a host and return more accurate and critical risk information. Frequently these scans are used together. First, a *non-credentialed scan* is performed across large network segments using automated tools. Then, based on these preliminary results, more detailed credentialed scans are run on machines with the most promise for vulnerabilities.

EXAM TIP Credentialed scans are more involved, requiring credentials and extra steps to log in to a system, whereas non-credentialed scans can be done more quickly across multiple machines using automation. Credentialed scans can reveal additional information over non-credentialed scans.

Intrusive vs. Non-Intrusive

Vulnerability scans can be intrusive or non-intrusive to the system being scanned. A *non-intrusive* scan is typically a simple scan of open ports and services, where an *intrusive* scan attempts to leverage potential vulnerabilities through an exploit to demonstrate the vulnerabilities. This intrusion can result in system crashes and is therefore referred to as intrusive.

Application

Applications are the software programs that perform data processing on the information in a system. Being the operational element with respect to the data, as well as the typical means of interfacing between users and the data, applications are common targets of attackers. Vulnerability scans assess the strength of a deployed application against the desired performance of the system when being attacked. Application vulnerabilities represent some of the riskier problems in the enterprise because the applications are necessary, and there are fewer methods to handle miscommunications of data the higher up the stack one goes.

Web Application

Web applications are just applications that are accessible across the web. This method of accessibility brings convenience and greater potential exposure to unauthorized activity. All the details of standard applications still apply, but the placing of the system on the web adds additional burdens on the system to prevent unauthorized access and keep web-based risks under control. From a vulnerability scan perspective, a web application is like an invitation to explore how well it is secured. At greatest risk are homegrown web applications because they seldom have the level of input protections needed for a hostile web environment.

Network

The *network* is the element that connects all the computing systems together, carrying data between the systems and users. The network can also be used in vulnerability scanning to access connected systems. The most common vulnerability scans are performed across the network in a sweep where all systems are scanned, mapped, and enumerated per the ports and services. This information can then be used to further target specific scans of individual systems in a move-detailed fashion, using credentials and potentially intrusive operations.

Common Vulnerabilities and Exposures (CVE)/ Common Vulnerability Scoring System (CVSS)

The *Common Vulnerabilities and Exposures (CVE)* enumeration is a list of known vulnerabilities in software systems. Each vulnerability in the list has an identification number, description, and reference. This list is the basis for most vulnerability scanner systems, as the scanners determine the software version and look up known or reported vulnerabilities. The *Common Vulnerability Scoring System (CVSS)* is a scoring system to determine how risky a vulnerability can be to a system. The CVSS score ranges from 0 to 10. As the CVSS score increases, so does the severity of risk from the vulnerability. Although the CVSS can't take into account where the vulnerability is in an enterprise, it can help determine severity using metrics such as whether it's easy to exploit, whether it requires user intervention, what level of privilege is required, and so on. Together, these two sets of information can provide a lot of information on the potential risk associated with a specific software system.

CVSS scores and their associated risk severity are as follows:

Risk Rating	CVSS Score
Low	0.1–3.9
Medium	4.0–6.9
High	7.0–8.9
Critical	9.0–10

EXAM TIP Know that Common Vulnerabilities and Exposures (CVE) is a list of known vulnerabilities, each with an identification number, description, and reference. The Common Vulnerability Scoring System (CVSS) determines how risky a vulnerability can be to a system. The CVSS score ranges from 0 to 10. As it increases, so does the severity of risk from the vulnerability.

Configuration Review

System configurations play a significant role in system security. Misconfigurations leave a system in a more vulnerable state, sometimes even causing security controls to be bypassed completely. Verification of system configurations is an important vulnerability check item; if you find a misconfiguration, the chances are high that it exposes a vulnerability. *Configuration reviews* are important enough that they should be automated and performed on a regular basis. There are protocols and standards for measuring and validating configurations. The Common Configuration Enumeration (CCE) and Common Platform Enumeration (CPE) guides, as part of the National Vulnerability Database (NVD) maintained by NIST, are places to start for details.

Syslog/Security Information and Event Management (SIEM)

Syslog stands for System Logging Protocol and is a standard protocol used in Linux systems to send system log or event messages to a specific server, called a syslog server. A wide variety of devices, such as printers, networking equipment, and systems across many platforms, use the syslog standard. The value in syslog is the separation of a system from error reports, allowing both for the security functions of logging to be separate from the system being monitored and for the aggregation of multiple log streams on a common server. A syslog server listens on either UDP port 514 or TCP port 6514. Syslog is for more than just errors; it is the standard for remote logging on Linux systems. Ubuntu stores global activity and startup messages in /var/log/syslog. Applications can use it as well.

The information in a syslog server is just tables of raw data. To make this information easier to use, a system called *security information and event management (SIEM)* is employed to collect, aggregate, and apply pattern matching to the volumes of data. This turns tables of data into meaningful actionable information based on rules established by an organization. The first step of processing in a SIEM is to collect data into a series of structured tables. This allows different data sources with different data elements to potentially work together. These data tables are then enriched using lookups and other joining features to provide greater context to the data that has been collected. The system can then examine this time-related data for event correlations that can be used to trigger incident response actions.

EXAM TIP Remember that syslog can be used for log aggregation on network devices and Linux operating systems. A syslog server listens for and logs messages from syslog clients. SIEM systems collect, aggregate, and apply pattern matching to the volumes of data to produce human-readable information.

Review Reports

The primary means of providing output from a SIEM is either an alert or a report. These are predetermined conditions that trigger a specific output of information based on rules in the system. These reports can then be reviewed to determine whether an incident exists or is a false alarm.

Packet Capture

Packet captures have been a staple of network engineers for as long as networks have existed. Diagnosing and understanding network communication problems is easier when one can observe how packets flow through a network. More recently, the concept of continuous packet captures to monitor a segment of network has become a tool in the security professional's toolbox. Most security alerting occurs after the fact. Something happens, a rule fires, and data is generated, causing an investigation into the rule. Although this can be done quickly with automation, the packets involved are long since gone. Enter continuous packet captures. In key areas of a network, where the ability to play back traffic from a previous period of time is important, a continuous collection of the packets can provide that opportunity. This typically will consume significant storage, so the placement and duration of collection can be very important.

Using a SIEM, coupled with smart appliances like next-generation firewalls, when a rule is fired, the network capture appliance can automatically collect and ship off a predetermined amount of traffic for later analysis. With the relative low cost of storage and proper placement, this method of capturing key data can be done with commodity hardware.

Data Inputs

The *data inputs* to a SIEM are as varied as the systems they are used to protect. While a modern network can generate extremely large quantities of log data, what is important in a SIEM is to determine what information is needed to support what decisions. One can collect everything, but that incurs a lot of cost and generates a lot of reports that no one needs. What is important is to define the outputs desired from the SIEM and then trace the necessary inputs from firewalls, network appliances, key servers, and so on to support those determinations. As a SIEM matures, more data sources are identified and included, and ones that are not used are removed. A SIEM is tuned by the security personnel to answer the questions relative to their environment and their risks.

User Behavior Analysis

SIEMS are systems built to apply rules to sets of data with respect to specific patterns. Traditionally this meant network- and server-type events, failures, and other conditions that alerted an operator that the system was not responding in a normal manner. Correlating events between systems can show patterns of activity that are either normal and expected or abnormal and require investigation. Advances in *user behavioral analysis* has provided another interesting use of the SIEM: monitoring what people do with their systems and how they do it. If every day, upon beginning work, the accountants start the same programs, then when an accountant account logs in and does something totally different, like accesses a system they have never accessed before, this indicates a behavioral change worth looking into. Many modern SIEMs have modules that analyze end-user behaviors, looking for anomalous behavior patterns that indicate a need for analysis.

Sentiment Analysis

The same systems that are used to pattern-match security issues can be adapted to match patterns of data indicating specific sentiments. Approximations of sentiment can be determined by using inputs such as e-mails, chats, feedback collection mechanisms, and social media communications, coupled with AI systems that can interpret text communications. Is the communicator happy, sad, mad, or frustrated? These sentiments and more can be determined by how people communicate.

EXAM TIP Sentiment analysis is used to identify and track patterns in human emotions, opinions, or attitudes that may be present in data.

Security Monitoring

Security monitoring is the process of collecting and analyzing information to detect suspicious behavior or unauthorized changes on your network and connected systems. This implies a process of defining which types of behavior should trigger alerts. Early SIEM devices focused on the collection of the information needed. Later SIEMs advanced into managing the event data associated with the detected events. Today, security orchestration, automation, and response (SOAR) systems complete the move to full cycle automation of security processes. Because of the complexity of modern IT systems and enterprises, together with the complexity of attacks and patterns of behaviors, without automated systems like SIEM and SOAR, security monitoring is just not possible.

Log Aggregation

Log aggregation is the process of combining logs together. This is done to allow different formats from different systems to work together. Log aggregation works to allow multiple independent sources of information to be connected together in a more comprehensive picture of the system state than a single data source could provide. During the process of aggregation, the log entries can be parsed, modified, and have key fields extracted or modified based on lookups or rules. The objective of log aggregation is to take multiple different data sources and condition the data into a form that is searchable and useable for specific purposes.

Log Collectors

Log collectors are pieces of software that function to gather data from multiple independent sources and feed it into a unified source such as a SIEM. Different sources may have differing formats, and log collectors can harmonize these different field elements into a comprehensive data stream.

Security Orchestration, Automation, and Response (SOAR)

Threat hunting is a data-intensive task. Enterprises possess a lot of security-related data. This data comes from a myriad of network appliances, intrusion detection systems, firewalls, and other security devices. This data is typically fed into a security information and event management (SIEM) system that can collect, aggregate, and apply pattern matching to the volumes of data. Alerts can then be processed by security personnel. However, this is far from complete integration. *Security orchestration, automation, and response (SOAR)* systems take SIEM data as well as data from other sources and assist in the creation of runbooks and playbooks.

Threat hunters use this information, both in raw form from the SOAR and SIEM systems and its processed form from runbooks and playbooks, to examine an enterprise as an attacker would, charting attack paths to the valuable information assets. Then, using this information, a threat hunter can narrow where they look for attackers to narrow paths of opportunity that they have identified as probable methods of access and attack.

This information is also useful to security assessors, as it lays out the security defenses in an easy-to-understand and -examine format. Gaps can be identified by examining the structure and content of the runbooks and playbooks. More information on SOAR as well as runbooks and playbooks are found in Chapter 29, "Mitigation Techniques and Controls."

EXAM TIP SOAR systems combine data and alarms from integrated platforms throughout the enterprise and place them in a single location where automated responses can then address threats and vulnerabilities.

Chapter Review

In this chapter, you became acquainted the tools and techniques employed in security assessments. The chapter opened with a section on threat hunting. In this section, the topics of intelligence fusion, threat feeds, advisories and bulletins, and maneuvering were covered. The next section covered vulnerability scans. This section began with an examination of false positives and false negatives. Then log reviews were covered, followed by credentialed vs. non-credentialed and intrusive vs. non-intrusive scans. Examinations of applications, web applications, and network scans were also provided. The section concluded with an examination of the Common Vulnerabilities and Exposures (CVE) and Common Vulnerability Scoring System (CVSS) systems, as well as configuration reviews.

The next section covered syslog and security information and event management (SIEM) systems. In this section, the topics included review reports, packet captures, data inputs, user behavioral analysis, and sentiment analysis. The topics of security monitoring, log aggregation, and log collectors completed the section. The chapter closed with an analysis of security orchestration, automation, and response (SOAR) systems.

Questions

To help you prepare further for the CompTIA Security+ exam, and to test your level of preparedness, answer the following questions and then check your answers against the correct answers at the end of the chapter.

1. If a system sends an alert that a user account is being hacked because of too many password failures, but analysis shows that the person's device had cached an old password, triggering the failures, what is this an example of?
   - **A.** False negative
   - **B.** False positive
   - **C.** Measurement error
   - **D.** Analysis failure

2. Anti-malware software fails to detect a ransomware attack that is supposed to be within its capabilities of detecting. What is this an example of?
   - **A.** False negative
   - **B.** False positive
   - **C.** Measurement error
   - **D.** Analysis failure
3. What is the primary limitation of a credentialed scan on a network?
   - **A.** Speed
   - **B.** Examining too deeply into individual boxes
   - **C.** The inability to scale across multiple systems
   - **D.** Slowing down your network with ancillary traffic
4. You desire to prove a vulnerability can be a problem. The best method would be to use a(n) ______________ scan?
   - **A.** credentialed
   - **B.** non-intrusive
   - **C.** non-credentialed
   - **D.** intrusive
5. Which of the following best describes what CVE is?
   - **A.** A place to report errors and vulnerabilities
   - **B.** A measure of the severity of a vulnerability
   - **C.** A list of known vulnerabilities
   - **D.** A list of systems that have vulnerabilities
6. Which of the following is not associated typically with SIEM processes?
   - **A.** Applications
   - **B.** Syslog
   - **C.** Log capture
   - **D.** Log aggregation
7. Which of the following is not part of SIEM processes?
   - **A.** Data collection
   - **B.** Event correlation
   - **C.** Alerting/reporting
   - **D.** Incident investigation

8. Threat hunting involves which of the following? (Choose all that apply.)
    A. Analysis of adversarial actions
    B. Interpretation of threats to other companies
    C. Compliance reporting
    D. Understanding how data flows in an enterprise
9. Which process allows log files to be enriched with additional data to provide context?
    A. Log aggregation
    B. Log collectors
    C. Log reviews
    D. Syslog
10. Which of the following are not typically scanned during a vulnerability scan?
    A. End users
    B. Network
    C. Applications
    D. Web applications

Answers

1. **B.** This is a false positive, as the report was positive that something had happened, when in fact it had not.
2. **A.** Failing to report on a known reportable event is a false negative.
3. **C.** Because a credentialed scan requires credentials for each system it is examining, and these credentials will change across a network, this type of scan is less scalable with automation.
4. **D.** An intrusive scan attempts to exercise a vulnerability. This presents risk in that it might upset the system, but if it works, it is clear proof of the risk associated with a vulnerability.
5. **C.** Common Vulnerabilities and Exposures is an enumeration or list of known vulnerabilities.
6. **A.** Applications may be all over the network and may provide data to a SIEM, but they are not typically part of the SIEM process.
7. **D.** Incident investigations occur after and as a result of SIEM processes but are not typically part of them.

8. **A, B,** and **D.** Threat hunting involves analyzing adversarial actions, interpreting the threats to other companies, and understanding how data flows in an enterprise so adversaries can be caught maneuvering.
9. **A.** During the process of aggregation, the log entries can be parsed, modified, and have key fields extracted or modified based on lookups or rules.
10. **A.** End users are not part of a vulnerability scan; they are air gapped from the system and are not part of the elements that are searched for vulnerabilities.

CHAPTER 8

Penetration Testing

In this chapter, you will

- Learn penetration testing concepts
- Learn about types of passive and active reconnaissance
- Explore various team exercise types associated with penetration testing

Penetration testing is a structured form of testing defenses using the methodologies employed by attackers. These exercises can be performed in a variety of different ways, which will be explored in the sections that follow.

Certification Objective This chapter covers CompTIA Security+ exam objective 1.8: Explain the techniques used in penetration testing.

Penetration Testing

Penetration testing simulates an attack from a malicious outsider—probing your network and systems for a way in (often *any* way in). Penetration tests, or *pen tests* for short, are often the most aggressive form of security testing and can take on many forms, depending on what is considered "in" or "out" of scope. For example, some pen tests simply seek to find a way into the network—any way in. This can range from an attack across network links, to social engineering, to having a tester physically break into the building. Other pen tests are limited—only attacks across network links are allowed, with no physical attacks.

Regardless of the scope and allowed methods, the goal of a pen test is always the same: to determine if an attacker can bypass your security and access your systems. Unlike a vulnerability assessment, which typically just catalogs vulnerabilities, a pen test attempts to exploit vulnerabilities to see how much access they allow. Penetration tests are very useful in the following ways:

- They can show relationships between a series of "low-risk" items that can be sequentially exploited to gain access (making them a "high-risk" item in the aggregate).

- They can be used to test the training of employees, the effectiveness of your security measures, and the ability of your staff to detect and respond to potential attackers.
- They can often identify and test vulnerabilities that are difficult or even impossible to detect with traditional scanning tools.

EXAM TIP Penetration tests are focused efforts to determine the effectiveness of the security controls used to protect a system.

An effective penetration test offers several critical elements. First, it focuses on the most commonly employed threat vectors seen in the current threat environment. Using zero-day threats that no one else has does not help a firm understand its security defenses against the existing threat environment. It is important to mimic real-world attackers if that is what the company wants to test its defenses against. Second, an effective penetration test focuses on real-world attacker objectives, such as getting to and stealing intellectual property (IP). Just bypassing defenses, but not obtaining the attacker's objectives, again, does not provide a full exercise of security capabilities.

Numerous penetration test methodologies are employed by penetration testers to manage the process of a penetration test. The most recognized is the Open Source Security Testing Methodology Manual (OSSTMM) method. For web applications, the Open Web Application Security Project (OWASP) is the most recognized standard in the industry. The National Institute of Standards and Technology (NIST) has released SP 800-115, "Technical Guide to Information Security Testing and Assessment," which includes the basic process diagram shown in Figure 8-1. The Penetration Testing Methodologies and Standards framework (PTES) and the Information System Security Assessment Framework (ISSAF) are two additional popular frameworks. All of these frameworks define a process, with the NIST model being the simplest. The importance of the process model is to have a plan that all team members can use to understand where they are in the process and the relationships between major tasks.

Figure 8-1 NIST Penetration Test process model from SP 800-115

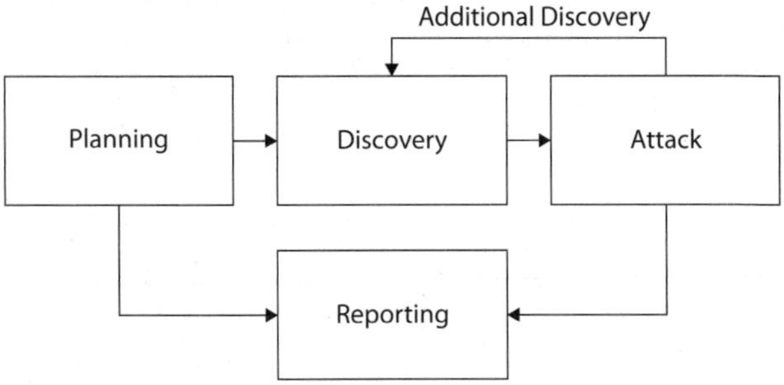

Known Environment

Known environment (white box) testing is almost the polar opposite of unknown environment (black box) testing (discussed next). Sometimes called *clear box testing,* white box techniques test the internal structures and processing within an application for bugs, vulnerabilities, and so on. A white box tester will have detailed knowledge of the application they are examining—they'll develop test cases designed to exercise each path, decision tree, input field, and processing routine of the application.

Known environment testing is often used to test paths within an application (if X, then go do this; if Y, then go do that), data flows, decision trees, and so on. Sometimes the term *white box testing* is applied to network assessments where the tester will have detailed knowledge of the network, including but not limited to IP addresses, network routes, and valid user credentials.

Unknown Environment

Unknown environment (black box) testing is a software-testing technique that consists of finding implementation bugs using malformed/semi-malformed data injection in an automated fashion. Unknown environment techniques test the functionality of the software, usually from an external or user perspective. Testers using black box techniques typically have no knowledge of the internal workings of the software they are testing. They treat the entire software package as a "black box"—they put input in and look at the output. They have no visibility into how the data is processed inside the application, only the output that comes back to them. Test cases for unknown environment testing are typically constructed around intended functionality (what the software is supposed to do) and focus on providing both valid and invalid inputs.

Unknown environment software testing techniques are very useful for examining any web-based applications, which are typically subjected to a barrage of valid, invalid, malformed, and malicious input from the moment they are exposed to public traffic. By performing unknown environment testing before an application is released, developers can potentially find and correct errors in the development or testing stage.

Unknown environment testing can also be applied to networks or systems. Pen tests and vulnerability assessments are often performed from a purely external perspective, where the testers have no inside knowledge of the network or systems they are examining.

Partially Known Environment

So, what happens when you mix a bit of known environment testing and a bit of unknown environment testing? You get partially known environment (gray box) testing. In a *partially known environment* test, the testers typically have some knowledge of the software, network, or systems they are testing. For this reason, partially known environment testing can be very efficient and effective because testers can often quickly eliminate entire testing paths, test cases, and toolsets and can rule out things that simply won't work and are not worth trying.

EXAM TIP The key difference between known, partially known, and unknown environment testing is the perspective and knowledge of the tester. Unknown environment testers have no knowledge of the inner workings and perform their tests from an external perspective. Known environment testers have detailed knowledge of the inner workings and perform their tests from an internal perspective. Partially known environment testers have partial knowledge. This is separate from the authorization element: authorized (white hat) versus unauthorized (black hat) activities.

Rules of Engagement

The *rules of engagement* associated with a penetration test are critical for several reasons. First and foremost, the activities associated with a penetration test are illegal if not authorized, and the rules of engagement specify the legal authority that the penetration testers have in performing their duties. The rules of engagement also establish the boundaries associated with the test so that it is actually exercising the functions desired by the customer. If a penetration tester performs activities outside the rules of engagement, they may be of no value to the enterprise and are thus wasted effort, and in many cases can cause problems. In cases where the enterprise incident response function is either part of the test or is informed to ignore specific activities, having this information coordinated via rules of engagement and proper on-site management is essential. Having an incident response (IR) team activated and spending energy when not part of the test is wasteful to a larger group than just the penetration team.

Typical rules of engagement will include a boundary of what is in scope and what is not. If machine IP addresses are being given to the penetration testing team, then a list of in- and out-of-bounds addresses should be provided. If the machines in scope are to be discovered, then a clear notation of what is not in bounds is needed. Other items might be elements such as time of testing activity. Performing a test during a busy business period might not be advised because of bandwidth and processing load issues. The scope of activities to be performed should obviously be nondestructive, but what constitutes proof of compromise needs to be determined. Any changes to the environment should be noted and either removed or clearly provided to the blue team. How the penetration testers should interact with other employees when discovered should also be included, as should a complete contact list of whom to call when something happens that requires immediate enterprise attention.

Lateral Movement

Lateral movement, sometimes referred to as *network lateral movement,* refers to the process used by attackers to move deeper into a network to get to the target data. In most cases, the initial entry into a system is via a user account that does not have access to the desired material, nor does the account have the appropriate levels of permissions. Through a series of specific activities, an attacker can elevate their level of privilege, as shown in the next section, and also move to other machines deeper in the network. This process of moving across a network is referred to as lateral movement and is a common event for advanced attackers. It also represents one of the points where defenders can catch an attacker, because in most cases these lateral movements are not normal activities for the user account being used.

Privilege Escalation

Privilege escalation is the process of gaining increased privileges for an account. This can be done in a variety of ways—sometimes legitimate, sometimes via a bug or vulnerability. Gaining root or admin access is always a goal for an attacker, because this gives them additional powers on a system that makes their job easier and opens up pathways that are otherwise closed to them. The pathways to privilege escalation for a penetration tester include things such as using a local administrator account, stealing credentials to an account that has administrative rights, and exploitation of a vulnerability that results in privilege escalation.

Some of these paths are easy to block—blocking local administrator accounts and significantly limiting the number of users with native administrative ability are important. Also, monitoring some administrative events such as account creation and account escalation can enable defenders to see when an attacker uses an elevated privilege for specific actions.

There are two types of privilege escalation: horizontal and vertical. In horizontal privilege escalation, the attacker expands their privileges by taking over another account and misusing the legitimate privileges granted to the other user. This is frequently done with lateral movement. This is also why restricting accounts with administrative access is vital, as it reduces the targets for horizontal privilege escalation.

In vertical privilege escalation, the attacker attempts to gain more permissions or access with an existing account they have already compromised. An attacker using a regular user-level account on a network can attempt to gain administrative permissions via exploiting vulnerabilities in processes or services running with administrative privilege. This is why restricting the number of processes or services with administrative permission is important, as it reduces this attack surface area. Vertical privilege escalation requires more sophistication and is the main technique employed by advanced persistent threats (APTs).

Persistence

Persistence is the ability to exist beyond a machine reboot or after disconnection. The term *advanced persistent threat (APT)* refers to a methodology that is focused first and foremost about maintaining persistence. This means the attacker can and will come back into the network, and with the use of good persistence mechanisms and different accounts, it will not be obvious when they reenter. Persistence can be achieved via a variety of mechanisms, such as by creating fake accounts, installing backdoors, using bots that call out through the network to allow the attacker a means of returning back into the network, and manipulating OS items such as Dynamic Link Libraries (DLLs) or permissions.

EXAM TIP Lateral movement, privilege escalation, and persistence are common tools in the toolbox of attackers and penetration testers. They are frequently used together, but each has its unique characteristics. For questions involving them, be sure to examine to which unique characteristic the question is referring in order to pick the correct answer.

Cleanup

Attacking a system can leave a lot of evidence laying around. Testing vulnerabilities and trying access control systems creates a pile of failed events associated with pen testing and attacking a system. One of the important steps that can be taken to avoid detection is cleaning up what messes you make. *Cleanup,* or covering one's tracks, is an essential step in a professional's toolkit. Clearing logs, blocking remote logging, messing with system history, and using reverse shells and Internet Control Message Protocol (ICMP) tunnels to avoid detection and logging are some of the methods employed. The use of rootkits or trojans to modify the OS so that specific account-based activities are not logged is one of the methods used by APT attacks. As an attacker moves laterally within the network and escalates privileges, covering their tracks behind them makes it very difficult for defenders to find the attacker once they have moved to a different account or a different machine.

Bug Bounty

Bug bounty programs are mechanisms where companies pay hackers for revealing the details of vulnerabilities that they discover, providing the companies an opportunity to correct the issues. Most bug bounties pay some form of cash reward, with several major companies like Microsoft, Apple, and Google paying up to six-digit rewards for very critical vulnerabilities. One of the important elements to understand is that for bug hunting to be legal, the firm must have an established bug bounty program, and the hunting activity must be in accordance with that program. Accessing a system and exploiting vulnerabilities on another person's or company's network without permission is a crime, and the bug bounty program can provide such permission if it is followed properly. Finding a vulnerability and attempting to sell it to a company without a bug bounty program is often met with a very strong legal response and potentially a criminal investigation.

EXAM TIP Remember that a bug bounty program is a formal approach to identifying bugs. These programs are often open to the public, and the firm that runs the program sets the rules of engagement.

Pivoting

Pivoting is a technique similar to lateral movement. In pivoting, one moves to a new location in a network and begins the attack process over again, performing scans to see machines that were not visible from the outside. The whole purpose of lateral movement is to go to where the data is, and pivoting is one of the key methods of learning where to move next. The process works as follows: Gain an initial foothold based on what you can see and do from outside the network. Then, from this new machine inside the network, begin the process over again and move deeper. Rinse and repeat. To cross a screened subnet (DMZ) takes a couple of pivots. To move into a protected enclave takes another pivot or two. Pivot, move, pivot again, move again—this is how an attacker or a pen tester gets deeper in the network.

One of the giveaways of this activity is internal scanning. Although it is common to see multiple scans occurring outside the network, once an attacker is inside the network in an area where there is no legitimate reason for scanning activity, a scan reveals that someone is "looking." Slowing down their scans is one method an attacker can use to avoid detection, but this stretches out their engagement, which is a cost factor for pen testers but not necessarily one for APTs.

EXAM TIP Lateral movement and pivoting work hand in hand. The purpose of lateral movement is to go to where the data is, and pivoting is one of the key methods of learning where to move next.

Passive and Active Reconnaissance

Reconnaissance can be one of two types: passive or active. *Passive reconnaissance* is performed using methods to gain information about targeted computers and networks without actively engaging with the target systems and thus avoiding detection. Using Google searches and third-party data repositories like DNS and IP registration records are techniques the attacker can use to provide a lot of information without ever touching the targets, thus completely avoiding detection.

In *active reconnaissance,* the attacker engages with the target system, typically conducting a port scan to find any open ports. Active reconnaissance involves using packets that can be traced; it involves engaging services that can be logged. Also, when active reconnaissance hits a machine set up as a honey trap, it provides evidence of activity that might look legit but isn't, because these devices are specifically not used as part of the enterprise—other than as a trap.

Passive reconnaissance has limits on how much an attacker can learn, but it's completely stealthy. Active reconnaissance is much more informative, but it tells the machines they are being "attacked." The key is to use passive reconnaissance first, and only use active reconnaissance as necessary to get a job done. When an attacker is sneaking into a network, being quiet can be important.

EXAM TIP Be sure to know the differences between active and passive reconnaissance techniques, as this is an easy test question. Passive reconnaissance is stealthy and doesn't actively engage the target system. Active reconnaissance engages the system or network and can gather much more information, but it can also be traced.

Drones

Drones are unmanned aerial platforms capable of carrying cameras, mobile devices, and other items across normal boundaries such as walls, fences, and checkpoints. This provides pen testers a means of getting closer to signals such as wireless networks and then recording traffic. While the use of drones to capture network traffic may seem esoteric, this technique has a name, war flying, and it is described in the next section.

War Flying

Using a drone to fly over a facility and capture wireless network traffic is called *war flying*. For example, if an office on the 28th floor of a building, with restricted elevators and physical access, flying a drone up to just outside the windows can provide pen testers access to wireless signals not available on the ground. And while flying a drone over a sensitive site such as a military base might be unadvisable, doing so in urban settings to gain access, including visual access via windows, is not as uncommon as one might imagine. What you can use drones for is limited mainly by your imagination. Just imagine if you could position your workstation where you place a drone—what might you see and interact with? You might be able to capture packets with passwords, for example, because at 28 stories in the air, no one is worried about eavesdroppers. You can capture machine names, IP addresses, and so much.

War Driving

War driving is the same concept as war flying, but rather than using a drone to capture the traffic, one simply drives past the points of access. Mapping the access points, including geographic information, has become a common activity, with many such maps already published online. Whether the target of a pen test is within the mapped area or you use anonymous access points to hide your own location, finding and using open access points is a useful tool in your pen tester toolkit. Numerous software packages support the functions of war driving, and the feature set of some of these packages has become fairly extensive, including adding geolocation information as well as building databases of the associated metadata with an open access point.

War driving is a follow-on technique of war chalking, which is the marking of curbs and sidewalks with chalk to create symbolic representations of observed open wireless networks in the area. This is a modern-day set of hobo markings, providing information to fellow travelers of the location and availability of open wireless networks.

Another variant of these attack methods is war shipping, where the attacker ships a specially set up mobile phone to a location. This device has a large external battery and special software. The phone is constantly running and collecting network data, and at periodic intervals, it uses its cellular capability to package and send out bursts of collected data. If you ship a phone to someone while they are on vacation, for example, the box can sit for days on the victim's desk, unopened, while the eavesdropping device records and sends out traffic for days. Again, this is a method of bypassing gates and guards, and is easily thwarted if a central mail room opens all packages and inspects their contents.

Footprinting

Footprinting, also called *reconnaissance,* is the first step in gaining active information on a network. Using footprinting, a pen tester can gather information about computer systems and the entities they belong to, and in some cases user information as well. The primary method of gathering this information is via network sniffing and the use of scanning software. Once a network is mapped via footprinting, the pen tester can make decisions about which machines to perform vulnerability mapping on, and in some cases, which machines to avoid, such as honeypots.

EXAM TIP Footprinting is the first step in gaining active information on a network during the reconnaissance process.

OSINT

OSINT (open source intelligence) is the technique of using publicly available information sources to gather information on a system. OSINT is not a single method but rather an entire set of both qualitative and quantitative methods that can be used to collect useful information. If an attack is going to employ social engineering methods, then the OSINT steps are used to gain information about the users and find methods that will improve the odds of a successful campaign. If the targets are network machines, then it can be useful to gather information from sites such as IP address registrars, DNS servers for mail server addresses, and other external-facing systems that require their addresses be known in order to function.

Items such as PR notices from a company about its adoption of new software can provide pen testers with valuable information about the systems they will be looking at. From employee postings on social media to HR postings of job openings, the list of potential sources and levels of detail associated with the information can be significant and, in many cases, extremely useful. At the beginning, a pen tester may have zero knowledge of a system and its components, but after some OSINT work, the level of information can increase significantly, thus changing an unknown environment (black box) type of encounter to at least a partially known environment (gray box) type of encounter.

EXAM TIP OSINT describes using public information sources to gain information about a target and find methods that will improve the odds of a successful campaign.

Exercise Types

Security *exercise types* include those focused on offense, defense, or a mix of offense and defense. Different colors are used to denote the different teams that participate in an exercise. These exercises can be created to test different aspects—from technical to managerial to top-level management actions. The objective of the exercises is to test capability, practice skills, learn options, and develop strategies in a nonthreatening environment.

Red Team

Red teams are composed of members who are focused on offense. Red team members use their skills to mimic a real-world threat environment and provide a test of a firm's defensive capabilities. Red teams are frequently third-party contractors, as their skill set is specialized and the required skill level is high. Depending on the scope of an exercise, red team members may vary based on the systems and protocols being tested, and having a large pool of experienced personnel is another reason most red team work is outsourced to firms that specialize in it and keep large teams for contracts.

Blue Team

The *blue team* is the defense team and, as such, is typically an in-house operation, unless the defensive efforts are outsourced. When you outsource your defense, this adds a layer of complexity to the use of exercises, as this activity has to be negotiated and contracted with your outsourced security provider as well. Blue team members come from the IT and security operations departments, and they typically perform two functions. The first is establishing defenses, configuring defensive elements such as firewalls and security appliances, managing permissions, and logging. The second involves monitoring and incident response functions. In this role, they are on the lookout for attacks and manage the system's responses to any unauthorized behaviors observed.

White Team

When an exercise involves scoring and/or a competition perspective, the team of judges is called the *white team*. If the exercise is such that it requires an outside set of coordinators to manage it, independent of the defending team, these coordinators are also called the white team. White team members are there to ensure that the actual exercise stays on track and employs the desired elements of a system.

Purple Team

A *purple team* is composed of both red team and blue team members. These team members work together to establish and test defenses. Many times, when you engage a third-party red team, it will include a couple blue team members to help manage your team's responses to the attack vectors being used. At times it may also be useful to have a red team member working with your blue team, helping them understand the next steps from a red team (attacker) perspective. The objective of all exercise teams is to improve a firm's cybersecurity posture, and having the right experts on both sides to help train a firm's overall blue team operations and strategies is an efficient method of advancing defensive capabilities.

EXAM TIP Remember that the red team is the attacker, the blue team is the defender, the white team is the exercise manager/judge, and the purple team is composed of a combination of red and blue team members.

Chapter Review

In this chapter, you became acquainted with the tools and techniques of penetration testers. The chapter opened with an examination of penetration testing and the characteristics of the environment. The first section included information on known, unknown, and partially known environments and the characteristics of each. Then rules of engagement were covered, followed by the techniques of lateral movement and privilege escalation. The topics of persistence and cleanup were also covered. Bug bounty programs and pivoting concluded the first major section.

An examination of the tools and techniques of active and passive reconnaissance was provided in the major next section. Topics included drones, war flying, war driving, and footprinting. This section ended with a discussion of open source intelligence (OSINT).

The chapter closed with an examination of the different exercise types and the teams used in these exercises. This section covered the composition and use of red, blue, white, and purple teams.

Questions

To help you prepare further for the CompTIA Security+ exam, and to test your level of preparedness, answer the following questions and then check your answers against the correct answers at the end of the chapter.

1. Which of the following teams is commonly used for active pen testing?
   - **A.** Red team
   - **B.** Black team
   - **C.** White team
   - **D.** Green team
2. War flying is a term to describe which of the following?
   - **A.** Pen testing networks on commercial planes
   - **B.** The use of aerial platforms to gain access to wireless networks
   - **C.** Driving around and sampling open Wi-Fi networks
   - **D.** The use of pen testing techniques against the Defense Department
3. When an attacker moves to a new machine and rescans the network to look for machines not previously visible, what is this technique called?
   - **A.** Lateral movement
   - **B.** Privilege escalation
   - **C.** Persistence
   - **D.** Pivoting

4. What is the most important first step in a penetration test?
   A. OSINT
   B. Rules of engagement
   C. Reconnaissance
   D. Privilege escalation
5. Covering one's tracks to prevent discovery is also known as what?
   A. Lateral movement
   B. OSINT
   C. Cleanup
   D. Pivoting
6. When a pen tester uses OSINT to gain information on a system, the type of environment can be changed from ______ to _______.
   A. closed, open
   B. unknown, known
   C. secure, vulnerable
   D. unknown, partially known
7. Which team involves members who emulate both attackers and defenders?
   A. Purple team
   B. Gold team
   C. Blue team
   D. White team
8. OSINT involves which of the following?
   A. Passive reconnaissance
   B. Active reconnaissance
   C. Port scanning
   D. Persistence
9. Which of the following is a formal approach to identifying system or network weaknesses and is open to the public?
   A. Active reconnaissance
   B. Passive reconnaissance
   C. OSINT
   D. Bug bounty

10. What is the purpose of a white team?
    A. To represent senior management
    B. To provide judges to score or rule on a test
    C. To represent parties that are targets in a pen test
    D. To provide a set of team members with offense and defensive skills (all stars)

Answers

1. **A.** The red team is a team of offense actors used in penetration testing.
2. **B.** War flying is the use of drones, airplanes, and other flying means of gaining access to wireless networks that are otherwise inaccessible.
3. **D.** The key part of the question is the rescanning. Pivoting involves the rescanning of network connections to find unknown or previously unseen connections.
4. **B.** The rules of engagement describe the scope of an engagement and provide important information regarding contacts and permissions. Obtaining these rules is essential before any pen test work begins.
5. **C.** Cleanup involves the steps of clearing logs and other evidence to prevent one from being easily discovered.
6. **D.** OSINT provides information about systems and their addresses and connections, including applications. This takes the status of a system from a completely unknown environment to a partially known environment.
7. **A.** Purple teams have both offensive (red) and defensive (blue) personnel to provide a balanced response.
8. **A.** OSINT is a passive activity, so passive reconnaissance is the correct answer. All of the other answers involve active measures.
9. **D.** Bug bounty programs can open up vulnerability discovery to the public with a set of rules that manages the disclosure process and the engaging of the systems.
10. **B.** When an exercise involves scoring and/or a competition perspective, the team of judges is called the white team. If the exercise is such that it requires an outside set of coordinators to manage it, independent of the defending team, they are also called a white team. White team members are there to ensure that the actual exercise stays on track and involves the desired elements of a system.

PART II

Architecture and Design

CHAPTER 9

Enterprise Security Architecture

In this chapter, you will

- Examine configuration management concepts
- Study data sovereignty and protection methods
- Examine a wide range of technologies used in architectures to protect data
- Examine methods utilized to protect data, including site resiliency and data deception techniques

Enterprises are different from simple single computers. When you have multiple systems that work together, there are architectural concerns to ensure that the elements can reliably and safely work together. Enterprise architects are all about establishing and following a standardized form for their systems, defining configurations and interfaces so that systems can work together. Numerous options are available for many things when configuring a system, and the enterprise architecture is there to guide people in making configuration choices that assist interoperability as well as security.

Certification Objective This chapter covers CompTIA Security+ exam objective 2.1: Explain the importance of security concepts in an enterprise environment.

Configuration Management

Proper configurations are essential in the enterprise. *Configuration management* is essential to secure the system using the specific configuration the implementation intended. Alterations to configurations can add functionality, remove functionality, and even completely change system functionality by altering elements of a program to include outside code. Monitoring and protecting a system from unauthorized configuration changes is important for security.

A wide range of resources exist to provide guidance for setting up and operating computer systems to a secure level that is understood and documented. Because all enterprises are different, it is essential for each enterprise to define the standards and frameworks it uses to guide configuration management. There are numerous sources for these guides, but three main sources exist for a large number of these systems. You can get benchmark guides from manufacturers of the software, from the government, and from an independent organization called Center for Internet Security (CIS). Not all systems have benchmarks, nor do all sources cover all systems, but having them defined for the enterprise and following the correct configuration and setup directives can go a long way in establishing security.

Diagrams

Diagrams are commonly used in architectural specifications to communicate how the enterprise is configured—from network diagrams that describe physical and logical connections, to annotated diagrams that provide essential settings. Graphical diagrams are used because they can be easier to follow at times and pictures can provide ready access to more information in most situations. Also, in the content-rich environment of specification lists, it is easier to digest and understand relationships when presented via diagram.

Baseline Configuration

The *baseline configuration* is the starting point for all future baseline assessments. This baseline is originally created at system creation and is a representation of how the system is supposed to be configured. As time goes on and updates are applied, this configuration will require updating, making it current with the desired system configuration. Baselining is the measuring of a system's current state of security readiness. Various tools are available that you can use to examine a system to see if it has specific weaknesses that make it vulnerable to attack—weaknesses like default passwords, issues with permissions, and so forth. The way baselining is supposed to work is simple: you set up a system, measure the baseline, fix the issues, and declare the resulting system configuration as your baseline. Then, in the future, after changing applications and such, you can measure the baseline again and look for any deviations. Whenever you update, patch, or add an application, it is possible to measure the security risk gap based on before and after baseline measurements.

A baseline deviation is a change from the original baseline value. This change can be positive, lowering risk, or negative, increasing risk. If the change increases risk, then you need to evaluate this new risk level for possible remediation. The biggest challenge is in running the baseline scans, or automating them, to determine when deviations occur.

Standard Naming Conventions

Standard naming conventions are important in an enterprise so that communications can be clear and understood. Enterprises adopt standard naming conventions to reduce sources of error and improve the clarity of communications. Having a set of rules for what one names everything—from files, to devices, to objects, including users—in Active Directory improves the communication and recognition of elements during work. If all servers are randomly named using 20-character alphanumeric sequences, then talking about which server to fix becomes a chore. Having them named in a manner that facilitates clear communication eliminates errors.

Internet Protocol (IP) Schema

Internet Protocol addresses in version 4 are 32-bit numbers—hardly useful for someone to comprehend. Therefore, a notation dividing the number into four sets of 8 bits, represented as xxx.xxx.xxx.xxx, where x is between 0 and 255, was created. The actual address is composed of two portions: a network portion and a host portion. Determining how to divide these up to maximize the utilization of an address space is the process of subnetting. There are two main addressing schemes: the Class A/B/C scheme and the CIDR notation method. The Class A/B/C scheme breaks the network and host at the decimal points of the notation listed earlier. The CIDR schema is more granular, with the address of the network portion being listed in bits preceded by a / symbol.

For an IP address that is broken into a Class A network, the leading bit by definition is 0, followed by 7 bits for the network space and 24 bits for hosts. This allows 128 networks of 16,777,216 hosts and is denoted as /8 in CIDR notation. Class B networks begin with 10 for the first two bits, and then 14 bits for networks (total of 16,384) and 16 bits for hosts (for a total of 65,536), or /16 in CIDR notation. The CIDR notation makes annotating network diagrams easy to understand and comprehend how the network is laid out. The key to this working is advanced planning and definition of the addressing schema, thus preventing illogical network segmentation schemes that waste space.

EXAM TIP Configuration management includes developing physical and logical diagrams, establishing secure baselines, creating understandable standard naming conventions, and implementing secure IP schemas.

Data Sovereignty

Data sovereignty is a relatively new type of legislation several countries have enacted recently that mandates data stored within their borders is subject to their laws, and in some cases that data originating within their borders must be stored there. In today's multinational economy, with the Internet's lack of borders, this has become a problem. Several high-tech firms have changed their business strategies and offerings in order to comply with data sovereignty rules and regulations. For example, LinkedIn, a business social network site, recently was told by Russian authorities that it needed to store all of its data on Russian citizens on servers in Russia. LinkedIn took the business decision that the cost was not worth the benefit and has since abandoned the Russian market. Data sovereignty can drive architectural decisions in enterprises that are multinational in origin. Some countries have strong regulations on where data on their citizens can be stored and processed. This will drive database and data application architectures and design.

EXAM TIP Remember that data sovereignty laws apply to data that is stored in a specific country. For example, if data is stored in the EU, then EU laws and privacy regulations apply to how that data is stored and handled.

Data Protection

Data protection is the set of policies, procedures, tools, and architectures used to ensure proper control over the data in the enterprise. Different data elements require different levels of protection and for different reasons. Customer data is subject to a wide array of legal and regulatory rules designed to protect customer data. Other sensitive data needs protection as well, as items such as intellectual property can result in significant business damage if lost. A wide range of techniques is employed as part of a data protection scheme, and these techniques are highlighted in the following sections.

Data is the most important element to protect in the enterprise. Equipment can be purchased, replaced, and shared without consequence; it is the information that is being processed that has the value. *Data security* refers to the actions taken in the enterprise to secure data, wherever it resides: in transit/motion, at rest, or in processing.

Data Loss Prevention (DLP)

Data loss prevention (DLP) solutions serve to prevent sensitive data from leaving the network without notice. Chapter 18, "Host and Application Security," covers the issues of checking for data loss at the endpoints, but the enterprise needs DLP protections as well. As data is stored in the enterprise, typically in databases, it is thus subject to loss directly from these points. This has led to enterprise-level DLP monitoring, where file activity is reported to centralized systems and to specialized DLP offerings such as the content DLP appliances offered by numerous security companies. Designing these security solutions into an enterprise architecture is part of the security architecture of a modern enterprise.

EXAM TIP DLP solutions are designed to protect data in transit/motion, at rest, or in processing from unauthorized use or exfiltration.

Masking

Data *masking* involves the hiding of data by substituting altered values. A mirror version of a database is created, and data modification techniques such as character shuffling, encryption, and word or character substitution are applied to change the data. Another form is to physically redact elements by substituting a symbol such as * or **x**. This is seen on credit card receipts, where the majority of the digits are removed in this fashion. Data masking makes reverse engineering or detection impossible. The use of data masking to make data sets for testing and to load honeypots with usable-yet-fake data is a common practice.

Encryption

Data encryption continues to be the best solution for data security. Properly encrypted, the data is not readable by an unauthorized party. There are numerous ways to enact this level of protection in the enterprise.

Encryption is the use of sophisticated mathematical techniques to prevent persons with unauthorized access to data from actually reading the data. The good news is that this can be done with standardized methods and applications, including built-in functions in database servers. Having key fields encrypted in storage prevents their loss, as any disclosure is unreadable. Developing the policies and procedures to ensure that the correct data fields are properly encrypted and that the business applications that need to use the data are configured to read the data is part of the overall enterprise architecture scheme. Employing encryption is one of the elements an enterprise can take that, when properly deployed, makes the loss of data a non-event. However, this requires specific architectural elements to employ.

Encryption, including its use and science, is covered in detail in Chapter 16, "Cryptographic Concepts."

At Rest

Data at rest refers to data being stored. Data is stored in a variety of formats: in files, in databases, and as structured elements. Whether in ASCII, XML, JavaScript Object Notation (JSON), or a database, and regardless of what media it is stored on, data at rest still requires protection commensurate with its value. Again, as with data in transit, encryption is the best means of protection against unauthorized access or alteration.

In Transit/Motion

Data has value in the enterprise, but for the enterprise to fully realize the value, data elements need to be shared and moved between systems. Whenever data is *in transit/motion,* being moved from one system to another, it needs to be protected. The most common method of this protection is via encryption. What is important is to ensure that data is always protected in proportion to the degree of risk associated with a data security failure.

In Processing

Data is processed in applications, is used for various functions, and can be at risk when in system memory or even in the act of processing. *Data in processing* is data that is actively being used, either in a processor or other computational element. Protecting data while in use is a much trickier proposition than protecting it in transit or in storage. While encryption can be used in these other situations, it is not practical to perform operations on encrypted data. This means that other means need to be taken to protect the data. Protected memory schemes and address space layout randomization are two tools that can be used to prevent data security failures during processing. Secure coding principles, including the definitive wiping of critical data elements once they are no longer needed, can assist in protecting data that is in processing.

EXAM TIP Remember the three important states of data and how it is protected at rest, in transit/motion, and in processing.

Tokenization

Tokenization is the use of a random value to take the place of a data element that has traceable meaning. A good example of this is the credit card approval process; you do not need to keep a record of the card number, the cardholder's name, or any of the sensitive data concerning the card verification code (CVC) because the transaction agent returns an approval code, which is a unique token to that transaction. You can store this approval code, the token, in your system, and if there comes a time you need to reference the original transaction, this token provides you with complete traceability to it. Yet, if it is disclosed to an outside party, it reveals nothing.

Tokens are used all the time in data transmission systems involving commerce because they protect sensitive information from being reused or shared, yet they maintain the desired nonrepudiation characteristics of the event. Tokenization is not an encryption step because encrypted data can be decrypted. By substituting a nonrelated random value, tokenization breaks the ability for any outside entity to "reverse" the action because there is no connection.

The use of tokenization in creating and testing data sets is another common use of this technology. The tokenization process preserves relational integrity, yet the tokens hold no meaning for other use.

EXAM TIP Tokenization uses a random value to take the place of a data element that has traceable meaning.

Rights Management

Protecting data has many different meanings in different contexts. *Rights management* is the systematic establishment of rules and order to the various rights that users can invoke over digital objects. For example, at the file level, there is read, write, and other access control options. At a context level, the options go further, including control over granular aspects such as editing, printing, copying, replaying, and so on. Digital rights management (DRM) is the term used to describe typical rights scenarios associated with various types of media files, including playing them, copying them, editing them, and saving them to your own device. These rights are designed to prevent unauthorized redistribution or use of digital content. Rights management goes further when you add items such as text documents. Who can edit, copy, delete, or move the material in corporate documents or databases is an enterprise concern. Developing a corporate-level set of policies and procedures to manage rights is essential when the enterprise has significant needs in this area. An ad hoc approach will lead to gaps and failures in what an enterprise-level solution can bring. Major content platforms have the ability to manage rights on an enterprise-level scale; what is needed, however, is the definition of the rights scheme desired.

Geographical Considerations

The Internet is a worldwide connection of systems, and once connected to the Internet, you are literally connected to the world. This makes *geographical considerations* a real topic, as there are a wide range of laws and regulations that do not stop at physical borders. Want to store information on EU citizens in the U.S.? The elements of GDPR can still apply if you do business with them. Want to store data on people in a foreign country? Their data protection laws may mandate certain data elements are stored on servers within their national borders. Researching and understanding the geographical implications and architecting the appropriate geographical considerations to ensure compliance are not just for large multinational companies.

With the mass migration to teleconferencing as a result of the pandemic in 2020, there has been much scrutiny over where data is stored and transmitted. Zoom, a major provider in the teleconferencing market, faced significant backlash over data being routed through servers in China. This adds the dimension of market forces and public opinion to the geographic consideration arena, and one that should be addressed before it becomes a business-impacting issue.

Response and Recovery Controls

Enterprises are designed with infrastructure that enables data to be the lifeblood of a modern organization. But with this infrastructure comes a need for operational guidance to make it function. Two of the elements that have to be designed into the enterprise are disaster recovery (DR) and business continuity (BC). Having backups is great, but they are of no use if you cannot recover and restore them. The creation of incident response programs, together with DR and BC efforts, is greatly facilitated by the inclusion of appropriate response and recovery controls as part of the enterprise. As stated earlier, backing up the data is half of the problem. Having mechanisms in place to restore data from backups and resume normal operations are elements that need to be designed into the enterprise. These elements require special sequencing; you need structures and permissions before data, as well as bandwidth for massive data restorations. In many cases, a complete data recovery can be a multiday effort, and one that has to be designed in place to begin while still operating in DR/BC modes and then switch back once the data is synced up.

Secure Sockets Layer (SSL)/Transport Layer Security (TLS) Inspection

The use of Transport Layer Security (TLS) in an enterprise can provide a lot of protections to data, but it also can prevent security tools from inspecting data for exfiltration and other concerns. The TLS protocol is designed to allow applications to communicate across a network to ensure the confidentiality and integrity of the communication. To inspect data that has been encrypted requires a point where the data can be decrypted and inspected before continuing its journey. Many security appliances are designed to include TLS inspection services so that the use of SSL/TLS encryption does not stop the appliance from doing its job. To perform the task of *Secure Sockets Layer (SSL)/Transport Layer Security (TLS) inspection*, the appliance must receive a set of proper keys to the encryption. The appliance can then receive the data, decrypt the data, perform its security task, re-encrypt the data using the same keys, and send the data on its way to the destination.

It is common for next-generation firewalls (NGFWs) to have TLS inspection built in, providing this level of protection for both inbound and outbound data. TLS inspection consists of two connections: server protection and client protection. The server protection inspects incoming connections to servers. The client protection inspects TLS outgoing connections initiated by clients inside the network. To perform TLS inspection requires two separate secure connections: one from the client to the firewall and one from the firewall to the server. You can use client protection alone, server protection alone, or client and server protection together. By decrypting the data communication at the firewall, the appliance is able to perform deep packet inspection and other security functions before re-encrypting the data and sending it on its way if it is an allowed transmission. This feature prevents encrypted channels from bypassing security elements in a network.

Hashing

Hashing is a technology whereby the uniqueness of a data element can be represented in a fixed-length string. Hashing has a lot of uses in an enterprise, representing data elements, yet not giving up the contents of the element to others. The cryptographic technology behind hashing is covered in Chapter 16, "Cryptographic Concepts." From an enterprise architecture point of view, one should look at hashing as a means of enabling data protection while still enabling the use of the underlying data. The hash value of a data element can act as a replacement for the data, and, if disclosed, the hash value cannot be reversed back to the data.

EXAM TIP A hash function is a special mathematical function that performs one-way encryption, which means that once the algorithm is processed, there is no feasible way to use the ciphertext to retrieve the plaintext that was used to generate it.

API Considerations

The application programming interface, or API, is a critical element in digital enterprises, allowing a method of integrating connections between different applications. However, with this greater ease of connectivity comes increased risk, and API security is often disregarded, resulting in security issues. APIs are like the doors and windows of modern applications. They provide access to applications and the data behind them. Insecure or poorly implemented APIs can be equated to malfunctioning doors and windows, which make protection of the valuable items in the house much more difficult. We can't just ban APIs because they are a common method of data connection in our systems. We need to consider the security implications of them—especially in an enterprise where access can expand dramatically with network size and complexity—and use security controls to mitigate risks from APIs that allow access to our systems. Designing in the correct set of authentication and authorization protocols is essential to enable this needed technology with the ability to function reliably and securely in the enterprise.

Site Resiliency

Resiliency of a site should include consideration of sites used to continue operations. *Site resiliency* considerations can be connected to the idea of restoration sites and their availability. Related to the location of backup storage is where the restoration services will be located. If the organization has suffered physical damage to its facility, having offsite data storage is only part of the solution. This data will need to be processed somewhere, which means that computing facilities similar to those used in normal operations are required. These sites are referred to as recovery sites. The recovery problem can be approached in a number of ways, including hot sites, warm sites, and cold sites.

Hot Sites

A *hot site* is a fully configured environment, similar to the normal operating environment that can be operational immediately or within a few hours, depending on its configuration and the needs of the organization.

Warm Sites

A *warm site* is partially configured, usually having the peripherals and software but perhaps not the more expensive main processing computer. It is designed to be operational within a few days.

Cold Sites

A *cold site* will have the basic environmental controls necessary to operate but few of the computing components necessary for processing. Getting a cold site operational may take weeks.

EXAM TIP Alternate sites have been highly tested on the CompTIA Security+ exam. It is important to know whether the data is available or not at each location. For example, a hot site has duplicate data or a near-ready backup of the original site. A cold site has no current or backup copies of the original site data. A warm site has backups, but they are typically several days or weeks old.

Deception and Disruption

Deception and disruption have become tools in the defender's arsenal against advanced threats. Because a threat actor has limited information about how a system is architected, the addition of deceptive elements such as honeypots/nets can lead to situations where the adversary is discovered. Once an adversary is discovered, a campaign can be waged against them, including the use of additional deception elements to disrupt the attacker's attack methodology. Deception adds a fake layer to your enterprise by placing decoy assets, fake data, and other artifacts in your enterprise. This fake technology is not part of your enterprise configurations, so no system or person should ever touch something fake unless they are actively seeking something or there is a misconfiguration.

Honeypots

A *honeypot* is a server that is designed to act like a real server on a corporate network, but rather than having real data, the honeypot possesses fake data. Honeypots serve as attractive targets to attackers. A honeypot acts as a trap for attackers, as traffic in the honeypot can be assumed to be malicious. Multiple honeypots can be connected in a honeynet, making an attractive target for hackers to discover during their reconnaissance phase.

Honeyfiles

A *honeyfile* is a file that is designed to look like a real file on a server, but the data it possesses is fake. Honeyfiles serve as attractive targets to attackers. A honeyfile acts as a trap for attackers, and the data in the file can contain triggers to alert DLP solutions. Access to the files can be monitored as well. A variation of a honeyfile is a honeyrecord in a database. These records serve the same purpose: they are fake and are never used, but if they are ever copied, you know there is unauthorized activity.

Honeyfiles and honeyrecords can be comingled with legitimate files and records, making their discovery and exploitation more likely. These elements act as tripwires and can be tracked to alert to unauthorized activity.

Honeynets

A *honeynet* is a network designed to look like a corporate network but is made attractive to attackers. A honeynet is a collection of honeypots. It looks like the corporate network, but because it is known to be a false copy, all of the traffic is assumed to be illegitimate. This makes it easy to characterize the attacker's traffic and also to understand where attacks are coming from. Honeynets will not be visited or used by legitimate systems, as legitimate systems have connections to the real servers, so any traffic on a honeynet is presumed to be that of an attacker, or a misconfigured system.

Fake Telemetry

When you are on a system and you realize there is no other traffic, the first thought is you are no longer in the enterprise network. To prevent a lack of "normal" traffic from being a dead giveaway that you have entered a fake part of the network, fake telemetry is used. *Fake telemetry* is synthetic network traffic that resembles genuine communications, delivered at an appropriate volume to make honeynets and honeypots look real.

EXAM TIP Fake telemetry is a deception technology used to make honeynets and honeypots look real and appealing to would-be attackers.

DNS Sinkhole

A *DNS sinkhole* is a DNS provider that returns specific DNS requests with false results. This results in the requester being sent to the wrong address, usually a nonroutable address. When a computer visits a DNS server to resolve a domain name, the server will give a result, if available; otherwise, it will send the resolution request to a higher-level DNS server for resolution. This means that the higher a DNS sinkhole is in this chain, the more requests it will affect and the more beneficial effect it can provide. A typical DNS sinkhole is a standard DNS server that has been configured to return nonroutable addresses for all domains in the sinkhole list so that every request will result in failure to get access to the real site. Some of the larger botnets have been rendered unusable by top-level domain (TLD) sinkholes that can span the entire Internet. DNS sinkholes are a useful tool for blocking malicious traffic, and they are used to combat bots and other malware that relies on DNS responses to communicate. A famous example of this was the use of a DNS sinkhole to block the WannaCry malware in 2017.

EXAM TIP A DNS sinkhole is a deception and disruption technology that returns specific DNS requests with false results. DNS sinkholes can be used in both destructive and constructive ways. When used in a constructive fashion, a DNS sinkhole prevents users from accessing malicious domains.

Chapter Review

In this chapter, you became acquainted with the elements of security concepts in an enterprise environment. The chapter opened with the topic of configuration management. Under configuration management, the subtopics of diagrams, baseline configurations, standard naming conventions, and Internet protocol (IP) schemas were covered. The next topic was data sovereignty.

Data privacy was the third section, with subtopics of data loss prevention, masking, and encryption. The subtopics continued with a description of data at rest, in transit/motion, and in processing. The data protection section finished with a discussion of tokenization and rights management. The chapter then continued with a series of standalone topics, including geographic considerations, response and recovery controls, and Secure Sockets Layer (SSL)/Transport Layer Security (TLS) inspection. This part of the chapter concluded with hashing and API considerations.

The last two sections of the chapter were site resiliency, where hot, warm, and cold sites are covered, followed by detection and disruption technologies. In the detection and disruption section, the topics of honeypots, honeyfiles, and honeynets were presented. The last two items in this section were fake telemetry and DNS sinkholes.

Questions

To help you prepare further for the CompTIA Security+ exam, and to test your level of preparedness, answer the following questions and then check your answers against the correct answers at the end of the chapter.

1. Which of the following is not a state of data in the enterprise?
   A. At rest
   B. In storage
   C. In processing
   D. In transit/motion
2. Creating fake network traffic to deceive attackers in segments of the network designed to deceive them is called what?
   A. DNS sinkhole
   B. Honeytraffic
   C. Fake telemetry
   D. Masking
3. If end-to-end encryption is used, which of the following technologies facilitates security monitoring of encrypted communication channels?
   A. Fake telemetry
   B. Tokenization
   C. Hashing
   D. TLS inspections
4. Enterprises can employ ____________ to block malicious command-and-control traffic from malware.
   A. encryption
   B. honeyfiles
   C. DNS sinkholes
   D. honeynets
5. Which of the following can provide complete traceability to an original transaction without revealing any personal information if disclosed to an outside party?
   A. Tokenization
   B. Data sovereignty

C. Rights management

D. Baseline configuration

6. A system that is ready for immediate use in the event of an outage is called what?

A. Standby system

B. Disaster recovery site

C. Backup site

D. Hot site

7. Data protection includes all of the following topics except which ones? (Choose all that apply.)

A. Honeypots

B. Masking

C. Tokenization

D. DNS sinkholes

8. Which of the following is important to consider when specifically examining configuration management?

A. Data loss prevention

B. Standard naming conventions

C. Rights management

D. Hashing

9. What is masking?

A. The use of stand-in data to replace real-time data

B. The marking of regions where data is not allowed by policy

C. The use of backups to preserve data during disruptive events

D. Redacting portions of data using a covering symbol such as * or x

10. What is the purpose of deception in an enterprise? (Choose all that apply.)

A. To trick attackers into stealing fake data

B. To identify misconfigured systems

C. To permit easy identification of unauthorized actors

D. To provide a place to test new systems without impacting regular operations

Answers

1. **B.** In storage is not a correct term used in describing the states of data. The correct states are at rest, in transit/motion, and in processing.

2. **C.** Fake telemetry is the name for fake network traffic in a deception-based environment.

3. **D.** TLS inspection systems allow TLS channels to be broken and re-established, permitting monitoring of secure traffic.
4. **C.** DNS sinkholes can prevent communications on command-and-control systems associated with malware and botnets by blocking the destination address through the intentional misrouting of traffic to a dead end.
5. **A.** Tokenization is the use of a random value to take the place of a data element that has traceable meaning. This provides complete traceability to the original transaction, and yet if disclosed to an outside party, it reveals nothing. Data sovereignty relates to a country's specific laws regarding the storage and transmission of personal data. Rights management is the systematic establishment of rules and order to the various rights that users can invoke over digital objects. A baseline configuration is originally created at system creation and is a representation of how the system is supposed to be configured.
6. **D.** A hot site is one that is ready for immediate use in the event of a failure. All of the other options are names created using distractor words.
7. **A and D.** Honeypots and DNS sinkholes are part of deception and disruption activities, not data protection.
8. **B.** Standard naming conventions improve the communication of critical elements, thus enabling better configuration management activities.
9. **D.** Masking is the marking over of portions of information to prevent disclosure (for example, using x's for all but the last four numbers of a credit card).
10. **A, B, and C.** Deception techniques such as honeynets and honeypots can trick attackers into stealing fake data and make them easier to find in the network. These techniques can also help in determining systems that are misconfigured.

CHAPTER 10

Virtualization and Cloud Security

In this chapter, you will

- Become familiar with cloud concepts
- Explore virtualization concepts

Virtualization and cloud services are becoming common enterprise tools to manage cost, capacity, complexity, and risk. You need to understand how these services contribute to a security solution in today's enterprise, as described in this chapter.

Certification Objective This chapter covers CompTIA Security+ exam objective 2.2: Summarize virtualization and cloud computing concepts.

Cloud Models

There are many different *cloud deployment models*. Clouds can be created by many entities, both internal and external to an organization. Many commercial cloud services are available from a variety of firms, ranging from Google and Amazon to smaller, local providers. Internally, an organization's own services can replicate the advantages of cloud computing while improving the utility of limited resources. The promise of cloud computing is improved utility and is marketed under the concepts of Platform as a Service (PaaS), Software as a Service (SaaS), and Infrastructure as a Service (IPaaS).

There are pros and cons to cloud-based computing. And for each use, the economic factors may differ (issues of cost, contracts, and so on). However, for someone standing up a test project for which they might not want to incur hardware costs associated with buying servers that may live beyond the test project, then "renting" space in the cloud makes sense. When multiple sites are involved and the issue of distributing data and backup solutions is a concern, cloud services offer advantages. However, with less control comes other costs, such as forensics, incident response, archiving data, long-term contracts, and network connectivity. For each case, a business analysis must be performed to determine the correct choice between cloud options and on-premises computing.

Infrastructure as a Service (IaaS)

Infrastructure as a Service (IaaS) is a marketing term used to describe cloud-based systems that are delivered as a virtual solution for computing. Rather than firms needing to build data centers, IaaS allows them to contract for utility computing as needed. IaaS is specifically marketed on a pay-per-use basis, scalable directly with need.

Platform as a Service (PaaS)

Platform as a Service (PaaS) is a marketing term used to describe the offering of a computing platform in the cloud. Multiple sets of software working together to provide services, such as database services, can be delivered via the cloud as a platform. PaaS offerings generally focus on security and scalability, both of which are characteristics that fit with cloud and platform needs.

Software as a Service (SaaS)

Software as a Service (SaaS) is the offering of software to end users from within the cloud. Rather than installing software on client machines, SaaS acts as software on demand, where the software runs from the cloud. This has a couple advantages: updates can be seamless to end users, and integration between components can be enhanced. Common examples of SaaS are products offered via the Web as subscription services, such as Microsoft Office 365 and Adobe Creative Suite.

Anything as a Service (XaaS)

With the growth of cloud services, applications, storage, and processing, the scale provided by cloud vendors has opened up new offerings that are collectively called *Anything as a Service (XaaS)*. The wrapping of the previously mentioned SaaS and IaaS components into a particular service (say, Disaster Recovery as a Service) creates a new marketable item.

EXAM TIP Be sure you understand the differences between the cloud computing service models Platform as a Service, Software as a Service, Infrastructure as a Service, and Anything as a Service.

Level of Control in the Hosting Models

One way to examine the differences between the cloud models and on-premises computing is to look at who controls what aspect of the model. In Figure 10-1, you can see that the level of control over the systems goes from complete self-control in on-premises computing to complete vendor control in XaaS.

Public

The term *public cloud* refers to a cloud service that is rendered over a system open for public use. In most cases, there is little operational difference between public and private

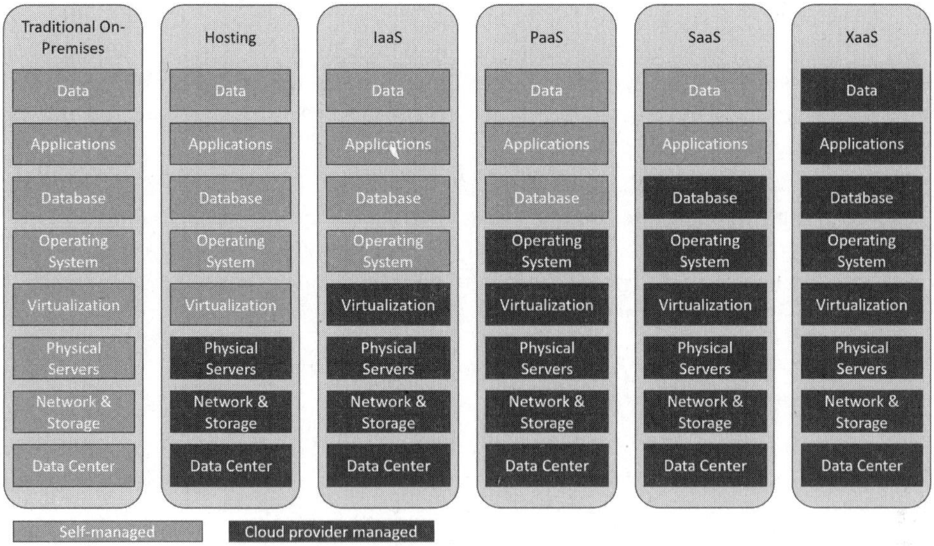

Figure 10-1 Comparison of the level of control in the various hosting models

cloud architectures, but the security ramifications can be substantial. Although public cloud services will separate users with security restrictions, the depth and level of these restrictions, by definition, will be significantly less in a public cloud.

Community

A *community cloud* system is one where several organizations with a common interest share a cloud environment for the specific purposes of the shared endeavor. For example, local public entities and key local firms may share a community cloud dedicated to serving the interests of community initiatives. This can be an attractive cost-sharing mechanism for specific data-sharing initiatives.

Private

If your organization is highly sensitive to sharing resources, you may wish to use a *private cloud*. Private clouds are essentially reserved resources used only by your organization—your own little cloud within the cloud. This setup will be considerably more expensive, but it should also carry less exposure and should enable your organization to better define the security, processing, and handling of data and so on that occurs within your cloud.

Hybrid

A *hybrid cloud* structure is one where elements from private, public, and community cloud structures are combined. When considering a hybrid structure, you need to remain cognizant that, operationally, these differing environments are not actually *joined* together but rather are *used* together. For example, sensitive information can be stored in a private cloud and issue-related information can be stored in the community cloud, yet all of this information is accessed by an application. This makes the overall system a hybrid cloud system.

EXAM TIP Be sure to understand and recognize the different cloud systems—private, public, hybrid, and community—because you may see all four as answer choices for a cloud question. The best answer will typically depend on a single factor or detail in the question.

Cloud Service Providers

Cloud service providers (CSPs) come in many sizes and shapes, with a myriad of different offerings, price points, and service levels. There are the mega-cloud providers, Amazon, Google, Microsoft, and Oracle, which have virtually no limit to the size they can scale to when needed. There are smaller firms, with some offering reselling from the larger clouds and others hosting their own data centers. Each of these has a business offering, and the challenge is determining which offering best fits the needs of your project or company. Many issues have to be resolved around which services are being provided and which are not, as well as price points and contractual terms. One important thing to remember: if something isn't in the contract, it won't be done. Take security items, for example: if you want the cloud provider to offer specific security functionality, it must be in the package you subscribe to; otherwise, you won't receive this functionality.

Managed Service Provider (MSP) / Managed Security Service Provider (MSSP)

A *managed service provider (MSP)* is a company that remotely manages a customer's IT infrastructure. A *managed security service provider (MSSP)* does the same thing as a third party that manages security services. For each of these services, the devil is in the details. The scope of the engagement, what is in the details of the contract, is what is being provided by the third party, and nothing else. For example, if you don't have managing backups as part of the contract, either you do it yourself or you have to modify the contract. Managed services provide the strength of a large firm but at a fraction of the cost that a small firm would have to pay to achieve the scale advantages of a large firm. So, obviously, there are advantages. However, the downside is flexibility, as there is no room for change without renegotiating the contract for services.

On-Premises vs. Off-Premises

Systems can exist in a wide array of places—from on-premises, to hosted, to in the cloud. *On-premises* means the system resides locally in the building of the organization. Whether it's a virtual machine (VM), storage, or even a service, if the solution is locally hosted and maintained, it is referred to as "on-premises." The advantage is that the organization has total control of the system and generally has high connectivity to it. The disadvantage is that it requires local resources and is not necessarily easy to scale. *Off-premises* or *hosted* services refer to having the services hosted somewhere else, commonly in a shared environment. Using a third party for hosted services provides you a set cost based on the amount of those services you use. This has cost advantages, especially when scale is included—does it make sense to have all the local infrastructure, including personnel, for a small, informational-only website? Of course not; you would have that website hosted. Storage works the opposite with scale. Small-scale storage needs are easily met in-house, whereas large-scale storage needs are typically either hosted or in the cloud.

EXAM TIP *On-premises* means the system is on your site. *Off-premises* means it is somewhere else—a specific location. The phrase "in the cloud" refers to having the system distributed across a remotely accessible infrastructure via a network, with specific cloud characteristics, such as scalability and so on. This is true for both on- and off-premises.

Fog Computing

Cloud computing has been described by pundits as using someone else's computer. If this is the case, then *fog computing* is using someone else's computers. Fog computing is a distributed form of cloud computing, in which the workload is performed on a distributed, decentralized architecture. Originally developed by Cisco, fog computing moves some of the work into the local space to manage latency issues, with the cloud being less synchronous. In this form, it is similar to edge computing, which is described in the next section.

Fog computing is an architecture where devices mediate processing between local hardware and remote servers. It regulates which information is sent to the cloud and which is processed locally, with the results sent to the user immediately and to the cloud with its latency. One can view fog computing as using intelligent gateways that handle immediate needs while managing the cloud's more efficient data storage and processing. This makes fog computing an adjunct to cloud, not a replacement.

Edge Computing

Edge computing refers to computing performed at the edge of a network. Edge computing has been driven by network vendors who have processing power on the network and wish new markets rather than just relying on existing markets. Edge computing is similar to fog computing in that it is an adjunct to existing computing architectures—one that is designed for speed. The true growth in edge computing has occurred with the Internet of Things (IoT) revolution. This is because edge computing relies on what one defines as "the edge," coupled with the level of processing needed. In many environments, the actual edge is not as large as one might think, and what some would call edge computing is better accomplished using fog computing. But when you look at a system such as IoT, where virtually every device may be an edge, then the issue of where to do computing comes into play—on the tiny IoT device with limited resources or at the nearest device with computing power. This has led networking companies to create devices that can manage the data flow and do the computing on the way.

EXAM TIP Remember that edge computing brings processing closer to the edge of the network, which optimizes web applications and IoT devices.

Thin Client

A *thin client* is a lightweight computer, with limited resources, whose primary purpose is to communicate with another machine. Thin clients can be very economical when they are used to connect to more powerful systems. Rather than having 32 GB of memory, a top-level processor, a high-end graphics card, and a large storage device on every desktop, where most of the power goes unused, the thin client allows access to a server where the appropriate resources are available and can be shared. With cloud computing and virtualization, where processing, storage, and even the apps themselves exist on servers in the cloud, what is needed is a device that connects to that power and acts as an input/output device.

Containers

Virtualization enables multiple OS instances to coexist on a single hardware platform. The concept of *containers* is similar, but rather than having multiple independent OSs, a container holds the portions of an OS that it needs separate from the kernel. Therefore, multiple containers can share an OS, yet have separate memory, CPU, and storage threads, guaranteeing that they will not interact with other containers. This allows multiple instances of an application or different applications to share a host OS with virtually no overhead. This also allows portability of the application to a degree separate from the OS stack. Multiple major container platforms exist, such as Docker. Rather than adopt a specific industry solution, the industry has coalesced around a standard form called the Open Container Initiative (OCI), designed to enable standardization and the market stability of the environment. Different vendors in the container space have slightly different terminologies, so you need to check with your specific implementation by vendor to understand the exact definition of container and cell in their environment.

You can think of containers as the evolution of the VM concept to the application space. A container consists of an entire runtime environment bundled into one package: an application, including all its dependencies, libraries, and other binaries, and the configuration files needed to run it. This eliminates the differences between development, test, and production environments, as the differences are in the container as a standard solution. By containerizing the application platform, including its dependencies, any differences in OS distributions, libraries, and underlying infrastructure are abstracted away and rendered moot.

EXAM TIP Containers are a form of operating system virtualization. They are a packaged-up combination of code and dependencies that help applications run quickly in different computing environments.

Microservices/API

An *application programming interface (API)* is a means for specifying how one interacts with a piece of software. Let's use a web service as an example: if it uses the representational state transfer (REST) API, then the defined interface is a set of four actions expressed in HTTP:

- **GET** Get a single item or a collection.
- **POST** Add an item to a collection.
- **PUT** Edit an item that already exists in a collection.
- **DELETE** Delete an item in a collection.

Microservices is a different architectural style. Rather than defining the inputs and outputs, microservices divide a system into a series of small modules that can be coupled together to produce a complete system. Each of the modules in a microservices architecture is designed to be lightweight, with simple interfaces and structurally complete. This allows for more rapid development and maintenance of code.

Infrastructure as Code

Infrastructure as code is the use of machine-readable definition files as well as code to manage and provision computer systems. By making the process of management programmable, there are significant scalability and flexibility advantages. Rather than having to manage physical hardware configurations using interactive configuration tools, infrastructure as code allows for this to be done programmatically. A good example of this is in the design of software-defined networking.

Software-Defined Networking (SDN)

Software-defined networking (SDN) is a network architecture where the control plane and the data plane are separated. This allows for networking hardware to be under programmatic control, even while processing data. Traditional network architectures have the data plane and the control plane coexisting, and one of the results is the reduced flexibility of changing the network. This comes as a result of the scope of communications with respect to data. Where a data stream doesn't go has only limited programmability options. With SDN, a complete network programming stack exists, separate from data flows and programmable across the entire network. This provides significant flexibility and programmability in SDN networks, although at the cost of complexity. A key element of SDN is network function virtualization (NFV). NFV is an architecture that virtualizes network services, such as routers, firewalls, and load balancers, as opposed to running them on dedicated, specific hardware. Together, SDN and NFV create a fully functional network under the infrastructure as code architectural model.

Software-Defined Visibility (SDV)

For a network device to operate on data, it must see the data flow. Firewalls can't manage data they don't see, so firewalls are physically positioned throughout the network in line with the system's physical architecture. Just as software-defined networking has changed how networks are managed, *software-defined visibility (SDV)* is an extension of this infrastructure as code idea for the network visibility problem. Rather than the next-generation firewall (NGFW) being positioned strategically in line with data flows physically, it is done via code through the SDN fabric. This allows flexibility in design and the ability to reconfigure networks on the fly, including the security components.

Serverless Architecture

When an infrastructure is established "on premises," the unit of computing power is a server. To set up e-mail, you set up a server. To set up a website, you set up a server. The same issues exist for storage: Need storage? Buy disks. Yes, these disks can all be shared, but in the end, computing is servers, storage is disks. With the cloud, this all changes. The cloud is like the ultimate shared resource, and with many large providers, you don't specify servers or disks, you specify capacity. The provider then spins up the required resources. This *serverless architecture* simplifies a lot of things and adds significant capabilities. By specifying the resources needed in terms of processing power, the cloud provider can spin up the necessary resources. Because you are in essence renting from a large pool of resources, this gives you the ability to have surge capacity, where for a period of time you increase capacity for some specific upturn in usage. One of the operational advantages of this is that cloud providers can make these changes via automated scripts that can occur almost instantaneously, as opposed to the on-premises problem of procurement and configuration. This architecture also supports service integration, thus expanding the utility of computing to the business.

EXAM TIP Know that serverless architecture is a way to develop and run applications and services without owning and managing an infrastructure. Servers are still used, but they are owned and managed "off-premises."

Services Integration

Services integration is the connection of infrastructure and software elements to provide specific services to a business entity. Connecting processing, storage, databases, web, communications, and other functions into an integrated comprehensive solution is the goal of most IT organizations. Cloud-based infrastructure is the ideal environment to achieve this goal. Through predesigned scripts, the cloud provider can manage services integration in a much more scalable fashion than individual businesses. For a business, each integration is a one-off creation, whereas the cloud services provider can capitalize on the reproducibility of doing the same integrations for many customers. And with this scale and experience comes cost savings and reliability.

Resource Policies

When you are specifying the details of a cloud engagement, how much processing power, what apps, what security requirements, how much storage, and access control are all resources. Management of these items is done via *resource policies*. Each cloud service provider has a different manner of allowing you to interact with their menu of services, but in the end, you are specifying the resource policies you wish applied to your account. Through resource policies you can define what, where, or how resources are provisioned. This allows your organization to set restrictions, manage the resources, and manage cloud costs.

Transit Gateway

A *transit gateway* is a network connection that is used to interconnect virtual private clouds (VPCs) and on-premises networks. Using transit gateways, organizations can define and control communication between resources on the cloud provider's network and their own infrastructure. Transit gateways are unique to each provider and are commonly implemented to support the administration of the provider's cloud environment.

Virtualization

Virtualization technology is used to enable a computer to have more than one OS present and, in many cases, operating at the same time. Virtualization is an abstraction of the OS layer, creating the ability to host multiple OSs on a single piece of hardware. To enable virtualization, a hypervisor is employed. A *hypervisor* is a low-level program that allows multiple operating systems to run concurrently on a single host computer. Hypervisors use a thin layer of code to allocate resources in real time. The hypervisor acts as the traffic cop that controls I/O and memory management. One of the major advantages of virtualization is the separation of the software and the hardware, creating a barrier that can improve many system functions, including security. The underlying hardware is referred to as the host machine, and on it is a host OS. Either the host OS has built-in hypervisor capability or an application is needed to provide the hypervisor function to manage the virtual machines (VMs). The virtual machines are typically referred to as guest OSs. Two types of hypervisors exist: Type I and Type II.

EXAM TIP A hypervisor is the interface between a virtual machine and the host machine hardware. Hypervisors comprise the layer that enables virtualization.

Type I

Type I hypervisors run directly on the system hardware. They are referred to as a native, bare-metal, or embedded hypervisors in typical vendor literature. Type I hypervisors are designed for speed and efficiency, as they do not have to operate through another OS layer. Examples of Type I hypervisors include KVM (Kernel-based Virtual Machine, a Linux implementation), Xen (Citrix Linux implementation), Microsoft Windows Server Hyper-V (a headless version of the Windows OS core), and VMware's vSphere/ESXi platforms. All of these Type I hypervisors are designed for the high-end server market in enterprises and are designed to allow multiple VMs on a single set of server hardware. These platforms come with management tool sets to facilitate VM management in the enterprise.

Type II

Type II hypervisors run on top of a host operating system. In the beginning of the virtualization movement, Type II hypervisors were most popular. Administrators could buy the VM software and install it on a server they already had running. Typical Type II hypervisors include Oracle's VirtualBox and VMware's VMware Player. These are designed for limited numbers of VMs, typically running in a desktop or small server environment.

Virtual Machine (VM) Sprawl Avoidance

Sprawl is the uncontrolled spreading and disorganization caused by lack of an organizational structure when many similar elements require management. Just as you can lose track of a file in a large file directory and have to hunt for it, you can lose track of a VM among many others that have been created. VMs basically are files that contain a copy of a working machine's disk and memory structures. Creating a new VM is a simple process. If an organization has only a couple of VMs, keeping track of them is relatively easy. But as the number of VMs grows rapidly over time, sprawl can set in. VM sprawl is a symptom of a disorganized structure. An organization needs to implement *VM sprawl avoidance* through policy. It can avoid VM sprawl through naming conventions and proper storage architectures so that the files are in the correct directory/folder, making finding the correct VM easy and efficient. But as in any filing system, it works only if everyone routinely follows the established policies and procedures to ensure that proper VM naming and filing are performed.

One of the strongest business cases for an integrated VM management tool such as ESXi Server from VMware is its ability to enable administrators to manage VMs and avoid sprawl. Being able to locate and use resources when required is an element of security, specifically availability, and sprawl causes availability issues.

VM Escape Protection

When multiple VMs are operating on a single hardware platform, one concern is *VM escape,* where software, either malware or an attacker, escapes from one VM to the underlying OS. Once the VM escape occurs, the attacker can attack the underlying OS or resurface in a different VM. When you examine the problem from a logical point of view, both VMs use the same RAM, the same processors, and so forth; the difference is one of timing and specific combinations. While the VM system is designed to provide protection, as with all things of larger scale, the devil is in the details. Large-scale VM environments have specific modules designed to detect escape and provide *VM escape protection* to other modules.

EXAM TIP Virtual environments have several specific concepts that the exam may address. Understand the differences between VM sprawl and VM escape and the issues each poses. Expect questions for which you are given several of these terms as options and have to choose the correct one.

Chapter Review

In this chapter, you became acquainted with virtualization and cloud services. The chapter opened with a description of the different cloud models, including Infrastructure as a Service, Platform as a Service, Software as a Service, and Anything as a Service. The models of private, public, hybrid, and community clouds were also explored. Next, the topics of cloud service providers, managed service providers, and managed security service providers were covered, followed by issues associated with on-premises, hosted, and cloud-based provisioning.

Next, the architectural elements of fog, edge, and thin client computing were covered, and containers and API/microservices were explored. Managing cloud resources via infrastructure as code, serverless architectures, services integration, resource policies, and transit gateways was covered. The chapter concluded with an examination of virtualization, hypervisors, both Types I and II, and the problems with VM sprawl and VM escape.

Questions

To help you prepare further for the CompTIA Security+ exam, and to test your level of preparedness, answer the following questions and then check your answers against the list of correct answers at the end of the chapter.

1. How does a hypervisor enable multiple guest operating systems to run concurrently on a host computer?
   - **A.** Via a specialized driver package
   - **B.** By abstracting the hardware from the guest operating system
   - **C.** By providing specific virtual hardware to each guest OS
   - **D.** By hiding the underlying Linux operating system

2. You have deployed a network of Internet-connected sensors across a wide geographic area. These sensors are small, low-power IoT devices, and you need to perform temperature conversions and collect the data into a database. The calculations would be best managed by which architecture?
   - A. Fog computing
   - B. Edge computing
   - C. Thin client
   - D. Decentralized database in the cloud
3. Your new application has multiple small processes that provide services to the network. You want to make this application run more efficiently by virtualizing it. What is the best approach for virtualization of this application?
   - A. Type II hypervisor
   - B. Linux KVM
   - C. Containerization
   - D. Type I hypervisor
4. Why is VM sprawl an issue?
   - A. VM sprawl uses too many resources on parallel functions.
   - B. The more virtual machines in use, the harder it is to migrate a VM to a live server.
   - C. Virtual machines are so easy to create, you end up with hundreds of small servers only performing a single function.
   - D. When servers are no longer physical, it can be difficult to locate a specific machine.
5. When doing incident response for your company, you review the forensics of several virtual servers and you see the attacker on the web server injecting code into uninitialized memory blocks. What attack is the attacker likely attempting?
   - A. Denial-of-service attack on the hypervisor
   - B. VM escape
   - C. Containerization attack
   - D. Crashing the CASB
6. You are planning to move some applications to the cloud, including your organization's accounting application, which is highly customized and does not scale well. Which cloud deployment model is best for this application?
   - A. SaaS
   - B. PaaS
   - C. IaaS
   - D. None of the above

7. You need to move to the cloud a specific customer service module that has a web front end. This application is highly scalable and can be provided on demand. Which cloud deployment model is best for this application?

   A. SaaS

   B. PaaS

   C. IaaS

   D. None of the above

8. One of the primary resources in use at your organization is a standard database that many applications tie into. Which cloud deployment model is best for this kind of application?

   A. SaaS

   B. PaaS

   C. IaaS

   D. None of the above

9. Which cloud deployment model has the fewest security controls?

   A. Private

   B. Public

   C. Hybrid

   D. Community

10. What is the primary downside of a private cloud model?

   A. Restrictive access rules

   B. Cost

   C. Scalability

   D. Lack of vendor support

Answers

1. **B.** The hypervisor abstracts the hardware from the guest operating system to enable multiple guest operating systems to run concurrently on a host computer.
2. **B.** Edge computing on the way to the cloud would be the best fit given the lightweight processing capability of the IoT devices.
3. **C.** Containerization runs small applications on a host OS with virtually no overhead.
4. **D.** VM sprawl is an issue because when virtual machines proliferate, they can be easily moved and potentially easily copied to random locations. This can make finding a specific machine difficult without a carefully constructed and consistently managed organizational structure.

5. **B.** Although all hypervisors actively try to prevent it, any flaw in memory handling could allow code that is maliciously placed in a block to be read by the hypervisor or another machine. This is known as VM escape. The scenario states virtual server, eliminating answers C and D, and operational code blocks in uninitialized memory would not cause a denial of service, eliminating answer A.
6. **C.** Infrastructure as a Service is appropriate for highly customized, poorly scaling solutions that require specific resources to run.
7. **A.** Software as a Service is suitable for delivering highly scalable, on-demand applications without installing endpoint software.
8. **B.** Platform as a Service is suitable for standard resources in use by many other applications.
9. **B.** The shared environment of a public cloud has the least amount of security controls.
10. **B.** A private cloud model is considerably more expensive, as it is a dedicated resource, negating some of the advantages of outsourcing the infrastructure in the first place.

CHAPTER 11

Secure Application Development, Deployment, and Automation Concepts

In this chapter, you will

- Learn to implement secure application development
- Understand secure development concepts
- Explore the addition of security to automated/agile development processes

Software development is a complex process with many different issues, from design, to coding, to testing and deployment, that need to be considered and managed to achieve the desired goals of secure software. Developing and using a security-inclusive application development process is essential. Expanding that process to include delivery and post-deployment issues is essential, and one of the key tools to achieve these objectives is the use of automation and scripting. This chapter covers these issues with respect to the Security+ Version 6 exam objectives.

Certification Objective This chapter covers CompTIA Security+ exam objective 2.3: Summarize secure application development, deployment, and automation concepts.

Environment

Most organizations have multiple, separate computing *environments* designed to provide isolation between the functions of development, test, staging, and production. The primary purpose of having these separate environments is to prevent security incidents arising from untested code ending up in the production environment. The hardware of these environments is segregated, and access control lists are used to prevent users from accessing more than one environment at a time. Moving code between environments requires a special account that can access both, minimizing issues of cross-contamination.

Development

The *development environment* is sized, configured, and set up for developing applications and systems. Unlike production hardware, the development hardware does not have to be scalable, and it probably does not need to be as responsive for given transactions. The development platform does need to use the same OS type and version as used in the production environment, for developing on Windows and deploying to Linux is fraught with difficulties that can be avoided by matching the environments in terms of OS type and version. After code is successfully developed, it is moved to a test system.

Test

The *test environment* fairly closely mimics the production environment—same versions of software, down to patch levels, same sets of permissions, same file structures, and so forth. The purpose of the test environment is to test a system fully prior to deploying it into production to ensure that it is bug-free and will not disrupt the production environment. The test environment may not scale like production, but from the viewpoint of the software/hardware footprint, it will look exactly like production. This is important to ensure that system-specific settings are tested in an environment identical to that in which they will be run.

Staging

The *staging environment* is an optional environment, but it is commonly used when an organization has multiple production environments. After passing testing, the system moves into staging, from where it can be deployed to the different production systems. The primary purpose of staging is to serve as a sandbox after testing, so the test system can test the next set while the current set is deployed across the enterprise. One method of deployment is a staged deployment, where software is deployed to part of the enterprise and then a pause occurs to watch for unseen problems. If none occur, the deployment continues, stage by stage, until all of the production systems are changed. By moving software in this manner, you never lose the old production system until the end of the move, giving you time to monitor and catch any unforeseen problems. This also prevents the total loss of production to a failed update.

Production

The *production environment* is where the systems work with real data, doing the business that the system is intended to perform. This is an environment where, by design, very few changes occur, and those that do must first be approved and tested via the system's change management process.

EXAM TIP Understand the structure and purpose of the different environments so that when given a scenario and asked to identify which environment is appropriate, you can pick the best answer: development, test, staging, or production.

Quality Assurance (QA)

Quality assurance (QA) is a common step in any manufacturing process, and software is no exception. Ensuring that quality is in a product is a process issue, not an inspection issue. Yes, testing is still needed, but the current state of the art is to drive security and quality issues via the actual software build process, not to have a series of inspectors after it is built. This being said, there is still a role for people who focus on quality and security issues in maintaining the bug register (a listing of all bugs) and helping the correct people on the team get the correct information with respect to building secure software.

Provisioning and Deprovisioning

Provisioning is the process of assigning permissions or authorities to objects. Users can be provisioned into groups, and computer processes or threads can be provisioned to higher levels of authority when executing. *Deprovisioning* is the removal of permissions or authorities. In secure coding, the practice is to provision a thread to an elevated execution permission level (for example, root) only during the time that the administrative permissions are needed. After those steps have passed, the thread can be deprovisioned back to a lower access level. This combination lowers the period of time an application is at an increased level of authority, thus reducing the risk exposure should the program get hijacked or hacked.

Integrity Measurement

Integrity is defined in the security field as a determination that data has no unauthorized changes. In a software development and deployment environment, this is a very important issue because even little changes can cause huge issues and can be difficult to detect. Maintaining control over a codebase means that two things are happening. First, you have control over the copies in such a way that people are only working on a legitimate codebase. Nothing ruins a day faster than learning your all-day programming session was performed on a set of code that's not being updated—in other words, you worked on the wrong copy. While not as disastrous as painting the wrong house (you don't have to paint it back), the work is in essence lost. When code is undergoing constant change from multiple authors, this is not as simple as it seems, and some form of version control is required. Second, you maintain a log of the changes and a method of identifying the versions. The version control system you use should keep track of the versions, but to clearly identify a set of code requires a different tool. A hash algorithm creates a unique hash value for each unique item it operates on, and codebases are digital objects. Maintaining a directory of hash values that denote the different versions of the codebase is how integrity controls are annotated within the code. If you have a version of the code, you can hash it and look up in the version table to see which version you have. This is superior to labeling in the code with metadata because the labels can be changed, but the hash is tied to the code. When code is released for deployment, it is typically signed digitally, and again the hash values ensure users that the code has not been changed.

Secure Coding Techniques

Software security begins with code that is secure and free of vulnerabilities. Unfortunately, all code has weaknesses and vulnerabilities, so instantiating the code in a manner that has effective defenses to prevent the exploitation of vulnerabilities can help maintain a desired level of security. Proper handling of configurations, errors and exceptions, and inputs can assist in the creation of a secure application. Testing the application throughout the system lifecycle can determine the actual security risk profile of a system.

There are numerous individual elements in the secure development lifecycle (SDL) that can assist a team in developing secure code. Correct SDL processes, such as input validation, proper error and exception handling, and cross-site scripting and cross-site request forgery mitigations, can improve the security of code. Process elements such as security testing, fuzzing, and patch management also help to ensure applications meet a desired risk profile.

Normalization

Normalization is an initial step in the input validation process. Specifically, it is the process of creating the canonical form, or simplest form, of a string before processing. Strings can be encoded using Unicode and other encoding methods. This makes byte-by-byte comparisons meaningless when trying to screen user input of strings. Checking to see whether the string is "rose" can be difficult when "A Rose is a rose is a r%6fse." The process of normalization converts all of these to "rose," where they can then be screened as valid input.

Different libraries exist to assist developers in performing this part of input validation. Developers should always normalize their inputs prior to validation steps to remove Unicode and other encoding issues. Per the Unicode standard, "When implementations keep strings in a normalized form, they can be assured that equivalent strings have a unique binary representation."

A Rose is a rose is a r%6fse

Canonical form refers to simplest form and, because of the many encoding schemes in use, can be a complex issue. Characters can be encoded in ASCII, Unicode, hex, UTF-8, and even combinations of these. So, if the attacker desires to obfuscate a response, then several things can happen.

By URL-encoding URL strings, it may be possible to circumvent filter security systems and intrusion detection systems. For example, the URL

```
http://www.myweb.com/cgi?file=/etc/passwd
```

can become the following:

```
http://www.myweb.com/cgi?file=/
%2F%65%74%63%2F%70%61%73%73%77%64
```

Double-encoding can complicate the matter even further. Thus, the round 1 decoding

```
scripts/..%255c../winnt
```

becomes the following:

```
scripts/..%5c../winnt
(%25 = "%" Character)
```

And the round 2 decoding

```
scripts/..%5c../winnt
```

becomes the following:

```
scripts/..\../winnt
```

The bottom line is simple: know that encoding can be used and plan for it when designing input-verification mechanisms. Expect encoded transmissions to be used to attempt to bypass security mechanisms.

Stored Procedures

Stored procedures are methods of interfacing with database engines. Stored procedures are precompiled scripted methods of data access that offer many advantages. First is speed. Because they are precompiled, they can run much more efficiently in the production environment. But because they are scripted in advance, they offer much less flexibility than other methods such as using parameterized queries or building and executing SQL statements on the fly in an application program.

EXAM TIP A stored procedure is a group of one or more statements stored within a database. Stored procedures are used in programming languages such as SQL, Java, C++, and C.

Obfuscation/Camouflage

Obfuscation or *camouflage* is the hiding of obvious meaning from observation. While obscurity is not considered adequate security under most circumstances, adding obfuscation or camouflage to a system to make it harder for an attacker to understand and exploit is a good thing. Numbering your e-mail servers email1, email2, email3, . . . tells an attacker what namespace to explore. Removing or hiding these hints makes the work harder and offers another layer of protection.

This works well for data names and other exposed elements that have to be exposed to the outside. Where this does not work well is in the construction of code. Obfuscated code, or code that is hard or even nearly impossible to read, is a ticking time bomb. The day will come when someone will need to read the code, figure out how it works so it can be modified, or determine why it is not working. If programmers have issues reading and understanding the code, including how it functions and what it is supposed to do, how can they contribute to its maintenance?

Code Reuse and Dead Code

Modern software development includes the extensive reuse of components. From component libraries to common functions across multiple components, there is significant opportunity to reduce development costs through reuse. This can also simplify a system through the reuse of known elements. The downside of massive reuse is associated with a monoculture environment, which is where a failure has a larger footprint because of all the places it is involved with.

During the design phase, decisions should be made as to the appropriate level of reuse. For some complex functions, such as in cryptography, reuse is the preferred path. In other cases, where the lineage of a component cannot be established, the risk of use may outweigh the benefit. Additionally, the inclusion of previous code, sometimes referred to as *legacy code,* can reduce development efforts and risk.

EXAM TIP The use of legacy code in current projects does not exempt that code from security reviews. All code should receive the same scrutiny, especially legacy code that may have been developed prior to the adoption of software development lifecycle (SDLC) processes.

Dead code is code that, while it may be executed, obtains results that are never used elsewhere in the program. There are compiler options that can remove dead code, called *dead code elimination,* but these must be used with care. Assume you have a section of code that you put in specifically to set a secret value to all zeros. The logic is as follows: generate a secret key, use the secret key, set the secret key to zero. You set the secret key to zero to remove the key from memory and keep it from being stolen. But along comes the dead code removal routine. It sees you set the value of secretkey == 0, but then you never use it again. So, the compiler, in optimizing your code, removes your protection step.

Server-Side vs. Client-Side Execution and Validation

In a modern client/server environment, data can be checked for compliance with input/output requirements either on the server or on the client. There are advantages to verifying data elements on a client before sending them to the server—namely, efficiency. Doing checks on the client saves a round trip, and its delays, before the user is alerted to a problem. This can improve the usability of software interfaces.

The client is not a suitable place to perform any critical value checks or security checks. The reasons for this are twofold. First, the client can change anything after the check. Second, the data can be altered while in transit or at an intermediary proxy. For all checks that are essential, either for business reasons or for security, the verification steps should be performed on the server side, where the data is free from unauthorized alterations. Input validation checks can be safely performed only on the server side.

EXAM TIP All input validation should be performed on the server side of the client–server relationship, where it is free from outside influence and change.

Memory Management

Memory management encompasses the actions used to control and coordinate computer memory, assigning memory to variables, and reclaiming it when it is no longer being used. Errors in memory management can result in a program that has a memory leak, and it can grow over time, consuming more and more resources. The routine to clean up memory that has been allocated in a program but is no longer needed is called *garbage collection*. In the C programming language and C++, where there is no automatic garbage collector, the programmer must allocate and free memory explicitly. One of the advantages of newer programming languages such as Java, C#, Python, and Ruby is that they provide automatic memory management with garbage collection. This may not be as efficient as specifically coding in C, but it is significantly less error prone.

Use of Third-Party Libraries and Software Development Kits (SDKs)

Programming today is to a great extent an exercise in using *third-party libraries* and *software development kits (SDKs)*. This is because once code has been debugged and proven to work, rewriting it is generally not a valuable use of time. Also, some fairly complex routines, such as encryption, have vetted, proven library sets that remove a lot of risk from programming these functions.

EXAM TIP Software developers use packaged sets of software programs and tools called SDKs to create apps for specific vender platforms.

Data Exposure

Data exposure is the loss of control over data from a system during operations. Data must be protected during storage, during communication, and even at times during use. It is up to the programming team to chart the flow of data through a system and ensure it is protected from exposure throughout the process. Data can be lost to unauthorized parties (a failure of confidentiality) and, equally dangerous, can be changed by an unauthorized party (a failure of integrity).

EXAM TIP The list of elements under secure coding techniques is long and specific in the CompTIA S+ exam objectives. It is important to understand the differences so you can recognize which one best fits the context of the question.

Open Web Application Security Project (OWASP)

The *Open Web Application Security Project (OWASP)* is a nonprofit foundation dedicated to improving web-based application software security. Best known for its top ten list of software vulnerabilities associated with website applications, OWASP also has a multitude of useful guidelines on its website, www.owasp.org. OWASP is a resource that should be actively used by web application programmers to prevent vulnerabilities that are common in web applications. This site has tons of resources to assist developers in producing better and more secure apps.

Software Diversity

Software is not a single product. There are many different forms, and these can be characterized by a wide range of differentiators. Software can be categorized by elements such as platform (PC, server, mobile, IoT device, cloud), programming language, interfaces (web, API, messaging, direct connections), purpose, and a whole host of other factors. One can say that each project in the end is unique. But, the fact that someone can point to why their software is different or special does not diminish the fact that it is a series of instructions for a computer to operate on, and that based on design decisions, coding decisions, and environment decisions, it can and will have vulnerabilities that could enable an attacker to do things that are not desired outcomes. Hence, all software needs security. Having a proper security process as part of the development process is important to reduce vulnerabilities and manage security issues as they are uncovered.

Another key aspect of software diversity is the issue of monoculture avoidance. As many systems in an enterprise have common elements, such as the operating system, key libraries, and so on, there exists the possibility for common vulnerabilities to affect many components. A consequence of software systems sharing common vulnerabilities is an increased susceptibility to malware and other attacks with common methods. The primary method of beating this systemic risk is through *software diversity*, having different components with different software elements.

Compilers

Compilers take computer programs written in one language and convert them to a set of codes that can run on a specific set of hardware. Modern compilers can take high-level, platform-agnostic code and convert it to machine language code that actually can run on a given platform. In the process of doing this transformation, compilers can manage various aspects of a program, such as memory, code efficiency, and more.

Binaries

Ultimately in the end, all digital computer systems are binary machines. *Binary* machines operate in one of two states: on (1) or off (0). Grouping these signals (the 1s and 0s) together into words and larger memory and processing structures is what makes computers capable of doing their work. But one interesting aspect of all of this is reproducibility. Two identical computers can run the exact same thing, and the signals and the memory structures will all be identical, because that is how computers work. This leads to another form of important diversity: randomization. Although all computer memory is a collection of 1s and 0s, how these signals are arranged has implications. Having two machines, or more, with completely identical memory layouts again provides attackers a reproducible target. This has led to defenses that include randomizing memory layouts, where the pattern is specific to each boot of the machine and is only known to the machine.

Binary diversity is the creation of identically functioning binary images, but with different specific instantiations. Different locations for memory variables, different pointer offsets, and different layouts in computer memory can all be done today and yet completely preserve functionality. This type of defense makes it difficult for an attacker to bypass controls and inject something directly into memory.

NOTE Taking binary diversity to the extreme, one can run a set of variants simultaneously in a multivariant execution environment (MVEE). The system then unifies inputs/outputs and monitors the operation, enabling detection of when variants diverge in behavior. This indicates abnormal behavior and enables the system to react and recover from a bad result stream.

Automation/Scripting

Automation through scripting and other programmable means has great utility in software development. The use of these technology-backed methods has led to a field of development known as DevOps. DevOps is a combination of *development* and *operations*—in other words, a blending of tasks performed by a company's application development and systems operations teams. DevOps emphasizes communication and collaboration between product management, software development, and operations professionals to facilitate continuous development, continuous integration, continuous delivery, and continuous monitoring processes. DevOps can be considered the anti-waterfall model because rather than going from phase to phase, in DevOps, as small changes are ready to advance, they advance. This leads to many small incremental changes but less time between updates and less time to fix or change things. Secure DevOps is the addition of security steps to the DevOps process. Just as you can add security steps to the waterfall model, or any other software development model, you can add them to DevOps as well, resulting in a secure DevOps outcome.

Automated Courses of Action

One of the key elements of DevOps is automation. DevOps relies on automation for much of its efficiencies. *Security automation* can do the same for security that automation has in DevOps. Automating routines and extensive processes allows fewer resources to cover more of the environment in a more effective and efficient manner. Automation removes manual labor costs, especially for skilled cybersecurity personnel. Rather than replacing the personnel with scripts, the use of automation allows the personnel to spend their time doing value-added analysis work.

EXAM TIP The implications of continuous monitoring/validation/integration/delivery/deployment will likely depend on the details of the question, the context, and the specific question being asked. To determine which aspect is correct requires careful examination of the context of the question. Learn the differences, not just the context of "continuous."

Continuous Monitoring

Continuous monitoring is the term used to describe the technologies and processes employed to enable rapid detection of compliance issues and security risks. More than just a buzzword, continuous monitoring is one of the most important tools available for risk management. Automation and scripts are commonly used as part of a continuous monitoring framework, as they can provide 24/7/365 monitoring of processes and conditions, feeding alerts into the organization's monitoring system for review and action by security personnel.

Continuous Validation

Continuous validation is the extension of testing to support the continuous process of software development that occurs in DevOps. As code is changed in the DevOps process, the new code must be tested with the existing codebase to ensure functionality and stability. Making this process part of the continuous development process is essential to keeping development on a timely trajectory.

Continuous Integration

Continuous integration is the DevOps manner of continually updating and improving the production codebase. By using high levels of automation and safety nets of automated back-out routines, continuous integration allows for testing and updating even minor changes without a lot of overhead. This means that rather than several large updates, with many integrated and many potentially cross-purpose update elements, all squeezed into a single big package, a whole series of smaller single-purpose integrations is run. Thus, when testing, you have isolated the changes to a small manageable number, without the significance of multiple potential interactions. This reduces interaction errors and other types of errors that are time-consuming to chase down.

Continuous Delivery

Continuous delivery is a natural extension of continuous integration so you can quickly release new changes to production in a sustainable way. Continuous delivery relies on automated testing and is an automated release process that enables the delivery of updates when they are complete, at any point of time, as opposed to a fixed release schedule. When code is ready to be released to production, continuous delivery is the automation of that step, but still under specific operator control.

Continuous Deployment

Continuous deployment is continuous delivery on autopilot. It goes one step further than continuous delivery in that the release is automatic. With this practice, every change that passes all stages of your production pipeline is released to production. There's no human intervention, and when all gates are met (that is, there are no failed tests), continuous deployment automatically sends the code to production.

EXAM TIP Continuous deployment goes one step further than continuous delivery—every change that passes all stages of your production pipeline is automatically released to customers.

Elasticity

Elasticity is the characteristic that something is capable of change without breaking. One of the strengths of cloud computing is its elasticity. One can add or subtract resources to or from a cloud environment almost automatically without issue. Elasticity in software works in the same fashion—how resilient the software is to changes in its environment while remaining secure. For software to be elastic, it needs to be able to run under a variety of different conditions. Legacy software that runs in a single thread, although easier to write, is not elastic. When single-threaded software gets employed in an environment of VMs, multiple processors, and cloud environments, its performance is limited to a single thread. Multithreaded software can scale and adapt better, but this also increases the complexity, bringing in issues such as race conditions. For scalability to be stable and sustainable, the software needs to be elastic.

Scalability

Scalability is the characteristic of a software system to process higher workloads on its current resources (scale up) or on additional resources (scale out) without interruption. Scalability is important in web systems, databases, application engines, and cloud systems. Workloads can vary, and cloud/container systems can add processing and storage, but the software must be capable of addressing the changes in an environment. While this seems obvious, the devil is in the details. Timing loops can affect the ability of software to run on faster hardware, as the system can only run as fast as its slowest link. Scaling out to multiple machines brings in issues of synchronization and coordination. All of these issues can be solved, but this has to happen during design and development, not after delivery.

Version Control

Programs are developed, released, and used, and then changes are needed, either to alter functionality, to fix errors, or to improve performance. This leads to multiple versions of programs. *Version control* is as simple as tracking which version of a program is being worked on, whether in dev, test, or production. Versioning tends to use the first whole number to indicate major releases and uses numbers after a decimal point to indicate minor changes.

Having the availability of multiple versions brings into focus the issue of *change management*. How does a firm manage which versions are currently being used, and how do they coordinate changes as they are released by a manufacturer? In traditional software publishing, a new version required a new install and fairly significant testing because the level of change could be drastic and call into question issues of compatibility, functionality, and even correctness. DevOps turned the tables on this equation by introducing the idea that developers and production work together and create in essence a series of micro-releases so that any real problems are associated with single changes and not bogged down by interactions between multiple module changes.

Whether you are in traditional software publishing or operating in the DevOps world, you still need a change management process that ensures all changes in production are authorized, properly tested, and rolled back if they fail, and you must maintain current and accurate documentation.

Chapter Review

In this chapter, you became acquainted with secure application development, deployment, and automation concepts. The chapter opened with a discussion of the environment, including development, test, staging, production, and quality assurance elements. It then examined provisioning and deprovisioning, and integrity management.

The chapter then moved on to secure coding techniques. These include normalization, stored procedures, obfuscation/camouflage, and code reuse and dead code. This section included a discussion of server-side versus client-side validation elements and it closed with memory management, the use of third-party libraries and software development kits, and data exposure.

The Open Web Application Security Project (OWASP) and software diversity were discussed next. Under software diversity, issues of compiler and binary diversity are covered. The chapter then moved on to the issues from the world of DevOps or automation and scripting as applied to software development. The topics in this section included automated courses of action, continuous monitoring, continuous validation, continuous integration, continuous delivery, and continuous deployment.

The chapter closed with an examination of elasticity and scalability followed by version control.

Questions

To help you prepare further for the exam, and to test your level of preparedness, answer the following questions and then check your answers against the correct answers at the end of the chapter.

1. To develop secure software that prevents attackers from directly injecting attacks into computer memory and manipulating the application's process, one should employ which method?
   - **A.** Elasticity
   - **B.** Dead code
   - **C.** Normalization
   - **D.** Software diversity
2. Problems in which phase will specifically stop continuous deployment but not necessarily continuous delivery?
   - **A.** Continuous integration
   - **B.** Continuous monitoring
   - **C.** Continuous validation
   - **D.** Continuous development
3. Why is memory management important in software development?
   - **A.** A program can grow and consume other program spaces.
   - **B.** Memory is expensive.
   - **C.** Memory can be a speed issue.
   - **D.** None of the above.
4. When a program is installed and needs permissions, what is this called?
   - **A.** Staging
   - **B.** Provisioning
   - **C.** Continuous integration
   - **D.** Version control

5. Which of the following statements concerning elasticity and scalability are true?
   - **A.** Scalability requires elasticity.
   - **B.** Elasticity involves enabling software to use more processors to do more work.
   - **C.** Elasticity means being prepared to take advantage of scalability.
   - **D.** All of the above.
6. To protect software from reverse engineering by attackers, developers can use which of the following?
   - **A.** Dead code
   - **B.** Obfuscation
   - **C.** Binary diversity
   - **D.** Stored procedures
7. To manage various releases of software over time, the organization uses which of the following?
   - **A.** Staging environment
   - **B.** Provisioning and deprovisioning steps
   - **C.** Version control
   - **D.** Continuous integration
8. Which of the following environments is used to test compatibility against multiple target environments?
   - **A.** Production
   - **B.** Test
   - **C.** Quality assurance
   - **D.** Staging
9. The fact that there are multiple methods of representing an object in a computer system can lead to issues when logical comparisons are needed. What can be used to ensure accuracy of comparison elements?
   - **A.** Normalization
   - **B.** Stored procedures
   - **C.** Third-party libraries
   - **D.** Third-party software development kits
10. What is the only sure method of ensuring input is valid before use on a server?
    - **A.** Use of third-party libraries and software development kits
    - **B.** Server-side validation
    - **C.** Stored procedures
    - **D.** Client-side validation

PART II

Answers

1. **D.** Software diversity in the form of diverse binaries will prevent direct memory attacks against known software structures.
2. **C.** Continuous validation is required to ensure error-free software, and errors will stop continuous deployment.
3. **A.** Memory management failures can lead to a program growing in size when executing. This can result in either its own failure or the diminishing of memory resources for other programs.
4. **B.** Provisioning is the assignment of permissions or authorities to objects.
5. **D.** All of the above is the correct answer. Scalability requires elasticity to scale, elasticity involves enabling software to use more processors to do more work, and elasticity means developing software that is prepared to take advantage of scalability.
6. **B.** Obfuscation is the technique of hiding properties to prevent examination. Making code hard to decompile and not storing any specific clues in the source code can make reverse engineering a challenge.
7. **C.** Version control comprises the processes and procedures employed to manage different releases of software over time.
8. **D.** The staging environment can be used to manage software releases against different targets to ensure compatibility.
9. **A.** Normalization is the process of reducing items to a canonical form before comparisons to ensure appropriate logical matching.
10. **B.** Server-side validation is the only sure validation method for inputs to the application.

CHAPTER 12

Authentication and Authorization

In this chapter, you will

- Learn how to identify and implement authentication methods, factors, and attributes
- Learn about authorization design concepts and requirements

One of the core tenets of computer security is the concept that all actions will be controlled via a system of approvals; for example, only authorized parties can perform the actions of accessing a resource, operating on a resource, and storing an item. Identity and access management systems are the mechanisms by which this is accomplished. This chapter examines the foundational elements behind authentication systems.

Certification Objective This chapter covers CompTIA Security+ exam objective 2.4: Summarize authentication and authorization design concepts.

Authentication Methods

Authentication is the process of verifying an identity previously established in a computer system. There are a variety of methods of performing this function, each with its advantages and disadvantages, as detailed in the following sections.

Directory Services

A *directory* is a data storage mechanism similar to a database, but it has several distinct differences designed to provide efficient data-retrieval services compared to standard database mechanisms. A directory is designed and optimized for reading data, offering very fast search and retrieval operations. The types of information stored in a directory tend to be descriptive attribute data. A directory offers a static view of data that can be changed without a complex update transaction. The data is hierarchically described in a treelike structure, and a network interface for reading is typical. Common uses of directories include e-mail address lists, domain server data, and resource maps of network resources. The *Lightweight Directory Access Protocol (LDAP)* is commonly used to handle user authentication and authorization and to control access to Active Directory (AD) objects.

To enable interoperability, X.500 was created as a standard for directory services. The primary method for accessing an X.500 directory is through the Directory Access Protocol (DAP), a heavyweight protocol that is difficult to implement completely, especially on PCs and more constrained platforms. This led to LDAP, which contains the most commonly used functionality. LDAP can interface with X.500 services and, most importantly, can be used over TCP with significantly less computing resources than a full X.500 implementation. LDAP offers all of the functionality most directories need and is easier and more economical to implement; hence, LDAP has become the Internet standard for directory services. LDAP standards are governed by two separate entities, depending on use: the International Telecommunication Union (ITU) governs the X.500 standard, and LDAP is governed for Internet use by the Internet Engineering Task Force (IETF). Many RFCs apply to LDAP functionality, but some of the most important are RFCs 4510 through 4519.

When integrating with cloud-based systems, you might find managing credentials across the two different domains challenging. Different vendors have created directory-based technologies to address this, such as AWS Directory Service for Microsoft Active Directory, also known as AWS Managed Microsoft AD. This service enables your directory-aware workloads and AWS resources to use a managed Active Directory in the AWS Cloud. Because AWS Managed Microsoft AD is built on the actual Microsoft Active Directory, you can use standard Active Directory administration tools and take advantage of built-in Active Directory features, such as Group Policy and single sign-on (SSO) features.

EXAM TIP A client starts an LDAP session by connecting to an LDAP server, called a Directory System Agent (DSA), which is by default on TCP and UDP port 389 or on port 636 for LDAPS (LDAP over SSL).

Federation

Federation, or *identity federation,* defines policies, protocols, and practices to manage identities across systems and organizations. Federation's ultimate goal is to allow users to seamlessly access data or systems across domains. Federation is enabled through the use of industry standards such as Security Assertion Markup Language (SAML), discussed in Chapter 24, "Implement Authentication and Authorization."

EXAM TIP Federated identity access management systems allow users to authenticate and access resources across multiple enterprises using a single credential. But don't confuse this with single sign-on (SSO), which allows users access to multiple resources within a single organization or enterprise.

Attestation

Attestation is the supplying of proof or evidence of some fact. In the case of authentication, attestation can be done by a service that checks the credentials supplied, and if they are correct and match the required values, the service can attest that the entry is valid or correct. Attestation is used throughout cybersecurity whenever a third party or entity verifies an object as valid or an item as correct in value.

Technologies

There are multiple ways to perform authentication, and multiple technologies can be employed to assist in the effort.

Time-based One-Time Password (TOTP)

The *Time-based One-Time Password (TOTP)* algorithm is a specific implementation of an HOTP (discussed next) that uses a secret key with a current timestamp to generate a one-time password (OTP). It is described in RFC 6238 (May 2011).

HMAC-based One-Time Password (HOTP)

HMAC-based One-Time Password (HOTP) is an algorithm that can be used to authenticate a user in a system by using an authentication server. (HMAC stands for hash-based message authentication code.) It is defined in RFC 4226 (December 2005).

EXAM TIP HOTP passwords can remain valid and active for an unknown time period. TOTP passwords are considered more secure because they are valid for short amounts of time and change often.

Short Message Service (SMS)

The use of *Short Message Service (SMS)*, or text messaging, in a cell phone provides a second authentication factor that is sent to a preidentified number. The message that is sent provides a code that the user enters into the system. This code typically has an expiration time, as shown in Figure 12-1. This is a way of verifying that the first credential, usually a password, was entered by the person expected—assuming they have control over the cell phone. This is a practical example of multifactor authentication, which is discussed later in this chapter.

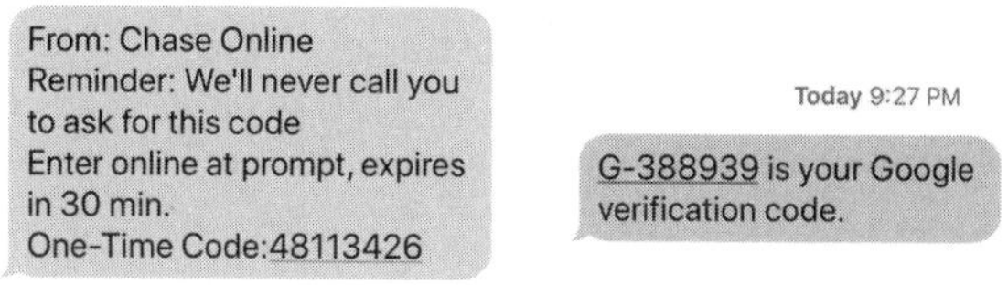
From: Chase Online
Reminder: We'll never call you
to ask for this code
Enter online at prompt, expires
in 30 min.
One-Time Code:48113426
Today 9:27 PM
G-388939 is your Google
verification code.

Figure 12-1 Sample SMS verification codes

Figure 12-2 Token authenticator from Blizzard Entertainment

Token Key

Token keys are physical devices that carry a digital token used to identify the user. This is a "something you have" element in a multifactor authentication scheme. The format of the actual token can vary from a smart card, to a keyboard fob, to a USB device. Proximity cards used in physical access systems are token-carrying devices.

As in all "something you have" elements, tokens are a proof of possession type of event, and to prevent their use if lost, they are backstopped with a PIN code. Different tokens can carry different forms of keys. The keys can be dynamic, changing over time, or static. Dynamic tokens add security in that the value changes over time and cannot be captured and replayed. An example of a commercial token is shown in Figure 12-2.

Static Codes

Static codes are just that—codes that do not change, or are static in nature. There are many use cases where these are essential, such as devices without user intervention. Devices that do not have user intervention are widely deployed in many systems. An example would be a smart electric meter, a device that needs to communicate with other systems and authenticate its identity. The use of static codes has a weakness in that, if compromised, the keys are no longer valid. The standard is to use cryptographic protection of all transmission of static codes, making the code unreadable even if the communication channel data is copied.

Authentication Applications

Need a second factor for authentication? We have an app for that. And this is not just a joke, but an increasingly common method of authentication that works by verifying that a user has a given mobile device in their possession. An *authentication application* functions by accepting user input, and if the user input is correct, it can pass the appropriate credentials to the system requesting authentication. This can be in the form of either a stored digital value or a one-time code in response to a challenge. Authentication applications exist for a variety of platforms—from Android to iOS, Linux, and Windows—and there are multiple vendors for each platform. The use of the application on the device is a second factor of authentication and is part of a multifactor authentication scheme.

Push Notifications

Push notification authentication supports user authentication by pushing a notification directly to an application on the user's device. The user receives the alert that an authentication attempt is taking place, and they can approve or deny the access via the user interface on the application. The push notification itself is not a secret; it is merely a means by which the user can authenticate and approve access. This is an out-of-band communication and demonstrates a second communication channel, thus making account hacking significantly more challenging.

Phone Call

Another form of authenticating a user has an interaction with the system via a phone call. The authentication *phone call* is delivered from the authentication system to a specified phone number, which then can verify that the user is in possession of the actual mobile device.

EXAM TIP Tokens represent something you have with respect to authentication as well as devices that can store more information than a user can memorize, which makes them very valuable for access control. The details in the scenario preceding a question will provide the necessary criteria to pick the best token method for the question.

Smart Card Authentication

A *smart card* (also known as an *integrated circuit card [ICC]* or *chip card*) is a credit card–sized card with embedded integrated circuits that is used to provide identification security authentication. Smart cards can increase physical security because they can carry long cryptographic tokens that are too long to remember and too large a space to guess. Also, because of the manner in which smart cards are employed and used, copying the number is not a practical option. Smart cards can be used in a variety of situations where you want to combine something you know (a PIN or password) with something you have (and can't be duplicated, such as a smart card). Many standard corporate-type laptops come with smart card readers installed, and their use is integrated into the Windows user access system.

Biometrics

Biometric factors are measurements of certain biological factors to identify one specific person from others. These factors are based on parts of the human body that are unique. The most well-known of these unique biological factors is the fingerprint. Fingerprint readers have been available for several years in laptops and other mobile devices, on keyboards, and as stand-alone USB devices.

However, many other biological factors can be used, such as the retina or iris of the eye, the geometry of the hand, and the geometry of the face. When these are used for authentication, there is a two-part process: enrollment and then authentication. During enrollment, a computer takes the image of the biological factor and translates it to a numeric value, called a template. When the user attempts to authenticate, the biometric feature is scanned by the reader, and the computer computes a value in the same fashion as the template and then compares the numeric value being read to the one stored in the database. If they match, access is allowed. Since these physical factors are unique, theoretically only the actual authorized person would be allowed access.

In the real world, however, the theory behind biometrics breaks down. Tokens that have a digital code work very well because everything remains in the digital realm. A computer checks your code, such as 123, against the database; if the computer finds 123 and that number has access, the computer opens the door. Biometrics, however, take an analog signal, such as a fingerprint or a face, and attempt to digitize it, and it is then matched against the digits in the database. The problem with an analog signal is that it might not encode the exact same way twice. For example, if you came to work with a bandage on your chin, would the face-based biometrics grant you access or deny it? Because of this, the templates are more complex in a manner where there can be a probability of match, or closeness measurement.

Fingerprint

A *fingerprint* scanner measures the unique pattern of a person's fingerprint and translates that pattern into a numerical value, or template, as discussed in the previous section. Fingerprint readers can be enhanced to ensure that the pattern is a live pattern—one with circulating blood or other detectable biological activity—to prevent simple spoofing with a Play-Doh mold of the print. Fingerprint scanners are cheap to produce and have widespread use in mobile devices. One of the challenges of fingerprint scanners is that they don't function if the user is wearing gloves (for example, medical gloves) or has worn off their fingerprints through manual labor, as many involved in the sheetrock trade do through normal work.

Retina

A retinal scanner examines blood vessel patterns in the back of the eye. Believed to be unique and unchanging, the *retina* is a readily detectable biometric. Retinal scanning does suffer from lack of user acceptance, as it involves a laser scanning the inside of the user's eyeball, which raises some psychological issues for some users who are wary of letting a laser scan the inside of their eye. This detection requires the user to be right in front of the device for it to work. It is also more expensive because of the precision of the detector and the involvement of lasers and users' vision.

Iris

An *iris* scanner works in a manner similar to a retinal scanner in that it uses an image of a unique biological measurement (in this case, the pigmentation associated with the iris of the eye). This can be photographed and measured from a distance, removing the psychological impediment of placing one's eye up close to a scanner. The downside to being able to capture an iris scan at a distance is that it's easy to do without a person's knowledge, and even to construct contact lenses that mimic a pattern. There are also some other issues associated with medical conditions such as pregnancy and some diseases that can be detected by changes in a person's iris and, if revealed, would be a privacy violation.

PART II

Facial

Facial recognition was mostly the stuff of sci-fi until it was integrated into various mobile phones. A sensor that recognizes when you move the phone into a position to see your face, coupled with a state of not being logged in, turns on the forward-facing camera, causing the system to look for its enrolled owner. This system has proven to have fairly high discrimination and works fairly well, with only one drawback: another person can move the phone in front of the registered user and it can unlock. In essence, another user can activate the unlocking mechanism when the user is unaware. The other minor drawback is that for certain transactions, such as positive identification for financial transactions, the position of the phone on an NFC location, together with the user's face needing to be in a certain orientation with respect to the phone, leads to some awkward positions. In other words, having to put your face in a proper position on the phone to identify you while holding it against the counter-height NFC credit card reader can be awkward.

Voice

Voice recognition is the use of unique tonal qualities and speech patterns to identify a person. Long the subject of sci-fi movies, this biometric has been one of the hardest to develop into a reliable mechanism, primarily because of problems with false acceptance and rejection rates, which will be discussed a bit later in the chapter.

Vein

A different biometric is the use of blood *vein* patterns to identify a user. Humans have a common vascular system, but the individual elements can vary in size and microstructure, and these fine-grained patterns are believed to be unique. Sensors can measure these patterns and use them to identify a user. Three common vascular pattern locations are used: palms, fingers, and the veins in the retina. This measurement is done via spectral analysis of the tissue, using frequencies that detect the hemoglobin in the blood. These are noninvasive measurements, but they do require close proximity to the user's item under measurement.

Gait Analysis

Gait analysis is the measurement of the pattern expressed by a person as they walk. An analysis of the gait, its length, the speed, and the rate of movement of specific points provides a unique signature that can be recorded and compared to previous samples. Even when not used for authentication, as a previous sample is required, gait analysis can be used to identify a suspect in a group of others, enabling the tracking of individuals in a crowd. From an access control perspective, in high-security situations, a camera can record the gait of incoming personnel and compare it to known values, providing a remote and early additional factor in determining identity.

Efficacy Rates

Biometric measurements have a level of uncertainty, and thus the efficacy of biometric solutions has been an issue since they were first developed. As each generation of sensor improved the accuracy of the measurements, the errors have been reduced to what is now a manageable level. For biometrics to be effective, they must have both low false positive rates and low false negative rates. The terms *false acceptance rate (FAR)* and *false rejection rate (FRR)* describe the chance that an incorrect user will be falsely accepted or a correct user will be falsely rejected, respectively, as covered in detail in the next sections. These two measures are different, and while a low false rejection rate is important for usability, a low false acceptance rate is more important from a security perspective. Users having to repeat trying to authenticate is bad, but having authentication occur for unauthorized users is worse.

The FIDO Alliance, a leading authentication standards and certification body, has specifications for error rates. FRR should be below 3 percent (no more than three errors in 100 attempts) and FAR should be below 0.01 percent (no more than one error in 10,000 attempts). As in all defense-in-depth scenarios, the backstop is a lockout function where devices will lock after a certain number of failed attempts. This makes the FAR more secure than just the simple percentage.

False Acceptance

The false acceptance rate (FAR) determines what level of false positives is allowed in the system. A *false acceptance* (or false positive) is demonstrated by the grayed-out area in Figure 12-3. In this area, the two curves overlap, and the decision has been made that at this threshold (or better) an accept signal will be given. Thus, if you are not a match, but your measured value falls on the upper end of the nonmatch curve (in the gray area), you will be considered a match, and hence become a false positive. The false acceptance rate is expressed as the probability that the system incorrectly identified a match between the biometric input and the stored template value.

When selecting the threshold value, the designer must be cognizant of two factors. One is the rejection of a legitimate biometric—the area on the match curve below the

Figure 12-3 False acceptance rate

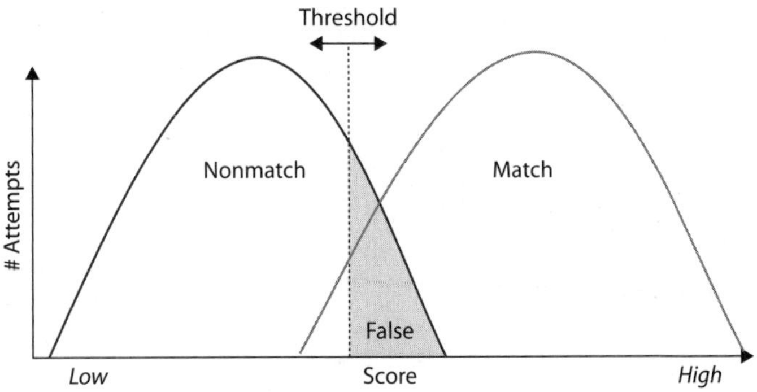

Figure 12-4 False rejection rate

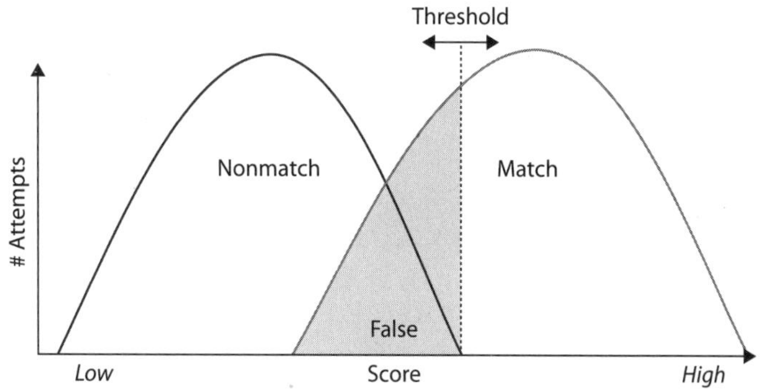

threshold value. The second is the acceptance of false positives. The more the curves overlap, the larger the problem, because once a threshold is chosen, that number defines the FAR. Setting the threshold higher will decrease false positives but increase false negatives or rejections. This would increase the false rejection rate, discussed in the next section.

False Rejection

The false rejection rate (FRR) determines what level of false negatives, or rejections, are going to be allowed in the system. A *false rejection* is demonstrated by the grayed-out area in Figure 12-4. In this section, the curves overlap, and the decision has been made that at this threshold (or lower), a reject signal will be given. Thus, if you are on the lower end of the match curve (in the gray area), you will be rejected, even if you should be a match. The false rejection rate is expressed as the probability that the system incorrectly rejected a legitimate match between the biometric input and the stored template value.

When comparing the FAR and the FRR, one realizes that, in most cases, whenever the curves overlap, they are related. This brings up the issue of the crossover error rate. Both the FAR and the FRR are set by choosing the threshold value. This is done when the system is set up and reflects the choice of which error rate is more important. If you want to make it harder for a false positive to occur, you will cause many failed authorizations of legitimate users because they will be seen by the system as on the other curve. If you want to make sure all legitimate users do not experience trouble during scans, then some unauthorized users will get accepted (false positives) because they will be interpreted by the system as being on the wrong curve based on where the threshold is set.

Crossover Error Rate

The *crossover error rate (CER)* is where both accept and reject error rates are equal. This is the desired state for the most efficient operation, and it can be managed by manipulating the threshold value used for matching. In practice, the values may not be exactly the same, but they will typically be close to each other. Figure 12-5 demonstrates the relationship between the FAR, FRR, and CER.

Figure 12-5 FRR, FAR, and CER compared

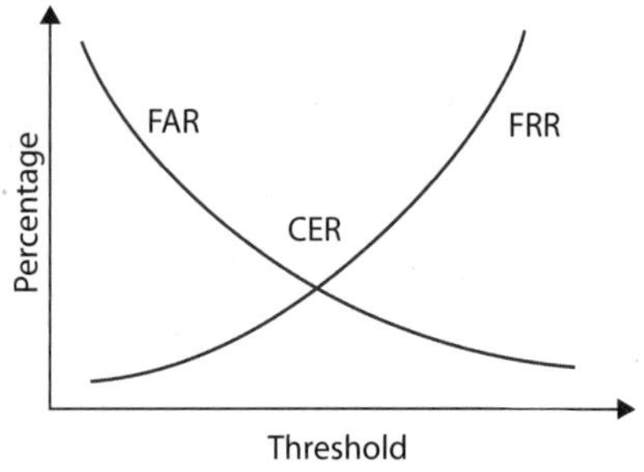

EXAM TIP Remember that the crossover error rate (CER) is the percentage at which the false acceptance rate (FAR) and false rejection rate (FRR) are equal.

Multifactor Authentication (MFA) Factors and Attributes

Multifactor authentication (or multiple-factor authentication) is simply the combination of two or more types of authentication. Five broad categories of authentication can be used: what you are (for example, biometrics), what you have (for instance, tokens), what you know (passwords and other information), somewhere you are (location), and something you do (physical performance). Two-factor authentication combines any two of these before granting access. An example would be a card reader that then turns on a fingerprint scanner—if your fingerprint matches the one on file for the card, you are granted access. Three-factor authentication would combine three types, such as a smart card reader that asks for a PIN before enabling a retina scanner. If all three, card (physical), PIN (knowledge), and scan (biometric), correspond to a valid user in the computer database, access is granted.

EXAM TIP Two-factor authentication combines any two methods, matching items such as a token with a biometric. Three-factor authentication combines any three, such as a passcode, biometric, and a token.

Multifactor authentication methods greatly enhance security by making it very difficult for an attacker to obtain all the correct materials for authentication. They also protect against the risk of stolen tokens, as the attacker must have the correct biometric, password, or both. More important, multifactor authentication enhances the security of biometric systems by protecting against a spoofed biometric. Changing the token makes the biometric useless unless the attacker can steal the new token. It also reduces false positives by trying to match the supplied biometric with the one that is associated with the supplied token. This prevents the computer from seeking a match using the entire database of biometrics. Using multiple factors is one of the best ways to ensure proper authentication and access control.

Factors

Factors are the specific elements that comprise an item of proof. These items can be grouped into three classes: something you know (passwords), something you have (token), and something you are (biometrics). Each of these has advantages and disadvantages, as discussed in the following sections.

Something You Know

The most common example of *something you know* is a password. One of the challenges with using something you know as an authentication factor is that it can be "shared" (or duplicated) without you knowing it. Another concern with using something you know is that because of the vast number of different elements a typical user has to remember, they do things to assist with memory, such as repeating passwords, making slight changes to a password, such as incrementing the number from password1 to password2, and writing them down. These are all common methods used to deal with password sprawl, yet they each introduce new vulnerabilities.

Another form of authentication via something you know is identity-driven authentication. In identity-driven authentication, you contact someone to get access, and they respond with a series of challenge questions. Sometimes the questions are based on previously submitted information, and sometimes the questions are based on publicly known information, such as previous addresses, phone numbers, cars purchased/licensed, and so on. Again, the proper respondent will know these answers, whereas an imposter will not. These tests are timed, and if the respondent takes too long (for example, taking the time to perform a lookup), they will fail.

Something You Have

Something you have specifically refers to security tokens and other items that a user can possess physically. One of the challenges with using something you have as an authentication factor is that you have to have it with you whenever you wish to be authenticated, and this can cause issues. It also relies on interfaces that may not be available for some systems, such as mobile devices, although interfaces, such as one-time password (OTP) generators, are device independent. OTP generators create new passwords on demand, against a sequence that is known only to the OTP generator and the OTP element on the system accepting the password.

One of the challenges of something you have is the concept of "something you lost," such as something you left in a briefcase, at home, and so on. Just as leaving your key ring with your office key can force a return trip back home to get it, so can leaving a dongle or other security element that is "something you have" in nature. And if something you have becomes something you had stolen, the implications are fairly clear—you don't have access and you have to re-identify yourself to get access again.

Something You Are

Something you are specifically refers to biometrics. One of the challenges with using "something you are" artifacts as authentication factors is that typically they are hard to change; once assigned, they inevitably become immutable, as you can change fingers, but only a limited number of times, and then you run out of changes. Another challenge with biometrics is that cultural or other issues associated with measuring things on a person may exist. For example, people in some cultures object to having their pictures taken. Another example is that physical laborers in some industries tend to lack scannable fingerprints because they are worn down. Some biometrics are not usable in certain environments; for instance, in the case of medical workers, or workers in clean-room environments, their personal protective gear inhibits the use of fingerprint readers and potentially other biometric devices.

Attributes

Attributes are collections of artifacts, like the factors previously presented, but rather than focus on the authentication item, they focus on elements associated with the user. Common attributes include the user's location, their ability to perform a task, or something about the user themselves. These attributes are discussed in the following sections.

Somewhere You Are

One of the more discriminant authentication factors is your location, or *somewhere you are*. When a mobile device is used, GPS can identify where the device is currently located. When you are logged on to a local, wired desktop connection, it shows you are in the building. Both of these can be compared to records to see if you are really there or should be there. If you are badged into your building, and at your desk on a wired PC, then a second connection with a different location would be suspect, as you can only be in one place at a time.

With geofencing (see Chapter 21, "Secure Mobile Solutions," for details), location becomes a big thing for marketing services pushing content to devices when in specific locations. Location services on mobile devices, coupled with geofencing, can alert others when you are in a specific area—not specifically authentication, but leading toward it.

Something You Can Do

Something you can do specifically refers to a physical action that you perform uniquely. An example of this is a signature; the movement of the pen and the two-dimensional output are difficult for others to reproduce. This makes it useful for authentication, but challenges exist in capturing the data, as signature pads are not common peripherals on machines. Gait analysis, presented earlier, is another example of this attribute. Something you can do is one of the harder artifacts to capture without specialized hardware, making it less ubiquitous as a method of authentication.

Something You Exhibit

Something you exhibit is a special case of a biometric. An example would be a brainwave response to seeing a picture. Another example would be the results of a lie detector test. The concept is to present a trigger and measure a response that cannot be faked. As sensors improve, tracking eye movement and sensing other aspects of responses will become forms that can be used to assist in authentication.

Someone You Know

Just as passwords relate to possession of knowledge, *someone you know* relates to a specific memory, but in this case an individual. This is the classic "having someone vouch for you" attribute. Electronically, this can be done via a chain of trust model, and it was commonly used in the past as a result of people signing each other's keys, indicating trust.

EXAM TIP Be able to differentiate between the three factors for authentication (something you know, have, and are) as well as the four attributes (somewhere you are, something you can do and exhibit, and someone you know). These are easily tested on the exam. Be sure you recognize examples for each factor to match to a scenario-type question.

Authentication, Authorization, and Accounting (AAA)

Authentication is the process of verifying an identity previously established in a computer system. There are a variety of methods for performing this function, each with its advantages and disadvantages. Authentication methods and their advantages and disadvantages were described throughout the chapter.

Authorization is the process of permitting or denying access to a specific resource. Once identity is confirmed via authentication, specific actions can be authorized or denied. Many types of authorization schemes are used, but the purpose is the same: determine whether a given user who has been identified has permissions for a particular object or resource being requested. This functionality is frequently part of the operating system and is transparent to users.

Accounting is the process of ascribing resource usage by account for the purpose of tracking resource utilization. This is a basic accounting function that is still used by some enterprises.

The separation of tasks, from identification to authentication to authorization, has several advantages. Many methods can be used to perform each task, and on many systems several methods are concurrently present for each task. Separation of these tasks into individual elements allows combinations of implementations to work together. Any system or resource, be it hardware (router or workstation) or a software component (database system), that requires authorization can use its own authorization method once authentication has occurred. This makes for efficient and consistent application of these principles.

EXAM TIP Authentication is the process of validating an identity. Authorization is the process of permitting or denying access to resources. Accounting is the process of keeping track of the resources a user accesses. Together, they make up the AAA framework for identity access security.

Cloud vs. On-premises Requirements

Authentication to *cloud versus on-premises requirements* is basically a revisiting of the identity and authentication problem all over again. When establishing either a cloud or on-premises system, you use identity and authentication as the foundation of your security effort. Whether you use an Active Directory methodology or other system to manage identities on premises, when you're establishing a cloud-based system, the options need to be completely reviewed and appropriate choices made based on the use of the cloud in the enterprise. Simple methods include a completely new independent system, although this increases costs and reduces usability when the number of users grows. Solutions such as federated authentication and single sign-on exist, and the proper determination of authentication processes should rest on data criticality and who needs access.

Chapter Review

In this chapter, you became acquainted with design concepts associated with authentication and authorization. The chapter opened with an examination of the authentication methods, including directory services, federation, attestation, and technologies. The technologies we examined were time-based one-time passwords, HMAC-based one-time passwords, Short Message Service, token keys, static codes, authentication applications, push notifications, and phone calls. The initial section closed with a discussion of smart card–based authentication.

The discussion of biometrics included both factors and usage. You learned about several different biometric technologies: fingerprint scanning, retinal scanning, iris scanning, facial recognition, voice recognition, vein patterns, and gait analysis. The methods and analytics covered included efficacy rates: false acceptance rate, false rejection rate, and crossover error rate.

The chapter continued with an examination of multifactor authentication factors and attributes. The three factors presented were something you know, something you have, and something you are. Four attributes followed: something you are, something you can do, something you exhibit, and someone you know. The chapter concluded with an examination of authentication, authorization, and accounting as well as cloud versus on-premises requirements.

Questions

To help you prepare further for the CompTIA Security+ exam, and to test your level of preparedness, answer the following questions and then check your answers against the correct answers at the end of the chapter.

1. During a visit to a hosting center where your organization keeps some offsite servers, you see a door with an odd-looking panel next to it. You see people approaching the panel and placing their eyes into a hooded viewer. A few seconds after they've done this, the door unlocks. What type of biometric scanner might this be?

   A. Voice recognition scanner

   B. Retinal scanner

C. Fingerprint scanner

D. Facial recognition scanner

2. You've spent the last week tweaking a fingerprint-scanning solution for your organization. Despite your best efforts, roughly 1 in 50 attempts will fail, even if the user is using the correct finger and their fingerprint is in the system. Your supervisor says 1 in 50 is "good enough" and tells you to move on to the next project. Your supervisor just defined which of the following for your fingerprint scanning system?

A. False rejection rate

B. False acceptance rate

C. Critical threshold

D. Failure acceptance criteria

3. Which of the following algorithms uses a secret key with a current timestamp to generate a one-time password?

A. Hash-based Message Authentication Code

B. Date-Hashed Message Authorization Password

C. Time-based One-Time Password

D. Single sign-on

4. With regard to authentication, an access token falls into which factor category?

A. Something you are

B. Something you have

C. Something you know

D. Something you see

5. Which of the following is *not* a common form of hardware token?

A. Proximity card

B. Common access card

C. USB token

D. Iris scan

6. While depositing cash from a charity fundraiser at a local bank, you notice bank employees are holding up cards next to a panel near a door. A light on the panel turns green and the employees are able to open the door. The light on the panel is normally red. What type of electronic door control is this bank using?

A. Iris scanner

B. Hardware token

C. Proximity card

D. Symmetric key token

7. Your colleague is telling you a story she heard about a way to trick fingerprint scanners using gummy bears. She heard that if you press a gummy bear against an authorized user's finger, you can then use that gummy bear as their fingerprint to fool a fingerprint scanner. If this works, the result is an example of which of the following?
   A. False negative
   B. False positive
   C. Crossover positive
   D. Crossover negative
8. To ensure customers entering credentials in your website are valid and not someone with stolen credentials, your team is tasked with designing multifactor authentication. Which of the following would *not* be a good choice?
   A. Static code
   B. Phone call
   C. Authentication application
   D. Short Message Service
9. When you're designing and tweaking biometric systems, the point where both the accept and reject error rates are equal is known as which of the following?
   A. Crossover acceptance rate
   B. Accept-reject overlap rate
   C. Crossover error rate
   D. Overlap acceptance rate
10. Which of the following is *not* a term used in multifactor authentication?
   A. Someone you know
   B. Somewhere you are
   C. Something you have
   D. Something you see

Answers

1. **B.** This is most likely a retinal scanner. Retinal scanners examine blood vessel patterns in the back of the eye. Retinal scanning must be done at short distances; the user has to be right at the device for it to work.
2. **A.** Your supervisor just defined the false rejection rate (FRR) for your system. The FRR is the level of false negatives, or rejections, that are going to be allowed in the system. In this case, your supervisor is willing to accept one false rejection for every 50 attempts.

3. **C.** The Time-based One-Time Password (TOTP) algorithm is a specific implementation of an HOTP that uses a secret key with a current timestamp to generate a one-time password. Note that *timestamp* is the key clue in the question.
4. **B.** An access token is a physical object that identifies specific access rights, and in authentication it falls into the "something you have" factor category.
5. **D.** An iris scan would be considered a biometric technique and is not a hardware token. A hardware token is a physical item the user must be in possession of to access their account or certain resources.
6. **C.** The bank employees are using proximity cards, which are contactless access cards that provide information to the electronic door control system. Proximity cards just need to be close enough to the scanner to work—they do not need to actually touch the scanner.
7. **B.** This is an example of a false positive. A false positive occurs when a biometric is scanned and allows access to someone who is not authorized.
8. **A.** Static codes can be captured and replayed and are not well suited for systems with active users.
9. **C.** The crossover error rate (CER) is the rate where both accept and reject error rates are equal. This is the desired state for the most efficient operation of a biometric system, and it can be managed by manipulating the threshold value used for matching.
10. **D.** Something you see is neither a factor (something you know, something you have, or something you are) nor an attribute (somewhere you are, something you can do, something you exhibit, or someone you know).

CHAPTER 13

Cybersecurity Resilience

In this chapter, you will

- Examine the elements that create redundancy
- Understand the types of backups and the roles they play in resilience

Systems are designed to operate for a purpose, and we use the term *risk* to describe the outcomes when issues degrade performance from an optimal state. For a variety of reasons, expecting a system to run flawlessly, at all times, is unreasonable. We can put defenses in place to mitigate the issues that occur when a system is degraded, but it still raises the question of how one gets back to full performance. This is where resiliency comes in. A resilient system is one that can return to proper operating conditions after having something go wrong. And in today's increasingly hostile environment, this is an important security measure.

Certification Objective This chapter covers CompTIA Security+ exam objective 2.5: Given a scenario, implement cybersecurity resilience.

Redundancy

Redundancy is the use of multiple, independent elements to perform a critical function, so that if one element fails, there is another that can take over the work. When developing a resiliency strategy for ensuring that an organization has what it needs to keep operating, even if hardware or software fails or if security is breached, you should consider other measures involving redundancy and spare parts. Some common applications of redundancy include the use of redundant servers, redundant connections, and redundant ISPs. The need for redundant servers and connections may be fairly obvious, but redundant ISPs may not be so, at least initially. Many ISPs already have multiple accesses to the Internet on their own, but by having additional ISP connections, an organization can reduce the chance that an interruption of one ISP will negatively impact the organization. Ensuring uninterrupted access to the Internet by employees or access to the organization's e-commerce site for customers is becoming increasingly important.

Many organizations don't see the need for maintaining a supply of spare parts. After all, with the price of storage dropping and the speed of processors increasing, why replace a broken part with older technology? However, a ready supply of spare parts can ease the process of bringing the system back online. Replacing hardware and software with newer versions can sometimes lead to problems with compatibility. An older version of some piece of critical software may not work with newer hardware, which may be more capable in a variety of ways. Having critical hardware (or software) spares for critical functions in the organization can greatly facilitate maintaining business continuity in the event of software or hardware failures.

EXAM TIP Redundancy is an important factor in both security and reliability. Make sure you understand the many different areas that can benefit from redundant components.

Geographic Dispersal

An important element to factor into the cost of the backup strategy is the expense of storing the backups. A simple strategy might be to store all your backups together for quick and easy recovery actions. This is not, however, a good idea. Suppose the catastrophic event that necessitated the restoration of backed-up data was a fire that destroyed the computer system the data was processed on. In this case, any backups that were stored in the same facility might also be lost in the same fire.

The solution is to keep copies of backups in separate locations. The most recent copy can be stored locally, as it is the most likely to be needed, while other copies can be kept at other locations. Depending on the level of security your organization desires, the storage facility itself could be reinforced against possible threats in your area (such as tornados or floods). A more recent advance is online backup services. A number of third-party companies offer high-speed connections for storing data in a separate facility. Transmitting the backup data via network connections alleviates some other issues with physical movement of more traditional storage media, such as the care during transportation (tapes do not fare well in direct sunlight, for example) or the time that it takes to transport the tapes.

Disk

Disks are the primary storage mechanism in a system, whether composed of physical hard drives with spinning platters or solid-state memory devices. The term *disk* refers to the spinning platter historically, but more and more storage is being handled by solid-state memory. Also, the logical construct of a disk can be mapped across multiple physical storage elements.

Redundant Array of Inexpensive Disks (RAID) Levels

A common approach to increasing reliability in disk storage is employing a *redundant array of inexpensive disks (RAID)*. RAID takes data that is normally stored on a single disk and spreads it out among several others. If any single disk is lost, the data can be recovered from the other disks where the data also resides. With the price of disk storage decreasing, this approach has become increasingly popular to the point that many individual users even have RAID arrays for their home systems. RAID can also increase the speed of data recovery as multiple drives can be busy retrieving requested data at the same time instead of relying on just one disk to do the work.

Several different RAID approaches can be considered:

- **RAID 0** (striped disks) simply spreads the data that would be kept on the one disk across several disks. This decreases the time it takes to retrieve data because the data is read from multiple drives at the same time, but it does not improve reliability because the loss of any single drive will result in the loss of all the data (since portions of files are spread out among the different disks). With RAID 0, the data is split across all the drives with no redundancy offered.
- **RAID 1** (mirrored disks) is the opposite of RAID 0. RAID 1 copies the data from one disk onto two or more disks. If any one disk is lost, the data is not lost since it is also copied onto the other disk(s). This method can be used to improve reliability and retrieval speed, but it is relatively expensive when compared to other RAID techniques.
- **RAID 2** (bit-level error-correcting code) is not typically used, as it stripes data across the drives at the bit level as opposed to the block level. It is designed to be able to recover the loss of any single disk through the use of error-correcting techniques.
- **RAID 3** (byte-striped with error check) spreads the data across multiple disks at the byte level with one disk dedicated to parity bits. This technique is not commonly implemented because input/output operations can't be overlapped due to the need for all to access the same disk (the disk with the parity bits).
- **RAID 4** (dedicated parity drive) stripes data across several disks but in larger stripes than in RAID 3, and it uses a single drive for parity-based error checking. RAID 4 has the disadvantage of not improving data retrieval speeds since all retrievals still need to access the single parity drive.
- **RAID 5** (block-striped with error check) is a commonly used method that stripes the data at the block level and spreads the parity data across the drives. This provides both reliability and increased speed performance. This form requires a minimum of three drives.

RAID 0 through 5 are the original techniques, with RAID 5 being the most common method used, as it provides both the reliability and speed improvements. Additional methods have been implemented, such as duplicating the parity data across the disks (RAID 6) and a stripe of mirrors (RAID 10). Some levels can be combined to produce a two-digit RAID level. RAID 10, then, is a combination of levels 1 (mirroring) and 0 (striping), which is why it is also sometimes identified as RAID 1 + 0. Mirroring is writing data to two or more hard disk drives (HDDs) at the same time—if one disk fails, the mirror image preserves the data from the failed disk. Striping breaks data into "chunks" that are written in succession to different disks.

EXAM TIP Knowledge of the basic RAID structures by number designation is a testable element and should be memorized for the exam. RAID 0 and RAID 1 both require a two-drive minimum. Both RAID 3 and RAID 5 have a three-drive minimum. RAID 10 (also called 1+0) requires four drives at a minimum.

Multipath

Between the storage systems and the server/computer is an I/O interface. This I/O interface converts the information from the computer to a form that works for the specific storage system. There are different interfaces for different types of storage systems (for example, RAID, SCSI, Fiber Channel, and SATA), each designed to deal with the necessary data transfers. When a storage element is connected by multiple adapters, this provides redundancy in the event of a problem with one of the adapters. This is referred to as a *multipath* connection and is commonly employed in high-reliability servers and critical systems. Figure 13-1 shows a server with two host bus adapters (HBAs), along with two storage area network (SAN) switches and two RAID controllers. This provides two independent paths from server to data.

Network

A network is the infrastructure element that connects all the IT components in the enterprise. A network can serve as a point of failure, or it can be a system of redundant connections that can be resilient under various traffic loads and connectivity conditions. Having a properly architected network that has multiple independent pathways and infrastructure elements designed to increase redundancy is important. Two major elements to consider are load balancers and network interface card (NIC) teaming to remove some of the common modes of network-related traffic failures.

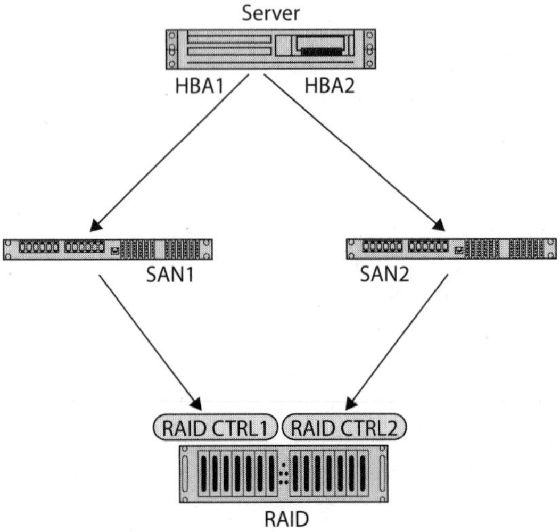

Figure 13-1 Multipath configuration of a RAID device to a server

Load Balancers

Certain systems, such as servers, are more critical to business operations and should therefore be the object of fault-tolerance measures. A common technique used in fault tolerance is load balancing through the use of a *load balancer,* which moves loads across a set of resources in an effort not to overload individual servers. This technique is designed to distribute the processing load over two or more systems. It is used to help improve resource utilization and throughput but also has the added advantage of increasing the fault tolerance of the overall system since a critical process may be split across several systems. Should any one system fail, the others can pick up the processing it was handling. While there may be an impact to overall throughput, the operation does not go down entirely. Load balancing is often utilized for systems handling websites, high-bandwidth file transfers, and large Internet Relay Chat (IRC) networks. Load balancing works by a series of health checks that tell the load balancer which machines are operating and by a scheduling mechanism that spreads the work evenly. Load balancing is best for stateless systems, as subsequent requests can be handled by any server, not just the one that processed the previous request.

Network Interface Card (NIC) Teaming

If a server has multiple network interface cards (NICs) connecting it to a switch or router, it will have multiple addresses, one for each NIC. *NIC teaming* is an alternative means of connecting used by servers that have multiple network interface cards and wish to enjoy the benefits of load balancing, fault tolerance, and failover without requiring added infrastructure to do it. When NIC teaming is used, the OS combines the NICs into a virtual NIC from the OS perspective. If one or more of the connections have traffic issues or connectivity issues, the other NICs can carry the load. Using NIC teaming allows your server to have redundancy and increased bandwidth, even in the event any of your physical adapters or cabling fails.

EXAM TIP NIC teaming groups multiple NICs together to form a logical network device called a bond. This provides for load balancing and fault tolerance.

Power

Power is required for all machines to operate, and having a reliable and resilient source of electrical power is critical for continued operations of enterprise computing. Servers and networking equipment are always on, and even occasional outages due to equipment failures need to be planned for and managed to provide an appropriate level of service. In a modern enterprise, equipment such as uninterruptible power supplies, generators, dual supplies, and managed power distribution all support having the proper levels of electricity available to the networking equipment all the time.

Uninterruptible Power Supply (UPS)

Uninterruptible power supplies (UPSs) are power supply systems that can function using a temporary battery backup in the event of a power failure. UPSs typically do not have sufficient battery backup capability to last for long, but they are designed to keep equipment running while backup power, such as from a generator, is connected. In an enterprise system, most UPSs are designed and rated for typically 20 minutes of runtime. This is enough time for the backup generators to start, or in the event that power cannot be restored, for the servers to transfer to a secondary site as part of a continuity of operations plan and then to gracefully shut down.

Generator

Backup *generators* are used to provide power when normal sources of electricity are lost. The power for these devices is either natural gas or diesel, and they produce sufficient electrical power to cover the desired services during a power outage. Generators come with a host of requirements, including maintenance and testing, and they require significant electrical architecture work to isolate the desired circuits. The objective typically isn't to provide power to everything that the normal power source supplies, as the scale of generation can be costly in some instances. The circuits energized by the backup generator are separate circuits that provide power to the desired components. Sizing of the backup generator is done with respect to the load, and because of the physical infrastructure, it is not easy or cost efficient to continuously resize the backup power. The other issue is that when long-term use happens in the case of diesel generators, a resupply of fuel needs to be managed. As these systems are typically used during natural disasters, having contracts in place that function during the disaster are important for refueling and maintenance operations.

Dual Supply

Individual pieces of equipment have power supplies in them to convert the line power in the facility to the voltages and currents used by the devices. The individual power supplies are one of the weakest links in a piece of equipment, as they tend to fail at a much higher rate than the lower-voltage equipment that they supply power to; hence, a plan needs to be in place for these when they fail. In cases where a minor outage is okay, having spare power supplies that can be replaced offline works.

For servers and other pieces of critical infrastructure, however, having a redundant, dual-supply system is essential. A *dual supply* is a system where two independent power supply units, either capable of handling the load, are used. In the event that either supply is lost, the other continues to carry the load. Typically, these devices are also made to be hot swappable, so in the event of a failure, the bad supply can be replaced without powering down the unit.

Managed Power Distribution Units (PDUs)

A *managed power distribution unit (PDU)* is a device designed to handle the electrical power for server racks. A fully populated server rack can use as much as 30kVA, or 10 times the amount of electricity for a typical home. This is why server rooms need special HVAC to handle the heat distribution, and they use managed power distribution units to efficiently handle the electrical side. A PDU can take three-phase 440/240VAC power in and convert it to either single-phase 110VAC or 48VDC power. The objective of a PDU is to efficiently convert the power, and manage the heat from the conversion, while producing a power flow that is conditioned from spikes and over/under voltage conditions. Most PDUs offer extensive monitoring capability, so entire racks of servers can have their power remotely monitored for conditions that might cause issues.

EXAM TIP Given a scenario, you should understand how each device is used to manage power and provide cybersecurity resilience.

Replication

Replication is a simple form of redundancy—that is, having another copy of something should something happen to the original. Dual power supplies replicate the power. Having a redundant array of disks to store data is another form of replication, as are backups and having offsite alternate operations for business continuity purposes. In situations where having something specific is essential, hearing someone say "two is one, and one is none" is a commonplace. Common ways of seeing replication in everyday enterprise operations include the use of storage area networks and virtual machine technologies.

Storage Area Network (SAN)

A *storage area network (SAN)* is a dedicated network that connects compute elements to storage elements. This network can be optimized for the types of data storage needed, in terms of size and data rates, in terms of format, and in terms of access criteria. Having the old-school model of the data stored on disks attached directly to a machine represents a failure mode when the machine fails. It also has issues when scaling to large quantities such as enterprise databases with multiple users. The SAN resolves this point of failure by making the data storage independent of any individual computer and can even interface to multiple redundant storage systems to allow redundancy on the side of data storage as well.

VM

Virtual machine (VM) technologies can enable replication of processing units that can be manipulated between different computers. Having a website with multiple identical servers to handle the load still has the issues associated with failures of individual servers and the rebuilding of those server components on the software side. VM technology resolves that by allowing multiple copies of a specific instance to be used on different hardware and with centralized monitoring and management. Need an extra web server because of the current system load? Just start another VM. It takes seconds as opposed to provisioning and building a server—a process measured in hours or days. VMs have revolutionized corporate computing operations because they allow administrators to manage the compute side easily by pointing and clicking to add or remove capacity and processing power using known-good images. Should a particular instance be modified by an unauthorized actor, a known-good replacement image can be established quickly, returning capacity to the enterprise. Also, the proper deployment of VMs and server technologies can provide hardware independence for specific operating images, enabling efficient use of server resources.

On-premises vs. Cloud

When you're examining redundancy, one factor to consider is location. Is the work going to happen on the premises or is it being done in the cloud? By itself, this does not provide redundancy, but once the determination of location is made, then factors can be employed to ensure appropriate levels of redundancy based on risk.

Backup Types

A key element in business continuity/disaster recovery (BC/DR) plans is the availability of *backups*. This is true not only because of the possibility of a disaster but also because hardware and storage media will periodically fail, resulting in loss or corruption of critical data. An organization might also find backups critical when security measures have failed and an individual has gained access to important information that may have become corrupted or at the very least can't be trusted. Data backup is thus a critical element in these plans, as well as in normal operation. There are several factors to consider in an organization's data backup strategy:

- How frequently should backups be conducted?
- How extensive do the backups need to be?
- What is the process for conducting backups?
- Who is responsible for ensuring backups are created?
- Where will the backups be stored?
- How long will backups be kept?
- How many copies will be maintained?

Keep in mind that the purpose of a backup is to provide valid, uncorrupted data in the event of corruption or loss of the original file or the media where the data was stored. Depending on the type of organization, legal requirements for maintaining backups can also affect how it is accomplished.

There are four main forms of backups: full, incremental, differential, and snapshot. Each of these has advantages and disadvantages in terms of time to back up and restore as well as complexity. These backup types are described in the upcoming sections.

Understanding the purpose of the archive bit is important when you read about the backup types. The archive bit is used to indicate whether a file has (1) or has not (0) changed since the last backup. The bit is set (changed to a 1) if the file is modified, or in some cases, if the file is copied, the new copy of the file has its archive bit set. The bit is reset (changed to a 0) when the file is backed up. The archive bit can be used to determine which files need to be backed up when using methods such as the differential backup method.

EXAM TIP When learning about the following backup types, be sure to pay attention to the details concerning how many backups are needed for a restore. Here's a typical exam question: "With this type of backup (differential or incremental) and a seven-day backup scheme, how many backup tapes are needed for a restore?" Note that this is not a simple case of memorization because you need the details from the scenario to answer the question. Also, you need to know the "order of restoration" of the backups.

Full

The easiest type of backup to understand is the full backup. In a *full backup*, all files and software are copied onto the storage media. Restoration from a full backup is similarly straightforward—you must copy all the files back onto the system. This process can take a considerable amount of time. Consider the size of even the average home PC today, for which storage is measured in tens and hundreds of gigabytes. Copying this amount of data takes time. In a full backup, the archive bit is cleared.

EXAM TIP A full backup copies all data and clears/resets the archive bit. This process takes considerable time to complete but allows for a complete restore with one tape.

Incremental

The *incremental backup* is a variation on a differential backup, with the difference being that instead of copying all files that have changed since the last full backup, the incremental backup backs up only files that have changed since the last full *or* incremental backup occurred, thus requiring fewer files to be backed up. With incremental backups, even less information will be stored in each backup. Just as in the case of the differential backup, the incremental backup relies on the occasional full backup being accomplished. After that, you back up only files that have changed since the last backup of any sort was conducted. To restore a system using this type of backup method requires quite a bit more work. You first need to go back to the last full backup and reload the system with this data. Then you have to update the system with every incremental backup that has occurred since the full backup. The advantage of this type of backup is that it requires less storage and time to accomplish. The disadvantage is that the restoration process is more involved. Assuming that you don't frequently have to conduct a complete restoration of your system, however, the incremental backup is a valid technique. An incremental backup will clear the archive bit.

EXAM TIP To perform a restore from incremental backup, you need the last full backup and every incremental tape since the last full backup.

Snapshot

A *snapshot is* a copy of a virtual machine at a specific point in time. A snapshot is created by copying the files that store the virtual machine. One of the advantages of a virtual machine over a physical machine is the ease with which the virtual machine can be backed up and restored—the ability to revert to an earlier snapshot is as easy as clicking a button and waiting for the machine to be restored via a change of the files.

Differential

In a *differential backup,* only the files that have changed since the last full backup was completed are backed up. This also implies that periodically a full backup needs to be accomplished. The frequency of the full backup versus the interim differential backups depends on your organization and needs to be part of your defined strategy. Restoration from a differential backup requires two steps: the last full backup first needs to be loaded and then the last differential backup performed can be applied to update the files that have been changed since the full backup was conducted. Again, this is not a difficult process, but it does take some time. The amount of time to accomplish the periodic differential backup, however, is much less than that for a full backup, and this is one of the advantages of this method. Obviously, if a lot of time has passed between differential backups, or if most files in your environment change frequently, then the differential backup does not differ much from a full backup. It should also be obvious that to accomplish the differential backup, the system has to have a method to determine which files have been changed since some given point in time. The archive bit is not cleared in a differential backup since the key for a differential is to back up all files that have changed since the last full backup.

EXAM TIP To perform a restore from differential backup, you need the last full backup and the most recent differential backup tape.

The amount of data that will be backed up, and the time it takes to accomplish this, has a direct bearing on the type of backup that should be performed. The following table outlines the three basic types of backups that can be conducted, the amount of space required for each, and the ease of restoration using each strategy.

	Full	Differential	Incremental
Amount of Space	Large	Medium	Medium
Restoration	Simple	Simple	Involved

There are times when each of these methods makes sense. If you have a large amount of data, but most is static (changes slowly if ever), then the small changes are best captured with differentials. If the whole data structure is changing, then full backups make more sense. Understanding the data is part of the key to understanding the correct mechanisms for backup and restore.

Tape

Tape drives are an older form of data storage mechanism, and they are characterized by their sequential read/write access. A disk allows you to directly access specific elements randomly, whereas a tape system stores everything in one long structure, requiring you to physical move the tape if you wish to access an element halfway through the storage. For general-purpose storage, this sequential access mechanism tends to create significant performance issues. But for backups and restores, these operations are sequential in nature, and thus tape is still well suited for this type of operation. For bulk storage of backups, tape is still a viable alternative in terms of cost and performance.

Disk

The term *disk* refers to either a physical hard drive with spinning platters or a solid-state memory device. Backing up a disk is a common operation for a single computer because most computers have very few disks, and this is a logical structure to maintain and restore. For client-based PCs, a disk backup can make sense, and many systems can perform a full, incremental, snapshot, or differential backup of a disk.

Copy

Copying is the simplest form of backup for a file or set of files. Users can use this option with ease, as the scope of their data backup requirement is typically small (for example, saving a copy of a critical document or an important picture). However, this method breaks down when the scope expands to larger and larger sets of data, and for large-scale backups, one of the previous methods is more efficient both for backing up and restoring. One of the advantages of having users make copies of critical documents is the ability to do a quick restore in the event of an overwrite error.

Network Attached Storage (NAS)

Network attached storage (NAS) is the use of a network connection to attach external storage to a machine. This is a simple method of extending storage, and the connection can be managed over either a USB connection or the Ethernet network connection. In either case, NAS is a simple extension of data storage to an external system, and typically these devices do not transfer data fast enough for regular operations. However, they do work well as an external site for data-backup-and-recover solutions on a smaller, single-machine scale.

Storage Area Network (SAN)

As mentioned previously, a storage area network (SAN) is a dedicated network that connects compute elements to storage elements. This network can be optimized for the types of data storage needed, in terms of size and data rates, in terms of format, and in terms of access criteria. Using a SAN as part of a backup solution is a good example of using technology to solve complex problems. Multiple different servers across the enterprise can connect via a SAN to a backup array, enabling efficient and effective backups in a manageable and flexible manner.

EXAM TIP NAS is a single storage device that serves files over the network to a machine. It's a simple form of external storage. A SAN, on the other hand, is a network of multiple devices designed to manage large and complex sets of data in real time at processor speed.

Cloud

Just as NAS and SANs can be used as locations to store data backups, so can the cloud. Numerous cloud-based backup security vendors and products place the data storage of a backup in the cloud. The advantages are all of the cloud advantages: offsite, can have multiple redundant copies, and available via the Web for recovery. The disadvantages are the same: the backup is on another box and it is protected only by the legal agreement between the user and the backup vendor. Also, these contracts tend to favor the backup vendor, not the client. So while the cloud can result in less on-premises administration of data, it can increase security concerns because someone else is protecting the data, under the guidelines of a contractual document that may or may not reflect current risk postures.

It is important to realize that cloud storage has invaded the desktop of many users. The wide range of basic cloud sync providers includes Dropbox, Box, Microsoft OneDrive, Google Drive, and iCloud, as well as many lesser-known entities. Understanding the risk associated with data in these situations matters in a corporate environment because what might be convenient or seem like a good idea from a user perspective might put data at risk of disclosure.

Image

An image-based backup is a specific structure of the backup file to match that of the system being backed up. This may take more time and space, but it is also guaranteed not to miss anything because it backs up everything, including the deleted data and free space. For critical systems, this provides a complete capture of the system as it was at the time of backup, including all nonpersistent data associated with the OS. Image backups can provide extra levels of assurance when certain types of failures (due to a malware attack, for example) leave a system unusable.

Online vs. Offline

Online backups are those that are stored in a location that is accessible via the Internet. This provides flexibility in recovery by making the backup data available anywhere there is a network connection. Offline backups are those stored on an offline system that is not accessible via the Internet. Online backups have the advantage of providing geographic separation of the backups from the original system.

Offsite Storage

Offsite backups are ones stored in a location separate from the system being backed up. This can be important in regard to problems that affect an area larger than a single room. A building fire, a hurricane, a tornado—these are all disasters that occur frequently and typically affect more than just a single room or building. Having backups offsite alleviates the risk of losing the backups to the same problem. In today's high-speed network world with cloud services, storing backups in the cloud is an option that can resolve many of the risks and issues associated with backup availability.

Distance Considerations

The *distance* associated with an offsite backup is a logistics problem. If you need to restore a system and the backup is stored hours away by car, that increases the recovery time. The delay resulting from physical movement of backup tapes has been alleviated in many systems through networks that move the data at the speed of the network. Distance is also critical when examining the reach of a disaster. It is important that the offsite location is far enough away that it is not affected by the same incident. This includes the physical location of a cloud storage provider's servers. If your business is in Puerto Rico and so is your cloud provider's servers, for example, Hurricane Maria likely made your data unavailable for a long time.

Nonpersistence

Nonpersistence refers to system items that are not permanent and can change. An example of something that is nonpersistent is the registry in Microsoft Windows, which is a dynamic list of configuration criteria. Nonpersistence needs to be appropriately managed, and systems that have this characteristic typically have mechanisms built in to manage this diversity. For VMs, where the current state of the system is continually changing, and thus the image is changing, we have snapshots. Snapshots provide a copy of the system at a point in time that you can then persist to use as a recovery point or backup.

EXAM TIP In the event of a failure in a nonpersistent system, all data is lost. The resilience and recovery of those conditions must occur from external sources. Think memory when you turn off your computer; it must be reloaded when you restart.

Revert to Known State

Things eventually go wrong, and when something goes wrong, you want to recover to a known point. Having the ability to recover to a known state is referred to as *reverting to a known state*. Modern OSs are a prime example of nonpersistence; they are regularly changing with new data, new software, new configurations, new drivers, and so on. While data backups can bring back the data elements of a system, bringing back the configuration of a system, including driver files and patches, is more complicated. How do you recover a system after a patch goes awry, or a new driver brings a level of instability?

Many OSs have the ability to roll back to a previous known configuration: both servers and desktops can be rolled back, restoring the system to a previous point in time while leaving the files intact—back to a condition where the OS previously worked properly.

Last Known-Good Configuration

When you have a system without persistence, you need a means to recover to a known-good state. On a boot failure, Microsoft Windows can give you an option to revert to the *last known-good configuration,* which is a means of reverting to a known state. In Windows 7, this was a direct menu option. In Windows 10, this option is buried under the Windows Recovery system. The methods of accessing it vary based on the type of issue, and whether or not you can get into Windows itself. If Windows fails on three subsequent boots in sequence, it will present you with recovery options rather than trying to boot again.

Live Boot Media

One means of beginning with a known configuration and a known state is to boot to *live boot media,* which is a bootable flash drive or DVD source that contains a complete bootable image of the OS. Using this as a means of starting in a known state is common in digital forensics investigations.

High Availability

One of the objectives of security is the availability of data and processing power when an authorized user desires it. *High availability* refers to the ability to maintain the availability of data and operational processing (services) despite a disrupting event. Generally this requires redundant systems, both in terms of power and processing, so that should one system fail, the other can take over operations without any break in service. High availability is more than data redundancy; it requires that both data and services be available.

EXAM TIP Fault tolerance and high availability are similar in their goals, yet they are separate in application. *High availability* refers to maintaining both data and services in an operational state, even when a disrupting event occurs. *Fault* tolerance is a design objective to achieve high availability should a fault occur.

Scalability

Scalability is a design element that enables a system to accommodate larger workloads by adding resources either making hardware stronger (scaling up) or adding additional nodes (scaling out). This term is commonly used in server farms and database clusters, as these both can have scale issues with respect to workload. Both elasticity and scalability have an effect on system availability and throughput, which can be significant security- and risk-related issues.

EXAM TIP Elasticity and scalability seem to be the same thing, but they are different. *Elasticity* is related to dynamically scaling a system with workload (scaling out), whereas *scalability* is a design element that enables a system both to scale up to more capable hardware and to scale out to more instances.

Restoration Order

Data restoration operations are designed to take an alternative copy of the data and put it back into a working system. If you back up a database and then later need to use the backup to restore the database, this is data restoration. But the order of restoration can make a difference. If you have a large database that takes days to back up and restore, then having a backup solution that allows you to restore the selected parts most needed faster can be a lifesaver. This is not just a technology issue; it requires planning and coordination because the most important data needs to be identified and then backed up in a manner that facilitates its quick restore. Developing a restoration plan, along with an order of what needs to be restored first, second, and so on, is important because this will drive certain operations when backing up the data in the first place.

Diversity

Most failures come from a series of common causes, either in the environment or the equipment. If you have a bunch of identical equipment, the advantage is you can have spares for the commonly known issues. The disadvantage is that these commonly known problems tend to affect all of the systems. Having a monoculture of all OSs being identical adds efficiency to patching, but it also adds risk in common failure modes across the entire enterprise. Having diversity in technologies, vendors, processes, and controls can assist in resiliency through differences in failure modes. The virus that hurts one OS typically has no effect on another. Building diversity into systems to allow parallel operations using different technologies, vendors, processes, and controls can provide a means to continue operation even during times of systems failures.

Technologies

The security industry has multiple technologies that can be employed across the enterprise in an effort to mitigate security risk. Employing the concept of defense in depth, it is best practice not to use a single technology, but to use several different technologies in an overlapping fashion, forcing an attacker to bypass them all to achieve their objective. Having firewalls, ACLs, bastion hosts in a screened subnet (DMZ), and network monitoring is an example of multiple technologies designed to detect unauthorized network activity. Having a diverse set of these elements improves the chances of catching an attacker, even when they can beat one or two control elements.

Vendors

Different vendors approach security problems with different methodologies, different toolsets, different policies and procedures, and different technologies. Adversaries have developed methods of beating different vendors, but if multiple vendors are brought into play, this makes it all that much more difficult for an adversary to bypass all of the employed options. Having diversity in the vendors used for security prevents vendor-specific forms of single points of failure and creates a more robust set of defensive capabilities.

Crypto

For cryptographic solutions to work, both sides must agree on algorithms, keys, and other parameters, but diversity can still exist in this environment. A prime example is in the TLS cipher suite, a set of different crypto protocols, preassigned to facilitate flexibility in establishing a connection. When you establish a TLS-enabled connection, the server and client both negotiate a selection of protocol parameters from the preassigned list, enabling a secure connection to be established. The same server with a different host, doing the same exercise, can end up with different crypto choices, but in the end it's still a secure connection. Having multiple options configured and available enables the removal of one if something affects it, while still providing a means of connecting via alternative options.

Controls

Defense in depth is a security principle where multiple layers of different security mechanisms are used to ensure catching a risk. This is the use of diversity in controls. Modern networks employ not just a firewall but also a screened subnet (DMZ), bastion hosts, and ACLs, all working together in a coordinated fashion to make bypassing the entire suite of controls nearly impossible.

EXAM TIP Diversity is about having multiple different sets of controls to provide for risk mitigation. Diversity should be practiced in all aspects and used to enhance security. A performance-based question that considers diversity should be examined in light of which element is most efficient to manipulate—technologies, vendors, crypto, or controls—and the answer is found in the specifics of the question.

Chapter Review

In this chapter, you became acquainted with the aspects of cybersecurity resilience. The chapter opened with an examination of elements that lead to redundancy, such as geographic dispersal; disks, including RAID and multipath solutions; network redundancy from load balancers and NIC teaming; and power supply concerns, including UPSs, generators, dual supplies, and PDUs. The issues around replication using both SAN and VMs were covered, as was a comparison of on-premises and the cloud.

The topic of backups was covered, including the backup methodologies of full, incremental, snapshot, and differential. Backup technologies of tape, disk, copy, NAS, SAN, cloud, and image were presented as well. An examination of online versus offline backup locations was provided, including offsite storage and distance considerations.

The issues associated with nonpersistence, including reverting to a known state, last known-good configuration, and live boot media, were covered. An examination of high availability and scalability as well as restoration order followed. The chapter concluded with a consideration of diversity and how diversity in technology, vendors, crypto, and controls can be used to mitigate risk.

Questions

To help you prepare further for the exam, and to test your level of preparedness, answer the following questions and then check your answers against the correct answers at the end of the chapter.

1. Which backup strategy includes only the files and software that have changed since the last full backup?
   - A. Incremental
   - B. Full
   - C. Snapshot
   - D. Differential
2. Which backup strategy focuses on copies of virtual machines?
   - A. Incremental
   - B. Full
   - C. Snapshot
   - D. Differential
3. When discussing location for storage of backups, which of the following statements are true? (Choose all that apply.)
   - A. The most recent copy should be stored offsite, as it is the one that is most current and is thus the most valuable.
   - B. Offsite storage is generally not necessary, except in cases where the possibility of a break-in at the main facility is high.
   - C. Offsite storage is a good idea so that you don't lose your backup to the same event that caused you to lose your operational data and thus need the backup.
   - D. The most recent copy can be stored locally, as it is the most likely to be needed, while other copies can be kept at other locations.

4. To deal with nonpersistence in a system, which of the following items offer risk mitigation? (Choose all that apply.)
   A. Image backups
   B. Cloud
   C. Last known-good configuration
   D. Revert to a known state
5. To have easily available quick backup of critical user documents, which of the following is recommended for backing these items up?
   A. Differential
   B. Snapshot
   C. Copy
   D. NAS
6. You have offices in six locations across town and wish to utilize a common backup restore methodology. Which would be the most efficient solution for your small offices?
   A. SAN
   B. NAS
   C. Cloud
   D. Offline
7. Which of the following statements is true about redundancy?
   A. It prevents failures.
   B. It is complicated and expensive to do.
   C. It applies only to hardware.
   D. It can be done across many systems.
8. What distinguishes high availability systems?
   A. The ability to change with respect to usage conditions
   B. The ability to process, even in times of disruption
   C. Automated backups and recovery functions
   D. The use of diversity to mitigate single threats
9. The continual changing of information in a system is referred to as what?
   A. Nonpersistence
   B. Snapshots
   C. Differentials
   D. Images

10. A PDU provides management of what in an enterprise?
    - A. Redundant backup processing
    - B. Power distribution to servers
    - C. Improved network connection to data storage
    - D. Load balancing

Answers

1. **D.** In a differential backup, only the files and software that have changed since the last full backup was completed are backed up. The incremental backup is a variation on a differential backup, with the difference being that instead of copying all files that have changed since the last full backup, the incremental backup backs up only files that have changed since the last full *or* incremental backup occurred, thus requiring fewer files to be backed up. In a full backup, all files and software are copied onto the storage media. Snapshots refer to copies of virtual machines.
2. **C.** Snapshots refer to copies of virtual machines. The incremental backup is a variation on a differential backup, with the difference being that instead of copying all files that have changed since the last full backup, the incremental backup backs up only files that have changed since the last full *or* incremental backup occurred, thus requiring fewer files to be backed up. In a full backup, all files and software are copied onto the storage media. In a differential backup, only the files and software that have changed since the last full backup was completed are backed up.
3. **C** and **D.** Offsite storage is a good idea so that you don't lose your backup to the same event that caused you to lose your operational data and thus need the backup. Additionally, the most recent copy can be stored locally, as it is the most likely to be needed, while other copies can be kept at other locations.
4. **A, C,** and **D.** Image backups capture the nonpersistence of the OS. Also, reverting to a known state and using the last known-good configuration both can resolve nonpersistence issues. Cloud (answer B) is not a direct answer, as by itself, the cloud does not offer persistence to a nonpersistent system. An image backup has everything, so restoring from it can resolve a persistence problem. For the cloud to be involved, it would be as a secondary item (that is, a place to store an image backup), but then it is not actually directly involved.
5. **C.** User-managed copies on external media of critical documents can make it very easy for the end user to manage recovery in a quick manner.
6. **C.** Cloud backup solutions can be ideal for small offices, and with the different offices, centralized administration can be added.

7. **D.** A wide range of options are associated with creating redundant systems—some as simple as configuration elements and system choices.
8. **B.** High availability systems continue to process data even when disrupting events occur.
9. **A.** Nonpersistence refers to system items such as memory and registry elements that are not permanent and can change over time, even while running.
10. **B.** Power distribution units provide a centralized means of managing and monitoring the power delivered to servers in a rack.

CHAPTER 14

Embedded and Specialized Systems

In this chapter, you will

- Explore the security implications of embedded systems
- Explore the security implications of smart devices/IoT
- Explore the security implications of SCADA systems

Cybersecurity is not just limited to IT systems in the enterprise. A significant number of embedded systems and specialized systems produce and consume data to achieve functionality. These systems require cybersecurity as well if their functionality is to be protected from adverse risk. This chapter covers the unique nature of these systems and how that relates to providing protection for them.

Certification Objective This chapter covers CompTIA Security+ exam objective 2.6: Explain the security implications of embedded and specialized systems.

Embedded Systems

Embedded systems is the name given to computers that are included as an integral part of a larger system, typically hardwired in. From computer peripherals like printers, to household devices like smart TVs and thermostats, to the car you drive, embedded systems are everywhere. Embedded systems can be as simple as a microcontroller with fully integrated interfaces (a system on a chip) or as complex as the dozens of interconnected embedded systems in a modern automobile. Embedded systems are designed with a single control purpose in mind and have virtually no additional functionality, but this does not mean that they are free of risk or security concerns. The vast majority of security exploits involve getting a device or system to do something it is capable of doing, and technically designed to do, even if the resulting functionality was never an intended use of the device or system.

The designers of embedded systems typically are focused on minimizing costs, with security seldom seriously considered as part of either the design or the implementation. Because most embedded systems operate as isolated systems, the risks have not been significant. However, as capabilities have increased, and these devices have become networked together, the risks have increased significantly. For example, smart printers have been hacked as a way into enterprises, and as a way to hide from defenders. Also, when next-generation automobiles begin to talk to each other, passing traffic and other information between them, and begin to have navigation and other inputs beamed into systems, the risks will increase and security will become an issue. This has already been seen in the airline industry, where the separation of in-flight Wi-Fi, in-flight entertainment, and cockpit digital flight control networks has become a security issue.

Raspberry Pi

The *Raspberry Pi* is a highly successful, low-cost, single-board computer. Millions of these devices have found their way into a wide range of applications—from use by hobbyists to prototype engineers, and even as production elements in some cases. This low-cost (less than $50) highly capable computing device offers a lot of features and connectivity. A quad-core ARM processor, 8 GB of RAM, connectivity via Ethernet, Bluetooth, USB, 2.4GHz and 5GHz Wi-Fi, and host of connectivity options for displays, I/O, and storage all make this a versatile platform. Securing a Raspberry Pi is similar to securing any other system. One has to consider the environment in which it will be deployed, how it is connected to other users, and what data and sensitive information is involved. Also, remember that this is, in most cases, a full Linux environment that requires permissions and other basic security elements.

A Raspberry Pi running a science fair project with no connectivity to the Web has a completely different scope than one that is connected to the Internet and being used to log sensitive data necessary for production in an enterprise setting. Determining the risk profiles and addressing them as appropriate is still a needed and important task.

Field Programmable Gate Arrays (FPGAs)

Field programmable gate arrays (FPGAs) are electronic circuits that are programmed to perform a specific function. These semiconductor devices are based around a matrix of configurable logic blocks (CLBs) that are connected via programmable interconnects, and in essence the logic is programmed before use. FPGAs are designed to be reprogrammed to the desired functionality requirements after manufacturing, and they can typically be reprogrammed as designs of the functionality evolve. Although not as fast as application-specific integrated circuits (ASICs), which are custom manufactured for specific design tasks, the programmability and reprogrammability capabilities of FPGAs provide significant design flexibility. FPGAs and ASICs are found in a lot of custom devices, where a full-blown computer with an operating system (OS) and all that it entails is not needed.

Arduino

The *Arduino* is a single-board microcontroller, not a full-fledged computer like the Raspberry Pi. The Arduino is simpler, designed to provide computer control to hardware projects without the overhead of a full computer, OS, and so on. While a Raspberry Pi is designed as a computer, the Arduino is designed as a controller, specifically for interfacing with sensors and devices. The Arduino can respond to sensor levels and actuate devices based on programming that is loaded onto the device. This coding works when power is applied; if power is lost, once it is restored, the device can begin functioning again—unlike a computer, which would have to reboot and start over. Expansion of the Arduino platform is done via a series of boards called shields that can add specific functionality in networking, display, data collection, and so on.

EXAM TIP Understand static environments—systems in which the hardware, OS, applications, and networks are configured for a specific function or purpose. These systems are designed to remain unaltered through their lifecycle, rarely requiring updates.

Supervisory Control and Data Acquisition (SCADA) / Industrial Control System (ICS)

SCADA is an acronym for *supervisory control and data acquisition,* a system designed to control automated systems in cyber-physical environments. SCADA systems have their own smart components, each of which is an example of an embedded system. Together they form a SCADA system, which can control manufacturing plants, traffic lights, refineries, energy networks, water plants, building automation and environmental controls, and a host of other systems. A SCADA system is also known as a distributed control system (DCS) or an industrial control system (ICS), depending on the industry and the configuration. Where computers control a physical process directly, a SCADA system likely is involved.

Most SCADA systems involve multiple components networked together to achieve a set of functional objectives. These systems frequently include a human–machine interface (HMI), where an operator can exert a form of directive control over the operation of the system under control. SCADA systems historically have been isolated from other systems, but the isolation is decreasing as these systems are being connected across traditional networks to improve business functionality. Many older SCADA systems were air gapped from the corporate network; that is, they shared no direct network connections. This meant that data flows in and out were handled manually and took time to accomplish. Modern systems removed this constraint and added direct network connections between the SCADA networks and the enterprise IT networks. These connections increase the attack surface and the risk to the system; the more they resemble an IT networked system, the greater the need for security functions.

SCADA systems have been drawn into the security spotlight with the Stuxnet attack on Iranian nuclear facilities, initially reported in 2010. Stuxnet is malware designed to attack a specific SCADA system and cause failures, resulting in plant equipment damage. This attack was complex and well designed, crippling nuclear fuel processing in Iran for a significant period of time. This attack raised awareness of the risks associated with SCADA systems, whether connected to the Internet or not (Stuxnet crossed an air gap to hit its target).

Facilities

SCADA systems find many uses in *facilities,* ranging from the building automation systems of the HVAC system, to pumps for water pressure, escalators and elevators, and fire alarms—the lists just keep going on. Many of these systems are independent systems where data is collected from sensors and used for a specific purpose (elevator scheduling based on buttons on floors, for instance). Others, such as building access controls, locked/secured doors, and fire alarm systems, may be interconnected to ensure safety under specific conditions and security under other conditions. Some of these systems are connected via the Internet for remote monitoring or control. As for all systems, understanding how to get access to a system and securing those access points is key for securing this type of SCADA employment.

Industrial

Industrial facilities have some of the same needs as other facilities—the computer control of various processes, such as security, environmental monitoring, fire alarms, and more. The key element is to understand that virtually any facility has a data collection–data response system, whether it's a simple HVAC or thermostat system or a more complex system such as a surveillance or fire alarm system. Each of these systems can stand alone, be partially integrated with other systems, fully integrated with others, or connected to the Internet; the combinations are almost endless and are tailored to meet the requirements of the facility.

Manufacturing

Manufacturing systems add another layer of computer-controlled processes to the industrial/facility mix—those of the actual manufacturing process itself. Manufacturing equipment is commonly computer controlled, using devices such as programmable logic controllers (PLCs), to execute a process-specific set of instructions based on sensor readings and actuator settings. These systems can be differentiated by a wide range of specific attributes, but the term SCADA is commonly used to cover them.

These systems may be connected to the Internet or have outside access for third-party vendors. Because the SCADA systems that are running your manufacturing are typically very critical to your enterprise, these systems require protection from attackers. The standard practice for this is one of strict network segmentation.

Energy

Energy systems range from electrical to chemical, petroleum, pipelines, nuclear, solar, hydrothermal, and more. Each of these systems has multiple systems under computer control, typically using the same types of SCADA components as other categories already discussed. In the case of energy distribution, such as pipelines and electricity, a further complication is the distributed nature of these elements, where they are geographically spread out (in many cases in our communities). This distribution of components "outside the corporate walls" adds a unique physical security aspect to these systems.

Logistics

Logistics systems are the systems that move material from point A to point B. These systems can involve sea, surface (roads and rail), and air transport. There are two basic elements that will be under control: the transport system itself and the material being moved.

EXAM TIP When examining SCADA systems, you have three things to worry about: the value of the information being protected, physical access to the system, and logical (typically network) access to the data. When examining the question, parse the question for the specific detail that matters.

Internet of Things (IoT)

The *Internet of Things (IoT)* is a term used to describe a wide range of devices that connect directly via the Internet to create a distributed sensor and processing system to achieve a specific function. As opposed to general-purpose devices, like computers and networking equipment, IoT devices are purpose built; they are designed to do a specific task. All these devices have a couple similarities. They all have a network interface because connectivity is their purpose as a smart device or a member of the Internet of Things club. On that network interface is some form of compute platform. With complete computer functionality now included on the system on a chip platform (covered in a later section), these tiny devices can have a complete working computer for just a few dollars in cost. The use of a Linux-type kernel as the core engine makes programming easier, as the base of programmers is very large. These devices also can be mass produced and at relatively low cost. The scaling of the software development over literally millions of units makes costs scalable. Functionality is king, meaning that security or anything that might impact new expanded functionality has to take a backseat.

Sensors

Sensors are devices that measure some physical item and return data that can be used by a system. Sensors come in an endless array of sizes, shapes, and physical constraints. Sensors can be used to measure temperatures, pressures, voltages, positions, humidity levels—the list goes on. Sensors can return the data as either a digital or analog signal. Analog sensors require an analog-to-digital conversion before the data can be used by a computer, although many interface boards do this translation automatically. When designing a system, you need to determine what needs to be measured, over what range, and at what precision, as well as environmental and other conditions; these factors all shape the specification for a sensor and determine the cost.

Smart Devices

Smart devices and devices that comprise the IoT have taken the world's markets by storm. From key fobs that can track the location of items via GPS, to cameras that can provide surveillance, to connected household appliances, TVs, dishwashers, refrigerators, crock pots, washers, and dryers—anything with a microcontroller now seems to be connected to the Web so that it can be controlled remotely. Artificial intelligence (AI) has also entered into the mix, enabling even greater functionality, embodied in products such as Amazon Echo, Google Home, Microsoft Cortana, and Apple Siri. Computer-controlled light switches, LED light bulbs, thermostats, and baby monitors—the smart home has become a reality, connecting everything to the Internet. You can carry a key fob that your front door recognizes, unlocking itself before you get to it. Of course, the security camera sees you first and alerts the system that someone is coming up the driveway. The only thing that can be said with confidence about this revolution is someone will figure out a how and a why to connect virtually anything to the network.

Wearables

Wearable technologies include everything from biometric sensors measuring heart rate, to step counters measuring how far one walks, to smart watches that combine all these functions and more. By measuring biometric signals, such as pulse rate, and body movements, it is possible to measure fitness and even sleep. These wearable devices are built using very small computers that run a real-time operating system, usually built from a stripped-down Linux kernel. As with all information-containing devices, how does one protect the data? As wearables learn more and more of your personal data, they become a source of interest for hackers. Protecting the data is the security objective for these devices.

Things you can do to start protecting personal data include checking the default settings, checking the privacy settings, turning off location tracking, reading the privacy policies, and, where possible, using a passcode to protect your personal information (PI).

Facility Automation

Low-cost sensors in an IoT package offer several advantages, including but not limited to, network delivery of data, significant data collection capability, and cost advantages with scale. In large facilities, this means security systems, HVACs, fire sensors, and so on can provide large-scale coverage, enabling automation of data collection that used to be done manually via a person walking around. Automation is more than just remote operation; apps such as IFTTT (If This Then That) systems can respond to changing conditions and use multiple indicators, including dates and times. Automation can improve risk because it removes errors and improves speed of response.

Weak Defaults

Whenever items are manufactured or produced in large quantities, specific specializations such as default credentials are a challenge. The typical process is to have default credentials on a device and then expect the user to change them. This expectation of a user changing credentials commonly results in poor security. *Weak defaults* are a condition where default conditions are generally known, including admin account and password, leaving the system completely vulnerable to an attacker. But even if the password is changed, in cases where large numbers of devices are deployed, is it reasonable to expect they all got the default credentials changed to unique passwords? One of the challenges of IoT deployment and security is managing literally thousands or millions of devices—and the credentials.

EXAM TIP The Internet of Things is all about connectivity of low-cost (relative) items at scale. Deployments of hundreds, thousands, and even millions of devices have been done, and the data can provide great insights that can only be seen with data at scale. However, with that scale comes the challenge of managing and securing the large number of devices.

Specialized Systems

As the name indicates, *specialized systems* are systems designed for special purposes. Four primary types of specialized systems targeted by CompTIA are the systems in medical devices, vehicles, aircraft, and smart meters. Each of these categories has significant computer systems providing much of the functionality control for the device, and each of these systems has its own security issues.

Medical Systems

Medical systems is a very diverse group—from small implantable devices, such as pacemakers, to multi-ton MRI machines. In between is a wide range of devices, from those that measure vital signs to those that actually control vital functions. Each of these has several interesting characteristics, and they all have an interesting caveat—they can have a direct effect on a human's life. This makes security of these devices also a safety function.

Medical devices such as lab equipment and infusion pumps have been running on computer controls for years. The standard of choice has been an embedded Linux kernel that has been stripped of excess functionality and pressed into service in the embedded device. One of the problems with this approach is how to patch this kernel when vulnerabilities are found. Another, related problem is that as the base system gets updated to a newer version, the embedded system stays trapped on the old version. This requires regression testing for problems, and most manufacturers will not undertake such labor-intensive chores.

Medical devices are manufactured under strict regulatory guidelines that are designed for static systems that do not need patching, updating, or changes. Any change would force a requalification—a lengthy, time-consuming, and expensive process. As such, these devices tend to never be patched. With the advent of several high-profile vulnerabilities, including Heartbleed and Bash shell attacks, most manufacturers simply recommended that the devices be isolated and never connected to an outside network. In concept, this is fine, but in reality, this can never happen, as all the networks in a hospital or medical center are connected.

A recent recall of nearly a half million pacemakers in 2017 for a software vulnerability that would allow a hacker to access and change the performance characteristics of the device is proof of the problem. The good news is that the devices can be updated without removing them, but it will take a doctor's visit to have the new firmware installed.

Vehicle Systems

A modern *vehicle* has not a single computer in it, but actually hundreds of them, all interconnected on a bus. The controller area network (CAN) bus is designed to allow multiple microcontrollers to communicate with each other without a central host computer. Before the CAN bus was invented, individual microcontrollers were used to control the engine, emissions, transmission, braking, heating, electrical, and other systems, and the wiring harnesses used to interconnect everything became unwieldy. Robert Bosch developed the CAN bus for cars, specifically to address the wiring harness issue, and when first deployed in 1986 at BMW, the weight reduction was over 100 pounds.

Since 2008, all new U.S. and European cars must use a CAN bus, per SAE regulations—a mandate engineers have willingly embraced as they continue to add more and more subsystems. The CAN bus has a reference protocol specification, but recent auto hacking discoveries have shown several interesting things. First, in defending allegations that some of its vehicles could suddenly accelerate without driver action, Toyota claimed that the only way to make a vehicle accelerate quickly is to step on the gas pedal—that software alone won't do it. However, this was proven to be false. Hackers have demonstrated almost complete control over all functions of the Toyota Prius using computers and CAN bus commands. Second, every automobile manufacturer has interpreted/ignored the reference protocol specification to varying degrees. Finally, as demonstrated by hackers at DEF CON, it is possible to disable cars in motion, over the Internet, as well as fool around with the entertainment console settings and other systems.

The bottom line is that, to function properly, newer vehicles rely on multiple computer systems, all operating semi-autonomously and with very little security. The U.S. Department of Transportation is pushing for vehicle-to-vehicle communication technology, so that vehicles can tell each other when traffic is changing ahead of them. Couple that with the advances in self-driving technology, and the importance of stronger security in the industry is clear. There is evidence that this is beginning, that security is improving, but the pace of improvement is slow when compared to typical computer innovation speeds.

Aircraft Systems

Aircraft also have a significant computer footprint inside, as most modern jets have what is called an "all-glass cockpit," meaning the old individual gauges and switches have been replaced with a computer display that includes a touchscreen. This enables greater functionality and is more reliable than the older systems. But as with vehicles, the connecting of all of this equipment onto busses that are then eventually connected to outside networks has led to a lot of security questions for the aviation industry. And, as is true of medical devices, patching the OS for aircraft systems is a difficult process because the industry is heavily regulated, with strict testing requirements. This makes for systems that, over time, will become vulnerable as the base OS has been thoroughly explored and every vulnerability mapped and exploited in non-aviation systems, and these use cases can port easily to aircraft.

Recent revelations have shown that the in-flight entertainment systems, on standard Linux distros, are separated from flight controls not by separate networks, but by a firewall. This has led hackers to sound the alarm over aviation computing safety.

Smart Meters

Smart meters is the common name for the advanced metering infrastructure, a program initiated by the Department of Energy to bring the functionality of remote automation to meters in utilities. Real-time two-way communications, computing infrastructure to analyze the data, and a whole host of new policies and procedures to take advantage of the automation have provided a revolution in utility operations. For electricity, this means real-time (with a granularity measured in minutes, not a month like previous manual reads) usage data that enables matching of supply and demand with greater efficiency. For all utilities, the ability to read meters, change service, disconnect, reconnect, and detect and manage outages provides cost savings and levels of service never possible with the old manually managed meters. Managing the large-scale deployment of infrastructure in a secure fashion requires an extensive cryptographic setup, with some meters having multiple passwords for different levels of operation. Multiply this by millions of meters, and this is not a trivial task to manage. However, there are software packages designed to automate these elements as well.

EXAM TIP Specialized systems are custom built to serve a purpose, and the required level of security goes along with the purpose. If the data needs protecting, then the same problems and solutions used to fix them apply. In most specialized systems, the risks are significant and cryptographic solutions are designed into the system to limit access to authorized users.

Voice over IP (VoIP)

Voice over IP—the transmission of voice communications over IP networks—is now a commonplace method of providing telephone services. VoIP makes telephone management as easy as an app in the enterprise, but it also brings security risks and vulnerabilities. VoIP systems require protections from standard traffic-based attacks such as denial of service, but also need protections from spoofing. Suppose you get an internal phone call from Ms. Jones, the company's CFO, and your screen says "Ms. Jones," but how do you know who is on the line? If you have never heard Ms. Jones speak before, do you trust the voice, the screen, or what? Authentication and the protection of the communication channels have been the province of the telephone company, but in VoIP there is no overarching phone company to manage these risks.

Additional risks include outsiders using your VoIP to connect to international telephony services and offering free phone calls or using your phone service to robocall people. Just as we have to secure systems like e-mail from outside, unauthorized users, we need to do the same with VoIP services.

Heating, Ventilation, Air Conditioning (HVAC)

Building-automation systems, climate-control systems, and *HVAC (heating, ventilation, and air conditioning)* systems are all examples of systems that are managed by embedded systems. Although these systems used to be independent and stand-alone systems, the rise of hyper-connectivity has shown value in integrating them. Having a "smart building" that reduces the use of building resources in accordance with the number and distribution of people inside increases efficiency and reduces costs. Interconnecting these systems and adding in Internet-based central control mechanisms does increase the risk profile from outside attacks. These outside attacks could result in HVAC malfunction or failure, rendering a major office building uninhabitable due to heat and safety.

Although not specific to the HVAC system in one sense, Target corporation's 2014 hack was begun when an HVAC vendor was compromised, leading to a compromise of the Target network and access to its point-of-sale network. The story of the hack made the news and cost Target hundreds of millions of dollars and resulted in a significant number of executive changes. Cloud security service provider Qualys said that its researchers have discovered that most of about 55,000 HVAC systems connected to the Internet over the past two years have flaws that can be easily exploited by hackers.

Drones

Drones, or *unmanned aerial vehicles (UAVs)*, represent the next frontier of flight. These machines range from the small *drones* that hobbyists can play with for under $300 to full-size aircraft that can fly across oceans. What makes these systems different from regular aircraft is that the pilot is on the ground, flying the device via remote control. UAVs have cameras, sensors, and processors to manage the information, and even the simple hobbyist versions have sophisticated autopilot functions. Because of the remote connection, UAVs are networked and operated either under direct radio control (rare) or via a networked system (much more common).

Multifunction Printers (MFPs)

Multifunction printers (MFPs), which combine a printer, scanner, and fax, have embedded compute power to act as a print server, manage the actual printing or scanning process, and allow complete network connectivity. These devices communicate in a bidirectional fashion, accepting print jobs and sending back job status, printer status, and other information to the computer. This has decoupled printing from the computer, making the printer a stand-alone entity. The system that runs all these functions was designed to provide maximum functionality for the device, and security is more of an afterthought than a design element. As such, these devices have been shown to be hackable and capable of passing malware from the printer to the computer. These attacks still exist primarily as a proof of concept as opposed to a real-world threat, which is fortunate, because the current generation of security software does not monitor printer activity to and from the computer very well.

Real-time Operating Systems (RTOSs)

Real-time operating systems (RTOSs) are designed for devices where the processing must occur in real time and data cannot be queued or buffered for any significant length of time. RTOSs are not general-purpose machines but are programmed for a specific purpose. They still have to deal with contention, and they have scheduling algorithms to deal with timing collisions, but in general an RTOS processes each input as it is received, or within a specific time slice defined as the response time. Examples of RTOSs range from something as common as an anti-lock braking computer system in a car to something as complex as a robotic system used on an assembly line.

Most general-purpose computer operating systems are capable of multitasking by design. This includes Windows and Linux. Multitasking systems make poor real-time processors, primarily because of the overhead associated with separating tasks and processes. Windows and Linux may have interrupts, but these are the exception, not the rule, for the processor. RTOS-based software is written in a completely different fashion, designed to emphasize the thread in processing rather than handling multiple threads.

The security implications surrounding real-time operating systems lie in their timing. Should an event do something that interferes with the system's ability to respond within its time allotment, then the system itself can fail in its task. Real-time operating systems also tend to be specific to the degree that updates and patches tend not to be common, as the manufacturer of the system does not provide that level of support. As items such as cars become more networked, these weaknesses are becoming apparent, and one can expect this situation to change over time.

Surveillance Systems

Digital *surveillance systems* have entered the computing world through a couple of different portals. First, there is the world of high-end digital cameras that have networking stacks, image processors, and even 4K video feeds. These are used in enterprises such as news organizations, which rely on getting the data live without extra processing delays. What is important to note is that most of these devices, although they are networked into other networks, have built-in virtual private networks (VPNs) that are always on, because the content is considered valuable enough to protect as a feature.

The next set of cameras reverses the quantity and quality characteristics. Where the high-end devices are fairly small in number, there is a growing segment of video surveillance cameras, including cameras for household surveillance, baby monitoring, and the like. Hundreds of millions of these devices are sold, and they all have a sensor, a processor, a network stack, and so forth. These are part of the Internet of Things revolution, where millions of devices connect together either on purpose or by happenstance. It was a network of these devices, along with a default username and password, that led to the Mirai botnet that actually broke the Internet for a while in the fall of 2016. The true root cause was a failure to follow a networking RFC concerning source addressing, coupled with the default username and password and remote configuration that enabled the devices to be taken over. Two sets of fails, working together, created weeks' worth of problems.

EXAM TIP VoIP, HVAC, drones/UAVs, MFPs, and surveillance systems have one weakness in common: access via the Internet. The same vector can be used against any connected system, and without defenses, these are typically very insecure systems. They have to be connected for functionality, and hence they need basic protections like passwords.

System on a Chip (SoC)

System on a chip (SoC) refers to a complete computer system miniaturized on a single integrated circuit, designed to provide the full functionality of a computing platform on a single chip. This includes networking and graphics display. Some SoC solutions come with memory, while others have the memory separate. SoCs are very common in the mobile computing market (both phones and tablets) because of their low power consumption and efficient design. Some SoC brands have become household names because mobile phone companies have advertised their inclusion in a system, such as the Snapdragon processor in Android devices. Quad-core and eight-core SoC systems are already in place, and they even have advanced designs such as quad plus one, where the fifth processor is slower and designed for simple processes and uses extremely small amounts of power. So when the quad cores are not needed, there is not significant energy usage.

The programming of SoC systems can occur at several different levels. Dedicated OSs and applications can be written for them, such as the Android fork of Linux, which is specific to the mobile device marketplace. Because these devices represent computing platforms with billions of devices worldwide, they have become a significant force in the marketplace. The security implications of SoC-based systems is associated not with the specifics of SoC, but in the fact that they are ubiquitous in our technology-driven lives. Security issues are handled by the device, not the specific SoC aspect itself.

Communication Considerations

Embedded and specialized systems are useful for a purpose, and many times those purposes require communications across a network for other resources. The *communication considerations* for embedded and specialized systems are dependent on the service, what task it is doing, and the resources needed. The methods of communication are wide and varied, and the choice is usually dependent on the range needed and with whom the communication is needed. For short-distance, local communications, certain technologies can excel. For worldwide communications, others would work better. Adopting technology already employed by users has advantages as well; for instance, why use a specialty radio circuit in an environment that already has Wi-Fi?

5G

5G is the latest generation mobile radio-based network. It is designed to connect virtually everyone and everything together, including machines, objects, and devices, with a focus on higher data speeds and bandwidth. 5G networks are more than just bigger pipes; the standard has many functional elements to improve both performance and efficiencies. 5G is in the process of being rolled out worldwide, and connectivity is via a cellular circuit—either a phone, modem, or a chipset designed in a product.

Just as having a full-blown server is overkill for a simple sensor, 5G may be overkill for many communication needs. If worldwide range, large bandwidth, and low latency are important, then 5G may be warranted, but if not, there are lower-cost alternatives.

Narrow-Band Radio

Narrow-band radio communications use narrow bands of frequencies for low-data-rate communications. While a low data rate may seem to be a big problem, not all systems have high-data-rate needs, and narrow-band radio offers advantages in range and power utilization. Lower-power transmitters are the norm, as are significantly longer ranges. So, if a company has a bunch of drilling rigs over a large geographic area and needs to move relative small quantities of data between them, then narrow-band radio can be the ideal solution.

Baseband Radio

Baseband refers to the original bandwidth produced by a signal. For typical audio signals, it is 20–20,000 Hz. For a signal to be transmitted over a radio circuit, it is usually encoded or modulated in a manner that can then be blended with the radio wave, carrying the information in the changes on a radio wave. *Baseband radio* refers to the signal that is being transmitted and represents a single channel of communication. Broadband radio is when multiple signals are bundled together for transmission, and equipment is typically required to separate out the individual communications. Baseband radio, by design, is very simple, as it only carries a single channel to manage communications across.

Subscriber Identity Module (SIM) Cards

A *subscriber identity module (SIM) card* is a device used to hold key information needed to conduct communications across telecommunication networks. A SIM card provides a means of identifying users and other key items of information when using telecommunication networks. When accessing a telecommunication network, one has to identify themselves for billing purposes. The SIM card provides the information needed by the network to attribute the call. Elements such as provider, serial numbers, and keys are stored on a universal integrated circuit card that acts as a standard for storing and managing this information on devices. SIM cards are important because they can contain user data and authentication information as well as provide identity services. When one moves a SIM card from one phone to another, the new hardware acts like the old hardware with respect to connectivity and, to a degree, stored data.

Zigbee

Zigbee is a low-power mesh radio service used to connect sensors and basic devices.

EXAM TIP Communication needs are common among a lot of devices, but the methods vary. Understanding the limitations of the different methods and the security options is important.

Constraints

Specialized and embedded systems have a different set of constraints that they are designed to operate under. Typical constraints for these devices include limitations on power, compute capacity, network throughput and bandwidth, cryptography, and cost. Additional issues in items like authentication and trust can also be driving factors. As these devices are built for a specific purpose, these limitations are actually design elements and are part of the ability of the system to perform its task in the expected environment.

Power

Electronic circuits take *power* to operate, and it comes from one of several sources: a power supply connected to the grid, a battery, solar, or another type of device. Power is a key driver in many embedded and specialized systems because it is a true limiter. When the power supply is interrupted and no backup power supply exists, the device stops functioning. Rechargeable lithium-ion batteries have come a long way in the past few years, and for mobile devices they form the primary supply. Power drives many design elements because extra functionality that is not needed, including speed, only uses power and does not add to the functionality of the unit.

Compute

The *compute* capability of embedded and specialized systems is another key component that is matched to the task the device is designed to accomplish. Compute performance is one of the major elements in the power equation, and excess compute capacity results in more power drain and less useful life on a battery charge. Microcontrollers, field programmable gate arrays (FPGAs), and application-specific integrated circuits (ASICs), all discussed earlier in the chapter, are valid options for the compute segment of a design, and each of these comes with a wide range of capabilities. From tiny microcontrollers the size of a grain of rice with very limited capabilities, to the ASICs designed for visual/lidar processing in modern self-driving cars, the range of capabilities is wide. The key point to remember is that compute power, power capacity, and useful lifetime without external power are all locked in a battle, each taking from the other two.

Network

Network limitations are due to constraints from power and connectivity. Without direct connectivity, networking requires a radio transceiver, and this increases power demands. Therefore, where networking is needed, it comes at a cost. There are a variety of methods used for networking, and the one chosen will be the cheapest and best solution for the networking needs available at the time of system design.

Leaving single-unit considerations aside, networking is the key value component behind the Internet of Things revolution. The utility of networking power is related to an exponential function associated with the number of nodes. Hence, the greater the number of nodes, the larger the utility, and this growth is exponential in nature. Larger deployments (think smart meters in a major metropolitan area) deliver tremendous quantities of data, via a network, to a data center on a regular and timely basis. Managing large data flows places a burden on the central site, which if not properly planned for and executed becomes a constraint on the overall system operation.

Cryptographic Functions

Cryptographic functions can be essential to secure data during transmission, but this functionality comes at a price. The level of computational resources for crypto functions can be substantial, thus becoming a constraint on the overall system. Lightweight cryptographic algorithms are being developed to specifically address these challenges, and these are covered in Chapter 16, "Cryptographic Concepts."

Inability to Patch

The *inability to patch* an item represents a security risk and a constraint. This is typically caused by a series of design decisions predicated on producing items that are not computers but rather single-purpose devices. While Raspberry Pi's and Arduinos may get patches from their developers, the embedded controller in a surveillance camera is another story altogether. Simply put, the ecosystem for most embedded devices is missing the means, the culture, and in many cases the sheer ability to manage the patch process.

Authentication

Authentication is an important predicate to security functionality. The definitions of confidentiality, integrity, and many other security attributes have the term *authenticated user* in them. This make authentication an important property, but given the non-computer ecosystem in which most specialized and embedded devices function, there is a problem with directly adopting the concept of authentication. This is not as significant a limitation as it may seem, however, because unlike computers, which perform a multitude of different functions for different users, specialized and embedded systems tend to perform a singular function with an undefined user by design. There may be a need for an administrative interface for some functions, but enabling this with a simple PIN is not problematic, especially if defaults were taken into account during the design and deployment. For more information on this topic, review "Weak Defaults," earlier in the chapter.

Range

In most cases, *range* is a function of power—one of the true limitations of many specialized and embedded systems. One of the challenges of IoT deployments is getting them to the Internet, because there range is unlimited. However, this comes at the cost of security/risk.

Cost

The whole purpose behind developing specialized/embedded systems is that the value is there. The functionality return for the *cost* of the unit justifies the design and deployment, so cost is to a degree baked in. So, rather than viewing cost as a constraint, it is the factor that drives the creation of these solutions. However, cost is also an economic issue because extra functionality leads to extra cost, and if this functionality isn't needed in the final solution, money is wasted.

Implied Trust

Implied trust, by definition, is trust that has not been specifically set up but yet exists. This is almost a given in many specialized systems because they are not intended or designed to be general-purpose compute devices; therefore, the thought processes associated with regular trust vis-à-vis computers and the Internet do not exist. This makes for easier connectivity, but also opens doors for an attacker.

EXAM TIP When questioned about constraints and specialized systems (not general-purpose computers), remember the ecosystem that the device is intended to run in and consider that when formulating the answer. Many times it is different for specialized/embedded systems than for a general-purpose computer.

Chapter Review

In this chapter, you became acquainted with the security implications of embedded systems, which have become ubiquitous in our everyday lives. The chapter opened with a discussion of embedded systems in the form of the Raspberry Pi, field programmable gate array (FPGA), and the Arduino microcontroller platform. The chapter then presented the SCADA/ICS space and how operational technology is its own world and one of significant size. Examinations of these systems in facilities as well as industrial, manufacturing, energy, and logistics settings were covered. The chapter then moved to the world of smart devices and the Internet of Things, including sensors, smart devices, wearable technology, facility automation, and weak defaults.

The chapter then covered specialized systems, including medical systems, vehicles, aircraft, and smart meters. A discussion of Voice over IP, HVAC systems, drones, and multifunction printers followed. Next, we looked at real-time operating systems, surveillance systems, and system on a chip, followed by communication considerations for embedded and specialty systems such as 5G, narrow band, baseband, SIM cards, and Zigbee. The chapter closed with an examination of system constraints in these systems, including power, compute performance, network functions, cryptographic functions, the inability to patch, authentication, range, cost, and implied trust.

Questions

To help you prepare further for the exam, and to test your level of preparedness, answer the following questions and then check your answers against the correct answers at the end of the chapter.

1. Which of the following statements is *not* true?
   - **A.** Embedded systems are designed with a single control purpose in mind and typically have no additional functionality.
   - **B.** Embedded systems are free of risk and security concerns.
   - **C.** *Embedded* is the name given to a computer that is included as an integral part of a larger system.
   - **D.** Embedded systems can be as complex as the dozens of interconnected embedded systems in a modern automobile.
2. Which of the following statements is true regarding the risk of next-generation vehicles?
   - **A.** There are minimal risks when next-generation automobiles share information.
   - **B.** Passing traffic and other information between vehicles does not increase security risks.
   - **C.** The sharing of navigation and other inputs between vehicles presents a potential security issue.
   - **D.** Time-to-market and cost minimization have minimal impact on potential risks being exploited.
3. Which of the following properly defines supervisory control and data acquisition (SCADA)?
   - **A.** A scaled-down version of Linux designed for use in an embedded system
   - **B.** The standard used for communicating between intelligent car systems
   - **C.** The risk created by connecting control systems in buildings
   - **D.** A system designed to control automated systems in cyber-physical environments

4. Which of the following statements is true about smart devices and the Internet of Things (IoT)?
   - **A.** The use of a Linux-type kernel as the core engine makes programming more complex.
   - **B.** Mass production introduces significant security risks.
   - **C.** The scaling of the software development over large numbers of units makes costs scalable, and functionality is paramount.
   - **D.** Security or anything that might impact new expanded functionality is considered early and gets the focus and resources necessary.
5. Which of the following statements is true about HVAC and building automation systems?
   - **A.** They have not been exploited to any significant degree yet.
   - **B.** Interconnecting these systems and using Internet-based central control mechanisms increases the risk profile from outside attacks.
   - **C.** Having a "smart building" that reduces the use of building resources in accordance with the number and distribution of people inside has not increased efficiency or reduced costs.
   - **D.** The rise of hyper-connectivity has introduced no additional security concerns.
6. Which of the following statements is *not* true about system on a chip?
   - **A.** It provides the full functionality of a computing platform on a single chip.
   - **B.** It typically has low power consumption and efficient design.
   - **C.** Programming of SoC systems can occur at several different levels, and thus potential risks are easily mitigated.
   - **D.** Because SoC represents computing platforms with billions of devices worldwide, it has become a significant force in the marketplace.
7. What distinguishes real-time operating systems (RTOSs) from general-purpose operating systems?
   - **A.** Unlike RTOSs, most general-purpose operating systems handle interrupts within defined time constraints.
   - **B.** Unlike general-purpose OSs, most RTOSs are capable of multitasking by design.
   - **C.** Unlike RTOSs, most general-purpose operating systems are multitasking by design.
   - **D.** Unlike general-purpose OSs, RTOSs are designed to handle multiple threads.

8. Which of the following statements is true about printers and multifunction devices?
   - A. They rely on the computer to manage the printing and scanning processes.
   - B. Because of their long history and widespread use, security is designed into these products.
   - C. These devices communicate in a bidirectional fashion, accepting print jobs and sending back job status, printer status, and so forth.
   - D. So far, they have not been shown to be hackable or capable of passing malware to the computer.
9. Which of the following is a very important aspect to always remember when dealing with security of medical devices?
   - A. They are still relatively new in their usage.
   - B. They can directly affect human life.
   - C. Security is not related to safety.
   - D. They are almost exclusively stand-alone devices, without Internet connectivity.
10. Which of the following poses a significant potential risk of unmanned aerial vehicles?
    - A. They have sophisticated autopilot functions.
    - B. They have cameras, sensors, and payloads.
    - C. Some models have a low price.
    - D. Because they are pilotless, their remote-control systems may be networked and therefore vulnerable to potential risks.

Answers

1. **B.** Embedded systems are *not* free of risk or security concerns, as hackers have demonstrated.
2. **C.** The sharing of navigation and other inputs presents a potential security issue for next-generation vehicles. False information, when shared, can cause problems.
3. **D.** SCADA is a system designed to control automated systems in cyber-physical environments.
4. **C.** The scaling of the software development over large numbers of units makes costs scalable, and functionality is paramount in smart devices and IoT.
5. **B.** Interconnecting HVAC and building automation systems and using Internet-based central control mechanisms to manage them increases the risk profile from outside attacks.

6. **C.** Programming of SoC systems can occur at several different levels, and thus potential risks are *difficult* to mitigate.
7. **C.** One thing that distinguishes real-time operating systems (RTOSs) from general-purpose operating systems is that most general-purpose operating systems are designed for multitasking.
8. **C.** Printers and multifunction devices communicate in a bidirectional fashion, accepting print jobs and sending back job status, printer status, and so forth.
9. **B.** A very important aspect to always remember when dealing with security of medical devices is that they can directly affect human life.
10. **D.** A significant potential risk of unmanned aerial vehicles is that, because they are pilotless, their remote-control systems may be networked and therefore vulnerable to potential risks.

CHAPTER 15

Physical Security Controls

In this chapter, you will

- Explore the importance of physical security controls
- Learn about important environment controls

Physical security is an important topic for businesses dealing with the security of networks and information systems. Businesses are responsible for managing their risk exposure, which requires securing a combination of assets: employees, product inventory, trade secrets, and strategy information. These and other important assets affect the profitability of a company and its future survival. Companies therefore perform many activities to attempt to provide physical security—locking doors, installing alarm systems, using safes, posting security guards, setting access controls, and more.

Environmental controls play an important role in the protection of the systems used to process information. Most companies today have invested a large amount of time, money, and effort in both network security and information systems security. In this chapter, you will learn about how the strategies for securing the network and for securing information systems are linked, and you'll learn several methods by which companies can minimize their exposure to physical security events that can diminish their network security.

Certification Objective This chapter covers CompTIA Security+ exam objective 2.7: Explain the importance of physical security controls.

Bollards/Barricades

The primary defense against a majority of physical attacks is the *barricades* between the assets and a potential attacker—walls, fences, gates, and doors. Barricades provide the foundation upon which all other security initiatives are based, but the security must be designed carefully, as an attacker has to find only a single gap to gain access. Barricades can also be used to control vehicular access to and near a building or structure. The simple post-type barricade that prevents a vehicle from passing but allows people to walk past is called a *bollard*.

EXAM TIP Bollards are sturdy posts often made of concrete or galvanized or stainless steel. They are used to protect entry ways and prevent unauthorized entry or vehicle ramming attacks.

Walls may have been one of the first inventions of humans. Once we learned to use natural obstacles such as mountains to separate us from our enemies, we next learned to build our *own* mountain for the same purpose. Hadrian's Wall in England, the Great Wall of China, and the Berlin Wall are all famous examples of such basic physical defenses. The walls of any building serve the same purpose, but on a smaller scale: they provide barriers to physical access to company assets. In the case of information assets, as a general rule, the most valuable assets are contained on company servers. To protect the physical servers, you must look in all directions. Doors and windows should be safeguarded, and a minimum number of each should be used in a server room when they are all that separate the servers from the personnel allowed to access them. It is very important that any transparent windows or doors do not allow shoulder surfing from outside the server room. It is good to see people in the room, just not what they type on their screens. Less obvious entry points should also be considered: Is a drop ceiling used in the server room? Do the interior walls extend to the actual roof, raised floors, or crawlspaces? Access to the server room should be limited to the people who need access, not to all employees of the organization. If you are going to use a wall to protect an asset, make sure no obvious holes appear in that wall.

NOTE Windows or no windows? Windows provide visibility, allowing people to observe activities in the server room. This can provide security if those doing the observing have authority to see the activity in the server room. If those outside do not have this authority, then windows should be avoided.

Another method of preventing surreptitious access is through the use of windows. Many high-security areas have a significant number of windows so that people's activities within the area can't be hidden. A closed server room with no windows makes for a quiet place for someone to achieve physical access to a device without worry of being seen. Windows remove this privacy element that many criminals depend on to achieve their entry and illicit activities.

EXAM TIP All entry points to server rooms and wiring closets should be closely controlled, and, if possible, access should be logged through an access control system.

Access Control Vestibules

The implementation of a access control vestibule, also called a mantrap, is one way to combat tailgating. An *access control vestibule* is composed of two closely spaced doors that require the user to card through one and then the other sequentially. Mantraps make it nearly impossible to trail through a doorway undetected—if an intruder happens to catch the first door before it closes, he will be trapped in by the second door, as the second door remains locked until the first one closes and locks.

EXAM TIP An access control vestibule door arrangement can prevent unauthorized people from following authorized users through an access-controlled door, which is also known as *tailgating*.

Badges

As organizations grow in size, it is not possible for everyone to know everyone else by sight. Hence, some form of physical identification is needed to recognize employees. A badge with a picture on it can enable others to quickly determine if you are an employee or not. Visitors are given their own badge that identifies them as a visitor. Radio-frequency identification (RFID) uses electromagnetic fields to automatically identify and record information. RFID tags are widely used in identification badges, replacing earlier magnetic stripe cards and making them useable with just a swipe near a reader.

Alarms

Alarms serve to alert operators to abnormal conditions. Physical security can involve numerous sensors, intrusion alarms, motion detectors, switches that alert to doors being opened, video and audio surveillance, and more. Each of these systems can gather useful information, but it is only truly useful if it is acted upon. When one of these systems has information that can be of use to operational personnel, an alarm is the easiest method of alerting personnel to the condition. Alarms are not simple; if a company has too many alarm conditions, especially false alarms, then the operators will not react to the conditions as desired. Tuning alarms so that they provide useful, accurate, and actionable information is important if you want them to be effective.

EXAM TIP Lighting, signs, fencing, and alarms are all items readily associated with physical security. The proper answer to an exam question will be based on the specific details of the question—watch for the clues and pick the best answer based on the context of the question.

Signage

Signs act as informational devices and can be used in a variety of ways to assist in physical security. *Signage* can provide information as to areas that are restricted, or it can indicate where specific precautions, such as keeping doors locked, are required. A common use of signs in high-security facilities is to delineate where visitors are allowed versus secured areas where escorts are required. Visual security clues can assist in alerting users to the need for specific security precautions. Visual clues as to the types of protection required can take the form of different-color name badges that signify the level of access, visual lanyards that indicate visitors, colored folders, and so forth.

Cameras

Cameras are an important tool for security. The old adage "a picture is worth a thousand words" consistently rings true, and this is especially true in security. From recording evidence for later use, like taking pictures of equipment, serial number panels, and so on, to collecting evidence at crime scenes, *cameras* enable the re-creation of scenes at a later date. Cameras have been around for over 100 years, but with the invention of digital photography, followed by the addition of cameras to cell phones, today there are literally billions of cameras worldwide taking tens of billions of photos. One of the interesting uses of this technology is the ability to quickly share photos with others, allowing someone to "see" far beyond normal range of eyesight. In 2020, when riots broke out across the U.S., many protesters documented the police response using cell phone cameras. While they were using their cameras to document the police, they also captured images that law enforcement would later use to catch those responsible for crimes.

Video cameras offer an even greater range of surveillance capability, and closed-circuit TV cameras are covered in a later section.

Motion Recognition

Motion recognition is an important technology to limit the search time and recording space associated with video images. Infrared (IR) radiation is not visible to the human eye, but it can be used just like a light source to detect a range of things. Motion from living creatures can be seen because of the heat signatures of their bodies. Infrared detection is a technical means of looking for things that otherwise may not be noticed. At night, when it is dark, someone can hide in the shadows, but infrared light can point them out to IR-sensing cameras. Infrared detectors can sense differences in temperature, which can be from a person entering a room, even if that person is not visible due to darkness. IR alarms are used extensively to monitor movement of people in areas where there should be none.

Object Detection

Modern surveillance video systems come with some impressive software. Even cameras sold to homeowners can scan video for movement and detect people, cars, and other designated objects such as packages left on a porch. The use of video software for object detection does not replace the human eye, but it significantly enhances a guard's ability to effectively use large banks of cameras to cover a facility. The citywide video surveillance system in London was the primary source of evidence that identified the terrorists who set off a series of bombs across the city in 2005.

Closed-Circuit Television (CCTV)

Video surveillance is typically done through *closed-circuit television (CCTV)*. The use of CCTV cameras for surveillance purposes dates back to at least 1961, when cameras were installed in the London Transport train station. The development of smaller camera components and lower costs has caused a boon in the CCTV industry since then.

Figure 15-1 IP-based cameras leverage existing IP networks instead of needing a proprietary CCTV cable.

CCTV cameras are used to monitor a workplace for security purposes. These systems are commonplace in banks and jewelry stores—places with high-value merchandise that is attractive to thieves. As the expense of these systems dropped, they became practical for many more industry segments. Traditional cameras are analog based and require a video multiplexer to combine all the signals and make multiple views appear on a monitor. Digital, IP-based cameras have changed that, as most of them are stand-alone units that are viewable through a web browser, such as the camera shown in Figure 15-1.

These IP-based systems add useful functionality, such as the ability to check on the building from the Internet. This network functionality, however, makes the cameras subject to normal IP-based network attacks. A DoS attack launched at the CCTV system just as a break-in is occurring is the last thing that anyone would want (other than the criminals). For this reason, IP-based CCTV cameras should be placed on their own separate network that can be accessed only by security personnel. The same physical separation applies to any IP-based camera infrastructure. Older time-lapse tape recorders are slowly being replaced with digital video recorders. While the advance in technology is significant, be careful if and when these devices become IP-enabled, since they will become a security issue, just like everything else that touches the network.

If you depend on a CCTV system to protect your organization's assets, carefully consider camera placement and the type of cameras used. Different iris types, focal lengths, and color or infrared capabilities are all options that make one camera superior to another in a specific location.

Industrial Camouflage

Camouflage is the specific act of rendering an item not readily observable. Considered by many to be a military thing, camouflage began in nature, where insects and animals have patterns making them seem to be different than they really are. This same principle is used all the time to make things hide in plain sight. Cell phone towers built to look like trees make them less conspicuous—and generally improve the visual surroundings. In response to physical acts against electrical substations, many utilities have put walls around the substations, making the internal equipment no longer visible and less of a target.

NOTE If you want to see some industrial camouflage in action, use Street View in Google Maps and look at these locations:

- 58 Joralemon Street, New York City, is a ventilation shaft and emergency access to the New York subway.
- 640 Millwood Road, Toronto, Canada, is an electrical substation—one of 250 in the city.
- 51 W. Ontario Street, Chicago, Illinois, is another substation—this one by Commonwealth Edison. The doors are fake and don't open, and the windows are actually vents.

Personnel

Physical security should be a part of a firm's overall security program. Physical security measures are those taken to ensure the separation of items to be protected from all forms of physical risk. Personnel are an important part of this equation—from guards to lobby workers who act as gatekeepers for visitors and packages, people are part of the physical security system.

Guards

Security *guards* provide an excellent security measure, because guards are a visible presence with direct responsibility for security. Other employees expect security guards to behave a certain way with regard to securing the facility. Guards typically monitor entrances and exits and can maintain access logs of who has entered and departed the building. In many organizations, everyone who passes through security as a visitor must sign a log, which can be useful in tracing who was at what location and why.

Security personnel are helpful in physically securing the machines on which information assets reside, but to get the most benefit from their presence, they must be trained to take a holistic approach to security. The value of data typically can be many times that of the machines on which the data is stored. Security guards typically are not computer security experts, so they need to be educated about the value of the data and be trained in network security as well as physical security involving users. They are the company's eyes and ears for suspicious activity, so the network security department needs to train them to notice suspicious network activity as well. Multiple extensions ringing in sequence during the night, computers rebooting all at once, and strangers parked in the parking lot with laptop computers or other mobile computing devices are all indicators of a network attack that might be missed without proper training.

Robot Sentries

Guard duty is by and large boring work, and although guards aren't highly paid over time, having a number of guards can be expensive. Robot technology has progressed to the point where robots can now perform many simple tasks, and guard duty can be one of these tasks. *Robot sentries* can patrol empty buildings and using sensors can detect the presence of unauthorized people. Robot sentries can then report the issue to a manned station that can alert the proper authorities for a response.

Reception

Reception areas are used as buffer zones between different areas of a facility, segmenting the building into separate regions. Having a visitor check-in desk allows control over visitors as well as enables functions like logging visitors, managing deliveries, and providing escorts for visitors. In lower security environments, this reception area may simply be someone at a desk, with no physical barrier. In more secure facilities, the receptionist is not only responsible for keeping logs, issuing access badges, and notifying escorts, but also controls the door everyone must go through. In very highly controlled environments, the actual door control is done remotely from the other side of the door so that people can't force their way past the receptionist.

Two-Person Integrity/Control

When tasks are critical, or failures could involve significant risk, the organizational principle of separation of duties applies. This topic is fully covered in Chapter 33, "Organizational Policies." When there are physical tasks, such as opening the door mentioned in the previous section, having two people required to perform the task provides a means of checks and balances. *Two-person integrity/control* is this principle in action: it is when two different people have to perform respective tasks that are both necessary for the action to occur. Person 1 can initiate a process, check IDs, enter data in a log, and issue a visitor badge, while person 2 can control the door access. This way, a failure by either person does not expose the process.

EXAM TIP Be able to explain important physical security controls, including guards, robot sentries, reception, and two-person integrity/control.

Locks

Locks are a common security measure that are used with near ubiquity. Everyone is familiar with using a lock to secure something. Many different *lock types* are used in and around the computer security arena. There are types for laptops and other mobile devices, for desktops, and even servers. Just as locks can keep your car or bike from being stolen, they can secure computers as well. Laptops are popular targets for thieves and should be locked inside a desk when not in use, or secured with special computer lockdown cables. Laptop thefts from cars can occur in seconds, and thieves have been caught taking laptops from security screening areas at airports while the owners are distracted with the screening process. If an organization uses desktop towers, it should use computer desks that provide a space in which to lock the computer. In some cases, valuable media is stored in a safe designed for that purpose. All of these measures can improve the physical security of the computers themselves, but most of them can be defeated by attackers if users are not knowledgeable about the security program and do not follow it.

Biometrics

Biometrics is the measurement of biological attributes or processes with the goal of identification of a party possessing those measurements. The most well-known biometric factor is the fingerprint. Fingerprint readers have been available for several years in laptops and other mobile devices, as shown in Figure 15-2, and as stand-alone USB devices.

Other biometric measurements that can be used for physical security purposes include the retina or iris of the eye, the geometry of the hand, and the geometry of the face. When any of these are used for authentication, there is a two-part process: enrollment and then authentication. During enrollment, a computer takes the image of the biological factor and reduces it to a numeric value. When the user attempts to authenticate, his or her feature is scanned by the reader, and the computer compares the numeric value being read to the one stored in the database. If they match, access is allowed. Since these physical factors are unique, theoretically only the actual authorized person would be allowed access.

Biometrics are frequently used in physical security and are becoming nearly ubiquitous for controlling access to mobile devices, such as phones and tablets. For many physical security situations, the true question for access is, are you the correct person who should have access? Using biometrics to confirm the identity of the person being presented for access as the same person who went through the identification phase at enrollment is a good way to answer this question. You can't loan your fingerprints, iris, or retina for a scan, or your hand for its geometry. Biometrics bind the identification token to the person.

Biometrics are not foolproof. Some biometric measures can be duplicated to fool a sensor, and in many cases, the actual biometric is converted to a number that can also

Figure 15-2 Newer laptop computers often include a fingerprint reader.

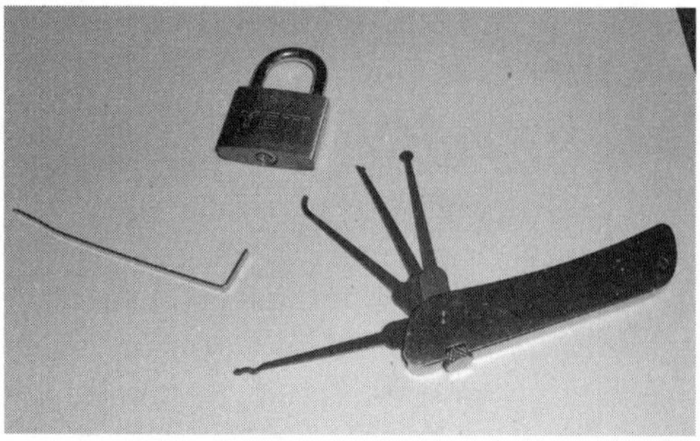

Figure 15-3 Lock-picking tools

be intercepted and used in a software attack. Safeguards exist for most biometric-bypass mechanisms, making them a usable security technology.

Electronic

Electronic locks are devices that impede a specific function unless a code is entered. This code is compared to a stored secret, and if the correct code is entered, the lock engages the mechanical stop and allows the mechanism to open. Electronic locks have an advantage in that they are not as susceptible to mechanical manipulation and bypass, yet they are still susceptible, in many cases via the mechanism that updates the secret "combination."

Physical

Physical locks have been used for hundreds of years; their design has not changed much: a metal "token" is used to align pins in a mechanical device. Physical locks have survived for years because they are low cost. Because all mechanical devices have tolerances, it is possible to sneak through these tolerances by "picking" the lock. Most locks can be easily picked with simple tools, some of which are shown in Figure 15-3.

Humans are always trying to build a better mousetrap, and that applies to locks as well. High-security locks, such as the one shown in Figure 15-4, have been designed to defeat attacks; these locks are more sophisticated than a standard home deadbolt system. Typically found in commercial applications that require high security, these locks are made to resist picking and drilling, as well as other common attacks such as simply

Figure 15-4 A high-security lock and its key

pounding the lock through the door. Another common feature of high-security locks is key control, which refers to the restrictions placed on making a copy of the key. For most residential locks, a trip to the hardware store will allow you to make a copy of the key. Key control locks use patented keyways that can only be copied by a locksmith, who will keep records on authorized users of a particular key.

High-end lock security is more important now that attacks such as "bump keys" are well known and widely available. A bump key is a key cut with all notches to the maximum depth, also known as "all nines." This key uses a technique that has be around a long time but has recently gained a lot of popularity. The key is inserted into the lock and then sharply struck, bouncing the lock pins up above the shear line and allowing the lock to open. High-security locks attempt to prevent this type of attack through various mechanical means such as nontraditional pin layout, sidebars, and even magnetic keys.

Combination locks, which work via a rotating dial, are common on high-end safes and can raise the security level substantially. In many cases, the only way to bypass one of these locks is to physically bypass the lock itself through drilling or other methods. Additional levels of safeguard exist, such as shatter plates, which when broken engage pins that prevent the door from opening.

Cable Locks

Portable equipment has a principal feature of being portable. This can also be a problem, as portable equipment—laptops, projectors, and the like—can be easily removed or stolen. *Cable locks* provide a simple means of securing portable equipment to furniture or another fixture in the room where the equipment resides. Cable locks can be used by road warriors to secure laptops from casual theft. They also can be used in open areas such as conference centers or rooms where portable equipment is exposed to a wide range of visitors.

USB Data Blocker

USB connectors on computers offer a pathway for data to enter into the system. Anyone who has physical access to a machine can plug in a USB device and execute code from the device. There are a variety of ways to block USB ports or render them inoperable, but in some cases, the USB port serves a secondary function as a power source for external devices. The USB connection has four conductors: two for power and two for data. If you block the data conductors, you can still charge your device from a USB source without giving that device any access to the data. When charging your phone in locations such as airports, or other unknown power sources, the use of a *USB data blocker* protects the phone but allows it to charge.

EXAM TIP A USB data blocker prevents attackers from infecting a device with malware or stealing data. Also remember that turning off the AutoPlay setting in the operating system will prevent malicious code from automatically running when you plug in a USB or other external media device.

Lighting

Proper *lighting* is essential for physical security. Unlit or dimly lit areas allow intruders to lurk and conduct unauthorized activities without a significant risk of observation by guards or other personnel. External building lighting is important to ensure that unauthorized activities cannot occur without being observed and responded to. Internal lighting is equally important because it enables more people to observe activities and see conditions that are not correct. As described earlier in the "Bollards/Barricades" section, windows can play an important role in assisting the observation of the premises. Having sensitive areas well lit and open to observation through windows prevents activities that would otherwise take place in secret. Unauthorized parties in server rooms are more likely to be detected if the servers are centrally located, surrounded in windows, and well lit.

Fencing

Fencing serves as a physical barrier around property. It can serve to keep people out or in, preventing the free movement across unauthorized areas. Fencing can be an important part of a physical security plan. Properly employed, it can help secure areas from unauthorized visitors. Outside of the building's walls, many organizations prefer to have a perimeter fence as a physical first layer of defense. Chain-link-type fencing is most commonly used, and it can be enhanced with barbed wire along the top. Anti-scale fencing, which looks like very tall vertical poles placed close together to form a fence, is used for high-security implementations that require additional scale and tamper resistance.

Inside a building, fencing can be used to provide a means of restricting entry into areas where separate physical security policies apply. Material storage, servers, networking gear, and other sensitive items can be separated from unauthorized access with simple chain link fences. These areas are typically called a *cage,* and entry/exit to the caged areas is via a *gate.* The gate allows controlled access and makes it easier to monitor who and what enters and leaves the controlled area. Gates are used for external fencing as well. Gates offer a monitoring point for ingress and egress from a controlled area.

Fire Suppression

According to the Fire Suppression Systems Association (www.fssa.net), 43 percent of businesses that close as a result of a significant fire never reopen. An additional 29 percent fail within three years of the event. The ability to respond to a fire quickly and effectively is thus critical to the long-term success of any organization. Addressing potential fire hazards and vulnerabilities has long been a concern of organizations in their risk analysis process. The goal obviously should be never to have a fire, but if one does occur, it is important to have mechanisms in place to limit the damage the fire can cause. *Fire suppression* systems are designed to provide protection against the damage from a fire that spreads in a facility. Because they are suppression systems, they don't prevent the fire from occurring per se, but they do stop it once it begins.

Water-Based Fire Suppression Systems

Water-based fire suppression systems have long been, and still are today, the primary tool to address and control structural fires. Considering the amount of electrical equipment found in today's office environment and the fact that, for obvious reasons, this equipment does not react well to large applications of water, it is important to know what to do with equipment if it does become subjected to a water-based sprinkler system. The 2017 *NFPA 75: Standard for the Protection of Information Technology Equipment* outlines measures that can be taken to minimize the damage to electronic equipment exposed to water.

Clean-Agent Fire Suppression Systems

Carbon dioxide (CO_2) has been used as a fire suppression agent for a long time. The Bell Telephone Company used portable CO_2 extinguishers in the early part of the 20th century. Carbon dioxide extinguishers attack all three necessary elements for a fire to occur. CO_2 displaces oxygen so that the amount of oxygen remaining is insufficient to sustain the fire. It also provides some cooling in the fire zone and reduces the concentration of "gasified" fuel.

Argon extinguishes fire by lowering the oxygen concentration below the 15 percent level required for combustible items to burn. Argon systems are designed to reduce the oxygen content to about 12.5 percent, which is below the 15 percent needed for the fire but is still above the 10 percent required by the EPA for human safety.

Inergen, a product of Ansul Corporation, is composed of three gases: 52 percent nitrogen, 40 percent argon, and 8 percent carbon dioxide. In a manner similar to pure argon systems, Inergen systems reduce the level of oxygen to about 12.5 percent, which is sufficient for human safety but not sufficient to sustain a fire.

Handheld Fire Extinguishers

Although computer security professionals typically do not have much influence over the type of fire suppression system that their office includes, they do need to be aware of what type has been installed, what they should do in case of an emergency, and what they need to do to recover after the release of the system. One area that they can influence, however, is the type of handheld fire extinguisher that is located in their area (see Table 15-1).

Class of Fire	Type of Fire	Examples of Combustible	Materials Example Suppression Method
A	Common combustibles	Wood, paper, cloth, plastics	Water or dry chemical
B	Combustible liquids	Petroleum products, organic solvents	CO_2 or dry chemical
C	Electrical	Electrical wiring and equipment, power tools	CO_2 or dry chemical
D	Flammable metals	Magnesium, titanium	Copper metal or sodium chloride

Table 15-1 Classes of Fires and Types of Suppression Methods

Automatic fire suppression systems designed to discharge when a fire is detected are not the only systems you should be aware of. If a fire can be caught and contained before the automatic systems discharge, it can mean significant savings to the organization in terms of both time and equipment costs (including the recharging of the automatic system). Handheld extinguishers are common in offices, but the correct use of them must be understood; otherwise, disaster can occur.

Fire Detection Devices

An essential complement to fire suppression systems and devices are fire detection devices (fire detectors). Detectors may be able to detect a fire in its very early stages, before a fire suppression system is activated, and sound a warning that potentially enables employees to address the fire before it becomes serious enough for the fire suppression equipment to kick in.

There are several different types of fire detectors. One type, of which there are two varieties, is activated by smoke. The two varieties of smoke detector are ionization and photoelectric. A photoelectric detector is good for potentially providing advance warning of a smoldering fire. This type of device monitors an internal beam of light. If something degrades the light (for example, by obstructing it), the detector assumes it is something like smoke and the alarm sounds. An ionization style of detector uses an ionization chamber and a small radioactive source to detect fast-burning fires. Shown in Figure 15-5, the chamber consists of two plates: one with a positive charge and one with a negative charge. Oxygen and nitrogen particles in the air become "ionized" (an ion is freed from the molecule). The freed ion, which has a negative charge, is attracted to the positive plate, and the remaining part of the molecule, now with a positive charge, is attracted to the negative plate. This movement of particles creates a very small electric current that the device measures. Smoke inhibits this process, and the detector will detect the resulting drop in current and sound an alarm.

Both of these devices are often referred to generically as smoke detectors, and combinations of both varieties are possible. For more information on smoke detectors, see http://home.howstuffworks.com/home-improvement/household-safety/fire/smoke2.htm. As both of these devices are triggered by the interruption of a signal, without regard to why, they can give false alarms. They are unable to distinguish the difference between the smoke from a kitchen fire and burned toast.

Figure 15-5
An ionization chamber for an ionization type of smoke detector

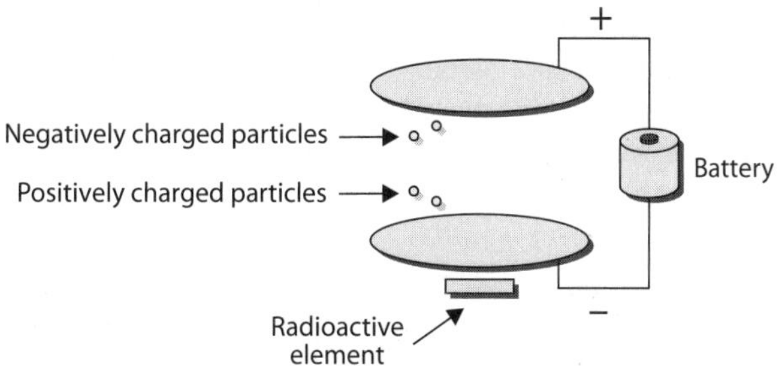

Another type of fire detector is activated by heat. These devices also come in two varieties. Fixed-temperature or fixed-point devices activate if the temperature in the area ever exceeds some predefined level. Rate-of-rise or rate-of-increase temperature devices activate when there is a sudden increase in local temperature that may indicate the beginning stages of a fire. Rate-of-rise sensors can provide an earlier warning but are also responsible for more false warnings.

A third type of detector is flame activated. This type of device relies on the flames from the fire to provide a change in the infrared energy that can be detected. Flame-activated devices are generally more expensive than the other two types but can frequently detect a fire sooner.

Sensors

One of the first items in the security equation is detection. Detection of a specific signal can then be compared to a reference as to if it is allowed or not. The sensor element provides the detection aspect to the security system, enabling decisions and resultant processes. For instance, a motion detector that is trained to detect oncoming traffic can sense someone going the wrong way in a tunnel or controlled exit space.

Motion Detection

When monitoring an area for unauthorized activity, one potentially useful tool is a *motion detector*. In areas where there is little or no expected traffic, a motion detector can alert an operator to activity in an area. Motion detectors come in a variety of types, but most are based on infrared (heat) radiation and can detect the changes of a warm body moving. They can be tuned for size, ignoring smaller movement such as small animals in outdoor settings. Although not useful in busy office buildings during normal daily use, motion detectors can be useful during off-hours, when traffic is minimal. Motion detectors can be used to trigger video systems, so they do not record large amounts of "empty" activity. Video monitoring of the loading dock area in the back of the building can be triggered in this fashion, using the motion detector to turn on cameras whenever activity is occurring.

Noise Detection

Noise detection is a sensor method that listens for specific sounds. Ordinary things can produce different sounds, and each of these can have a specific spectral signature that can be used to hear some items while ignoring others. Glass breakage has a specific sound, and sensors can be tuned to "hear" glass breakage and provide an alert when it occurs. The use of sensors that target events such as this and provide the information to a central alarm panel can greatly increase the effectiveness of security personnel in monitoring a larger facility.

Proximity Reader

Proximity readers are sensors that provide a signal at a specified distance. The most common application of these are card readers connected to doors: you "swipe" your card by placing it near the reader, and if the codes are correct, you are granted access. However, these devices have much greater utility. A series of proximity readers scattered throughout a facility can act as a reporting sensor, monitoring guards as they traverse their appointed rounds. Guards can check in to each point by interacting with the proximity reader, typically by swiping a card near the device, and the device records their presence at that spot at that time. With near field communication (NFC) and advanced Bluetooth via smartphones, the uses of proximity readers beyond just paying for things is growing exponentially. For example, proximity devices in bus stops can allow your smartphone to get an updated bus schedule. The ability to sense and communicate over short distances has almost endless possibilities.

Moisture Detection

Moisture, or water, can have significant detrimental effects on certain items. *Moisture detection* sensors provide a remote means of monitoring everything from water leaks to humidity problems. Water can cause damage to electronics, artwork, and many other items. Being able to monitor moisture levels provides the security team a means of detecting the potential for damage from items such as leaking sprinklers or water leaks. As in all sensors, the objective is to provide better "eyes and ears" for the security personnel, allowing 24/7 coverage of issues, many times in remote areas, for conditions that may require attention.

Cards

Controlling physical access to a small facility can be achieved through door locks and physical keys, but that solution is unwieldy for larger facilities with numerous people coming and going. Many organizations rely on a badging system using either *tokens* or *cards* that can be tied to automated ID checks and logging of entry/exit. This can provide much greater detail in tracking who is in a facility and when they have come and gone. Tokens and cards can provide a serialized ID for each user, enabling user-specific logging. Originally designed to augment payroll timecards, these electronic IDs have improved security through the logging of employees' in and out times. Tokens and cards offer the same function as keys, but the system can be remotely updated to manage access in real time, and users can have their privileges revoked without a company or admin having to recover the token or card.

Temperature

Temperature sensors do exactly what you'd think: they sense temperatures. Part of the physical security equation is preventing damage to the infrastructure in an organization, and servers can be an important part of that infrastructure. Server rooms are highly temperature-controlled areas, with hot and cold sides, as servers tend to generate heat, and that heat needs to be removed. Hot and cold aisles are covered in more detail in a later section in this chapter. Monitoring the current temperature in server rooms requires temperature sensors, properly placed to measure the actual temperature experienced by the servers. An analytical monitoring solution can then alert the appropriate personnel when certain temperature ranges are exceeded. In small facilities, one sensor for the entire room might be sufficient; in larger server farms, there may be a sensor per rack. In any case, the idea is the same: measure the temperature and report on exceptions.

EXAM TIP The use of sensors as part of an overall physical security solution is important. There are many things that need to be monitored, and using sensors with automation to assist the security team in seeing out-of-range conditions is important. The objective is to understand the importance of physical security, and that includes the specific details measured by sensors.

Drones

The use of *drones* has risen sharply in the past couple of years. From home/hobbyist models that can carry a small camera, to larger industrial rigs that can carry larger cameras for longer periods, these devices have revolutionized remote viewing of items. Drones are used by railroads to inspect tracks and used by electric companies to inspect power lines. Their ability to go almost anywhere and visually inspect things is a great resource. These offer interesting use cases for both offense and defense in cybersecurity, because they can be used to surveil physical facilities remotely, providing eyes on demand in a variety of places you might not want a person to go to and in a timeframe that can't be met any other way.

Visitor Logs

Physical security *visitor logs* provide the same utility as computer logs for a security investigation. They act as a record of what was observed at specific points in time. Having roving guards check in at various places across a shift via a log entry provides a record of the actual surveillance. Logs of visitors arriving and departing, equipment received and shipped out, and so forth serve as a record of the physical happenings in a facility.

Remote sensing of badges and equipment utilizing RFID tags can create an automatic log of equipment movement, including information about when, where, what, and who. Advanced capabilities such as these make inventory of movable equipment easier, as its location is tracked and it can be scanned remotely.

EXAM TIP Cameras, IR detection, motion detection, and logs are all methods associated with detection—and frequently after-the-fact detection at that. These devices and methods provide valuable attribution fact patterns, even after the actual event.

Faraday Cages

Electromagnetic interference (EMI) is an electrical disturbance that affects an electrical circuit. EMI is due to either electromagnetic induction or radiation emitted from an external source, either of which can induce currents into the small circuits that make up computer systems and cause logic upsets. EMI can plague any type of electronics, but the density of circuitry in the typical data center can make it a haven for EMI. The amount of sensitivity to an EMI field depends on a number of factors, including the length of the circuit, which can act like an antenna. EMI is grouped into two general types: narrowband and broadband. Narrowband is, by its nature, electromagnetic energy with a small frequency band and, therefore, typically sourced from a device that is purposefully transmitting in the specified band, such as a phone. Broadband covers a wider array of frequencies and is typically caused by some type of general electrical power use such as power lines or electric motors.

An example of shielding that can be employed is a *Faraday cage* or *Faraday shield,* which is an enclosure of conductive material that is grounded. This can be room-sized or built into a building's construction; the critical element is that there is no significant gap in the enclosure material. These measures can help shield EMI, especially in high-radio-frequency environments. Faraday cages can be item specific in size, so smaller systems that can encase just a single smartphone are available.

EXAM TIP When it comes to shielding, understand the difference between a Faraday cage (as a large open space) and EMI shielding on cables (very specific shielding) and which is appropriate based on what is being protected from EMI.

Air Gap

Air gap is a term used to describe the physical and logical separation of a network from all other networks. This separation is designed to prevent unauthorized data transfers to and from the network. The flaw in this logic is that users will move data by other means, such as a USB drive, to get their work done. Frequently called "sneaker net," this unauthorized bypassing of the air gap, although ostensibly for the purpose of mission accomplishment, increases system risk because it also bypasses checks, logging, and other processes important in development and deployment.

Screened Subnet

The concept of a screened subnet (previously known as a demilitarized zone [DMZ]) comes from military parlance where it represents an area that is not "owned" by either side. This concept is used in networking to indicate a zone where access controls are not as strict as the inside, or as open as the outside; it's a place of joint cooperation and controlled risk. This same concept works in physical structures, where the lobby is like the outside world and anyone can enter, then there are common hallways where employees mingle, and finally there are special offices and server rooms where access is tightly controlled. The common work areas are akin to the DMZ—an area of controlled risk.

Protected Cable Distribution

Cable runs between systems need to be protected from physical damage to the cables and subsequent communication failures. This is accomplished by *protected distribution/protected cabling* during the cable installation. This may be something as simple as metal tubes or as complex a concrete pipes to run buried cables. The objective is to prevent any physical damage to the physical layer portion of the system. Protected distribution/protected cabling provides physical safeguards to the cabling between systems, from all physical hazards, including interception and tapping. Shielding cables, such as shielded twisted pair cables, are designed to prevent electromagnetic interference from affecting the signals on the wires in the cable. The protection of entire systems is covered in the earlier section "Faraday Cages."

Secure Areas

Secure areas are those areas where specific preventative measures are taken to control access both to and from. Like many other physical security constructs, there is a wide range of levels for secure areas. From those created by a simple locked door, to those with special procedures and guards, secure areas can be tailored to the security needs of an enterprise. The overall idea behind a secure area is to limit information and people flow in and out of the area, and when it is permitted it is under the proper level of control. Transport Security Administration (TSA) creates a secure area when you go to an airport by allowing only certain materials and people to pass the checkpoint.

Air Gap

As previously mentioned, the term *air gap* is used to refer to a system where there is no direct connection to outside systems. An air-gapped network does not have a connection to outside networks. An air gap for a network extends to all physical connections, wired and wireless, and exists to protect a computer or network from outside influences or to keep data from leaving the system. Seemingly simple in principle, it is much harder in practice. If a system is air gapped, how does data get in? What do you do with the results? How do you maintain the system, provide updates, and so on? In practice, when air gaps are used, they have to be monitored for connections that occur around them, ensuring the system remains isolated.

EXAM TIP CompTIA lists air gap twice in Objective 2.7, so consider yourself warned. An air gap is a security measure implemented to ensure that systems within a secure network are totally isolated (not connected) from an unsecure network such as the Internet.

Vault

A *vault* is a secured area that is designed to provide a specific level of security for what is stored inside. This can be a physical space, with specific safeguards such as walls that cannot be penetrated and doors that can be secured. A vault is a larger item than most safes, typically room sized. For example, a bank vault is used to store large sums of money and other valuables.

Safe

Safes are physical storage devices that are intended to impede unauthorized access to their protected contents. Safes come in a wide variety of shapes, sizes, and costs. The higher the level of protection from the physical environment, the better the level of protection against unauthorized access. Safes are not perfect; in fact, they are rated in terms of how long they can be expected to protect the contents from theft or fire. The better the rating, the more expensive the safe.

There are times when a safe is overkill, providing a higher level of security than is really needed. A simpler solution is *secure cabinets* and *enclosures*. Secure cabinets and enclosures provide system owners a place to park an asset until its use. Most secure cabinets/enclosures do not offer all of the levels of protection that one gets with a safe, but they can be useful, especially when the volume of secure storage is large.

Secure enclosures can provide security against some forms of physical access, as in users, yet still provide the proper environmental controls and setting necessary for operation. Safes cannot typically provide these levels of controls.

Hot and Cold Aisles

The trend toward smaller, denser servers means more servers and devices per rack, putting a greater load on the cooling systems. This encourages the use of a hot aisle/cold aisle layout. A data center that is arranged into *hot and cold aisles* dictates that all the intake fans on all equipment face the cold aisle and that the exhaust fans all face the opposite aisle. The HVAC system is then designed to push cool air underneath the raised floor and up through perforated tiles on the cold aisle. Hot air from the hot aisle is captured by return air ducts for the HVAC system. The use of this layout is designed to control airflow, with the purpose being never to mix the hot and cold air. This requires the use of blocking plates and side plates to close open rack slots. The benefits of this arrangement are that cooling is more efficient and can handle higher density.

NOTE Understanding airflow allows you to understand hot and cold aisles. Cold air is produced by the HVAC equipment, and this cold air is sent to servers. The servers shed their heat, making air hot, which is removed. The aisles keep the hot air from mixing with the cold air, making the cooling efficient. You wouldn't leave a door open in summer with the air conditioning on, would you?

EXAM TIP Understand and be able to explain the importance of secure areas such as air gap, vault, safe, hot aisle, and cold aisle.

Secure Data Destruction

When data is no longer being used, whether it be on old printouts, old systems being discarded, or broken equipment, it is important to destroy the data before losing physical control over the media it is on. Many criminals have learned the value of dumpster diving to discover information that can be used in identity theft, social engineering, and other malicious activities. An organization must concern itself not only with paper trash, but also the information stored on discarded objects such as computers. Several government organizations have been embarrassed when old computers sold to salvagers proved to contain sensitive documents on their hard drives. It is critical for every organization to have a strong disposal and destruction policy and related procedures. This section covers *data destruction and media sanitization* methods.

Burning

Burning is considered one of the gold-standard methods of data destruction. Once the storage media is rendered into a form that can be destroyed by fire, the chemical processes of fire are irreversible and render the data lost forever. The typical method is to shred the material, even plastic discs and hard drives (including SSDs), and then put the shred in an incinerator and oxidize the material back to base chemical forms. When the material is completely combusted, the information that was on it is gone.

Shredding

Shredding is the physical destruction by tearing an item into many small pieces, which can then be mixed, making reassembly difficult if not impossible. Important papers should be shredded, and *important* in this case means anything that might be useful to a potential intruder or dumpster diver. It is amazing what intruders can do with what appears to be innocent pieces of information. Shredders come in all sizes, from little desktop models that can handle a few pages at a time, or a single CD/DVD, to industrial versions that can handle even phone books and multiple discs at the same time. The ultimate in industrial shredders can even shred hard disk drives, metal case and all. Many document destruction companies have larger shredders on trucks that they bring to their client's location and do on-site shredding on a regular schedule.

Pulping

Pulping is a process by which paper fibers are suspended in a liquid and recombined into new paper. If you have data records on paper, and you shred the paper, the pulping process removes the ink by bleaching, and recombines all the shred into new paper, completely destroying the physical layout of the old paper.

Pulverizing

Pulverizing is a physical process of destruction using excessive physical force to break an item into unusable pieces. Pulverizers are used on items like hard disk drives, destroying the platters in a manner that they cannot be reconstructed. A more modern method of pulverizing the data itself is the use of encryption. The data on the drive is encrypted and the key itself is destroyed. This renders the data nonrecoverable based on the encryption strength. This method has unique advantages of scale; a small business can pulverize its own data, whereas it would either need expensive equipment or a third party to pulverize the few disks it needs to destroy each year.

Degaussing

A safer method for destroying files on magnetic storage devices (that is, magnetic tape and hard drives) is to destroy the data magnetically, using a strong magnetic field to degauss the media. *Degaussing* realigns the magnetic particles, removing the organized structure that represented the data. This effectively destroys all data on the media. Several commercial degaussers are available for this purpose.

Purging

Data *purging* is a term that is commonly used to describe methods that permanently erase and remove data from a storage space. The key phrase is "remove data," for unlike deletion, which just destroys the data, purging is designed to open up the storage space for reuse. A circular buffer is a great example of an automatic purge mechanism. It stores a given number of data elements and then the space is reused. If a circular buffer holds 64 MB, for example, once it is full, it overwrites the oldest material as new material is added to the buffer.

Third-Party Solutions

Like many other elements of a security program, there are contractors that sell data destruction as a service. These vendors can take advantage of scale, increasing the capability while sharing the cost of equipment. However, this also introduces a new form of data loss, through the use of the third party that has access to the data before destruction. And, as with all third-party relationships, what counts is what is in the contract. Therefore, a good security review of the particulars in the contract is warranted, not just for legal issues but also technical ones.

EXAM TIP This section covers several methods of data/media destruction, a couple of which are used together. Learn the details of each method and look for nonsense answer choices to narrow down the possible correct answers, such as options that refer to pulping non-paper items or degaussing nonmagnetic media.

Chapter Review

In this chapter, you became acquainted with the principles of physical security controls, including environmental controls. The chapter began by discussing bollards/barricades, signage, cameras, CCTV, and industrial camouflage—all items designed to restrict, guide, or monitor physical movement. From there the chapter moved into security guards, robot sentries, locks, lighting, sensors, drones/UAVs, and protected distribution for cables. These elements further refine restrictions on movement and the ability to access system components. The chapter then examined Faraday cages, air gap, and DMZ. Secure areas including vaults, safes, hot aisles, and cold aisles were also covered.

The chapter closed with an examination of secure data destruction methods, including burning, shredding, degaussing, and third-party solutions.

Questions

To help you prepare further for the CompTIA Security+ exam, and to test your level of preparedness, answer the following questions and then check your answers against the correct answers at the end of the chapter.

1. Why is physical security important to protecting data?
   - **A.** Physical access to data will negate the security advantages of the cloud.
   - **B.** Information resides on physical assets, linking physical and information security.
   - **C.** Social engineering can negate any information security controls.
   - **D.** None of the above.
2. Why is proper interior and exterior lighting important?
   - **A.** It can detect people who are where they don't belong.
   - **B.** It shows who is in a restricted space.
   - **C.** It allows more people and activities to be observed.
   - **D.** It is needed for the use of closed-circuit television cameras.
3. Your organization has experienced multiple incidents of graffiti tagging and people loitering in the parking lot despite the chain-link fence surrounding it. What is the best solution to the issue?
   - **A.** "No Trespassing" signage
   - **B.** More guard stations
   - **C.** Additional external lighting
   - **D.** Changing the chain-link fencing to anti-scale fencing
4. After a physical security incident, what critical data can security guards commonly provide?
   - **A.** Employee ID information
   - **B.** Access logs of who has entered and exited the building
   - **C.** Alarm codes
   - **D.** Blueprints showing unmonitored areas of the building

5. Alarms are effective only if which of the following is true?
   A. They alert on abnormal conditions.
   B. Every entrance is monitored with a sensor.
   C. They are not tied to the information systems.
   D. They are tuned to provide accurate and useful alerts.
6. You are implementing a test lab at your organization for early alpha software development. To prevent any of the development code from inadvertently getting put on production computers, what should you implement?
   A. Air gap
   B. Strict firewalls
   C. Protected distribution
   D. Patch management
7. What is the security benefit of a Faraday cage?
   A. Prevents attack by EMP
   B. Prevents accessing a device using a wireless network or cell connection
   C. Works better than anti-scale fencing
   D. Prevents stack overflows by EMI
8. What is an example of a human-based screened subnet (DMZ)?
   A. A visitor's lobby that is separated from a company office by a receptionist
   B. Hallways between the company lobby and offices
   C. A server room with a locked door
   D. The networking cabinets in the facility
9. What is a primary problem with biometrics?
   A. Technically, biometrics are difficult to implement.
   B. The human body changes over time.
   C. Biometrics are easily faked.
   D. Biometrics can't be loaned or delegated.
10. What should you do to protect your IP-based CCTV system from a DDoS attack?
   A. Reconfigure your firewalls.
   B. Connect it to an intrusion detection system.
   C. Require multifactor authentication to access the CCTV system.
   D. Place all CCTV components on a separate network.

Answers

1. **B.** Information resides on physical assets, linking physical security with the security of information.
2. **C.** Proper lighting allows more people and activities to be observed.
3. **D.** A change from chain-link fencing to anti-scale fencing to prevent intruders from climbing the fence is the best solution.
4. **B.** Guards commonly have logs of who has entered and exited a building.
5. **D.** Alarms are effective only if they are tuned to provide accurate and useful alerting information.
6. **A.** A lab environment can be air gapped from the rest of the network to prevent software from being accidentally copied to production machines.
7. **B.** A Faraday cage can prevent accessing a device via radio frequency waves, either from a wireless network or cell radio.
8. **B.** The lobby is part of the outside environment, so the hallways are the better choice. Server rooms and networking rooms are the more secured spaces.
9. **B.** Some biometric features can change over time, or medical conditions can make them less reliable, thus forcing a re-identification phase to resync a user and their biometric.
10. **D.** The CCTV system should be on a completely separate network, air gapped if possible, with only security personnel having access.

CHAPTER 16

Cryptographic Concepts

In this chapter, you will

- Identify the different types of cryptography
- Learn about current cryptographic methods
- Understand how cryptography is applied for security
- Given a scenario, utilize general cryptography concepts
- Compare and contrast basic concepts of cryptography

Cryptography is the science of *encrypting*, or hiding, information—something people have sought to do since they began using language. Although language allowed them to communicate with one another, people in power attempted to hide information by controlling who was taught to read and write. Eventually, more complicated methods of concealing information by shifting letters around to make the text unreadable were developed. These complicated methods are cryptographic algorithms, also known as ciphers. The word *cipher* comes from the Arabic word *sifr*, meaning empty or zero.

Certification Objective This chapter covers CompTIA Security+ exam objective 2.8: Summarize the basics of cryptographic concepts.

General Cryptographic Concepts

Historical ciphers were simple to use and also simple to break. Because hiding information continued to be important, more advanced transposition and substitution ciphers were required. As systems and technology became more complex, ciphers were frequently automated by some mechanical or electromechanical device. A famous example of a modern encryption machine is the German Enigma machine from World War II. This machine used a complex series of substitutions to perform encryption, and interestingly enough, it gave rise to extensive research in computers.

When setting up a cryptographic scheme, it is important to use proven technologies. Proven cryptographic libraries and cryptographically correct random number generators are the foundational elements associated with a solid program. Homegrown or custom elements in these areas can greatly increase risk associated with a broken system. Developing your own cryptographic algorithms is beyond the abilities of most groups.

Algorithms are complex and difficult to create. Any algorithm that has not had public review can have weaknesses. Most good algorithms are approved for use only after a lengthy test and public review phase.

When material, called *plaintext*, needs to be protected from unauthorized interception or alteration, it is encrypted into *ciphertext*. This is done using an algorithm and a key, and the rise of digital computers has provided a wide array of algorithms and increasingly complex keys. The choice of specific algorithm depends on several factors, which will be examined in this chapter.

NOTE This chapter introduces many names, acronyms, and details that all work together to define cryptographic basics. The layout of the chapter is aligned with the Security+ objective, which makes lookup easier, but it means some terms will be described later in the chapter. You are advised to do a quick read through the chapter to learn where everything is and then read it again for content, knowing where topics are if you need to look them up.

Fundamental Methods

Modern cryptographic operations are performed using both an algorithm and a key. The choice of algorithm depends on the type of cryptographic operation that is desired. The subsequent choice of key is then tied to the specific algorithm. Cryptographic operations include encryption for the protection of confidentiality, hashing for the protection of integrity, digital signatures to manage nonrepudiation, and a bevy of specialty operations such as key exchanges.

While the mathematical specifics of these operations can be very complex and are beyond the scope of this level of material, the knowledge to properly employ them is not complex and is subject to being tested on the CompTIA Security+ exam. Encryption operations are characterized by the quantity and type of data, as well as the level and type of protection sought. Integrity protection operations are characterized by the level of assurance desired. Data is characterized by its usage: data in transit, data at rest, or data in use. It is also characterized in how it can be used, either in block form or stream form, as described next.

EXAM TIP The terms *data in transit*, *data at rest*, and *data in use* are industry-standard terms. In the Security+ objectives, such as 2.1 under "Data protection," slightly different terms are used. Security+ uses *at rest, in transit/motion*, and *in processing*. It is important to recognize and use the exam-specific terms on the exam.

Digital Signatures

A *digital signature* is a cryptographic implementation designed to demonstrate authenticity and identity associated with a message. Using public key cryptography, a digital signature allows traceability to the person signing the message through the use of their private key. The addition of hash codes allows for the assurance of integrity of the message as

Figure 16-1 Digital signature operation

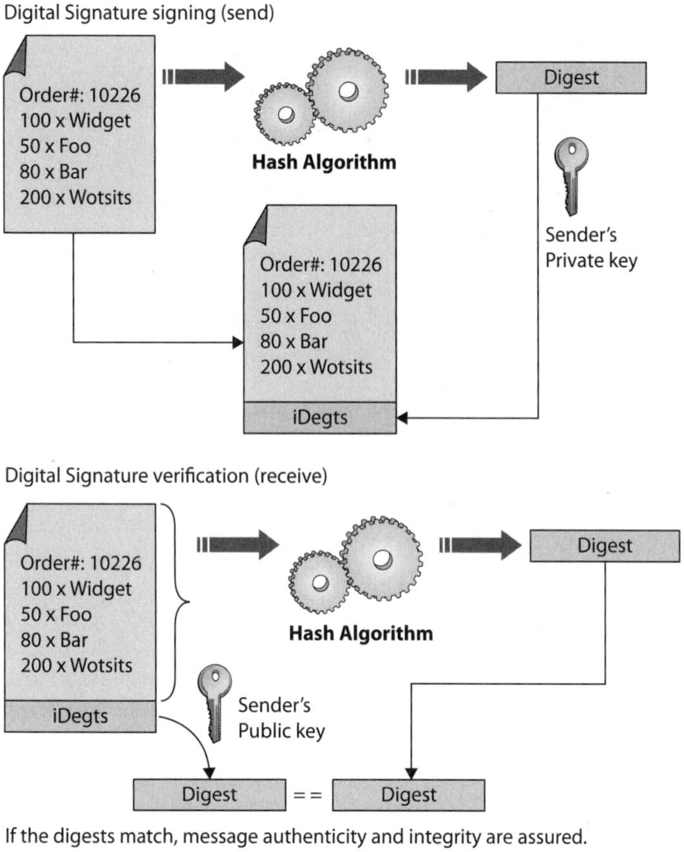

well. The operation of a digital signature is a combination of cryptographic elements to achieve a desired outcome. The steps involved in digital signature generation and use are illustrated in Figure 16-1. The message to be signed is hashed, and the hash is encrypted using the sender's private key. Upon receipt, the recipient can decrypt the hash using the sender's public key. If a subsequent hashing of the message reveals an identical value, two things are known: First, the message has not been altered. Second, the sender possessed the private key of the named sender and is therefore presumably the same person.

A digital signature does not by itself protect the contents of the message from interception. The message is still sent in the clear, so if confidentiality of the message is a requirement, additional steps must be taken to secure the message from eavesdropping. This can be done by encrypting the message itself, or by encrypting the channel over which it is transmitted.

EXAM TIP Know that a digital signature guarantees that the contents of a message have not been altered while in transit.

Key Length

The strength of a cryptographic function typically depends upon the strength of a key, where a larger key has more entropy and adds more strength to the encryption. Because different algorithms use different methods with a key, direct comparison of key strength between different algorithms is not easily done. Some cryptographic systems have fixed key lengths, such as Triple Digital Encryption Standard (3DES), while others, such as Advanced Encryption Standard (AES), have multiple lengths (for example, AES-128, AES-192, and AES-256).

Some algorithms offer choices in key lengths: as a general rule, a longer key length is more secure, but also will take longer to compute. With regard to finding the right balance between security and usability, here are some recommended minimum key lengths:

- Symmetric key lengths of at least 80 to 112 bits.
- Elliptic curve key lengths of at least 160 to 224 bits.
- RSA key lengths of at least 2048 bits. In particular, the CA/Browser Forum Extended Validation (EV) Guidelines require a minimum key length of 2048 bits.
- DSA key lengths of at least 2048 bits.

NOTE Cryptography is a discipline filled with acronyms; they are used for algorithms, methods, and processes. This may seem intimidating, but after a couple passes through the chapter, they will become more familiar to you.

Key Stretching

Key stretching is a mechanism that takes what would be weak keys and "stretches" them to make the system more secure against brute-force attacks. As computers have gained computational power, hash functions can be computed very quickly, leading to a need for a manner of increasing the workload when computing hashes; otherwise, an attacker can merely compute them all. In the case of a short key, the chance of randomly matching the hash function by use of computational guessing attacks has increased. To make matching the hash more difficult, one must increase the keyspace or slow down the computation. Key stretching involves increasing the computational complexity by adding iterative rounds of computations—rounds that cannot be done in parallel. When one wants to use a brute-force attack, the increase in computational workload becomes significant when done billions of times, making this form of attack much more expensive.

Salting

To provide sufficient entropy for low-entropy inputs to hash functions, a high-entropy piece of data can be concatenated with the material being hashed. The term *salt* refers to this initial data piece. Salts are particularly useful when the material being hashed is short and low in entropy. The addition of a high-entropy (say, a 30-character) salt to a three-character password greatly increases the entropy of the stored hash.

NOTE Entropy is an important term in cryptography; it refers to the level of randomness. Entropy will be covered in greater detail later in the chapter.

Another term used in this regard is *initialization vector*, or *IV*, and this is used in several ciphers, particularly in the wireless space, to achieve randomness, even with normally deterministic inputs. IVs can add randomness and are used in block ciphers to initiate modes of operation.

NOTE Initialization vectors will be covered in more detail in Chapter 4, "Network Attack Indicators." A *nonce* is a number used only once, and is similar to a salt, or an IV. However, because it is only used once, if it is needed again, a different value is used. Nonces provide random nondeterministic entropy into cryptographic functions and are commonly used in stream ciphers to break stateful properties when the key is reused.

Hashing

Hashing functions are commonly used encryption methods. A *hashing function* is a special mathematical function that performs one-way encryption, which means that once the algorithm is processed, there is no feasible way to use the ciphertext to retrieve the plaintext that was used to generate it. Also, ideally, there is no feasible way to generate two different plaintexts that compute to the same hash value. Figure 16-2 shows a generic hashing process.

Common uses of hashing algorithms are to store computer passwords and to ensure message integrity. The idea is that hashing can produce a unique value that corresponds to the data entered, but the hash value is also reproducible by anyone else running the same algorithm against the data. So you could hash a message to get a *message authentication code (MAC)*, and the computational number of the message would show that no intermediary has modified the message. This process works because hashing methods are typically public, and anyone can hash data using the specified method. It is computationally simple to generate the hash, so it is simple to check the validity or integrity of something by matching the given hash to one that is locally generated. HMAC, or

Figure 16-2
How hashes work

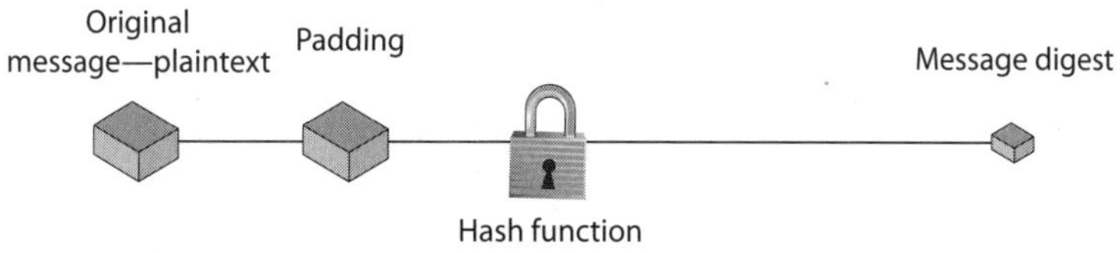

Hash-based Message Authentication Code, is a special subset of hashing technology. It is a hash algorithm applied to a message to make a MAC, but it is done with a previously shared secret. So, the HMAC can provide integrity simultaneously with authentication.

A hash algorithm can be compromised with what is called a *collision attack,* in which an attacker finds two different messages that hash to the same value. This type of attack is very difficult and requires generating a separate algorithm that will attempt to find a text that will hash to the same value of a known hash. This must occur faster than simply editing characters until you hash to the same value, which is a type of brute-force attack. The consequence of a hash function that suffers from collisions is that integrity is lost. If an attacker can make two different inputs purposefully hash to the same value, she might trick people into running malicious code and cause other problems. Popular hash algorithms are the Secure Hash Algorithm (SHA) series, the RIPEMD algorithms, and the Message Digest (MD) hash of varying versions (MD2, MD4, and MD5).

EXAM TIP Remember that a hash function is a special mathematical function that performs one-way encryption.

Hashing functions are very common, and they play an important role in the way information, such as passwords, is stored securely and the way in which messages can be signed. By computing a digest of the message, less data needs to be signed by the more complex asymmetric encryption, and this still maintains assurances about message integrity. This is the primary purpose for which the protocols were designed, and their success will allow greater trust in electronic protocols and digital signatures.

Key Exchange

Cryptographic mechanisms use both an algorithm and a key, with the key requiring communication between parties. In symmetric encryption, the secrecy depends on the secrecy of the key, so insecure transport of the key can lead to failure to protect the information encrypted using the key. *Key exchange* is the central foundational element of a secure symmetric encryption system. Maintaining the secrecy of the symmetric key is the basis of secret communications. In asymmetric systems, the key exchange problem is one of key publication. Because public keys are designed to be shared, the problem is reversed from one of secrecy to one of publicity.

EXAM TIP With symmetric encryption the message to be protected is encrypted and decrypted using the same secret key. Asymmetric encryption uses two separate keys to encrypt and decrypt the message.

Early key exchanges were performed by trusted couriers. People carried the keys from senders to receivers. One could consider this form of key exchange to be the ultimate in *out-of-band* communication. With the advent of digital methods and some mathematical algorithms, it is possible to pass keys in a secure fashion. This can occur even when all packets are subject to interception. The Diffie-Hellman key exchange is one example of this type of secure key exchange. The Diffie-Hellman key exchange depends on two random numbers, each chosen by one of the parties and kept secret. Diffie-Hellman key exchanges can be performed *in-band,* and even under external observation, as the secret random numbers are never exposed to outside parties.

Elliptic Curve Cryptography

Elliptic curve cryptography (ECC) works on the basis of elliptic curves. An *elliptic curve* is a simple function that is drawn as a gently looping curve on the *X, Y* plane. Elliptic curves are defined by this equation:

$$y^2 = x^3 + ax^2 + b$$

Elliptic curves work because they have a special property—you can add two points on the curve together and get a third point on the curve.

For cryptography, the elliptic curve works as a public key algorithm. Users agree on an elliptic curve and a fixed curve point. This information is not a shared secret, and these points can be made public without compromising the security of the system. The security of elliptic curve systems has been questioned, mostly because of lack of analysis. However, all public key systems rely on the difficulty of certain math problems. It would take a breakthrough in math for any of the mentioned systems to be weakened dramatically, but research has been done about the problems and has shown that the elliptic curve problem has been more resistant to incremental advances. Again, as with all cryptography algorithms, only time will tell how secure ECC implementations really are.

The big benefit of ECC systems is that they require less computing power for a given bit strength. This makes ECC ideal for use in low-power mobile devices. The surge in mobile connectivity has brought secure voice, e-mail, and text applications that use ECC and AES algorithms to protect a user's data.

EXAM TIP Elliptic curve cryptography can be used in several ways, including in a key exchange and a digital signature. Security+ has three acronyms you need to know in this area: ECC for elliptic curve cryptography, ECDHE for Elliptic Curve Diffie-Helman Ephemeral, and ECDSA for Elliptic Curve Digital Signatures Algorithm. It is important to have a working knowledge of the terms in the Security+ glossary.

Perfect Forward Secrecy

Perfect forward secrecy (PFS) is a property of a public key system in which a key derived from another key is not compromised, even if the originating key is compromised in the future. This is especially important in session key generation, where future communication sessions may become compromised; if perfect forward secrecy were not in place, then past messages that had been recorded could be decrypted.

Quantum Cryptography

Quantum cryptography is the use of quantum computing hardware to perform encryption and decryption processes. Quantum hardware is still in its early stages of development, and the immense computing power in these platforms will revolutionize cryptography. Most of the issues associated with quantum cryptography are still theoretical, as machines with sufficient power and programmability have yet to be constructed. But, like all technology races, when the ability to hack encryption with quantum machines arrive, new methods of encrypting using the same types of hardware will restore the balance between encryption strength and the ability to hack it.

Quantum principles have already been deployed into communication-related key exchanges through quantum key distribution (QKD). QKD does not actually encrypt communication but rather provides a means for users to securely distribute keys that are used for encrypting the communication channel.

NOTE Quantum computing will make changes in both computing and communications. In computing, quantum methods promise solutions to currently unsolvable problems. In communications, quantum methods offer new means of security, including key distribution, which is already available via quantum key distribution.

Quantum computing is one of the frontiers of computing and involves the creation of a whole new type of computer. Quantum computers use a new structure called *qubits,* which allow information to be represented differently than just "on" or "off" as binary bits do. In a fashion, qubits enable multiple paths of a problem to be computed simultaneously. Quantum computing is more than just hardware; it involves new forms of software, and there is significant development in this area as well. Recently, scientists have claimed to surpass conventional computing power with a quantum machine, but before you get all excited, this was not a general-purpose machine, but one dedicated to solving only a single, specific problem. In spite of all of the current limitations, quantum computing will bring significant breakthroughs in computing in the future.

Post-Quantum Era

As quantum computing presents a challenge for many of today's cryptographic algorithms, significantly reducing their strength, there is a movement to develop algorithms that are not easily solved via quantum methods. This is not a theoretical exercise, as government agencies and others have been working on practical solutions to have answers and substitute algorithms should any existing algorithm fail, whether by quantum computing or other problem.

There are currently several cryptographic algorithms that have been developed in response to quantum methods and are believed to be resistant to quantum computing–based decryption methods to a reasonable level. These methods use different mathematical properties, making simultaneous solution sets not as effective, thus limiting the power of quantum computing in solving this type of problem. As with all systems, there are trade-offs, and in this case the newer methods tend to use longer keys and require more computational power to employ.

Ephemeral Keys

Ephemeral keys are cryptographic keys that are used only once after generation. When an ephemeral key is used as part of the Diffie-Hellman scheme, it forms an Ephemeral Diffie-Hellman (EDH) key exchange. An EDH generates a temporary key for each connection, never using the same key twice. This provides for perfect forward secrecy. If this is constructed using an elliptic curve algorithm, it would be ECDHE, for Elliptic Curve Diffie-Helman Ephemeral, as mentioned previously.

EXAM TIP Ephemeral keys are cryptographic keys that are used only once after generation.

Modes of Operation

In symmetric or block algorithms, there is a need to deal with multiple blocks of identical data to prevent multiple blocks of cyphertext that would identify the blocks of identical input data. There are multiple methods of dealing with this, called *modes of operation.* The basic premise is to use some source of entropy before encrypting subsequent blocks so that identical blocks of plaintext produce differing blocks of ciphertext. These modes can be broken into three groups: authenticated, unauthenticated, and counter.

Authenticated

Authenticated encryption with associated data (AEAD) is a form of encryption designed to provide both confidentiality and authenticity services. A wide range of authenticated modes is available for developers, including GCM, OCB, and EAX.

NOTE Why do you need authenticated encryption? To protect against chosen ciphertext attacks such as POODLE, you need a second layer using a MAC implementation such as HMAC-SHA. This is done using the following steps:

- Compute the MAC on the ciphertext, not the plaintext.
- Use different keys: one for encryption and a different one for the MAC.

This specific, yet generic prescription adds steps and complications for developers. To resolve this, special modes for block ciphers called authenticated encryption (AE) and authenticated encryption with associated data (AEAD) were devised. These provide the same protection as the block cipher/MAC combination, but in a single function with a single key. AE(AD) modes were developed to make solutions easier for implementations, but adoption has been slow.

OCB is *Offset Codebook Mode,* a patented implementation that offers the highest performance, but because of patents, it's not included in any international standards. EAX solves the patent problem, but likewise has not been adopted by any international standards. This leaves GCM (Galois Counter Mode), which is described in the next section.

Counter

Counter mode (CTM) uses a "counter" function to generate a nonce that is used for each block encryption. Different blocks have different nonces, enabling parallelization of processing and substantial speed improvements. The sequence of operations is to take the counter function value (nonce), encrypt it using the key, then XOR it with plaintext. Each block can be done independently, resulting in the ability to multithread the processing. Note that CTM is also abbreviated as CTR in some circles.

CCM is a mode of operation involving CBC (cipher block chaining, described in the next section) with a MAC, or CBC-MAC. This method was designed for block ciphers with a length of 128 bits, where the length of the message and any associated data must be known in advance. This means it is not an "online" form of AEAD, which is characterized as allowing any length of input.

Galois Counter Mode (GCM) is an extension of CTM in that there's an addition of a Galois mode of authentication. This adds an authentication function to the cipher mode, and the Galois field used in the process can be parallelized, providing efficient operations. GCM is employed in many international standards, including IEEE 802.1ad and 802.1AE. NIST has recognized AES-GCM as well as GCM and GMAC. AES GCM cipher suites for TLS are described in IETF RFC 5288.

Unauthenticated

Unauthenticated modes use a non-identity-based source for the entropy element for subsequent blocks. In cipher block chaining (CBC), each block is XORed with the previous ciphertext block before being encrypted. To obfuscate the first block, an initialization vector (IV) is XORed with the first block before encryption. CBC is one of the most common modes used, but it has two major weaknesses. First, because there is a dependence on previous blocks, the algorithm cannot be parallelized for speed and efficiency. Second, because of the nature of the chaining, a plaintext block can be recovered from two adjacent blocks of ciphertext. An example of this is in the POODLE (Padding Oracle On Downgraded Legacy Encryption) attack on TLS. This type of padding attack works because a one-bit change to the ciphertext causes complete corruption of the corresponding block of plaintext and inverts the corresponding bit in the following block of plaintext, but the rest of the blocks remain intact.

Blockchain

Blockchains are lists of records, where each addition to the list is done by a cryptographic algorithm. While this may seem complex, it serves an important purpose: records in a blockchain are resistant to modification. This permits a distributed ledger that can record transactions and have both verification of additions and protection with respect to integrity. The strength of the integrity comes from both the signing of records and the distributed nature of the blockchain. While a record can be altered, it would require all records after it to also be altered, and thus would be detectable across the copies on the distributed storage of the chain. So, while records are technically alterable, in practicality the system is provably secure.

The concept of blockchains was invented to create the public transaction ledger of cryptocurrencies. A *cryptocurrency* is a currency system built on a finite set of "rare" numbers that are mined and then "created." As there is no central authority, numbers when mined are entered into the distributed ledger, marking their creation. All transactions are also entered into the ledger, preventing double-spending of the tokens. The use of the distributed public ledger provides the protections that physical tokens provide—only one person can control a given currency token at any given time, and all transactions are immutable.

NOTE While cryptocurrencies such as Bitcoin get the headlines, the true winner in blockchain technology has been the implementation of distributed public ledgers. *Public ledgers* have been used to resolve many challenging problems in tracking financial transactions, supply chains, and other ledger-based issues. Application for items such as music royalties, DNS systems, and tracking food from farm to table are all examples of blockchain technology solutions under development.

EXAM TIP Blockchain is the recordkeeping technology behind Bitcoin. It is a distributed and decentralized public record.

Cipher Suites

The term *cipher suite* refers to a set of algorithms used together in cryptography, with the most famous being the TLS cipher suite (see https://www.iana.org/assignments/tls-parameters/tls-parameters.xhtml). These combinations are predetermined to facilitate ease of application via TLS connection; rather than having to specify and agree on each parameter, a single number can represent a complete cipher set. The cipher suite will list the key exchange mechanism, the authentication protocol, the block/stream cipher, and message authentication.

Block

Block ciphers operate on input data in a series of blocks. In the TLS cipher suite, in TLS 1.2, several block ciphers are available, including AES, 3DES, and IDEA. With the introduction of TLS 1.3, this list is substantially trimmed to only ciphers that can support AEAD operations. This removes the CBC versions of AES. The implementation of AEAD schemes closes a series of potential loopholes that had been attacked in the past.

Stream

Stream ciphers operate on streams of data instead of blocks. Stream operations typically take place on a single byte at a time, using an XOR function and a pseudorandom key. The challenge is to produce a long pseudorandom string of bytes that can be used to both encrypt and decrypt the stream. Specific stream algorithms, such as A5 and RC4, have been used for years, but weaknesses have led to newer algorithms such as ChaCha20 and the use of AES-GCM in a key stream mode.

EXAM TIP A block cipher encrypts plaintext one block at a time. A stream cipher encrypts one byte at a time.

Symmetric vs. Asymmetric

Both symmetric and asymmetric encryption methods have their advantages and disadvantages. Symmetric encryption tends to be faster, is less computationally involved, and is better for bulk transfers. But it suffers from a key management problem in that keys must be protected from unauthorized parties. Asymmetric methods resolve the key secrecy issue with public keys, but they add significant computational complexity, which makes them less suited for bulk encryption.

Bulk encryption can be done using the best of both systems, by using asymmetric encryption to pass a symmetric key. By adding in ephemeral key exchange, you can achieve perfect forward secrecy, discussed earlier in the chapter. Digital signatures, a highly useful tool, are not practical without asymmetric methods. Table 16-1 compares symmetric and asymmetric methods.

EXAM TIP Know the differences between symmetric and asymmetric encryption. Symmetric uses one key, and it is faster but less secure. Asymmetric uses two keys, and it is slower but more secure.

Measure	Symmetric Encryption	Asymmetric Encryption
Primary use	Bulk encryption of large quantities	Exchanging of symmetric keys
Number of keys used	1; the same key encrypts and decrypts.	2; one key can encrypt, the other decrypts.
Common algorithms	AES, 3DES, RCA, IDEA	DSA, RSA, El Gamal, ECC, Diffie-Hellman
Pros	Fast. Can be used for large quantities of data.	Can be used without sharing a common secret. Used to exchange keys for symmetric encryption.
Cons	The common key that needs to be shared; if it is lost, protection is lost.	Slower, not good for large quantities of data.

Table 16-1 Comparison of Symmetric and Asymmetric Encryption

It is common for symmetric and asymmetric encryption to be used together. For instance, when you go to a website that is TLS protected (HTTPS), you need to exchange a symmetric key with the web server to protect the communication channel. This is done via asymmetric encryption methods, as they can create a secure key exchange between parties without the need for a predetermined common secret. This is used to exchange the symmetric key that then is used to encrypt and decrypt data, securing the communication channel. Another common joint usage of cryptographic elements is in digital signatures. Asymmetric encryption elements provide authentication services (that is, proof of who a sender is and nonrepudiation). The key, being small, is handled by asymmetric methods. The message, being large, is handled by the symmetric key and symmetric method, which is suited for bulk encryption. Understanding the differences and use of each type, including hashing, is important both for the exam and in the practice of security.

Lightweight Cryptography

In a world where computing devices gain power with every iteration of the CPU, it is hard to imagine the need for less compute-intensive cryptography. Enter the world of the Internet of Things (IoT), where small, portable, energy- and compute-resource-constrained devices abound. These devices are small, cheap, and number in the hundreds of millions to billions. They have a need to communicate securely and manage functions such as authentication. *Lightweight cryptography* is a specialized suite of cryptographic algorithms designed to operate in this resource-constrained environment.

Entire suites of lightweight algorithms designed for 8-bit processors have been developed, including hash functions, block and stream ciphers, and even asymmetric and signing functions. NIST has driven significant research in recent years, and an ISO/IEC standard series, ISO/IEC 29192, covers the methods and details.

Steganography

Steganography, an offshoot of cryptography technology, gets its meaning from the Greek word *steganos,* meaning covered. Invisible ink placed on a document and hidden by innocuous text is an example of a steganographic message. Another example is a tattoo placed on the top of a person's head, visible only when the person's hair is shaved off.

Hidden writing in the computer age relies on a program to hide data inside other data. The most common application is the concealing of a text message in a picture file. The Internet contains multiple billions of image files, allowing a hidden message to be located almost anywhere without being discovered. The nature of the image files also makes a hidden message difficult to detect. While it is most common to hide messages inside images, they can also be hidden in video and audio files.

The advantage to steganography over cryptography is that the messages do not attract attention, and this difficulty in detecting the hidden message provides an additional barrier to analysis. The data that is hidden in a steganographic message is frequently also encrypted, so should it be discovered, the message will remain secure. Steganography has many uses, but the most publicized uses are to hide illegal material, often pornography, or allegedly for covert communication by terrorist networks. While there is no direct evidence to support that terrorists use steganography, the techniques have been documented in some of their training materials.

Steganographic encoding can be used in many ways and through many different media. Covering them all is beyond the scope of this book, but we will discuss one of the most common ways to encode into an image file: *LSB encoding*. LSB, which stands for least significant bit, is a method of encoding information into an image while altering the actual visual image as little as possible. A computer image is made up of thousands or millions of pixels, all defined by 1s and 0s. If an image is composed of RGB (Red Green Blue) values, each pixel has an RGB value represented numerically from 0 to 255. For example, 0,0,0 is black, and 255,255,255 is white, which can also be represented as 00000000, 00000000, 00000000 for black and 11111111, 11111111, 11111111 for white. Given a white pixel, editing the least significant bit of the pixel to 11111110, 11111110, 11111110 changes the color. The change in color is undetectable to the human eye, but in an image with a million pixels, this creates a 125KB area in which to store a message.

Hidden content can be embedded in virtually any encoded data stream, where coding is used to represent the digital version of an image, an audio stream, or a video stream. Encoding the hidden information in aspects of the actual signal in a manner that unnoticeably alters the fidelity of the original signal is what provides the covert channel. To better protect the data from analysis, an encryption pass is made on the covert data, making the covert data to be embedded look like noise, which further protects the channel from simple discovery.

Homomorphic Encryption

One of the primary purposes of cryptography is to prevent unauthorized access to data. This is important for data at rest and data in transit, but it can be an issue for data in use. Data that is encrypted while stored or being moved is protected from observation or alteration by unauthorized parties. But this also forces authorized parties to perform decryption steps before performing computations, followed by additional re-encryption steps after computations, which represents a significant penalty for use. Enter the world of homomorphic encryption. *Homomorphic encryption* is a set of algorithms that allows operations to be conducted on encrypted data, without decrypting and re-encrypting. The concept is simple: create a system that allows operations on ciphertext that, when decrypted, will have the same result as if the operation was performed on plaintext.

Most of the operations associated with homomorphic-encrypted data involve work on numbers—specifically integers in the form of addition. While this may seem to be a limitation, it is a huge advance, as much of the data that is "changed" in systems is in fact numbers, or values in databases. What's more, if the number can be added to, then with multiple rounds of addition, multiplication can be achieved, and by using negative numbers, subtraction can be achieved. This makes the use of homomorphic methods valuable for many transactional-based systems.

Common Use Cases

Cryptographic services are being employed in more and more systems, and many common use cases are associated with them. Examples include implementations to support situations such as low power, low latency, and high resiliency, as well as supporting functions such as confidentiality, integrity, and nonrepudiation.

Low-Power Devices

Low-power devices, such as mobile phones and portable electronics, are commonplace, and these devices have needs for cryptographic functions. Cryptographic functions tend to take significant computational power, and special cryptographic functions, such as elliptic curve cryptography, are well suited for low-power applications.

Low-Latency Operations

Some use cases involve low-latency operations, which makes specialized cryptographic functions needed to support operations that have extreme time constraints. Stream ciphers are examples of low-latency operations.

High-Resiliency Systems

High-resiliency systems are characterized by functions that have the ability to resume normal operational conditions after an external disruption. The use of cryptographic modules can support resiliency through a standardized implementation of cryptographic flexibility.

Support for Confidentiality

Protecting data from unauthorized reading is the definition of confidentiality. Cryptography is the primary means of protecting data confidentiality—at rest, in transit, and in use.

Support for Integrity

Times arise when the integrity of data is needed (for instance, during transfers). Integrity can demonstrate that data has not been altered. Message authentication codes (MACs) supported by hash functions are an example of cryptographic services supporting integrity.

Support for Obfuscation

There are times when information needs to be obfuscated—that is, protected from causal observation. In the case of a program, obfuscation can protect the code from observation by unauthorized parties.

Supporting Authentication

Authentication is a property that deals with the identity of a party—be it a user, a program, or a piece of hardware. Cryptographic functions can be employed to demonstrate authentication, such as the validation that an entity has a specific private key associated with a presented public key, thus proving identity.

Support for Nonrepudiation

Nonrepudiation is a property that deals with the ability to verify that a message has been sent and received so that the sender (or receiver) cannot refute sending (or receiving) the information. An example of this in action is seen with the private key holder relationship. It is assumed that the private key never leaves the possession of the private key holder. Should this occur, it is the responsibility of the holder to revoke the key. Thus, if the private key is used, as evidenced by the success of the public key, then it is assumed that the message was sent by the private key holder. Thus, actions that are signed cannot be repudiated by the holder.

EXAM TIP Remember that nonrepudiation is the ability to verify that a message has been sent and received so that the sender (or receiver) cannot refute sending (or receiving) the information.

EXAM TIP Understanding the different common use cases and being able to identify the applicable use case given a scenario is a testable element associated with this section's objective.

Limitations

When you're examining the options for implementing cryptographic solutions, a wide range of constraints or limitations can become an issue. How much processing power, how much data, and what form of data (block or stream) are all important to consider. Also important to consider is how these choices impact or limit the effectiveness of your solution, such as how long your solution can protect data. There are several key issues to understand, such as speed, size, weak key implications, and more. These are described in the following sections.

Speed

Encryption and decryption speed can be an issue with various forms of communication. The more complex the algorithm, the more rounds that are performed and the stronger the encryption, but the slower the throughput. Computational efficiency is an important benchmark in modern cryptography and has led to algorithms such as ChaCha20 gaining favor, as it has a significant speed advantage over AES.

Size

In cryptography, size does matter, and this is related to key size. The bigger the key, the more data that can be throughput and the stronger the encryption. Size comes with a trade-off: speed. Longer keys take longer to generate, and the more rounds a system operates, the longer the time to encrypt/decrypt. So size is a means of approximating strength, at a cost of speed. This trade-off is a major consideration in developing algorithms for practical implementation.

Weak Keys

Cryptographic strength is a function of the algorithm strength and the strength of the key. As mentioned earlier, key length can be an important element in the strength of a cryptographic solution. But there is also the issue of weak keys, or keys that, despite length, for a given algorithm result in weaker encryption.

For some algorithms there are cases of key values that result in weaker encryption. A key value of all zeros, or all ones, is just another key value in the set of all possible values, but numbers such as these or those with patterns may cause weaknesses. A perfect algorithm would have no weak key values, but not all algorithms share this desired trait. Currently DES, RC4, IDEA, Blowfish, and GMAC algorithms can suffer from weak keys. Understanding the issue and eliminating the use of weak keys as part of the implementation of a specific algorithm is an important safeguard.

Time

Nothing lasts forever, even in cryptography. Given enough time, any encryption can be broken—one must simply try all the keys. This is referred to as a brute-force attack. So the objective of cryptography is to protect data for a long-enough period that brute-force decryption is not a factor in the security equation. With modern encryption algorithms such as AES, and conventional (non-quantum) computing, the time to brute force the problem is beyond human life spans, so the systems are considered secure. Older methods, such as DES, have proven to no longer provide long protection times due to modern computing speeds.

Longevity

The longevity of an encryption scheme must be measured not in today's computing ability, but in light of the increases in computing abilities over the expected protection time desired by the encryption. If we want to protect materials for the next 25 years, we need to consider what computing power will be available in the next 25 years—a challenge given advances in quantum computing. While we can accurately predict the raw computing power of current computing platforms for decades, new methods such as quantum computing call these predictions into question. This has led the drive behind government agencies working on next-generation encryption schemes that will be resistant to quantum computing efforts.

Predictability

The key element that makes cryptographic functions strong is a randomness function that eliminates any form of predictability. The use of cryptographic random numbers is important, as it removes the predictability problem of pseudorandom number generators. Computers will perform operations in a reproducible manner: given the same inputs, you get the same outputs. When it comes to creating random numbers, the sequence of random numbers produced by an algorithm will typically be reproducible, and while it may look random, statistically speaking, it really isn't because knowing one of the numbers will enable you to know later numbers in the sequence. This makes the use of a cryptographical random number generator crucial to the success of cryptographic solutions, as it removes the element of predictability.

Reuse

Reusing cryptographic keys is a sure way to result in failure. The more material that an attacker can get using the same key, the greater his ability to use cryptanalysis tools to break the scheme. This is how the Enigma and Purple machines failed during WWII. There are several built-in mechanisms to help prevent these problems. In block encryption, introducing a variable element of data between identical blocks prevents simple cryptanalysis. One name for this is an initialization vector (IV), which is a structural method of introducing randomness. It is important to use a long IV value so it doesn't repeat, as the repeated use of the IV over a series of messages was the primary cause of the failure of WEP. The use of ephemeral keys is another example of preventing reuse of a cryptographic element as ephemeral keys are used only once.

Entropy

The level or amount of randomness is referred to as *entropy*. Entropy is the measure of uncertainty associated with a series of values. Perfect entropy equates to complete randomness, such that given any string of bits, there is no computation to improve guessing the next bit in the sequence. A simple "measure" of entropy is in bits, where the bits are the power of 2, which represents the number of choices. Therefore, 2048 options would represent 11 bits of entropy. In this fashion, one can calculate the entropy of passwords and measure how "hard" they are to guess. There are specific mathematical formulas that can estimate entropy, and these provide a means of measuring the true randomness associated with a digital item.

EXAM TIP A lack of good entropy may leave a cryptosystem vulnerable and unable to securely encrypt data.

Computational Overhead

Different algorithms have differing means of computing the complexity that makes cryptographic solutions secure. One of the limitations of a cryptographic system is the level of computational overhead needed to generate the system. This concept has driven systems such as elliptic curve cryptographic systems, where the computations are based on addition, as opposed to RSA systems, which are based on large-number multiplication. As with all trade-offs, there are different advantages to each system, so they are not universally interchangeable, and computational overhead is one of many factors that must be considered when developing a solution.

Resource vs. Security Constraints

When using cryptography for protection of data, several factors need to be included in the implementation plan. One of the first decisions is in algorithm selection. Not only should you avoid deprecated algorithms, but you also need to match the algorithm to the intended use. This includes things like the resources available—is it an embedded system with low computing power or a server with dedicated cryptographic hardware? How much protection is needed? What is the data throughput rate? All of these factors need to be considered when weighing the selection of cryptographic solutions, as resources are seldom unlimited and security considerations can greatly vary.

Weak/Deprecated Algorithms

Over time, cryptographic algorithms fall to different attacks or just the raw power of computation. The challenge with these algorithms is understanding which ones have fallen to attacks and may yet still be available for use in software libraries, resulting in their inappropriate application in use. Although this list will continue to grow, it is important to consider this topic, because old habits die hard. The use of hash algorithms such as MD5 should be considered inappropriate, as manufactured collisions have been achieved. Even newer hash functions, such as SHA-1 and SHA-256, have issues because they are suspect to forced collisions. The Data Encryption Standard (DES), and its commonly used stronger form 3DES, have fallen from favor. The good news is that new forms of these functions are widely available, and in many cases, such as with AES and ChaCha20, they are computationally efficient, providing better performance.

EXAM TIP Understanding the different limitations of cryptographic solutions and being able to identify the implications given a use case scenario is a testable element associated with this section's objective.

Chapter Review

In this chapter, you became acquainted with the basics of cryptography. The chapter opened with a discussion of cryptographic concepts, followed by an examination of the topics of digital signatures, key length, key stretching, salting, hashing, key exchange, elliptic curve cryptography, perfect forward secrecy, quantum computing, and the post-quantum era. The chapter continued with the concepts of ephemeral elements, modes of operation for block ciphers, blockchains, and cipher suites. An examination of symmetric vs. asymmetric schemes, lightweight cryptography, steganography, and homomorphic encryption was presented. The chapter concluded with topics associated with common use cases and the limitations of cryptographic systems.

Questions

To help you prepare further for the CompTIA Security+ exam, and to test your level of preparedness, answer the following questions and then check your answers against the correct answers at the end of the chapter.

1. If you need to perform operations such as addition on encrypted elements, what type of encryption scheme would you use?
   - **A.** Asymmetric
   - **B.** Homomorphic
   - **C.** Stream
   - **D.** Lightweight
2. Which of the following is *not* a limitation associated with cryptographic solutions?
   - **A.** Speed
   - **B.** Computational overhead
   - **C.** Longevity
   - **D.** Entropy
3. What set of algorithms is designed for low-power devices such as the Internet of Things and embedded systems?
   - **A.** Lightweight
   - **B.** Hashing
   - **C.** Stream
   - **D.** Blockchain
4. How do you make a short secret, such as a password, become long enough for use?
   - **A.** Salting
   - **B.** Key elongation
   - **C.** Key stretching
   - **D.** Ephemeral operations
5. What is the best way to get the plaintext from a hash value?
   - **A.** Use linear cryptanalysis.
   - **B.** Use a reverse hash function.
   - **C.** You cannot get the plaintext out of a hash value.
   - **D.** Use an ephemeral key.

6. What does a salt provide?
   A. It tells the algorithm how many digits of primes to use.
   B. It primes the algorithm by giving it initial noncritical data.
   C. It adds additional rounds to the cipher.
   D. It provides additional entropy.
7. What makes a digitally signed message different from an encrypted message?
   A. The digitally signed message has encryption protections for integrity and nonrepudiation.
   B. The digitally signed message uses much stronger encryption and is harder to break.
   C. The encrypted message only uses symmetric encryption.
   D. There is no difference.
8. Steganography is commonly accomplished using which method?
   A. Encryption
   B. Initialization vectors (IVs)
   C. LSB encoding
   D. Entropy substitution
9. To prevent the loss of a single message due to accidental decryption from affecting other encrypted messages, which of the following properties is needed?
   A. Stream encryption
   B. Perfect forward secrecy
   C. Entropy
   D. Obfuscation
10. Given a large quantity of data in the form of a streaming video file, what is the best type of encryption method to protect the content from unauthorized live viewing?
   A. Symmetric block
   B. Hashing algorithm
   C. Stream cipher
   D. Asymmetric block

Answers

1. **B.** Homomorphic schemes allow computations on encrypted elements.
2. **D.** Entropy is a measure of randomness, not a limitation of a cryptographic solution.

3. **A.** Lightweight encryption algorithms are designed for resource-constrained systems.
4. **C.** Key stretching is a mechanism that takes what would be weak keys and "stretches" them to make the system more secure.
5. **C.** Hash ciphers are designed to reduce the plaintext to a small value and are built to not allow extraction of the plaintext. This is why they are commonly called "one-way" functions.
6. **D.** The salt adds additional entropy, or randomness, to the encryption key, specifically providing separation between equal inputs such as identical passwords on different accounts.
7. **A.** The digital signature includes a hash of the message to supply message integrity and uses asymmetric encryption to demonstrate nonrepudiation (the fact that the sender's private key was used to sign the message).
8. **C.** LSB, or least significant bit, is designed to place the encoding into the image in the least significant way to avoid altering the image.
9. **B.** Perfect forward secrecy (PFS) is a property of a public key system in which a key derived from another key is not compromised even if the originating key is compromised in the future.
10. **C.** Stream ciphers work best when the data is in very small chunks to be processed rapidly, such as live streaming video. Block ciphers are better when it comes to large chunks of data.

PART III

Implementation

CHAPTER 17

Secure Protocols

In this chapter, you will

- Learn to implement secure protocols for given scenarios
- Explore use cases for secure protocols

Protocols enable communication between components, independent of vendor, and act as a language that specifies how communications are to be conducted and what can be communicated. As is true of many communications technologies, protocols have both secure and nonsecure versions. This chapter examines common protocols that can be secured and their use cases.

Certification Objective This chapter covers CompTIA Security+ exam objective 3.1: Given a scenario, implement secure protocols.

This exam objective is a good candidate for performance-based questions, which means you should expect questions in which you must apply your knowledge of the topic to a scenario. The best answer to a question will depend on specific details in the scenario preceding the question, not just the question itself. The question may also involve tasks other than just picking the best answer from a list. Instead, it may involve actual simulation of steps to take to solve a problem.

Protocols

Protocols act as a common language, allowing different components to talk using a shared, known set of commands. Secure protocols are those that have built-in security mechanisms so that, by default, security can be enforced via the protocol. Many different protocols exist, all of which are used to achieve specific communication goals.

EXAM TIP During the exam, you should expect to be asked to implement common protocols and services when given a basic scenario. Pay very close attention to the protocol details and port numbers covered throughout this chapter!

Domain Name System Security Extensions (DNSSEC)

The Domain Name System (DNS) is a protocol for the translation of names into IP addresses. When a user enters a name such as www.example.com, DNS converts this name into the actual numerical IP address. DNS records are also used for e-mail delivery. The DNS protocol uses UDP over port 53 for standard queries, although TCP can be used for large transfers such as zone transfers. DNS is a hierarchical system of servers, ranging from local copies of records up through Internet providers to root-level servers. DNS is one of the primary underlying protocols used on the Internet and is involved in almost all addressing lookups. The problem with DNS is that requests and replies are sent in plaintext and are subject to spoofing.

DNSSEC (Domain Name System Security Extensions) is a set of extensions to the DNS protocol that, through the use of cryptography, enables origin authentication of DNS data, authenticated denial of existence, and data integrity but does not extend to availability or confidentiality. DNSSEC records are signed so that all DNSSEC responses are authenticated but not encrypted. This prevents unauthorized DNS responses from being interpreted as correct. Authenticated denial of existence also allows a resolver to validate that a certain domain name does not exist.

Data transfers over UDP port 53 are limited to 512 bytes in size, and DNSSEC packets can be larger. For this reason, DNSSEC typically uses TCP port 53 for its work. It is possible to extend UDP packet size to 4096 to cope with DNSSEC, and this is covered in RFC 2671.

EXAM TIP DNSSEC validates DNS data, thus providing integrity, but it does not provide controls for availability or confidentiality.

SSH

The *Secure Shell (SSH)* protocol is an encrypted remote terminal connection program used for remote connections to a server. SSH uses asymmetric encryption but generally requires an independent source of trust with a server, such as manually receiving a server key, to operate. SSH uses TCP port 22 as its default port.

EXAM TIP SSH uses public key cryptography for secure remote terminal access and was designed as a secure replacement for Telnet.

Secure/Multipurpose Internet Mail Extensions (S/MIME)

MIME (Multipurpose Internet Mail Extensions) is a standard for transmitting binary data via e-mail. E-mails are sent as plaintext files, and any attachments need to be encoded so as to fit the plaintext format. MIME specifies how this is done with Base64 encoding. Because it is plaintext, there is no security associated with the attachments; they can be seen by any machine between sender and receiver. *S/MIME (Secure/Multipurpose Internet*

Mail Extensions) is a standard for public key encryption and signing of MIME data in e-mails. S/MIME is designed to provide cryptographic protections to e-mails and is built into the majority of modern e-mail software to facilitate interoperability.

EXAM TIP Remember that S/MIME is the standard for e-mail encryption. It provides authentication, message integrity, and nonrepudiation in e-mails.

Secure Real-time Transport Protocol (SRTP)

The *Secure Real-time Transport Protocol (SRTP)* is a network protocol for securely delivering audio and video over IP networks. SRTP uses cryptography to provide encryption, message authentication and integrity, and replay protection to the Real-time Transport Protocol (RTP) data.

Lightweight Directory Access Protocol over SSL (LDAPS)

Lightweight Directory Access Protocol (LDAP) is the primary protocol for transmitting directory information. Directory services may provide any organized set of records, often with a hierarchical structure, and are used in a wide variety of situations, including Active Directory (AD) datasets. By default, LDAP traffic is transmitted insecurely. You can make LDAP traffic secure by using it with SSL/TLS, known as *LDAP over SSL (LDAPS)*. Commonly, LDAP is enabled over SSL/TLS by using a certificate from a trusted certificate authority (CA).

LDAPS uses an SSL/TLS tunnel to connect LDAP services. Technically, this method was retired with LDAPv2 and replaced with Simple Authentication and Security Layer (SASL) in LDAPv3. SASL (which is not listed in the exam objectives) is a standard method of using TLS to secure services across the Internet.

EXAM TIP LDAPS communication occurs over port TCP 636. LDAPS communication to a global catalog server occurs over TCP 3269. When connecting to port 636 or 3269, SSL/TLS is negotiated before any LDAP traffic is exchanged.

File Transfer Protocol, Secure (FTPS)

File Transfer Protocol, Secure (FTPS) is the implementation of FTP over an SSL/TLS secured channel. This supports complete FTP compatibility, yet provides the encryption protections enabled by SSL/TLS. FTPS uses TCP port 989 (data connection port) and port 990 (control connection port). As SSL has been deprecated, under RFC 7568, now only TLS is used in FTPS.

SSH File Transfer Protocol (SFTP)

SSH File Transfer Protocol (SFTP) is the use of FTP over an SSH channel. This leverages the encryption protections of SSH to secure FTP transfers. Because of its reliance on SSH, SFTP uses TCP port 22.

Simple Network Management Protocol, Version 3 (SNMPv3)

The *Simple Network Management Protocol, version 3 (SNMPv3)* is a standard for managing devices on IP-based networks. SNMPv3 was developed specifically to address the security concerns and vulnerabilities of SNMPv1 and SNMPv2. SNMP is an application-layer protocol, part of the IP suite of protocols, and can be used to manage and monitor devices, including network devices, computers, and other devices connected to the IP network. All versions of SNMP require ports 161 and 162 to be open on a firewall.

EXAM TIP If presented with a network device management scenario, remember the only secure version of SNMP is SNMPv3.

Hypertext Transfer Protocol over SSL/TLS (HTTPS)

Hypertext Transfer Protocol Secure (HTTPS) is the use of SSL or TLS to encrypt a channel over which HTTP traffic is transmitted. Because of issues with all versions of SSL, only TLS is recommended for use. HTTPS uses TCP port 443 and is the most widely used method to secure HTTP traffic.

Secure Sockets Layer (SSL) is a deprecated application of encryption technology developed for transport-layer protocols across the Web. This protocol used public key encryption methods to exchange a symmetric key for use in confidentiality and integrity protection as well as authentication. The last version, v3, is outdated, having been replaced by the IETF standard *TLS*. All versions of SSL have been deprecated due to security issues, and in the vast majority of commercial servers employing SSL/TLS, SSL has been retired. Because of the ubiquity of the usage of the term SSL, it will last for quite a while, but in function, encryption is now done via TLS.

Transport Layer Security (TLS) is an IETF standard for the employment of encryption technology and replaces SSL. Using the same basic principles, TLS updates the mechanisms employed by SSL. Although sometimes referred to as SSL, it is a separate standard. The standard port for SSL and TLS is undefined because it depends on what the protocol being protected uses; for example, port 80 for HTTP becomes port 443 when it is for HTTPS.

EXAM TIP HTTPS is used for secure web communications. Using port 443, it offers integrity and confidentiality.

IPSec

IPSec is a set of protocols developed by the IETF to securely exchange packets at the network layer (layer 3) of the OSI model (RFCs 2401–2412). Although these protocols work only in conjunction with IP networks, once an IPSec connection is established, it is possible to tunnel across other networks at lower levels of the OSI model. The set of security services provided by IPSec occurs at the network layer of the OSI model, so higher-layer protocols, such as TCP, UDP, Internet Control Message Protocol (ICMP), Border Gateway Protocol (BGP), and the like, are not functionally altered by the implementation of IPSec services.

The IPSec protocol series has a sweeping array of services it is designed to provide, including but not limited to access control, connectionless integrity, traffic-flow confidentiality, rejection of replayed packets, data security (encryption), and data origin authentication. IPSec has two defined modes—transport and tunnel—that provide different levels of security. IPSec also has three modes of connection: host-to-server, server-to-server, and host-to-host.

It is possible to use both methods at the same time, such as using transport within one's own network to reach an IPSec server, which then tunnels to the target server's network, connecting to an IPSec server there, and then using the transport method from the target network's IPSec server to the target host. IPSec uses the term *security association (SA)* to describe a unidirectional combination of specific algorithm and key selection to provide a protected channel. If the traffic is bidirectional, two SAs are needed and can in fact be different.

Authentication Header (AH) / Encapsulated Security Payload (ESP)

IPSec uses two protocols to provide traffic security:

- Authentication Header (AH)
- Encapsulating Security Payload (ESP)

IPSec does not define specific security algorithms, nor does it require specific methods of implementation. IPSec is an open framework that allows vendors to implement existing industry-standard algorithms suited for specific tasks. This flexibility is key in IPSec's ability to offer a wide range of security functions. IPSec allows several security technologies to be combined into a comprehensive solution for network-based confidentiality, integrity, and authentication. IPSec uses the following:

- Diffie-Hellman (RFC 3526) and ECDH (RFC 4753) key exchange between peers on a public network
- Public key signing of Diffie-Hellman key exchanges to guarantee identity and avoid man-in-the-middle attacks
- Cryptographic algorithms defined for use with IPsec:
  - HMAC-SHA1/SHA2 for integrity protection and authenticity
  - TripleDES-CBC for confidentiality
  - AES-CBC for confidentiality
  - AES-GCM for providing confidentiality and authentication together efficiently
  - ChaCha20 + Poly1305 for providing confidentiality and authentication together efficiently

- Authentication algorithms:
  - RSA
  - ECDSA (RFC 4754)
  - PSK (RFC 6617)
- Digital certificates to act as digital ID cards between parties

To provide traffic security, two header extensions have been defined for IP datagrams. The *AH*, when added to an IP datagram, ensures the integrity of the data and also the authenticity of the data's origin. By protecting the nonchanging elements in the IP header, the AH protects the IP address, which enables data origin authentication. The *ESP* provides security services for the higher-level protocol portion of the packet only, not the IP header.

EXAM TIP IPSec *AH* protects integrity, but it does not provide privacy because only the header is secured. IPSec *ESP* provides confidentiality, but it does not protect integrity of the packet. To cover both privacy and integrity, both headers can be used at the same time.

AH and ESP can be used separately or in combination, depending on the level and types of security desired. Both also work with the transport and tunnel modes of IPSec protocols.

Tunnel/Transport

The *transport* mode encrypts only the data portion of a packet, thus enabling an outsider to see source and destination IP addresses. The transport mode protects the higher-level protocols associated with a packet and protects the data being transmitted but allows knowledge of the transmission itself. Protection of the data portion of a packet is referred to as content protection.

Tunnel mode provides encryption of source and destination IP addresses as well as of the data itself. This provides the greatest security, but it can be done only between IPSec servers (or routers) because the final destination needs to be known for delivery. Protection of the header information is known as context protection.

EXAM TIP In *transport mode* (end-to-end), security of packet traffic is provided by the endpoint computers. In *tunnel mode* (portal-to-portal), security of packet traffic is provided between endpoint node machines in each network and not at the terminal host machines.

Post Office Protocol (POP) / Internet Message Access Protocol (IMAP)

Post Office Protocol (POP) / Internet Message Access Protocol (IMAP) refers to POP3 and IMAP4, respectively, using ports 110 for POP3 and 143 for IMAP. When POP and

IMAP are sent over an SSL/TLS session, secure POP3 utilizes TCP port 995 and secure IMAP4 uses TCP port 993. Encrypted data from the e-mail client is sent to the e-mail server over an SSL/TLS session. With the deprecation of SSL, TLS is the preferred protocol today. If e-mail connections are started in nonsecure mode, the STARTTLS directive tells the clients to change to the secure ports.

The other mail protocol, Simple Mail Transfer Protocol (SMTP), uses a variety of ports, depending on usage. SMTP servers' default port is TCP port 25. Mail clients use SMTP typically only when communicating with a mail relay server, and then they use TCP port 587 or, when SSL/TLS encrypted, TCP port 465 (RFC 8314).

EXAM TIP IMAP uses port 143, but secure IMAP4 uses port 993. POP3 uses port 110, but secure POP3 uses port 995.

EXAM TIP SMTP between servers is TCP port 25, but when clients are involved, it is TCP port 587 or, if encrypted, TCP port 465.

Use Cases

Protocols enable parties to have a common understanding of how communications will be handled, and they define the expectations for each party. Since different use cases have different communication needs, different protocols are used in different use cases. Various IETF working groups have been working to standardize some general-purpose security protocols, ones that can be reused over and over instead of inventing new ones for each use case. SASL, introduced earlier in the chapter, is an example of such an effort; SASL is a standardized method of invoking a TLS tunnel to secure a communication channel. This method is shown to work with a wide range of services—currently more than 15 and increasing.

This section examines some common use cases and the associated secure protocols used in them.

EXAM TIP This section covers how the various protocols are used in different use cases. Given a use case on the exam, you need to be able to identify the correct protocol(s) as well as be able to do the same in reverse: identify use cases for a given protocol.

Voice and Video

Voice and *video* are frequently streaming media and, as such, have their own protocols for the encoding of the data streams. To securely transfer this material, you can use the Secure Real-time Transport Protocol (SRTP), which securely delivers audio and video over IP networks. SRTP is covered in RFC 3711 (https://tools.ietf.org/html/rfc3711).

EXAM TIP Remember that SRTP is a secure version of RTP. It is often used for VoIP as well as multimedia application streaming.

Time Synchronization

Network Time Protocol (NTP) is the standard for *time synchronization* across servers and clients. NTP is transmitted over UDP port 123. NTP has no assurance against a man-in-the-middle attack, and although this has raised concerns over the implications, to date, nothing has been done to secure NTP directly, or to engineer an out-of-band security check. If you are hypersensitive to this risk, you could enclose all time communications using a TLS tunnel, although this is not an industry practice.

E-mail and Web

E-mail and the *Web* are both native plaintext-based systems. As discussed previously in this chapter, HTTPS, which relies on SSL/TLS, is used to secure web connections. Use of HTTPS is widespread and common. Keep in mind that SSL is no longer considered secure. E-mail is a bit more complicated to secure, and the best option is via S/MIME, also discussed previously in this chapter.

File Transfer

Secure *file transfer* can be accomplished via a wide range of methods, ensuring the confidentiality and integrity of file transfers across networks. FTP is not secure, but as previously discussed, SFTP and FTPS are secure alternatives that can be used.

Directory Services

Directory services use LDAP as the primary protocol. When security is required, LDAPS is a common option, as described previously. Directory services are frequently found behind the scenes with respect to logon information.

Remote Access

Remote access is the means by which users can access computer resources across a network. Securing remote access can be done via many means—some for securing the authentication process and others for the actual data access itself. As with many situations that require securing communication channels or data in transit, organizations commonly use SSL/TLS to secure remote access. Depending on the device being accessed, a variety of secure protocols exist. For networking equipment, such as routers and switches, SSH is the secure alternative to Telnet. For servers and other computer connections, access via VPN, or use of IPSec, is common.

Domain Name Resolution

Domain name resolution is performed primarily by the DNS protocol. DNS is a plaintext protocol and the secure version, DNSSEC, is not widely deployed as yet. For local deployments, DNSSEC has been available in Windows Active Directory domains since 2012. From an operational perspective, both TCP and UDP port 53 can be used for DNS, with the need of firewall protection between the Internet and TCP port 53 to prevent attackers from accessing zone transfers.

Routing and Switching

Routing and *switching* are the backbone functions of networking in a system. Managing the data associated with networking is the province of SNMPv3. SNMPv3 enables applications to manage data associated with networking and devices. Local access to the boxes may be accomplished by Telnet, although for security reasons SSH should be used instead.

Network Address Allocation

Managing *network address allocation* functions in a network requires multiple decision criteria, including the reduction of complexity and the management of device names and locations. SNMPv3 has many functions that can be employed to manage the data flows of this information to management applications that can assist administrators in network assignments.

IP addresses can be allocated either statically, which means manually configuring a fixed IP address for each device, or via DHCP, which allows for the automation of assigning IP addresses. In some cases, a mix of static and DHCP is used. IP address allocation is part of proper network design, which is crucial to the performance and expandability of a network. Learn how to properly allocate IP addresses for a new network—and know your options if you run out of IP addresses.

EXAM TIP The past several use cases are related but different. Pay careful attention to the exact wording of the question being asked when you have to choose among options such as domain name resolution, routing, and address allocation. These are all associated with IP networking, but they perform separate functions.

Subscription Services

Subscription services involve the management of data flows to and from a system based on either a push (publish) or pull (subscribe) model. Managing what data elements are needed by which nodes is a problem you can tackle by using directory services such as LDAP.

Another use of subscription services is the Software as a Service (SaaS) model, where software is licensed on a subscription basis. The actual software is hosted centrally, commonly in the cloud, and user access is based on subscriptions. This is becoming a common software business model.

Chapter Review

In this chapter, you became acquainted with secure protocols used in an enterprise and the use cases to which they apply. Specifically, you examined the following protocols; DNSSEC, SSH, S/MIME, SRTP, LDAPS, FTPS, SFTP, SNMPv3, HTTPS (SSL/TLS), IPSec, Authentication Header (AH) / Encapsulated Security Payload (ESP), tunnel/transport, and Secure POP3/IMAP4. The chapter then moved to which protocols apply in use cases involving voice and video, time synchronization, e-mail and the Web, file transfer, directory services, remote access, domain name resolution, routing and switching, network address allocation, and subscription services. The key element of this chapter is that it prepared you to choose the correct secure protocols for use cases when given a scenario on the CompTIA Security+ exam.

Questions

To help you prepare further for the CompTIA Security+ exam, and to test your level of preparedness, answer the following questions and then check your answers against the correct answers at the end of the chapter.

1. A user reports to the help desk that he is getting "cannot resolve address" error messages from his browser. Which port is likely a problem on his firewall?
   - **A.** 22
   - **B.** 53
   - **C.** 161
   - **D.** 162
2. What is a weakness of the DNS protocol?
   - **A.** Requests and replies are sent in plaintext.
   - **B.** It doesn't provide billing standardization in cloud infrastructures.
   - **C.** TCP can be used for large transfers such as zone transfers.
   - **D.** Its encryption capabilities are slow.
3. Which of the following is a benefit of DNSSEC?
   - **A.** Scalability
   - **B.** Lower expenditures from operations capital (OpsCap) expenditures
   - **C.** Enables origin authentication, authenticated denial of existence, and data integrity
   - **D.** Availability and confidentiality
4. What is the Secure Shell (SSH) protocol?
   - **A.** It is an encrypted remote terminal connection program used for remote connections to a server.
   - **B.** It provides dynamic network address translation.

C. It provides Software as a Service (SaaS).

D. It provides snapshots of physical machines at a point in time.

5. What is the purpose of the Secure/Multipurpose Internet Mail Extensions (S/MIME) protocol?

   A. It is used in audio encryption.

   B. It optimizes the use of ports 80 and 443.

   C. It encrypts HTTP traffic.

   D. It provides cryptographic protections to e-mails.

6. What is the purpose of Lightweight Directory Access Protocol Secure (LDAPS)?

   A. It leverages encryption protections of SSH to secure FTP transfers.

   B. It uses an SSL/TLS tunnel to connect LDAP services.

   C. It digitally signs DNS records.

   D. It provides both symmetric and asymmetric encryption.

7. Which port does FTPS use?

   A. 53

   B. 83

   C. 990

   D. 991

8. You are a security admin for XYZ company. You suspect that company e-mails using the default POP and IMAP e-mail protocols and ports are getting intercepted while in transit. Which of the following ports should you consider using?

   A. Ports 995 and 993

   B. Ports 53 and 22

   C. Ports 110 and 143

   D. Ports 161 and 16240

9. What is the purpose of the Simple Network Management Protocol version 3 (SNMPv3)?

   A. It provides asymmetric encryption values.

   B. It achieves specific communication goals.

   C. It provides a common language for developers.

   D. It is used to securely manage devices on IP-based networks.

10. What is the purpose of HTTPS?
    A. To allow enumeration and monitoring of network resources
    B. To use SSL or TLS to encrypt a channel over which HTTP traffic is transmitted
    C. To implement Single Sign-On
    D. To enhance communication protocols

Answers

1. **B.** Domain Name System (DNS) uses TCP and UDP port 53 for standard queries and responses. This port should be open on the firewall in this scenario. Secure Shell (SSH) uses TCP port 22 as its default port. All versions of SNMP require ports 161 and 162 to be open on a firewall.
2. **A.** A major weakness of the DNS protocol is that requests and replies are sent in plaintext.
3. **C.** A major benefit of DNSSEC is that it enables origin authentication, authenticated denial of existence, and data integrity.
4. **A.** The SSH protocol is an encrypted remote terminal connection program used for remote connections to a server.
5. **D.** The purpose of the S/MIME protocol is to provide cryptographic protections to e-mail and attachments.
6. **B.** LDAPS uses an SSL/TLS tunnel to connect LDAP services.
7. **C.** FTPS uses port 990.
8. **A.** The default POP3 and IMAP4 ports are 110 and 143, respectively. These are not secure. As a security admin, you should consider using secure POP using port 995 and secure IMAP using port 993.
9. **D.** The purpose of SNMPv3 is to securely manage devices on IP-based networks.
10. **B.** HTTPS uses SSL or TLS to encrypt a channel over which HTTP traffic is transmitted.

CHAPTER 18

Host and Application Security

In this chapter, you will

- Examine how to implement host-based security solutions
- Explore application security solutions

Computing involves the processing of data using machines and applications. Ensuring that both machines and the applications that run on them are as secure as possible is an important part of an enterprise security program. This chapter explores the steps used to secure both hardware and the applications that run on it to manage overall system risk.

Certification Objective This chapter covers CompTIA Security+ exam objective 3.2: Given a scenario, implement host or application security solutions.

Endpoint Protection

Endpoint protection is the concept of extending the security perimeter to the devices that are connecting to the network. A variety of endpoint protection solutions can be employed, including antivirus/anti-malware solutions, endpoint detection and response solutions, data loss prevention solutions, and firewalls. Host-based intrusion detection and prevention solutions can also be deployed at endpoints. Not all endpoints are the same with respect to either capability or the risks from attack, and endpoint solutions should be tailored to take those elements into account.

Antivirus

Antivirus (AV) products attempt to identify, neutralize, or remove malicious programs, macros, and files. These products were initially designed to detect and remove computer viruses, though many of the antivirus products are now bundled with additional security products and features. Most current antivirus software packages provide protection against a wide range of threats, including viruses, worms, Trojans, and other malware. Use of an up-to-date antivirus package is essential in the current threat environment.

Although antivirus products have had over two decades to refine their capabilities, the purpose of the antivirus products remains the same: to detect and eliminate computer viruses and malware. Most antivirus products combine the following approaches when scanning for viruses:

- **Signature-based scanning** Much like an intrusion detection system (IDS), the antivirus products scan programs, files, macros, e-mails, and other data for known worms, viruses, and malware. The antivirus product contains a virus dictionary with thousands of known virus signatures that must be frequently updated, as new viruses are discovered daily. This approach will catch known viruses but is limited by the virus dictionary—what it does not know about, it cannot catch.
- **Heuristic scanning (or analysis)** Heuristic scanning does not rely on a virus dictionary. Instead, it looks for suspicious behavior—anything that does not fit into a "normal" pattern of behavior for the operating system (OS) and applications running on the system being protected.

As signature-based scanning is a familiar concept, let's examine heuristic scanning in more detail. Heuristic scanning typically looks for commands or instructions that are not normally found in application programs, such as attempts to access a reserved memory register. Most antivirus products use either a weight-based system or a rule-based system in their heuristic scanning (more effective products use a combination of both techniques). A *weight-based system* rates every suspicious behavior based on the degree of threat associated with that behavior. If the set threshold is passed based on a single behavior or a combination of behaviors, the antivirus product will treat the process, application, macro, and so on that is performing the behavior(s) as a threat to the system. A *rule-based system* compares activity to a set of rules meant to detect and identify malicious software. If part of the software matches a rule, or if a process, application, macro, and so on performs a behavior that matches a rule, the antivirus software will treat that as a threat to the local system.

Some heuristic products are very advanced and contain capabilities for examining memory usage and addressing, a parser for examining executable code, a logic flow analyzer, and a disassembler/emulator so they can "guess" what the code is designed to do and whether or not it is malicious.

EXAM TIP Heuristic scanning is a method of detecting potentially malicious or "virus-like" behavior by examining what a program or section of code does. Anything that is "suspicious" or potentially "malicious" is closely examined to determine whether or not it is a threat to the system. Using heuristic scanning, an antivirus product attempts to identify new viruses or heavily modified versions of existing viruses before they can damage your system.

As with IDS/IPS products, encryption and obfuscation pose a problem for antivirus products: anything that cannot be read cannot be matched against current virus dictionaries or activity patterns. To combat the use of encryption in malware and viruses, many heuristic scanners look for encryption and decryption loops. As malware is usually designed to run alone and unattended, if it uses encryption, it must contain all the instructions to encrypt and decrypt itself, as needed. Heuristic scanners look for instructions such as the initialization of a pointer with a valid memory address, manipulation of a counter, or a branch condition based on a counter value. While these actions don't always indicate the presence of an encryption/decryption loop, if the heuristic engine can find a loop, it might be able to decrypt the software in a protected memory space, such as an emulator, and evaluate the software in more detail. Many viruses share common encryption/decryption routines that help antivirus developers.

Current antivirus products are highly configurable, and most offerings will have the following capabilities:

- **Automated updates** Perhaps the most important feature of a good antivirus solution is its ability to keep itself up to date by automatically downloading the latest virus signatures on a frequent basis. This usually requires that the system be connected to the Internet in some fashion and that updates be performed on a daily (or more frequent) basis.
- **Automated scanning** Most antivirus products allow for the scheduling of automated scans so that you can designate when the antivirus product will examine the local system for infected files. These automated scans can typically be scheduled for specific days and times, and the scanning parameters can be configured to specify what drives, directories, and types of files are scanned.
- **Media scanning** Removable media is still a common method for virus and malware propagation, and most antivirus products can be configured to automatically scan optical media, USB drives, memory sticks, or any other types of removable media as soon as they are connected to or accessed by the local system.
- **Manual scanning** Many antivirus products allow the user to scan drives, files, or directories (folders) "on demand."
- **E-mail scanning** E-mail is still a major method of virus and malware propagation. Many antivirus products give users the ability to scan both incoming and outgoing messages as well as any attachments.
- **Resolution** When the antivirus product detects an infected file or application, it can typically perform one of several actions. The antivirus product may quarantine the file, making it inaccessible. It may try to repair the file by removing the infection or offending code, or it may delete the infected file. Most antivirus products allow the user to specify the desired action, and some allow for an escalation in actions, such as cleaning the infected file if possible and quarantining the file if it cannot be cleaned.

Antivirus solutions are typically installed on individual systems (desktops, servers, and even mobile devices), but network-based antivirus capabilities are also available in many commercial gateway products. These gateway products often combine firewall, IDS/IPS, and antivirus capabilities into a single integrated platform. Most organizations will also employ antivirus solutions on e-mail servers, as that continues to be a very popular propagation method for viruses.

NOTE The intentions of computer virus writers have changed over the years—from simply wanting to spread a virus in order to be noticed, to creating stealthy botnets as a criminal activity. One method of remaining hidden is to produce viruses that can morph to lower their detection rates by standard antivirus programs. The number of variants for some viruses has increased from less than 10 to greater than 10,000. This explosion in signatures has created two issues: One, users must constantly (sometimes more than daily) update their signature file. Two, and more important, detection methods are having to change as the number of signatures becomes too large to scan quickly. For end users, the bottom line is simple: update signatures automatically, and at least daily.

While the installation of a good antivirus product is still considered a necessary best practice, there is growing concern about the effectiveness of antivirus products against developing threats. Early viruses often exhibited destructive behaviors; they were poorly written and modified files and were less concerned with hiding their presence than they were with propagation. We are seeing an emergence of viruses and malware created by professionals, sometimes financed by criminal organizations or governments, that go to great lengths to hide their presence. These viruses and malware are often used to steal sensitive information or turn the infected PC into part of a larger botnet for use in spamming or attack operations.

EXAM TIP Antivirus is an essential security application on all platforms. There are numerous compliance schemes that mandate antivirus deployment, including Payment Card Industry Data Security Standard (PCI DSS) and North American Electric Reliability Council Critical Infrastructure Protections (NERC CIP).

Anti-Malware

In the early days of PC use, threats were limited: most home users were not connected to the Internet 24/7 through broadband connections, and the most common threat was a virus passed from computer to computer via an infected floppy disk (much like the medical definition, a computer virus is something that can infect the host and replicate itself). But things have changed dramatically since those early days, and current threats pose a much greater risk than ever before. Automated probes from botnets and worms are not the only threats roaming the Internet—there are viruses and malware spread by e-mail, phishing, infected websites that execute code on your system when you visit them, adware, spyware, and so on. Anti-malware is the name of a product designed to protect your machine from malicious software or malware. Today, most anti-malware solutions are combined with antivirus solutions into a single product. Fortunately, as the threats increase in complexity and capability, so do the products designed to stop them. One of the most dangerous forms of malware is ransomware; it spreads quickly, encrypting a user's files and locking it until a ransom is paid. For more details on anti-malware products, reread the preceding "Antivirus" section and realize that malware is a different threat than a virus, but the defenses are the same.

Endpoint Detection and Response (EDR)

Endpoint detection and response (EDR) solutions are integrated solutions that combine individual endpoint security functions into a complete package. Having a packaged solution makes updating easier, and frequently these products are designed to integrate into an enterprise-level solution with a centralized management platform. Some of the common EDR components include antivirus, anti-malware, software patching, firewall, and DLP solutions. Unified endpoint management (UEM) is a newer security model that focuses on the managing and securing devices in an enterprise such as desktops, laptops, smartphones, and other devices from a single location. UEM is covered in Chapter 22.

DLP

Data loss prevention (DLP) solutions serve to prevent sensitive data from leaving the network without notice. What better place to check than at endpoints? Well, it is important to understand what an endpoint is. For e-mail, the endpoint really is the server, and this offers a scalable location against multiple mailboxes. Applying DLP across endpoints to chase items such as USB downloads of data can be an exercise fraught with heavy maintenance of DLP rulesets, heavyweight clients that affect endpoint performance, and a lack of discrimination that can cause productivity issues. This has led to endpoint DLP monitoring, where file activity is reported to centralized systems, and to specialized DLP offerings such as the content DLP being rolled out by Microsoft across the Microsoft 365 environment. These endpoint solutions do not provide complete or comprehensive coverage but taken together can achieve many of the objectives with less cost and complexity.

Next-Generation Firewall (NGFW)

Next-generation firewalls (NGFWs) act by inspecting the actual traffic crossing the firewall—not just looking at the source and destination addresses and ports, but also at the actual content being sent. This makes next-generation firewalls a potent player in the hunt for malicious content on the way in and company secrets on the way out. As with all of these rule-driven platforms, the challenge is in maintaining appropriate rulesets that catch the desired bad traffic.

Host-based Intrusion Detection System (HIDS)

Host-based intrusion detection systems (HIDSs) act to detect undesired elements in network traffic to and from the host. Because the intrusion detection system is tied to the host, it can be very specific with respect to threats to the host OS and ignore those that would have no effect. Being deployed at a specific endpoint, it can be tuned to the specifics of the endpoint and endpoint applications, providing greater levels of specific detection. The disadvantage of the HIDS is that it only detects the issues; it must rely on another component, typically through some logging or reporting mechanism, to act on the threat. This is resolved in a host-based intrusion prevention system, discussed in the next section.

Host-based Intrusion Prevention System (HIPS)

A *host-based intrusion prevention system (HIPS)* is a HIDS with additional components to permit it to respond automatically to a threat condition. The response can be as simple as dropping a packet, up to killing a connection. A HIPS has all the characteristics of the underlying HIDS, with the added advantage of being able to perform predefined actions in response to a threat.

EXAM TIP Remember that HIDS can only detect malicious activity and send alerts. HIPS, on the other hand, can detect and prevent attacks.

Host-based Firewall

Personal firewalls, or *host-based firewalls,* are host-based protective mechanisms that monitor and control traffic passing in to and out of a single system. Designed for the end user, software firewalls often have a configurable security policy that allows the user to determine which traffic is "good" and is allowed to pass and which traffic is "bad" and is blocked. The decision for good versus bad is based on the addresses being passed, both IP address and port combinations. Software firewalls are extremely commonplace—so much so that most modern OSs come with some type of personal firewall included. Having the firewall on the host OS provides the ability to tune the firewall to the usage pattern of the specific endpoint.

Linux-based OSs have had built-in software-based firewalls for a number of years, including TCP Wrapper, ipchains, and iptables. An example of a Linux firewall is shown in Figure 18-1.

TCP Wrapper is a simple program that limits inbound network connections based on port number, domain, or IP address and is managed with two text files called hosts.allow and hosts.deny. If the inbound connection is coming from a trusted IP address and destined for a port to which it is allowed to connect, then the connection is allowed.

Ipchains is a more advanced, rule-based software firewall that allows for traffic filtering, Network Address Translation (NAT), and redirection. Three configurable "chains" are used for handling network traffic: input, output, and forward. The input chain contains rules for traffic that is coming into the local system. The output chain contains rules for traffic that is leaving the local system. The forward chain contains rules for traffic that was received by the local system but is not destined for the local system. Iptables is the latest evolution of ipchains. Iptables uses the same three chains for policy rules and traffic handling as ipchains, but with iptables each packet is processed only by the appropriate chain. Under ipchains, each packet passes through all three chains for processing. With

Figure 18-1 Linux firewall

iptables, incoming packets are processed only by the input chain, and packets leaving the system are processed only by the output chain. This allows for more granular control of network traffic and enhances performance.

In addition to the "free" firewalls that come bundled with OSs, many commercial personal firewall packages are available. Many commercial software firewalls limit inbound and outbound network traffic, block pop-ups, detect adware, block cookies and malicious processes, and scan instant messenger traffic. While you can still purchase or even download a free software-based personal firewall, most commercial vendors are bundling the firewall functionality with additional capabilities such as antivirus and antispyware.

Microsoft Windows has had a personal software firewall since Windows XP SP2. Today, Windows Firewall is called Windows Defender Firewall (see Figure 18-2). It is enabled by default and provides warnings when disabled. Windows Defender Firewall is fairly configurable; it can be set up to block all traffic, to make exceptions for traffic you want to allow, and to log rejected traffic for later analysis.

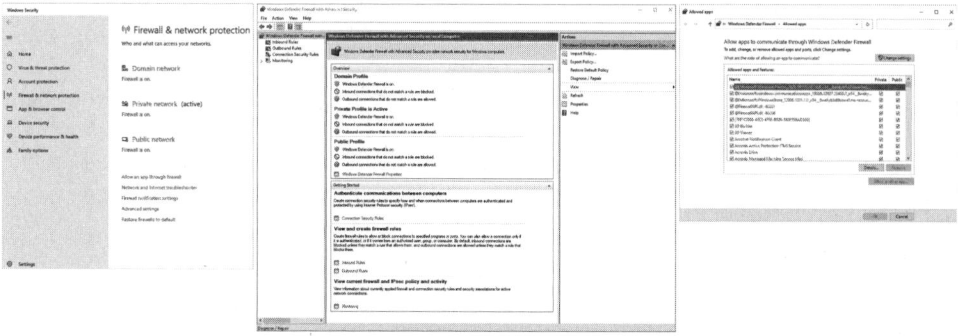

Figure 18-2 Windows Defender Firewall is enabled by default.

In Windows 10, Microsoft modified Windows Defender Firewall to make it more capable and configurable. More options were added to allow for more granular control of network traffic as well as the ability to detect when certain components are not behaving as expected. For example, if your Microsoft Outlook client suddenly attempts to connect to a remote web server, Windows Defender Firewall can detect this as a deviation from normal behavior and block the unwanted traffic.

EXAM TIP When examining endpoint security solutions, you'll see that one of the key differentiators is in what the system detects. There are single-purpose systems, such as antivirus, anti-malware, and DLP. Multipurpose systems such as EDR, firewalls, and HIDS/HIPS can look for a variety of types of items. The key to all this is in the definition of the rules for each product.

Boot Integrity

Booting a system is the process of getting a system powered up and the correct software loaded to move the system to a proper operating condition. *Boot integrity* is the characteristic of the intended hardware/firmware/software load for the system being in compliance with the expected state. Having a means to ensure boot integrity is a means of assuring that the hardware, firmware, and initial loading of software are free of any tampering. The term *trusted platform boot* includes the hardware and any associated BIOS, firmware, and hypervisor software.

Boot Security/Unified Extensible Firmware Interface (UEFI)

UEFI offers a solution to the problem of boot integrity, called *Secure Boot,* which is a mode that, when enabled, only allows signed drivers and OS loaders to be invoked. Secure Boot requires specific setup steps, but once enabled, it blocks malware that attempts to alter the boot process. Secure Boot enables the *attestation* that the drivers and OS loaders being used have not changed since they were approved for use. Secure Boot is supported by Microsoft Windows and all major versions of Linux.

One of the key characteristics of the UEFI BIOS as opposed to the legacy BIOS is that UEFI BIOS is designed to work with the hardware platform to ensure that the flash memory that holds the BIOS cannot be changed without the proper cryptographic credentials. This forms a Root of Trust in the contents of the flash memory, specifically in the UEFI BIOS. The key used to sign the BIOS is controlled by the equipment manufacturer, thus preventing unauthorized changes to the BIOS. The BIOS performs a countercheck on all updates prior to loading them, using a private key stored on the BIOS, ensuring all updates are properly signed by the manufacturer. These steps create the Root of Trust for the system.

Secure Boot operates by verifying digital signatures on all the steps in the boot process. The BIOS checks the loader, and the loader checks the kernel objects, each of these being digital signature checks with keys controlled by the manufacturer. This ensures that all components have not been tampered with and have the integrity of the original component.

Measured Boot

Measured boot is also a method of depending on the Root of Trust in starting a system, but rather than using signatures to verify subsequent components, a measured boot process hashes the subsequent processes and compares the hash values to known good values. This has the advantage that it can be extended beyond items covered by the manufacturer, as the signatures come from the manufacturer and thus are limited to only specific items. The known-good hash values must be stored in a secure location and the Trusted Platform Module (TPM) platform configuration registers (PCRs) comprise the secure location that is used.

Boot Attestation

One of the challenges in securing an OS is the myriad of drivers and other add-ons that hook into the OS and provide specific added functionality. If these additional programs are not properly vetted before installation, this pathway can provide a means by which malicious software can attack a machine. And because these attacks can occur at boot time, at a level below security applications such as antivirus software, they can be very difficult to detect and defeat.

Boot attestation is the reporting of the state of a system with respect to components and their relationship to the Root of Trust. Part of the UEFI/Root of Trust specification is the means of reporting via digital signatures of the verified integrity of the system components. This information can be used remotely by a server to determine if an OS is correct and has the correct patch level before allowing admission to a corporate VPN, as well as for other network admission activities.

EXAM TIP *Attestation* means verifying the authenticity of a platform or device based on a trusted record of evidence. Secure Boot, for example, ensures the system boots into a trusted configuration by having evidence of each step's authenticity verified.

Database

Major *database* engines have built-in encryption capabilities. The advantage to these encryption schemes is that they can be tailored to the data structure, protecting the essential columns while not impacting columns that are not sensitive. Properly employing database encryption requires that the data schema and its security requirements be designed into the database implementation. The advantage is in better protection against any database compromise, and the performance hit is typically negligible with respect to other alternatives.

Tokenization

Tokenization is the process of substituting a surrogate value, called a token, for a sensitive data element. This allows processing of the data, including referential integrity without disclosing the sensitive value. The concept of tokenization is widely used in industries like finance and healthcare to help reduce the risk of disclosure of sensitive data elements while data is used, and to minimize the risk of sensitive data being exposed via systems that do not need it. Think of a bank examining credit records for people and having elements such as their Social Security number. This data value, while sensitive, is essential to get the right credit information from the credit bureaus, but it also is meaningless to the loan officer. Using the real value to do the join with the credit bureau but using a token to represent it on subsequent reports protects the value when not needed.

Salting

Salting is the process of adding a random element to a value before performing a mathematical operation like hashing. This is done to add randomization and to also prevent identical original values from being hashed into an identical hash, which would indicate that the two users have the same values. Hashing is used to protect passwords when stored. Salting the hash functions protects identical inputs from producing identical outputs and thus revealing that two users have identical passwords.

Hashing

Hashing is a mathematical method of reducing a data element to a short form that is not reversible to the original form. Hashing sensitive data has the effect of creating a token, and hashes can be used as tokens in data structures.

EXAM TIP Know the differences between tokenization, salting, and hashing. *Tokenization* is the process of substituting a surrogate value, called a token, for a sensitive data element. *Salting* is the process of adding a random element to a value before performing a mathematical operation like hashing. *Hashing* is a mathematical method of reducing a data element to a short form that is not reversible to the original form.

Application Security

Applications are the reason for the computer equipment; it is the applications that do the work. Because the manufacturers of operating systems and infrastructure software have resolved the issues of the past with large numbers of vulnerabilities, the prime targets for attackers today are the applications. Applications come in two classes: commercial software and software that is built in-house. In-house apps are much less likely to have a serious security review as part of their build and are more likely to have vulnerabilities. The details behind secure application development is covered in detail in Chapter 11.

Input Validations

The avenue for an attacker to access an application is via its inputs. Having a stringent and comprehensive validation of inputs prior to processing them is essential to filter out specific attacks. If the input is going to be included in the SQL lookup, then ensuring the input is clean of unwanted SQL code is essential. *Input validation* is easy to explain: check everything before use. But in practice, it is time-consuming and detailed work that is often overlooked or corners are cut.

EXAM TIP Proper input validation prevents many different attack types by ensuring that input is properly formulated.

Secure Cookies

Cookies are text files sent with every request to a website. They have been used for a variety of functions, including maintaining state, preferences, usage parameters, and so on. An attribute in the cookie called the *secure attribute,* when set, instructs the browser and server to only transport the cookie over HTTPS channels. As cookies are transmitted in plaintext across the Web, if they are outside a protected HTTPS channel, they are subject to being read by unauthorized parties. Having the secure attribute set prevents the browser from sending that particular cookie over a non-secure connection. This does not end all risk because, if an attacker tampers with the cookie that is stored on the endpoint machine, the attribute can be changed back to allow the cookie to be sent over a non-secure connection.

Hypertext Transfer Protocol (HTTP) Headers

Browsers are the window to many applications, acting as a means of providing user input and receiving system responses. The HTTP has a large number of options and features that can be manipulated via a browser, to improve the usability of a site, but in some manipulative cases, they can result in security risks. The website can exert some control over browser behaviors via response headers that convey directives to the browser. Using a security-related set of response headers can alleviate such risks as protocol downgrade attacks, clickjacking, cookie hijacking and other attacks. An example is the HTTP Strict Transport Security (HSTS) directive:

```
Strict-Transport-Security: max-age 3600; includeSubDomains
```

This directive declares that browsers should only interact via HTTPS, never HTTP, with a max time of 3600 seconds, and that all subdomains are included in this directive. There are numerous additional response headers used in HTTP, and the best place to learn details, although they are beyond the Security+ exam, is on the OWASP project website.

Code Signing

An important factor in ensuring that software is genuine and has not been altered is a method of testing the software integrity. From a baseline-hardening point of view, how can you be sure that the code you are using is genuine and has not been tampered with? The answer is a process known as *code signing,* which involves applying a digital signature to code, providing a mechanism where the end user can verify the code integrity.

In addition to verifying the integrity of the code, digital signatures provide evidence as to the source of the software.

Code is signed by the manufacturer, either the commercial vendor or the in-house team. This digital signature contains the hash of the code, allowing its integrity to be verified at any time. If the hash of the code and the one on record match, and the signatures are valid, then the code is trustworthy with respect to its lineage.

EXAM TIP Code signing ensures that code has not been changed since being signed.

Allow List

Applications can be controlled at the OS at start time via block lists or allow lists. *Allow lists* are lists of applications that are permitted to run on the OS. Allow listing is easier to employ from the aspect of the identification of applications that are allowed to run—hash values can be used to ensure the executables are not corrupted. The challenge in allow listing is the number of potential applications that are run on a typical machine. For a single-purpose machine, such as a database server, allow listing can be relatively easy to employ. For multipurpose machines, it can be more complicated.

Block List/Deny List

The *block list/deny list* is essentially a list noting which applications should not be allowed to run on the machine. This is basically a permanent "ignore" or "call block" type of capability. Blocking in this fashion is difficult to use against dynamic threats, as the identification of a specific application can easily be avoided through minor changes.

EXAM TIP An *allow list* is a list of approved applications. A *block/deny list* is a list of applications that should not be allowed to run.

Secure Coding Practices

Application security begins with code that is secure and free of vulnerabilities. Unfortunately, all code has weaknesses and vulnerabilities, so instantiating the code in a manner that has effective defenses to prevent the exploitation of vulnerabilities can maintain a desired level of security. Software creation is a manufacturing type of process that should be guided and managed by policies and procedures. Instantiating the necessary steps to ensure secure code is being generated requires adherence to a set of secure coding practices, including the proper handling of configurations, errors and exceptions, and inputs, which can assist in the creation of a secure application. Testing of the application throughout the software development lifecycle can determine the actual security risk profile of a system.

There are numerous individual elements in a software development lifecycle methodology (SDLM) that can assist a team in developing secure code. Correct SDLM processes, such as input validation, proper error and exception handling, and cross-site scripting and cross-site request forgery mitigations, can improve the security of code. Process elements such as security testing, fuzzing, and patch management also help to ensure applications meet a desired risk profile.

The two main enumerations of common software errors are the Top 25 list, maintained by MITRE, and the OWASP Top Ten list for web applications. Depending on the type of application being evaluated, these lists provide a solid starting point for security analysis of known error types. MITRE is the repository of the industry-standard list for standard programs, and the OWASP list is for web applications. Because the causes of common errors do not change quickly, these lists are not updated every year.

Static Code Analysis

Static code analysis is when the code is examined without being executed. This analysis can be performed on both source code and object code bases. The term *source code* is typically used to designate the high-level language code, although, technically, source code is the original code base in any form, from high-level language to machine code. Static analysis can be performed by humans or tools, although humans are limited to the high-level language, while tools can be used against virtually any form of code base.

Static code analysis is frequently performed using automated tools. These tools are given a variety of names but are commonly called static code analyzers or source code analyzers. Sometimes, extra phrases, such as "binary scanners" and "bytecode scanners," are used to differentiate the tools. Static tools use a variety of mechanisms to search for weaknesses and vulnerabilities. Automated tools can provide advantages when checking syntax, using approved function/library calls, and examining rules and semantics associated with logic and calls. They can catch elements a human could overlook.

Manual Code Review

Code can also be reviewed manually. A *manual code review* can be done in one of two fashions: either directed or undirected. In an undirected review, a programmer examines the code to see what it does and how it does it. This is like proofreading a paper, although a code review is typically a team effort. A directed review is one where the code author walks through the code, explaining each line to the rest of the team. This ensures more eyes examine syntax and structures for errors and weaknesses.

Dynamic Code Analysis

Dynamic code analysis is performed while the software is executed, either on a target system or an emulated system. The system is fed specific test inputs designed to produce specific forms of behaviors. Dynamic analysis can be particularly important on systems such as embedded systems, where a high degree of operational autonomy is expected. As a case in point, the failure to perform adequate testing of software on the Ariane rocket program led to the loss of an Ariane 5 booster during takeoff. Subsequent analysis showed that if proper software testing had been performed, the error conditions could have been detected and corrected without the loss of the flight vehicle. Many times, you can test software in use without the rest of the system, and for some use cases, where failure costs are high, extensive testing before actual use is standard practice.

Dynamic analysis requires specialized automation to perform specific testing. Among the tools available are dynamic test suites designed to monitor operations for programs that have a high degree of parallel functions, thread-checking routines to ensure multi-core processors and software are managing threads correctly, and programs designed to detect race conditions and memory-addressing errors.

EXAM TIP Static code analysis is when the code is examined without being executed. Dynamic code analysis analyzes the code during execution.

Fuzzing

Fuzzing (or *fuzz testing*) is a brute force method of addressing input validation issues and vulnerabilities. The basis for fuzzing a program is the application of large numbers of inputs to determine which inputs cause faults and which ones might be vulnerable to exploitation. Fuzz testing can be applied to anywhere data is exchanged to verify that input validation is being performed properly. Network protocols can be fuzzed, file protocols can be fuzzed, and web protocols can be fuzzed. The vast majority of browser errors are found via fuzzing. Fuzz testing works well in known environments, unknown environments, and partially known environments, as it can be performed without knowledge of the specifics of the application under test.

Hardening

The key management issue behind running a secure system setup is to identify the specific needs of a system for its proper operation and enable only the items necessary for those functions. Keeping all other services and users off the system improves system throughput and increases security. Reducing the attack surface area associated with a system reduces the vulnerabilities now and in the future as updates are required.

Open Ports and Services

Services on machines are accessed through either TCP or UDP ports. For services that are being used, it is important that the port be open and not blocked by a firewall, which would stop the traffic to the service. But for security, any service that is not going to be used on a system should be disabled, and the ports should be blocked by the firewall. This has the effect of reducing the attack surface on a target and eliminating any vulnerability-based risk from services that are not needed. Blocking unneeded open ports and disabling unused services are both easy and should be applied to virtually every machine. This is one of the cheapest defenses and should be one of the first applied because of the breadth of issues it heads off.

Attackers use active reconnaissance and tools such as Nmap to scan and view open ports. As a security analyst, you can use the same tools, including netstat, to quickly ascertain listening ports and active connections. These should all be mapped to required services or else turned off and blocked.

EXAM TIP Any service that is not going to be used on a system should be disabled, and any unnecessary ports should be blocked by the firewall.

Registry

The Registry in Microsoft Windows systems acts as a repository of all information related to configurations. Configuration options for the OS are located in the Registry. Configuration options for applications are also located in the Registry. Using a structural hierarchical model to manage all of these parameters in one place resolves the housekeeping mess of having configuration information scattered all over a system, with access control issues for each and every location.

The Windows Registry is not a structure to be casually modified or changed. One security task you can do is periodically making a backup of the Registry to a secure location, as this will be important if something alters the current Registry. While Windows has mechanisms to protect the Registry, this is a key part of the OS-application interface; if it's lost, applications would have to be reloaded and reconfigured. Registry-editing tools can also be limited by group policies under a domain-based system.

Disk Encryption

Hardening a system also means protecting the information in the system. *Disk encryption* can provide data protection even if the disk is removed from one system and placed in another. Having the data encrypted on the disk renders it unusable without the proper keys. The best solutions for disk encryption today are built in to the operating system and use hardware encryption on the disk itself and store the keys in the TPM PCR. This makes the data easy for the OS to access when properly booted and logged in to, yet nearly impossible to bypass, even by removing the disk and putting it in another machine.

OS

Many different systems have the need for an *operating system (OS)*. Hardware in networks requires an operating system to perform the networking function. Servers and workstations require an OS to act as the interface between applications and the hardware. Specialized systems such as kiosks and appliances, both of which are forms of automated single-purpose systems, require an OS between the application software and hardware.

Servers require an operating system to bridge the gap between the server hardware and the applications being run. Currently, server OSs include Microsoft Windows Server, many flavors of Linux, and more and more VM/hypervisor environments.

For performance reasons, Linux has a significant market share in the realm of server OSs, although Windows Server with its Active Directory (AD) technology has made significant inroads into that market share.

The OS on a workstation exists to provide a functional working space for a user to interact with the system and its various applications. Because of the high level of user interaction on workstations, it is very common to see Windows in this role. In large enterprises, the ability of Active Directory to manage users, configurations, and settings easily across the entire enterprise has given Windows client workstations an advantage over Linux.

Appliances are standalone devices, wired into the network and designed to run an application to perform a specific function on traffic. These systems operate as headless servers, preconfigured with applications that run and perform a wide range of security services on the network traffic they see. For reasons of economics, portability, and functionality, the vast majority of appliances are built on top of a Linux-based system. As these are often customized distributions, keeping them patched becomes a vendor problem because this sort of work is outside the scope or ability of most IT people to properly manage.

Kiosks are standalone machines, typically operating a browser instance on top of a Windows OS. These machines are usually set up to automatically log in to a browser instance that is locked to a website that allows all of the functionality desired. Kiosks are commonly used for interactive customer service applications, such as interactive information sites, menus, and so on. The OS on a kiosk needs to be able to be locked down to minimal functionality, have elements such as automatic login, and provide an easy way to construct the applications.

Mobile devices began as phones with limited additional capabilities, but as the Internet and functionality spread to mobile devices, the capabilities of these devices have expanded as well. From smartphones to tablets, today's mobile system is a computer, with virtually all the compute capability one could ask for—with a phone attached. The two main mobile OSs in the market today are Apple's iOS and Google's Android system.

No matter what the OS, updates and patches should be applied where and when possible. Any nonessential services and software should be disabled and/or removed. Unnecessary open ports should be blocked or closed. All users should implement strong passwords and change them on a regular basis. Access policies and permissions should be implemented based on least privilege, where appropriate. Privileged user accounts should be used only when necessary, and there should be no local administrative accounts on Windows boxes. Also, logging should be implemented. In domain-based environments, group policies should be deployed to maintain security settings.

Patch Management

Patch management is the process used to maintain systems in an up-to-date fashion, including all required patches. Every OS, from Linux to Windows, requires software updates, and each OS has different methods of assisting users in keeping their systems up to date.

In Windows 10 forward, Microsoft has adopted a new methodology treating the OS as a service and has dramatically updated its servicing model. Windows 10 now has a twice-per-year feature update release schedule, aiming for March and September, with an 18-month servicing timeline for each release. Applying all Microsoft patches is highly recommended, as once the patches are released, attackers will know the vulnerabilities.

How you patch a Linux system depends a great deal on the specific version in use and the patch being applied. In some cases, a patch will consist of a series of manual steps requiring the administrator to replace files, change permissions, and alter directories. In other cases, the patches are executable scripts or utilities that perform the patch actions automatically. Some Linux versions, such as Red Hat, have built-in utilities that handle the patching process. In those cases, the administrator downloads a specifically formatted file that the patching utility then processes to perform any modifications or updates that need to be made.

Regardless of the method you use to update the OS, it is critically important to keep systems up to date. New security advisories come out every day, and while a buffer overflow may be a "potential" problem today, it will almost certainly become a "definite" problem in the near future. Much like the steps taken to baseline and initially secure an OS, keeping every system patched and up to date is critical to protecting the system and the information it contains.

Vendors typically follow a hierarchy for software updates:

- **Hotfix** This term refers to a (usually) small software update designed to address a specific problem, such as a buffer overflow in an application that exposes the system to attacks. Hotfixes are typically developed in reaction to a discovered problem and are produced and released rather quickly.
- **Patch** This term refers to a more formal, larger software update that can address several or many software problems. Patches often contain enhancements or additional capabilities as well as fixes for known bugs. Patches are usually developed over a longer period of time.
- **Service pack** This refers to a large collection of patches and hotfixes rolled into a single, rather large package. Service packs are designed to bring a system up to the latest known-good level all at once, rather than requiring the user or system administrator to download dozens or hundreds of updates separately.

Third-Party Updates

Maintaining up-to-date software is a problem the scales poorly. As more and more applications are added, from a wider and wider selection of vendors, the process of keeping track of what software is up to date and which programs require updating is a challenge. To solve this challenge, a wide range of vendors offer services that can check for updates and even update your applications for you. The key to making this work is to ensure that (1) the solution chosen covers the apps you use, and (2) you properly enroll the apps with the program so it knows what to update.

Auto-Update

Updating software is a maintenance task that sits near the bottom of everyone's list. It is relatively simple: you just have to look up and see if there are updates, download them if they are there, and update. And then repeat for every piece of software on your system. Time consuming and boring, this is clearly a task for automation. What's more, this task is actually important enough that automating the patching process is itself a security control in the NIST 800-53 series. Using an auto-update function to keep software up to date solves more problems than it creates. Many software vendors now equip their software with an *auto-update* function that calls home, gets the update, and installs it automatically. Yes, there is a risk that a new update will not function correctly, but that could only be discovered with extensive testing, and with the exception of specialized systems in highly critical operations, the testing will never occur.

Self-Encrypting Drive (SED)/ Full Disk Encryption (FDE)

Self-encrypting drives (SEDs) and *full disk encryption (FDE)* are methods of implementing cryptographic protection on hard drives and other similar storage media with the express purpose of protecting the data, even if the drive is removed from the machine. Portable machines, such as laptops, have a physical security weakness in that they are relatively easy to steal and then can be attacked offline at the attacker's leisure. The use of modern cryptography, coupled with hardware protection of the keys, makes this vector of attack much more difficult. In essence, both of these methods offer a transparent, seamless manner of encrypting the entire hard drive using keys that are only available to someone who can properly log in to the machine.

Opal

FDE and SED began as software-only proprietary solutions, but a hardware-based standard called Opal has been created. Developed by the Trusted Computing Group (TCG), Opal is used for applying hardware-based encryption to mass storage devices, hard drives (rotating media), solid state drives, and optical drives. Having a standard has the advantages of interoperability between vendors and can be OS independent. Having it in hardware improves performance and increases security. The encryption/decryption keys are stored in the hard drive controller and are never loaded into system memory, keeping them safe from attack.

EXAM TIP SED, FDE, and Opal are methods of implementing encryption on hard drives.

Hardware Root of Trust

A *hardware root of trust* is the concept that if one has trust in a source's specific security functions, this layer can be used to promote security to higher layers of a system. Because roots of trust are inherently trusted, they must be secure by design. This is usually accomplished by keeping them small and limiting their functionality to a few specific tasks. Many roots of trust are implemented in hardware that is isolated from the OS and the rest of the system so that malware cannot tamper with the functions they provide. Examples of roots of trust include TPM chips in computers and Apple's Secure Enclave coprocessor in its iPhones and iPads. Apple also uses a signed Boot ROM mechanism for all software loading.

With respect to UEFI and Secure Boot, previously covered in this chapter, the term *Root of Trust* refers to a condition by which the hardware and BIOS work together to ensure the integrity of the BIOS and all subsequent software and firmware loads. Once complete, this forms a Root of Trust that can be attested to via the TPM chip.

Trusted Platform Module (TPM)

The *Trusted Platform Module (TPM)* is a hardware solution on the motherboard, one that assists with key generation and storage as well as random number generation. When the encryption keys are stored in the TPM, they are not accessible via normal software channels and are physically separated from the hard drive or other encrypted data locations. This makes the TPM a more secure solution than storing the keys on the machine's normal storage.

The TPM platform also supports other security functions through a series of protected storage locations called platform configuration registers (PCRs). These locations are cryptographically protected from unauthorized reading and writing and serve as a location for critical information such as the data that forms the basis for the Root of Trust.

Sandboxing

Sandboxing refers to the quarantine or isolation of a system from its surroundings. It has become standard practice for some programs with an increased risk surface to operate within a sandbox, limiting the interaction with the CPU and other processes, such as memory. This works as a means of quarantine, preventing problems from getting out of the sandbox and onto the OS and other applications on a system.

Virtualization can be used as a form of sandboxing with respect to an entire system. You can build a VM, test something inside the VM, and, based on the results, make a decision with regard to stability or whatever concern was present.

Chapter Review

In this chapter, you became acquainted with the aspects of implementing host or application security solutions. The chapter began with an exploration of endpoint protection solutions. These solutions included antivirus, anti-malware, endpoint detection and response, data loss prevention, next-generation firewalls, host-based intrusion detection systems, host-based intrusion prevention systems, and host-based firewalls. The next major topic was boot integrity where boot security/UEFI, measured boot, and boot attestation were covered. The topic of database security followed, and in this section the elements of tokenization, salting, and hashing were covered.

The topic of application security was a significant part of this chapter. The section covered the topics of input validation, secure cookies, Hypertext Transfer Protocol (HTTP) headers, and code signing. This topic continued with allow lists and block list/deny lists. Then it moved into secure coding practices, static code analysis (including manual code review), dynamic code analysis, and fuzzing.

The next major section was on system hardening. Here we covered open ports and services, registry, disk encryption, OS, patch management, third-party updates, and auto-update. The chapter finished with a discussion of self-encrypting drives (SEDs) and full disk encryption (FDE), including Opal, hardware root of trust, Trusted Platform Module (TPM), and sandboxing.

Questions

To help you prepare further for the CompTIA Security+ exam, and to test your level of preparedness, answer the following questions and then check your answers against the correct answers at the end of the chapter.

1. Fuzz testing works best in which of the following testing environments?
   - **A.** Known environment testing
   - **B.** Partially known environment testing
   - **C.** Unknown environment testing
   - **D.** Fuzz testing works equally well in all of the above.
2. Which code analysis method is performed while the software is executed, either on a target system or an emulated system?
   - **A.** Static analysis
   - **B.** Runtime analysis
   - **C.** Sandbox analysis
   - **D.** Dynamic analysis
3. Which of the following are associated with endpoint protection? (Choose all that apply.)
   - **A.** EDR
   - **B.** TPM
   - **C.** DLP
   - **D.** HTTP headers
4. You have a series of web servers that you wish to harden. Which of the following is the best solution for this case?
   - **A.** A block list/deny list
   - **B.** An allow list
   - **C.** Secure cookies
   - **D.** Code signing

5. You are examining the server infrastructure and wish to harden the machines in your server farm. Which is the first task you should perform across all of your servers?
   A. Apply a block list/deny list.
   B. Apply an allow list.
   C. Block open ports and disable unused services.
   D. Employ disk encryption.
6. Databases can use which of the following for security? (Choose all that apply.)
   A. Tokenization
   B. Salting
   C. Code signing
   D. Secure cookies
7. When you're creating a website, which of the following will provide protection against user attacks against your site? (Choose all that apply.)
   A. Tokenization
   B. HTTP headers
   C. Code signing
   D. Fuzzing
8. Your firm has 200 desktops in three sites, split among a dozen business departments. Which of the following would be the first that you should ensure is working correctly to reduce risk?
   A. Application security
   B. Secure Boot
   C. Patch management
   D. Secure cookies
9. You have a database full of very sensitive data. Salespeople need to access some of this sensitive data when onsite with a customer. The best method to prevent leakage of critical data during these access sessions would be to employ which of the following?
   A. Salting
   B. Hashing
   C. Block list
   D. Tokenization
10. Which of the following elements is not part of the Root of Trust?
   A. Registry
   B. UEFI
   C. TPM PCR
   D. Digital signatures

Answers

1. **D.** Fuzz testing works well in known environment, unknown environment, and partially known environment testing, as it can be performed without knowledge of the specifics of the application under test.
2. **D.** Dynamic analysis is performed while the software is executed, either on a target system or an emulated system. Static analysis is when the code is examined without being executed. Sandboxing refers to the execution of computer code in an environment designed to isolate the code from direct contact with the target system. Runtime analysis is descriptive of the type of analysis but is not the term used in the industry.
3. **A** and **C.** Endpoint detection and response (EDR) is the combination of several individual endpoint protection mechanisms into a common management framework. Data loss prevention (DLP) is the checking for sensitive data before exfiltration. Both of these are associated with endpoint security. The Trusted Platform Module (TPM), while involved in many security technologies, does not play a direct role in endpoint protection. Nor do HTTP headers, which are associated with the server serving up the web content.
4. **B.** Allow lists are ideally suited for single-purpose servers, as the applications that are to be allowed to execute are known in advance.
5. **C.** Because the server farm may have multiple different types of systems, elements such as allow lists become more complicated, as the results do not scale across different server types. All machines benefit from blocking of unused ports and disabling of unused services.
6. **A** and **B.** Databases can use tokens to represent unique sensitive data, allowing joins between tables and records without exposing the data. Salting can be used to ensure that hashed values of identical input fields will not reveal the fact that two records share the same data.
7. **B** and **D.** HTTP headers prevent browsers from performing some activities that are allowed (by protocol) but not advised by site rules. Fuzzing will provide input as to input validation errors.
8. **C.** Patch management reduces the attack surface on the operating systems and application components. Automating this process is an important early step in the security journey because of the number of items it addresses.
9. **D.** The use of tokens to join records while hiding sensitive fields is common practice for views on database tables.
10. **A.** The Windows Registry is where configuration parameters for the OS and applications are stored. It is not associated with the Root of Trust, as it is not even accessible during the establishment of this trust chain.

CHAPTER 19

Secure Network Design

In this chapter, you will

- Learn the essential elements of secure network design
- Explore the various devices used to secure a network

Networks connect the components of an enterprise IT system, carrying signals and data and enabling the IT system to function in the desired manner for the business. Having minimal risk come from the network is important, and the methods to achieve this are through secure network system design. This chapter explores the Security+ elements of secure network design.

Certification Objective This chapter covers CompTIA Security+ exam objective 3.3: Given a scenario, implement secure network designs.

EXAM TIP Preparing for scenario-based questions requires more than simply learning the terms associated with network-based security solutions such as routers, switches, proxies, and load balancers. You should be familiar with how and when to configure each device based on a given scenario.

Load Balancing

Certain systems, such as servers, are more critical to business operations and should therefore be the object of fault-tolerance measures. A common technique that is used in fault tolerance is load balancing through the use of a load balancer. *Load balancing* involves the use of devices that move loads across a set of resources in an effort not to overload individual servers. This technique is designed to distribute the processing load over two or more systems. It is used to help improve resource utilization and throughput but also has the added advantage of increasing the fault tolerance of the overall system since a critical process may be split across several systems. Should any one system fail, the others can pick up the processing it was handling. While there may be an impact to overall throughput, the operation does not go down entirely. Load balancing is often utilized for systems handling websites, high-bandwidth file transfers, and large Internet Relay Chat (IRC) networks. Load balancing works by a series of health checks that tell the load balancer which machines are operating, and by a scheduling mechanism to spread the work evenly. Load balancing is best for stateless systems, as subsequent requests can be handled by any server, not just the one that processed the previous request.

Active/Active

In an *active/active* scheme, all the load balancers are active, sharing the load-balancing duties. Active/active load balancing can have performance efficiencies, but it is important to watch the overall load. If the overall load cannot be covered by $N - 1$ load balancers (that is, one fails), then the failure of a load balancer will lead to session interruption and traffic loss. Without a standby passive system to recover the lost load, the system will trim the load based on capacity, dropping requests that the system lacks capacity to service.

EXAM TIP Two or more servers work together to distribute the load in an active/active load-balancing configuration. If a server fails, service interruption or traffic loss may result.

Active/Passive

For high-availability solutions, having a single load balancer creates a single point of failure (SPOF). It is common to have multiple load balancers involved in the balancing work. In an *active/passive* scheme, the primary load balancer is actively doing the balancing while the secondary load balancer passively observes and is ready to step in any time the primary system fails.

EXAM TIP All traffic is sent to the active server in an active/passive configuration. If the active server fails, the passive server is promoted to active.

Scheduling

When a load balancer moves loads across a set of resources, it decides which machine gets a request via a *scheduling* algorithm. There are a couple of commonly used scheduling algorithms: affinity-based scheduling and round-robin scheduling.

Affinity

Affinity-based scheduling is designed to keep a host connected to the same server across a session. Some applications, such as web applications, can benefit from affinity-based scheduling. The method used by affinity-based scheduling is to have the load balancer keep track of where it last balanced a particular session and direct all continuing session traffic to the same server. If it is a new connection, the load balancer establishes a new affinity entry and assigns the session to the next server in the available rotation.

Round-Robin

Round-robin scheduling involves sending each new request to the next server in rotation. All requests are sent to servers in equal amounts, regardless of the server load. Round-robin schemes are frequently modified with a weighting factor, known as weighted round-robin, to take the server load or other criteria into account when assigning the next server.

EXAM TIP Round-robin and weighted round-robin are scheduling algorithms used for load-balancing strategies.

Virtual IP

In a load balanced environment, the IP addresses for the target servers of a load balancer will not necessarily match the address associated with the router sending the traffic. Load balancers handle this through the concept of virtual IP addresses, or *virtual IPs,* that allow for multiple systems to be reflected back as a single IP address.

Persistence

Persistence is the condition where a system connects to the same target in a load-balanced system. This can be important for maintaining state and integrity of multiple round-trip events. Persistence is achieved through affinity-based scheduling of server assets in load balancing. This was discussed in the "Affinity" section earlier in this chapter.

Network Segmentation

Network segmentation is where you have configured the network devices to limit traffic access across different parts of a network. This can be done to prevent access to sensitive machines, but also aids in network traffic management. A group of database servers that never need direct connection to the Internet can be located on a network segment where routing rules will not allow direct connection from outside of the protected enclave. Dividing a network into segments generally does not take more equipment, but rather is done in how the networking equipment is configured to communicate across the defined segments. A screened subnet (DMZ) is an example of a segment, one that is accessible from the Internet, and from the internal network, but cannot be crossed directly.

Virtual Local Area Network (VLAN)

A LAN is a set of devices with similar functionality and similar communication needs, typically co-located and operated off a single switch. This is the lowest level of a network hierarchy and defines the domain for certain protocols at the data link layer (layer 2) for communication. A virtual LAN (VLAN) is a logical implementation of a LAN and allows computers connected to different physical networks to act and communicate as if they were on the same physical network. A VLAN has many of the same characteristic attributes as a LAN and behaves much like a physical LAN but is implemented using switches and software. This very powerful technique allows significant network flexibility, scalability, and performance and allows administrators to perform network reconfigurations without having to physically relocate or re-cable systems.

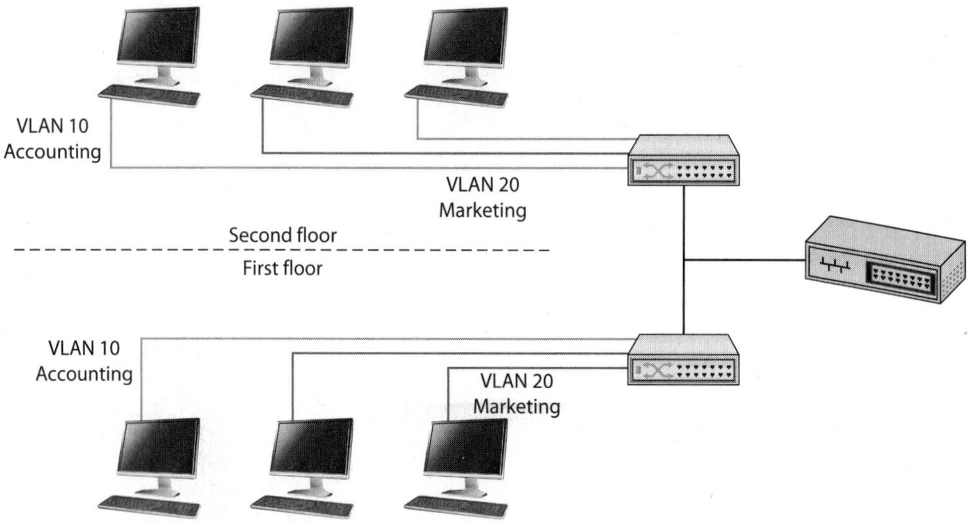

Figure 19-1 VLANs and trunks

Trunking is the process of spanning a single VLAN across multiple switches. A trunk-based connection between switches allows packets from a single VLAN to travel between switches, as shown in Figure 19-1. Two trunks are shown in the figure: VLAN 10 is implemented with one trunk, and VLAN 20 is implemented with the other. Hosts on different VLANs cannot communicate using trunks and thus are switched across the switch network. Trunks enable network administrators to set up VLANs across multiple switches with minimal effort. With a combination of trunks and VLANs, network administrators can subnet a network by user functionality without regard to host location on the network or the need to re-cable machines.

VLANs are used to divide a single network into multiple subnets based on functionality. This permits the accounting and marketing departments, for example, to share a switch because of proximity yet still have separate traffic domains. The physical placement of equipment and cables is logically and programmatically separated so that adjacent ports on a switch can reference separate subnets. This prevents unauthorized use of physically close devices through separate subnets that are on the same equipment. VLANs also allow a network administrator to define a VLAN that has no users and map all of the unused ports to this VLAN (some managed switches allow administrators to simply disable unused ports as well). Then, if an unauthorized user should gain access to the equipment, that user will be unable to use unused ports, as those ports will be securely defined to nothing. Both a purpose and a security strength of VLANs is that systems on separate VLANs cannot directly communicate with each other.

EXAM TIP Physical segregation requires creating two or more physical networks, each with its own servers, switches, and routers. Logical segregation uses one physical network with firewalls and/or routers separating and facilitating communication between the logical networks.

Screened Subnet (Previously Known as Demilitarized Zone)

The zone that is between the untrusted Internet and the trusted internal network is called the *screened subnet*. This was previously known by the term *demilitarized zone (DMZ)*, after its military counterpart of the same name, where neither side has any specific controls. Within the inner, secure network, separate branches are frequently carved out to provide specific functional areas.

A screened subnet in a computer network is used in the same way; it acts as a buffer zone between the Internet, where no controls exist, and the inner, secure network, where an organization has security policies in place. To demarcate the zones and enforce separation, a firewall is used on each side of the screened subnet. The area between these firewalls is accessible from either the inner, secure network or the Internet. Figure 19-2 illustrates these zones as caused by firewall placement. The firewalls are specifically designed to prevent direct access across the screened subnet from the Internet to the inner, secure network.

Special attention is required for the security settings of devices placed in the screened subnet, as you should consider them to always be compromised by unauthorized users. Machines whose functionality is locked down to preserve security are commonly called *hardened operating systems* in the industry. This lockdown approach needs to be applied to the machines in the screened subnet, and although it means that their functionality is limited, such precautions ensure that the machines will work properly in a less-secure environment.

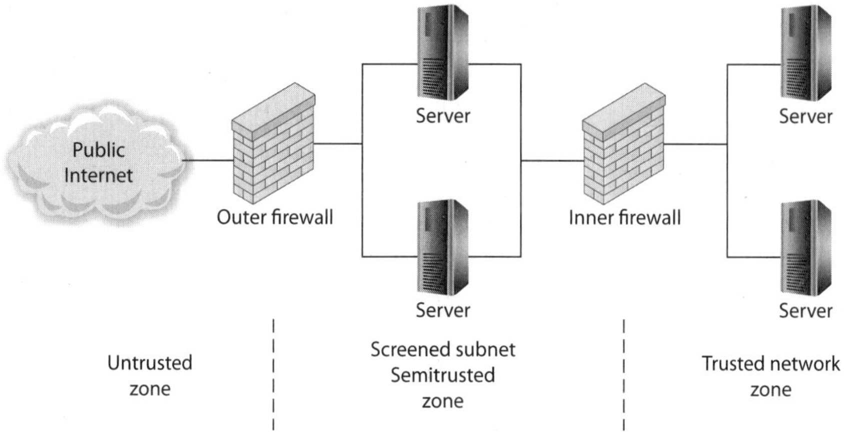

Figure 19-2 The screened subnet and zones of trust

Many types of servers belong in the screened subnet, including web servers that are serving content to Internet users, as well as remote-access servers and external e-mail servers. In general, any server directly accessed from the outside, untrusted Internet zone needs to be in the screened subnet. Other servers should not be placed in the screened subnet. Domain name servers for your inner, trusted network and database servers that house corporate databases should not be accessible from the outside. Application servers, file servers, print servers—all of the standard servers used in the trusted network—should be behind both the inner and outer firewalls, along with the routers and switches used to connect these machines.

The idea behind the use of the screened subnet topology is to force an outside user to make at least one hop in the screened subnet before he can access information inside the trusted network. If the outside user makes a request for a resource from the trusted network, such as a data element from a database via a web page, then this request needs to follow this scenario:

1. A user from the untrusted network (the Internet) requests data via a web page from a web server in the screened subnet.
2. The web server in the screened subnet requests the data from the application server, which can be in the screened subnet or in the inner, trusted network.
3. The application server requests the data from the database server in the trusted network.
4. The database server returns the data to the requesting application server.
5. The application server returns the data to the requesting web server.
6. The web server returns the data to the requesting user from the untrusted network.

This separation accomplishes two specific, independent tasks. First, the user is separated from the request for data on a secure network. By having intermediaries do the requesting, this layered approach allows significant security levels to be enforced. Users do not have direct access or control over their requests, and this filtering process can put controls in place. Second, scalability is more easily realized. The multiple-server solution can be made to be very scalable, literally to millions of users, without slowing down any particular layer.

EXAM TIP Screened subnets act as a buffer zone between unprotected areas of a network (the Internet) and protected areas (sensitive company data stores), allowing for the monitoring and regulation of traffic between these two zones.

East-West Traffic

Data flows in an enterprise can be described in patterns, such as north-south and east-west. Data flowing into and out of a data center or enterprise is called north-south traffic. *East-west traffic* is the data flow pattern between devices within a portion of the enterprise (that is, between functionally related boxes to support north-south traffic). The levels of east-west traffic are important to network engineers, as the networking infrastructure must be able to sustain operational loads.

EXAM TIP *East-west traffic* refers to network data flows within an enterprise network. *North-south traffic* refers to data flowing between the enterprise network or data center and the outside of the network.

Extranet

An *extranet* is an extension of a selected portion of a company's intranet to external partners. This allows a business to share information with customers, suppliers, partners, and other trusted groups while using a common set of Internet protocols to facilitate operations. Extranets can use public networks to extend their reach beyond a company's own internal network, and some form of security, typically virtual private networking (VPN), is used to secure this channel. The use of the term *extranet* implies both privacy and security. Privacy is required for many communications, and security is needed to prevent unauthorized use and events from occurring. Both of these functions can be achieved through the use of technologies described in this chapter and other chapters in this book. Proper firewall management, remote access, encryption, authentication, and secure tunnels across public networks are all methods used to ensure privacy and security for extranets.

EXAM TIP An extranet is a semiprivate network that uses common network technologies (HTTP, FTP, and so on) to share information and provide resources to business partners. Extranets can be accessed by more than one company because they share information between organizations.

Intranet

An *intranet* describes a network that has the same functionality as the Internet for users but lies completely inside the trusted area of a network and is under the security control of the system and network administrators. Typically referred to as campus or corporate networks, intranets are used every day in companies around the world. An intranet allows a developer and a user the full set of protocols—HTTP, FTP, instant messaging, and so on—that is offered on the Internet, but with the added advantage of trust from the network security. Content on intranet web servers is not available over the Internet to untrusted users. This layer of security offers a significant amount of control and regulation, allowing users to fulfill business functionality while ensuring security.

Two methods can be used to make information available to outside users: Duplication of information onto machines in the screened subnet can make it available to other users. Proper security checks and controls should be made prior to duplicating the material to ensure security policies concerning specific data availability are being followed. Alternatively, extranets (discussed in the previous section) can be used to publish material to trusted partners.

EXAM TIP An intranet is a private, internal network that uses common network technologies (HTTP, FTP, and so on) to share information and provide resources to internal organizational users.

Should users inside the intranet require access to information from the Internet, a proxy server can be used to mask the requestor's location. This helps secure the intranet from outside mapping of its actual topology. All Internet requests go to the proxy server. If a request passes the filtering requirements, the proxy server, assuming it is also a cache server, looks in its local cache of previously downloaded web pages. If it finds the page in its cache, it returns the page to the requestor without needing to send the request to the Internet. If the page is not in the cache, the proxy server, acting as a client on behalf of the user, uses one of its own IP addresses to request the page from the Internet. When the page is returned, the proxy server relates it to the original request and forwards it on to the user. This masks the user's IP address from the Internet. Proxy servers can perform several functions for a firm; for example, they can monitor traffic requests, eliminating improper requests such as inappropriate content for work. They can also act as a cache server, cutting down on outside network requests for the same object. Finally, proxy servers protect the identity of internal IP addresses using Network Address Translation (NAT), although this function can also be accomplished through a router or firewall using NAT as well. Proxy servers and NAT are covered in detail later in this chapter.

Zero Trust

Traditional IT network security is based on the castle-and-moat model. In the castle-and-moat model, it is hard to obtain access from outside the network because of walls and the moat, with the only access being the gate where IDs are checked. Once you're inside, trust is conveyed by the fact you passed the gate check. This approach has been used for years because it is simple to implement, but the problem with this approach is that once an attacker gains access to the network, they have access to everything inside.

Zero trust is a security model centered on the belief that you should not trust any request without verifying authentication and authorization. Zero trust implementations require strict identity verification for every account trying to access resources, regardless of their location. Zero trust security requires a holistic approach to security that incorporates several additional layers of defense and technologies.

Virtual Private Network (VPN)

Virtual private network (VPN) technologies allow two networks to connect securely across an unsecure stretch of network by tunneling across the intermediate connections. These technologies are achieved with protocols discussed in multiple chapters throughout this book, such as IPSec, L2TP, SSL/TLS, and SSH. At this level, you should understand that these technologies enable two sites, such as a remote worker's home network and the corporate network, to communicate across unsecure networks, including the Internet, at a much lower risk profile. The two main uses for tunneling/VPN technologies are site-to-site communications and remote access to a network.

VPNs work because only the endpoints have the information to decrypt the packets being sent across the network. At all of the intermediate hops, if a packet is intercepted, it cannot be read. This enables secure network communication between two endpoints of a circuit.

Always On

One of the challenges associated with VPNs is the establishment of the secure connection. In many cases, this requires additional end-user involvement, in the form of launching a program, entering credentials, or both. This acts as an impediment to use, as users avoid the extra steps. *Always-on VPNs* are a means to avoid this issue through the use of pre-established connection parameters and automation. Always-on VPNs can self-configure and connect once an Internet connection is sensed and provide VPN functionality without user intervention.

EXAM TIP When an Internet connection is made, an always-on VPN client automatically establishes a VPN connection.

Split Tunnel vs. Full Tunnel

Split tunnel is a form of VPN where not all traffic is routed via the VPN. Split tunneling allows multiple connection paths, some via a protected route such as the VPN, whereas other traffic from, say, public Internet sources is routed via non-VPN paths. The advantage of split tunneling is the ability to avoid bottlenecks from all traffic having to be encrypted across the VPN. A split tunnel would allow a user private access to information from locations over the VPN and less secure access to information from other sites. The disadvantage is that attacks from the non-VPN side of the communication channel can affect the traffic requests from the VPN side. A *full tunnel* solution routes all traffic over the VPN, providing protection to all networking traffic.

EXAM TIP For performance-based questions, simply learning the terms associated with VPNs and IPSec in particular is insufficient. You should be familiar with the configuration and use of IPSec components, including the types of configurations and their use to support organizational security.

Remote Access vs. Site-to-Site

Site-to-site communication links are network connections to two or more networks across an intermediary network layer. In almost all cases, this intermediary network is the Internet or some other public network. To secure the traffic that is going from site to site, encryption in the form of either a VPN or a tunnel can be employed. In essence, this makes all of the packets between the endpoints in the two networks unreadable to nodes between the two sites.

Remote access is when a user requires access to a network and its resources but is not able to make a physical connection. Remote access via a tunnel or VPN has the same effect as directly connecting the remote system to the network—it's as if the remote user just plugged a network cable directly into their machine. So, if you do not trust a machine to be directly connected to your network, you should not use a VPN or tunnel, for if you do, that is what you are logically doing.

EXAM TIP Tunneling/VPN technology is a means of extending a network either to include remote users or to connect two sites. Once the connection is made, it is like the connected machines are locally on the network.

IPSec

IPSec is a set of protocols developed by the IETF to securely exchange packets at the network layer (layer 3) of the OSI reference model (RFCs 2401–2412). Although these protocols work only in conjunction with IP networks, once an IPSec connection is established, it is possible to tunnel across other networks at lower levels of the OSI model. The set of security services provided by IPSec occurs at the network layer of the OSI model, so higher-layer protocols, such as TCP, UDP, Internet Control Message Protocol (ICMP), Border Gateway Protocol (BGP), and the like, are not functionally altered by the implementation of IPSec services.

The IPSec protocol series has a sweeping array of services it is designed to provide, including but not limited to access control, connectionless integrity, traffic-flow confidentiality, rejection of replayed packets, data security (encryption), and data-origin authentication. IPSec has two defined modes—transport and tunnel—that provide different levels of security. IPSec also has three modes of connection: host-to-server, server-to-server, and host-to-host.

The transport mode encrypts only the data portion of a packet, thus enabling an outsider to see source and destination IP addresses. The transport mode protects the higher-level protocols associated with a packet and protects the data being transmitted but allows knowledge of the transmission itself. Protection of the data portion of a packet is referred to as content protection.

Tunnel mode provides encryption of source and destination IP addresses, as well as of the data itself. This provides the greatest security, but it can be done only between IPSec servers (or routers) because the final destination needs to be known for delivery. Protection of the header information is known as context protection.

EXAM TIP In *transport mode* (end-to-end), security of packet traffic is provided by the endpoint computers. In *tunnel mode* (portal-to-portal), security of packet traffic is provided between endpoint node machines in each network and not at the terminal host machines.

It is possible to use both methods at the same time, such as using transport within one's own network to reach an IPSec server, which then tunnels to the target server's network, connecting to an IPSec server there, and then using the transport method from the target network's IPSec server to the target host. IPSec uses the term *security association (SA)* to describe a unidirectional combination of specific algorithm and key selection to provide a protected channel. If the traffic is bidirectional, two SAs are needed and can in fact be different.

SSL/TLS

Secure Sockets Layer (SSL)/Transport Layer Security (TLS) is an application of encryption technology developed for transport-layer protocols across the Web. This protocol uses public key encryption methods to exchange a symmetric key for use in confidentiality and integrity protection as well as authentication. All versions of SSL have been deprecated due to security issues, and in the vast majority of commercial servers employing SSL/TLS, SSL has been retired. Because of its ubiquity, the term SSL will last for quite a while, but in function, it is now done via TLS. TLS can be used to affect a VPN between a client browser and the web server and is one of the most common methods of protecting web traffic.

The standard port for SSL and TLS is undefined because it depends on what the protocol being protected uses; for example, port 80 for HTTP becomes port 443 when it is for HTTPS. If the connection is for FTP, then FTPS uses TCP ports 989 and 990.

HTML5

HTML5 is the current version of the HTML protocol standard, and this version was developed to handle the modern web content of audio and video as well as to enhance the ability of a browser to function without add-ins such as Flash, Java, and browser helper objects for common functions. One of the areas this has enhanced is the ability to connect to a VPN by implementing a secure HTML5-based remote access solution. This does not require Java or other plugins, thus removing compatibility and updating of accessories issues. As HTML5 was designed to operate across a wide range of devices, including mobile platforms, functionality such as this can advance security across multiple platforms.

EXAM TIP HTML5 doesn't require browser plugins and is considered a secure remote access alternative to using SSL/TLS VPNs.

Layer 2 Tunneling Protocol (L2TP)

Layer 2 Tunneling Protocol (L2TP) is an Internet standard and came from the Layer 2 Forwarding (L2F) protocol, a Cisco initiative designed to address issues with Point-to-Point Tunneling Protocol (PPTP). Whereas PPTP is designed around Point-to-Point Protocol (PPP) and IP networks, L2F (and hence L2TP) is designed for use across all kinds of networks, including ATM and Frame Relay. Additionally, whereas PPTP is designed to be implemented in software at the client device, L2TP was conceived as a hardware implementation using a router or a special-purpose appliance. L2TP can be configured in software and is in Microsoft's Routing and Remote Access Service (RRAS), which uses L2TP to create a VPN.

L2TP works in much the same way as PPTP, but it opens up several items for expansion. For instance, in L2TP, routers can be enabled to concentrate VPN traffic over higher-bandwidth lines, creating hierarchical networks of VPN traffic that can be more efficiently managed across an enterprise. L2TP also has the ability to use IPSec and encryption protocols, providing a higher level of data security. L2TP is also designed to work with established AAA services such as RADIUS and TACACS+ to aid in user authentication, authorization, and accounting. L2TP is established via UDP port 1701, so this is an essential port to leave open across firewalls supporting L2TP traffic.

DNS

The *Domain Name System (DNS)* is a protocol for the translation of names into IP addresses. When users enter a name such as www.example.com, the DNS system converts this name into the actual numerical IP address. DNS records are also used for e-mail delivery. The DNS protocol uses UDP over port 53 for standard queries, although TCP can be used for large transfers such as zone transfers. DNS is a hierarchical system of servers, from local copies of records, up through Internet providers to root-level servers. DNS is one of the primary underlying protocols used on the Internet and is involved in almost all addressing lookups. The problem with DNS is that requests and replies are sent in plaintext and are subject to spoofing.

DNSSEC (Domain Name System Security Extensions) is a set of extensions to the DNS protocol that, through the use of cryptography, enables origin authentication of DNS data, authenticated denial of existence, and data integrity but does not extend to availability or confidentiality. DNSSEC records are signed so that all DNSSEC responses are authenticated but not encrypted. This prevents unauthorized DNS responses from being interpreted as correct. Authenticated denial of existence also allows a resolver to validate that a certain domain name does not exist.

Data transfers over UDP port 53 are limited to 512 bytes in size, and DNSSEC packets can be larger. For this reason, DNSSEC typically uses TCP port 53 for its work. It is possible to extend UDP packet size to 4096 bytes to cope with DNSSEC, and this is covered in RFC 6891.

Network Access Control (NAC)

Networks comprise connected workstations and servers. Managing security on a network involves managing a wide range of issues related not only to the various connected hardware but also to the software operating those devices. Assuming that the network is secure, each additional connection involves risk. Managing the endpoints on a case-by-case basis as they connect is a security methodology known as *network access control (NAC)*. Two main competing methodologies exist: Network Access Protection (NAP) is a Microsoft technology for controlling network access to a computer host, and Network Admission Control (NAC) is Cisco's technology for controlling network admission.

Microsoft's NAP system is based on measuring the system health of the connecting machine, including patch levels of the OS, antivirus protection, and system policies. NAP was first utilized in Windows XP Service Pack 3, Windows Vista, and Windows Server 2008, and it requires additional infrastructure servers to implement the health checks. The system includes enforcement agents that interrogate clients and verify admission criteria. The client side is initiated whenever network connections are made. Response options include rejection of the connection request and restriction of admission to a subnet.

Cisco's NAC system is built around an appliance that enforces policies chosen by the network administrator. A series of third-party solutions can interface with the appliance, allowing the verification of a whole host of options, including client policy settings, software updates, and client security posture. The use of third-party devices and software makes this an extensible system across a wide range of equipment.

Neither Cisco NAC nor Microsoft NAP is widely adopted across enterprises. The client pieces are all in place, but enterprises have been slow to fully deploy the server side of this technology. The concept of automated admission checking based on client device characteristics is here to stay, as it provides timely control in the ever-changing network world of today's enterprises. With the rise of "bring your own device" (BYOD) policies in organizations, there is renewed interest in using network access control to assist in protecting the network from unsafe devices.

EXAM TIP For the Security+ exam, NAC refers to *network access control.* The Microsoft and Cisco solutions referenced in this section are examples of this type of control—their names and acronyms are not relevant to the Security+ exam. The concept of network access control (NAC) and what it accomplishes is relevant and testable.

Agent and Agentless

In recognition that deploying agents to machines can be problematic in some instances, vendors have also developed agentless solutions for NAC. Rather than have the agent wait on the host for activation and use, the agent can operate from within the network itself, rendering the host in effect agentless. In *agent*-based solutions, code is stored on the host machine for activation and use at time of connection. In *agentless* solutions, the code resides on the network and is deployed to memory for use in a machine requesting connections, but since it never persists on the host machine, it is referred to as agentless. In most instances, there is no real difference in the performance of agent versus agentless solutions when properly deployed. The real difference comes in the issues of having agents on boxes versus persistent network connections for agentless.

Agentless NAC is often implemented in a Microsoft domain through an Active Directory (AD) controller. For example, NAC code verifies devices are in compliance with access policies when a domain is joined by a user or when they log in or log out. Agentless NAC is also often implemented through the use of intrusion prevention systems.

EXAM TIP NAC agents are installed on devices that connect to networks in order to produce secure network environments. With agentless NAC, the NAC code resides not on the connecting devices, but on the network, and it's deployed to memory for use in a machine requesting connection to the network.

Out-of-Band Management

Management of a system across the network can be either in-band or out-of-band. In in-band management systems, the management channel is the same channel as the data channel. This has an advantage in physical connection simplicity and a disadvantage that if a problem occurs due to data flows, the management commands may not be able to access the device. For important network devices and services, an out-of-band management channel is recommended. *Out-of-band management* channels are physically separate connections, via separate interfaces that permit the active management of a device even when the data channel is blocked for some reason.

Port Security

Switches can perform a variety of security functions. Switches work by moving packets from inbound connections to outbound connections. While moving the packets, it is possible for switches to inspect the packet headers and enforce security policies. *Port security* is a capability provided by switches that enables you to control which devices and how many of them are allowed to connect via each port on a switch. Port security operates through the use of MAC addresses. Although not perfect—MAC addresses can be spoofed—port security can provide useful network security functionality.

Port address security based on Media Access Control (MAC) addresses can determine whether a packet is allowed or blocked from a connection. This is the very function that a firewall uses for its determination, and this same functionality is what allows an 802.1X device to act as an "edge device."

Port security has three variants:

- **Static learning** A specific MAC address is assigned to a port. This is useful for fixed, dedicated hardware connections. The disadvantage is that the MAC addresses need to be known and programmed in advance, making this good for defined connections but not good for visiting connections.
- **Dynamic learning** Allows the switch to learn MAC addresses when they connect. Dynamic learning is useful when you expect a small, limited number of machines to connect to a port.
- **Sticky learning** Also allows multiple devices to a port, but also stores the information in memory that persists through reboots. This prevents the attacker from changing settings through power cycling the switch.

Broadcast Storm Prevention

One form of attack is a flood. There are numerous types of flooding attacks: ping floods, SYN floods, ICMP floods (Smurf attacks), and traffic flooding. Flooding attacks are used as a form of denial of service (DoS) to a network or system. Detecting flooding attacks is relatively easy, but there is a difference between detecting the attack and mitigating the attack. Flooding can be actively managed through dropping connections or managing traffic. *Flood guards* act by managing traffic flows. By monitoring the traffic rate and percentage of bandwidth occupied by broadcast, multicast, and unicast traffic, a flood guard can detect when to block traffic to manage flooding.

EXAM TIP Flood guards are commonly implemented in firewalls and IDS/IPS solutions to prevent DoS and DDoS attacks.

Bridge Protocol Data Unit (BPDU) Guard

To manage the Spanning Tree Protocol (STP), devices and switches can use Bridge Protocol Data Units (BPDUs) packets. These are specially crafted messages with frames that contain information about the Spanning Tree Protocol. The issue with BPDU packets is, while necessary in some circumstances, their use results in a recalculation of the STP, and this consumes resources. An attacker can issue multiple BPDU packets to a system to force multiple recalculations that serve as a network denial of service attack. To prevent this form of attack, edge devices can be configured with *Bridge Protocol Data Unit (BPDU) guards* that detect and drop these packets. While this eliminates the use of this functionality from some locations, the resultant protection is worth the minor loss of functionality.

Loop Prevention

Switches operate at layer 2 of the OSI reference model, and at this level there is no countdown mechanism to kill packets that get caught in loops or on paths that will never resolve. This means that a mechanism is needed for *loop prevention*. On layer 3, a time-to-live (TTL) counter is used, but there is no equivalent on layer 2. The layer 2 space acts as a mesh, where potentially the addition of a new device can create loops in the existing device interconnections. Open Shortest Path First (OSPF) is a link-state routing protocol that is commonly used between gateways in a single autonomous system. To prevent loops, a technology called spanning trees is employed by virtually all switches. STP allows for multiple, redundant paths, while breaking loops to ensure a proper broadcast pattern. STP is a data link layer protocol and is approved in IEEE standards 802.1D, 802.1w, 802.1s, and 802.1Q. It acts by trimming connections that are not part of the spanning tree connecting all of the nodes. STP messages are carried in BPDU frames described in the previous section.

EXAM TIP Remember that BPDU guards, MAC filtering, and loop detection are all mechanisms used to provide port security. Understand the differences in their actions. MAC filtering verifies MAC addresses before allowing a connection, BPDU guards prevent tampering with BPDU packets, and loop detection detects loops in local networks.

Dynamic Host Configuration Protocol (DHCP) Snooping

When an administrator sets up a network, they usually assign IP addresses to systems in one of two ways: statically or dynamically through DHCP. A static IP address assignment is fairly simple: the administrator decides what IP address to assign to a server or PC, and that IP address stays assigned to that system until the administrator decides to change it. The other popular method is through the Dynamic Host Configuration Protocol (DHCP). Under DHCP, when a system boots up or is connected to the network, it sends out a broadcast query looking for a DHCP server. All available DHCP servers reply to this request. Should there be more than one active DHCP server within the network, the client uses the one whose answer reaches them first. From this DHCP server, the client then receives the address assignment. DHCP is very popular in large user environments where the cost of assigning and tracking IP addresses among hundreds or thousands of user systems is extremely high.

The weakness of using the first response received allows a rogue DNS server to reconfigure the network. A rogue DHCP server can route the client to a different gateway, an attack known as DHCP spoofing. Attackers can use a fake gateway to record data transfers, obtaining sensitive information, before sending data on to its intended destination, which is known as a man-in-the-middle attack. Incorrect addresses can lead to a DoS attack blocking key network services. *Dynamic Host Configuration Protocol (DHCP) snooping* is a defensive measure against an attacker that attempts to use a rogue DHCP device. DHCP snooping prevents malicious DHCP servers from establishing contact by examining DHCP responses at the switch level and not sending those from unauthorized DHCP servers. This method is detailed in RFC 7513, co-authored by Cisco and adopted by many switch vendors.

Media Access Control (MAC) Filtering

MAC filtering is the selective admission of packets based on a list of approved Media Access Control (MAC) addresses. Employed on switches, this method is used to provide a means of machine authentication. In wired networks, this enjoys the protection afforded by the wires, making interception of signals to determine their MAC addresses difficult. In wireless networks, this same mechanism suffers from the fact that an attacker can see the MAC addresses of all traffic to and from the access point, and then can spoof the MAC addresses that are permitted to communicate via the access point.

EXAM TIP MAC filtering can be employed on wireless access points but can be bypassed by attackers observing allowed MAC addresses and spoofing the allowed MAC address for the wireless card.

Network Appliances

Network appliances are machines that provide services across a network. Many network-based functionalities can be effectively managed via network appliances. Security functions such as jump servers, network-based intrusion detection systems, VPN endpoints, collectors, and aggregators are some common examples. The next sections contain information on those specifically identified in Security+ objectives.

Jump Servers

A *jump server* is a hardened system on a network specifically used to access devices in a separate security zone. For someone outside the network to access protected resources inside the network, they first connect to the jump host, and their activities to the internal services are performed via that connection. Because of specific monitoring and hardening, a jump server can act as a safer alternative than allowing direct outside access. The level of functionality via a jump host can be controlled, and the activity can be specifically monitored to detect and stop attacks.

EXAM TIP Jump servers are hardened systems often used to protect and provide a means to access resources in a screened subnet, for example.

Proxy Servers

Though not strictly a security tool, a *proxy server* can be used to filter out undesirable traffic and prevent employees from accessing potentially hostile websites. A proxy server takes requests from a client system and forwards them to the destination server on behalf of the client. Different types of proxy servers are described in the following sections.

Deploying a proxy solution within a network environment is usually done either by setting up the proxy and requiring all client systems to configure their browsers to use the proxy or by deploying an intercepting proxy that actively intercepts all requests without requiring client-side configuration.

From a security perspective, proxies are most useful in their ability to control and filter outbound requests. By limiting the types of content and websites employees can access from corporate systems, many administrators hope to avoid loss of corporate data, hijacked systems, and infections from malicious websites. Administrators also use proxies to enforce corporate acceptable use policies and track use of corporate resources.

Forward

Proxies can operate in two directions. A *forward proxy* operates to forward requests to servers based on a variety of parameters, as described in the other portions of this section. Forward proxies can be used to bypass firewall restrictions, act as a cache server, and change your IP address (more useful before widespread adoption of NAT). Forward proxies can be deployed by attackers to get users to use them for "caching purposes" under the guise of speeding up connections, when, in fact, they actually slow down the connection and create a man-in-the-middle attack scenario.

Reverse

A *reverse proxy* is typically installed on the server side of a network connection, often in front of a group of web servers, and intercepts all incoming web requests. It can perform a number of functions, including traffic filtering, Secure Sockets Layer (SSL)/Transport Layer Security (TLS) decryption, serving of common static content such as graphics, and performing load balancing.

EXAM TIP A forward proxy is Internet-facing and acts on behalf of the client. It protects the client. A reverse proxy is internally facing and acts on behalf of the server, which it protects.

Network-based Intrusion Detection System (NIDS)/ Network-based Intrusion Prevention System (NIPS)

Network-based intrusion detection systems (NIDSs) are designed to detect, log, and respond to unauthorized network or host use, both in real time and after the fact. NIDSs are available from a wide selection of vendors and are an essential part of network security. These systems are implemented in software, but in large systems, dedicated hardware is required as well.

A *network-based intrusion prevention system (NIPS)* has as its core an intrusion detection system. However, whereas a NIDS can only alert when network traffic matches a defined set of rules, a NIPS can take further actions. A NIPS can take direct action to block an attack, with its actions governed by rules. By automating the response, a NIPS significantly shortens the response time between detection and action.

EXAM TIP Recognize that a NIPS has all the same characteristics as a NIDS but, unlike a NIDS, can automatically respond to certain events (for example, by resetting a TCP connection) without operator intervention.

Whether network-based or host-based, an IDS will typically consist of several specialized components working together, as illustrated in Figure 19-3. These components are

Figure 19-3 Logical depiction of IDS components

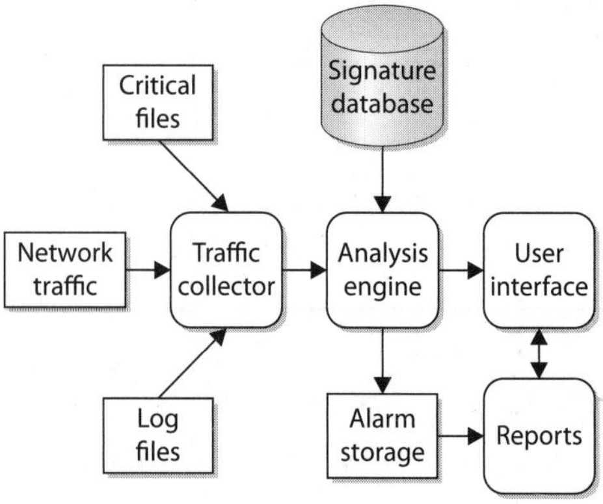

often logical and software-based rather than physical and will vary slightly from vendor to vendor and product to product. Typically, an IDS will have the following logical components:

- **Traffic collector (or sensor)** This component collects activity/events for the IDS to examine. On a host-based IDS, this could be log files, audit logs, or traffic coming to or leaving a specific system. On a network-based IDS, this is typically a mechanism for copying traffic off the network link—basically functioning as a sniffer. This component is often referred to as a sensor.
- **Analysis engine** This component examines the collected network traffic and compares it to known patterns of suspicious or malicious activity stored in the signature database. The analysis engine is the "brains" of the IDS.
- **Signature database** The signature database is a collection of patterns and definitions of known suspicious or malicious activity.
- **User interface and reporting** This component interfaces with the human element, providing alerts when appropriate and giving the user a means to interact with and operate the IDS.

Most IDSs can be tuned to fit a particular environment. Certain signatures can be turned off, telling the IDS not to look for certain types of traffic. For example, if you are operating in a pure Linux environment, you may not wish to see Windows-based alarms, as they will not affect your systems. Additionally, the severity of the alarm levels can be adjusted depending on how concerned you are over certain types of traffic. Some IDSs will also allow the user to exclude certain patterns of activity from specific hosts. In other words, you can tell the IDS to ignore the fact that some systems generate traffic that looks like malicious activity, because it really isn't.

NIDSs/NIPSs can be divided into three categories based on primary methods of detection used: signature based, heuristic/behavioral based, and anomaly based. These are described in the following sections.

Signature Based

This model relies on a predefined set of patterns (called *signatures*). The IDS has to know what behavior is considered "bad" ahead of time before it can identify and act upon suspicious or malicious traffic. *Signature-based* systems work by matching signatures in the network traffic stream to defined patterns stored in the system. Signature-based systems can be very fast and precise, with low false-positive rates. The weakness of signature-based systems is that they rely on having accurate signature definitions beforehand, and as the number of signatures expand, this creates an issue in scalability.

EXAM TIP False negatives often happen when alerts that should be generated aren't. False positives occur when expected behavior is identified as malicious.

Heuristic/Behavior

The *behavioral* model relies on a collected set of "normal behavior"—what should happen on the network and is considered "normal" or "acceptable" traffic. Behavior that does not fit into the "normal" activity categories or patterns is considered suspicious or malicious. This model can potentially detect zero-day or unpublished attacks but carries a high false-positive rate because any new traffic pattern can be labeled as "suspect."

The *heuristic* model uses artificial intelligence (AI) to detect intrusions and malicious traffic. This is typically implemented through algorithms that help an IDS decide whether or not a traffic pattern is malicious. For example, a URL containing a character repeated 10 times may be considered "bad" traffic as a single signature. With a heuristic model, the IDS will understand that if 10 repeating characters is bad, 11 is still bad, and 20 is even worse. This implementation of fuzzy logic allows this model to fall somewhere between signature-based and behavior-based models.

Anomaly

This detection model is similar to behavior-based methods. The IDS is first taught what "normal" traffic looks like and then looks for deviations from those "normal" patterns. An *anomaly* is a deviation from an expected pattern or behavior. Specific anomalies can also be defined, such as Linux commands sent to Windows-based systems and implemented via an AI-based engine to expand the utility of specific definitions.

EXAM TIP Anomaly detection identifies deviations from normal behavior.

Inline vs. Passive

The distinction between in-band and out-of-band NIDS/NIPS is similar to the distinction between inline and passive sensors. An *in-band* NIDS/NIPS is an inline sensor coupled to a NIDS/NIPS that makes its decisions "in band" and enacts changes via the sensor. This has the advantage of high security, but it also has implications related to traffic levels and traffic complexity. In-band solutions work great for protecting network segments that have high-value systems and a limited number of traffic types, such as in front of a set of database servers with serious corporate data, where the only types of access would be via database connections.

An out-of-band system relies on a *passive* sensor, or set of passive sensors, and has the advantage of greater flexibility in detection across a wider range of traffic types. The disadvantage is the delay in reacting to the positive findings, as the traffic has already passed to the end host.

HSM

A *hardware security module (HSM)* is a device used to manage or store encryption keys. It can also assist in cryptographic operations such as encryption, hashing, or the application of digital signatures. HSMs are typically peripheral devices, connected via USB or a network connection. HSMs have tamper-protection mechanisms to prevent physical access to the secrets they safeguard. Because of their dedicated design, they can offer significant performance advantages over general-purpose computers when it comes to cryptographic operations. When an enterprise has significant levels of cryptographic operations, HSMs can provide throughput efficiencies.

EXAM TIP Storing private keys anywhere on a networked system is a recipe for loss. HSMs are designed to allow the use of the key without exposing it to the wide range of host-based threats.

Sensors

Sensors are devices that capture data and act upon it. There are multiple kinds of sensors and various placement scenarios. Each type of sensor is different, and no single type of sensor can sense everything. Sensors can be divided into two types based on where they are placed: network and host. Network-based sensors can provide coverage across multiple machines, but are limited by traffic engineering to systems that packets pass them. They may have issues with encrypted traffic because if the packet is encrypted and they cannot read it, they are unable to act upon it. On the other hand, network-based sensors have limited knowledge of what hosts they see are doing, so the sensor analysis is limited in their ability to make precise decisions on the content. Host-based sensors provide more specific and accurate information in relation to what the host machine is seeing and doing, but they are limited to just that host. A good example of the differences in sensor placement and capabilities is seen in the host-based intrusion detection and network-based intrusion detection systems.

Sensors have several different actions they can take: they can report on what they observe, they can use multiple readings to match a pattern and create an event, and they can act based on proscribed rules. Not all sensors can take all actions, and the application of specific sensors is part of a monitoring and control deployment strategy. This deployment strategy must consider network traffic engineering, the scope of action, and other limitations.

Collectors

Collectors are sensors, or concentrators that combine multiple sensors, that collect data for processing by other systems. Collectors are subject to the same placement rules and limitations as sensors.

Aggregators

An *aggregator* is a device that takes multiple inputs and combines them to a single output. Think of it as a many-to-one type of device. It is placed upstream from the multitude of devices and can take the place of a router or a much larger switch. Assume you have ten users on each of three floors. You can place a 16-port switch on each floor, and then consume three router ports. Now make that ten floors of ten users, and you are consuming ten ports on your router for the ten floors. An aggregate switch will reduce this to one connection, while providing faster switching between users than the router would. These traffic management devices are located based on network layout topologies to limit unnecessary router usage.

Firewalls

A *firewall* can be hardware, software, or a combination of both whose purpose is to enforce a set of network security policies across network connections. It is much like a wall with a window: the wall serves to keep things out, except those permitted through the window (see Figure 19-4). Network security policies act like the glass in the window: they permit some things to pass, such as light, while blocking others, such as air. The heart of a firewall is the set of security policies that it enforces. Management determines what is allowed in the form of network traffic between devices, and these policies are used to build rulesets for the firewall devices used to filter network traffic across the network.

Security policies are rules that define what traffic is permissible and what traffic is to be blocked or denied. These are not universal rules, and many different sets of rules are created for a single organization with multiple connections. A web server connected to the Internet may be configured to allow traffic only on port 80 for HTTP and have all other ports blocked, for example. An e-mail server may have only necessary ports for e-mail open, with others blocked. The network firewall can be programmed to block all traffic to the web server except for port 80 traffic, and to block all traffic bound to the mail server except for port 25. In this fashion, the firewall acts as a security filter, enabling control over network traffic, by machine, by port, and in some cases based on application-level detail. A key to setting security policies for firewalls is the same as for

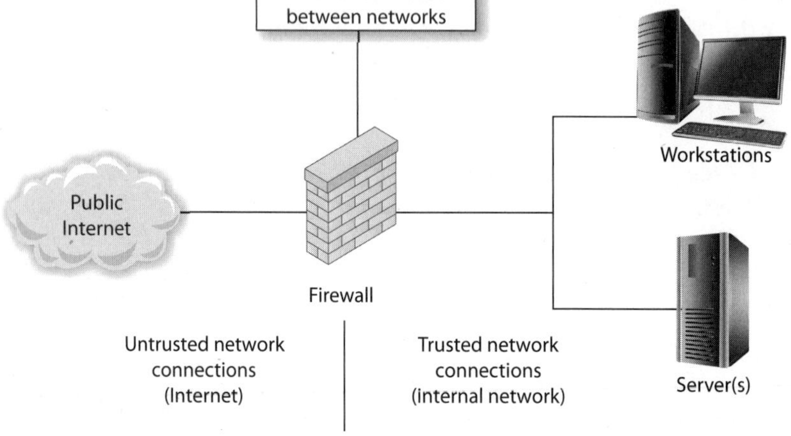

Figure 19-4 How a firewall works

other security policies—the principle of least access: allow only the necessary access for a function; block or deny all unneeded functionality. How an organization deploys its firewalls determines what is needed for security policies for each firewall.

As will be discussed later, the security topology will determine what network devices are employed at what points in a network. At a minimum, your organization's connection to the Internet should pass through a firewall. This firewall should block all network traffic except that specifically authorized by the organization. Blocking communications on a port is simple—just tell the firewall to close the port. The issue comes in deciding what services are needed and by whom, and thus which ports should be open and which should be closed. This is what makes a security policy useful. The perfect set of network security policies, for a firewall, is one that the end user never sees and that never allows even a single unauthorized packet to enter the network. As with any other perfect item, it will be rare to find the perfect set of security policies for firewalls in an enterprise. When developing rules for a firewall, the principle of least access is best to use; you want the firewall to block as much traffic as possible, while allowing the authorized traffic through.

To develop a complete and comprehensive security policy, you first need to have a complete and comprehensive understanding of your network resources and their uses. Once you know how the network will be used, you will have an idea of what to permit. In addition, once you understand what you need to protect, you will have an idea of what to block. Firewalls are designed to block attacks before they reach a target machine. Common targets are web servers, e-mail servers, DNS servers, FTP services, and databases. Each of these has separate functionality, and each has unique vulnerabilities. Once you have decided who should receive what type of traffic and what types should be blocked, you can administer this through the firewall.

EXAM TIP The Security+ exam objectives list many firewall types—from web application firewalls to appliance, host-based, and virtual firewalls. Be able to distinguish them from each other and know how they might be implemented in a given scenario.

Web Application Firewall (WAF)

A *web application firewall (WAF)* is a device that performs restrictions based on rules associated with HTTP/HTTPS traffic. By definition, web application firewalls are a form of content filter, and their various configurations allow them to provide significant capabilities and protections. The level of specificity in what can be allowed or blocked can be as precise as "allow Facebook but block Facebook games." WAFs can detect and block disclosure of critical data, such as account numbers, credit card numbers, and so on. WAFs can also be used to protect websites from common attack vectors such as cross-site scripting, fuzzing, and buffer overflow attacks.

You can configure a web application firewall to examine inside a TLS session. This is important if an attacker is attempting to use an encrypted channel such as TLS to mask their activity. Because legitimate TLS channels are instantiated by the system, you can pass the appropriate credentials internally to the WAF to enable TLS inspection.

NGFW

Advanced firewalls employ stateful packet filtering to prevent several types of undesired communications. To distinguish these firewalls from firewalls that act only on address and port information, they are called *next-generation firewalls (NGFWs)*. Next-generation firewalls can keep track of the state associated with a communication, and they can filter based on behaviors that are not properly associated with the state of the communication. For instance, should a packet coming from outside the network attempt to pretend that it is a response to a message from inside the network, the next-generation firewall will have no record of it being requested and can discard it, blocking the undesired external access attempt.

Stateful

A *stateful* packet inspection firewall can act upon the state condition of a conversation—is this a new conversation or a continuation of a conversation, and did it originate inside or outside the firewall? This provides greater capability, but at a processing cost that has scalability implications. To look at all packets and determine the need for each and its data requires stateful packet filtering. Stateful means that the firewall maintains, or knows, the context of a conversation. In many cases, rules depend on the context of a specific communication connection. For instance, traffic from an outside server to an inside server may be allowed if it is requested but blocked if it is not. A common example is a request for a web page. This request is actually a series of requests to multiple servers, each of which can be allowed or blocked. As many communications will be transferred to high ports (above 1023), stateful monitoring will enable the system to determine which sets of high port communications are permissible and which should be blocked. A disadvantage of stateful monitoring is that it takes significant resources and processing to perform this type of monitoring, and this reduces efficiency and requires more robust and expensive hardware.

Stateless

The typical network firewall operates on IP addresses and ports, in essence a *stateless* interaction with the traffic. The most basic firewalls simply shut off either ports or IP addresses, dropping those packets upon arrival. While useful, they are limited in their abilities as many services can have differing IP addresses, and maintaining the list of allowed IP addresses is time consuming and, in many cases, not practical. But for internal systems (say, a database server) that have no need to connect to a myriad of other servers, having a simple IP-based firewall in front can limit access to the desired set of machines.

Unified Threat Management (UTM)

Unified threat management (UTM) is a marketing term used to describe all-in-one devices employed in network security. UTM devices typically provide a wide range of services, including switching, firewall, IDS/IPS, anti-malware, anti-spam, content filtering, and traffic shaping. These devices are designed to simplify security administration and are targeted for small and midsized networks. Because of the wide range of services UTMs provide, they are typically located at the edge of the network, managing traffic in and out of the network. When a UTM sends an alert, it is best to treat the alert like any other action that triggers an incident response and investigate the cause. Different firms can stack different security appliances together as part of their UTM offering, and the throughput and functionality can vary from vendor to vendor based on the workload the stack creates on processing incoming packets.

EXAM TIP UTM devices provide a wide range of services, including switching, firewall, IDS/IPS, anti-malware, anti-spam, content filtering, and traffic shaping. This can simplify administration. However, a UTM device can also be single point of failure (SPOF).

Network Address Translation (NAT) Gateway

If you're thinking that a 32-bit address space that's chopped up and subnetted isn't enough to handle all the systems in the world, you're right. While IPv4 address blocks are assigned to organizations such as companies and universities, there usually aren't enough Internet-visible IP addresses to assign to every system on the planet a unique, Internet-routable IP address. To compensate for this lack of available IP address space, organizations use *Network Address Translation (NAT)*, which translates private (nonroutable) IP addresses into public (routable) IP addresses.

Certain IP address blocks are reserved for "private use," and not every system in an organization needs a direct, Internet-routable IP address. Actually, for security reasons, it's much better if most of an organization's systems are hidden from direct Internet access. Most organizations build their internal networks using the private IP address ranges (such as 10.1.1.X) to prevent outsiders from directly accessing those internal networks. However, in many cases those systems still need to be able to reach the Internet. This is accomplished by using a NAT device (typically a firewall or router) that translates the many internal IP addresses into one of a small number of public IP addresses.

For example, consider a fictitious company, ACME.com. ACME has several thousand internal systems using private IP addresses in the 10.X.X.X range. To allow those IP addresses to communicate with the outside world, ACME leases an Internet connection and a few public IP addresses, and deploys a NAT-capable device. ACME administrators configure all their internal hosts to use the NAT device as their default gateway. When internal hosts need to send packets outside the company, they send them to the NAT device. The NAT device removes the internal source IP address out of the outbound packets and replaces it with the NAT device's public, routable address and sends the packets on their way. When response packets are received from outside sources, the device performs NAT in reverse, stripping off the external, public IP address from the destination address field and replacing it with the correct internal, private IP address before sending the packets into the private ACME.com network. Figure 19-5 illustrates this NAT process.

In Figure 19-5, we see an example of NAT being performed. An internal workstation (10.10.10.12) wants to visit a website at 199.181.132.250. When the packet reaches the NAT device, the device translates the 10.10.10.12 source address to the globally routable 63.69.110.110 address, the IP address of the device's externally visible interface.

PART III

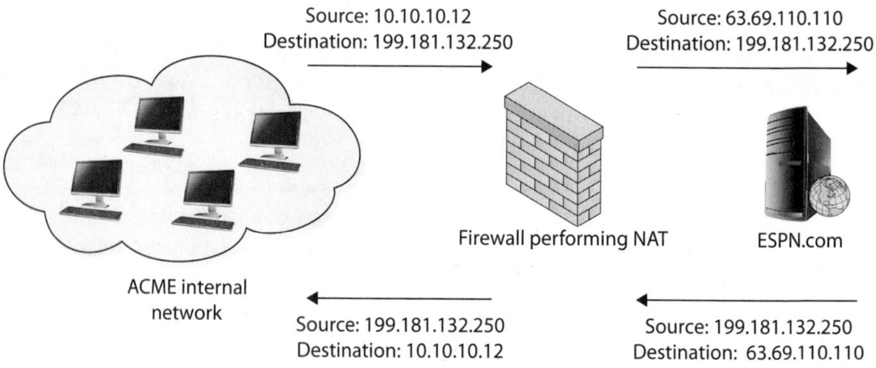

Figure 19-5 Logical depiction of NAT

When the website responds, it responds to the device's address just as if the NAT device had originally requested the information. The NAT device must then remember which internal workstation requested the information and route the packet to the appropriate destination.

While the underlying concept of NAT remains the same, there are actually several different approaches to implementing NAT, including the following:

- **Static NAT** Maps an internal, private address to an external, public address. The same public address is always used for that private address. This technique is often used when hosting something you wish the public to be able to get to, such as a web server, behind a firewall.
- **Dynamic NAT** Maps an internal, private IP address to a public IP address selected from a pool of registered (public) IP addresses. This technique is often used when translating addresses for end-user workstations and the NAT device must keep track of internal/external address mappings.
- **Port Address Translation (PAT)** Allows many different internal, private addresses to share a single external IP address. Devices performing PAT replace the source IP address with the NAT IP address and replace the source port field with a port from an available connection pool. PAT devices keep a translation table to track which internal hosts are using which ports so that subsequent packets can be stamped with the same port number. When response packets are received, the PAT device reverses the process and forwards the packet to the correct internal host. PAT is a very popular NAT technique and in use at many organizations.

Content/URL Filter

Content/URL filters are used to limit specific types of content across the Web to users. A common use is to block sites that are not work related such as Facebook and online games. Content filters can also examine the actual content being returned to a browser, looking for a list of restricted terms or items and blocking not based on URL but on returned content. Like all other policy enforcement devices, content filters rely on a set of rules, and rule maintenance is an issue. One of the most common issues with content filters is too broad of a blocking. In a medical environment, blocking the word "breast" will not work, nor will it in a chicken plant. There needs to be a mechanism in place to lift blocks easily and quickly if a user objects and it is easy to determine they should have access.

Open Source vs. Proprietary

Firewalls come in many forms and types, and one method of differentiating them is to separate them into *open source* and *proprietary* (commercial) solutions. Open source firewalls are exemplified by iptables, a built-in functionality in Linux systems. Iptables and other open source solutions have the cost advantage of being free, but the initial cost of a firewall solution is not the only factor. Ease of maintenance and rule management are the key drivers for long-term use, and many proprietary solutions have worked to increase the utility of their offerings through improving these interfaces.

One of the most common firewalls employed is Microsoft Windows Defender firewall, a proprietary firewall built into the Windows OS.

Hardware vs. Software

Firewalls can be physical devices, hardware, or a set of software services running on a system. For use on a host, a software solution like Microsoft Windows Defender or iptables on a Linux host may well fit the bill. For use in an enterprise setting at a network level, with a need to separate different security zones, a dedicated hardware device is more efficient and economical.

Appliance vs. Host Based vs. Virtual

Firewalls can be located on a host, either as a separate application or part of the operating system itself. In software-defined networking (SDN) networks, firewalls can be instantiated as virtual network functions, providing all of the features under a virtual software solution. Firewalls can also be instantiated via an appliance, acting as a network segregation device, separating portions of a network based on firewall rules.

Access Control List (ACL)

Access controls lists provide the system information as to what objects are permitted which actions. In the case of networks, ACLs can control who gets to change the network parameters via configurations, who gets to pass specific firewalls, and a host of other decisions. The concept of having a list of allowed users, or ACL, is widely used by networks to manage the network security aspects.

Route Security

Routing is the basis of interconnecting networks that comprise the Internet. Packets cross the networks to move information from source to destination. Depending on where the source and destination are with respect to each other, the route a packet takes can be wide ranging, from simple and short to complex and long. The protocols used to connect the various networks range from simple, like the Internet Protocol (IP), to more complex, such as BGP, IS-IS, OSPF, EIGRP, and RIPv2. Maintaining route security is part of the function of each of these protocols, and each serves to fulfill a specific needed functionality in connecting networks. From a Security+ perspective, the details behind each of these protocols is out of scope, but understanding that they work together both to enable network functionality and secure packet transfers is important.

Quality of Service (QoS)

Quality of Service (QoS) is the use of specific technologies on a network to guarantee its ability to manage traffic based on a variety of indicators. High-bandwidth, real-time traffic, such as Voice over IP (VoIP), video conferencing, and video-on-demand, has a high sensitivity to network issues such as latency and jitter. QoS technologies are used to manage network conditions such as bandwidth (throughput), latency (delay), jitter (variance in latency), and error rates. They do this by providing differentiated handling and capacity allocation to specific flows based on packet type and source. QoS enables network administrators to assign the priority in which packets are handled as well as the amount of bandwidth afforded to that application or traffic flow.

Implications of IPv6

The most commonly noted change with IPv6 over IPv4 is the increased addressing range, from 32-bit addresses to 128-bit addresses, offering virtually an unlimited address space, but this is far from the only advance. IPv6 has many implications for secure network designs—some good, some problematic. IPv6 enables end-to-end encryption, which is great for communication security but bad for network monitoring. IPv6 uses the Secure Neighbor Discovery (SEND) protocol, which alleviates ARP poisoning attacks. IPv6 utilizes its wide address space in a manner different from IPv4—there is no NAT in IPv6, so networks will need to be redesigned to take advantage of the increased space and the inherent benefits of the new versions of supporting protocols like ICMPv6, DHCPv6, and so on. In short, IPv6 is a complete reinvention of the networking field with many new advantages—and fewer problems. The challenge is in learning the new protocols and their specific implications. As one of the IPv6 architects explained at a public event, IPv6 is not just window dressing on an old protocol; it is a completely new protocol—backward compatible in some respects, but one that opens up a whole new world of networking.

Port Spanning/Port Mirroring

Most enterprise switches have the ability to copy the activity of one or more ports through a Switch Port Analyzer (SPAN) port, also known as a *port mirror*. This traffic can then be sent to a device for analysis. Port mirrors can have issues when traffic levels get heavy, as the aggregate SPAN traffic can exceed the throughput of the device. For example, a 16-port switch, with each port running at 100 Mbps, can have traffic levels of 1.6 GB if all circuits are maxed, which gives you a good idea of why this technology can have issues in high-traffic environments.

Port Taps

A *test access point (TAP)* is a passive signal-copying mechanism installed between two points on the network. The TAP can copy all packets it receives, rebuilding a copy of all messages. TAPs provide the one distinct advantage of not being overwhelmed by traffic levels, at least not in the process of data collection. The primary disadvantage is that a TAP is a separate piece of hardware and adds to network costs. Unauthorized TAPs can present a security threat, as they make a connection available for monitoring and altering traffic as a man-in-the-middle attack.

EXAM TIP Port taps, when placed between sending and receiving devices, can be used to carry out man-in-the-middle attacks. Thus, when placed by an unauthorized party, they can be a security risk.

Monitoring Services

Network security monitoring (NSM) is the process of collecting and analyzing network data to detect unauthorized activity. NSM is not a way to prevent intrusions, but when deployed inside a network, it can detect where other defenses have failed. It is like having a local security guard patrolling inside a closed building. NSM can be deployed as a service, and many firms have an offering to support monitoring services that give an enterprise a means of detecting unauthorized activity. Having defenses is important, but watching to see when those defenses are failing is the purpose of NMS and monitoring services.

File Integrity Monitors

File integrity monitors are a series of internal processes that can validate the integrity of OS and application files. There are OS utilities that can be automated to do this as well as applications to manage this critical task. Some forms of whitelisting solutions perform this same task, doing a hash check against a known-good value before allowing a program to launch.

Whenever you download a file from an online source, even if from the vendor of the file, you should perform a file integrity check to ensure that the file has not been tampered with in any fashion. This will alert you to a changed binary, even if the hosting agent of the file doesn't know about the specific issue. File integrity checks operate by taking a hash of the file and comparing this value to an offline store of correct values. If the hashes match, then the file is unaltered.

On Microsoft Windows machines, a system file integrity check can be performed using the command-line command **sfc /scannow**. On Debian Linux systems, the command **debsums** is used to verify hash values of installed package components.

EXAM TIP To work properly, every security device covered in this section must be placed inline with the traffic flow that it is intended to interact with. If there are network paths around the device, it will not perform as designed. Understanding the network architecture is important when placing devices.

Chapter Review

In this chapter, you became acquainted with the principles behind secure network design. The chapter opened with an examination of load balancing, including active/active, active/passive, scheduling methodologies, virtual IP, and persistence. The next section dealt with network segmentation, including discussions on virtual local area networks (VLANs), screened subnets, east-west traffic flows, extranets, intranets, and the concept of zero trust.

The next section examined virtual private networks (VPNs). The concepts of always on, split tunnel versus full tunnel, remote access versus site-to-site, IPSec, SSL/TLS instantiations, HTML5 implications, and Layer 2 Tunneling Protocol (L2TP) were presented. The next section was on DNS, followed by network access control (NAC), including both agent and agentless forms. Out-of-band management was covered, followed by a section on port security. Under port security, the topics of broadcast storm prevention, Bridge Protocol Data Unit (BPDU) guards, loop prevention, Dynamic Host Configuration Protocol (DHCP) snooping, and media access control (MAC) filtering were covered.

The next major section covered network appliances. Under this section, jump servers and proxy servers, both forward and reverse, were covered. An examination of network-based intrusion detection systems (NIDSs) and network-based intrusion prevention systems (NIPSs) followed, including sections on signature-based systems, heuristic/behavior systems, anomaly-based systems, and inline versus passive placement options. Additional network appliances covered included HSM devices, sensors, collectors, and aggregators. The next major section on network appliances covered firewalls. In this area, the topics of web application firewalls (WAFs), next-generation firewalls (NGFWs), stateful versus stateless traffic, unified threat management (UTM) systems, Network Address Translation (NAT) gateways, content/URL filters, open source versus proprietary firewall implementations, hardware versus software implementations, and appliance versus host-based versus virtual systems were covered.

The topics of access control lists (ACLs), route security, Quality of Service (QoS), and the implications of IPv6 followed. The chapter concluded with sections on port spanning/port mirroring, including port TAPs, monitoring services, and file integrity monitors.

Questions

To help you prepare further for the CompTIA Security+ exam, and to test your level of preparedness, answer the following questions and then check your answers against the correct answers at the end of the chapter.

1. A network-based intrusion prevention system (NIPS) relies on what other technology at its core?
   - A. VPN
   - B. IDS
   - C. NAT
   - D. ACL
2. You have been asked to prepare a report on network-based intrusion detection systems that compares the NIDS solutions from two potential vendors your company is considering. One solution is signature based and one is behavior based. Which of the following lists what your report will identify as the key advantage of each?
   - A. Behavioral: low false-negative rate; Signature: ability to detect zero-day attacks
   - B. Behavioral: ability to detect zero-day attacks; Signature: low false-positive rates
   - C. Behavioral: high false-positive rate; Signature: high speed of detection
   - D. Behavioral: low false-positive rate; Signature: high false-positive rate
3. How can proxy servers improve security?
   - A. They use TLS-based encryption to access all sites.
   - B. They can control which sites and content employees access, lessening the chance of malware exposure.
   - C. They enforce appropriate use of company resources.
   - D. They prevent access to phishing sites.
4. What technology can check the client's health before allowing access to the network?
   - A. DLP
   - B. Reverse proxy
   - C. NIDS/NIPS
   - D. NAC
5. What kind of device provides tamper protection for encryption keys?
   - A. HSM
   - B. IPSec
   - C. Jump server
   - D. HTML5

6. What is the purpose of the DNS protocol?
   A. It provides a function for charging SaaS on a per-use basis.
   B. It supports the networking infrastructure.
   C. It translates names into IP addresses.
   D. It defines tenants in a public cloud.
7. A user reports to the help desk that he is getting "cannot resolve address" error messages from his browser. Which port is likely a problem on his firewall?
   A. 22
   B. 553
   C. 440
   D. 53
8. What is the primary purpose of a screened subnet?
   A. To prevent direct access to secure servers from the Internet
   B. To provide a place for corporate servers to reside so they can access the Internet
   C. To create a safe computing environment next to the Internet
   D. To slow down traffic coming and going to the network
9. What is the best tool to ensure network traffic priorities for video conferencing are maintained?
   A. QoS
   B. VLAN
   C. Network segmentation
   D. Next-generation firewall
10. If you wish to monitor 100 percent of the transmissions from your customer service representatives to the Internet and other internal services, which is the best tool to use?
   A. SPAN port
   B. TAP
   C. Mirror port
   D. Aggregator switches

Answers

1. **B.** A NIPS relies on the technology of an intrusion detection system (IDS) at its core to detect potential attacks.

2. **B.** The key advantage of a behavior-based NIDS is its ability to detect zero-day attacks, whereas the key advantage of a signature-based NIDS is low false-positive rates.
3. **B.** Proxy servers can improve security by limiting the sites and content accessed by employees, thus limiting the potential access to malware.
4. **D.** NAC, or network access control, is a technology that can enforce the security health of a client machine before allowing it access to the network.
5. **A.** A hardware security module (HSM) has tamper protections to prevent the encryption keys it manages from being altered.
6. **C.** The Domain Name System (DNS) translates names into IP addresses.
7. **D.** The Domain Name System (DNS) uses TCP and UDP port 53 for standard queries and responses.
8. **A.** The primary purpose of a screened subnet is to provide separation between the untrusted zone of the Internet and the trusted zone of enterprise systems. It does so by preventing direct access to secure servers from the Internet.
9. **A.** Quality of Service (QoS) solutions can manage traffic flows by type to provide guaranteed access and priority for specific traffic flows.
10. **B.** A test access point (TAP) is required to monitor 100 percent of the transmissions from your customer service representatives to the Internet and other internal services.

CHAPTER 20

Wireless Security

In this chapter, you will

- Learn about wireless cryptographic and authentication protocols
- Learn about methods and installation considerations

Wireless is increasingly the way people access the Internet. Because wireless access is considered a consumer benefit, many businesses add wireless access points to lure customers into their shops. With the rollout of fifth-generation (5G) cellular networks, people are also increasingly accessing the Internet from their mobile phones. The massive growth in popularity of nontraditional computers such as netbooks, e-readers, and tablets has also driven the popularity of wireless access.

As wireless use increases, the security of the wireless protocols has become a more important factor in the security of the entire network. As a security professional, you need to understand wireless network applications because of the risks inherent in broadcasting a network signal where anyone can intercept it. Sending unsecured information across public airwaves is tantamount to posting your company's passwords by the front door of the building. This chapter looks at several current wireless protocols and their security features.

Certification Objective This chapter covers CompTIA Security+ exam objective 3.4: Given a scenario, install and configure wireless security settings.

Cryptographic Protocols

Wireless networks, by their very nature, make physical security protections against rogue connections difficult. This lack of a physical barrier makes protection against others eavesdropping on a connection also a challenge. *Cryptographic protocols* are the standards used to describe cryptographic methods and implementations to ensure interoperability between different vendors' equipment.

The history of cryptographic protocols in wireless begins with Wired Equivalent Privacy (WEP) and then transitions to Wi-Fi Protected Access (WPA), but both of these fell to poor design. The designers of the 802.11 protocol attempted to maintain confidentiality in wireless systems by introducing WEP, which uses a cipher to encrypt the data as it is transmitted through the air. WEP was initially a success, but over time several weaknesses were discovered in this protocol. WEP encrypts the data traveling across the network with an RC4 stream cipher, attempting to ensure confidentiality. The flaw in WEP was that the initialization vector was of insufficient length to protect the channel.

The first standard to be used in the market to replace WEP was WPA. This standard uses the flawed WEP algorithm with the Temporal Key Integrity Protocol (TKIP). TKIP works by using a shared secret combined with the card's MAC address to generate a new key, which is mixed with the initialization vector (IV) to make per-packet keys that encrypt a single packet using the same RC4 cipher used by traditional WEP. This overcomes the WEP key weakness, as a key is used on only one packet.

Although both WEP and WPA were flawed, they led to WPA2, and eventually WPA3, both of which are in use today. If you find the older protocols still in use, understand that they do not provide any substantial level of security and should be upgraded.

NOTE WEP and WPA are no longer listed under Security+ exam objectives, but the facts and background are relevant to WPA2 and illustrate how we got to where we are.

Wi-Fi Protected Access 2 (WPA2)

IEEE 802.11i is the standard for security in wireless networks and is also known as *Wi-Fi Protected Access 2 (WPA2)*. It uses 802.1X to provide authentication and uses Advanced Encryption Standard (AES) as the encryption protocol. WPA2 uses the AES block cipher, a significant improvement over WEP and WPA's use of the RC4 stream cipher. WPA2 specifies the use of the Counter Mode with CBC-MAC Protocol (in full, the Counter Mode with Cipher Block Chaining–Message Authentication Codes Protocol, or simply CCMP). CCMP is described later in this chapter.

While WPA2 addressed the flaws in WPA and was the de facto standard for many years on wireless networks that were serious about security, it too fell to a series of issues, leading to the development of WPA3. WPA2 comes with a variety of methods to set up the shared key elements, and those are described later in the chapter. The WPA2-Personal passphrase can be cracked using brute force attacks. Even worse, once a hacker captures the data from the airwaves, the actual password cracking can occur offline on a more powerful, dedicated machine. Any encrypted messages they recorded can then be decrypted later, thus yielding passwords and other sensitive data.

WPA2 comes in two flavors: WPA2-Personal and WPA2-Enterprise. WPA2-Personal is also called WPA2-PSK because it uses authentication based on a pre-shared key (PSK), which allows home users without an enterprise authentication server to manage the keys. To use WPA2-PSK on a network, the router is given the pre-shared key, typically a plain-English passphrase between 8 and 63 characters long. WPA2-Personal then uses TKIP to combine that passphrase with the network Service Set Identifier (SSID) to generate unique encryption keys for each wireless client. WPA2-Enterprise replaces the pre-shared key with IEEE 802.1X, which is discussed in its own section later in this chapter. By eliminating the PSK element, WPA2-Enterprise can create stronger keys, and the information is not subject to capture.

In WPA2, an attacker can record the 4-way handshake between a client and the access point and use this data to crack the password. This will then crack all the keys that have been used or will be used in the future. Because of the ability to break future messages based on past messages, forward secrecy is not provided by WPA2.

Wi-Fi Protected Access 3 (WPA3)

Wi-Fi Protected Access 3 (WPA3) is the successor to WPA2. Developed in 2018, it strives to resolve the weaknesses found in WPA2. WPA3 improves the security of the encryption by using Simultaneous Authentication of Equals (SAE) in place of the PSK authentication method used in prior WPA versions. SAE is described in detail later in this chapter. This change allows WPA3-Personal networks to employ simple passphrases that are significantly more time consuming to break than was the case with WPA/WPA2.

WPA3-Enterprise brings a whole host of upgrades, including 192-bit minimum-strength security protocols and cryptographic tools such as the following:

- **Authenticated encryption** 256-bit Galois/Counter Mode Protocol (GCMP-256)
- **Key derivation and confirmation** 384-bit Hashed Message Authentication Code (HMAC) with Secure Hash Algorithm (HMAC-SHA-384)
- **Key establishment and authentication** Elliptic Curve Diffie-Hellman (ECDH) exchange and Elliptic Curve Digital Signature Algorithm (ECDSA) using a 384-bit elliptic curve
- **Robust management frame protection** 256-bit Broadcast/Multicast Integrity Protocol Galois Message Authentication Code (BIP-GMAC-256)

WPA3 integrates with the back-end enterprise authentication infrastructure, such as a RADIUS server. It can use elliptic curve Diffie-Hellman exchanges and elliptic curve Digital Signature Algorithm (DSA) protocols to provide a method of strong authentication. The WPA3 protocol makes use of a Quick Response (QR) code for users to connect their devices to the "Wi-Fi CERTIFIED Easy Connect" network, which allows them to scan a QR code on a device with their smartphone. WPA3 offers forward secrecy based on its method of encryption; previous messages do not enable future decryption.

EXAM TIP WPA2 uses pre-shared keys; WPA3 does not. If SAE is used, it is for WPA3-level authentication. Forward secrecy is only provided by WPA3.

Counter Mode/CBC-MAC Protocol (CCMP)

CCMP stands for *Counter Mode with Cipher Block Chaining–Message Authentication Code Protocol* (or *Counter Mode with CBC-MAC Protocol*). CCMP is a data encapsulation encryption mechanism designed for wireless use. CCMP is actually the mode in which the AES cipher is used to provide message integrity. Unlike WPA/TKIP, WPA2/CCMP requires new hardware to perform the AES encryption.

Simultaneous Authentication of Equals (SAE)

Simultaneous Authentication of Equals (SAE) is a password-based key exchange method developed for mesh networks. Defined in RFC 7664, it uses the Dragonfly protocol to perform a key exchange and is secure against passive monitoring. SAE is not a new protocol; it has been around for more than a decade, but its incorporation as part of enterprise-level wireless protocols is relatively new. It is well suited for this because it creates a cryptographically strong shared secret for securing other data. Because of its zero-knowledge key generation method, it is resistant to active, passive, and dictionary attacks. As a peer-to-peer protocol, it does not rely on other parties, so it is an alternative to using certificates or a centralized authority for authentication. To configure SAE, you must set the security parameter k to a value of at least 40, per the recommendation in RFC 7664, "Dragonfly Key Exchange," for all groups to prevent timing leaks.

Authentication Protocols

Wireless networks have a need for secure authentication protocols. The following authentication protocols should be understood for the Security+ exam: EAP, PEAP, EAP-FAST, EAP-TLS, EAP-TTLS, IEEE 802.1X, and RADIUS Federation.

Extensible Authentication Protocol (EAP)

The *Extensible Authentication Protocol (EAP)* is a protocol for wireless networks that expands on authentication methods used by the Point-to-Point Protocol (PPP). PPP is a protocol that was commonly used to directly connect devices to each other. EAP is defined in RFC 2284 (obsoleted by 3748). EAP can support multiple authentication mechanisms, including tokens, smart cards, certificates, one-time passwords, and public key encryption authentication. EAP has been expanded into multiple versions, some of which are covered in the following sections.

Protected Extensible Authentication Protocol (PEAP)

PEAP, or *Protected EAP,* was developed to protect EAP communication by encapsulating it with Transport Layer Security (TLS). This is an open standard developed jointly by Cisco, Microsoft, and RSA. EAP was designed assuming a secure communication channel. PEAP provides that protection as part of the protocol via a TLS tunnel. PEAP is widely supported by vendors for use over wireless networks. The Wi-Fi Alliance added PEAP to its list of supported protocols for WPA/WPA2/WPA3.

EAP-FAST

EAP-FAST (EAP Flexible Authentication via Secure Tunneling) is described in RFC 4851 and proposed by Cisco to be a replacement for LEAP, a previous Cisco version of EAP. It offers a lightweight tunneling protocol to enable authentication. The distinguishing characteristic is the passing of a Protected Access Credential (PAC) that is used to establish a TLS tunnel through which client credentials are verified. The Wi-Fi Alliance added EAP-FAST to its list of supported protocols for WPA/WPA2/WPA3.

EAP-TLS

EAP-TLS is an Internet Engineering Task Force (IETF) open standard (RFC 5216) that uses the TLS protocol to secure the authentication process. EAP-TLS relies on TLS, an attempt to standardize the Secure Sockets Layer (SSL) structure to pass credentials. This is still considered one of the most secure implementations, primarily because common implementations employ client-side certificates. This means that an attacker must also possess the key for the client-side certificate to break the TLS channel. The Wi-Fi Alliance added EAP-TLS to its list of supported protocols for WPA/WPA2/WPA3.

EXAM TIP The Security+ exam has used questions concerning certificates and authentication protocols in the past. EAP-TLS for mutual authentication requires client and server certificates. PEAP and EAP-TTLS eliminate the requirement to deploy or use client certificates. EAP-FAST does not require certificates.

EAP-TTLS

EAP-TTLS (which stands for *EAP–Tunneled TLS)* is a variant of the EAP-TLS protocol. EAP-TTLS works much the same way as EAP-TLS, with the server authenticating to the client with a certificate, but the protocol tunnels the client side of the authentication, allowing the use of legacy authentication protocols such as Password Authentication Protocol (PAP), Challenge-Handshake Authentication Protocol (CHAP), Microsoft Challenge Handshake Authentication Protocol (MS-CHAP), and MS-CHAP-V2. In EAP-TTLS, the authentication process is protected by the tunnel from man-in-the-middle attacks, and although client-side certificates can be used, they are not required, making this easier to set up than EAP-TLS to clients without certificates. The Wi-Fi Alliance added EAP-TTLS to its list of supported protocols for WPA/WPA2/WPA3.

NOTE WPA3 is designed to work together with a variety of EAP methods in an enterprise. A WPA3 station performs server certificate validation when using EAP-TTLS, EAP-TLS, EAP, and PEAP methods.

EXAM TIP There are two key elements concerning EAP. First, it is only a framework to secure the authentication process, not an actual encryption method. Second, many variants exist, and understanding the differences, and how to recognize them in practice, between EAP, PEAP, EAP-FAST, EAP-TLS, and EAP-TTLS is important for the exam.

IEEE 802.1X

IEEE 802.1X is an authentication standard that supports port-based authentication services between a user and an authorization device, such as an edge router. IEEE 802.1X is commonly used on wireless access points as a port-based authentication service prior to admission to the wireless network. WPA2-Enterprise uses IEEE 802.1X to establish a secure connection between devices. IEEE 802.1X over wireless uses either IEEE 802.11i or an EAP-based protocol such as EAP-TLS or PEAP-TLS.

Remote Authentication Dial-in User Service (RADIUS) Federation

Using a series of RADIUS servers in a federated connection has been employed in several worldwide *RADIUS federation* networks. One example is the project eduroam (short for *education roaming*), which connects users of education institutions worldwide. The process is relatively simple in concept, although the technical details to maintain the hierarchy of RADIUS servers and routing tables is daunting at a worldwide scale. A user packages their credentials at a local access point using a certificate-based tunneling protocol method. The first RADIUS server determines which RADIUS server to send the request to, and from there the user is authenticated via their home RADIUS server, and the results are passed back, permitting the joining to the network.

Because the credentials must pass multiple different networks, the EAP methods are limited to those with certificates and credentials to prevent loss of credentials during transit. This type of federated identity at global scale demonstrates the power of RADIUS and EAP methods.

EXAM TIP RADIUS federation allows users to use their normal credentials across trusted networks. This allows users in one organization to authenticate and access resources on another trusted organization's network using one set of credentials.

Methods

Authentication methods are used to provide authentication services (in the case of wireless networks, remotely) through the configuration of the protocols used to protect the communication channel. This section covers the configuration of the systems so that the protocols can be employed in a secure manner.

Pre-shared Key (PSK) vs. Enterprise vs. Open

When building out a wireless network, you must decide how you are going to employ security on the network. Specifically, you need to address who will be allowed to connect, and what level of protection will be provided in the transmission of data between devices and the access point.

Both WPA and WPA2, discussed in detail earlier in the chapter, have two methods to establish a connection: PSK and Enterprise. *PSK* stands for pre-shared key, which is a secret that's shared between users. A PSK is typically entered as a passphrase of up to 63 characters. This key must be securely shared between users, as it is the basis of the security provided by the protocol. The PSK is converted to a 256-bit key that is then used to secure all communications between the device and access point. PSK has one particular vulnerability: simple and short PSKs are at risk of brute force attempts. Keeping the PSK at least 20 random characters long or longer should mitigate this attack vector.

In *Enterprise* mode, the devices use IEEE 802.1X and a RADIUS authentication server to enable a connection. This method allows the use of usernames and passwords and provides enterprise-class options such as network access control (NAC) integration and multiple random keys, instead of everyone sharing the same PSK. If everyone has the same PSK, then secrecy between clients is limited to other means, and in the event of one client failure, others could be compromised.

In WEP-based systems, there are two options: Open System authentication and shared key authentication. *Open System authentication* is not truly authentication; instead, it is merely a sharing of a secret key based on the SSID. The process is simple: the mobile client matches the SSID with the access point and requests a key (called authentication) to the access point. Then the access point generates an authentication code (the key, as there is no specific authentication of the client), which is a random number intended for use only during that session. The mobile client uses the authentication code and joins the network. The session continues until disassociation either by request or loss of signal.

EXAM TIP Understand the differences between PSK, Enterprise, and Open System authentication.

Wi-Fi Protected Setup (WPS)

Wi-Fi Protected Setup (WPS) is a network security standard created to provide users with an easy method of configuring wireless networks. Designed for home networks and small business networks, this standard involves the use of an eight-digit PIN to configure wireless devices. WPS consists of a series of EAP messages and has been shown to be susceptible to a brute force attack. A successful attack can reveal the PIN, and subsequently the WPA/WPA2 passphrase, and allow unauthorized parties to gain access to the network. Currently, the only effective mitigation is to disable WPS. The Wi-Fi Alliance, when deprecating WPS, added the Easy Connect method to replace it and eliminated the weaknesses of WPS.

Captive Portals

Captive portal refers to a specific technique of using an HTTP client to handle authentication on a wireless network. Frequently employed in public hotspots, a captive portal opens a web browser to an authentication page. This occurs before the user is granted admission to the network. The access point uses this simple mechanism by intercepting all packets and returning the web page for login. The actual web server that serves up the authentication page can be in a walled-off section of the network, blocking access to the Internet until the user successfully authenticates.

EXAM TIP Captive portals are common in coffee shops, airports, hotels, and stores. The user accepts the offered conditions, views, and advertisement, provides an e-mail address or other authentication requirement, and is granted access to the portal.

Installation Considerations

Wireless systems are more than just protocols. Putting up a functional wireless system in a house is as easy as plugging in a wireless access point and connecting. However, in an enterprise, where multiple access points will be needed, the configuration takes significantly more work. Site surveys are needed to determine proper access point and antenna placement, as well as channels and power levels.

Elements that have to be considered are based on signal propagation and interference. Signal propagation is a function of antennas, signal strength, and the physical layout of a facility, including intervening structures. These are all addressed using site surveys, Wi-Fi analyzers, and software to optimize access point placement.

Site Surveys

When developing a coverage map for a complex building site, you need to take into account a wide variety of factors—particularly walls, interfering sources, and floor plans. A *site survey* involves several steps: mapping the floor plan, testing for RF interference, testing for RF coverage, and analyzing material via software. The software can suggest placement of access points. This is an example of a predictive site survey analysis.

After deploying the APs, you survey the site again, mapping the results versus the predicted analysis while watching signal strength and signal-to-noise ratios. One of the results of this is a heat map, or graphical representation of signal strength. This is discussed in the next section, and Figure 20-1 illustrates what the heat map portion of a site survey looks like. This actual signal strength analysis is called an onsite analysis site survey and is used to validate the predictive analysis. If necessary, access points can be moved to improve signal strengths in problem areas.

Another important use of site surveys is the auditing of existing wireless networks to find areas of degraded performance or even rogue access points. Both of these circumstances represent risk to wireless networks, and the only way to find these conditions is to periodically monitor for them.

EXAM TIP Wireless networks are dependent on radio signals to function. It is important to understand that antenna type, placement, and site surveys are used to ensure proper coverage of a site, including areas blocked by walls, interfering signals, and echoes.

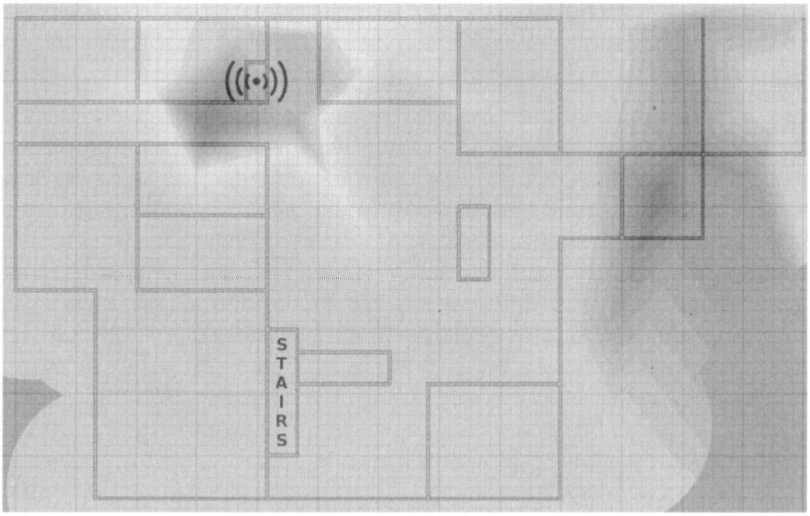

Figure 20-1 A sample Wi-Fi heat map

Heat Maps

A Wi-Fi *heat map* is a map of wireless signal coverage and strength. Typically, a heat map shows a layout of a room, floor, or facility overlaid by a graphical representation of a wireless signal. Heat maps are created using a Wi-Fi analyzer and software to allow the analysis of Wi-Fi signal strength in the form of a graphical layout. This allows network administrators to find areas of weak signals and consider alternative access point placement. An example of a heat map is shown in Figure 20-1. The different shades indicate signal strength, showing where reception is strong and where it is weak.

EXAM TIP A site survey is a process for determining Wi-Fi signal strengths; the heat map is one of the outcomes and is part of the survey.

Wi-Fi Analyzers

Wi-Fi analyzers provide a means of determining signal strength and channel interference. A Wi-Fi analyzer is an RF device used to measure signal strength and quality. It can determine if the Wi-Fi signal strength is sufficient, and if there are competing devices on a particular channel. This enables an engineer to allocate signals both in strength and channel to improve Wi-Fi performance.

Channel Overlays

Wi-Fi radio signals exist at specific frequencies: 2.4 GHz and 5.0 GHz. Each of these signals is broken into a series of channels, and the actual data transmissions occur across these channels. Wi-Fi versions of IEEE 802.11 (a, b, g, n) work with channel frequencies of 2400 MHz and 2500 MHz, hence the term 2.4 GHz for the system. The 100 MHz in between is split into 14 channels of 20 MHz each. As a result, each channel overlaps with up to four other channels. If you used nearby channels, this overlapping makes wireless network throughput quite poor. For this reason, most 2.4 GHz systems use channels 1, 6, and 11. When multiple access points are in close proximity, there can be issues with competing signals. In an apartment, if you find that your neighbors are using channels 2 and 10, then you would want to switch your devices to 6 to improve signal strength in your channel. Most wireless routers use an auto function to manage this function, but in cases where congestion is occurring, learning the distribution of signals via a site survey and partitioning your devices into available channels will improve performance.

Beyond just improving channel overlay issues, the Wi-Fi Alliance has improved system throughput through the use of newer standards, including 802.11ac and 802.11ax. These systems use a set of different encoding mechanisms and frequency allocations to increase throughput in dense Wi-Fi environments such as large public gatherings. These methods are referred to as Wi-Fi 6 or, in the case of 802.11ax specifically, High Efficiency Wireless (HEW).

Wireless Access Point (WAP) Placement

Wireless access point (WAP) placement is seemingly simple. Perform a site survey, determine the optimum placement based on RF signal strength, and you are done. But not so fast. Access points also need power, so the availability of power to the placement can be an issue. And if the access point is going to be connected to the network, then availability of a network connection is also a consideration. These issues can actually be more challenging in a home environment because home users are not likely to incur the expense of running dedicated power and network connections to the access point. To help solve this issue in home and small networks, many vendors have mesh-based Wi-Fi extenders that enable Wi-Fi radio frequency (RF) signals to be extended via relays, but this can come at a throughput cost if the network becomes congested with devices.

For security reasons, you should be aware that Wi-Fi signals go through walls, so placing access points where they produce large areas of coverage outside a facility may lead to outsiders accessing your system. Protecting the access point from physical access is also important. Coordinating AP placement with site surveys is important to address issues of poor placement leading to bad coverage, signal bleed, and throughput costs associated with adding too many APs or extenders.

Controller and Access Point Security

Wireless access points are physical connections to your network infrastructure and should be guarded as such. Proper *controller and access point security* provisions include both physical and logical security precautions. The case of logical security has been the main focus of this chapter, keeping unauthorized users from accessing the channels. Physical security is just as important, if not more so, and the actual devices and network connections should be placed in a location that is not readily accessible to an attacker. This is especially true for exterior connections where no one would observe someone physically manipulating the device.

Chapter Review

In this chapter, you became acquainted wireless security. The chapter opened with an examination of some of the cryptographic protocols used in wireless communications, including the WPA2, WPA3, CCMP, and SAE protocols. The next section was on authentication protocols. In this section, we explored the EAP series, including PEAP, EAP-FAST, EAP-TLS, and EAP-TTLS. Next was IEEE 802.1X and RADIUS.

The next section examined methods of configuring wireless services. In this section, the topics of pre-shared key versus enterprise versus open methods, Wi-Fi protected setup, and captive portals were covered. The chapter concluded with a section on installation considerations, including site surveys, heat maps and Wi-Fi analyzers. Channel overlays, wireless access point placement, and controller and access point security concerns completed the chapter.

Questions

To help you prepare further for the CompTIA Security+ exam, and to test your level of preparedness, answer the following questions and then check your answers against the correct answers at the end of the chapter.

1. The use of an eight-digit PIN to set up a wireless connection is part of which of the following?
   - **A.** WPA
   - **B.** SAE
   - **C.** WPA3
   - **D.** WPS
2. What is the role of EAP in wireless connections?
   - **A.** It is a framework for establishing connectivity.
   - **B.** It is a framework for passing authentication information.
   - **C.** It is a framework to secure the authentication process.
   - **D.** It is an actual encryption method used during authentication.
3. What is the primary difference between WPA2-Personal and WPA2-Enterprise?
   - **A.** The use of a pre-shared secret
   - **B.** The number of concurrent supported users
   - **C.** Licensing costs on a per-user basis
   - **D.** The use of SAE for connections

4. You are setting up a Wi-Fi hotspot for guest visitors. What is the best method of establishing connections?
   A. Open access
   B. A posted password visually available on site
   C. Use of a PSK solution
   D. Captive portal
5. What is the most secure means of establishing connectivity to a Wi-Fi access point?
   A. CCMP
   B. SAE protocol
   C. WPA2
   D. IEEE 802.1X
6. A site survey will reveal all of the following except which one?
   A. Optimal access point placement
   B. Captive portal location
   C. Channel allocations
   D. Link speeds across the site
7. Forward secrecy exists for which of the following protocols?
   A. WPS
   B. WPA2
   C. WPA3
   D. All of the above
8. Your boss has asked you to set up wireless connectivity at a new company location. However, she is concerned about planning, coverage, and security regarding AP placement. She wants you to ensure coverage and address security concerns. Which of the following should you consider using while setting up this new location? (Select three.)
   A. RADIUS federation
   B. Site survey
   C. Wi-Fi analyzer
   D. Heat map
9. You are using EAP-TTLS, which includes what unique aspect?
   A. It cannot be used in WPA3.
   B. It requires client-side certificates.
   C. It cannot be used with CHAP.
   D. It is easier to set up than other EAP schemes.

10. Which protocol allows the passing of legacy authentication protocols such as PAP, CHAP, and MS-CHAP?
    A. EAP-TTLS
    B. EAP-TLS
    C. SAE
    D. CCMP

Answers

1. **D.** Wi-Fi Protected Setup (WPS) uses an eight-digit PIN to establish a connection between devices.
2. **C.** EAP is only a framework to secure the authentication process, not an actual encryption method.
3. **A.** WPA2-Personal uses a PSK, whereas WPA2-Enterprise does not.
4. **D.** A captive portal is a method of having users log on to your system. These are common in coffee shops, airports, hotels, and stores.
5. **B.** The use of SAE, part of WPA3, is currently the most secure way to establish a connection via wireless.
6. **B.** Captive portals are software-driven locations a user is pointed to, not part of the physical Wi-Fi configuration.
7. **C.** Forward secrecy is only available via WPA3. This is because the method of establishing the connection is not observable.
8. **B, C,** and **D**. Professional site surveys, Wi-Fi analyzers, and heat maps for wireless network installations and proper access point (AP) placement are used to ensure coverage area and security concerns. Answers A is incorrect because RADIUS federation allows users to use their normal credentials across trusted networks.
9. **D.** EAP-TTLS is easier to set up than other EAP networks because of its ability to operate without client-side certificates.
10. **A.** The EAP-TTLS protocol tunnels the client side of the authentication, allowing the use of legacy authentication protocols such as Password Authentication Protocol (PAP), Challenge-Handshake Authentication Protocol (CHAP), MS-CHAP, and MS-CHAP-V2.

CHAPTER 21

Secure Mobile Solutions

In this chapter, you will

- Understand the connection methods of mobile devices
- Understand the different types of mobile devices and their management
- Be introduced to mobile device policies and procedures
- Examine some deployment models of mobile devices

There has been an amazing convergence of business and individual usage of mobile devices. The convergence of cloud storage capabilities and Software as a Service (SaaS) is dramatically changing the landscape of mobile device usage. The ubiquitous presence of mobile devices and the need for continuous data access across multiple platforms have led to significant changes in the way mobile devices are being used for personal and business purposes. In the past, companies provided mobile devices to their employees for primarily business usage, but they were available for personal usage. With continuously emerging devices and constantly changing technologies, many companies are allowing employees to bring their own devices for both personal and business usage.

Certification Objective This chapter covers CompTIA Security+ exam objective 3.5: Given a scenario, implement secure mobile solutions.

Connection Methods and Receivers

Mobile devices, by their mobile nature, require a non-wired means of connection to a network. Typically, this connection on the enterprise side is via the Internet, but on the mobile device side a wide range of options exist for connectivity. Where and how mobile devices connect to a network can be managed by the enterprise by architecting the mobile connection aspect of its wireless network. This section will cover the common methods of connecting, including cellular, Wi-Fi, Bluetooth, NFC, infrared, and USB. The connection methods of point-to-point and point-to-multipoint are explained. Specialized receivers, such as GPS and RFID, are covered at the end of the section.

Cellular

Cellular connections use mobile telephony circuits, today typically fourth-generation (4G) or LTE in nature, although some 3G services still exist. One of the strengths of cellular is that robust nationwide networks have been deployed, making strong signals available virtually anywhere with reasonable population density. The corresponding weakness is that gaps in cellular service still exist in remote areas.

As this book is being written, the telecommunications world is moving to 5G, the newest form of cellular. This change will occur in densely populated areas first and then move across the globe. 5G is more than just a newer, faster network; it is a redesign to improve network communications through greater throughput, lower latency, better quality-of-service controls, and service differentiations. It is designed to handle streaming video downloads, standard audio calls, and data transfers from a myriad of smaller Internet of Things (IoT) devices, all with appropriate service levels. 5G will enable network services that facilitate the move to widespread data connectivity and transfers over the cellular networks. 5G is much more than just a better cellphone; it is the network for the data connectivity era.

Wi-Fi

Wi-Fi refers to the radio communication methods developed under the Wi-Fi Alliance. These systems exist on 2.4- and 5-GHz frequency spectrums, and networks are constructed by both the enterprise you are associated with and third parties. This communication methodology is ubiquitous with computing platforms and is relatively easy to implement and secure. Securing Wi-Fi networks is covered extensively in Chapter 20, "Wireless Security."

Bluetooth

Bluetooth is a short-to-medium range, low-power wireless protocol that transmits in the 2.4-GHz band, which is the same band used for 802.11. The original concept for this short-range (approximately 32 feet) wireless protocol is to transmit data in personal area networks (PANs). Bluetooth transmits and receives data from a variety of devices, the most common being mobile phones, laptops, printers, and audio devices. The mobile phone has driven a lot of Bluetooth growth and has even spread Bluetooth into new cars as a mobile phone hands-free kit. Advances in transmitter power, antenna gain, and operating environment uses have expanded the range up to 3800 meters in some outdoor applications.

Bluetooth has gone through several releases. Version 1.1 was the first commercially successful version, with version 1.2 released in 2007 and correcting some of the problems found in 1.1. Version 1.2 allows speeds up to 721 Kbps and improves resistance to interference. Version 1.2 is backward compatible with version 1.1. With the rate of advancement and the life of most tech items, Bluetooth 1 series is basically extinct. Bluetooth 2.0 introduced enhanced data rate (EDR), which allows the transmission of up to 3.0 Mbps. Bluetooth 3.0 has the capability to use an 802.11 channel to achieve speeds up to 24 Mbps. The current version is the Bluetooth 4.0 standard, with support for three modes: Classic, High Speed, and Low Energy.

Bluetooth 4 introduced a new method to support collecting data from devices that generate data at a very low rate. Some devices, such as medical devices, may only collect and transmit data at low rates. This feature, called Bluetooth Low Energy (BLE), was designed to aggregate data from various sensors, like heart rate monitors, thermometers, and so forth, and carries the commercial name Bluetooth Smart. Bluetooth 5 continues the improvements of BLE, increasing BLE's data rate and range.

As Bluetooth became popular, people started trying to find holes in it. Bluetooth features easy configuration of devices to allow communication, with no need for network addresses or ports. Bluetooth uses pairing to establish a trust relationship between devices. To establish that trust, the devices advertise capabilities and require a passkey. To help maintain security, most devices require the passkey to be entered into both devices; this prevents a default passkey–type attack. The Bluetooth's protocol advertisement of services and pairing properties is where some of the security issues start. Bluetooth should always have discoverable mode turned off unless you're deliberately pairing a device. The following table displays Bluetooth versions and speeds.

Bluetooth Version	Maximum Range	Maximum Data Rate
3.0 (Classic)	< 200 feet	25 Mbps
4.X	200 feet / 60 meters	25 Mbps
5.X	985 feet / 300 meters	50 Mbps

In the Bluetooth versions of 5.X, different data rates correspond to differing ranges, with higher rates at lower ranges supporting more data-rich devices, and lower rates having longer ranges to support lower-data-rate IoT devices. Bluetooth 5 uses a different frequency spectrum, requiring new hardware and limiting backward compatibility, but it is designed for local networks of the future with low power consumption, inexpensive hardware, small implementations, and scalable data rates versus range considerations.

NFC

Near field communication (NFC) is a set of wireless technologies that enables smartphones and other devices to establish radio communication when they are within close proximity to each other—typically a distance of 10 cm (3.9 in) or less. This technology did not see much use until recently when it started being employed to move data between cell phones and in mobile payment systems. NFC is likely to become a high-use technology in the years to come as multiple uses exist for the technology, and the next generation of smartphones is sure to include this as a standard function. Currently, NFC relies to a great degree on its very short range for security, although apps that use it have their own security mechanisms as well.

Infrared

Infrared (IR) is a band of electromagnetic energy just beyond the red end of the visible color spectrum. IR has been used in remote-control devices for years. IR made its debut in computer networking as a wireless method to connect to printers. Now that wireless keyboards, wireless mice, and mobile devices exchange data via IR, it seems to be everywhere. IR can also be used to connect devices in a network configuration, but it is slow compared to other wireless technologies. IR cannot penetrate walls but instead bounces off them. Nor can it penetrate other solid objects; therefore, if you stack a few items in front of the transceiver, the signal is lost. Because IR can be seen by all in range, any desired security must be on top of the base transmission mechanism.

USB

Universal Serial Bus (USB) has become the ubiquitous standard for connecting devices with cables. Mobile phones can transfer data and charge their battery via USB. Laptops, desktops, even servers have USB ports for a variety of data connection needs. Many devices, such as phones, tablets, and IoT devices, also use USB ports, although many are moving to the newer and smaller USB type C (USB-C) connector. USB ports have greatly expanded users' ability to connect devices to their computers. USB ports automatically recognize a device being plugged into the system and usually work without the user needing to add drivers or configure software. This has spawned a legion of USB devices, from music players to peripherals to storage devices—virtually anything that can consume or deliver data connects via USB.

The most interesting of these devices, for security purposes, are the USB flash memory–based storage devices. USB drive keys, which are basically flash memory with a USB interface in a device typically about the size of your thumb, provide a way to move files easily from computer to computer. When plugged into a USB port, these devices automount and behave like any other drive attached to the computer. Their small size and relatively large capacity, coupled with instant read-write capability, present security problems. They can easily be used by an individual with malicious intent to conceal the removal of files or data from the building or to bring malicious files into the building and onto the company network.

USB connectors come in a wide range of sizes and shapes. For mobile use, there is USB mini, USB micro, and now USB-C, which is faster and reversible (does not care which side is up). There are also type A and type B connectors, with different form factors. The original USB provided data rates up to 480 Mbps, with USB 3 raising it to 5 Gbps, 3.1 to 10 Gbps, and 3.2 to 20 Gbps. USB 4 provides speeds up to 40 Gbps.

Point-to-Point

Radio signals travel outward from an antenna, and eventually are received by a receiving antenna. *Point-to-point* communications are defined as communications with one endpoint on each end—a single transmitter talking to a single receiver. This terminology transferred to networking, where a communications channel between two entities in isolation is referred to as point-to-point. Examples of point-to-point communications include Bluetooth, where this is mandated by protocol, and USB, where it is mandated by physical connections.

Point-to-Multipoint

Point-to-multipoint communications have multiple receivers for a transmitted signal. When a message is sent in broadcast mode, it has multiple receivers and is called a point-to-multipoint communication. Most radio-based and networked systems are potentially point-to-multipoint, from a single transmitter to multiple receivers, limited only by protocols.

EXAM TIP Remember that a point-to-point connection is between two devices (one to one) while point-to-multipoint connections are one (device) to many (devices).

Global Positioning System (GPS)

The *Global Positioning System (GPS)* is a series of satellites that provide nearly global coverage of highly precise time signals that, when multiple signals are combined, can produce precise positional data in all three dimensions. GPS receivers, operating in the 6-GHz band, are small, cheap, and have been added to numerous mobile devices, becoming nearly ubiquitous. The ability to have precise time, precise location, and, using differential math, precise speed has transformed many mobile device capabilities. GPS enables geolocation, geofencing, and a whole host of other capabilities.

RFID

Radio frequency identification (RFID) tags are used in a wide range of use cases. From tracking devices to tracking keys, the unique serialization of these remotely sensible devices has made them useful in a wide range of applications. RFID tags come in several different forms and can be classified as either active or passive. Active tags have a power source, whereas passive tags utilize the RF energy transmitted to them for power. RFID tags are used as a means of identification and have the advantage over bar codes that they do not have to be visible, just within radio wave range—typically centimeters to 200 meters, depending on tag type. RFID tags are used in a range of security situations, including contactless identification systems such as smart cards.

RFID tags have multiple security concerns; first and foremost, because they are connected via RF energy, physical security is a challenge. Security was recognized as an important issue for RFID tag systems because they form a means of identification and there is a need for authentication and confidentiality of the data transfers. Several standards are associated with securing the RFID data flow, including ISO/IEC 18000 and ISO/IEC 29167 for cryptography methods to support confidentiality, untraceability, tag and reader authentication, and over-the-air privacy, whereas ISO/IEC 20248 specifies a digital signature data structure for use in RFID systems.

Several different attack types can be performed against RFID systems. The first is against the RFID devices themselves—the chips and readers. A second form of attack goes against the communication channel between the device and the reader. The third category of attack is against the reader and back-end system. This last type is more of a standard IT/IS attack, depending on the interfaces used (web, database, and so on) and therefore is not covered any further. Attacks against the communication channel are relatively easy because the radio frequencies are known and devices exist to interface with tags. Two main attacks are replay and eavesdropping. In a replay attack, the RFID information is recorded and then replayed later; in the case of an RFID-based access badge, it could be read in a restaurant from a distance and then replayed at the appropriate entry point to gain entry. In the case of eavesdropping, the data can be collected, monitoring the movement of tags for whatever purpose needed by an unauthorized party. Both of these attacks are easily defeated using the aforementioned security standards.

If eavesdropping is possible, then what about man-in-the-middle attacks? These are certainly possible because they would be a combination of a sniffing (eavesdropping) action, followed by a replay (spoofing) attack. This leads to the question as to whether RFID can be cloned. And again, the answer is yes, if the RFID information is not protected via a cryptographic component.

EXAM TIP The various mobile device connection methods are conducive to performance-based questions, which means you need to pay attention to the scenario presented and choose the best connection methodology. Consider data rate, purpose, distances, and so forth in picking the best choice.

Mobile Device Management (MDM)

Knowledge of *mobile device management (MDM)* concepts is essential in today's environment of connected devices. MDM began as a marketing term for a collective set of commonly employed protection elements associated with mobile devices. When it's viewed as a comprehensive set of security options for mobile devices, every corporation should have and enforce an MDM policy. The policy should require the following:

- Device locking with a strong password
- Encryption of data on the device
- Device locking automatically after a certain period of inactivity
- The capability to remotely lock the device if it is lost or stolen
- The capability to wipe the device automatically after a certain number of failed login attempts
- The capability to remotely wipe the device if it is lost or stolen

Password policies should extend to mobile devices, including lockout and, if possible, the automatic wiping of data. Corporate policy for data encryption on mobile devices should be consistent with the policy for data encryption on laptop computers. In other words, if you don't require encryption of portable computers, then should you require it for mobile devices? There is not a uniform answer to this question because mobile devices are much more mobile in practice than laptops, and more prone to loss.

This is ultimately a risk question that management must address: what is the risk and what are the costs of the options employed? This also raises a bigger question: which devices should have encryption as a basic security protection mechanism? Is it by device type or by user based on what data would be exposed to risk? Fortunately, MDM solutions exist, making the choices manageable.

EXAM TIP Mobile device management (MDM) is a marketing term for a collective set of commonly employed protection elements associated with mobile devices. In enterprise environments, MDM allows device enrollment, provisioning, updating, tracking, policy enforcement, and app management capabilities.

Application Management

Mobile devices use applications to perform their data processing. The method of installing, updating, and managing the applications is done though a system referred to as *application management* software. Different vendor platforms have different methods of managing this functionality, with the two major players being the Google Store for Android devices and the Apple App Store for iOS devices. Both Apple and Android devices have built-in operations as part of their operating system (OS) to ensure seamless integration with their respective stores and other MDM solutions.

Content Management

Applications are not the only information moving to mobile devices. Content is moving as well, and organizations need a means of content management for mobile devices. For instance, it might be fine to have, and edit, some types of information on mobile devices, whereas other, more sensitive information should be blocked from mobile device access. *Content management* is the set of actions used to control content issues, including what content is available and to what apps, on mobile devices. Most organizations have a data ownership policy that clearly establishes their ownership rights over data, regardless of whether the data is stored on a device owned by the organization or a device owned by the employee. But enterprise content management goes a step further, examining what content belongs on specific devices and then using mechanisms to enforce these rules. Again, MDM solutions exist to assist in this security issue with respect to mobile devices.

Remote Wipe

Today's mobile devices are ubiquitous and are very susceptible to loss and theft. When enterprise data exists on these devices, management of the data, even if the device is lost, is a concern. Further, it is unlikely that a lost or stolen device will be recovered by the owner, thus making even encrypted data stored on a device more vulnerable to decryption. If the thief can have your device for a long time, they can take all the time they want to try to decrypt your data. Therefore, many companies prefer to just remotely wipe a lost or stolen device. *Remote wiping* a mobile device typically removes data stored on the device and resets the device to factory settings. There is a dilemma in the use of BYOD devices that store both personal and enterprise data. Wiping the device usually removes all data, both personal and enterprise. Therefore, a corporate policy that requires wiping a lost device may mean the device's user loses personal photos and data. The software controls for separate data containers, one for business and one for personal, have been proposed but are not a mainstream option yet.

For most devices, remote wipe can only be managed via apps on the device, such as Outlook for e-mail, calendar and contacts, and MDM solutions for all data. For Apple and Android devices, the OS also has the ability to set the device up for remote locking and factory reset, which effectively wipes the device.

Geofencing

Geofencing is the use of the Global Positioning System (GPS) and/or radio frequency identification (RFID) technology to create a virtual fence around a particular location and detect when mobile devices cross the fence. This enables devices to be recognized by others, based on location, and have actions taken. Geofencing is used in marketing to send messages to devices that are in a specific area, such as near a point of sale, or just to count potential customers. Geofencing has been used for remote workers, notifying management when they have arrived at remote work sites, allowing things like network connections to be enabled for them. The uses of geofencing are truly only limited by one's imagination.

Turning off geofencing is possible via the device. On Apple devices, just turn off location services. Although to completely prevent tracking of the device, you must turn off the radio using Airplane mode.

Geolocation

Most mobile devices are now capable of using GPS for tracking device location. Many apps rely heavily on GPS location, such as device-locating services, mapping applications, traffic monitoring apps, and apps that locate nearby businesses such as gas stations and restaurants. Such technology can be exploited to track movement and location of the mobile device, which is referred to as *geolocation*. This tracking can be used to assist in the recovery of lost devices.

EXAM TIP Know the difference between geofencing and geolocation. These make great distractors.

Screen Locks

Most corporate policies regarding mobile devices require the use of the mobile device's *screen-locking* capability. This usually consists of entering a passcode or PIN to unlock the device. It is highly recommended that screen locks be enforced for all mobile devices. Your policy regarding the quality of the passcode should be consistent with your corporate password policy. However, many companies merely enforce the use of screen-locking.

Figure 21-1
iOS lock screens

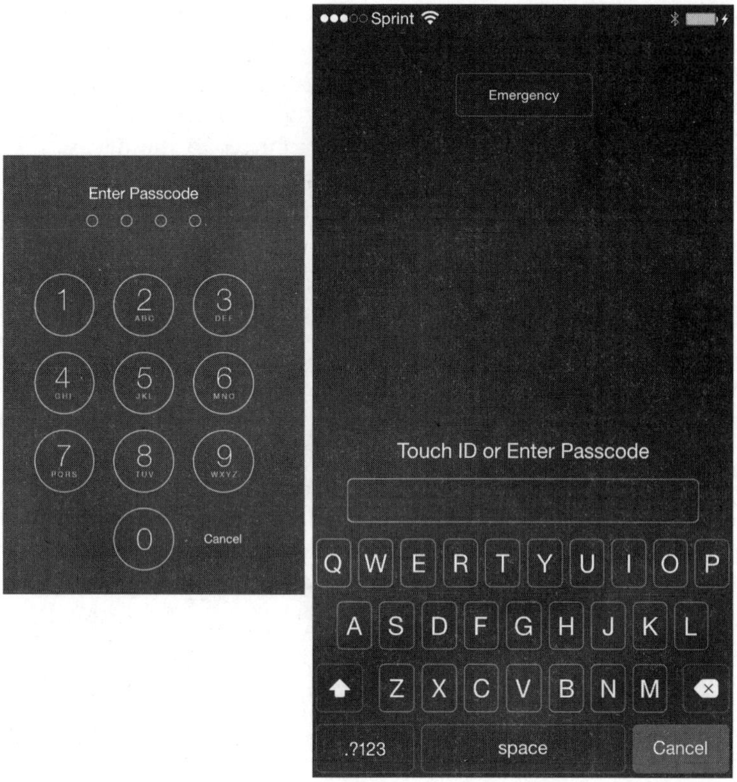

Thus, users tend to use convenient or easy-to-remember passcodes. Some devices allow complex passcodes. As shown in Figure 21-1, the device screen on the left supports only a simple iOS passcode, limited to four numbers, while the device screen on the right supports a passcode of indeterminate length and can contain alphanumeric characters.

Some more advanced forms of screen locks work in conjunction with device wiping. If the passcode is entered incorrectly a specified number of times, the device is automatically wiped. Apple has made this an option on iOS devices. Apple also allows remote locking of a device from the user's iCloud account. Android devices have a wide range of options, including the use of apps as screen locks.

EXAM TIP Mobile devices require basic security mechanisms of screen locks, lockouts, device wiping, and encryption to protect sensitive information contained on them.

Push Notification Services

Push notification services are services that deliver information to mobile devices without a specific request from the device. Push notifications are used by a lot of apps in mobile devices to indicate that content has been updated. Push notification methods are typically unique to the platform, with Apple Push Notification service for Apple devices and Android Cloud to Device Messaging as examples. Many other back-end server services have similar server services for updating their content. As push notifications enable the movement of information from external sources to the device, this has some security implications, such as device location, and potential interaction with the device. For instance, it is possible to push the device to emit a sound, even if the sound is muted on the device.

Passwords and PINs

Passwords and *PINs* are common security measures used to protect mobile devices from unauthorized use. These are essential tools and should be used in all cases and mandated by company policy. The rules for passwords covered throughout this book apply to mobile devices as well; in fact, maybe even more so. Having a simple gesture-based swipe on the screen as a PIN can at times be discovered by looking at the oil pattern on the screen. If the only swipes are for unlocking the phone, then the pattern can be seen, and security is lost via this method. Either cleaning or dirtying the whole screen is the obvious solution.

Biometrics

Biometrics are used across a wide range of mobile devices as a means of access control. Many of these devices have less-than-perfect recognition, and various biometric sensors have proven to be hackable, as demonstrated in many security presentations at conferences. The newest biometric method, facial recognition, is based on a camera image of the user's face while they are holding their phone. Because these biometric sensors have been shown to be bypassable, they should be considered convenience features, not security features. Management policies should reflect this fact and should dictate that these methods not be relied on for securing important data.

Context-Aware Authentication

Context-aware authentication is the use of contextual information—who the user is, what resource they are requesting, what machine they are using, how they are connected, and so on—to make the authentication decision as to whether to permit the user access to the requested resource. The goal is to prevent unauthorized end users, devices, or network connections from being able to access corporate data. This approach can be used, for example, to allow an authorized user to access network-based resources from inside the office but deny the same user access if they are connecting via a public Wi-Fi network.

Containerization

Containerization on mobile devices refers to dividing the device into a series of containers—one container holding work-related materials, the other personal. The containers can separate apps, data—virtually everything on the device. Some mobile device management (MDM) solutions support remote control over the work container. This enables a much stronger use case for mixing business and personal matters on a single device. Most MDM solutions offer the ability to encrypt the containers, especially the work-related container, thus providing another layer of protection for the data.

Storage Segmentation

On mobile devices, it can be very difficult to keep personal data separate from corporate data. *Storage segmentation* is similar to containerization in that it represents a logical separation of the storage in the unit. Some companies have developed capabilities to create separate virtual containers to keep personal data separate from corporate data and applications. For devices that are used to handle highly sensitive corporate data, this form of protection is highly recommended.

EXAM TIP Remember that containerization and storage segmentation are technologies to keep personal data separate from corporate data on devices.

Full Device Encryption

Just as laptop computers should be protected with whole disk encryption to protect the data in case of loss or theft, you may need to consider *full device encryption (FDE)* for mobile devices used by your organization's employees. Mobile devices are much more likely to be lost or stolen, so you should consider encrypting data on your organization's mobile devices. More and more, mobile devices are used when accessing and storing business-critical data or other sensitive information. Protecting the information on mobile devices is becoming a business imperative. This is an emerging technology, so you'll need to complete some rigorous market analysis to determine what commercial product meets your needs.

EXAM TIP Protection of data on a mobile device is accomplished via multiple tools and methods. For the exam, pay careful attention to the details of the question to determine which protection method is applicable, as each defends against a different issue. Full device encryption offers completely different protection from screen locks, and the details of the question will steer you to the correct answer. Don't jump on the choice that appears to be obvious; take a moment to understand the details.

Mobile Devices

Mobile devices can bring much to the enterprise in terms of business functionality, but with this increased utility comes additional risks. There are a variety of ways to manage the risk, including the use of encryption and endpoint protections designed for mobile devices. You can use several different methodologies to manage mobile devices, and these are covered in the following sections.

MicroSD Hardware Security Module (HSM)

A *MicroSD HSM* is a hardware security module in a MicroSD form factor. This device allows you a portable means of secure storage for a wide range of cryptographic keys. These devices come with an application that manages the typical HSM functions associated with keys, including backup, restore, and many PKI functions.

MDM/Unified Endpoint Management (UEM)

MDM software is an application that runs on a mobile device and, when activated, can manage aspects of the device, including connectivity and functions. The purpose of an MDM application is to turn the device into one where the functionality is limited in accordance with the enterprise policy. *Unified endpoint management (UEM)* is an enterprise-level endpoint management solution that can cover all endpoints, from PCs to laptops, from phones to other mobile devices, tablets, and even some wearables. The idea behind UEM is to extend the function set from MDM to encompass all endpoint devices, including bringing more functionality under enterprise control. A UEM can manage the deployment of corporate resources onto an endpoint, providing control over things such as application and resource access, remote control of the device, and monitoring of device activity. MDM and UEM solutions also assist with asset management, including location and tracking.

Mobile Application Management (MAM)

Mobile devices bring a plethora of applications along with them into an enterprise. While MDM solutions can protect the enterprise from applications installed on a device, there is also a need to manage corporate applications on the device. The deployment, updating, and configuration of applications on devices requires an enterprise solution that is scalable and provides for the installation, updating, and management of in-house applications across a set of mobile devices. *Mobile application management (MAM)* tool suites provide these capabilities in the enterprise.

EXAM TIP Distinguishing between MDM, UEM, and MAM applications is done by functionality. MAM controls in-house applications on devices. MDM controls the data on the device, segregating it from the general data on the device. UEM is a complete endpoint control solution that works across virtually every form of endpoint, mobile or not.

SEAndroid

Security Enhanced Android (SEAndroid) is a mobile version of the Security Enhanced Linux (SELinux) distribution that enforces mandatory access control (MAC) over all processes, even processes running with root/superuser privileges. SELinux has one overarching principle: default denial. This means that anything that is not explicitly allowed is denied.

Enforcement and Monitoring

Your organization's policies regarding mobile devices should be consistent with your existing computer security policies. Your training programs should include instruction on mobile device security. Disciplinary actions should be consistent. Your monitoring programs should be enhanced to include monitoring and control of mobile devices.

Third-Party Application Stores

Many mobile devices have manufacturer-associated app stores from which apps can be downloaded to their respective devices. These app stores are considered by an enterprise to be *third-party application stores*, as the contents they offer come from neither the user nor the enterprise. Currently there are two main app stores: the Apple App Store for iOS devices and Google Play for Android devices. The Apple App Store is built on the principle of exclusivity, and stringent security requirements are highly enforced for the apps that are offered. Google Play has fewer restrictions, which has translated into some security issues stemming from apps. Managing what apps a user can add to the device is essential because many of these apps can create security risks for an organization. This issue becomes significantly more complex with employee-owned devices and access to corporate data stores. The segmentation options discussed earlier to separate work and personal spaces are offered on a limited number of mobile devices, so the ability to control this access becomes problematic. Virtually all segmentation is done via an additional app—the MDM solution. Devices permitted access to sensitive corporate information should be limited to company-owned devices, allowing more stringent control.

Rooting/Jailbreaking

A common hack associated with mobile devices is the jailbreak. *Jailbreaking* is a process by which the user escalates their privilege level, bypassing the operating system's controls and limitations. The user still has the complete functionality of the device, but also has additional capabilities, bypassing the OS-imposed user restrictions. There are several schools of thought concerning the utility of jailbreaking, but the important issue from a security point of view is that running any device with enhanced privileges can result in errors that cause more damage, because normal security controls are typically bypassed. Jailbreaking an Apple iOS device can also void the manufacturer's warranty, as well as render the device no longer usable with the App Store.

Rooting a device is a process by which OS controls are bypassed, and this is the term frequently used for Android devices. Whether the device is rooted or jailbroken, the effect is the same: the OS controls designed to constrain operations are no longer in play and the device can do things it was never intended to do, either good or bad.

EXAM TIP Rooting is used to bypass OS controls on Android, and jailbreaking is used to escalate privileges and do the same on iOS devices. Both processes stop OS controls from inhibiting user behaviors.

Sideloading

Sideloading is the process of adding apps to a mobile device without using the authorized store associated with the device. Currently, sideloading only works on Android devices, as Apple has not enabled execution of any apps except those coming through the App Store. Sideloading is an alternative means of instantiating an app on the device without having to have it hosted on the requisite app store. The downside, simply put, is that without the vendor app store screening, one is at greater risk of installing malicious software in the guise of a desired app.

Custom Firmware

Custom firmware is firmware for a device that has been altered from the original factory settings. This firmware can bring added functionality, but it can also result in security holes. Custom firmware should be used only on devices that do not have access to critical information.

Carrier Unlocking

Most mobile devices in the United States come locked to a carrier, while in other parts of the world they are unlocked, relying upon a subscriber identity module (SIM) for connection and billing information. This is a byproduct of the business market decisions made early in the mobile phone market lifecycle and has remained fairly true to date. If you have a carrier-locked device and you attempt to use a SIM from another carrier, the device will not accept it unless you unlock the device. *Carrier unlocking* is the process of programming the device to sever itself from the carrier. This is usually done through the inputting of a special key sequence that unlocks the device.

Firmware OTA Updates

Firmware essentially is software. It may be stored in a chip, but like all software, it sometimes requires updating. With mobile devices being literally everywhere, the scale does not support bringing the devices to a central location or connection for updating. *Firmware OTA (over-the-air) updates* are a solution to this problem. Similar to adding or updating an app from an app store, you can tap a menu option on a mobile device to connect to an app store and update the device firmware. All major device manufacturers support this model because it is the only real workable solution.

Camera Use

Many mobile devices include on-board cameras, and the photos/videos they take can divulge information. This information can be associated with anything the camera can image—whiteboards, documents, and even the location of the device when the photo/video was taken via geo-tagging (discussed in the upcoming "GPS Tagging" section). Another challenge presented by mobile devices is the possibility that they will be used for illegal purposes. This can create liability for the company if it is a company-owned device. Despite all the potential legal concerns, possibly the greatest concern of mobile device users is that their personal photos will be lost during a device wipe originated by the company.

SMS/Multimedia Message Service (MMS)/Rich Communication Services (RCS)

Short Message Service (SMS) and *Multimedia Messaging Service (MMS)* are standard protocols used to send messages, including multimedia content in the case of MMS, to and from mobile devices over a cellular network. SMS is limited to short, text-only messages of fewer than 160 characters and is carried over the signaling path of the cellular network when signaling data is not being sent. SMS dates back to the early days of mobile telephony in the 1980s, while MMS is a more recent development designed to support sending multimedia content to and from mobile devices. Because of the content connections that can be sent via MMS in particular, and SMS in certain cases, it is important to at least address these communication channels in relevant policies.

Rich Communication Services (RCS) is a protocol that is currently used alongside SMS and MMS. RCS operates between the mobile device and the carrier and requires RCS-capable apps on both ends of the communication. RCS supports modern methods of communication, like adding user-desired features such as integration with stickers, video, images, groups, and other modern mobile data formats. RCS is intended to eventually replace both SMS and MMS.

External Media

External media refers to any item or device that can store data. From flash drives to hard drives, music players, smartphones, and even smart watches, if it can store data, it is a pathway for data exfiltration. External media can also deliver malware into the enterprise. The risk is evident: these devices can carry data into and out of the enterprise, yet they have become synonymous with today's tech worker. The key is to develop a policy that determines where these devices can exist and where they should be banned, and then follow the plan with monitoring and enforcement.

USB On-The-Go (USB OTG)

Universal Serial Bus is a common method of connecting mobile devices to computers and other host-based platforms. Connecting mobile devices directly to each other required changes to USB connections. Enter *USB On-The-Go (USB OTG)*, an extension of USB technology that facilitates direct connection between USB OTG–enabled mobile devices. USB OTG allows those devices to switch back and forth between the roles of host and device, including deciding which provides power (host) and which consumes power across the interface. USB OTG also allows the connection of USB-based peripherals, such as keyboards, mice, and external storage, to mobile devices. Although USB OTG is relatively new, most mobile devices made since 2015 are USB OTG compatible.

Recording Microphone

Many of today's electronic devices—from smartphones and smart watches to devices such as the online assistants from Amazon and Google, and even toys—have the ability to record audio information. *Recording microphones* can be used to record conversations, collecting sensitive data without the parties under observation even being aware of the activity. As with other high-tech gadgets, the key is to determine the policy of where recording microphones can be used and the rules for their use.

GPS Tagging

Photos taken on mobile devices or with cameras that have GPS capabilities can have location information embedded in the digital photo. This is called *GPS tagging* by CompTIA and *geo-tagging* by others. Posting photos with geo-tags embedded in them has its use, but it can also unexpectedly publish information that users may not want to share. For example, if you use your smartphone to take a photo of your car in the driveway and then post the photo on the Internet in an attempt to sell your car, if geo-tagging was enabled on the smartphone, the location of where the photo was taken is embedded as metadata in the digital photo. Such a posting could inadvertently expose where your home is located. There has been much public discussion on this topic, and geo-tagging can be disabled on most mobile devices. It is recommended that it be disabled unless you have a specific reason for having the location information embedded in the photo.

Wi-Fi Direct/Ad Hoc

Wi-Fi typically connects a Wi-Fi device to a network via a wireless access point. Other methods exist, namely Wi-Fi direct and Wi-Fi ad hoc. In *Wi-Fi direct*, two Wi-Fi devices connect to each other via a single-hop connection. In essence, one of the two devices acts as an access point for the other device. The key element is the single-hop nature of a Wi-Fi direct connection. Wi-Fi direct connects only two devices, but these two devices can be connected with all of the bells and whistles of modern wireless networking, including WPA2.

Wi-Fi direct uses a couple of services to establish secure connections between two devices. The first is Wi-Fi Direct Device and Service Discovery. This protocol provides a way for devices to discover each other based on the services they support before connecting. A device can see all compatible devices in the area and then narrow down the list to only devices that allow a specific service (say, printing) before displaying to the user a list of available printers for pairing. The second protocol used is WPA2. This protocol is used to protect the connections and prevent unauthorized parties from pairing to Wi-Fi direct devices, or intercepting communications from paired devices.

The primary difference with *Wi-Fi ad hoc* is that in the ad hoc network, multiple devices can communicate with each other, with each device capable of communicating with all other devices. WPA2 as well as other Wi-Fi standards are covered in detail in Chapter 20.

Tethering

Tethering involves connecting a device to a mobile device that has a means of accessing a network for the purpose of sharing the network access. Connecting a mobile phone to a laptop to charge the phone's battery is not tethering. Connecting a mobile phone to a laptop so that the laptop can use the phone to connect to the Internet is tethering. When you tether a device, you create additional external network connections.

Hotspot

The term *hotspot* can refer to a specific piece of network equipment, an endpoint for a wireless solution, or in other respects the physical area in which it provides connectivity. Typically, a Wi-Fi endpoint, a hotspot provides a set of users a method of connecting to a network. These can be used for employees, customers, guests, or combinations thereof based on access control mechanisms employed at the endpoint device. A network engineer will refer to a hotspot as the physical equipment that provides services over a specified geographic area, while a user will refer to it as a place they can connect to the network.

EXAM TIP Tethering involves the connection of a device to a mobile device to gain network connectivity. A hotspot can be tethered if the actual device is mobile, but if the device is fixed, it is not tethering.

Payment Methods

Twenty years ago, *payment methods* were cash, check, or charge. Today we have new intermediaries: smart devices with near field communication (NFC) linked to credit cards offer a convenient alternative form of payment. While the actual payment is still a credit/debit card charge, the payment pathway is through the digital device. Utilizing the security features of the device, NFC, and biometrics/PIN, this form of payment has some advantages over the other methods because it allows additional specific security measures, such as biometric-based approval for the transaction, before accessing the payment method.

EXAM TIP This section contains topics that can be tested with performance-based questions. It is not enough to simply learn the terms associated with the material. You should be familiar with how to determine the correct enforcement and monitoring solution based on a given scenario. The scenario will provide the necessary information to determine the best answer to the question. You should understand the differences between the items—from app stores, to OS protections, to connectivity options—sufficiently to be able to select the correct item based on the stated scenario.

Deployment Models

When determining how to incorporate mobile devices securely in your organization, you need to consider a wide range of issues, including how security will be enforced, how all the policies will be enforced, and, ultimately, what devices will be supported. You can choose from a variety of device deployment models to support your security strategy, ranging from a pure employee-owned model (BYOD) to a strict corporate-owned model, with several hybrid models in between. Each of these models has advantages and disadvantages.

EXAM TIP Be prepared for performance-based questions that ask you to determine the correct mobile deployment model based on a given scenario.

Bring Your Own Device (BYOD)

The *bring your own device (BYOD)* deployment model has many advantages in business, and not just from the perspective of minimizing device cost for the organization. Users tend to prefer to have a single device rather than carry multiple devices. Users have less of a learning curve on devices they already know how to use or have an interest in learning. This model is popular in small firms and in organizations that employ a lot of temporary workers. The big disadvantage is that employees will not be eager to limit their use of their personal device based on corporate policies, so corporate control will be limited.

Corporate-Owned, Personally Enabled (COPE)

In the *corporate-owned, personally enabled (COPE)* deployment model, employees are supplied a mobile device that is chosen and paid for by the organization, but they are given permission to use it for personal activities. The organization can decide how much choice and freedom employees get with regard to personal use of the device. This allows the organization to control security functionality while dealing with the employee dissatisfaction associated with the traditional method of device supply, corporate-owned, business only (COBO).

Choose Your Own Device (CYOD)

The *choose your own device (CYOD)* deployment model is similar to BYOD in concept in that it gives users a choice in the type of device. In most cases, the organization constrains this choice to a list of acceptable devices that can be supported in the organization. Because the device is owned by the organization, it has greater flexibility in imposing restrictions on device use in terms of apps, data, updates, and so forth.

Corporate-Owned

In the *corporate-owned* deployment model, also known as corporate-owned, business only (COBO), the company supplies employees with a mobile device that is restricted to company-only use. The disadvantage of this model is that employees have to carry two devices—one personal and one for work—and then separate functions between the devices based on purpose of use in each instance. The advantage is that the corporation has complete control over its devices and can apply any security controls desired without interference from other device functionality.

EXAM TIP Expect performance-based questions for the different deployment models: BYOD, CYOD, COPE, and corporate-owned. The correct answer to the question will lie in the details of the scenario, so look carefully at the details to determine the best answer.

Virtual Desktop Infrastructure (VDI)

While it seems the deployment models are only associated with phones, this is really not the case, because personal computers can also be external mobile devices requiring connections at times. In the case of laptops, a *virtual desktop infrastructure (VDI)* solution can bring control to the mobile environment associated with non-corporate-owned equipment. The enterprise can set up virtual desktop machines that are fully security compliant and contain all the necessary applications needed by the employee and then let the employee access the virtual machine via either a virtual connection or a remote desktop connection. This can solve most if not all of the security and application functionality issues associated with mobile devices. It does require an IT staff that is capable of setting up, maintaining, and managing the VDI in the organization, which is not necessarily a small task, depending on the number of instances needed. Interaction with these VDIs can be accomplished easily on many of today's mobile devices because of their advanced screens and compute power.

Chapter Review

In this chapter, you became acquainted with the elements required to deploy mobile devices securely. The chapter opened with a description of the various communication connection methods. Specifically, the chapter covered cellular, Wi-Fi, Bluetooth, NFC, infrared, and USB connection methods. The methods of point-to-point and point-to-multipoint were covered. Global positioning and RFID technologies were also covered.

From there, the chapter explored the concept of mobile device management. In this section, the topics included application and content management, remote wiping, geofencing and geolocation, screen locks, push notification services, passwords and PINs, biometrics, context-aware authentication, containerization, storage segmentation, and full device encryption. The next section looked at MicroSD HSM, MDM/UEM solutions, MAM, and SEAndroid systems.

The chapter next examined the enforcement and monitoring requirements for third-party app stores, rooting/jailbreaking, sideloading, custom firmware, carrier unlocking, firmware OTA updates, camera use, SMS/MMS, external media, USB OTG, recording microphones, GPS tagging, Wi-Fi direct/ad hoc, tethering, hotspots, and payment methods. The chapter closed with a discussion of the deployment models, including BYOD, CYOD, COPE, corporate-owned, and VDI.

Questions

To help you prepare further for the CompTIA Security+ exam, and to test your level of preparedness, answer the following questions and then check your answers against the correct answers at the end of the chapter.

1. Which of the following is a weakness of cellular technology?
   - **A.** Multiple vendors in a nationwide network
   - **B.** Less availability in rural areas
   - **C.** Multiple cell towers in close proximity in urban areas
   - **D.** Strong signals in areas of reasonable population

2. What frequency spectrum does Bluetooth use?
   A. 1.7 GHz
   B. 2.4 GHz
   C. 5 GHz
   D. 6.4 GHz
3. You need to use cryptographic keys between several devices. Which of the following can manage this task?
   A. MAM solutions
   B. Firmware OTA updates
   C. USB OTG
   D. MicroSD HSM
4. Which of the following are the three modes supported by Bluetooth 4.0?
   A. Classic, Low Speed, High Energy
   B. Enhanced Data Rate, Backward Compatible, High Energy
   C. Classic, High Speed, Low Energy
   D. Synchronous, High Speed, Low Energy
5. What is the primary use of near field communication (NFC)?
   A. Establishing radio communications over a short proximity
   B. Communication in sparsely populated areas
   C. Long-distance connectivity
   D. Communication in noisy industrial environments
6. You need to manage a whole host of different endpoints in the enterprise, including mobile devices, iPads, printers, PCs and phones. Which of the following is the most comprehensive solution?
   A. COPE-based solutions
   B. MAM solutions
   C. MDM solutions
   D. UEM solutions
7. What is a disadvantage of infrared (IR) technology?
   A. It has a high data rate.
   B. It cannot penetrate solid objects.
   C. It can penetrate walls.
   D. It uses a slow encryption technology.

8. What is the main security concern with Universal Serial Bus (USB) technology?
   - **A.** It connects to cell phones for easy charging.
   - **B.** It uses proprietary encryption.
   - **C.** It automounts and acts like a hard drive attached to the computer.
   - **D.** It uses older encryption technology.
9. Why is it important to establish policies governing remote wiping of mobile devices?
   - **A.** Mobile devices typically do not mix personal and business data.
   - **B.** Mobile devices are more easily secured.
   - **C.** Thieves cannot decrypt mobile devices.
   - **D.** They are more susceptible to loss than other devices.
10. What is the purpose of geofencing?
    - **A.** It can be used to remotely wipe a lost device.
    - **B.** It makes securing the mobile device simpler.
    - **C.** It enables devices to be recognized by location and have actions taken.
    - **D.** It can enforce device locking with a strong password.

Answers

1. **B.** A weakness of cellular technology is that it is less available in rural areas.
2. **B.** Bluetooth uses the 2.4-GHz frequency spectrum.
3. **D.** MicroSD HSM facilitates HSM functionality via a MicroSD connection. It can be connected via an adapter to any USB device.
4. **C.** The three modes supported by Bluetooth 4.0 are Classic, High Speed, and Low Energy.
5. **A.** The primary use of NFC is to establish radio communications over a short proximity.
6. **D.** UEM (unified endpoint management) solutions can address a wider range of devices in a more comprehensive manner than MDM and MAM solutions.
7. **B.** A disadvantage of IR technology is that it cannot penetrate solid objects.
8. **C.** The main security concern with USB technology is that it automounts and acts like a hard drive attached to the computer.
9. **D.** It is important to establish policies governing the remote wiping of mobile devices because they are more susceptible to loss than other devices.
10. **C.** The purpose of geofencing is to enable devices to be recognized by location and have actions taken.

CHAPTER 22

Implementing Cloud Security

In this chapter, you will

- Explore cloud security controls
- Compare and contrast cloud security solutions
- Learn about cloud-native controls versus third-party solutions

Cloud computing is becoming more and more prevalent because of multiple business factors. It has many economic and technical advantages over traditional IT in many use cases, but that is not to say it comes without problems. Securing cloud systems is in one respect no different from securing a traditional IT system: protect the data from unauthorized reading and manipulation. But the tools, techniques, and procedures vary greatly from standard IT, and while clouds can be secure, it is by the application of the correct set of security controls, not by happenstance.

Certification Objective This chapter covers CompTIA Security+ exam objective 3.6: Given a scenario, apply cybersecurity solutions to the cloud.

Cloud Security Controls

Cloud security controls are a shared issue—one that is shared between the user and the cloud provider. Depending on your terms of service with your cloud provider, you will share responsibilities for software updates, access control, encryption, and other key security controls. In the section "Cloud Models" in Chapter 10, Figure 10-1 illustrated the differing levels of shared responsibility in various cloud models. What is important to remember is to define the requirements up front and have them written into the service agreement with the cloud provider, because unless they are part of the package, they will not occur.

High Availability Across Zones

Cloud computing environments can be configured to provide nearly full-time availability (that is, a high availability system). This is done using redundant hardware and software that make the system available despite individual element failures. When something experiences an error or failure, the failover process moves the processing performed by the failed component to the backup component elsewhere in the cloud. This process is transparent to users as much as possible, creating an image of a high availability system to users. Architecting these failover components across zones provides *high availability across zones*. As with all cloud security issues, the details are in your terms of service with your cloud provider; you cannot just assume it will be high availability. It must be specified in your terms and architected in by the provider.

EXAM TIP Remember that zones can be used for replication and provide load balancing as well as high availability.

Resource Policies

Cloud-based resources are controlled via a set of policies. This is basically your authorization model projected into the cloud space. Different cloud vendors have different mechanisms to define the groups, types of resources allowed, and assignments by location or compartment. The integration between the enterprise identity access management (IAM) system and the cloud-based IAM system is a configuration element of utmost importance when setting up the cloud environment. The policies set the permissions for the cloud objects. Once the resource policies from the enterprise are extended into the cloud environment and set up, they must be maintained. The level of integration between the cloud-based IAM system and the enterprise-based IAM system will determine the level of work required for regular maintenance activities.

Secrets Management

Data that is in the cloud is still data that is on a server and is therefore, by definition, remotely accessible. Hence, it is important to secure the data using encryption. A common mistake is to leave data unencrypted on the cloud. It seems hardly a week goes by without a report of unencrypted data being exposed from a cloud instance. Fingers always point to the cloud provider, but in most cases the blame is on the end user. Cloud providers offer encryption tools and management services, yet too many companies don't implement them, which sets the scene for a data breach.

Secrets management is the term used to denote the policies and procedures employed to connect the IAM systems of the enterprise and the cloud to enable communication with the data. Storing sensitive data, or in most cases virtually any data, in the cloud without putting in place appropriate controls to prevent access to the data is irresponsible and dangerous. Encryption is a failsafe—even if security configurations fail and the data falls into the hands of an unauthorized party, the data can't be read or used without the keys. It is important to maintain control of the encryption keys. The security of the keys, which can be done outside the primary cloud instance and elsewhere in the enterprise, is how the secrecy is managed.

Secrets management is an important aspect of maintaining cloud security. The secrets used for system-to-system access should be maintained separately from other configuration data and handled according to the strictest principles of confidentiality because these secrets allow access to the data in the cloud.

EXAM TIP Use of a secrets manager can enable secrets management by providing a central trusted storage location for certificates, passwords, and even application programming interface (API) keys.

Integration and Auditing

The integration of the appropriate level and quantity of security controls is a subject that is always being audited. Are the controls appropriate? Are they placed and used correctly? Most importantly, are they effective? These are standard IT audit elements in the enterprise. The moving of computing resources to the cloud does not change the need or intent of audit functions.

Cloud computing audits have become a standard as enterprises are realizing that unique cloud-based risks exist with their data being hosted by other organizations. To address these risks, organizations are using specific cloud computing audits to gain assurance and to understand the risk of their information being lost or released to unauthorized parties. These cloud-specific audits have two sets of requirements: one being an understanding of the cloud security environment as deployed, and the second being related to the data security requirements. The result is that cloud computing audits can be in different forms, such as SOC 1 and SOC 2 reporting, HITRUST, PCI, and FedRAMP. For each one of these data-specific security frameworks, additional details are based on the specifics of the cloud environment and the specifics of the security controls employed by both the enterprise and the cloud vendor.

Storage

Cloud-based data *storage* was one of the first uses of cloud computing. Security requirements related to storage in the cloud environment are actually based on the same fundamentals as in the enterprise environment. Permissions to access and modify data need to be defined, set, and enforced. A means to protect data from unauthorized access is generally needed, and encryption is the key answer, just as it is in the enterprise. The replication of data across multiple different systems as part of the cloud deployment and the aspects of high availability elements of a cloud environment can complicate the securing of data.

Permissions

Permissions for data access and modifications are handled in the same manner as in an on-premises IT environment. Identity access management (IAM) systems are employed to manage the details of who can do what with each object. The key to managing this in the cloud is the integration of the on-premises IAM system with the cloud-based IAM system.

Encryption
Encryption of data in the cloud is one of the foundational elements to securing one's data when it is on another system. Data should be encrypted when stored in the cloud, and the keys should be maintained by the enterprise, not the cloud provider. Keys should be managed in accordance with the same level of security afforded keys in the enterprise.

Replication
Data may replicate across the cloud as part of a variety of cloud-based activities. From shared environments to high availability systems, including their backup systems, data in the cloud can seem to be fluid, moving across multiple physical systems. This level of *replication* is yet another reason that data should be encrypted for security. The act of replicating data across multiple systems is part of the resiliency of the cloud, in that single points of failure will not have the same effects that occur in the standard IT enterprise. Therefore, this is one of the advantages of the cloud.

High Availability
High availability storage works in the same manner as high availability systems described earlier in the chapter. Having multiple different physical systems working together to ensure your data is redundantly and resiliently stored is one of the cloud's advantages. What's more, the cloud-based IAM system can use encryption protections to keep your data secret, while high availability keeps it available.

Network
Cloud-based systems are made up of machines connected using a network. Typically this network is under the control of the cloud service provider (CSP). While you may be given network information, including addresses, the networks you see might actually be encapsulated on top of another network that is maintained by the service provider. In this fashion, many cloud service providers offer a virtual network that delivers the required functions without providing direct access to the actual network environment.

Virtual Networks
Most networking in cloud environments is via a virtual network operating in an overlay on top of a physical network. The *virtual network* can be used and manipulated by users, whereas the actual network underneath cannot. This gives the cloud service provider the ability to manage and service network functionality independent of the cloud instance with respect to a user. The virtual network technology used in cloud environments can include software-defined networking (SDN) and network function virtualization (NFV) as elements that make it easier to perform the desired networking tasks in the cloud.

Public and Private Subnets
Just as in traditional IT systems, there is typically a need for public-facing subnets, where the public/Internet can interact with servers, such as mail servers, web servers, and the like. There is also a need for private subnets, where access is limited to specific addresses, preventing direct access to secrets such as datastores and other important information

assets. The cloud comes with the capability of using both public-facing and private subnets; in other words, just because something is "in the cloud" does not change the business architecture of some having machines connected to the Internet and some not. Now, being "in the cloud" means that, in one respect, the Internet is used for all access. However, in the case of private subnets, the cloud-based IAM system can determine who is authorized to access which parts of the cloud's virtual network.

Segmentation

Segmentation is the network process of separating network elements into segments and regulating traffic between the segments. The presence of a segmented network creates security barriers for unauthorized accessors through the inspection of packets as they move from one segment to another. This can be done in a multitude of ways—via MAC tables, IP addresses, and even tunnels, with devices such as firewalls and secure web gateways inspecting at each connection. The ultimate in segmentation is the zero-trust environment, where microsegmentation is used to continually invoke the verification of permissions and controls. All of these can be performed in a cloud network. Also, as with the other controls already presented, the details are in the service level agreement (SLA) with the cloud service provider.

API Inspection and Integration

APIs are software interfaces that allow various software components to communicate with each other. This is true in the cloud just as it is in the traditional IT enterprise. Because of the nature of cloud environments, accepting virtually all requests across the web, there is a need for verifying information before it can be used. One key element in this solution is presented later in the chapter—the next-generation secure web gateway. This system analyzes information transfers at the application layer to verify authenticity and correctness.

Content inspection refers to the examination of the contents of a request to an API by applying rules to determine whether a request is legitimate and should be accepted. As APIs act to integrate one application to another, errors in one application can be propagated to other components, thus creating bigger issues. The use of *API content inspection* is an active measure to prevent errors from propagating through a system and causing trouble.

EXAM TIP Cloud security controls provide the same functionality as normal network security controls; they just do it in a different environment. The cloud is not a system without controls.

Compute

The cloud has become a service operation where applications can be deployed, providing a form of cloud-based computing. The *compute* aspects of a cloud system have the same security issues as a traditional IT system; in other words, the fact that a compute element is in the cloud does not make it any more or less secure. What has to happen is that security requirements need to be addressed as data comes and goes from the compute element.

Security Groups

Security groups are composed of the set of rules and policies associated with a cloud instance. These rules can be network rules, such as rules for passing a firewall, or they can be IAM rules with respect to who can access or interact with an object on the system. Security groups are handled differently by each cloud service provider, but in the end they provide a means of managing permissions in a limited granularity mode. Different providers have different limits, but in the end the objective is to place users into groups rather than to perform individual checks for every access request. This is done to manage scalability, which is one of the foundational elements of cloud computing.

Dynamic Resource Allocation

A cloud-based system has certain hallmark characteristics besides just being on another computer. Among these characteristics is providing scalable, reliable computing in a cost-efficient manner. Having a system whose resources can grow and shrink as the compute requirements change, without the need to buy new servers, expand systems, and so on, is one of the primary advantages of the cloud. Cloud service providers offer more than just bare hardware. One of the values associated with the cloud is its ability to grow as the load increases and to shrink (thus saving costs) as the load decreases. Cloud service providers manage this using *dynamic resource allocation* software that monitors the levels of performance. In accordance with the service agreement, they can act to increase resources incrementally as needed.

Instance Awareness

Just as enterprises have moved to the cloud, so have attackers. Command-and-control networks can be spun up in cloud environments, just as they are on real enterprise hardware. This creates a situation where a cloud is communicating with another cloud, and how does the first cloud understand if the second cloud is legit? *Instance awareness* is the name of a capability that must be enabled on firewalls, secure web gateways, and cloud access security brokers (CASBs) to determine if the next system in a communication chain is legitimate or not. Take a cloud-enabled service such as Google Drive, or Microsoft OneDrive, or Box, or any other cloud-based storage. Do you block them all? Or do you determine by instance which is legit and which is not? This is a relatively new and advanced feature, but one that is becoming increasingly important to prevent data disclosures and other issues from integrating cloud apps with unauthorized endpoints.

Virtual Private Cloud (VPC) Endpoint

A *virtual private cloud endpoint* allows connections to and from a virtual private cloud instance. VPC endpoints are virtual elements that can scale. They are also redundant and typically highly available. A VPC endpoint provides a means to connect a VPC to other resources without going out over the Internet. View it as a secure tunnel to directly access other cloud-based resources without exposing the traffic to other parties. VPC endpoints can be programmable to enable integration with IAM and other security solutions, enabling cross-cloud connections securely.

EXAM TIP A VPC endpoint provides a means to connect a VPC to other resources without going out over the Internet. In other words, you don't need additional VPN connection technologies or even an Internet gateway.

Container Security

Container security is the process of implementing security tools and policies to ensure your container is running as intended. Container technology allows applications and their dependencies to be packaged together into one operational element. This element, also commonly called a *manifest,* can be version-controlled, deployed, replicated, and managed across an environment. Containers can contain all the necessary OS elements for an application to run; they can be considered self-contained compute platforms. Security can be designed into the containers, as well as enforced in the environment in which the containers run. Running containers in cloud-based environments is a common occurrence because the ease of managing and deploying the containers fits the cloud model well. Most cloud providers have container-friendly environments that enable the necessary cloud environment security controls as well as allow the container to make its own security decisions within the container.

EXAM TIP Cloud-based computing has requirements to define who can do what (security groups) and what can happen and when (dynamic resource allocation) as well as to manage the security of embedded entities such as containers. Some of these controls are the same (security groups and containers) while other controls are unique to the cloud environment (dynamic resource allocations).

Solutions

Cloud security solutions are similar to traditional IT security solutions in one simple way: there is no easy, magic solution. Security is achieved through multiple actions designed to ensure the security policies are being followed. Whether in the cloud or in an on-premises environment, security requires multiple activities, with metrics, reporting, management, and auditing to ensure effectiveness. With respect to the cloud, some specific elements need to be considered, mostly in interfacing existing enterprise IT security efforts with the methods employed in the cloud instance.

CASB

A *cloud access security broker (CASB)* is a security policy enforcement point that is placed between cloud service consumers and cloud service providers to manage enterprise security policies as cloud-based resources are accessed. A CASB can be an on-premises or cloud-based item; the key is that it exists between the cloud provider and customer connection, thus enabling it to mediate all access. Enterprises use CASB vendors to address cloud service risks, enforce security policies, and comply with regulations. A CASB solution works wherever the cloud services are located, even when they are beyond the enterprise perimeter and out of the direct control of enterprise operations. CASBs work at both the bulk and microscopic scale. They can be configured to block some types of access like a sledgehammer, while also operating as a scalpel, trimming only specific elements. They do require an investment in the development of appropriate strategies in the form of data policies that can be enforced as data moves to and from the cloud.

EXAM TIP Remember that a CASB is a security policy enforcement point that is placed between cloud service consumers and cloud service providers to manage enterprise security policies as cloud-based resources are accessed.

Application Security

When applications are provided by the cloud, application security is part of the equation. Again, this immediately becomes an issue of potentially shared responsibility based on the cloud deployment model chosen. If the customer has the responsibilities for securing the applications, then the issues are the same as in the enterprise, with the added twist of maintaining software on a different platform—the cloud. Access to the application for updating as well as auditing and other security elements must be considered and factored into the business decision behind the model choice.

If the cloud service provider is responsible, there can be economies of scale, and the providers have the convenience of having their own admins maintain the applications. However, with that comes the cost, and the issues of auditing to ensure it is being done correctly. At the end of the day, the concepts of what needs to be done with respect to application security does not change just because it is in the cloud. What does change is who becomes responsible for it, and how it is accomplished in the remote environment. As with other elements of potential shared responsibilities, this is something that needs to be determined before the cloud agreement is signed; if it is not in the agreement, then it is solely on the user to provide the responses.

Next-Generation Secure Web Gateway (SWG)

A *next-generation secure web gateway (SWG)* is a network security service located between the users and the Internet. SWGs work by inspecting web requests against company policy to ensure malicious applications and websites are blocked and inaccessible. An SWG solution includes essential security technologies such as URL filtering, application control, data loss prevention, antivirus, and HTTPS inspection rolled into a comprehensive service to deliver strong web security.

Secure web gateways and next-generation firewalls (NGFWs) are similar because they both provide advanced network protection and are able to identify friendly versus malicious traffic. The strength of SWGs lies in their ability to use application layer inspection to identify and protect against advanced Internet-based attacks.

Firewall Considerations in a Cloud Environment

Firewalls are needed in cloud environments in the same manner they are needed in traditional IT environments. In cloud computing, the network perimeter has essentially disappeared; it is a series of services running outside the traditional IT environment and connected via the Internet. To the cloud, the user's physical location and the device they're using no longer matter. The cloud needs a firewall blocking all unauthorized connections to the cloud instance. In some cases, this is built into the cloud environment; in others, it is up to the enterprise or cloud customer to provide this functionality.

Cost

The first question on every manager's mind is *cost*—what will this cost me? There are cloud environments that are barebones and cheap, but they also don't come with any built-in security functionality, such as a firewall, leaving it up to the customer to provide. Therefore, this needs to be included in the cost comparisons to cloud environments with built-in firewall functionality. The cost of a firewall is not just in the procurement but also the deployment and operation. And all of these factors need to be included, not only for firewalls around the cloud perimeter, but internal firewalls used for segmentation as well.

Need for Segmentation

As previously discussed, segmentation can provide additional opportunities for security checks between critical elements of a system. Take the database servers that hold the crown jewels of a corporation's data, be that intellectual property (IP), business information, customer records; each enterprise has its own flavor, but all have critical records that the loss of or disclosure of would be a serious problem. Segmenting off this element of the network and only allowing access to a small set of defined users at the local segment is a strong security protection against attackers traversing your network. It can also act to keep malware and ransomware from hitting these critical resources. Firewalls are used to create the segments, and the need for them must be managed as part of the requirements package for designing and creating the cloud environment.

Open Systems Interconnection (OSI) Layers

The *open systems interconnection (OSI) layers* act as a means of describing the different levels of communication across a network. From the physical layer (layer 1) to the network layer (layer 3) is the standard realm of networking. Layer 4, the transport layer, is where TCP and UDP function, and through level 7, the application layer, is where applications work. This is relevant with respect to firewalls because most modern application-level attacks do not occur at layers 1–3, but rather happen in layers 4–7. This makes traditional IT firewalls inadequately prepared to see and stop most modern attacks. Modern next-generation firewalls and secure web gateways operate higher in the OSI model, including up to the application layer, to make access decisions. These devices are more powerful and require significantly more information and effort to effectively use, but with integrated security orchestration, automation, and response (SOAR) frameworks and systems, they are becoming valuable components in the security system. As cloud networking is a virtualized function, many of the old network-based attacks will not function on the cloud network, but the need is still there for the higher-level detection of the next-generation devices. These are the typical firewall and security appliances that are considered essential in cloud environments.

EXAM TIP Modern next-generation firewalls and secure web gateways operate higher in the OSI model, using application layer data to make access decisions.

Cloud-Native Controls vs. Third-Party Solutions

When one is looking at cloud security automation and orchestration tools, there are two sources. First is the set provided by the cloud service provider. These cloud-native controls vary by provider and by specific offering that an enterprise subscribes to as part of the user agreement and service license. Third-party tools also exist that the customer can license and deploy in the cloud environment. The decision is one that should be based on a comprehensive review of requirements, including both capabilities and cost of ownership. This is not a simple binary A or B choice; there is much detail to consider. How will each integrate with the existing security environment? How will the operation be handled, and who will have to learn what tools to achieve the objectives? This is a complete review of the people, processes, and technologies, because any of the three can make or break either of these deployments.

Chapter Review

In this chapter, you first became acquainted with cloud security controls. In the first section, the topics of high availability across zones, resource policies, secrets management, integration, and auditing were covered. Next was storage with considerations for permissions, encryption, replication, and high availability. A discussion of networking followed, with subsections on virtual networks, public and private subnets, segmentation, and API inspection and integration. The last subsection under security controls was about the compute aspects of a cloud system, where the topics of security groups, dynamic resource allocations, instance awareness, virtual private cloud endpoints, and container security were covered.

The chapter wrapped up with an examination of the solutions involved in cloud security. In this section, cloud access security brokers (CASBs), application security, next-generation secure web gateways (SWGs), and firewall considerations in a cloud environment were presented. The chapter closed with a section on cloud-native controls versus third-party solutions.

Questions

To help you prepare further for the CompTIA Security+ exam, and to test your level of preparedness, answer the following questions and then check your answers against the correct answers at the end of the chapter.

1. The policies and procedures employed to connect the IAM systems of the enterprise and the cloud to enable communication with the data are referred to as what?

A. API inspection and integration
B. Secrets management
C. Dynamic resource allocation
D. Container security

2. Which of the following terms is not related to storage security in the cloud?
A. Permissions
B. High availability
C. Segmentation
D. Encryption

3. Resource policies involve all of the following except?
A. Permissions
B. IAM
C. Cost
D. Access

4. Virtual networking in a cloud environment can include all of the following except?
A. VPC endpoint
B. Public subnets
C. Private subnets
D. Network function virtualization

5. What structure is used to manage users in cloud environments?
A. Permissions
B. Incident awareness
C. Dynamic resource allocations
D. Security groups

6. Which of the following is a security policy enforcement point placed between cloud service consumers and cloud service providers to manage enterprise security policies as cloud-based resources are accessed?
A. SWG
B. VPC endpoint
C. CASB
D. Resource policies

7. Secure web gateways operate by inspecting at what point in the communication channel?
   - **A.** Security group membership
   - **B.** Application layer
   - **C.** Instance awareness
   - **D.** API inspection
8. Which of the following are critical in cloud security? (Choose all that apply.)
   - **A.** Firewalls
   - **B.** Integration and auditing
   - **C.** Secrets management
   - **D.** Encryption
9. High availability is dependent on which of the following?
   - **A.** Secrets management
   - **B.** Dynamic resource allocation
   - **C.** Container security
   - **D.** CASB
10. Which is the most critical element in understanding your current cloud security posture?
    - **A.** Cloud service agreement
    - **B.** Networking security controls
    - **C.** Encryption
    - **D.** Application security

Answers

1. **B.** Secrets management is the name used to denote the policies and procedures employed to connect the IAM systems of the enterprise and the cloud to enable communication with the data.
2. **C.** Segmentation is a network issue, separate from storage.
3. **C.** Cost is not part of the resource policies. Resource policies describe how the elements of IAM, both in the enterprise and in the cloud, work together to provision resources.
4. **A.** VPC endpoints are not part of the virtual network; although they are virtual applications, they are not part of the network per se.
5. **D.** Security groups are used to manage users in the cloud environment.

6. **C.** The definition of a cloud access security broker (CASB) is a security policy enforcement point that is placed between cloud service consumers and cloud service providers to manage enterprise security policies as cloud-based resources are accessed.
7. **B.** SWGs operate at the application layer, making application layer determinations of suitability.
8. **A, B, C, and D.** All of these play important roles in securing cloud environments.
9. **B.** High availability depends on the ability of the cloud to reallocate resources in the event of a failure; this is one of the functions of dynamic resource allocation.
10. **A.** While many things are involved in cloud security, they all start on the foundation of the cloud services agreement, which describes all of the terms of service.

CHAPTER 23

Identity and Account Management Controls

In this chapter, you will

- Examine identity concepts and practices
- Examine account types
- Review different account policies used to manage accounts
- Given a scenario, implement identity and account management controls

Identity forms part of the foundation of authentication in computer systems. The second part of this foundation is the use of accounts that are managed by a series of policies to enforce a level of rational risk associated with their use. This chapter explores the topic of identity, accounts, and the related policies to manage these entities in the enterprise.

Certification Objective This chapter covers CompTIA Security+ exam objective 3.7: Given a scenario, implement identity and account management controls.

Identity

Identification is the process of ascribing a computer ID to a specific user, computer, network device, or computer process. The identification process is typically performed only once, when a user ID is issued to a particular user. User identification enables authentication and authorization to form the basis for accountability. For accountability purposes, user IDs should not be shared, and for security purposes, user IDs should not be descriptive of job function. This practice enables you to trace activities to individual users or computer processes so that users can be held responsible for their actions. Identification usually takes the form of a logon ID or user ID. A required characteristic of such IDs is that they must be unique.

Identity Provider (IdP)

The term *identity provider (IdP)* is used to denote a system or service that creates, maintains, and manages identity information. IdPs can range in scale and scope—from operating for a single system to operating across an enterprise. Additionally, they can be operated locally, distributed, or federated, depending on the specific solution. Multiple standards have been employed to achieve these services, including those built on the Security Assertion Markup Language (SAML), OpenID, and OAuth. These standards are covered in Chapter 24, "Implement Authentication and Authorization."

EXAM TIP The identity provider (IdP) creates, manages, and is responsible for authenticating identity.

Attributes

How would you describe the elements of an identity? Identity *attributes* are the specific characteristics of an identity—name, department, location, login ID, identification number, e-mail address, and so on—that are used to accurately describe a specific entity. These elements are needed if one is to store identity information in some form of directory, such as an LDAP directory. The particulars of a schema need to be considered to include attributes for people, equipment (servers and devices), and services (apps and programs), as any of these can have an identity in a system. The details of schemas have already been taken care of via Active Directory, various IdPs, and so on, so this is not something that needs to be created; however, it does need to be understood.

Certificates

Certificate-based authentication is a means of proving identity via the presentation of a certificate. Certificates offer a method of establishing authenticity of specific objects such as an individual's public key or downloaded software. A *digital certificate* is a digital file that is sent as an attachment to a message and is used to verify that the message did indeed come from the entity it claims to have come from. Using a digital certificate is a verifiable means of establishing possession of an item (specifically, the certificate). When the certificate is held within a store that prevents tampering or extraction, this becomes a reliable means of identification, especially when combined with an additional factor such as something you know or a biometric. The technical details behind digital certificates are covered in Chapter 25, "Public Key Infrastructure."

Tokens

An access *token* is a physical object that identifies specific access rights and, in authentication, falls into the "something you have" factor. Your house key, for example, is a basic physical access token that allows you access into your home. Although keys have been used to unlock devices for centuries, they do have several limitations. Keys are paired exclusively with a lock or a set of locks, and they are not easily changed. It is easy to add an authorized user by giving the user a copy of the key, but it is far more difficult to give that user selective access unless that specified area is already set up as a separate key. It is also difficult to take access away from a single key or key holder, which usually requires a rekey of the whole system.

In many businesses, physical access authentication has moved to contactless radio frequency cards and proximity readers. When passed near a card reader, the card sends out a code using radio waves. The reader picks up this code and transmits it to the control panel. The control panel checks the code against the reader from which it is being read and the type of access the card has in its database. The advantages of this kind of token-based system include the fact that any card can be deleted from the system without affecting any other card or the rest of the system. In addition, all doors connected to the system can be segmented in any form or fashion to create multiple access areas, with different permissions for each one. The tokens themselves can also be grouped in multiple ways to provide different access levels to different groups of people. All of the access levels or segmentation of doors can be modified quickly and easily if building space is repurposed. Newer technologies are adding capabilities to the standard token-based systems. Smart cards can also be used to carry identification tokens. The primary drawback of token-based authentication is that only the token is being authenticated. Therefore, the theft of the token could grant anyone who possesses the token access to what the system protects.

The risk of theft of the token can be offset by the use of multifactor authentication (described in Chapter 12, "Authentication and Authorization"). One of the ways that people have tried to achieve multifactor authentication is to add a biometric factor to the system. A less expensive alternative is to use hardware tokens in a challenge/response authentication process. In this way, the token functions as both a "something you have" and "something you know" authentication mechanism.

Several variations on this type of device exist, but they all work on the same basic principles. The device has an LCD screen and may or may not have a numeric keypad. Devices without a keypad will display a password (often just a sequence of numbers) that changes at a constant interval, usually about every 60 seconds. When an individual attempts to log in to a system, they enter their own user ID number and then the number that is displayed on the LCD. These two numbers are either entered separately or concatenated. The user's own ID number is secret, and this prevents someone from using a lost device. The system knows which device the user has and is synchronized with it so that it will know the number that should have been displayed. Since this number is constantly changing, a potential attacker who is able to see the sequence will not be able to use it later, since the code will have changed. Devices with a keypad work in a similar fashion (and may also be designed to function as a simple calculator). The individual who wants to log in to the system will first type their personal identification number into the calculator. They will then attempt to log in. The system will then provide a challenge; the user must enter that challenge into the calculator and press a special function key. The calculator will then determine the correct response and display it. The user provides the response to the system they are attempting to log in to, and the system verifies that this is the correct response. Since each user has a different PIN, two individuals receiving the same challenge will have different responses. The device can also use the date or time as a variable for the response calculation so that the same challenge at different times will yield different responses, even for the same individual.

SSH Keys

SSH keys are access credentials used by the Secure Shell (SSH) protocol. They function like usernames and passwords, but SSH keys are primarily used for automated processes and services. SSH keys are also used in implementing single sign-on (SSO) systems used by system administrators. SSH keys are exchanged using public key cryptography, and the keys themselves are digital keys. The concepts of public key cryptography are covered in Chapter 16, "Cryptographic Concepts."

Smart Cards

Smart cards are devices that store cryptographic tokens associated with an identity. The form factor is commonly a physical card, credit card sized, that contains an embedded chip that has various electronic components to act as a physical carrier of information.

The U.S. federal government has several smart card solutions for identification of personnel. The Personal Identity Verification (PIV) card is a U.S. government smart card that contains the cardholder's credential data used to determine access to federal facilities and information systems. The Common Access Card (CAC) is a smart card used by the U.S. Department of Defense (DoD) for active-duty military, Selected Reserve members, DoD civilians, and eligible contractors. Like the PIV card, it is used for carrying the cardholder's credential data, in the form of a certificate, and to determine access to federal facilities and information systems.

EXAM TIP Remember the various uses for tokens, keys, and smart cards. An access token is a physical object that identifies specific access rights and, in authentication, falls into the "something you have" factor. SSH keys are primarily used for automated processes and services. A PIV card is a smart card used for federal employees and contractors. CAC cards are used by the U.S. DoD for active-duty military, Selected Reserve members, DoD civilians, and eligible contractors.

Account Types

To manage the privileges of many different people effectively on the same system, a mechanism for separating people into distinct entities (users) is required, so you can control access on an individual level. It's convenient and efficient to be able to lump users together when granting many different people (groups) access to a resource at the same time. At other times, it's useful to be able to grant or restrict access based on a person's job or function within the organization (role). While you can manage privileges on the basis of users alone, managing user, group, and role assignments together is far more convenient and efficient.

User Account

The term *user account* refers to the account credentials used when accessing a computer system. In privilege management, a user is a single individual, such as "John Forthright" or "Sally Jenkins." This is generally the lowest level addressed by privilege management and the most common area for addressing access, rights, and capabilities. When accessing a computer system, each user is generally given a user ID—a unique alphanumeric identifier they will use to identify themselves when logging in or accessing the system. User IDs are often based on some combination of the user's first, middle, and last names and often include numbers as well. When developing a scheme for selecting user IDs, you should keep in mind that user IDs must be unique to each user, but they must also be fairly easy for the user to remember and use. Because the user ID is used to identify the person who performed specific actions, it is important not to have generic or shared credentials. Either of these situations makes traceability to an authorized user difficult, if not impossible.

EXAM TIP Having unique, nonshared user IDs for all users of a system is important when it comes time to investigate access control issues.

With some notable exceptions, in general a user wanting to access a computer system must first have a user ID created for them on the system they wish to use. This is usually done by a system administrator, security administrator, or other privileged user, and this is the first step in privilege management—a user should not be allowed to create their own account.

Once the account is created and a user ID is selected, the administrator can assign specific permissions to that user. Permissions control what the user is allowed to do on the system—which files they may access, which programs they may execute, and so on. Whereas PCs typically have only one or two user accounts, larger systems such as servers and mainframes can have hundreds of accounts on the same system.

Account policy enforcement is an important part of user credential systems. Managing credentials begins with policies that state the desired objectives. Key elements of a policy include prohibition of sharing accounts and of generic accounts not assigned to a user. For users who have multiple roles, multiple accounts may be necessary, but these need to be delineated by policy rather than on an ad hoc basis. Credential management rules, such as password policy, should be enacted, including lockout and recovery procedures. When users no longer are authorized, such as when they leave the firm or change jobs, their accounts should be disabled, not removed.

Shared and Generic Accounts/Credentials

Shared accounts go against the specific premise that accounts exist so that user activity can be tracked. This said, there are times that shared accounts are used for groups like guests (guest accounts are covered in the next section). Sometimes the shared accounts are called *generic accounts* and exist only to provide a specific set of functionalities, such as in a PC running in kiosk mode, with a browser limited to accessing specific sites as an information display. Under these circumstances, being able to trace the activity to a user is not particularly useful.

A common form of a shared account is one created to run nightly batch operations. As every action must be associated to a user account, a shared account in the name of a batch user can be used to run batch jobs. This is a generic set of *credentials,* not actually associated with a single person but rather associated with a particular type of process (batch jobs, backups, and so on). These credentials are maintained by administrators but are reserved for specific uses, such as executing batch jobs. Because these accounts are in essence local and are being used to run tasks, they can be restricted in function (not permitted to log in, for instance), thus lowering their usefulness for an attacker.

A typical example found in many enterprises resembles the following scenario:

Problem: Organizations use a single account and password for multiple people: for example, the local global administrator account for Office 365 or the root account in Salesforce.

Risk: Commonly shared accounts are distributed and often the credentials (username and password) are put in a shared location. This is a serious no-no by security standards because you can't tell from auditing who exactly accessed what and when they did it. You can see the account, but you have no idea which user was performing the actions.

Modern solution: An Azure AD administrator configures which applications a user can access by using the Access Panel and choosing the type of single sign-on best suited for that application. Using the password-based single-sign on type allows Azure AD to act as a kind of "broker" during the sign-on process for that app.

Guest Accounts

Guest accounts are frequently used on corporate networks to provide visitors access to the Internet and to some common corporate resources, such as projectors, printers in conference rooms, and so forth. Again, like generic accounts, these types of accounts are restricted in their network capability to a defined set of machines, with a defined set of access, much like a user visiting the company's public-facing website via the Internet. As such, logging and tracing activity have little to no use, so the overhead of establishing a unique account does not make sense.

EXAM TIP Guest accounts are granted limited permissions and access. They are used primarily for visitors. It is common practice to disable guest accounts as well as other default accounts when not in use.

Service Accounts

Service accounts are accounts that are used to run processes that do not require human intervention to start, stop, or administer. From running batch jobs in the data center to executing simple tasks that an organization must complete for purposes of regulatory compliance, many reasons exist for running processes with service accounts that don't require an account holder. From a security perspective, administrators can configure service accounts to minimize risks associate with them. For example, in Windows systems, administrators can prevent service accounts from logging in to the system. This limits some of the attack vectors that can be applied to these accounts. Another security provision that can be applied to service accounts that run batch jobs at night is to restrict when they can run. Any service account that has to run in an elevated privilege mode can also be designated to receive extra monitoring and scrutiny.

EXAM TIP Service accounts run without human intervention and are granted only enough permission to run the services they support.

Account Policies

The key method used to control access to most systems is still one based on passwords. In conjunction with a strongly enforced account policy that prohibits sharing of passwords and credentials, use of passwords forms the foundation to support the concept that each user ID should be traceable to a single person's activity. Passwords need to be managed to provide appropriate levels of protection. They need to be strong enough to resist attack, and yet not too difficult for users to remember. An *account policy* can act to ensure that the necessary steps are taken to enact a secure password solution, both by users and by the password infrastructure system.

Password Complexity

Every organization should have defined *password complexity* requirements that passwords must meet. Typical requirements specify that the password must meet the minimum length requirement and have characters from at least three of the following four groups: English uppercase characters (A through Z), English lowercase characters (a through z), numerals (0 through 9), and nonalphabetic characters (such as !, $, #, and %).

EXAM TIP You may be aware of new research from NIST that indicates that password complexity rules designed to force entropy into passwords do so at the risk of other, less-desirable password behaviors by users, such as writing them down or versioning them with an increasing number element. The latest NIST guidance (Special Publication 800-63B, June 2017) is that long passphrases offer the best protection. However, SP 800-63B was published after CompTIA released its Security+ exam objectives, so for the exam, you should know the tried-and-true password complexity requirements listed here.

NOTE Strong passwords aren't enough these days. Computing power allows cybercriminal to run sophisticated programs to obtain or try massive numbers of credentials. That's why relying on passwords alone is no longer sufficient. Specifically, companies should adopt tools like single sign-on (SSO) and multifactor authentication (MFA), also known as two-factor authentication.

Password History

Password history refers to passwords previously used by an account. It is good security policy to prohibit reuse of passwords, at least for a set number of passwords. In Windows, under Local Security Policy (under Local Group policies), you can set three elements that work together to manage password history:

- **Enforce password history** Tells the system how many passwords to remember and does not allow a user to reuse an old password in that list
- **Maximum password age** Specifies the maximum number of days a password may be used before it must be changed
- **Minimum password age** Specifies the minimum number of days a password must be used before it can be changed again

The minimum password age is to prevent a user from changing their password 20 times in a row to recycle back to the previous or current password. An example of account password management in Microsoft Windows is shown in Figure 23-1.

Password Reuse

Password reuse is a bad idea in that it reopens an exposure to an adversary who has previously obtained a password. Official guidance is passwords should not be reused for at least a year, and for at least a half-dozen changes, whichever comes last. Practically, we should never reuse passwords—for a single account or between accounts. As breaches have released many e-mails and passwords into the open domain, people should never expect old passwords to be secure. Adopting a policy of no reuse makes good sense from a risk perspective. This is to minimize the opportunity for an adversary to take advantage

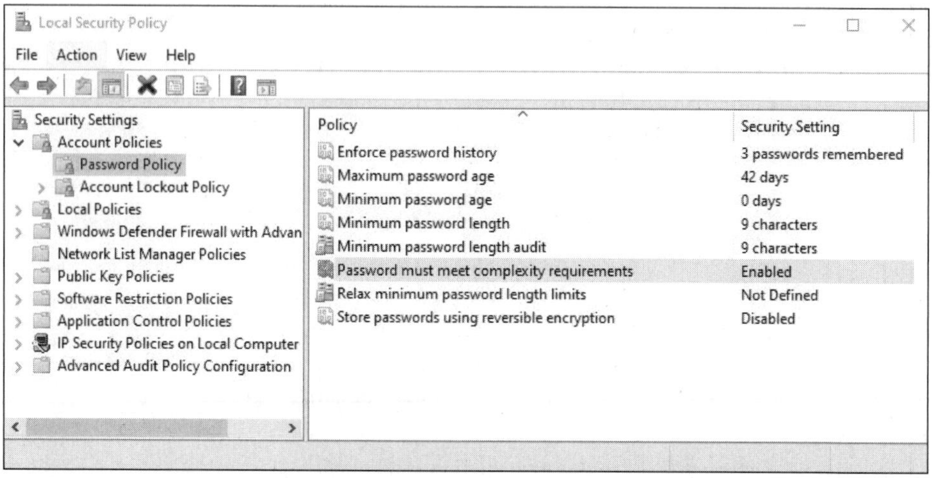

Figure 23-1 Applying password policies by GPO

of a reuse case. As described in the previous section, you can restrict password reuse in Windows under local group policies.

EXAM TIP Strong password policies and settings can help prevent password-cracking attempts such as brute force and dictionary attacks.

Time of Day

Creating *time-of-day* restrictions for access can solve many account management problems. For the majority of workers who work set shifts, having a system whereby their accounts are not active during their nonworking hours reduces the surface of user accounts available for attackers to use. This is even more important for privileged users, as their elevated accounts offer greater risk, and if an authorized user of an account is not working, there is no reason to have it authorized. As with all policies, provisions need to be made for change and emergencies, whereby authorized users can obtain access when needed, even if outside normal working hours.

You can set logon time limits for a user in Windows using an administrative command prompt with the following syntax:

```
net user <username> /time:<day>,<time>
```

Alternatively, in a domain environment, you can also set logon hour restrictions in Active Directory through Group Policy and Group Policy Objects (GPOs).

Network Location

Having restrictions for accounts based on the *network location* can be a very powerful tool in limiting attack surfaces against privileged accounts. Prohibiting specific types of access based on where on the network a user is currently located will prevent someone from using the CFO's credentials from the manufacturing floor, or the head of HR from a kiosk in the lobby. While this might on rare occasion prevent the legitimate user from performing actions under these circumstances, this is a small price to pay for the blanket protection of privileged account access.

Geofencing

Geofencing is the use of the Global Positioning System (GPS) and/or radio frequency identification (RFID) technology to create a virtual fence around a particular location and detect when mobile devices cross the fence. This enables devices to be recognized by others, based on location, and have actions taken. Geofencing is used in marketing to send messages to devices that are in a specific area such as near a point of sale, or just to count potential customers. Geofencing has been used for remote workers, notifying management when they have arrived at remote work sites, allowing things like network connections to be enabled for them. The uses of geofencing are truly only limited by one's imagination.

Turning off geofencing is possible via the device. On Apple devices, just turn off Location Services. Although to completely prevent tracking of the device, you must turn off the radio using Airplane Mode.

Geotagging

Geotagging is the process of applying geotags (location information) to a specific item. The actual geotags can be in a variety of formats but are typically some form of an encoding of latitude and longitude. All sorts of digital data can be geotagged, including but not limited to photographs, videos, websites, and items posted on social media sites. Closely related is the concept of geocoding, which refers to the use of non-coordinate-based geographic metadata elements such as physical street addresses or building locations. Together these elements can provide a significant level of utility to various services, allowing them to customize things based on the location of the device, service, or user.

Geotags have been used in many investigations, as many photos have geotag information embedded in the metadata at the time of creation. This data can be read by special utilities that can read the exchangeable image file (EXIF) or extensible metadata platform (XMP) formats.

Geolocation

Most mobile devices are now capable of using GPS for tracking device location. Many apps rely heavily on GPS location, such as device-locating services, mapping applications, traffic-monitoring apps, and apps that locate nearby businesses such as gas stations and restaurants. Such technology can be exploited to track movement and location of the mobile device, which is referred to as *geolocation*. This tracking can be used to assist in the recovery of lost devices.

EXAM TIP Know the difference between geofencing and geolocation. These make great distractor answer choices for each other in exam questions.

Time-based Logins

Time-based logins are the implementation of time-based authentication, and the proper deployment of this method requires appropriate policies and procedures. Making time-based logins function properly requires the integration of location information as well as time information into an integrated system that can lead to a fine-grained and highly secure assurance of a user being the person they say they are. Time-based exclusions also assist in security, blocking account usage outside of normal working hours.

Access Policies

Access policies are a set of policies to assist in the management of the access control system. From simple policies covering password use, password length, expiration, and lockout, to more complex issues such as account expiration, recovery, and disablement, these directives provide the guidance for security personnel to manage access systems.

Password policies are needed to cover the details of items such as password length, complexity, reuse, and history. Password length and complexity may seem to be forever-increasing targets, but defining them is important to prevent people from using simple, easy-to-crack passwords. Having a formal policy that prohibits sharing of passwords or logging in to another person's account (even with permission) may seem superfluous, but it will be needed when this policy is not in place and something goes wrong. Password reuse for users with both regular and elevated accounts can be an issue; if they use the same password for both accounts, is either really secure? Again, a policy provides appropriate guidance and rules.

Account expiration should occur when a user is no longer authorized to use a system. This requires coordination between those who manage the accounts and those who manage the need for access. The best solution is for the managers of the workers requiring access to manage the need—they are close to the situation, understand the need, and are generally the first to know when access is no longer necessary (for example, when an employee transfers or quits).

Managers should be the first ones to notify the security team as to any changes in permissions, and human resources (HR) should play a backup role. Having frontline management initiate permissions issues also enables the proper continuation of permissions when a person departs. Who assumes ownership over files that the previous person was the sole owner of?

NOTE In Windows systems, user account expiration is a built-in feature that allows you to create a temporary user account that will expire automatically on the specified date. Upon reaching the expiration date, the user account is expired and the user is unable to log on to Windows after that date. This can be good for temporary and contract workers.

Account recovery seems like an esoteric topic until you lose the password on your laptop and have no way back in. This is even more serious if you lose administrator account passwords to key elements of your infrastructure. Having a recovery plan for accounts in case something happens to the people who know the passwords is important in order for the enterprise to continue after the loss of a resource. Rather than focus on all the ways the organization can lose a resource—being fired, leaving on one's own accord, stepping in front of a bus, and so on—focus instead on a simple recovery method like an envelope containing a list of accounts and passwords, put in a safe governed by a different senior executive. Public key infrastructure (PKI) systems have key-recovery mechanisms that are there for a reason—to be used when emergencies happen. Account recovery is no different: you need to have a plan and execute it in order to prepare for an emergency when you need to put the plan into action. Because if you wait until you need a plan, it is too late to create it.

EXAM TIP Accounts have many facets that are governed by both action and policy. Remember, policy directs actions, and the specifics of the question give the context by which you can choose the best answer.

Account Permissions

With one user and one machine, permissions are easy: you are administrator and can access everything. But with more users and more machines, the calculus of who should have what permissions over which objects is what has led to the various access control strategies covered in the next chapter (Chapter 24). As the numbers of users and objects increase, the simple methods of access control become difficult to manage without guidance. Developing a policy for *account permissions* provides just that guidance to those who are implementing the access control schemes. Data owners may wish to determine who has what rights to their data, but trying to keep up with the details, on an account-by-account basis, is a pathway to failure. This has led to groups, roles, and rules being used to manage the details, but these are guided by policies.

An example of a policy would be that users who are acting as database administrators are assigned to a group of database administrators, to facilitate easier management. Once in the group, the group permissions solve the detail by user. Similarly, system administrators may be assigned to a group, to control their permissions. System administrators may have multiple groups so that an administrator cannot access the logs from the systems they can access. Those systems belong to a different group of administrators. A good policy can enforce separation of duties as well as manage the detail associated with the granularity of permissions.

A common differentiation of types of users is:

- **Administrator** An administrator account has full control of the files, directories, services, and other resources on the local computer. The administrator account can create other local users, assign user rights, and assign permissions. The administrator account can take control of local resources at any time simply by changing the user rights and permissions. In Linux systems, the root account is used for administrative purposes, while in Windows the account is called either Administrator or Local Administrator.
- **Standard user** Standard accounts are the basic accounts you use for normal, everyday tasks. As a standard user, you can do just about anything you would need to do, such as running software and personalizing your desktop. Standard users may be limited from installing new programs.
- **Guest** The guest account should be disabled by default on installation. The guest account lets occasional or one-time users who do not have an account on the computer temporarily sign in to the local server or client computer with limited user rights. Guest accounts make the logging and identification of users impossible.

Other systems may have differing groups of users, such as power users that exist between standard users and administrators. Each enterprise can make these determinations on their own and enforce via policies.

Account Audits

Account audits are like all other audits—they are an independent verification that the policies associated with the accounts are being followed. An independent auditor can check all of the elements of policies. Passwords can be checked using a password cracker—if it breaks a password, odds are the user wasn't following the rules. The various restrictions, such as account lockout, and reuse can be checked. An auditor can verify that all the authorized users are still with the firm or are operating in an authorized capacity. Audits work to ensure the implementation of policies is actually working to specification.

Impossible Travel Time/Risky Login

Correct logins to an account can record many elements of information, including where the login came from. This "where" can be a machine in a network, or even a geographic location. Using this metadata, some interesting items can be calculated. Should a login occur from a separate location where the user is already logged in, is it possible for the user to be in two locations at the same time? Likewise, if the second login occurs from a geographically separate location, is there time to actually travel this far in the time between the logins? These are all cases of *risky logins* or examples of *impossible travel time.* There are applications that can detect these anomalies and present this information to you to make decisions as to whether or not the second login should be allowed. What should govern these decisions is a policy that specifically addresses these conditions.

Elements of the policy are not simple, because while a remote login from a continent away might be easy to deny, what of the two logins in the same building overlapping? Is it against policy to have one system logged in, with the screen locked, and then go to a different system? In some high-security instances, this second occurrence might be blocked by policy, whereas in less security instances, the usability of multiple logins might be allowed. This is why a policy is needed—to coordinate management across all of these differing conditions, not leaving it up to a security technician's discretion as they configure appliances and access control systems.

Lockout

Account *lockout* is akin to disablement, although lockout typically refers to temporarily blocking the user's ability to log in to a system. For example, if a user mistypes their password a certain number of times, they may be forced to wait a set amount of time while their account is locked out before attempting to log in again. These lockouts can be automated on most systems and provide a series of increasing time hurdles for an attacker, while minimizing the inconvenience to legitimate users who have credential problems. Users might mistype their password a couple of times, so at worst a minimal lockout hits a legitimate user on the rare occasion. An attacker, trying a set of possible passwords, will hit the lockouts multiple times. Lockout after three attempts allows for a reasonable error rate and balances risk.

EXAM TIP An account lockout policy is used to disable a user account when an incorrect password is used a specified number of times over a certain period of time. This is especially useful for slowing down brute force attempts at cracking a password.

Disablement

Account *disablement* is a step between the account having access and the account being removed from the system. Whenever an employee leaves a firm, all associated accounts should be disabled to prevent further access by the ex-employee. Disabling is preferable to removal, as removal may result in permission and ownership problems. Removing an account can orphan items that remain without other forms of ownership, making it more difficult to share the former employee's files. Periodic audits of user accounts to ensure they still need access is also a good security measure. Disabling an account is reversible, but it prohibits the account from being used until the issue that resulted in the disabling is resolved. Account disablement can be an automatic response from a security system if it detects that the account is under attack (say, from brute force password guessing).

EXAM TIP Accounts have many facets that are governed by both action and policy. Remember, policy directs actions, and the specifics of the question give the context by which you can choose the best answer. There is a lot of detail in this section, and it is all testable in this manner.

Chapter Review

This chapter opened with an examination of the concepts surrounding identity for account management and access control. In the first section, the topics of identity providers (IdPs), attributes, certificates, and tokens were presented. The section finished with SSH keys and smart cards. The next section examined different account types, including user accounts, shared and generic accounts/credentials, guest accounts, and service accounts.

The bulk of the chapter was formed around account policies. This section began with policies associated with passwords: password complexity, history, and reuse. The next topics were time-of-day policies. Location-related policies, including network location, geofencing, geotagging, and geolocation, were covered next. Time-based logins were also explained, followed by general account policies covering access policies, account permissions, and account audits.

The chapter wrapped up with a look at the impossible travel time/risky login issues, followed by lockout and disablement policies.

Questions

To help you prepare further for the CompTIA Security+ exam, and to test your level of preparedness, answer the following questions and then check your answers against the correct answers at the end of the chapter.

1. A friend of yours who works in the IT department of a bank tells you that tellers are allowed to log in to their terminals only from 9 A.M. to 5 P.M., Monday through Saturday. What is this restriction an example of?
   - **A.** User auditing
   - **B.** Least privilege
   - **C.** Time-of-day restrictions
   - **D.** Account verification
2. Your organization is revamping its account management policies and you've been asked to clarify the difference between account disablement and account lockout. Which of the following statements best describes that difference?
   - **A.** Account disablement removes the user and all their data files; account lockout does not.
   - **B.** Account lockout typically only affects the ability to log in; account disablement removes all privileges.
   - **C.** Account lockout is permanent; account disablement is easily reversible.
   - **D.** Account disablement requires administrative privileges to execute; account lockout can be performed by any user.
3. Password policies are needed for all of the following except?
   - **A.** Password complexity
   - **B.** Password history
   - **C.** Password reuse
   - **D.** Password language
4. Which of the following is used to identify when a device is within a specified distance of a location?
   - **A.** Geofencing
   - **B.** Geoproximity
   - **C.** Geodistance
   - **D.** Geotagging

5. Account audits are used for all of the following except?
   - **A.** Testing password strength
   - **B.** Verification of user training
   - **C.** Verification of user employment/authorization
   - **D.** Testing for password policy enforcement
6. Which of the following represents the greatest risk when used?
   - **A.** Service accounts
   - **B.** User accounts
   - **C.** Guest accounts
   - **D.** Shared accounts
7. When a new login request comes from a geographically distant location, for a user with a history of recent local logins, what policy can best help address legitimacy?
   - **A.** Impossible travel time
   - **B.** Geolocation
   - **C.** Network location
   - **D.** Time-of-day restrictions
8. You wish to tokenize account credentials so people can carry their passwords with them and not have to remember or type in long passwords. The best solution would involve which of the following?
   - **A.** Identity providers (IdPs)
   - **B.** SSH keys
   - **C.** Smart card
   - **D.** Password managers
9. On a web-facing interface, where your employees can gain access to the network, you wish to employ security against brute force attacks. One of the most cost-effective tools is to enforce which of the following?
   - **A.** Geofencing policy
   - **B.** Password complexity policy
   - **C.** Account lockout policy
   - **D.** Certificates

10. Which type of policy sets the direction for the security team to manage who can access what resources in a system?
    A. Account permissions policy
    B. Time-based login policies
    C. Password policies
    D. Time-of-day restriction policies

Answers

1. **C.** Time-of-day restrictions are often used to limit the hours during which a user is allowed to log in to or access a system. This helps prevent unauthorized access outside that user's normal working hours.
2. **B.** Account disablement is a step down from removing an account completely. While the account (and associated data files) still exist on the system, the account itself is disabled and has no privileges to access the system. Account lockout typically only affects logon privileges. Performing a temporary account lockout is a common approach to thwarting brute force password-guessing attacks.
3. **D.** The language used in the creation of passwords is not an issue, especially given that most passwords are ideally strings of random characters.
4. **A.** Geofencing is an electronic distance-based perimeter used to detect specific devices when they cross within a certain geographic area.
5. **B.** User training would not be examined during an account audit. Account audits are focused on the authentication system policies and implementations.
6. **D.** Shared accounts are the greatest risk because you don't know who is using them.
7. **A.** When a subsequent account access request is received and there is not adequate time for the user to physically move to the new location, it is likely a fraudulent attempt.
8. **C.** Smart cards enable employees to easily carry cryptographic keys.
9. **C.** Account lockout is a temporary measure to slow down brute force attempts at cracking a password.
10. **A.** Developing a policy for account permissions provides guidance to those who are implementing the access control schemes.

CHAPTER 24

Implement Authentication and Authorization

In this chapter, you will

- Examine authentication management concepts
- Explore different authentication methods
- Examine different access control schemes

Authentication and authorization are important to control who has access to computer systems and resources. Principles of controlling access and properly authenticating apply to both internal access and remote access. Remote access requirements are more rigorous, but the same principles can be applied to internal access.

Access control mechanisms work together with accounts and account policies to determine the proper level of access for users on systems. The chapter will examine authentication management, authentication methods, and access control schemes.

Certification Objective This chapter covers CompTIA Security+ exam objective 3.8: Given a scenario, implement authentication and authorization solutions.

Authentication Management

Authentication is one of the foundational elements of establishing and maintaining security. Authentication management is achieved through a combination of hardware and software elements, including passwords, password keys, vaults, Trusted Platform Module (TPM) and hardware security module (HSM) solutions, as well as alternative authentication methods such as knowledge-based systems.

Password Keys

Passwords represent a secret between a user and an authentication system. One of the challenges in maintaining passwords is for a user to have a system that maintains passwords, as secrets, and does so securely. The usual method involves managing the group of passwords collectively via a password manager solution, which encrypts the passwords with a key. This *password key* represents the access pathway to the passwords and changes the myriad of different passwords, which can be unique for every site or use, into a single secret represented by the password key. The user maintains the secrecy of the password key, and the password manager manages the other passwords.

Password Vaults

Password vaults are software mechanisms designed to manage the problem of users having multiple passwords for the myriad of different systems. Vaults provide a means of storing the passwords until they are needed, and many password manager programs include additional functionality such as password generation and password handling via a browser. Vaults do represent a single point of failure in that if an attacker gets the password key, or master password, they have access to all of the user's passwords. Cryptographic protections should remedy this, but it also introduces another issue with vaults—what to do when the user losses their master password. Any recovery mechanism would represent a major risk for the system, so in most systems it is incumbent on the user to maintain this information somewhere else as a backup.

Another form of password vaults is the systems built into software and operating systems (OSs) to securely hold credentials. Examples of these are the Keychain in macOS and iOS and the Credential Manager in Microsoft Windows. The use of browser-based password storage is much less secure, as numerous utilities exist that can get the passwords out of most of them, making these solutions less secure and an obvious target for attackers. The OS-based Keychain and Credential Manager solutions are much more robust and can limit overall risk.

TPM

The *Trusted Platform Module (TPM)* is a hardware solution on the motherboard, one that assists with key generation and storage as well as random number generation. When the encryption keys are stored in the TPM, they are not accessible via normal software channels and are physically separated from the hard drive or other encrypted data locations. This makes the TPM a more secure solution than keeping the keys in the machine's normal storage.

EXAM TIP A TPM acts as a secure cryptoprocessor. It is a hardware solution that assists with key generation and secure, encrypted storage.

HSM

A *hardware security module (HSM)* is a device used to manage or store encryption keys. It can also assist in cryptographic operations such as encryption, hashing, or the application of digital signatures. HSMs typically are peripheral devices connected via USB or a network connection. HSMs have tamper-protection mechanisms to prevent physical access to the secrets they protect. Because of their dedicated design, they can offer significant performance advantages over general-purpose computers when it comes to cryptographic operations. When an enterprise has significant levels of cryptographic operations, HSMs can provide throughput efficiencies.

EXAM TIP Storing private keys anywhere on a networked system is a recipe for loss. HSMs are designed to allow the use of keys without exposing them to the wide range of host-based threats.

Knowledge-based Authentication

Knowledge-based authentication is a method where the identity of a user is verified via a common set of knowledge. This is a very useful method for verifying the identity of a user without having a stored secret in advance. The standard methodology associated with authentication is an identity and a common secret that are previously recorded in a system, and then upon later use verified by recall on the user's part and lookup by the system. But what if the user has never accessed the site to establish their identity? How can it be established on the fly, so to speak? Knowledge-based authentication relies on a set of knowledge that, while it may be available to many, is from such a vast set of information that the recall only will work for the user themselves.

A good example is when accessing a site such as a credit bureau to obtain information on yourself. The site has a vast array of knowledge associated with you, and it can see if you can identify an address you have lived at (out of a list of four addresses), a car you owned (out of a list of four cars), a car or mortgage payment amount, or a credit card account. In a timed quiz, to eliminate extensive lookups, the user is presented with a series of multiple-choice options. If they get them all correct, then odds are that they are the person they represent themselves to be. The last time the author went through one of these tests, the range of time for the knowledge covered was greater than 20 years, making the breadth of knowledge to choose from large indeed.

Authentication

Authentication protocols are the standardized methods used to provide authentication services, and in the case of wireless networks, these are provided remotely. Wireless networks have a need for secure authentication protocols. The following sections cover several key authentication protocols and methods in use today.

EAP

The *Extensible Authentication Protocol (EAP)* is a protocol for wireless networks that expands on authentication methods used by the Point-to-Point Protocol (PPP). PPP is a protocol that was commonly used to directly connect devices to each other. EAP is designed to support multiple authentication mechanisms, including tokens, smart cards, certificates, one-time passwords, and public key encryption authentication. EAP has been expanded into multiple versions, some of which are covered in the following sections. EAP is defined in RFC 2284 (obsoleted by 3748).

PEAP, or *Protected EAP,* was developed to protect the EAP communication by encapsulating it with Transport Layer Security (TLS). This is an open standard developed jointly by Cisco, Microsoft, and RSA. EAP was designed assuming a secure communication channel. PEAP provides that protection as part of the protocol via a TLS tunnel. PEAP is widely supported by vendors for use over wireless networks.

The Wi-Fi Alliance added EAP-FAST to its list of supported protocols for WPA/WPA2 in 2010, and to WPA3 in 2018. *EAP-FAST (EAP Flexible Authentication via Secure Tunneling)* is described in RFC 4851 and proposed by Cisco to be a replacement for LEAP, a previous Cisco version of EAP. It offers a lightweight tunneling protocol to enable authentication. The distinguishing characteristic is the passing of a Protected Access Credential (PAC) that is used to establish a TLS tunnel through which client credentials are verified. The Wi-Fi Alliance also added EAP-TLS to its list of supported protocols for WPA/WPA2 in 2010, and WPA3 was added in 2018. *EAP-TLS* is an IETF open standard (RFC 5216) that uses the TLS protocol to secure the authentication process. EAP-TLS relies on TLS, an attempt to standardize the SSL structure to pass credentials. This is still considered one of the most secure implementations, primarily because common implementations employ client-side certificates. This means that an attacker must also possess the key for the client-side certificate to break the TLS channel.

The Wi-Fi Alliance also added EAP-TTLS to its list of supported protocols for WPA/WPA2 in 2010, and WPA3 in 2018. EAP-TTLS (the acronym stands for EAP–Tunneled TLS protocol) is a variant of the EAP-TLS protocol. EAP-TTLS works much the same way as EAP-TLS, with the server authenticating to the client with a certificate, but the protocol tunnels the client side of the authentication, allowing the use of legacy authentication protocols such as Password Authentication Protocol (PAP), Challenge-Handshake Authentication Protocol (CHAP), MS-CHAP, and MS-CHAP-V2. In EAP-TTLS, the authentication process is protected by the tunnel from man-in-the-middle attacks, and although client-side certificates can be used, they are not required, making this easier to set up than EAP-TLS to clients without certificates.

NOTE WPA3 was released by the Wi-Fi Alliance in 2018, and it specifically is designed to address WPA2 weaknesses, while still allowing older methods. Per the WPA3 specification, a WPA3 station shall perform server certificate validation when using EAP-TTLS, EAP-TLS, EAP-PEAPv0 or EAP-PEAPv1 EAP methods.

EXAM TIP There are two key elements concerning EAP. First, it is only a framework to secure the authentication process. Second, it can support multiple methods and itself is not an actual encryption method.

Challenge-Handshake Authentication Protocol (CHAP)

Challenge-Handshake Authentication Protocol (CHAP) is used to provide authentication across a point-to-point link using PPP. In this protocol, authentication after the link has been established is not mandatory. CHAP is designed to provide authentication periodically through the use of a challenge/response system sometimes described as a three-way

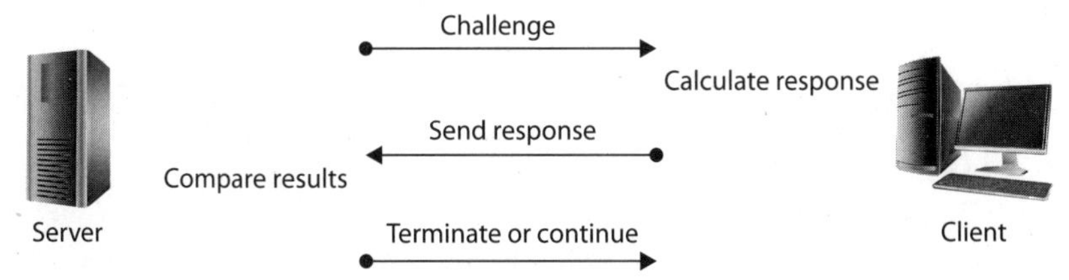

Figure 24-1 The CHAP challenge/response sequence

handshake, as illustrated in Figure 24-1. The initial challenge (a randomly generated number) is sent to the client. The client uses a one-way hashing function to calculate what the response should be and then sends this back. The server compares the response to what it calculated the response should be. If they match, communication continues. If the two values don't match, then the connection is terminated. This mechanism relies on a shared secret between the two entities so that the correct values can be calculated.

EXAM TIP CHAP uses PPP, which supports three functions:
—Encapsulate datagrams across serial links
—Establish, configure, and test links using LCP (Link Control Protocol)
—Establish and configure different network protocols using NCP (Network Control Protocol)

PPP supports two authentication protocols:
—Password Authentication Protocol (PAP)
—Challenge-Handshake Authentication Protocol (CHAP)

Password Authentication Protocol (PAP)

Password Authentication Protocol (PAP) authentication involves a two-way handshake in which the username and password are sent across the link in clear text. PAP authentication does not provide any protection against playback and line sniffing. PAP is now a deprecated standard.

EXAM TIP PAP is a cleartext authentication protocol and hence is subject to interception. CHAP uses a challenge/response handshake protocol to secure the channel.

802.1X

802.1X is an authentication standard that supports port-based authentication services between a user and an authorization device, such as an edge router. 802.1X is commonly used on wireless access points as a port-based authentication service prior to admission to the wireless network. 802.1X over wireless uses either 802.11i or an EAP-based protocol, such as EAP-TLS or PEAP-TLS.

RADIUS

Remote Authentication Dial-In User Service (RADIUS) is a protocol that was developed as an AAA protocol. It was submitted to the IETF as a series of RFCs: RFC 2058 (RADIUS specification), RFC 2059 (RADIUS accounting standard), and updated RFCs 2865–2869 and 3579 are now standard protocols. The IETF AAA Working Group has proposed extensions to RADIUS (RFC 2882) and a replacement protocol called Diameter (RFC 7075).

RADIUS is designed as a connectionless protocol utilizing User Datagram Protocol (UDP) as its transport-level protocol. Connection-type issues, such as timeouts, are handled by the RADIUS application instead of the transport layer. RADIUS utilizes UDP ports 1812 for authentication and authorization and 1813 for accounting functions.

RADIUS is a client/server protocol. The RADIUS client is typically a network access server (NAS). The RADIUS server is a process or daemon running on a Linux or Windows Server machine. Communications between a RADIUS client and RADIUS server are encrypted using a shared secret that is manually configured into each entity and not shared over a connection. Hence, communications between a RADIUS client (typically a NAS) and a RADIUS server are secure, but the communications between a user (typically a PC) and the RADIUS client are subject to compromise. This is important to note because if the user's machine (the PC) is not the RADIUS client (the NAS), then communications between the PC and the NAS are typically not encrypted and are passed in the clear.

EXAM TIP Using UDP transport to a centralized network access server, RADIUS provides client systems with authentication and access control within an enterprise network.

Single Sign-On (SSO)

Single sign-on (SSO) is a form of authentication that involves the transferring of credentials between systems. As more and more systems are combined in daily use, users are forced to have multiple sets of credentials. A user may have to log in to three, four, five, or even more systems every day just to do her job. Single sign-on allows a user to transfer her credentials so that logging in to one system acts to log her in to all of them. This has the advantage of reducing login hassles for the user. It also has the disadvantage of combining the authentication systems in such a way that if one login is compromised, then all of the user's logins are compromised.

Security Assertion Markup Language (SAML)

Security Assertion Markup Language (SAML) is a single sign-on capability used for web applications to ensure user identities can be shared and are protected. It defines standards for exchanging authentication and authorization data between security domains. It is becoming increasingly important with cloud-based solutions and with Software as a Service (SaaS) applications, as it ensures interoperability across identity providers.

SAML is an XML-based protocol that uses security tokens and assertions to pass information about a "principal" (typically an end user) to a SAML authority (an "identity provider" or IdP) and the service provider (SP). The principal requests a service from the SP, which then requests and obtains an identity assertion from the IdP. The SP can then grant access or perform the requested service for the principal.

EXAM TIP By allowing identity providers to pass on credentials to service providers, SAML allows you log in to many different websites using one set of credentials.

Terminal Access Controller Access Control System Plus (TACACS+)

The *Terminal Access Controller Access Control System Plus (TACACS+)* protocol is the current generation of the TACACS family. TACACS+ has extended attribute control and accounting processes.

One of the fundamental design aspects is the separation of authentication, authorization, and accounting in this protocol. Although there is a straightforward lineage of these protocols from the original TACACS, TACACS+ is a major revision and is not backward compatible with previous versions of the protocol series.

TACACS+ uses TCP as its transport protocol, typically operating over TCP port 49. This port is used for the login process. Both UDP and TCP port 49 are reserved for the TACACS+ login host protocol.

TACACS+ is a client/server protocol, with the client typically being a network access server (NAS) and the server being a daemon process on a UNIX, Linux, or Windows server. This is important to note because if the user's machine (usually a PC) is not the client (usually a NAS), then communications between the PC and NAS are typically not encrypted and are passed in the clear. Communications between a TACACS+ client and TACACS+ server are encrypted using a shared secret that is manually configured into each entity and is not shared over a connection. Hence, communications between a TACACS+ client (typically a NAS) and a TACACS+ server are secure, but the communications between a user (typically a PC) and the TACACS+ client are subject to compromise.

EXAM TIP TACACS+ is a protocol that takes a client/server model approach and handles authentication, authorization, and accounting (AAA) services. It is similar to RADIUS but uses TCP (port 49) as a transport method.

OAuth

OAuth (Open Authorization) is an open protocol that allows secure, token-based authorization on the Internet from web, mobile, and desktop applications via a simple and standard method. OAuth is used by companies such as Google, Facebook, Microsoft, and Twitter to permit users to share information about their accounts with third-party applications or websites. OAuth 1.0 was developed by a Twitter engineer as part of the Twitter OpenID implementation. OAuth 2.0 (not backward compatible) has taken off with support from most major web platforms. OAuth's main strength is that it can be used by an external partner site to allow access to protected data without having to re-authenticate the user.

OAuth was created to remove the need for users to share their passwords with third-party applications, instead substituting a token. OAuth 2.0 expanded this into also providing authentication services, so it can eliminate the need for OpenID.

OpenID

OpenID is a simple identity layer on top of the OAuth 2.0 protocol, just discussed. OpenID allows clients of all types, including mobile, JavaScript, and web-based clients, to request and receive information about authenticated sessions and end users. OpenID is intended to make the process of proving who you are easier, the first step in the authentication–authorization ladder. To do authorization, a second process is needed, and OpenID is commonly paired with OAuth 2.0. OpenID was created for federated authentication that lets a third party, such as Google or Facebook, authenticate your users for you, by using accounts that the users already have.

EXAM TIP OpenID and OAuth are typically used together, yet have different purposes. OpenID is used for authentication, whereas OAuth is used for authorization.

Kerberos

Developed as part of MIT's project Athena, *Kerberos* is a network authentication protocol designed for a client/server environment. The current release at the time of writing is Kerberos version 5, release 1.18.5, which is supported by all major operating systems. Kerberos securely passes a symmetric key over an insecure network using the Needham-Schroeder symmetric key protocol. Kerberos is built around the idea of a trusted third party, termed a *key distribution center (KDC)*, which consists of two logically separate parts: an authentication server (AS) and a ticket-granting server (TGS). Kerberos communicates via "tickets" that serve to prove the identity of users.

Taking its name from the three-headed dog of Greek mythology, Kerberos is designed to work across the Internet, an inherently insecure environment. Kerberos uses strong encryption so that a client can prove its identity to a server, and the server can in turn authenticate itself to the client. A complete Kerberos environment is referred to as a Kerberos realm. The Kerberos server contains user IDs and hashed passwords for all users that will have authorizations to realm services. The Kerberos server also has shared secret keys with every server to which it will grant access tickets.

The basis for authentication in a Kerberos environment is the ticket. Tickets are used in a two-step process with the client. The first ticket is a ticket-granting ticket (TGT) issued by the AS to a requesting client. The client can then present this ticket to the Kerberos server with a request for a ticket to access a specific server. This client-to-server ticket is used to gain access to a server's service in the realm. Since the entire session can be encrypted, this will eliminate the inherently insecure transmission of items such as a password that can be intercepted on the network. Tickets are timestamped and have a lifetime, so attempting to reuse a ticket will not be successful.

The steps involved in Kerberos authentication are as follows:

1. The user presents credentials and requests a ticket from the Key Distribution Server (KDS).
2. The KDS verifies credentials and issues a TGT.
3. The user presents a TGT and request for service to the KDS.
4. The KDS verifies authorization and issues a client-to-server ticket.
5. The user presents a request and a client-to-server ticket to the desired service.
6. If the client-to-server ticket is valid, service is granted to the client.

To illustrate how the Kerberos authentication service works, think about the common driver's license. You have received a license that you can present to other entities to prove you are who you claim to be. Because other entities trust the state in which the license was issued, they will accept your license as proof of your identity. The state in which the license was issued is analogous to the Kerberos authentication service realm, and the license acts as a client-to-server ticket. It is the trusted entity both sides rely on to provide valid identifications. This analogy is not perfect, because we all probably have heard of individuals who obtained a phony driver's license, but it serves to illustrate the basic idea behind Kerberos.

EXAM TIP Kerberos is a third-party authentication service that uses a series of tickets as tokens for authenticating users. The steps involved are protected using strong cryptography.

Access Control Schemes

The term *access control* describes a variety of protection schemes. It sometimes refers to all security features used to prevent unauthorized access to a computer system or network. In this sense, it may be confused with *authentication*. More properly, *access* is the ability of a subject (such as an individual or a process running on a computer system) to interact with an object (such as a file or hardware device). Authentication, on the other hand, deals with verifying the identity of a subject.

To understand the difference, consider the example of an individual attempting to log in to a computer system or network. Authentication is the process used to verify to the computer system or network that the individual is who he claims to be. The most common method to do this is through the use of a user ID and password. Once the individual has verified his identity, access controls regulate what the individual can actually do on the system—just because a person is granted entry to the system does not mean that he should have access to all data the system contains.

Consider another example. When you go to your bank to make a withdrawal, the teller at the window will verify that you are indeed who you claim to be by asking you to provide some form of identification with your picture on it, such as your driver's license. You might also have to provide your bank account number. Once the teller verifies your identity, you will have proved that you are a valid (authorized) customer of this bank. This does not, however, mean that you have the ability to view all information that the bank protects—such as your neighbor's account balance. The teller will control what information, and funds, you can access and will grant you access only to the information that you are authorized to see. In this example, your identification and bank account number serve as your method of authentication and the teller serves as the access control mechanism.

In computer systems and networks, access controls can be implemented in several ways. An access control matrix provides the simplest framework for illustrating the process and is shown in Table 24-1. In this matrix, the system is keeping track of two processes, two files, and one hardware device. Process 1 can read both File 1 and File 2 but can write only to File 1. Process 1 cannot access Process 2, but Process 2 can execute Process 1. Both processes have the ability to write to the printer.

While simple to understand, the access control matrix is seldom used in computer systems because it is extremely costly in terms of storage space and processing. Imagine the size of an access control matrix for a large network with hundreds of users and thousands of files. The actual mechanics of how access controls are implemented in a system varies, though access control lists (ACLs) are common. An ACL is nothing more than a list that contains the subjects that have access rights to a particular object. The list identifies not only the subject but the specific access granted to the subject for the object. Typical types of access include read, write, and execute, as indicated in the sample access control matrix.

No matter what specific mechanism is used to implement access controls in a computer system or network, the controls should be based on a specific *model* of access. Several different models are discussed in security literature and listed under exam objective 3.8, including attribute-based access control (ABAC), role-based access control (RBAC), rule-based access control (also RBAC), mandatory access control (MAC), and discretionary access control (DAC).

Attribute-Based Access Control (ABAC)

Attribute-based access control (ABAC) is a form of access control based on attributes. These attributes can be in a wide variety of forms, such as user attributes, resource or object attributes, and environmental attributes. For instance, a doctor can access medical

	Process 1	**Process 2**	**File 1**	**File 2**	**Printer**
Process 1	Read, write, execute		Read, write	Read	Write
Process 2	Execute	Read, write, execute	Read, write	Read, write	Write

Table 24-1 An Access Control Matrix

records, but only for patients to which she is assigned, or only when she is on shift. The major difference between ABAC and role-based access control (discussed next) is the ability to include Boolean logic in the access control decision.

EXAM TIP The ABAC process of authorization evaluates specific rules and policies against attributes associated with a subject or object. ABAC is often used in large enterprises that use a federated structure. It is somewhat more complicated and costly to implement than other access control models.

Role-Based Access Control

ACLs can be cumbersome and can take time to administer properly. Another access control mechanism that has been attracting increased attention is *role-based access control (RBAC)*. In this scheme, instead of each user being assigned specific access permissions for the objects associated with the computer system or network, each user is assigned a set of roles that he or she may perform. The roles are in turn assigned the access permissions necessary to perform the tasks associated with those roles. Users will thus be granted permissions to objects in terms of the specific duties they must perform—not according to a security classification associated with individual objects.

Rule-Based Access Control

The first thing you might notice is the ambiguity introduced with this access control method also using the acronym RBAC. *Rule-based access control* also uses objects such as ACLs to help determine whether or not access should be granted. In this case, a series of rules is contained in the ACL, and the determination of whether to grant access will be made based on these rules. An example of such a rule is one that states that no employee may have access to the payroll file after hours or on weekends. As with MAC (discussed next), users are not allowed to change the access rules, and administrators are relied on for this. Rule-based access control can actually be used in addition to or as a method of implementing other access control methods. For example, MAC methods can utilize a rule-based approach for implementation.

EXAM TIP Do not become confused between rule-based and role-based access controls, even though they both have the same acronym. The name of each is descriptive of what it entails and will help you distinguish between them.

MAC

A less frequently employed system for restricting access is *mandatory access control (MAC)*. This system, generally used only in environments in which different levels of security classifications exist, is much more restrictive regarding what a user is allowed to do. As defined by the "Orange Book," a Department of Defense (DoD) document that at one time was the standard for describing what constituted a trusted computing system, a mandatory access control is "a means of restricting access to objects based on the sensitivity (as represented by a label) of the information contained in the objects and the formal authorization (i.e., clearance) of subjects to access information of such sensitivity." In this case, the owner or subject can't determine whether access is to be granted to another subject; it is the job of the operating system to decide.

EXAM TIP Common information classifications include High, Medium, Low, Confidential, Private, and Public.

In MAC, the security mechanism controls access to all objects, and individual subjects cannot change that access. The key here is the label attached to every subject and object. The label will identify the level of classification for that object and the level to which the subject is entitled. Think of military security classifications such as Secret and Top Secret. A file that has been identified as Top Secret (has a label indicating that it is Top Secret) may be viewed only by individuals with a Top Secret clearance. It is up to the access control mechanism to ensure that an individual with only a Secret clearance never gains access to a file labeled as Top Secret. Similarly, a user cleared for Top Secret access will not be allowed by the access control mechanism to change the classification of a file labeled as Top Secret to Secret or to send that Top Secret file to a user cleared only for Secret information. The complexity of such a mechanism can be further understood when you consider today's windowing environment. The access control mechanism will not allow a user to cut a portion of a Top Secret document and paste it into a window containing a document with only a Secret label. It is this separation of differing levels of classified information that results in this sort of mechanism being referred to as *multilevel security*.

Finally, just because a subject has the appropriate level of clearance to view a document does not mean that she will be allowed to do so. The concept of least privilege, sometimes called "need to know," which is a DAC concept (discussed next), also exists in MAC mechanisms. Least privilege means that a person is given access only to information that she needs in order to accomplish her job or mission.

Discretionary Access Control (DAC)

Both *discretionary access control (DAC)* and mandatory access control are terms originally used by the military to describe two different approaches to controlling an individual's access to a system. Per the "Orange Book," DACs are "a means of restricting access to objects based on the identity of subjects and/or groups to which they belong. The controls are discretionary in the sense that a subject with a certain access permission is capable of passing that permission (perhaps indirectly) on to any other subject." While this might appear to be confusing "government-speak," the principle is rather simple. In systems that employ DACs, the owner of an object can decide which other subjects can have access to the object and what specific access they can have. One common method to accomplish this is the permission bits used in Linux-based systems. The owner of a file can specify what permissions (read/write/execute) members in the same group can have and also what permissions all others can have. ACLs are also a common mechanism used to implement DAC.

EXAM TIP If you are trying to remember the difference between MAC and DAC, just remember that MAC is associated with multilevel security labels such as Top Secret and Secret, whereas DAC uses ACLs.

Conditional Access

Conditional access is an access control scheme where specific conditions are examined before access is given. A condition could be the user location when accessing resources: if local, then grant access; if remote, then deny access. The list of conditions can be broad and follows this general form:

If { condition } **then** { action }

Some examples follow:

- **If** { client is using legacy authentication } **then** { block access }
- **If** { device is not compliant } **then** { block access }
- **If** { user is an admin } **then** { enable multifactor authentication }

Conditional access can be very useful when an entity has a wide array of different systems with differing access needs.

Privileged Access Management

Privileged accounts are any accounts with greater-than-normal user access. Privileged accounts are typically root- or administrative-level accounts and represent risk in that they are unlimited in their powers. These accounts require regular real-time monitoring, if at all possible, and should always be monitored when operating remotely. Administrators may need to perform tasks via a remote session in certain scenarios, but when they do, they first need to identify the purpose and get approval.

Privileged access management is a combination of the policies, procedures, and technologies for controlling access to and use of elevated or privileged accounts. This enables the organization to log and control privileged access across the entire environment. The primary purpose is to limit the attack surface that these accounts have, and to minimize exposure based on current operational needs and conditions.

File System Permissions

Files need security on systems, to prevent unauthorized access and unauthorized alterations. File system security is the set of mechanisms and processes employed to ensure this critical function. Using a connection of file storage mechanisms, along with access control lists and access control models, provides a means by which this can be done. You need a file system capable of supporting user-level access differentiation—something NTFS does but FAT32 does not. Next, you need to have a functioning access control model—MAC, DAC, ABAC, or other, as previously described in this chapter. Then you need a system to apply the users' permissions to the files, which can be handled by the OS, although administering and maintaining this can be a challenge.

If multiple users share a computer system, the system administrator likely needs to control who is allowed to do what when it comes to viewing, using, or changing system resources. Although operating systems vary in how they implement these types of controls, most operating systems use the concepts of permissions and rights to control and safeguard access to resources. *Permissions* control what a user is allowed to do with objects on a system, and *rights* define the actions a user can perform on the system itself. Let's examine how the Windows operating systems implement this concept.

The Windows operating systems use the concepts of permissions and rights to control access to files, folders, and information resources. When using the NTFS file system, administrators can grant users and groups permission to perform certain tasks as they relate to files, folders, and Registry keys. The basic categories of NTFS permissions are as follows:

EXAM TIP Permissions can be applied to a specific user or group to control that user or group's ability to view, modify, access, use, or delete resources such as folders and files.

- **Full Control** A user/group can change permissions on the folder/file, take ownership if someone else owns the folder/file, delete subfolders and files, and perform actions permitted by all other NTFS folder permissions.
- **Modify** A user/group can view and modify files/folders and their properties, can delete and add files/folders, and can delete properties from or add properties to a file/folder.
- **Read & Execute** A user/group can view the file/folder and can execute scripts and executables, but they cannot make any changes (files/folders are read-only).
- **List Folder Contents** A user/group can list only what is inside the folder (applies to folders only).
- **Read** A user/group can view the contents of the file/folder and the file/folder properties.
- **Write** A user/group can write to the file or folder.

Figure 24-2 shows the permissions on a folder called Data from a Windows Server system. In the top half of the Permissions window are the users and groups that have permissions for this folder. In the bottom half of the window are the permissions assigned to the highlighted user or group.

Under UNIX operating systems, file permissions consist of three distinct parts:

- **Owner permissions (read, write, and execute)** The owner of the file
- **Group permissions (read, write, and execute)** The group to which the owner of the file belongs
- **World permissions (read, write, and execute)** Anyone else who is not the owner and does not belong to the group to which the owner of the file belongs

Figure 24-2 Permissions for the Data folder

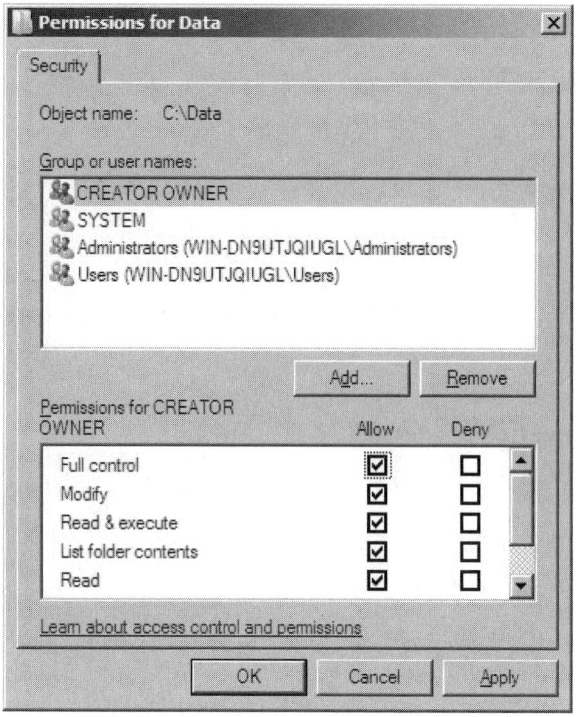

EXAM TIP Discretionary access control restricts access based on the user's identity or group membership.

For example, suppose a file called *secretdata* has been created by the owner of the file, Luke, who is part of the Engineering group. The owner permissions on the file would reflect Luke's access to the file (as the owner). The group permissions would reflect the access granted to anyone who is part of the Engineering group. The world permissions would represent the access granted to anyone who is not Luke and is not part of the Engineering group.

In Linux, a file's permissions are usually displayed as a series of nine characters, with the first three characters representing the owner's permissions, the second three characters representing the group permissions, and the last three characters representing the permissions for everyone else (that is, for the world). This concept is illustrated in Figure 24-3.

Figure 24-3 Discretionary file permissions in the UNIX environment

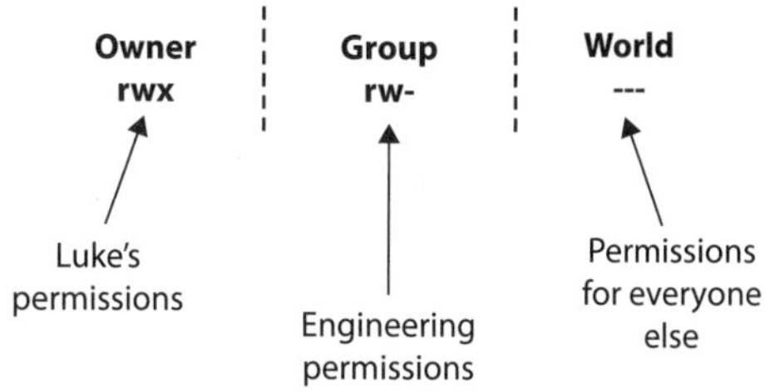

Suppose the file secretdata is owned by Luke with group permissions for Engineering (because Luke is part of the Engineering group), and the permissions on that file are rwx, rw-, and ---, as shown in Figure 24-3. This would mean the following:

- Luke can read, write, and execute the file (rwx).
- Members of the Engineering group can read and write the file but not execute it (rw-).
- The world has no access to the file and can't read, write, or execute it (---).

Remember that under the DAC model, the file's owner, Luke, can change the file's permissions any time he wants.

Chapter Review

In this chapter, you became acquainted with how to implement authentication and authorization solutions. The chapter opened with an examination of authentication management, including password keys, password vaults, TPM and HSM solutions, and knowledge-based authentication.

The next section covered forms of authentication solutions, starting with the EAP, CHAP, and PAP protocols. Then it moved into IEEE 802.1X, RADIUS, and single sign-on solutions. A description of Security Assertion Markup Language (SAML) was the next item covered, followed by a discussion of Terminal Access Controller/Access Control System Plus (TACACS+). The methods of OAuth and OpenID were discussed next, and the section closed with a discussion of Kerberos.

The last section of the chapter covered access control schemes. It opened with a discussion of attribute-based access control (ABAC), role-based access control (RBAC), rule-based access control (also RBAC), mandatory access control (MAC), and discretionary access control (DAC). The section closed with a discussion of conditional access control, privilege access management, and file system permissions.

Questions

To help you prepare further for the CompTIA Security+ exam, and to test your level of preparedness, answer the following questions and then check your answers against the correct answers at the end of the chapter.

1. Your organization needs a system for restricting access to files based on the sensitivity of the information in those files. You might suggest which of the following access control systems?

   A. Discretionary access control

   B. Mandatory access control

C. Confidential access control

D. File-based access control

2. Which of the following describes a major difference between NTFS and FAT32 file systems?

A. NTFS supports user-level access differentiation.

B. FAT32 supports group-level access differentiation.

C. FAT32 natively encrypts files and directories.

D. NTFS logs all file access using secure tokens.

3. Your organization has grown too large to support assigning permissions to users individually. Within your organization, you have large groups of users who perform the same duties and need the same type and level of access to the same files. Rather than assigning individual permissions, your organization may wish to consider using which of the following access control methods?

A. Group-based access control

B. Shift-based access control

C. Role-based access control

D. File-based access control

4. A ticket-granting server is an important element in which of the following authentication models?

A. 802.1X

B. RADIUS

C. TACACS+

D. Kerberos

5. Which of the following is an open standard that uses security tokens and assertions and allows you to access multiple websites with one set of credentials?

A. PAP

B. CHAP

C. SSO

D. SAML

6. What protocol is used for RADIUS?

A. UDP

B. NetBIOS

C. TCP

D. Proprietary

7. What are accounts with greater than "normal" user access called?
   A. Privileged accounts
   B. System accounts
   C. Superuser accounts
   D. Audit accounts
8. You have to implement an OpenID solution. What is the typical relationship with existing systems?
   A. OpenID is used for authentication, OAuth is used for authorization.
   B. OpenID is used for authorization, OAuth is used for authentication.
   C. OpenID is not compatible with OAuth.
   D. OpenID only works with Kerberos.
9. You wish to create an access control scheme that enables the CFO to access financial data from his machine, but not from the machine in the reception area of the lobby. Which access control model is best suited for this?
   A. Role-based access control
   B. Conditional access control
   C. Mandatory access control
   D. Discretionary access control
10. You need to design an authentication system where users who have never connected to the system can be identified and authenticated in a single process. Which is the best solution?
    A. RADIUS
    B. Password vault-based authentication
    C. TPM-based authentication
    D. Knowledge-based authentication

Answers

1. **B.** Mandatory access control (MAC) is a system used in environments with different levels of security classifications. Access to objects (like files) is based on the sensitivity of the information contained in those objects and the authorization of the user to access information with that level of sensitivity.
2. **A.** NTFS supports user-level access differentiation and allows you to assign user permissions to files and folders.

3. **C.** Your organization could consider role-based access control. In role-based access control, instead of each user being assigned specific access permissions for the objects associated with the computer system or network, each user is assigned a set of roles that he or she may perform. The roles are in turn assigned the access permissions necessary to perform the tasks associated with the roles. Users will thus be granted permissions to objects in terms of the specific duties they must perform—not according to a security classification associated with individual objects.
4. **D.** Kerberos uses ticket-granting servers to manage the issuance of tickets granting various permissions on the system.
5. **D.** SAML is an XML-based protocol that uses security tokens and assertions to pass information about a "principal" (typically an end user) to a SAML authority (an "identity provider" or IdP) and the service provider (SP). In simpler terms, by allowing identity providers to pass on credentials to service providers, SAML allows you can log in to many different websites using one set of credentials.
6. **A.** RADIUS has been officially assigned UDP port 1812 for RADIUS authentication and port 1813 for RADIUS accounting by the Internet Assigned Numbers Authority (IANA). However, previously, ports 1645 (authentication) and 1646 (accounting) were used unofficially and became the default ports assigned by many RADIUS client/server implementations of the time. The tradition of using 1645 and 1646 for backward compatibility continues to this day. For this reason, many RADIUS server implementations monitor both sets of UDP ports for RADIUS requests. Microsoft RADIUS servers default to 1812 and 1813, but Cisco devices default to the traditional 1645 and 1646 ports.
7. **A.** Privileged accounts are any accounts with greater-than-normal user access. Privileged accounts are typically root- or admin-level accounts and represent risk in that they are unlimited in their powers.
8. **A.** Typically OpenID is used for authentication, and OAuth is used for authorization.
9. **B.** Conditional access control models allow differing access control schemes based on specific conditions beyond just user account.
10. **D.** Knowledge-based authentication schemes allow the authentication of users who have not previously established their identity via a combined identification and authentication methodology.

CHAPTER 25

Public Key Infrastructure

In this chapter, you will

- Learn about the different components of a PKI system
- Learn about the concepts to employ a PKI system
- Understand how certificates are used as part of a security solution
- Implement public key infrastructure components

A *public key infrastructure (PKI)* provides all the components necessary for different types of users and entities to be able to communicate securely and in a predictable manner. A PKI is made up of hardware, applications, policies, services, programming interfaces, cryptographic algorithms, protocols, users, and utilities. These components work together to allow communication to manage asymmetric keys facilitating the use of public key cryptography for digital signatures, data encryption, and integrity. Although many different applications and protocols can provide the same type of functionality, constructing and implementing a PKI boils down to establishing a level of trust.

Certification Objective This chapter covers CompTIA Security+ exam objective 3.9: Given a scenario, implement public key infrastructure.

This objective is a good candidate for performance-based questions, which means you should expect questions in which you must apply your knowledge of the topic to a scenario. The best answer to a question will depend on specific details in the scenario preceding the question, not just the question. The questions may also involve tasks other than just picking the best answer from a list. Instead, you may be instructed to order items on a diagram, put options in rank order, match two columns of items, or perform a similar task.

Public Key Infrastructure (PKI)

A PKI is composed of several components, all working together to handle the distribution and management of keys in a public key cryptosystem. Keys are carried via a digital structure known as a *certificate*. Other components, such as certificate authorities and registration authorities, exist to manage certificates. Working together, these components enable seamless use of public key cryptography between systems.

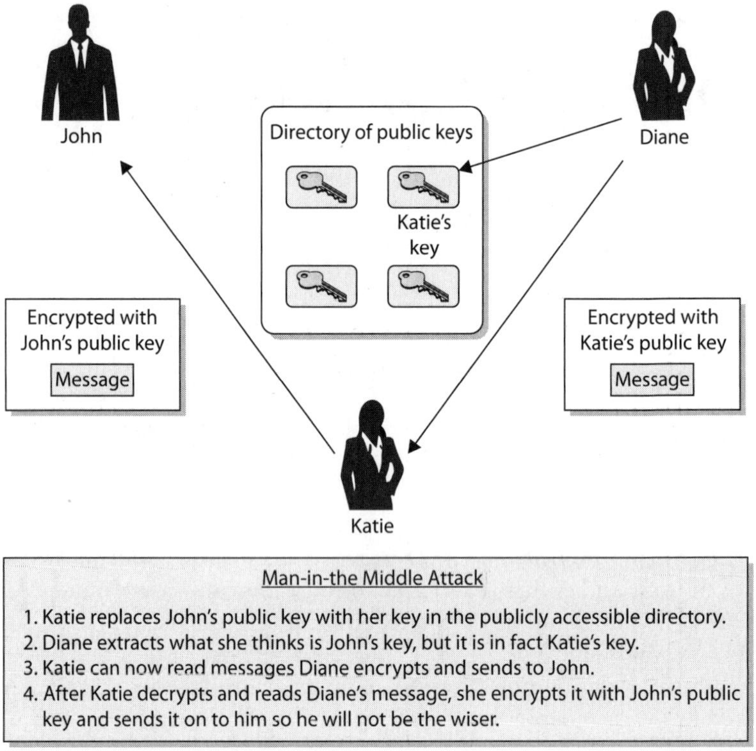
John
Diane
Directory of public keys
Katie's key
Encrypted with John's public key
Message
Encrypted with Katie's public key
Message
Katie
Man-in-the Middle Attack
1. Katie replaces John's public key with her key in the publicly accessible directory.
2. Diane extracts what she thinks is John's key, but it is in fact Katie's key.
3. Katie can now read messages Diane encrypts and sends to John.
4. After Katie decrypts and reads Diane's message, she encrypts it with John's public key and sends it on to him so he will not be the wiser.

Figure 25-1 Without PKIs, individuals could spoof others' identities, a man-in-the-middle attack.

If, for example, John and Diane want to communicate securely, John can generate his own public/private key pair and send his public key to Diane, or he can place his public key in a directory (folder) that is available to everyone. If Diane receives John's public key, either from him or from a public directory, how does she know it really came from John? Maybe another individual is masquerading as John and has replaced John's public key with her own, as shown in Figure 25-1. If this took place, Diane would believe that her messages could be read only by John and that the replies were actually from him. However, she would actually be communicating with Katie. What is needed is a way to verify an individual's identity, to ensure that a person's public key is bound to their identity and thus ensure that the previous scenario (and others) cannot take place.

In PKI environments, entities called registration authorities (RAs) and certificate authorities (CAs) provide services similar to those of the Department of Motor Vehicles (DMV). When John goes to register for a driver's license, he has to prove his identity to the DMV by providing his passport, birth certificate, or other identifying documentation. If the DMV is satisfied with the proof John provides (and John passes a driving test), the DMV will create a driver's license that can then be used by John to prove his identity. Whenever John needs to identify himself, he can show his driver's license. Although many people may not trust John to identify himself truthfully, they do trust the third party, the DMV.

In the PKI context, while some variations exist in specific products, the RA will require proof of identity from the individual requesting a certificate and will validate this information. The RA will then advise the CA to generate a certificate, which is analogous to a driver's license. The CA will digitally sign the certificate using its private key. The use of the private key assures the recipient that the certificate came from the CA. When Diane receives John's certificate and verifies that it was actually digitally signed by a CA that she trusts, she will believe that the certificate is actually John's—not because she trusts John, but because she trusts the entity that is vouching for his identity (the CA).

EXAM TIP A registration authority (RA) verifies digital certificate requests and forwards them to a certificate authority (CA). The CA is a trusted organization that validates and issues digital certificates.

This is commonly referred to as a *third-party trust model*. Public keys are components of digital certificates, so when Diane verifies the CA's digital signature, this verifies that the certificate is truly John's and that the public key the certificate contains is also John's. This is how John's identity is bound to his public key.

This process allows John to authenticate himself to Diane and others. Using the third-party certificate, John can communicate with her, using public key encryption, without prior communication or a preexisting relationship. Once Diane is convinced of the legitimacy of John's public key, she can use it to encrypt and decrypt messages between herself and John, as illustrated in Figure 25-2.

Numerous applications and protocols can generate public/private key pairs and provide functionality similar to what a PKI provides, but no trusted third party is available for both of the communicating parties. For each party to choose to communicate this

Figure 25-2 Public keys are components of digital certificates.

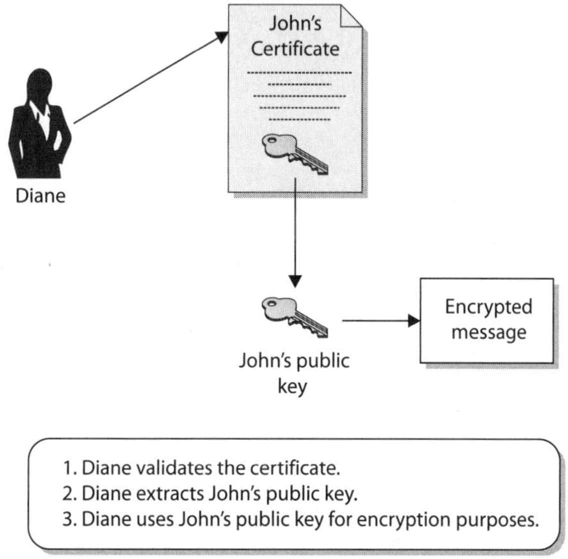
John's Certificate
Diane
John's public key
Encrypted message
1. Diane validates the certificate.
2. Diane extracts John's public key.
3. Diane uses John's public key for encryption purposes.

way without a third party vouching for the other's identity, the two must choose to trust each other and the communication channel they are using. In many situations, it is impractical and dangerous to arbitrarily trust an individual you do not know, and this is when the components of a PKI must fall into place—to provide the necessary level of trust you cannot provide, or choose not to provide, on your own.

What does the "infrastructure" in "public key infrastructure" really mean? An infrastructure provides a sustaining groundwork upon which other things can be built. So an infrastructure works at a low level to provide a predictable and uniform environment that allows other, higher-level technologies to work together through uniform access points. The environment that the infrastructure provides allows these higher-level applications to communicate with each other and gives them the underlying tools to carry out their tasks.

EXAM TIP Make sure you understand the role of PKI in managing certificates and trust associated with public keys.

Key Management

The whole purpose for PKI is to provide the structure and components necessary for an organization to manage cryptographic keys that need to be shared between entities. A digital key is just a digital number, simply data. Metadata elements about the keys—who made them, what they are used for, how long they are valid, and a host of other questions—need to be stored with the key. Hence, the invention of a certificate, which is a simple text file that contains vital information about a key. In addition to this metadata, other important elements surrounding key management include policies on key protection, storage, key escrow, and key recovery. Cryptographic keys are important and critical to the functioning cryptographic solutions in an enterprise. Some keys need to be shared to be effective; others need to be kept private. Key management is the set of activities that an organization must undertake to ensure that keys enable proper cryptography and do not cause security issues.

NOTE The security associated with the use of public key cryptography revolves around the security of the private key. Nonrepudiation depends on the principle that the private key is only accessible to the holder of the key. If another person has access to the private key, they can impersonate the proper key holder.

Certificate Authority (CA)

As previously described, the *certificate authority (CA)* is the trusted authority that certifies individuals' identities and creates electronic documents indicating that individuals are who they say they are. The electronic document is referred to as a *digital certificate,* and it establishes an association between the subject's identity and a public key. The private key that is paired with the public key in the certificate is stored separately.

The CA is more than just a piece of software, however; it is actually made up of the software, hardware, procedures, policies, and people involved in validating individuals' identities and generating the certificates. This means that if one of these components is compromised, it can negatively affect the CA overall and can threaten the integrity of the certificates it produces.

Every CA should have a certification practices statement (CPS) that outlines how identities are verified; the steps the CA follows to generate, maintain, and transmit certificates; and why the CA can be trusted to fulfill its responsibilities. It describes how keys are secured, what data is placed within a digital certificate, and how revocations will be handled. If a company is going to use and depend on a public CA, the company's security officers, administrators, and legal department should review the CA's entire CPS to ensure that it will properly meet the company's needs, and to make sure that the level of security claimed by the CA is high enough for their use and environment. A critical aspect of a PKI is the trust between the users and the CA, so the CPS should be reviewed and understood to ensure that this level of trust is warranted.

The certificate server is the actual service that issues certificates based on the data provided during the initial registration process. The server constructs and populates the digital certificate with the necessary information and combines the user's public key with the resulting certificate. The certificate is then digitally signed with the CA's private key.

Intermediate CA

Intermediate CAs function to transfer trust between different CAs. These CAs are also referred to as subordinate CAs because they are subordinate to the CA that they reference. The path of trust is walked up from the subordinate CA to the higher-level CA; in essence, the subordinate CA is using the higher-level CA as a reference.

Registration Authority (RA)

A *registration authority (RA)* is the PKI component that accepts a request for a digital certificate and performs the necessary steps of registering and authenticating the person requesting the certificate. The authentication requirements differ depending on the type of certificate being requested. Most CAs offer a series of classes of certificates with increasing trust by class.

Each higher class of certificate can carry out more powerful and critical tasks than the one below it. This is why the different classes have different requirements for proof of identity. If you want to receive a Class 1 certificate, you may only be asked to provide your name, e-mail address, and physical address. For a Class 2 certificate, you may need to provide the RA with more data, such as your driver's license, passport, and company information that can be verified. To obtain a Class 3 certificate, you will be asked to provide even more information and most likely will need to go to the RA's office for a face-to-face meeting. Each CA will outline the certification classes it provides and the identification requirements that must be met to acquire each type of certificate.

Certificate Revocation List (CRL)

The CA provides protection against bad certificates by maintaining a *certificate revocation list (CRL)*, a list of serial numbers of certificates that have been revoked. The CRL also contains a statement indicating why the individual certificates were revoked and a date when the revocation took place. The list usually contains all certificates that have been revoked within the lifetime of the CA. Certificates that have expired are not the same as those that have been revoked. If a certificate has expired, it means that its end validity date was reached.

The CA is the entity responsible for the status of the certificates it generates; it needs to be told of a revocation, and it must provide this information to others. The CA is responsible for maintaining the CRL and posting it in a publicly available directory.

EXAM TIP The certificate revocation list is an essential item to ensure a certificate is still valid. CAs post CRLs in publicly available directories to permit automated checking of certificates against the list before certificate use by a client. A user should never trust a certificate that has not been checked against the appropriate CRL.

What if Stacy wants to get revenge against Joe for something, and she attempts to revoke Joe's certificate herself? If she is successful, Joe's participation in the PKI can be negatively affected because others will not trust his public key. Although we might think Joe deserves this, we need to have some system in place to make sure people cannot arbitrarily have others' certificates revoked, whether for revenge or for malicious purposes.

When a revocation request is submitted, the individual submitting the request must be authenticated. Otherwise, this could permit a type of denial-of-service attack, in which someone has another person's certificate revoked. The authentication can involve an agreed-upon password that was created during the registration process, but authentication should not be based on the individual proving that he has the corresponding private key, because it may have been stolen, and the CA would be authenticating an imposter.

The CRL's integrity needs to be protected to ensure that attackers cannot modify data pertaining to a revoked certification from the list. If this were allowed to take place, anyone who stole a private key could just delete that key from the CRL and continue to use the private key fraudulently. The integrity of the list also needs to be protected to ensure that bogus data is not added to it. Otherwise, anyone could add another person's certificate to the list and effectively revoke that person's certificate. The only entity that should be able to modify any information on the CRL is the CA.

The mechanism used to protect the integrity of a CRL is a *digital signature*. The CA's revocation service creates a digital signature for the CRL. To validate a certificate, the user accesses the directory where the CRL is posted, downloads the list, and verifies the CA's digital signature to ensure that the proper authority signed the list and to ensure that the list was not modified in an unauthorized manner. The user then looks through the list to determine whether the serial number of the certificate that he is trying to validate is listed. If the serial number is on the list, the private key should no longer be trusted, and the public key should no longer be used.

One concern is how up to date the CRL is—how often is it updated and does it actually reflect *all* the certificates currently revoked? The actual frequency with which the list is updated depends on the CA and its CPS. It is important that the list is updated in a timely manner so that anyone using the list has the most current information. CRL files can be requested by individuals who need to verify and validate a newly received certificate, or the files can be periodically pushed down (sent) to all users participating within a specific PKI. This means the CRL can be pulled (downloaded) by individual users when needed or pushed down to all users within the PKI on a timed interval.

The actual CRL file can grow substantially, and transmitting this file and requiring PKI client software on each workstation to save and maintain it can use a lot of resources; therefore, the smaller the CRL the better. It is also possible to first push down the full CRL, and after that initial load, the following CRLs pushed down to the users are delta CRLs, meaning that they contain only the changes to the original or base CRL. This can greatly reduce the amount of bandwidth consumed when updating CRLs.

In implementations where the CRLs are not pushed down to individual systems, the users' PKI software needs to know where to look for the posted CRL that relates to the certificate it is trying to validate. The certificate might have an extension that points the validating user to the necessary CRL distribution point. The network administrator sets up the distribution points, and one or more points can exist for a particular PKI. The distribution point holds one or more lists containing the serial numbers of revoked certificates, and the user's PKI software scans the list(s) for the serial number of the certificate the user is attempting to validate. If the serial number is not present, the user is assured that it has not been revoked. This approach helps point users to the right resource and also reduces the amount of information that needs to be scanned when checking that a certificate has not been revoked.

One last option for checking distributed CRLs is an online service. When a client user needs to validate a certificate and ensure that it has not been revoked, he can communicate with an online service that will query the necessary CRLs available within the environment. This service can query the lists for the client instead of pushing down the full CRL to each and every system. So if Alice receives a certificate from Bob, she can contact an online service and send it the serial number listed in the certificate Bob sent. The online service would query the necessary CRLs and respond to Alice by indicating whether or not that serial number was listed as being revoked.

Certificate Attributes

A digital certificate binds an individual's identity to a public key, and it contains all the information a receiver needs to be assured of the identity of the public key owner. The certificates are created and formatted based on the X.509 standard, which outlines the necessary fields of a certificate and the possible values that can be inserted into the fields. The latest version of X.509 is v3, and the fields it contains are described in the Table 25-1.

Field Name	**Field Description**
Certificate Version	X.509 version used for this certificate: Version 1 = 0 Version 2 = 1 Version 3 = 2
Serial Number	A nonnegative integer assigned by the certificate issuer that must be unique to the certificate.
Signature Algorithm Parameters (optional)	The algorithm identifier for the algorithm used by the CA to sign the certificate. The optional Parameters field is used to provide the cryptographic algorithm parameters used in generating the signature.
Issuer	Identification for the entity that signed and issued the certificate. This must be a Distinguished Name within the hierarchy of CAs.
Validity Not valid before time Not valid after time	Specifies a period of time during which the certificate is valid, using a "not valid before" time and a "not valid after" time (expressed in UTC or in a generalized time).
Subject	The Distinguished Name for the certificate owner. This can contain the Common Name and other elements, such as Organization, Location, State, and Country: CN = *.google.com, O = Google LLC, L = Mountain View, S = California, C = US
Subject Public Key Info	An encryption algorithm identifier followed by a bit string for the public key.
Issuer Unique ID	Optional for versions 2 and 3. This is a unique bit-string identifier for the CA that issued the certificate.
Subject Unique ID	Optional for versions 2 and 3. This is a unique bit-string identifier for the subject of the certificate.
Extensions Extension ID Critical Extension Value	Optional for version 3. The Extensions area consists of a sequence of extension fields containing an extension identifier, a Boolean field indicating whether the extension is critical, and an octet string representing the value of the extension. Extensions can be defined in standards or defined and registered by organizations or communities.
Thumbprint Algorithm Algorithm Parameters (optional)	Identifies the algorithm used by the CA to sign this certificate. This field must match the algorithm identified in the Signature Algorithm field.
Thumbprint	The signature is the bit-string hash value obtained when the CA signed the certificate. The signature certifies the contents of the certificate, binding the public key to the subject.

Table 25-1 X.509 Certificate Fields

Figure 25-3 shows the actual values of the different certificate fields for a particular certificate. The version of this certificate is v3 (X.509 v3) and the serial number is also listed—this number is unique for each certificate that is created by a specific CA. The CA used the SHA-1 hashing algorithm to create the message digest value and then signed it using the CA's private key using the RSA algorithm.

Figure 25-3 Fields within a digital certificate

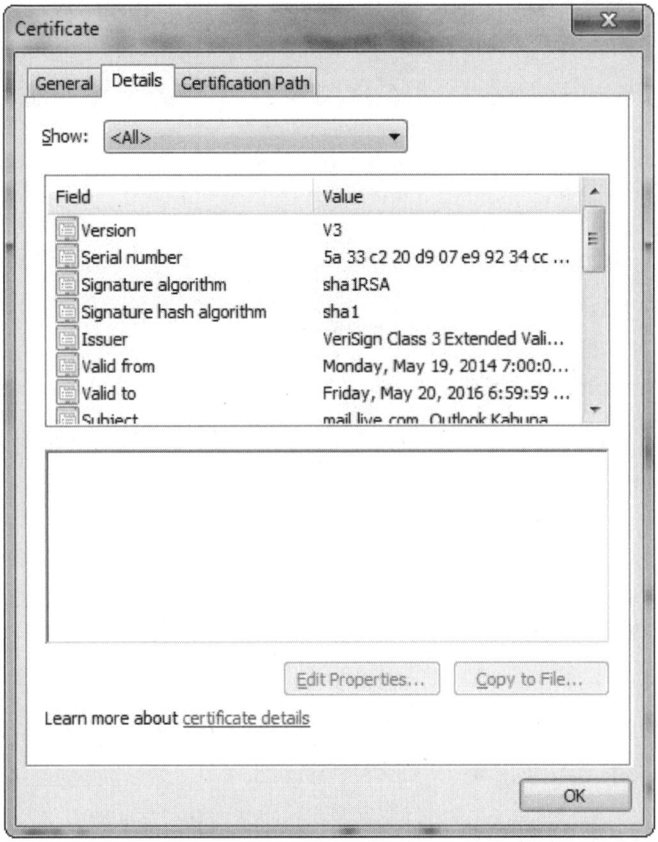

Online Certificate Status Protocol (OCSP)

One of the protocols used for online revocation services is the *Online Certificate Status Protocol (OCSP)*, a request and response protocol that obtains the serial number of the certificate that is being validated and reviews CRLs for the client. The protocol has a responder service that reports the status of the certificate back to the client, indicating whether it has been revoked, it is valid, or its status is unknown. This protocol and service save the client from having to find, download, and process the right lists.

EXAM TIP Certificate revocation checks are done either by examining the CRL or using OCSP to see if a certificate has been revoked.

Certificate Signing Request (CSR)

A *certificate signing request (CSR)* is the actual request to a CA containing a public key and the requisite information needed to generate a certificate. The CSR contains all the identifying information that is to be bound to the key by the certificate-generation process.

CN

The *Common Name (CN)* field is represented in the Subject field of the certificate and is the fully qualified domain name (FQDN) for which the certificate is valid. A common representation in the subject line of a certificate may contain the Common Name and other elements, such as Organization, Location, State, and Country: CN = *.google.com, O = Google LLC, L = Mountain View, S = California, C = US. The O is organization, L is location, S is state, and C is country.

Distinguished Name (DN) is a term that describes the identifying information in a certificate and is part of the certificate itself. A certificate contains DN information for both the owner or requestor of the certificate (called the Subject DN) and the CA that issues the certificate (called the Issuer DN).

Subject Alternative Name (SAN)

Subject Alternative Name (SAN) is a field (extension) in a certificate that has several uses. In certificates for machines, it can represent the FQDN of the machine. For users, it can be the user principal name (UPN) or, in the case of an SSL certificate, it can indicate multiple domains across which the certificate is valid. Figure 25-4 shows the multiple

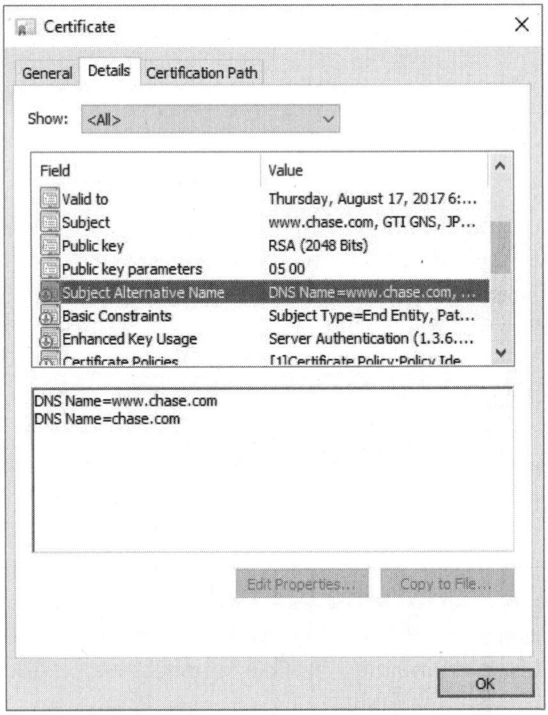

Figure 25-4 Subject Alternative Name

domains covered by the certificate in the box below the field details. SAN is an extension that is used to a significant degree, as it has become a standard method used in a variety of circumstances.

NOTE SAN certificates allow you to secure a primary domain and then add additional domains to the Subject Alternative Name field of the certificate. For example, you can secure all these domains with a single SAN certificate:

- www.example.com
- email.example.com
- intranet.example.com
- www.example.net

More information on Subject Alternative Names and certificates will be presented in a later section.

Expiration

A certificate itself has a lifetime that can be different from the key pair's lifetime. The certificate's lifetime is specified by the validity dates inserted into the digital certificate. These are beginning and ending dates indicating the time period during which the certificate is valid. The certificate cannot be used before the start date, and once the end date is met, the certificate is expired and a new certificate will need to be issued. Examining Figure 25-3 from earlier in the chapter, what can you say about the status of this certificate?

Types of Certificates

Four main types of certificates are used:

- End-entity certificates
- CA certificates
- Cross-certification certificates
- Policy certificates

End-entity certificates are issued by a CA to a specific subject, such as Joyce, the Accounting department, or a firewall, as illustrated in Figure 25-5. An end-entity certificate is the identity document provided by PKI implementations.

A *CA certificate* can be self-signed, in the case of a stand-alone or root CA, or it can be issued by a superior CA within a hierarchical model. In the model in Figure 25-5, the superior CA gives the authority and allows the subordinate CA to accept certificate requests and generate the individual certificates itself. This may be necessary when a company needs to have multiple internal CAs, and different departments within an organization need to have their own CAs servicing their specific end-entities (users, network

Figure 25-5 End-entity and CA certificates

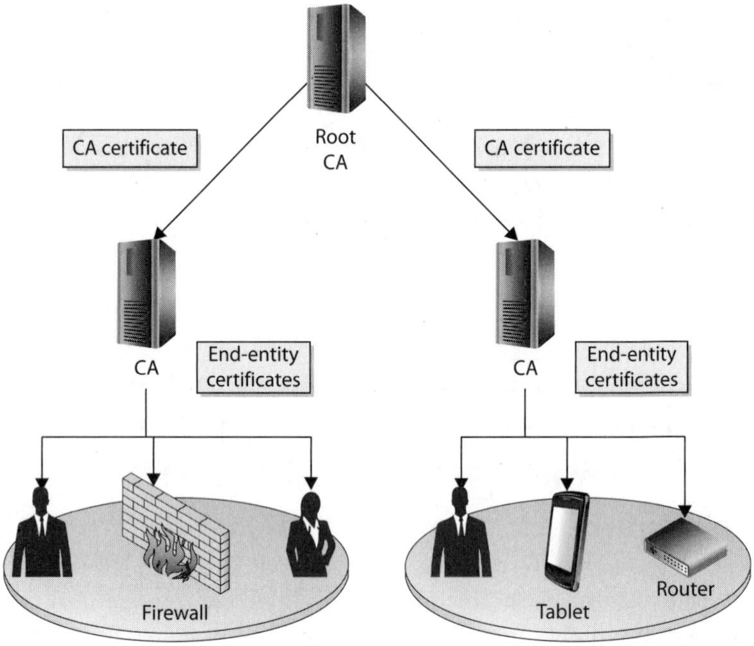

devices, and applications) in their sections. In these situations, a representative from each department requiring a CA registers with the more highly trusted CA and requests a CA certificate.

Cross-certification certificates, or *cross-certificates,* are used when independent CAs establish peer-to-peer trust relationships. Simply put, they are a mechanism through which one CA can issue a certificate allowing its users to trust another CA.

Within sophisticated CAs used for high-security applications, a mechanism is required to provide centrally controlled policy information to PKI clients. This is often done by placing the policy information in a *policy certificate.*

Wildcard Certificates

Certificates can be issued to an entity such as example.com. But what if there are multiple entities under example.com that need certificates? There are two choices: issue distinct certificates for each specific address or use *wildcard* certificates. Wildcard certificates work exactly as one would expect. A certificate issued for *.example.com would be valid for one.example.com as well as two.example.com.

EXAM TIP Wildcard certificates include an asterisk and period before the domain name. SSL certificates commonly extend encryption to subdomains through the use of wildcards.

Subject Alternative NameSAN

As mentioned earlier in the chapter, *Subject Alternative Name (SAN)* is a field (extension) in a certificate that has several uses. In certificates for machines, it can represent the fully qualified domain name (FQDN) of the machine; for users, it can be the user principal name (UPN). In the case of an SSL certificate, it can indicate multiple domains across which the certificate is valid. Figure 25-6 shows the two domains covered by the certificate in the box below the Field details. SAN is an extension that is used to a significant degree because it has become a standard method used in a variety of circumstances.

Code-Signing Certificates

Certificates can be designated for specific purposes, such as code signing. This is to enable the flexibility of managing certificates for specific functions and to reduce the risk in the event of compromise. *Code-signing certificates* are designated as such in the certificate itself, and the application that uses the certificate adheres to this policy restriction to ensure proper certificate usage.

Certificate
General
Details
Certification Path
Certificate Information
This certificate is intended for the following purpose(s):
• Proves your identity to a remote computer
• Ensures software came from software publisher
• Protects software from alteration after publication
• Allows data on disk to be encrypted
• Protects e-mail messages
• Allows secure communication on the Internet
Issued to: GlobalSign
Issued by: GlobalSign
Valid from 12/15/2006 to 12/15/2021
Issuer Statement
OK

Figure 25-6 Code Signing Certificate

Self-Signed Certificates

Certificates are signed by a higher-level CA, providing a root of trust. As with all chains, there is a final node of trust: the root node. Not all certificates have to have the same root node. A company can create its own certificate chain for use inside the company, and thus it creates its own root node. This company-created "root certificate" is an example of a CA certificate, mentioned earlier, and must be *self-signed,* as there is no other "higher" node of trust. What prevents one from signing their own certificates? The trust chain would begin and end with the certificate, and the user would be presented with the dilemma of whether or not to trust the certificate because, in the end, all a certificate does is detail a chain of trust to some entity that an end user trusts. Self-signing is shown for the root certificate in Figure 25-7 (the upper-left certificate).

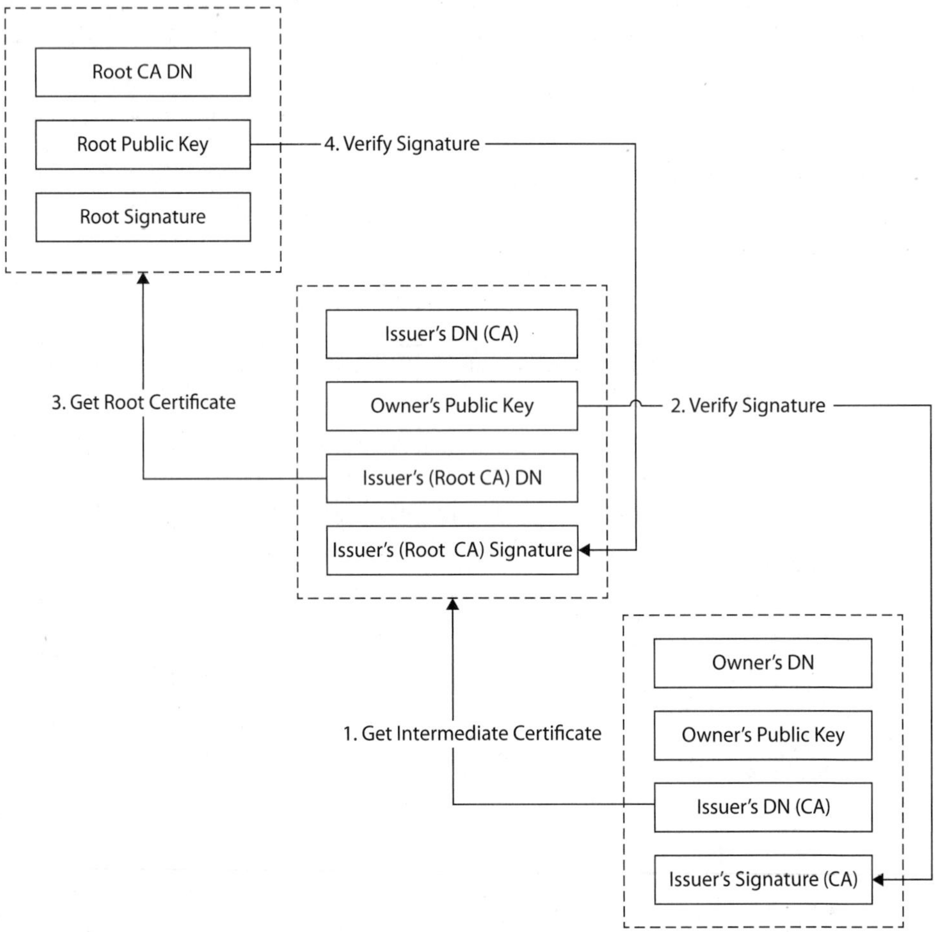

Figure 25-7 Certificate chaining

Machine/Computer

Certificates bind identities to keys and provide a means of authentication, which at times is needed for computers. Active Directory Domain Services (AD DS) can keep track of machines in a system via machines identifying themselves using *machine certificates,* also known as *computer certificates*. When a user logs in, the system can use either the machine certificate, identifying the machine, or the user certificate, identifying the user—whichever is appropriate for the desired operation. This is an example of an end-entity certificate.

E-mail

Digital certificates can be used with e-mail systems for items such as digital signatures associated with e-mails. Just as other specialized functions such as code signing have their own certificates, it is common for a separate *e-mail certificate* to be used for identity associated with e-mail. This is an example of an end-entity certificate.

User

User certificates are just that—certificates that identify a user. They are an example of an end-entity certificate.

NOTE User certificates are employed by users for encrypted file systems (EFS), e-mail, and client authentications, whereas computer certificates help computers to authenticate to the network.

Root

A *root certificate* is a certificate that forms the initial basis of trust in a trust chain. All certificates are signed by the CA that issues them, and CAs can be chained together in a trust structure. Following the chain, one climbs the tree of trust until they find a self-signed certificate, indicating it is a root certificate. What determines whether or not a system trusts a root certificate is whether or not the root certificate is in the system's store of trusted certificates. Different vendors, such as Microsoft and Apple, have trusted root certificate programs that determine by corporate policy which CAs they will label as trusted. Root certificates, because they form anchors of trust for other certificates, are examples of CA certificates, as explained earlier.

Domain Validation

Domain validation is a low-trust means of validation based on an applicant demonstrating control over a DNS domain. Domain validation is typically used for TLS and has the advantage that it can be automated via checks against a DNS record. A domain validation–based certificate, which is typically free, offers very little in assurance that the identity has not been spoofed because the applicant doesn't need to directly interact with the issuer. Domain validation scales well and can be automated with little to no real interaction between an applicant and the CA, but in return it offers little assurance. Domain validation is indicated differently in different browsers, primarily to separate it from extended validation certificates, described next.

Extended Validation

Extended validation (EV) certificates are used for HTTPS websites and software to provide a high level of assurance as to the originator's identity. EV certificates use the same methods of encryption to protect certificate integrity as do domain- and organization-validated certificates. The difference in assurance comes from the processes used by a CA to validate an entity's legal identity before issuance. Because of the additional information used during the validation, EV certificates display the legal identity and other legal information as part of the certificate. EV certificates support multiple domains, but do not support wildcards.

To assist users in identifying EV certificates and the enhanced trust, several additional visual clues are provided to users when EVs are employed. When implemented in a browser, the legal entity name is displayed, in addition to the URL and a lock symbol, and in most instances, the entire URL bar is green. All major browser vendors provide this support, and because the information is included in the certificate itself, this function is web server agnostic.

EXAM TIP Know the various types of certificates discussed in this section and what they are used for.

Certificate Formats

Digital certificates are defined in *RFC 5280: Internet X.509 Public Key Infrastructure Certificate and Certificate Revocation List (CRL) Profile.* This RFC describes the X.509 v3 digital certificate format in detail. There are numerous ways to encode the information in a certificate before instantiation as a file, and the different methods result in different file extensions. Common extensions include .der, .pem, .crt, .cer, .pfx, .p12, and .p7b. Although they all can contain certificate information, they are not all directly interchangeable. While in certain cases some data can be interchanged, the best practice is to identify how your certificate is encoded and then label it correctly.

KEY

A *KEY* file, denoted by the file extension .key, can be used both for public and private PKCS#8 keys. The keys may be encoded as binary DER or as ASCII PEM.

Distinguished Encoding Rules (DER)

Distinguished Encoding Rules (DER) is one of the Abstract Syntax Notation One (ASN.1) encoding rules that can be used to encode any data object into a binary file. With respect to certificates, the data associated with the certificate, a series of name-value pairs, needs to be converted to a consistent format for digital signing. DER offers a consistent mechanism for this task. A DER file (.der extension) contains binary data and can be used for a single certificate.

Privacy-Enhanced Mail (PEM)

Privacy-Enhanced Mail (PEM) is the most common format used by certificate authorities when issuing certificates. PEM comes from RFC 1422 and is a Base64-encoded ASCII file that begins with "-----BEGIN CERTIFICATE-----", followed by the Base64 data, and ends with "-----END CERTIFICATE-----". A PEM file supports multiple digital certificates, including a certificate chain. A PEM file can contain multiple entries, one after another, and can include both public and private keys. Most platforms, however, such as web servers, expect the certificates and private keys to be in separate files.

The PEM format for certificate data is used in multiple file types, including .pem, .cer, .crt, and .key files.

EXAM TIP If you need to transmit multiple certificates, or a certificate chain, use PEM for encoding. PEM encoding can carry multiple certificates, whereas DER can only carry a single certificate.

Personal Information Exchange (PFX)

A PKCS#12 file is a portable file format with a .pfx extension. It is a binary format for storing the server certificate, intermediate certificates, and the private key in one file. *Personal Information Exchange (PFX)* files are typically used on Windows machines to import and export certificates and private keys.

CER

The .cer file extension is used to denote an alternative form, from Microsoft, of CRT files. The .cer/.crt extension is used for certificates and may be encoded as binary DER or as ASCII PEM. The .cer and .crt extensions are nearly synonymous. The .cer extension is most commonly associated with Microsoft Windows systems, whereas .crt is associated with UNIX systems.

NOTE The only time .crt and .cer can safely be interchanged is when the encoding type can be identical (for example, PEM-encoded CRT is the same as PEM-encoded CER).

EXAM TIP The file extension .cer is an SSL certificate file format used by web servers to help verify the identity and security of the site in question.

P12

P12 is an alternative file extension for a PKCS#12 file format, a binary format for storing the server certificate, intermediate certificates, and the private key in one encrypted file.

These files usually have an extensions such as .pfx or .p12. They are typically used on Windows machines to import and export certificates and private keys.

P7B

The PKCS#7 or *P7B* format is stored in Base64 ASCII format and has a file extension of .p7b or .p7c. A P7B file begins with "-----BEGIN PKCS7-----" and only contains certificates and chain certificates (intermediate CAs), not the private key. The most common platforms that support P7B files are Microsoft Windows and Java Tomcat.

Concepts

PKI systems are composed of the items discussed in the first section, as well as methods of using and employing those items to achieve the desired functionality. When you are employing a PKI-based solution, it is important to understand that the security of the solution is as dependent upon how the elements are employed as it is on how they are constructed. This section describes several important operational elements, such as pinning, stapling, and certificate chaining, and it examines the various trust models.

Online vs. Offline CA

Certification servers must be online to provide certification services, so why would anyone have an offline server? The primary reason is security. If a given certificate authority is used only for periodic functions—for example, signing of specific certificates that are rarely reissued or signed—then keeping the server offline except when needed provides a significant level of security to the signing process. Other CA requests, such as CRL and validation requests, can be moved to a validation authority approved by the CA.

Stapling

Stapling is the process of combining related items to reduce communication steps. An example is when someone requests a certificate, stapling sends both the certificate and OCSP responder information in the same request to avoid the additional fetches the client would have to perform during path validations.

EXAM TIP Certificate stapling is considered a more efficient way to handle certificate verification. It minimizes the burden on the CA.

Pinning

When a certificate is presented for a host, either identifying the host or providing a public key, this information can be saved in an act called *pinning,* which is the process of associating a host with a previously provided X.509 certificate or public key. This can be important for mobile applications that move between networks frequently and are much more likely to be associated with hostile networks where levels of trust are low and risks of malicious data are high. Pinning assists in security through the avoidance of the use of DNS and its inherent risks when on less-than-secure networks.

The process of reusing a certificate or public key is called *key continuity*. This provides protection from an attacker, assuming that the attacker was not in position to attack on the initial pinning. If an attacker is able to intercept and taint the initial contact, then the pinning will preserve the attack. You should pin any time you want to be relatively certain of the remote host's identity, relying on your home network security, and you are likely to be operating at a later time in a hostile environment. If you choose to pin, you have two options: pin the certificate or pin the public key.

EXAM TIP Certificate pinning is the process of associating a host with its expected public key or X.509 certificate.

Trust Model

A *trust model* is a construct of systems, personnel, applications, protocols, technologies, and policies that work together to provide a certain level of protection. All of these components can work together seamlessly within the same trust domain because they are known to the other components within the domain and are trusted to some degree. Different trust domains are usually managed by different groups of administrators, have different security policies, and restrict outsiders from privileged access.

Most trust domains (whether individual companies or departments) are not usually islands cut off from the world—they need to communicate with other, less-trusted domains. The trick is to figure out how much two different domains should trust each other as well as how to implement and configure an infrastructure that would allow these two domains to communicate in a way that will not allow security compromises or breaches. This can be more difficult than it sounds.

One example of trust considered earlier in the chapter is the driver's license issued by the DMV. Suppose, for example, that Bob is buying a lamp from Carol and he wants to pay by check. Since Carol does not know Bob, she does not know if she can trust him or have much faith in his check. But if Bob shows Carol his driver's license, she can compare the name to what appears on the check, and she can choose to accept it. The trust anchor (the agreed-upon trusted third party) in this scenario is the DMV, since both Carol and Bob trust it more than they trust each other. Since Bob had to provide documentation to prove his identity to the DMV, that organization trusted him enough to generate a license, and Carol trusts the DMV, so she decides to trust Bob's check.

Consider another example of a trust anchor. If Joe and Stacy need to communicate through e-mail and would like to use encryption and digital signatures, they will not trust each other's certificate alone. But when each receives the other's certificate and sees that they both have been digitally signed by an entity they both do trust—the CA—then they have a deeper level of trust in each other. The trust anchor here is the CA. This is easy enough, but when we need to establish trust anchors between different CAs and PKI environments, it gets a little more complicated.

When two companies need to communicate using their individual PKIs, or if two departments within the same company use different CAs, two separate trust domains are involved. The users and devices from these different trust domains will need to communicate with each other, and they will need to exchange certificates and public keys. This means that trust anchors need to be identified, and a communication channel must be constructed and maintained.

A trust relationship must be established between two issuing authorities (CAs). This happens when one or both of the CAs issue a certificate for the other CA's public key, as shown in Figure 25-8. This means that each CA registers for a certificate and public key from the other CA. Each CA validates the other CA's identification information and generates a certificate containing a public key for that CA to use. This establishes a trust path between the two entities that can then be used when users need to verify other users' certificates that fall within the different trust domains. The trust path can be unidirectional or bidirectional, so either the two CAs trust each other (bidirectional) or only one trusts the other (unidirectional).

As illustrated in Figure 25-8, all the users and devices in trust domain 1 trust their own certificate authority (CA 1), which is their trust anchor. All users and devices in trust domain 2 have their own trust anchor, CA 2. The two CAs have exchanged certificates and trust each other, but they do not have a common trust anchor between them.

The trust models describe and outline the trust relationships between the different CAs and different environments, which will indicate where the trust paths reside. The trust models and paths need to be thought out before implementation to restrict and control access properly and to ensure that as few trust paths as possible are used. Several different trust models can be used: the hierarchical, peer-to-peer, and hybrid models are discussed in the following sections.

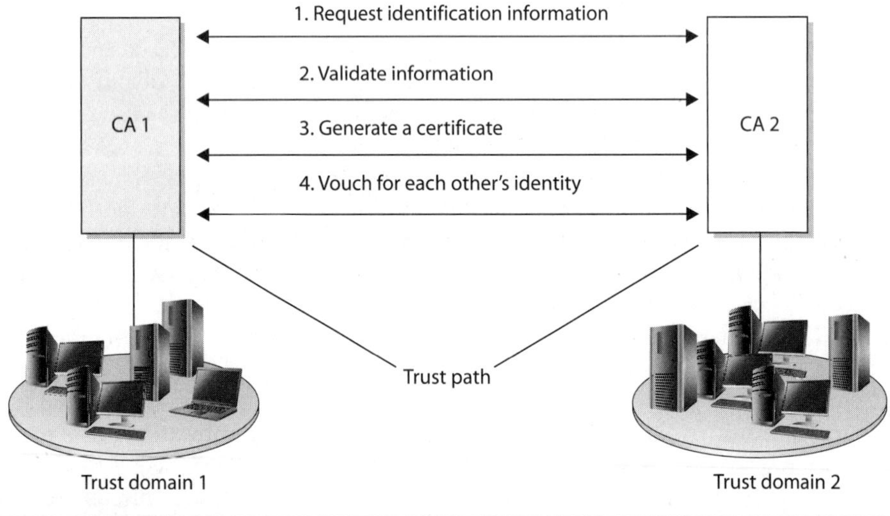

Figure 25-8 A trust relationship can be built between two trust domains to set up a communication channel.

Hierarchical Trust Model

The first type of trust model we'll examine is a basic hierarchical structure that contains a root CA, an intermediate CA, leaf CAs, and end-entities. The configuration is that of an inverted tree, as shown in Figure 25-9. The root CA is the ultimate trust anchor for all other entities in this infrastructure, and it generates certificates for the intermediate CAs, which in turn generate certificates for the leaf CAs, and the leaf CAs generate certificates for the end-entities.

As introduced earlier in the chapter, intermediate CAs function to transfer trust between different CAs. These CAs are referred to as subordinate CAs, as they are subordinate to the CA that they reference. The path of trust is walked up from the subordinate CA to the higher-level CA; in essence, the subordinate CA is using the higher-level CA as a reference.

As shown in Figure 25-9, no bidirectional trusts exist—they are all unidirectional trusts, as indicated by the one-way arrows. Since no other entity can certify and generate certificates for the root CA, it creates a self-signed certificate. This means that the certificate's issuer and subject fields hold the same information, both representing the root CA, and the root CA's public key will be used to verify this certificate when that time comes. This root CA certificate and public key are distributed to all entities within this trust model.

Walking the Certificate Path When a user in one trust domain needs to communicate with another user in another trust domain, one user will need to validate the other's certificate. This sounds simple enough, but what it really means is that each certificate for each CA, all the way up to a shared trusted anchor, also must be validated. If Debbie needs to validate Sam's certificate, as shown in Figure 25-9, she actually also needs to validate the Leaf D CA and Intermediate B CA certificates, as well as Sam's.

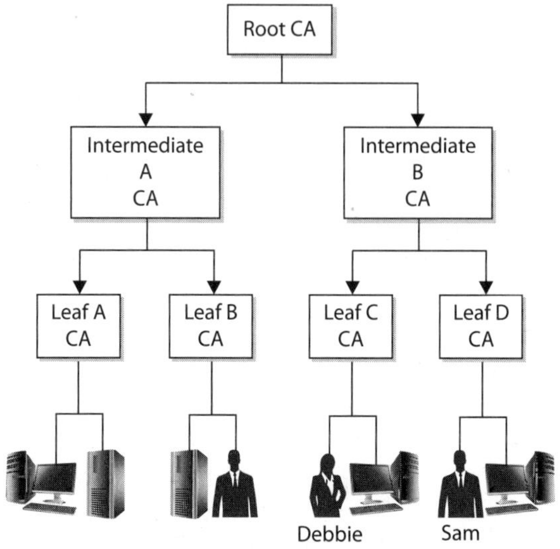

Figure 25-9 The hierarchical trust model outlines trust paths.

So in Figure 25-9, we have a user, Sam, who digitally signs a message and sends it and his certificate to Debbie. Debbie needs to validate this certificate before she can trust Sam's digital signature. Included in Sam's certificate is an issuer field, which indicates that the certificate was issued by Leaf D CA. Debbie has to obtain Leaf D CA's digital certificate and public key to validate Sam's certificate. Remember that Debbie validates the certificate by verifying its digital signature. The digital signature was created by the certificate issuer using its private key, so Debbie needs to verify the signature using the issuer's public key.

Debbie tracks down Leaf D CA's certificate and public key, but she now needs to verify this CA's certificate, so she looks at the issuer field, which indicates that Leaf D CA's certificate was issued by Intermediate B CA. Debbie now needs to get Intermediate B CA's certificate and public key.

Debbie's client software tracks this down and sees that the issuer for the Intermediate B CA is the root CA, for which she already has a certificate and public key. So Debbie's client software had to follow the *certificate path,* meaning it had to continue to track down and collect certificates until it came upon a self-signed certificate. A self-signed certificate indicates that it was signed by a root CA, and Debbie's software has been configured to trust this entity as her trust anchor, so she can stop there. Figure 25-10 illustrates the steps Debbie's software had to carry out just to be able to verify Sam's certificate.

This type of simplistic trust model works well within an enterprise that easily follows a hierarchical organizational chart, but many companies cannot use this type of trust model because different departments or offices require their own trust anchors. These demands can be derived from direct business needs or from inter-organizational politics. This hierarchical model might not be possible when two or more companies need to communicate with each other. Neither company will let the other's CA be the root CA, because each does not necessarily trust the other entity to that degree. In these situations, the CAs will need to work in a peer-to-peer relationship instead of in a hierarchical relationship.

Peer-to-Peer Trust Model

In a *peer-to-peer trust model,* one CA is not subordinate to another CA, and no established trusted anchor between the CAs is involved. The end-entities will look to their issuing CA as their trusted anchor, but the different CAs will not have a common anchor.

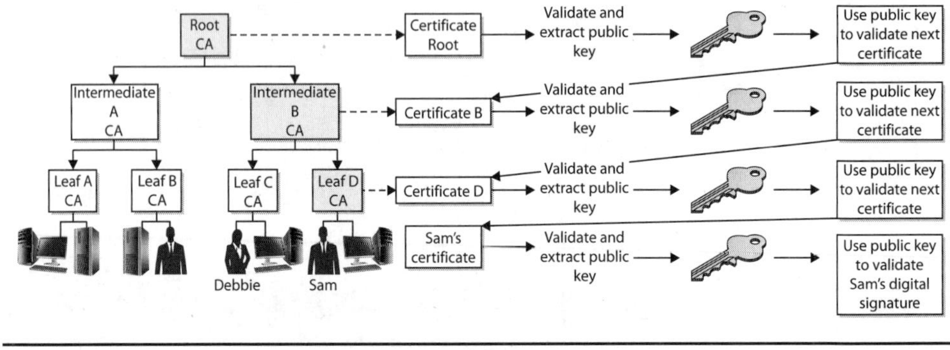

Figure 25-10 Verifying each certificate in a certificate path

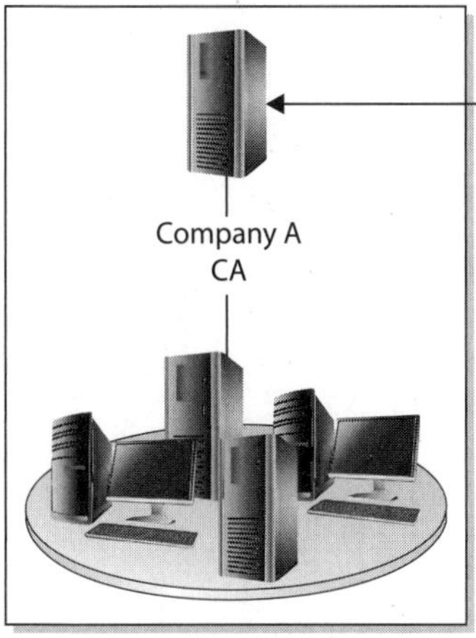

Figure 25-11 Cross-certification creates a peer-to-peer PKI model.

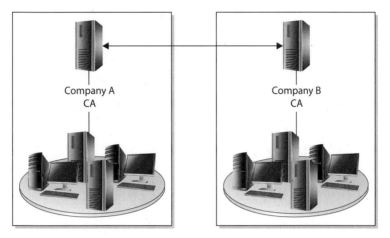

Figure 25-11 illustrates this type of trust model. The two different CAs will certify the public key for each other, which creates a bidirectional trust. This is referred to as *cross-certification* since the CAs are not receiving their certificates and public keys from a superior CA, but instead are creating them for each other.

One of the main drawbacks to this model is scalability. Each CA must certify every other CA that is participating, and a bidirectional trust path must be implemented, as shown in Figure 25-12. If one root CA were certifying all the intermediate CAs, scalability would not be as much of an issue. Figure 25-12 represents a fully connected mesh architecture, meaning that each CA is directly connected to and has a bidirectional trust relationship with every other CA. As you can see in this illustration, the complexity of this setup can become overwhelming.

Hybrid Trust Model

A company can be complex within itself, and when the need arises to communicate properly with outside partners, suppliers, and customers in an authorized and secured

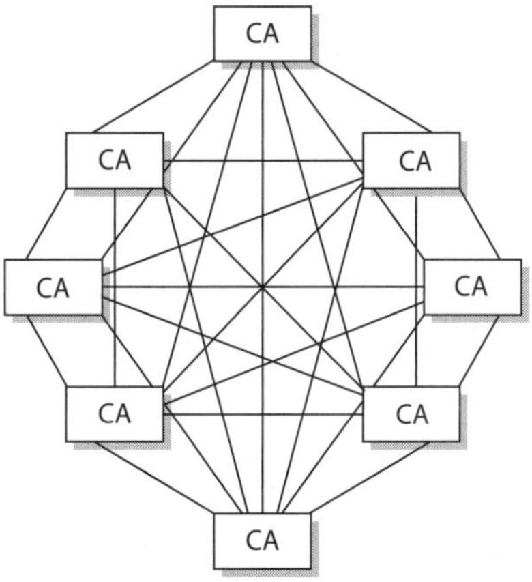

Figure 25-12 Scalability is a drawback in cross-certification models.

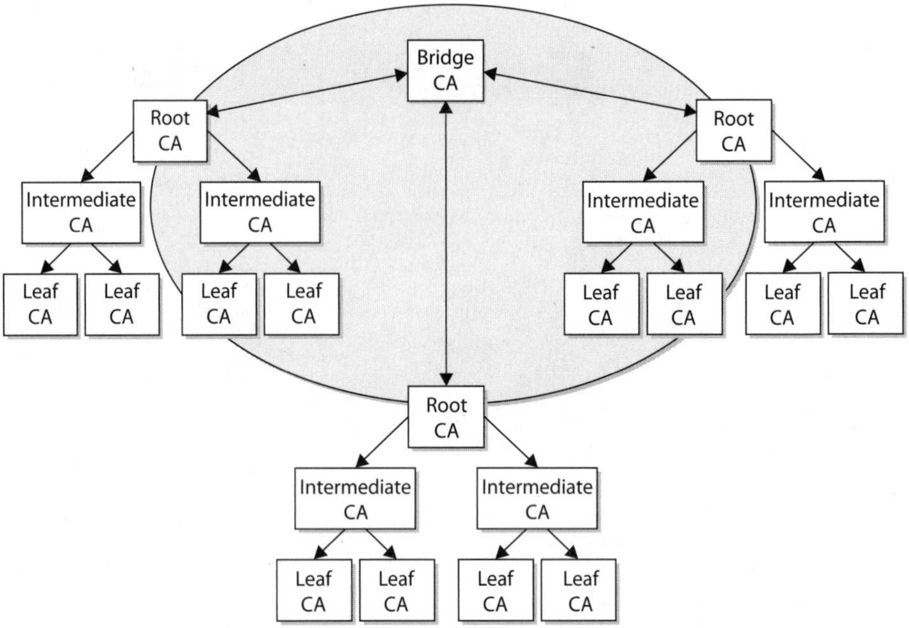

Figure 25-13 A bridge CA can control the cross-certification procedures.

manner, this complexity can make sticking to either the hierarchical or peer-to-peer trust model difficult, if not impossible. In many implementations, the different model types have to be combined to provide the necessary communication lines and levels of trust. In a *hybrid trust model,* the two companies have their own internal hierarchical models and are connected through a peer-to-peer model using cross-certification.

Another option in this hybrid configuration is to implement a *bridge CA.* Figure 25-13 illustrates the role that a bridge CA could play—it is responsible for issuing cross-certificates for all connected CAs and trust domains. The bridge CA is not considered a root or trust anchor, but merely the entity that generates and maintains the cross-certification for the connected environments.

EXAM TIP Three trust models exist: hierarchical, peer-to-peer, and hybrid. Hierarchical trust is like an upside-down tree. Peer-to-peer is a lateral series of references, and hybrid is a combination of hierarchical and peer-to-peer trust.

Key Escrow

The impressive growth of the use of encryption technology has led to new methods for handling keys. *Key escrow* is a system by which your private key is kept both by you and by a third party. Encryption is adept at hiding secrets, and with computer technology being affordable to everyone, criminals and other ill-willed people began using encryption to conceal communications and business dealings from law enforcement agencies. Because they could not break the encryption, government agencies began asking for key escrow. Key escrow in this circumstance is a system by which your private key is kept both by you and by the government. This allows people with a court order to retrieve your private key to gain access to anything encrypted with your public key. The data is essentially encrypted by your key and the government key, giving the government access to your plaintext data.

Key escrow is also used by corporate enterprises, as it provides a method of obtaining a key in the event that the key holder is not available. There are also key recovery mechanisms to do this, and the corporate policies will determine the appropriate manner in which to safeguard keys across the enterprise.

Key escrow that involves an outside agency can negatively impact the security provided by encryption, because the government requires a huge, complex infrastructure of systems to hold every escrowed key, and the security of those systems is less efficient than the security of you memorizing the key. However, there are two sides to the key escrow coin. Without a practical way to recover a key if or when it is lost or the key holder dies, for example, some important information will be lost forever. Such issues will affect the design and security of encryption technologies for the foreseeable future.

EXAM TIP Key escrow can solve many problems resulting from an inaccessible key, and the nature of cryptography makes the access of the data impossible without the key.

Certificate Chaining

Certificates are used to convey identity and public key pairs to users, but this raises the question: why trust the certificate? The answer lies in the *certificate chain,* a chain of trust from one certificate to another, based on signing by an issuer, until the chain ends with a certificate that the user trusts. This conveys the trust from the trusted certificate to the certificate that is being used. Examining Figure 25-7 from earlier in the chapter, we can look at the ordered list of certificates from the one presented to one that is trusted.

Certificates that sit between the presented certificate and the root certificate are called chain or intermediate certificates. The intermediate certificate is the signer/issuer of the presented certificate, indicating that it trusts the certificate. The root CA certificate is the signer/issuer of the intermediate certificate, indicating that it trusts the intermediate certificate. The chaining of certificates is a manner of passing trust down from a trusted root certificate. The chain terminates with a root CA certificate, which is always signed by the CA itself. The signatures of all certificates in the chain must be verified up to the root CA certificate.

Chapter Review

In this chapter, you became acquainted with the principles of public key infrastructure. The chapter opened with a description of the components of a PKI system, including certificate authority (CA), key management, intermediate CA, registration authority (RA), certificate revocation list (CRL), and certificate attributes. Next, the topics Online

Certificate Status Protocol (OCSP), certificate signing request (CSR), CN, SAN, and expiration were covered. The discussion continued with types of certificates, including wildcard, SAN, code-signing, self-signed, machine/computer, e-mail, user, root, domain validation, and extended validation certificates. The chapter continued with certificate formats, such as Distinguished Encoding Rules (DER), Privacy-Enhanced Mail (PEM), Personal Information Exchange (PFX), CER, P12, and P7B. The chapter concluded with a discussion of PKI concepts, including online versus offline CA, stapling, pinning, trust models, key escrow, and certificate chaining.

Questions

To help you prepare further for the CompTIA Security+ exam, and to test your level of preparedness, answer the following questions and then check your answers against the correct answers at the end of the chapter.

1. You are asked by the senior system administrator to refresh the SSL certificates on the web servers. The process is to generate a certificate signing request (CSR), send it to a third party to be signed, and then apply the return information to the CSR. What is this an example of?
   - **A.** Pinning
   - **B.** Borrowed authority
   - **C.** Third-party trust model
   - **D.** Stapling
2. A certificate authority consists of which of the following?
   - **A.** Hardware and software
   - **B.** Policies and procedures
   - **C.** People who manage certificates
   - **D.** All of the above
3. Your manager wants you to review the company's internal PKI system's CPS for applicability and verification and to ensure that it meets current needs. What are you most likely to focus on?
   - **A.** Revocations
   - **B.** Trust level provided to users
   - **C.** Key entropy
   - **D.** How the keys are stored
4. You are preparing an e-mail to send to a colleague at work, and because the message information is sensitive, you decide you should encrypt it. When you attempt to apply the certificate that you have for the colleague, the encryption fails. The certificate was listed as still valid for another year, and the certificate authority is still trusted and working. What happened to this user's key?

A. It was using the wrong algorithm.
B. You are querying the incorrect certificate authority.
C. It was revoked.
D. The third-party trust model failed.

5. Which of the following is a requirement for a CRL?
   A. It must have the e-mail addresses of all the certificate owners.
   B. It must contain a list of all expired certificates.
   C. It must contain information about all the subdomains covered by the CA.
   D. It must be posted to a public directory.

6. What does OCSP do?
   A. It reviews the CRL for the client and provides a status about the certificate being validated.
   B. It outlines the details of a certificate authority, including how identities are verified, the steps the CA follows to generate certificates, and why the CA can be trusted.
   C. It provides for a set of values to be attached to the certificate.
   D. It provides encryption for digital signatures.

7. The X.509 standard applies to which of the following?
   A. SSL providers
   B. Digital certificates
   C. Certificate revocation lists
   D. Public key infrastructure

8. You are browsing a website when your browser provides you with the following warning message: "There is a problem with this website's security certificate." When you examine the certificate, it indicates that the root CA is not trusted. What most likely happened to cause this error?
   A. The certificate was revoked.
   B. The certificate does not have enough bit length for the TLS protocol.
   C. The server's CSR was not signed by a trusted CA.
   D. The certificate has expired.

9. You are issued a certificate from a CA, delivered by e-mail, but the file does not have an extension. The e-mail notes that the root CA, the intermediate CAs, and your certificate are all attached in the file. What format is your certificate likely in?
   A. DER
   B. CER
   C. PEM
   D. PFX

10. Why is pinning more important on mobile devices?
    A. It uses elliptic curve cryptography.
    B. It uses less power for pinned certificate requests.
    C. It reduces network bandwidth usage by combining multiple CA requests into one.
    D. It allows caching of a known good certificate when roaming to low-trust networks.

Answers

1. **C.** This is an example of the third-party trust model. Although you are generating the encryption keys on the local server, you are getting these keys signed by a third-party authority so that you can present the third party as the trusted agent for users to trust your keys.
2. **D.** A certificate authority (CA) is the hardware and software that manage the actual certificate bits, the policies and procedures that determine when certificates are properly issued, and the people who make and monitor the policies for compliance.
3. **B.** You are most likely to focus on the level of trust provided by the CA to users of the system, as providing trust is the primary purpose of the CA.
4. **C.** The certificate has likely been revoked, or removed from that user's identity and no longer marked valid by the certificate authority.
5. **D.** Certificate revocation lists (CRLs) must be posted to a public directory so that all users of the system can query it.
6. **A.** Online Certificate Status Protocol (OCSP) is an online protocol that will look for a certificate's serial number on CRLs and provide a status message about the certificate to the client.
7. **B.** The X.509 standard is used to define the properties of digital certificates.
8. **C.** In this case, the server's certificate signing request (CSR) was not signed by a CA that is trusted by the endpoint computer, so no third-party trust can be established. This could be an indication of an attack, so the certificate should be manually verified before data is provided to the web server.
9. **C.** Because the certificate includes the entire certificate chain, it is most likely delivered to you in Privacy-Enhanced Mail (PEM) format.
10. **D.** Pinning is important on mobile devices because they are much more likely to be used on various networks, many of which have much lower trust than their home network.

PART IV

Operations and Incident Response

CHAPTER 26

Tools/Assess Organizational Security

In this chapter, you will

- Learn to use tools for network reconnaissance and discovery
- Learn to use tools for file manipulation
- Explore shell and script environments
- Learn to use tools for packet capture and replay
- Learn to use tools for forensics
- Explore the world of tools for accomplishing security-related tasks

Competency in performing many security functions involves the use of tools. The number, scope, and details for the tools used in the security industry could fill an entire book, but a basic understanding of a core set of tools is important. This chapter attempts to deliver on this premise and the Security+ objective for tool usage.

Certification Objective This chapter covers CompTIA Security+ exam objective 4.1: Given a scenario, use the appropriate tool to assess organizational security.

EXAM TIP This chapter is filled with hands-on commands that need to be used to be learned. The path to learning these commands is in using them. This is not a read-and-remember chapter, but rather a do-and-learn one. Linux commands can be a bit troublesome for some, so practice is advised. We suggest practicing with the Linux commands described and visiting Linux man pages, which are online refence manuals, for examples of a vast array of Linux commands: https://www.kernel.org/doc/man-pages/.

Network Reconnaissance and Discovery

Networks are like most infrastructure—you never see or care about it until it isn't working. And when you do want to look, how do you do it? A wide range of tools can be used to permit you to see the inner workings of a network, and they are covered in the sections that follow.

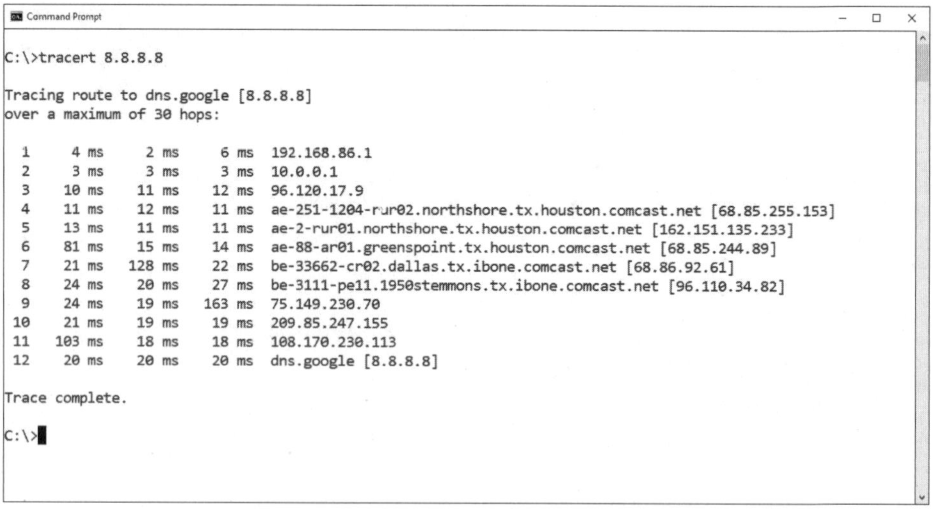

```
Command Prompt

C:\>tracert 8.8.8.8

Tracing route to dns.google [8.8.8.8]
over a maximum of 30 hops:

  1     4 ms     2 ms     6 ms  192.168.86.1
  2     3 ms     3 ms     3 ms  10.0.0.1
  3    10 ms    11 ms    12 ms  96.120.17.9
  4    11 ms    12 ms    11 ms  ae-251-1204-rur02.northshore.tx.houston.comcast.net [68.85.255.153]
  5    13 ms    11 ms    11 ms  ae-2-rur01.northshore.tx.houston.comcast.net [162.151.135.233]
  6    81 ms    15 ms    14 ms  ae-88-ar01.greenspoint.tx.houston.comcast.net [68.85.244.89]
  7    21 ms   128 ms    22 ms  be-33662-cr02.dallas.tx.ibone.comcast.net [68.86.92.61]
  8    24 ms    20 ms    27 ms  be-3111-pe11.1950stemmons.tx.ibone.comcast.net [96.110.34.82]
  9    24 ms    19 ms   163 ms  75.149.230.70
 10    21 ms    19 ms    19 ms  209.85.247.155
 11   103 ms    18 ms    18 ms  108.170.230.113
 12    20 ms    20 ms    20 ms  dns.google [8.8.8.8]

Trace complete.

C:\>
```

Figure 26-1 tracert example

tracert/traceroute

The *tracert* command is a Windows command for tracing the route that packets take over the network. The tracert command provides a list of the hosts, switches, and routers in the order in which a packet passes through them, providing a trace of the network route from source to target. As tracert uses Internet Control Message Protocol (ICMP), if ICMP is blocked, tracert will fail to provide information. On Linux and macOS systems, the command with similar functionality is traceroute. Figure 26-1 shows using the tracert command to trace the route from a Windows system on a private network to a Google DNS server.

EXAM TIP The tracert and traceroute commands display the route a packet takes to a destination, recording the number of hops along the way. These are excellent tools to use to see where a packet may get hung up during transmission.

nslookup/dig

The Domain Name System (DNS) is used to convert a human-readable domain name into an IP address. This is not a single system, but rather a hierarchy of DNS servers, from root servers on the backbone of the Internet, to copies at your Internet service provider (ISP), your home router, and your local machine, each in the form of a DNS cache. To examine a DNS query for a specific address, you can use the *nslookup* command. Figure 26-2 shows a series of DNS queries executed on a Windows machine. In the first request, the DNS server was with an ISP, while on the second request, the DNS

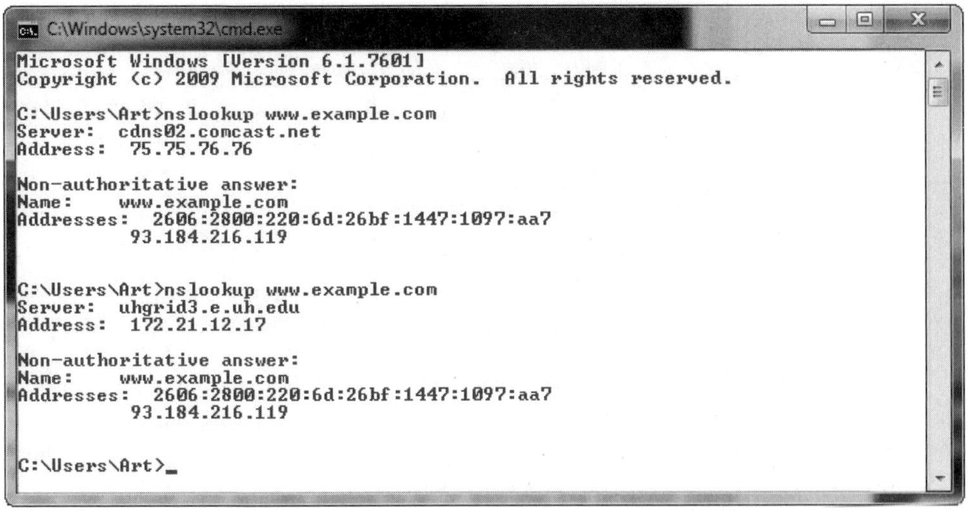

Figure 26-2 nslookup of a DNS query

server was from a virtual private network (VPN) connection. Between the two requests, the network connections were changed, resulting in different DNS lookups.

At times, nslookup will return a nonauthoritative answer, as shown in Figure 26-3. This typically means the result is from a cache as opposed to a server that has an authoritative (that is, known to be current) answer, such as from a DNS server.

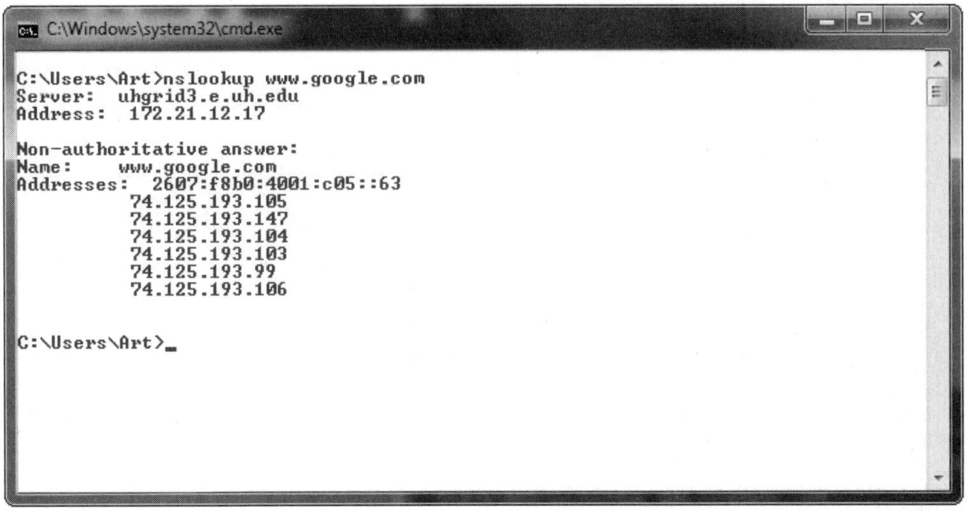

Figure 26-3 Cache response to a DNS query

While nslookup works on Windows systems, the command *dig*, which stands for Domain Information Groper, works on Linux systems. One difference is that dig is designed to return answers in a format that is easy to parse and include in scripts, which is a common trait of Linux command-line utilities.

ipconfig/ifconfig

Both *ipconfig* (for Windows) and *ifconfig* (for Linux) are command-line tools to manipulate the network interfaces on a system. They have the ability to list the interfaces and connection parameters, alter parameters, and release/renew connections. If you are having network connection issues, this is one of the first tools you should use, to verify the network setup of the operating system and its interfaces.

The ip command in Linux is used to show and manipulate routing, devices, policy routing, and tunnels. The ipconfig command is an important command for troubleshooting because it displays current TCP/IP configurations on a local system. The command displays adapter information such as MAC address, current IP addresses (both IPv4 and IPv6), subnet mask, default gateway, as well as DNS servers and whether DHCP is enabled. Figure 26-4 shows some of the information available from ipconfig on a Windows machine. This is an important troubleshooting tool because when you can't connect to something, it is the first place to start exploring network connections, as it gives you all of your settings.

nmap

Nmap is a is free, open source port scanning tool developed by Gordon Lyon and has been the standard network mapping utility for Windows and Linux since 1999.

```
Command Prompt

Wireless LAN adapter Wireless Network Connection:

   Connection-specific DNS Suffix  . : lan
   Description . . . . . . . . . . . : Intel(R) Dual Band Wireless-AC 7260
   Physical Address. . . . . . . . . : 48-51-B7-B7-7B-77
   DHCP Enabled. . . . . . . . . . . : Yes
   Autoconfiguration Enabled . . . . : Yes
   Link-local IPv6 Address . . . . . : fe80::d452:6002:630c:aeae%4(Preferred)
   IPv4 Address. . . . . . . . . . . : 192.168.86.76(Preferred)
   Subnet Mask . . . . . . . . . . . : 255.255.255.0
   Lease Obtained. . . . . . . . . . : Monday, November 23, 2020 10:12:49 AM
   Lease Expires . . . . . . . . . . : Tuesday, November 24, 2020 10:12:50 AM
   Default Gateway . . . . . . . . . : 192.168.86.1
   DHCP Server . . . . . . . . . . . : 192.168.86.1
   DHCPv6 IAID . . . . . . . . . . . : 357061047
   DHCPv6 Client DUID. . . . . . . . : 00-01-00-01-26-6E-0E-28-48-51-B7-B7-7B-77
   DNS Servers . . . . . . . . . . . : 192.168.86.1
   NetBIOS over Tcpip. . . . . . . . : Enabled
```

Figure 26-4 ipconfig example

The *nmap* command is the command to launch and run the nmap utility. Nmap is used to discover what systems are on a network and the open ports and services on those systems. This tool has many other additional functions, such as OS fingerprinting, finding rogue devices, and discovering services and even application versions. It operates via the command line, so it's very scriptable. It also has a GUI interface called Zenmap. Nmap works on a wide range of operating systems, including Microsoft Windows, Linux, and macOS. This is one of the top ten tools used by system administrators on a regular basis. Nmap includes a scripting engine using the Lua programming language to write, save, and share scripts that can automate different types of scans. All sorts of tasks can be automated, including regular checks for well-known network infrastructure vulnerabilities.

ping/pathping

The *ping* command sends echo requests to a designated machine to determine if communication is possible. The syntax is **ping** [***options***] ***targetname/address***. The options include items such as name resolution, how many pings, data size, TTL counts, and more. Figure 26-5 shows a ping command on a Windows machine.

Pathping is a TCP/IP-based utility that provides additional data beyond that of a ping command. Pathping will first display your path results as if you were using tracert or traceroute. Pathping then calculates loss information, as shown in Figure 26-6.

EXAM TIP The ping command is used to test connectivity between systems.

hping

Hping is a TCP/IP packet creation tool that allows a user to craft raw IP, TCP, UDP, and ICMP packets from scratch. This tool provides a means of performing a wide range of network operations; anything that you can do with those protocols can be crafted into a packet. This includes port scanning, crafting ICMP packets, host discovery, and more. The current version is hping3, and it is available on most operating systems, including Windows and Linux.

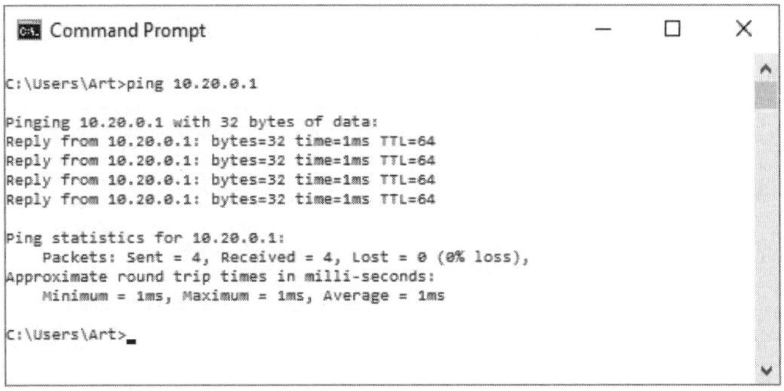

Command Prompt
C:\Users\Art>ping 10.20.0.1
Pinging 10.20.0.1 with 32 bytes of data:
Reply from 10.20.0.1: bytes=32 time=1ms TTL=64
Reply from 10.20.0.1: bytes=32 time=1ms TTL=64
Reply from 10.20.0.1: bytes=32 time=1ms TTL=64
Reply from 10.20.0.1: bytes=32 time=1ms TTL=64
Ping statistics for 10.20.0.1:
Packets: Sent = 4, Received = 4, Lost = 0 (0% loss),
Approximate round trip times in milli-seconds:
Minimum = 1ms, Maximum = 1ms, Average = 1ms
C:\Users\Art>_

Figure 26-5 ping command

```
C:\>pathping 96.120.17.9

Tracing route to 96.120.17.9 over a maximum of 30 hops

  0  Art-PC.lan [192.168.86.76]
  1  192.168.86.1
  2  10.0.0.1
  3  96.120.17.9

Computing statistics for 75 seconds...
            Source to Here   This Node/Link
Hop  RTT    Lost/Sent = Pct  Lost/Sent = Pct  Address
  0                                           Art-PC.lan [192.168.86.76]
                                0/ 100 =  0%   |
  1   14ms     0/ 100 =  0%     0/ 100 =  0%  192.168.86.1
                                0/ 100 =  0%   |
  2   19ms     0/ 100 =  0%     0/ 100 =  0%  10.0.0.1
                                1/ 100 =  1%   |
  3   26ms     1/ 100 =  1%     0/ 100 =  0%  96.120.17.9

Trace complete.

C:\>
```

Figure 26-6 Pathping example

Like all Linux commands, hping can be programmed in Bash scripts to achieve greater functionality. Outputs can also be piped to other commands. Hping also works with an embedded Tcl scripting functionality, which further extends its usefulness for system administrators. Between the range of options and the native scripting capability, hping offers a wide range of functions, including creating password-protected backdoors that are piped to other services. The power comes from the programmability, the options, and the creative work of system administrators.

netstat

The *netstat* command is used to monitor network connections to and from a system. The following are some examples of how you can use netstat:

- **netstat –a** Lists all active connections and listening ports
- **netstat –at** Lists all active TCP connections
- **netstat –an** Lists all active UDP connections

Many more options are available and useful. The netstat command is available on Windows and Linux, but availability of certain netstat command switches and other netstat command syntax may differ from operating system to operating system.

EXAM TIP The netstat command is useful for viewing all listening ports on a computer and determining which connections are active.

netcat

Netcat is the network utility designed for Linux environments. It has been ported to Windows but is not regularly used in Windows environments. The actual command to invoke netcat is **nc –options –address**.

The netcat utility is the tool of choice in Linux for reading from and writing to network connections using TCP or UDP. Like all Linux command-line utilities, it is designed for scripts and automation. Netcat has a wide range of functions. It acts as a connection to the network and can act as a transmitter or a receiver, and with redirection it can turn virtually any running process into a server. It can listen on a port and pipe the input it receives to the process identified.

EXAM TIP You should know what each of these tools looks like when being used. If presented with output from one of the tools, you should be able to identify the tool that was used and what action the tool is performing.

IP Scanners

IP scanners do just their name implies: they scan IP networks and can report on the status of IP addresses. There are a wide range of free and commercial scanning tools, and most come with significantly greater functionality than just reporting on address usage. If all you want are addresses, there are a variety of simple command-line network discovery tools that can provide those answers. For instance, if you only want to scan your local LAN, **arp – a** will do just that. If you want more functionality, you can use the nmap program covered earlier in the chapter. Another solution is Nessus, a commercial offering covered later in the chapter.

arp

The *arp* command is designed to interface with the operating system's Address Resolution Protocol (ARP) caches on a system. In moving packets between machines, a device sometimes needs to know where to send a packet using the MAC or layer 2 address. ARP handles this problem through four basic message types:

- **ARP request** "Who has this IP address?"
- **ARP reply** "I have that IP address; my MAC address is…"
- **Reverse ARP (RARP) request** "Who has this MAC address?"
- **RARP reply** "I have that MAC address; my IP address is…"

These messages are used in conjunction with a device's ARP table, where a form of short-term memory associated with these data elements resides. The commands are used as a simple form of lookup. When a machine sends an ARP request to the network, the reply is received and entered into all devices that hear the reply. This facilitates efficient address lookups, but also makes the system subject to attack.

The arp command allows a system administrator the ability to see and manipulate the ARP cache on a system. This way they can see if entries have been spoofed or if other problems, such as errors, occur.

route

The *route* command works in Linux and Windows systems to provide information on current routing parameters and to manipulate these parameters. In addition to listing the current routing table, it has the ability to modify the table. Figure 26-7 shows three examples of route on a Linux system. The first is a simple display of the kernel IP routing table. The second shows a similar result using the ip command. The last is the use of the ip command to get the details of the local table with destination addresses that are assigned to localhost.

curl

Curl is a tool designed to transfer data to or from a server, without user interaction. It support a long list of protocols (DICT, FILE, FTP, FTPS, Gopher, HTTP, HTTPS, IMAP, IMAPS, LDAP, LDAPS, MQTT, POP3, POP3S, RTMP, RTMPS, RTSP, SCP, SFTP, SMB, SMBS, SMTP, SMTPS, Telnet, and TFTP) and acts like a Swiss army knife for interacting with a server. Originally designed to interact with URLs, curl has expanded into a jack-of-all-trades supporting numerous protocols. It works on both Linux and Windows systems, although the command options are slightly different.

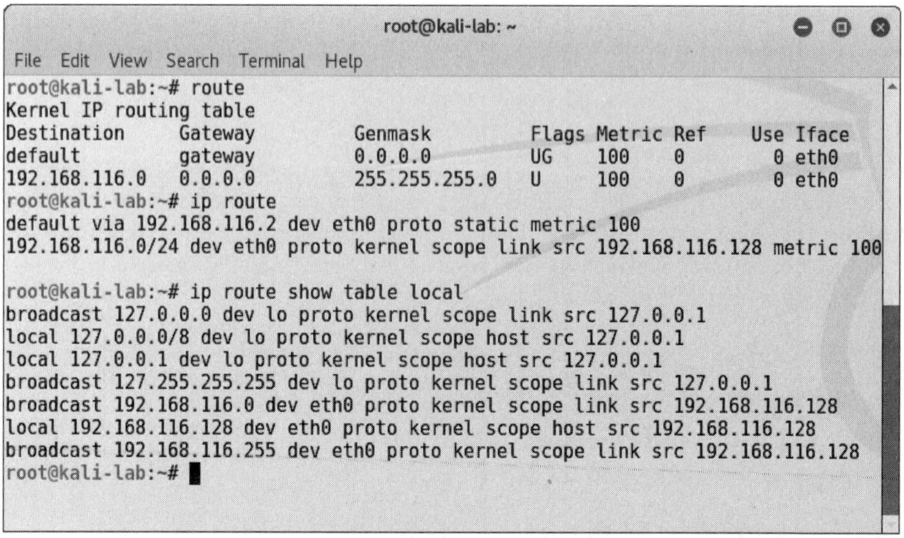
root@kali-lab: ~
File Edit View Search Terminal Help
root@kali-lab:~# route
Kernel IP routing table
Destination Gateway Genmask Flags Metric Ref Use Iface
default gateway 0.0.0.0 UG 100 0 0 eth0
192.168.116.0 0.0.0.0 255.255.255.0 U 100 0 0 eth0
root@kali-lab:~# ip route
default via 192.168.116.2 dev eth0 proto static metric 100
192.168.116.0/24 dev eth0 proto kernel scope link src 192.168.116.128 metric 100
root@kali-lab:~# ip route show table local
broadcast 127.0.0.0 dev lo proto kernel scope link src 127.0.0.1
local 127.0.0.0/8 dev lo proto kernel scope host src 127.0.0.1
local 127.0.0.1 dev lo proto kernel scope host src 127.0.0.1
broadcast 127.255.255.255 dev lo proto kernel scope link src 127.0.0.1
broadcast 192.168.116.0 dev eth0 proto kernel scope link src 192.168.116.128
local 192.168.116.128 dev eth0 proto kernel scope host src 192.168.116.128
broadcast 192.168.116.255 dev eth0 proto kernel scope link src 192.168.116.128
root@kali-lab:~#

Figure 26-7 The route and ip commands in Linux

Here's a simple example of using curl to simulate a GET request for a website URL:

```
curl https://www.example.com
```

theHarvester

theHarvester is a Python-based program designed to assist penetration testers in the gathering of information during the reconnaissance portion of a penetration test. This is a useful tool for exploring what is publicly available about your organization on the Web, and it can provide information on employees, e-mails, and subdomains using different public sources such as search engines, PGP key servers, and Shodan databases. Designed for Linux and included as part of Kali and other penetration testing distributions, theHarvester is shown in Figure 26-8 searching for the first 500 e-mails from the domain kali.org using Google.

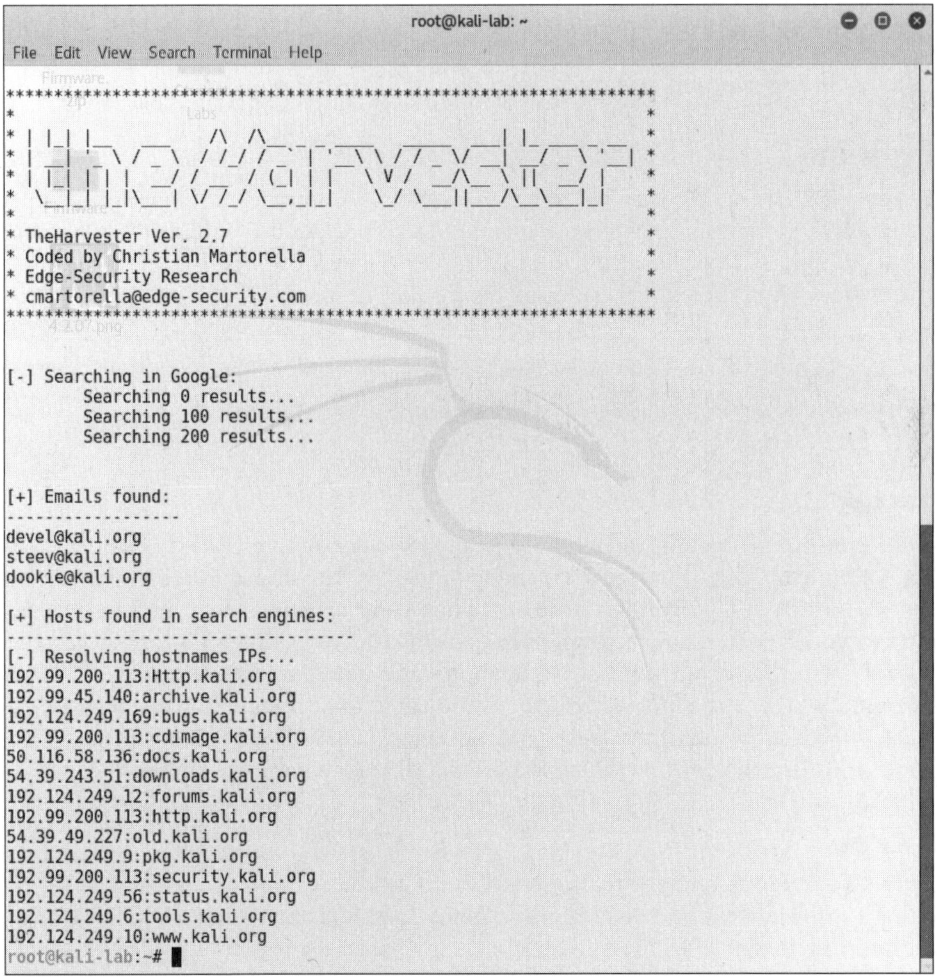

Figure 26-8 theHarvester

sn1per

Sn1per is a Linux-based tool used by penetration testers. Sn1per is an automated scanner designed to collect a large amount of information while scanning for vulnerabilities. It runs a series of automated scripts to enumerate servers, open ports, and vulnerabilities, and it's designed to integrate with the penetration testing tool Metasploit. Sn1per goes further than just scanning; it can also brute force open ports, brute force subdomains and DNS systems, scan web applications for common vulnerabilities, and run targeted nmap scripts against open ports as well as targeted Metasploit scans and exploit modules. This tool suite comes as a free community edition, with limited scope, as well as an unlimited professional version for corporations and penetration testers.

scanless

Scanless is a command-line utility to interface with websites that can perform port scans as part of a penetration test. When you use this tool, the source IP address for the scan is the website, not your testing machine. Written in Python, with a simple interface, scanless anonymizes your port scans.

dnsenum

Dnsenum is a Perl script designed to enumerate DNS information. Dnsenum will enumerate DNS entries, including subdomains, MX records, and IP addresses. It can interface with Whois, a public record that identifies domain owners, to gather additional information. Dnsenum works on Linux distros that support Perl.

EXAM TIP DNS enumeration can be used to collect information such as user names and IP addresses of targeted systems.

Nessus

Nessus is one of the leading vulnerability scanners in the marketplace. It comes in a free version, with limited IP address capability, and fully functional commercial versions. Nessus is designed to perform a wide range of testing on a system, including the use of user credentials, patch level testing, common misconfigurations, password attacks, and more. Designed as a full suite of vulnerability and configuration testing tools, Nessus is commonly used to audit systems for compliance to various security standards such as PCI DSS, SOX, and other compliance schemes. Nessus free version was the original source of the OpenVAS fork, which is a popular free vulnerability scanner.

Cuckoo

Cuckoo is a sandbox used for malware analysis. Cuckoo is designed to allow a means of testing a suspicious file and determining what it does. It is open source, free software that can run on Linux and Windows. Cuckoo is a common security tool used to investigate suspicious files, as it can provide reports on system calls, API calls, network analysis, and memory analysis.

EXAM TIP The Security+ exam will test your knowledge of the network reconnaissance and discovery tools previously detailed. Practice with each of them and, given a scenario, be able to identify and use the appropriate tool!

File Manipulation

In computer systems, most information can be represented as a file. Files are files, as are directories and even entire storage systems. The concept of a file is the basic interface to information. Because of this, file manipulation tools have the ability to manage a lot of tasks. As many operations are scripted, the ability to manipulate a file, returning specific elements or records, has great utility. This next section looks at a bunch of tools used to manipulate files in Linux systems.

head

Head is a utility designed to return the first lines of a file. A common option is the number of lines one wishes to return. For example, **head -5** returns the first five lines of a file.

tail

Tail is a utility designed to return the last lines of a file. A common option is the number of lines one wishes to return. For example, **tail -5** returns the last five lines of a file.

cat

Cat is a Linux command, short for concatenate, that can be used to create and manipulate files. It can display the contents of a file, handle multiple files, and can be used to input data from stdin, which is a stream of input, to a file if the file does not exist. Here is an example:

```
# cat textfile.txt
```

The **cat** command can be piped through **more** or **less** to limit scrolling of long files:

```
# cat textfile.txt | more
```

If you need line numbers in the output, you can add the **-n** option. The output can be piped through various other Linux commands, providing significant manipulation capability. For instance, you can combine four files and sort the output into a fifth file, like so:

```
# cat textfile1.txt textfile2.txt textfile3.txt textfile4.txt | sort >
textfile5.txt
```

grep

Grep is a Linux utility that can perform pattern-matching searches on file contents. The name grep comes from "Globally search for Regular Expression and Print the matching lines." Grep dates back to the beginning of the Unix OS and was written by Ken Thompson. Today, the uses of grep are many. It can count the number of matches, and it can find lines with matching expressions, either case sensitive or case insensitive. It can use anchors (matching based on beginning or ending of a word), wildcards, and negative searches (finding lines that do not contain a specified element), and it works with other tools through the redirection of inputs and outputs.

Grep has many options, including the use of regular expressions to perform matching. Here's a sampling of the more common options:

```
grep [options] pattern [files]
Options Description
-c : This prints only a count of the lines that match a pattern
-h : Display the matched lines, but do not display the filenames.
-i : Ignores, case for matching
-l : Displays list of a filenames only.
-n : Display the matched lines and their line numbers.
-v : This prints out all the lines that do not matches the pattern
-w : Match whole word
-o : Print only the matched parts of a matching line, with each such part on
a separate output line.
```

There are many other options, including the display of lines before and after matches. To get a full feel of the breadth of options, consult the man page for grep.

chmod

Chmod is the Linux command used to change access permissions of a file. The general form of the command is

```
chmod <options> <permissions> <filename>
```

Permissions can be entered either in symbols or octal numbers. Let's assume we want to set the following permissions: The user can read, write, and execute the file. Members of the group can read and execute it, and all others may only read it. In this case, we can use either of the following two commands, which are identical in function:

```
chmod u=rwx,g=rx,o=r <filename>
chmod 754 <filename>
```

The octal notation works as follows: 4 stands for "read," 2 stands for "write," 1 stands for "execute," and 0 stands for "no permission." Thus, for the user, 7 is the combination of permissions 4+2+1 (read, write, and execute). For the group, 5 is 4+0+1 (read, no write, and execute), and for all others, 4 is 4+0+0 (read, no write, and no execute).

logger

The Linux command *logger* is how you can add log file information to /var/log/syslog. The logger command works from the command line, from scripts, or from other files, thus providing a versatile means of making log entries. The syntax is simple:

```
logger <message to put in the log>
```

This command will put the text in the option into the syslog file.

EXAM TIP Know the purpose of the Linux file manipulation commands. Given a scenario, be prepared to implement the appropriate command.

Shell and Script Environments

One of the more powerful aspects of the Linux environment is the ability to create shell scripts. By combining a series of functions, and through the use of redirecting inputs and outputs, one can do significant data manipulation. Take a PCAP file for instance. Let's assume you need to extract specific data elements. You want only ping (echo) replies to a specific IP address. And for those records, you only want one byte in the data section. Using a series of commands in a shell script, you can create a dissector that takes the PCAP, reads it with tcpdump, extracts the fields, and then writes the desired elements to a file. You could do this with Python as well, and with some tools, you can get partway there. Bottom line: there is a lot you can do using the OS shell and scripts.

SSH

SSH (Secure Shell) is a cryptographically secured means of communicating and managing a network over an unsecured connection. It was originally designed as a replacement for the plaintext protocols of Telnet and other tools. When remotely accessing a system, it is important not to use a plaintext communication channel, as that would expose information such as passwords and other sensitive items to interception.

EXAM TIP SSH is a cryptographically secured means of communicating and managing a network. SSH uses port 22 and is the secure replacement for Telnet.

PowerShell

PowerShell is a Microsoft Windows-based task automation and configuration management framework, consisting of a command-line shell and scripting language. PowerShell is built on top of the .NET Common Language Runtime (CLR) and accepts and returns .NET objects. The commands used in PowerShell are called cmdlets, and they can be combined to process complex tasks. PowerShell can be run from a PowerShell Console prompt, or through the Windows PowerShell Integrated Scripting Environment (ISE), which is a host application for Windows PowerShell. The following example finds all executables within the Program Files folder that were last modified after October 1, 2005, and that are neither smaller than 1MB nor larger than 10MB:

```
Get-ChildItem -Path $env:ProgramFiles -Recurse -Include *.exe | Where-Object
-FilterScript {($_.LastWriteTime -gt '2005-10-01') -and ($_.Length -ge 1mb)
-and ($_.Length -le 10mb)} | out-host -paging
```

Because the Microsoft Windows object model is included, as well as numerous cmdlets designed to perform specific data access operations, PowerShell is an extremely powerful tool for managing Windows systems in an enterprise. With its latest release, PowerShell has been modified to run on multiple platforms, including Windows, macOS, and Linux.

EXAM TIP PowerShell is a powerful command-line scripting interface. PowerShell files use the .ps1 file extension.

Python

Python is a computer language commonly used for scripting and data analysis tasks facing system administrators and security personnel. Python is a full-fledged computer language. It supports objects, functional programming, and garbage collection, and most importantly has a very large range of libraries that can be used to bring functionality to a program. The downside is that it is interpreted, so speed is not a strong attribute. However, usability is high, and coupled with the library support, Python is a must-learn language for most security professionals.

EXAM TIP Python is a general-purpose computer programming language that uses the file extension .py.

OpenSSL

OpenSSL is a general-purpose cryptography library that offers a wide range of cryptographic functions on Windows and Linux systems. Designed to be a full-featured toolkit for the Transport Layer Security (TLS) and Secure Sockets Layer (SSL) protocols, it provides so much more for real-world daily challenges. OpenSSL can perform the following tasks in either scripts or programs, offering access to cryptographic functions without having to develop the code:

- Work with RSA and ECDSA keys
- Create certificate signing requests (CSRs)
- Verify CSRs

- Create certificates
- Generate self-signed certificates
- Convert between encoding formats (PEM, DER) and container formats (PKCS12, PKCS7)
- Check certificate revocation status
- And more

One can view OpenSSL as a Swiss army knife for all things involving cryptography functions.

Packet Capture and Replay

Computers communicate and exchange data via network connections by way of packets. Software tools that enable the capturing, editing, and replaying of the packet streams can be very useful for a security professional. Whether you're testing a system or diagnosing a problem, having the ability to observe exactly what is flowing between machines and being able to edit the flows is of great utility. The tools in this section provide this capability. They can operate either on live network traffic or recorded traffic in the form of packet capture (PCAP) files.

Tcpreplay

Tcpreplay is the name for both a tool and a suite of tools. As a suite, tcpreplay is a group of free, open source utilities for editing and replaying previously captured network traffic. As a tool, it specifically replays a PCAP file on a network. Originally designed as an incident response tool, tcpreplay has utility in a wide range of circumstances where network packets are used. It can be used to test all manner of security systems through the use of crafted PCAP files to trip certain controls. It is also used to test online services such as web servers. If you have a need to send network packets to another machine, tcpreplay suite has your answer.

Tcpdump

The *tcpdump* utility is designed to analyze network packets either from a network connection or a recorded file. You also can use tcpdump to create files of packet captures, called PCAP files, and perform filtering between input and output, making it a valuable tool to lessen data loads on other tools. For example, if you have a complete packet capture file that has hundreds of millions of records, but you are only interested in one server's connections, you can make a copy of the PCAP file containing only the packets associated with the server of interest. This file will be smaller and easier to analyze with other tools.

Wireshark

Wireshark is the gold standard for graphical analysis of network protocols. With dissectors that allow the analysis of virtually any network protocol, this tool can allow you to examine individual packets, monitor conversations, carve out files, and more. When it comes to examining packets, Wireshark is the tool. When it comes to using this functionality in a scripting environment, TShark provides the same processing in a scriptable form, producing a wide range of outputs, depending on the options set. Wireshark has the ability to capture live traffic, or it can use recorded packets from other sources.

EXAM TIP When you're examining packets, the differentiator is what do you need to do. Wireshark allows easy exploration. Tcpdump captures packets into PCAP files, and tcpreplay has a suite of editing tools.

Forensics

Digital forensics is the use of specific methods to determine who did what on a system at a specific time, or some variant of this question. Computers have a wide range of artifacts that can be analyzed to make these determinations. There are tools to collect these artifacts, and tools used to analyze the data collected. In this section, we examine some of the primary tools used in these efforts. Digital forensic processes and procedures are covered in detail in Chapter 30, "Digital Forensics." This is just an examination of some of the tools used.

dd

Data dump *(dd)* is a Linux command-line utility used to convert and copy files. On Linux systems, virtually everything is represented in storage as a file, and dd can read and/or write from/to these files, provided that function is implemented in the respective drivers. As a result, dd can be used for tasks such as backing up the boot sector of a hard drive, obtaining a fixed amount of random data, or copying (backing up) entire disks. The dd program can also perform conversions on the data as it is copied, including byte order swapping and conversion to and from the ASCII and EBCDIC text encodings. dd has the ability to copy everything, back up/restore a partition, and create/restore an image of an entire disk. Some common examples follow.

Here's how to back up an entire hard disk:

```
# dd if = /dev/sda of = /dev/sdb
```

Here, **if** represents input file and **of** represents output file. Therefore, the exact copy of /dev/sda will be available in /dev/sdb. If there are any errors, the preceding command will fail. If you give the parameter **conv=noerror**, it will continue to copy if there are read errors. Note that input file and output file should be checked very carefully because mistakes can overwrite data, causing you to lose all your data.

Here's how to create an image of a hard disk:

```
# dd if = /dev/hda of = ~/hdadisk.img
```

When doing a forensics data capture, rather than taking a backup of the hard disk, you should create an image file of the hard disk and save it on another storage device. There are many advantages to backing up your data to a disk image, one being the ease of use. Image files contain all the information on the associated source, including unused and previously used space.

memdump

Linux has a utility program called memory dumper, or *memdump*. This program dumps system memory to the standard output stream, skipping over any holes in memory maps. By default, the program dumps the contents of physical memory (/dev/mem). The output from memdump is in the form of a raw dump. Because running memdump uses memory, it is important to send the output to a location that is off the host machine being copied, using a tool such as netcat.

WinHex

WinHex is a hexadecimal file editor. This tool is very useful in forensically investigating files, and it provides a whole host of forensic functions such as the ability to read almost any file, display contents of the file, convert between character sets and encoding, perform hash verification functions, and compare files. As a native file reader/hex editor, it can examine specific application files without invoking the application and changing the data. WinHex is a commercial program that is part of the X-Ways forensic suite, which is a comprehensive set of digital forensic tools.

FTK Imager

FTK Imager is the company AccessData's answer to dd. FTK Imager is a commercial program, free for use, and is designed to capture an image of a hard drive (or other device) in a forensic fashion. Forensic duplications are bit-by-bit copies, supported by hashes to demonstrate that the copy and the original are exact duplicates in all ways. As with all forensically sound collection tools, FTK Imager retains the file system metadata (and the file path) and creates a log of the files copied. This process does not change file access attributes. FTK Imager is part of the larger, and commercial, FTK suite of forensic tools.

Autopsy

Autopsy is the open source answer for digital forensic tool suites. This suite, developed by Brian Carrier, has evolved over the past couple of decades into a community-supported open source project that can perform virtually all digital forensic functions. It runs on Windows and offers a comprehensive set of tools that can enable network-based collaboration and automated, intuitive workflows. It has tools to support hard drives, removable devices, and smartphones. It supports MD5 hash creation and lookup, deleted file carving, EXIF data extraction from JPEG images, indexed keyword searches, extension mismatch detections, e-mail message extractions, and artifact extractions from web browsers.

It has case management tools to support the functions of case analysis and reporting, including managing timelines.

EXAM TIP Be able to identify the various digital forensics tools discussed and know the purpose of each. For example, know that dd is a Linux command-line utility used to convert and copy files, whereas FTK Imager is a commercial program designed to capture an image of a hard drive (or other device) in a forensic fashion.

Exploitation Frameworks

Exploitation frameworks are toolsets designed to assist hackers in the tasks associated with exploiting vulnerabilities in a system. These frameworks are important because the exploitation path typically involves multiple steps, all done in precise order on a system to gain meaningful effect. The most commonly used framework is Metasploit, a set of "tools" designed to assist a penetration tester in carrying out the steps needed to exploit a vulnerability on a system. These frameworks can be used by security personnel as well, specifically to test the exploitability of a system based on existing vulnerabilities and employed security controls.

Password Crackers

Password crackers are used by hackers to find weak passwords. Why would a system administrator use one? Same reason. Running your system's password lists through a password cracker provides two things: an early warning of a crackable password, and peace of mind that your passwords are safe when you can't crack any in a reasonable period of time.

Password crackers work using dictionary lists and brute force. On the dictionary lists, they make passwords by combining words with each other, with numbers and special symbols, and test those against the system. They also can perform brute force attacks. Password crackers can work online against a live system, but then they can be subject to timeouts after a limited number of false entries. However, if they can steal the password file, they can operate at maximum speed until a match is found. On a modern Core i9 machine with a GPU, ten-character passwords will fall in roughly a week of work. With the use of multiple GPUs through a cloud vendor, this can fall to hours.

Data Sanitization

Data sanitization tools are tools used to destroy, purge, or otherwise identify for destruction specific types of data on systems. Before a system can be retired and disposed of, you need to sanitize the data needs. There are several approaches, the first being the whole disk approach. You can use a data sanitization tool to erase or wipe the entire storage of the system, making the data no longer recoverable. One method of doing this is to use self-encrypting disks, and the destruction of the key leaves the disk unrecoverable. A second, more targeted approach is to identify the sensitive data and deal with it specifically. Tools such as Identity Finder excel at this aspect of data sanitization. As with all tools, it is not the tool that provides the true value but rather the processes and procedures that ensure the work is done, and done correctly when required.

Chapter Review

In this chapter, you became acquainted with the tools used in security. The chapter began with a section on network reconnaissance and discovery. In this section, the tools tracert/traceroute, nslookup/dig, ipconfig/ifconfig, nmap, ping/pathping, hping, netstat, netcat, IP scanners, arp, route, curl, theHarvester, sn1per, scanless, dnsenum, Nessus, and Cuckoo were covered.

The next section covered tools used in file manipulation. In this section, the tools covered were head, tail, cat, grep, chmod, and logger. The next section was on shell and script environments. Here, SSH, PowerShell, Python, and OpenSSL were covered. The next section covered packet capture and replay, and the tools tcpreplay, tcpdump, and Wireshark were covered.

Digital forensic tools were covered in the next major section. Here, dd, memdump, WinHex, FTK Imager, and Autopsy were presented. The chapter concluded with an examination of exploitation frameworks, password crackers, and data sanitization tools.

Questions

To help you prepare further for the CompTIA Security+ exam, and to test your level of preparedness, answer the following questions and then check your answers against the correct answers at the end of the chapter.

1. To secure communications during remote access of a system, one can use which of the following tools?
   A. OpenSSL
   B. SSH
   C. dd
   D. tcpdump
2. Which of the following is not a packet capture/analysis tool?
   A. Wireshark
   B. tcpreplay
   C. tcpdump
   D. dd
3. To capture an image of the memory in a running system, one can use which of the following?
   A. grep
   B. dumpmem
   C. memdump
   D. logger

4. Which tools are used in IP address investigations? (Choose all that apply.)
   A. tracert
   B. theHarvester
   C. dnsenum
   D. chmod
5. To search through a system to find files containing a phrase, what would the best tool be?
   A. curl
   B. logger
   C. chmod
   D. grep
6. What does chmod do?
   A. Sets permission on a file
   B. Initiates a change modification entry in a log file
   C. Cryptographically hashes a file
   D. Lists the files in a working directory
7. You need to analyze previously collected packet data on a network, including editing some of the data. Which is the best tool to use?
   A. tcpreplay
   B. tcpdump
   C. netstat
   D. Wireshark
8. Which of these tools is used in penetration testing? (Choose all that apply.)
   A. nmap
   B. Nessus
   C. scanless
   D. theHarvester
9. To automate system administration across an enterprise Windows network, including using Windows objects, the best choice would be which of the following?
   A. Bash scripting
   B. Python
   C. Wireshark
   D. PowerShell

10. You think a file is malware. What is the first tool you should invoke?
    A. Cuckoo
    B. WinHex
    C. OpenSSL
    D. Autopsy

Answers

1. **B.** SSH encrypts the communication channel across the path its packets take.
2. **D.** The dd utility captures files from file systems, not packets on a network.
3. **C.** Memdump is a program used to copy what is currently in memory.
4. **A** and **C.** Tracert gives the IP addresses of a communication channel, and dnsenum gets information from a DNS server.
5. **D.** Grep is the pattern-matching tool that can be used to match patterns and search for matches.
6. **A.** Chmod is used to set/manage file permissions in a Linux environment.
7. **A.** Tcpreplay is the best tool to use in this case because the question requested packet editing.
8. **A, B, C,** and **D.** All of these tools are used in penetration testing. Nmap finds systems, Nessus scans for vulnerabilities, scanless hides the IP of the machine scanning, and theHarvester collects information on potential targets.
9. **D.** PowerShell is the best tool to use in this case. The key is the inclusion of Windows objects.
10. **A.** Cuckoo is a sandbox program designed to analyze malicious software, separating the software from direct connection to the OS.

CHAPTER 27

Incident Response Policies, Processes, and Procedures

In this chapter, you will

- Define incident response policies and plans
- Explore incident response processes and exercises
- Compare and contrast various incident response frameworks, procedures, plans, and policies

Normal operations in an IT enterprise include preparing for when things go wrong. One aspect of this is when things are not operating correctly, for reasons unknown, and the incident response (IR) process is used to determine the what, why, and where of the problem. A bigger problem is a disaster, where disaster recovery and continuity of operations are the pressing issues. Each of these situations requires preparation and readiness for the enterprise to navigate all of the complexities of these types of operations. This chapter looks at the concepts and procedures behind these specialized operations.

Certification Objective This chapter covers CompTIA Security+ exam objective 4.2: Summarize the importance of policies, processes, and procedures for incident response.

Incident Response Plans

An *incident response plan* describes the steps an organization performs in response to any situation determined to be abnormal in the operation of a computer system or network. The causes of incidents are many—from the environment (storms), to user error, to unauthorized actions by unauthorized users, to name a few. Although the causes may be many, the results can be classified into classes. A low-impact incident may not result in any significant risk exposure, so no action other than repairing the broken system is needed. A moderate-risk incident will require greater scrutiny and response efforts, and a high-level risk exposure incident will require the greatest scrutiny and response efforts. To manage incidents when they occur, an IT team needs to create an incident response plan that includes a table of guidelines to assist in determining the level of response.

Two major elements play a role in determining the level of response. Information criticality is the primary determinant, and this comes from the data classification and the quantity of data involved. For example, the loss of one administrator password is less serious than the loss of all of them and thus requires a lower level of response. The second factor is how the incident potentially affects the organization's operations. A series of breaches, whether minor or not, indicates a pattern that can have public relations and regulatory issues.

The incident response plan will cover a wide range of items, which are discussed in the next several sections. Although an incident response plan may cover more items in a given enterprise, the Security+ objectives examine incident response process steps, exercises, frameworks, plans, and policies.

Incident Response Process

The *incident response process* is the set of actions security personnel perform in response to a wide range of triggering events. These actions are broad and varied, as they have to deal with numerous causes and consequences. Incident response activities at times are closely related to other IT activities involving IT operations. Incident response activities can be similar to disaster recovery and business continuity operations. Incident response activities are not performed in a vacuum, but rather are intimately connected to many operational procedures, and this connection is key to overall system efficiency. The six phases of the incident response process and their sequencing are shown in Figure 27-1.

Figure 27-1 Incident response process

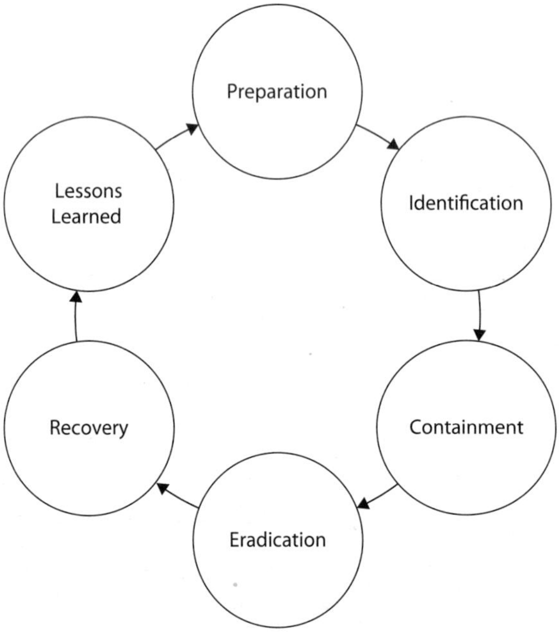

EXAM TIP Know the six phases of the incident response process and the order in which they are performed: preparation, identification, containment, eradication, recovery, and lessons learned.

Preparation

Preparation is the phase of incident response that occurs before a specific incident. Preparation includes all the tasks needed to be organized and ready to respond to an incident. Through the use of a structured framework coupled with properly prepared processes, incident response becomes a manageable task. Without proper preparation, this task can quickly become impossible or intractably expensive. Successful handling of an incident is a direct result of proper preparation. Items done in preparation include ensuring that the correct data events are being logged, the reporting of potential incidents is happening, and people are trained with respect to the IR process and their personal responsibilities.

Identification

Identification is the process where a team member suspects that a problem is bigger than an isolated incident and notifies the incident response team for further investigation. An incident is defined as a situation that departs from normal, routine operations. Whether an incident is important or not is the first point of decision as part of an incident response process. A single failed login is technically an incident, but if it is followed by a correct login, then it is not of any consequence. In fact, this could even be considered normal. But having 10,000 failed attempts on a system, or failures across a large number of accounts, is distinctly different and may be worthy of further investigation. The act of identification involves coming to a decision that the information related to the incident is worthy of further investigation by the IR team.

Identification can be done by many on the IT team, such as the help desk, admins, database personnel—in essence, anyone who finds something out of the ordinary that may be a real problem. Some training is required to prevent false alarms; a single failed file access, for instance, or a server that resets unexpectedly are just things that happen and are probably not a cause for IR alarm. But when single incidents become multiple incidents, then an investigation may be warranted and the conditions should be identified as a possible IR issue.

A key first step is to process the information and determine whether or not to invoke incident response processes. Incident information can come from a wide range of sources, including logs, employees, help desk calls, system monitoring, security devices, and more. The challenge is to detect that something other than simple routine errors is occurring. When evidence accumulates—or, in some cases, specific items such as security device logs indicate a potential incident—the next step is to escalate the situation to the IR team.

The IR team examines the information, gathering additional information if necessary, to determine the cause of the incident. If it meets the defined thresholds of the organization, an incident will be logged and fully investigated. Whatever the root cause, if it is truly more than a random error, the next step is containment.

Containment

Once the IR team has determined that an incident has in fact occurred and requires a response, their first step is to contain the incident and prevent its spread. For example, if the incident involves a virus or worm that is attacking database servers, then protecting uninfected servers is paramount. *Containment* is the set of actions taken to constrain the incident to a minimal number of machines. This preserves as much of production as possible and ultimately makes handling the incident easier. This can be complex because, in many cases, containing the problem requires fully understanding it as well as its root cause and the vulnerabilities involved.

Eradication

Once the IR team has contained a problem to a set footprint, the next step is to eradicate the problem. *Eradication* involves removing the problem, and in today's complex system environment, this may mean rebuilding a clean machine. A key part of operational eradication is the prevention of reinfection. Presumably, the system that existed before the problem occurred would be prone to a repeat infection, so this needs to be specifically guarded against. One of the strongest value propositions for virtual machines is the ability to rebuild quickly, making the eradication step relatively easy.

Recovery

After the issue has been eradicated, the recovery process begins. At this point, the investigation is complete and documented. *Recovery* is the process of returning the asset into the business function and restoring normal business operations. Eradication, the previous step, removed the problem, but in most cases the eradicated system will be isolated. The recovery process includes the steps necessary to return the system and applications to operational status. After recovery, the team moves to document the lessons learned from the incident.

Lessons Learned

A postmortem session should collect *lessons learned* and assign action items to correct weaknesses and to suggest ways to improve. To paraphrase a famous quote, those who fail to learn from history are destined to repeat it. The lessons learned phase serves two distinct purposes. The first is to document what went wrong and allowed the incident to occur in the first place. Failure to correct this means a sure repeat. The second is to examine the incident response process itself. Where did it go well, where did problems occur, and how can it be improved? Continuous improvement of the actual incident response process is an important task.

EXAM TIP The two main elements covered thus far overlap: incident response planning and the actual incident response process are both multistep items that can easily appear in questions on the exam. Be sure to pay attention to which element (either planning or process) is being discussed in the question as well as what aspect of that topic. In other words, first determine if the question concerns the planning process or the IR process and then pick the correct phase.

Exercises

One really doesn't know how well a plan is crafted until it is tested. *Exercises* come in many forms and functions, and doing a tabletop exercise where the planning and preparation steps are tested is an important final step in the planning process. Having a process and a team assembled is not enough unless the team has practiced the process on the systems of the enterprise.

EXAM TIP If you're given a scenario, the details of the scenario will point to the appropriate part of the planning process. Therefore, pay attention to the details for the best answer.

Tabletop

A *tabletop exercise* is one that is designed for the participants to walk through all the steps of a process, ensuring all elements are covered and that the plan does not forget a key dataset or person. This is typically a fairly high-level review, designed to uncover missing or poorly covered elements and gaps in communications, both between people and systems. This tabletop exercise is a critical final step because it validates the planning covered the needed elements. The steps in the exercise should be performed by the principal leaders of the business and IT functions to ensure that all steps are correct. Although this will take time from senior members, given the criticality of this business process, as it is being done for operations determined to be vital to the business, it hardly seems like overkill.

This exercise aspect is not a one-time thing; it should be repeated after major changes to systems that impact the continuity of the operations plan or other major changes such as personnel turnover. As such, major corporations regularly exercise these types of systems on a predetermined schedule, rotating through day and night shifts, primary and backup personnel, and various systems.

Walkthroughs

Walkthroughs examine the actual steps that take place associated with a process, procedure, or event. Walkthroughs are in essence a second set of eyes, where one party either explains or demonstrates the steps to perform a task while a second person observes. The observer's job is to examine the activity for compliance with applicable policies and directives. Is the task being accomplished correctly in terms of the process? Are the proper controls, processes, and procedures being followed? Walkthroughs can be done on elements such as computer code, where the person who wrote the code shows it to others on the team and walks them through the program, line by line. Explaining how it works and showing how it is coded allows for others to examine both syntax and process flow and provide valuable feedback on the code before it is implemented in a project. Having a supervisor observe the process for any function enables an independent determination as to whether their actions are in line with corporate security policies. Because the person doing the work relies upon training and repetitive practice, a periodic walkthrough provides evidence that proper procedures are actually being followed. Walkthroughs are commonly used by audit personnel to ensure proper processes are being followed.

Simulations

A *simulation* is an approximation of the operation of a process or system that is designed to represent the actual system operations over a period of time. The simulation can be used in place of systems or elements that are not practical to replicate during an exercise, such as a complex element like a chemical plant or a time-consuming activity like a backup operation. Simulations are used in exercises to provide context for the participants without the expense associated with the use of a real system.

EXAM TIP The different types of exercise elements, tabletop exercises, walkthroughs, and simulations can be used together as part of an exercise package.

Attack Frameworks

Attack frameworks provide a roadmap of the types of actions and sequence of actions used when attacking a system. Frameworks bring a sense of structure and order to the multidimensional problem associated with defending a variety of systems against multiple different types of attackers with various objectives. The objective of using a framework is to improve post-compromise detection of adversaries in enterprises by providing guidance on where an adversary's actions may be observable and where one can take specific actions. Organizations can use frameworks to identify holes in defenses and prioritize them based on the risk associated with actions an adversary is likely to take. Three different frameworks are described in the following sections: the MITRE ATT&CK framework, the Diamond Model of Intrusion Analysis, and the Cyber Kill Chain.

MITRE ATT&CK

The MITRE ATT&CK framework is a comprehensive matrix of attack elements, including the tactics and techniques used by attackers on a system. This framework can be used by threat hunters, red teamers, and defenders to better classify attacks and understand the sequential steps an adversary will be taking when attacking a system. This framework enables personnel to plan and defend, even during an attack, and further it acts as a useful tool in assessing an organization's risk.

The MITRE ATT&CK framework has a fairly simple design, with the top row of the matrix covering activities such as initial access, execution, persistence, privilege escalation, defense evasion, credential access, discovery, lateral movement, collection, command and control, exfiltration, and impact. Under each of these activities is a series of techniques and sub-techniques. Taken together, this matrix paints a comprehensive picture of paths through an organization's IT enterprise.

EXAM TIP The MITRE ATT&CK framework is a knowledgebase of various real-world observations and attack techniques. It is often used by organizations for threat modeling.

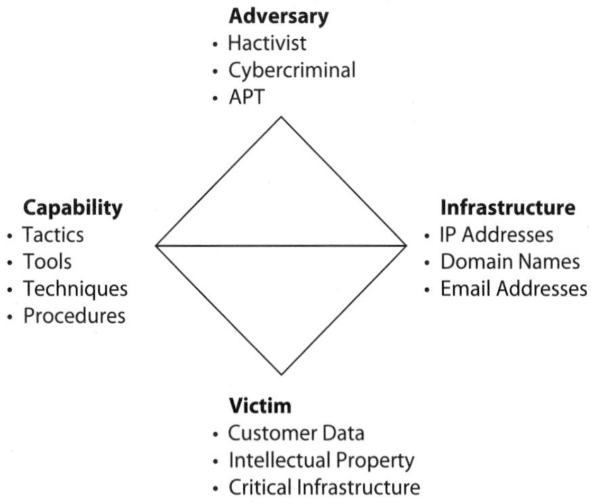

Figure 27-2 Diamond Model of Intrusion Analysis

The Diamond Model of Intrusion Analysis

The *Diamond Model of Intrusion Analysis* is a cognitive model used by the threat intelligence community to describe a specific event. It is based on the notion that an event has four characteristics, each comprising a corner of the diamond, as shown in Figure 27-2. Taken together, these elements describe an event. The four nodes that make up an event are adversary, infrastructure, capability, and victim. The adversary node is a description of the attacker and their data, including anything you know about them (e-mails, names, locations, handles, and so on). The infrastructure node is a description of what is being used in the attack, such as IP addresses, domain names, e-mail addresses, and so on. The victim node is the target, and the capability node is a description of what is being used (malware, stolen certificates/credentials, tools, exploits, and so on). As an example, a completed diamond could take the following form:

1. **Adversary** Whois is used to get an e-mail for the registrant—the possible attacker.
2. **Infrastructure** The C2 domain name resolves to an IP address.
3. **Capability** The response teams finds the C2 server domain name.
4. **Victim** A victim discovers malware and launches an incident response.

EXAM TIP The Diamond Model enables intrusion analysis by placing malicious activity at four points of the diamond: adversary, infrastructure, capability, and victim.

Cyber Kill Chain

The Cyber Kill Chain is a model developed by Lockheed Martin as a military form of engagement framework. This model has a series of distinct steps that an attacker uses during a cyberattack—from the early reconnaissance stages to the exfiltration of data. The use of the Cyber Kill Chain helps us understand and combat different forms of attack—from ransomware, to security breaches, and even advanced persistent threats (APTs).

The Cyber Kill Chain has slightly different steps depending on whose version you use, but the most common implementations include the following ones:

1. **Reconnaissance** Research and identify targets.
2. **Weaponization** Exploit vulnerabilities to enter.
3. **Delivery** Deliver the payload (evil content).
4. **Exploitation** Begin the payload attack on the system and gain entry.
5. **Installation** Implement backdoors, persistent access, bots, and so on.
6. **Command and Control** Communicate to outside servers for control purposes.
7. **Action on Objective** Obtain the objective of the attack (for example, steal intellectual property).

By understanding the progression of an attack, defenders can choose their point of defense, which enables them to react to an attack with a plan and a purpose.

EXAM TIP Developed by Lockheed Martin, the Cyber Kill Chain is a framework used to defend against the chain of events an attacker takes, from the beginning of an attack to the end of an attack.

Stakeholder Management

Stakeholders are the parties that have an interest in a process or the outcome of a process. Stakeholders can be internal or external to an organization. With respect to incident response scenarios, all levels of management and many different business functions can be involved internally, including corporate legal, communications, liaisons with regulators, customer support elements, and the operations personnel. Externally, there can be issues that involve vendors and customers, and there may be reporting requirements to regulators and other outside groups. With this wide range of involved parties, having a structure to manage communication with the various stakeholders is important to keep them properly informed and to separate the communication tasks from the operational tasks associated with responding to the incident. Having a *stakeholder management* process, including defined personnel roles and responsibilities, is essential for the management of the stakeholders and their relationships during incidents.

Communication Plan

Planning the desired reporting requirements, including escalation steps, is an important part of the operational plan for an incident. Who will talk for the incident response team and to whom, and what will they say? How does the information flow? Who needs to be involved? When does the issue escalate to higher levels of management? These are all questions best handled in the calm of a pre-incident planning meeting, where the procedures are crafted, rather than on the fly as an incident is occurring. A *communication plan* as part of the incident response effort that answers the preceding questions and defines responsibilities for communication is a key element to be developed during the preparation phase.

Reporting requirements can refer to industry, regulatory, and statutory requirements in addition to internal communications. Understanding the reporting requirements to external entities is part of the responsibility of the communications lead on the team. Having the correct information in the hands of the correct people at the correct time is an essential part of reporting, and a prime responsibility of the communications lead on the team.

Disaster Recovery Plan

No matter what event you are worried about—whether natural or person-made and whether targeted at your organization or more random—you can make preparations to lessen the impact on your organization and the length of time your organization will be out of operation. A *disaster recovery plan (DRP)* is critical for effective disaster recovery efforts. A DRP defines the data and resources necessary and the steps required to restore critical organizational processes.

Consider what your organization needs to perform its mission. This information provides the beginning of a DRP since it tells you what needs to be quickly restored. When considering resources, don't forget to include both the physical resources (such as computer hardware and software) and the personnel (the people who know how to run the systems that process your critical data).

To begin creating your DRP, first identify all critical functions for your organization and then answer the following questions for each of these critical functions:

- Who is responsible for the operation of this function?
- What do these individuals need to perform the function?
- When should this function be accomplished relative to other functions?
- Where will this function be performed?
- How is this function performed (what is the process)?
- Why is this function so important or critical to the organization?

By answering these questions, you can create an initial draft of your organization's DRP. The name often used to describe the document created by addressing these questions is *business impact assessment (BIA)*. Both the disaster recovery plan and the business impact assessment, of course, will need to be approved by management, and it is essential that they buy into the plan—otherwise your efforts will more than likely fail. The old adage "those who fail to plan, plan to fail" certainly applies in this situation.

A good DRP must include the processes and procedures needed in order for your organization to functioning properly and to ensure continued operation. What specific steps will be required to restore operations? These processes should be documented and, where possible and feasible, reviewed and exercised on a periodic basis. Having a plan with step-by-step procedures that nobody knows how to follow does nothing to ensure the continued operation of the organization. Exercising your DRP and processes before a disaster occurs provides you with the opportunity to discover flaws or weaknesses in the plan when there is still time to modify and correct them. It also provides an opportunity for key figures in the plan to practice what they will be expected to accomplish.

NOTE It is often informative to determine what category your various business functions fall into. You may find that certain functions currently being conducted are not essential to your operations and could be eliminated. In this way, preparing for a security event may actually help you streamline your operational processes.

Business Continuity Plan

As in most operational issues, planning is a foundational element to success. This is true in business continuity, and the *business continuity plan (BCP)* represents the planning and advanced policy decisions to ensure the business continuity objectives are achieved during a time of obvious turmoil. You might wonder what the difference is between a disaster recovery plan and a business continuity plan. After all, isn't the purpose of disaster recovery the continued operation of the organization or business during a period of disruption? Many times, these two terms are used synonymously, and for many organizations there may be no major difference between them. There are, however, real differences between a BCP and a DRP, one of which is the focus.

The focus of a BCP is the continued operation of the essential elements of the business or organization. Business continuity is not about operations as normal but rather about trimmed-down, essential operations only. In a BCP, you will see a more significant emphasis placed on the limited number of critical systems the organization needs to operate. The BCP will describe the functions that are most critical, based on a previously conducted business impact analysis, and will describe the order in which functions should be returned to operation. The BCP describes what is needed in order for the business to continue to operate in the short term, even if all requirements are not met and risk profiles are changed.

The focus of a DRP is on recovering and rebuilding the organization after a disaster has occurred. The recovery's goal is the complete operation of all elements of the business. The DRP is part of the larger picture, while the BCP is a tactical necessity until operations can be restored. A major focus of the DRP is the protection of human life, meaning evacuation plans and system shutdown procedures should be addressed. In fact, the safety of employees should be a theme throughout a DRP.

EXAM TIP Although the terms DRP and BCP may be used synonymously in small firms, in large firms, there is a difference in focus between the two plans. The focus of the BCP is on continued operation of a business, albeit at a reduced level or through different means during some period of time. The DRP is focused specifically on recovering from a disaster. In many cases, both of these functions happen at the same time, and hence they are frequently combined in small firms and in many discussions. The DRP is part of the larger BCP process.

Continuity of Operation Planning (COOP)

Ensuring continuity of operations is a business imperative, as it has been shown that businesses that cannot quickly recover from a disruption have a real chance of never recovering and going out of business. The overall goal of *continuity of operation planning (COOP)* is to determine which subset of normal operations needs to be continued during periods of disruption. Continuity of operations planning involves developing a comprehensive plan to enact during a situation where normal operations are interrupted. This includes identifying critical assets (including key personnel), critical systems, and interdependencies as well as ensuring their availability during a disruption.

Developing a continuity of operations plan is a joint effort between the business and the IT team. The business understands which functions are critical for continuity of operations, and which functions can be suspended. The IT team understands how this translates into equipment, data, and services and can establish the correct IT functions. Senior management will have to make the major decisions concerning balancing risk versus cost versus criticality when examining hot, warm, or cold site strategies.

EXAM TIP The COOP is focused on continuing business operation, whereas the BCP is focused on returning a business to functioning profitably, even if at a reduced level or capacity. Government agencies, where service is essential and costs can be dealt with later, focus on COOP, while many businesses have to focus on DRP and BCP.

Incident Response Team

The *cyber incident response team (CIRT)* is composed of the personnel who are designated to respond to an incident. The incident response plan should identify the membership and backup members, prior to an incident occurring. Once an incidence response begins, trying to find personnel to perform tasks only slows down the function, and in many cases would make it unmanageable. Whether a dedicated team or a group of situational volunteers, the planning aspect of incident response needs to address the topic of who is on the team and what their duties are.

Management needs to appoint the team members and ensure that they have time to be prepared for service. The team leader is typically a member of management who fully understands both the enterprise IT environment and IR process because their job is to lead the team with respect to the process. Subject matter experts (SMEs) on the various systems that are involved provide the actual working portion of the team, often in concert with operational IT personnel for each system. The team is responsible for all phases of the incident response process, which was covered previously in the chapter.

A critical step in the incident response planning process is to define the roles and responsibilities of the incident response team members. These roles and responsibilities may vary slightly based on the identified categories of incident, but defining them before an incident occurs empowers the team to perform the necessary tasks during the time-sensitive aspects of an incident. Permissions to cut connections, change servers, and start/stop services are common examples of actions that are best defined in advance to prevent time-consuming approvals during an actual incident.

There are several specific roles that are unique to all IR teams: the team leader, the team communicator, and an appropriate bevy of SMEs. The team leader manages the overall IR process, so they need to be a member of management so they can navigate the corporate chain of command. The team communicator is the spokesperson for the team to all other groups, inside and outside the company. IR team members are typically SMEs, and their time is valuable and should be spent on task. The team communicator shields these members from the time-consuming press interview portion as much as possible.

Retention Policies

Data retention is the storage of data records. One of the first steps in understanding data retention in an organization is the determination of what records require storage and for how long. Among the many reasons for retaining data, some of the most common are for the purposes of billing and accounting, contractual obligation, warranty history, and compliance with local, state, and national government regulations, such as IRS rules. Maintaining data stores for longer than is required is a source of risk, as is not storing the information long enough. Some information is subject to regulations requiring lengthy data retention, such as PHI for workers who have been exposed to specific hazards. Some data elements, such as the card verification code (CVC/CV2) element in a credit card transaction, are never stored as part of a transaction record. They are used for approval and destroyed to prevent loss after the transaction is concluded.

Failure to maintain the data in a secure state can also be a retention issue, as is not retaining it. In some cases, destruction of data, specifically data subject to legal hold in a legal matter, can result in adverse court findings and sanctions. Even if the data destruction is unintentional or inadvertent, it is still subject to sanction, as the firm had a responsibility to protect it. Legal hold can add significant complexity to data retention efforts, as it forces guaranteed separate storage of the data until the legal issues are resolved. Once data is on the legal hold track, its retention clock does not expire until the hold is lifted. This makes identifying, labeling, and maintaining the data subject to a legal hold an added dimension to normal storage considerations.

EXAM TIP Data retention policies differ by organization. However, some information such as PHI may be subject to regulations requiring specific data retention rules.

Chapter Review

In this chapter, you first became acquainted with incident response plans and processes. Under incident response processes, the model for preparation, identification, containment, eradication, recovery, and lessons learned was presented. The next major topic was exercises. In this portion of the discussion, the different types of exercises (tabletop, walkthroughs, and simulations) were presented.

The next major section looked at attack frameworks. The MITRE ATT&CK framework was presented, followed by the Diamond Model of Intrusion Analysis and the Cyber Kill Chain model. Stakeholder management was covered as well as plans for communication during an incident.

The chapter wrapped up with an examination of disaster recovery plans, business continuity plans, and continuity of operations plans. The composition of the incident response team was covered, and the retention policies associated with incident response data were presented.

Questions

To help you prepare further for the CompTIA Security+ exam, and to test your level of preparedness, answer the following questions and then check your answers against the correct answers at the end of the chapter.

1. Which phase of the incident response process occurs before an actual incident?
   - A. Preparation
   - B. Identification
   - C. Containment
   - D. Prevention
2. Which phase of the incident response process involves removing the problem?
   - A. Identification
   - B. Eradication
   - C. Recovery
   - D. Mitigation

3. What is the term used to describe the steps an organization performs after any situation determined to be abnormal in the operation of a computer system?
   A. Computer/network penetration incident plan
   B. Incident response plan
   C. Backup restoration and reconfiguration
   D. Cyber event response
4. What is the term for the set of steps needed to develop a comprehensive plan to enact during a situation where normal operations are interrupted?
   A. Disaster recovery
   B. Continuity of operations planning
   C. Incident response planning
   D. Restoration of business functions planning
5. In which phase of the incident response process are actions taken to constrain the incident to the minimal number of machines?
   A. Eradication
   B. Identification
   C. Containment
   D. Recovery
6. Which of the following is not part of the Diamond Model of Intrusion Analysis?
   A. Victim
   B. Infrastructure
   C. Adversary
   D. Vulnerability
7. For organizations that draw a distinction between a BCP and a DRP, which of the following statements is true?
   A. The BCP details the functions that are most critical and outlines the order in which critical functions should be returned to service to maintain business operations.
   B. The BCP is a subset of the DRP.
   C. The DRP outlines the minimum set of business functions required for the organization to continue functioning.
   D. The DRP is always developed first, and the BCP normally is an attachment to this document.

8. Which of the following are part of the Cyber Kill Chain? (Choose all that apply.)
   A. Reconnaissance
   B. Weaponization
   C. Anti-forensics
   D. Installation
9. Two major elements play a role in determining the level of response to an incident. Information criticality is the primary determinant. What is the other?
   A. Information sensitivity or the classification of the data
   B. The value of any data lost in the incident
   C. How the incident potentially affects the organization's operations
   D. Whether the organization wishes to pursue a legal settlement against the attacker(s)
10. What is the best way to deal with large, complex systems that have very expensive and lengthy process elements in an exercise?
   A. Tabletops
   B. Walkthroughs
   C. Simulations
   D. Just skip this element.

Answers

1. **A.** Preparation is the phase of incident response that occurs before a specific incident. Preparation includes all the tasks needed to be organized and ready to respond to an incident. The act of identification is coming to a decision that the information related to the incident is worthy of further investigation by the IR team. Containment is the set of actions taken to constrain the incident to the minimal number of machines. Prevention is not a phase of the incident response process.
2. **B.** Eradication involves removing the problem, and in today's complex system environment, this may mean rebuilding a clean machine. The act of identification is coming to a decision that the information related to the incident is worthy of further investigation by the IR team. The recovery process includes the steps necessary to return the systems and applications to operational status. Mitigation is not a phase in the incident response process.
3. **B.** Incident response plan is the term used to describe the steps an organization performs in response to any situation determined to be abnormal in the operation of a computer system.

4. **B.** Continuity of operations planning is the set of steps needed to develop a comprehensive plan to enact during a situation where normal operations are interrupted. Disaster recovery is the process that an organization uses to recover from events that disrupt normal operations. An incident response plan describes the steps an organization performs in response to any situation determined to be abnormal in the operation of a computer system. Restoration of business functions planning is not a standard term used in recovery planning.
5. **C.** Containment is the set of actions taken to constrain the incident to the minimal number of machines. Eradication involves removing the problem, and in today's complex system environment, this may mean rebuilding a clean machine. The act of identification is coming to a decision that the information related to the incident is worthy of further investigation by the IR team. The recovery process includes the steps necessary to return the systems and applications to operational status.
6. **D.** Vulnerability is not a formal node of the Diamond Model for Intrusion Analysis. The fourth node is capability.
7. **A.** Many organizations, particularly smaller ones, treat the two terms BCP and DRP synonymously, but for organizations that don't, the BCP outlines the business functions necessary for continued operation and may describe the order in which functions will be restored. The DRP outlines all processes and how they can be restored; the BCP acts as a companion document that describes which functions need to be restored and in which order.
8. **A, B,** and **D.** Reconnaissance, weaponization, and installation are steps in the Cyber Kill Chain. Anti-forensics is not; although these actions may occur, they are embedded in other steps.
9. **C.** The second factor involves a business decision on how an incident plays into current business operations. A series of breaches, whether minor or not, indicates a pattern that can have public relations and regulatory issues.
10. **C.** Simulation is a valuable tool to imitate parts of a process that can't be included in an exercise because of cost, time, resources, or other constraints.

CHAPTER 28

Investigations

In this chapter, you will

- Learn about the different sources of information used to support an investigation
- Learn how to incorporate appropriate data sources to support an investigation

Investigations are used to determine what happened, who did what, and what elements of an information system have been affected by some specific event or series of events. The elements that need to be investigated for unauthorized activity and changes include both the data elements in the system and the system itself. There can be a wealth of diagnostic and investigatory data collected as part of an ongoing security operation or developed in response to an incident. This chapter looks at how to utilize these sources of data to support an investigation and shed light on what actually happened to both the system and the data it processed.

Certification Objective This chapter covers CompTIA Security+ exam objective 4.3: Given an incident, utilize appropriate data sources to support an investigation.

Vulnerability Scan Output

Vulnerability scan output provides information as to the systems that are running, any additional services that are listening on the network, and what the known vulnerabilities are against each of these. This information is important in a couple of ways. First, it allows verification that the authorized systems are adequately patched. Systems with vulnerabilities act as entry points for attackers, and ensuring the entry points are closed is important. Second, and even more important, is the identification of additional services. These services may or may not be patched, and they too represent a pathway into a system for an attacker. Having extra services running that are not needed only increases the attack surface area, making it easier for attackers to get into a system. Bottom line: a vulnerability report provides you information on what is visible on your network, authorized or not.

SIEM Dashboards

SIEM (security information and event management) dashboards are the windows into the SIEM datastore, a collection of information that can tell you where attacks are occurring and provide a trail of breadcrumbs to show how the attacker got into the network and moved to where they are now. SIEM systems act as the information repository for information surrounding potential and actual intrusions. During an investigation, the SIEM system can provide a host of information concerning a user, what they have done, and so on. The fundamental purpose of a SIEM system is to provide alerts and relevant information to incident response teams that are investigating incidents. If something happens that initiates an investigation, and the SIEM system has no relevant information, then this suggests that the SIEM and its component elements need better tuning to provide meaningful surveillance of the system for potential problems.

EXAM TIP SIEMs allow you to identify, visualize, and monitor trends via alerts and a dashboard.

Sensor

Sensors are the devices that provide security data into the security datastore. Regardless of where that datastore is housed, the security information is important for investigators. Sensors don't just happen; they have to be placed in the correct location to collect information. Sensor placement begins with defining collection objectives. A study of where the data flows, where the information of value is in a network, and where adversaries can gain access, coupled with what information you wish to collect, are just some of the factors that go into designing sensor placement. Just as logs can provide a lot of useful information, they also can produce a lot of meaningless data. Sensors are no different. Packet capture sensors can record vital information for an investigation, but they have to be in the correct location (that is, have visibility with respect to the desired packets) while also avoiding common traffic areas where there is a lot of noise. To be properly prepared for future investigations, you need to properly design and place your sensors.

Sensitivity

Sensitivity is the quality of being quick to detect or respond to slight changes, signals, or influences. As the purpose of a SIEM system is to alert operators to changes that indicate significant events, sensitivity to those events is important. The biggest problem with SIEMs and sensitivity is the tradeoff between false positives and false negatives. If you alert on too many possible conditions, you increase false positives and create operator fatigue. Wait for too much data, and you miss some, creating a false negative and an impression that the SIEM system doesn't work. Adjusting the sensitivity until you have the right balance is a tough but important task.

Trends

Trends are a series of data points that indicate a change over time. Trends can be increasing, decreasing, cyclical, or related to variability. What is important is that trends indicate some form of change. Not all forms of change are relevant to the SIEM system's mission, and a key element is in understanding which changes are and which aren't. Some changes are important in a direct fashion, such as failed logins. If the average number of failed logins is 20 per day, and suddenly you are getting 10,000 in an hour, that indicates something has changed. An attacker? A script with an error? It will take some investigation to find. What if those same failures were spread across four users, all system admins? Trends matter, but so does the information behind them. This makes alerting on multiple items with good comprehensive reports more useful than just an alert stating "this number is too high." Context matters.

Alerts

Alerts are the primary method of communication between the SIEM system and operators. When conditions meet the rule requirements, the SIEM system can send an alert. The more information that can be provided in the alert (other related information, the context of the event, and so on), the better the alert. The key isn't to tell a security engineer "something happened, go find out what it is," but rather to steer the engineer in the correct direction with supplemental information that the operator can interpret and then devise a plan to investigate effectively.

Correlation

Correlation is the process of establishing a relationship between two variables. However, as a wise scientist once stated, correlation is not causation, meaning that just because measurements trend together doesn't mean one causes the other. There is frequently another element at play, some variable not being measured. Think about a series of failed logins coming from an IP address that was also rejected at a firewall for scanning activity. Or how about some access control failures, and activity such as a successful login with a different username from same IP address in a short time period? Or a UDP packet with port 67 as the destination port, but the destination address is not one of your DHCP servers? Correlation is a means for a SIEM system to apply rules to combine data sources to fine-tune event detection.

EXAM TIP SIEM event correlation logs are extremely useful because they can be used to identify malicious activity across a plethora of network devices and programs. This is data that otherwise may go unnoticed.

Log Files

Log files are a primary source of information during an investigation. Software can record in log files a wide range of information as it is operating. From self-health checks, to error-related data, to operational metadata supporting the events that are happening on a system, all this data ends up in log files. These log files act as a historical record of what happened on a system. Log files require configuration because if you don't log an event when it happens, you can't go back in time to capture it. By the same token, logging everything creates too much data—data that must be waded through during an investigation. The key is balance: record what you need to know to make determinations—no more, no less.

Network

Networks are filled with equipment that can provide valuable log information. Firewalls, routers, load balancers, and switches can provide a wealth of information as to what is happening on the network. *Network logs* tend to have a duplication issue as packets can traverse several devices, giving multiple, nearly identical records. Removing duplicate as well as extraneous data is the challenge with network logging, but the payoff can be big because proper logging can make tracing attackers easier.

System

Virtually every operating system creates *system logs*. These logs can provide a very detailed history of what actions were performed on a system. Login records that indicate failed logins can be important, but so can entries that show login success. Multiple failures followed by a success can be suspicious, especially when the number of failures and timing precludes a human operator typing. What about access permission failures? These can indicate an attempt to perform unauthorized activity. What about access successes? Logging these would swamp the database with a large number of irrelevant records. This is one of the challenges of logging things on a system—which logs produce meaningful answers and which just produce noise? Also, realize that the decision to log has to happen before an event occurs; in other words, you can't go back and have a do-over if you fail to log a crucial piece of evidence.

Application

Application logs are generated by the applications themselves as they run. Some applications provide extensive logging; others minimal or even no logging. Some applications allow configuration of what is logged; others do not. Many server applications—web servers, mail servers, and database servers—have extensive logging capability, including which user performed which action and when. Other systems merely log when they start and stop operations and may log errors.

Security

Security logs are logs kept by the OS for metadata associated with security operations. In Microsoft Windows, literally hundreds of different events can be configured to write to the Security log—system starting, system shutting down, permission failures, logins, failed logins, changing the system time, a new process creation, scheduled task changes, and more. These logs can be important, but to be important they need to be tuned to collect the information needed. In Windows, this is typically done through group policy objects. The driving force for what needs to be recorded is the system's audit policy, a statement about what records need to be kept.

EXAM TIP The Windows Event Viewer is used to look at Windows logs. The System log displays information related to the operating system. The Application log provides data related to applications that are run on the system. The Security log provides information regarding the success and failure of attempted logins as well as security-related audit events. Be ready to identify specific log file output on the exam!

Web

Web servers respond to specific, formatted requests for resources with responses, whether in the form of a web page or an error. And all of this activity can be logged. Web servers are specifically deployed to do this task, but they are also targets of attacks—attacks that try to run malicious scripts, perform DDoS attacks, perform injection and cross-site scripting attacks, and more. Web log files can help identify when these activities are occurring.

DNS

DNS logs, when enabled, can contain a record for every query and response. This can be a treasure trove of information for an investigator because it can reveal malware calling out to its command-and-control server, or data transfers to non-company locations. Analysis of DNS logs can show IP addresses and domain names that your systems should be communicating with as well as ones they shouldn't be communicating with. In cases where an attacker or malware is doing the communication, these communication channels may be next to invisible on the network, but the DNS system, as part of the network architecture, can log the activity. This is one of the reasons why DNS logs are some of the most valuable logs to import into a SIEM system.

Authentication

Authentication logs contain information about successful and failed authentication attempts. The most common source of authentication log information comes from the system's security logs, but additional sources exist as well. With the expansion of multifactor authentication services, applications that manage second factors also have logs. These logs are important, as they can show anomalies such as proper primary login data but failed second-factor data, indicating that the primary authentication information may have been disclosed.

Dump Files

Dump files are copies of what was in memory at a point in time—typically a point when some failure occurred. Dump files can be created by the operating system (OS) when the OS crashes, and these files can be analyzed to determine the cause of the crash. Dump files can also be created by several utilities and then shipped off to a third party for analysis when an application is not behaving correctly. Dump files can contain a wide range of sensitive information, including passwords, cryptographic keys, and more.

Care should be taken when handling dump files, and especially when sharing them for analysis. Several security vendors have tools that assist in the securing of sensitive information in dump files, but the risk of secret disclosure is still present. Because of the size and complexity involved in interpreting dump files, they are not a common investigative tool, except for narrow investigations such as why a system is crashing.

Attackers, on the other hand, love to get dump files and peruse them; therefore, setting systems to not persist dump files is common to prevent hackers from crashing a server and then coming back to get the subsequent dump file.

VoIP and Call Managers

Voice over IP (VoIP) solutions and *call manager* applications enable a wide range of audio and video communication services over the Internet. These systems can log a variety of data, including call information such as the number called (to and from), time of the call, and duration of the call. These records are called call detail records (CDRs). When combined with video and audio systems using VoIP, these logs can be enhanced with information as to how the information was encoded, including the codecs involved and the resolutions.

Session Initiation Protocol (SIP) Traffic

The Session Initiation Protocol (SIP) is a text-based protocol used for signaling voice, video, and messaging applications over IP. SIP provides information for initiating, maintaining, and terminating real-time sessions. *SIP traffic logs* are typically in the SIP Common Log Format (CLF), which mimics web server logs and captures the details associated with a communication (such as to and from).

Syslog/Rsyslog/Syslog-ng

Syslog stands for System Logging Protocol and is a standard protocol used in Linux systems to send system log or event messages to a specific server, called a syslog server. *Rsyslog* is an open source variant of syslog that follows the syslog specifications but also provides additional features such as content-based filtering. *Syslog-ng* is another open source implementation of the syslog standard. Syslog-ng also extends the original syslog model with elements such as content filtering. A primary advantage of syslog-ng over syslog and rsyslog is that it can tag, classify, and correlate in real time, which can improve SIEM performance. For Linux-based systems, these implementations are the de facto standard for managing log files. As log files are one of the primary artifact sources, investigations make significant use of log files and syslog-captured data to build histories of what actually happened on a system.

EXAM TIP Syslog, rsyslog, and syslog-ng all move data into log files on a log server. Rsyslog and syslog-ng both extend the original syslog standard by adding capabilities such as content filtering, log enrichment, and correlation of data elements into higher-level events.

Journalctl

On Linux systems, the initial daemon that launches the system is called systemd. When systemd creates log files, it does so through the systemd-journald service. Journalctl is the command that is used to view these logs. To see the various command options for journalctl, you should consult the man pages on the system. Here is an example of a journalctl command to view logs for a given system service:

```
journalctl -u ssh
```

EXAM TIP Understand the differences between journalctl and syslog. Journalctl is the command to examine logs on a server. Syslog (and the variants rsyslog and syslog-ng) is used to move logs to a log server and sometimes to manipulate the log file entries in transit.

NXLog

NXLog is a multiplatform log management tool designed to assist in the use of log data during investigations. This tool suite is capable of handling syslog-type data as well as other log formats, including Microsoft Windows. It has advanced capabilities to enrich log files through context-based lookups, correlations, and rule-based enrichments. NXLog has connectors to most major applications and can act as a log collector, forwarder, aggregator, and investigative tool for searching through log data. As logs are one of the most used data sources in investigations, tools such as NXLog can enable investigators to identify security issues, policy violations, and operational problems in systems.

Bandwidth Monitors

Bandwidth monitors are utilities designed to measure network bandwidth utilization over time. Bandwidth monitors can provide information as to how much bandwidth is being utilized, by service type, and how much remains. Bandwidth monitors can log this information over time and provide a historical record of network congestion problems, including by type of traffic in quality of service–enforced networks.

Metadata

Metadata is data about data. A file entry on a storage system has the file contents plus metadata, including the filename, creation, access, and update timestamps, size, and more. Microsoft Word files have the document contents and additional fields of associated metadata. JPEGs have the same fields of metadata, including the location of the capture and the device used to create the images. Tons of metadata exist on a system, and in many cases individual elements of metadata need to be correlated with other metadata to determine activities. Take, for example, when a USB is inserted into a system. This creates metadata, but for what user? Separate metadata can tell you who was logged in at that time. Collecting, analyzing, and correlating metadata are all part of almost every investigation.

EXAM TIP Remember that everything digital contains metadata, and correlating metadata is a part of almost every investigation.

E-Mail

E-mail is half metadata, half message. For short messages, the metadata can be larger than the message itself. E-mail metadata is in the header of the e-mail and includes routing information, the sender, receiver, timestamps, subject, and other information associated with the delivery of the message. The header of an e-mail includes information for the handling of the e-mail between mail user agents (MUAs), mail transfer agents (MTAs), and mail delivery agents (MDAs), as well as a host of other details. The entire message is sent via plain ASCII text, with attachments included using Base64 encoding. The e-mail header provides all of the information associated with an e-mail as it moves from sender to receiver. The following is a sample e-mail header:

```
Received: from smtp4.cc.uh.edu (129.7.234.211) by xFENode3B.mail.example.
net (129.7.40.150) with Microsoft SMTP Server id 8.2.255.0; Sat, 11 Apr 2020
18:54:42 -0500
Received: from smtp4.cc.uh.edu (smtp4.example.net [127.0.0.1]) by localhost
(Postfix) with SMTP id BC4DA1E004A  for <waconklin@example.com>; Sat, 11 Apr
2020 18:53:55 -0500 (CDT)
Received: from nm22.bullet.mail.ne1.yahoo.com (nm22.bullet.mail.ne1.yahoo.com

 [98.138.90.85]) by smtp4.example.net (Postfix) with ESMTP id  538C31E0034
for <waconklin@example.com>; Sat, 11 Apr 2020
 18:53:55 -0500 (CDT)
DKIM-Signature: v=1; a=rsa-sha256; c=relaxed/relaxed;
d=yahoo.com; s=s2048;
 t=1428796434; bh=esKcEn6Pe1DHaDx/5lqarnNbc5vZAFO5+z93Xt/06S0=;
h=Date:From:Reply-To:To:In-Reply-To:References:Subject:From:Subject;
b=OQTvNETmW6KKGn/cWXsQd43khwTbwsGpRFhpwB0iCopROLVxabwPryOB/6RpSb37JC5IYTxYrDj
rslDhaSBj1381Y8ior9CS83YyV3JnRzk6F+YrDQDUXAuG5vbhDo9lKUX0pNa/R4rdvK47T6uO9
2k7wf1++egSLATDeId5ccUFUZLBQpxBJx6WtLJbI6eValGPQLgLCNdhedkgGBEugp+Yfc0xDr97
5euYFsxwLDS36pi88etIkMso0FDbQLsGfk3SneIkm+o5wSDq7lAsWk3NX4p+yFjW16V
7OjQSg2Xf6KnNt9gUh9v98U+WW/Crwlq110xUHL1FjiP6oNsGkw==
Received: from [98.138.100.112] by nm22.bullet.mail.ne1.yahoo.com
with NNFMP;
 11 Apr 2020 23:53:54 -0000
Received: from [98.138.89.173] by tm103.bullet.mail.ne1.yahoo.com
with NNFMP;
 11 Apr 2020 23:53:53 -0000

Received: from [127.0.0.1] by omp1029.mail.ne1.yahoo.com with NNFMP;
11 Apr 2020 23:53:53 -0000
X-Yahoo-Newman-Property: ymail-5
X-Yahoo-Newman-Id: 880223.99814.bm@omp1029.mail.ne1.yahoo.com
X-YMail-OSG: NKvYQJkVM1kWuLmyDvNnFXECaMumy9LBgfZhcKRiubzkoq9_NVdEUqlT7hMlkOv
1oWFqcbcyiJwpOTgEmUZIsGX2ZpKSfNrUUzmQ3.ksRewbg9xRVVDqnQbdJksIfeePVCUGNJ26elD
Ts4mEjfkzWPGKiXkxmy8iNhDzszw0RmJpDOrRDymsdTE3ObnKA83ZXSj9w0CwXnkJ_UtmVSWtyl0
NLDv8KRSPl0IaW8APZeaAmmTKPO06z.8jJg.GOGWAZbonqsm_zXvMjcfmmQ8wd8PBOh2pFqzvwvn
```

```
cfwHL3.iDmOzcNBYrF5mNfbmdaoHAztYxA8edB2kFqN3vje3VJPkoPOCiOhq_c_wFIs8E6W02VjK
0gCJRLAPEwyo30kyz_QDyGgfpfv4GAXrz9bQet8sy_e2ztRyVnj9GDu.DHSYnU5TaTLzvRhMQO3p
082zOb2Qm_4Miilk36RzypHRAEWh_GlTxr3sRloz1RhsioTgMYqksk0E_7P2bBJOJb3HsTyG2o_i
swOuz7CIt8U67Fe1IlDoPsU5hJj8DXHlSK_pGUl3j

Received: by 98.138.105.206; Sat, 11 Apr 2020 23:53:53 +0000
Date: Sat, 11 Apr 2020 23:53:52 +0000
From: Sender Name SenderName@yahoo.com
Reply-To: Sender Name SenderName@yahoo.com
To: "Conklin, Wm. Arthur" waconklin@example.com
Message-ID: 517184424.1041513.1428796432644.JavaMail.yahoo@mail.yahoo.com
In-Reply-To: 9AF24FE2BE34BC42A10F1DE75C05D8871652896780@EXSERVER3.example.com
References: 9AF24FE2BE34BC42A10F1DE75C05D8871652896780@EXSERVER3.example.com
Subject: Re: Homework Lab 2
MIME-Version: 1.0
Content-Type: multipart/mixed;
        boundary="----=_Part_1041512_683422731.1428796432643"
X-PMX-Version: 6.0.3.2322014, Antispam-Engine: 2.7.2.2107409, Antispam-Data:
2015.4.11.234523
X-PerlMx-Spam: Gauge=IIIIIIII, Probability=8%, Report='
HTML_50_70 0.1, HTML_NO_HTTP 0.1, BODYTEXTH_SIZE_10000_LESS 0,
BODYTEXTP_SIZE_3000_LESS 0, BODY_SIZE_10000_PLUS 0, DKIM_SIGNATURE 0,
ECARD_KNOWN_DOMAINS 0, REFERENCES 0, WEBMAIL_SOURCE 0, __ANY_URI 0,
__BOUNCE_CHALLENGE_SUBJ 0, __BOUNCE_NDR_SUBJ_EXEMPT 0, __C230066_P1_5 0,
Return-Path: SenderName@yahoo.com
```

E-mail header data can be important in investigations because it can show details such as the following:

- **From** Contains information on where the message comes from (can easily be forged).
- **To** The receiving end of the e-mail (not necessarily the recipient's e-mail address).
- **Subject** Think of this as the "title" or the topic that the sender sets on their e-mail.
- **Date** This is the date and time when an e-mail is written.
- **Return-Path** Also known as Reply-To, this field contains the address where the reply to the e-mail will be sent.
- **Delivery Date** This is the timestamp when an e-mail client receives the e-mail.
- **Received** This line shows the servers an e-mail has gone through in order to arrive at the recipient's mailbox. To read it from a chronological point of view, you must start at the bottom (where the e-mail was originally sent from) and read to the top (the final destination of the e-mail).
- **DKIM Signature and Domain Key Signature** DKIM stands for DomainKeys Identified Mail. Along with the domain key signature, it is part of an e-mail signature identification system.
- **Message-ID** This is a combination of unique letters and numbers created when the e-mail was first written (also forgeable).

- **MIME-version** MIME is an Internet standard that extends the format and the functionality of an e-mail. You can attach videos, images, and other files using MIME. Attachments are in Base64.
- **Content-type** Tells you whether the e-mail is written as plaintext or HTML.
- **X-Spam status** Tells you the score of an e-mail. If it reaches more than the threshold, the e-mail will be considered spam.
- **X-Spam level** This level depends on the score of the e-mail's X-Spam status. For every point it gains, the X-Spam level will show one asterisk.
- **Message body** The actual message that was sent.

As you can see, an e-mail can be mostly metadata.

Mobile

Mobile devices generate, store, and transmit metadata. Common fields include when a call or text was made, whether it was an incoming or outgoing transmission, the duration of the call or the text message's length (in characters), and the phone numbers of the senders and recipients. Note that the message or audio signal is not part of the metadata, but how much can you get from the metadata alone? More than meets the eye. For example, numbers can be looked up, providing the identities of senders and receivers (such as a conversation with the doctor's office, followed by a call from a pharmacy).

Other sources of metadata include things like Wi-Fi access points connected to, GPS data in application logs, whether the device has a camera, and EXIF data (discussed later in the "File" section).

Web

The Web provides a means of moving information between browsers and servers. There are a variety of protocols involved and a variety of sources of metadata. The web pages themselves are full of metadata, and browsers store different metadata covering what pages were accessed and when. Browser metadata is a commonly used source of forensic information, because entries of what and when a browser has accessed data can be important. Did a user go to a specific web page? Did they use a web-based e-mail client, exposing actual e-mail information as well as the fact they used e-mail? How long were they on a site? If a user hits a site that displays an image tagged by one of the security appliances, did they stay on that page or immediately go to a different site? There can be a wealth of user behavior information with respect to web browsing.

File

File metadata comes in two flavors: system and application. The file system uses metadata to keep track of the filename as well as the timestamps associated with last access, creation, and last write. The system metadata will include items needed by the OS, such as ownership information, parent object, permissions, and security descriptors.

Application metadata in a file is part of the file data field and is used by the application. For instance, a Microsoft Word document contains a lot of metadata, including fields for author, company, number of times edited, last print time, and so on. Currently, Word has over 90 fields of metadata that can be used/modified by a user. A JPEG file, on the other hand, has metadata that's typically expressed in the form of EXIF data. The Exchangeable image file (EXIF) format is a standard that defines the formats of image, audio, and metadata tags used by cameras, phones, and other digital recording devices. Common EXIF metadata can include the following:

- The original filename
- Capture and last edited date and timestamps (with varying precision)
- GPS location coordinates (degrees of latitude and longitude)
- A small thumbnail of the original image
- The author's name and copyright details
- Compass heading
- Device information, including manufacturer and model
- Capture information, including lens type, focal range, aperture, shutter speed, and flash settings

EXIF data exists to assist applications that use these files and can be modified independently of the file contents.

EXAM TIP Metadata is a very valuable source of information during an investigation. Understanding what type of information and detail are present in each major category is important.

NetFlow/sFlow

NetFlow and *sFlow* are protocols designed to capture information about packet flows (that is, a sequence of related packets) as they traverse a network. NetFlow is a proprietary standard from Cisco. Flow data is generated by the network devices themselves, including routers and switches. The data that is collected and shipped off to data collectors is a simple set of metadata—source and destination IP addresses, source and destination ports, if any (ICMP, for example, doesn't use ports), and the protocol. NetFlow does this for all packets, while sFlow (sampled flow) does a statistical sampling. On high-throughput networks, NetFlow can generate large quantities of data—data that requires de-duplication. However, having all that data will catch the rare security event packets. sFlow is more suited for statistical traffic monitoring. Cisco added statistical monitoring to NetFlow on its high-end infrastructure routers to deal with the traffic volumes.

EXAM TIP Both NetFlow and sFlow collect packets from routers and switches. NetFlow data can be useful in intrusion investigations. sFlow is used primarily for traffic management, although it will help with DDoS attacks.

IPFIX

Internet Protocol Flow Information Export (IPFIX) is an IETF protocol that's the answer to the proprietary Cisco NetFlow standard. IPFIX is based on NetFlow version 9 and is highly configurable using a series of templates. The primary purpose of IPFIX is to provide a central monitoring station with information about the state of the network. IPFIX is a push-based protocol, where the sender sends the reports and receives no response from the receiver.

Protocol Analyzer Output

A protocol analyzer (also known as a *packet sniffer, network analyzer,* or *network sniffer*) is a piece of software or an integrated software/hardware system that can capture and decode network traffic. Protocol analyzers have been popular with system administrators and security professionals for decades because they are such versatile and useful tools for a network environment. From a security perspective, protocol analyzers can be used for a number of activities, such as the following:

- Detecting intrusions or undesirable traffic. (An IDS/IPS must have some type of capture and decode capabilities to be able to look for suspicious/malicious traffic.)
- Capturing traffic during incident response or incident handling.
- Looking for evidence of botnets, Trojans, and infected systems.
- Looking for unusual traffic or traffic exceeding certain thresholds.
- Testing encryption between systems or applications.

From a network administration perspective, protocol analyzers can be used for activities such as these:

- Analyzing network problems
- Detecting misconfigured applications or misbehaving applications
- Gathering and reporting network usage and traffic statistics
- Debugging client/server communications

Regardless of the intended use, a protocol analyzer must be able to see network traffic in order to capture and decode it. The output of the protocol analyzer is a human-readable format of the information being passed on the system. This information can provide insights into what exactly is or is not happening. Tools can be used to scan the output for specific items of interest, patterns, specific activities, and other elements of communication that might be of interest.

Chapter Review

In this chapter, you became acquainted with security elements associated with investigations. The chapter opened with a section on vulnerability scan outputs followed by one on SIEM dashboards. In the second section, the subtopics of sensors, sensitivity, trends, alerts, and correlations were covered. The next section covered log files, and the subjects of network, system, application, security, Web, DNS, and authentication were presented. These were followed by dump files, VoIP and call managers, and SIP traffic logs.

The topics of syslog/rsyslog/syslog-ng, journalctl, NXLog, retention, and bandwidth monitors were covered next. The next major section was on metadata, which described the e-mail, mobile, web, and file forms of metadata.

The chapter finished with a section on NetFlow/sFlow, where IPFIX was presented, and then a look at protocol analyzer outputs.

Questions

To help you prepare further for the CompTIA Security+ exam, and to test your level of preparedness, answer the following questions and then check your answers against the correct answers at the end of the chapter.

1. Which can be the most valuable log for finding malware in a system?

A. Network

B. Web

C. DNS

D. IPFIX

2. To best understand which machines are talking to each other, which of the following should be used?

A. DNS logs

B. NetFlow

C. Network logs

D. SIEM alerts

3. To remotely log information using a centralized log server, which of the following protocols should be used?

A. DNS

B. NetFlow

C. Syslog

D. IPFIX

4. IPFIX is used for what?
   A. Capturing which machines are in communication with each other
   B. Managing mobile messaging solutions
   C. Reading syslog files
   D. DNS logs
5. Where can you find metadata showing where a picture was taken?
   A. EXIF data
   B. IPFIX data
   C. E-mail metadata
   D. SIP CTL
6. Which of these is not associated with syslog files?
   A. Journalctl
   B. NXLog
   C. SIP CTL
   D. IPFIX
7. Correlation does what with SIEM data?
   A. Determines causes
   B. Provides background contextual information
   C. Allows rule-based interpretation of data
   D. All of the above
8. What is one of the challenges of NetFlow data?
   A. Proprietary format
   B. Excess data fields
   C. Record size
   D. Removing duplicate records along a path
9. What tool can be used to read system log data in Linux systems?
   A. Any text editor
   B. Journalctl
   C. Web browser
   D. Protocol analyzer

10. Which of the following are issues that need to be determined as part of setting up a SIEM solution? (Choose all that apply.)
    - **A.** Sensor placement
    - **B.** Log files and relevant fields
    - **C.** Desired alert conditions
    - **D.** DNS logging

Answers

1. **C.** DNS logs can see requests to communicate with malware command-and-control (C2) servers.
2. **B.** NetFlow data describes which machines are talking to which machines.
3. **C.** Syslog is the protocol used to move log files to remote servers.
4. **A.** IPFIX works like NetFlow, identifying which machines are communicating with each other.
5. **A.** EXIF is the metadata associated with image and video files.
6. **D.** IPFIX is not associated with syslog files.
7. **C.** Correlation allows different events to be combined to provide greater specificity in determining SIEM-based event detection. Correlation is a means for a SIEM system to apply rules to combine data sources to fine-tune event detection.
8. **D.** Although NetFlow is a proprietary standard, its format is published. It has a small record size, and data it can be repeated from multiple devices along a packet's path. Removing the duplicates (records) in a distributed system can be a challenge.
9. **B.** Journalctl can read system logs on Linux systems.
10. **A, B, C, and D.** Setting up a SIEM requires many steps, including identification of the data source, alerting conditions, which logs and fields to use, and more.

CHAPTER 29

Mitigation Techniques and Controls

In this chapter, you will

- Learn about the different mitigations that can be applied to systems
- Learn about the various controls that can be used to secure systems

Systems cannot be completely secure by design or use, but a series of elements can be used to increase the security posture of a system. These controls and mitigation elements work to reduce risk in the system. This chapter explores various controls and mitigations covered on the Security+ exam.

Certification Objective This chapter covers CompTIA Security+ exam objective 4.4: Given an incident, apply mitigation techniques or controls to secure an environment.

Reconfigure Endpoint Security Solutions

Endpoint security solutions are controls that can mitigate risk at the endpoint. Endpoint solutions must recognize the threat and then trigger a specific action to mitigate the risk. Antivirus/antimalware solutions are the typical endpoint protection most users think of, as are elements such as firewalls and intrusion protection elements.

More integrated endpoint elements can be part of the operating system, or they can work with the operating system (OS) to alter behaviors to enforce rules. Microsoft has two mechanisms that are part of the Windows OS to manage which applications can operate on their machines:

- **Software restrictive policies** Employed via group policies, software restrictive policies allow significant control over applications, scripts, and executable files. The primary mode is by machine and not by user account.
- **User account level control** Enforced via AppLocker, a service that allows granular control over which users can execute which programs. Through the use of rules, an enterprise can exert significant control over who can access and use installed software.

On a Linux platform, similar capabilities are offered from third-party vendor applications.

The last question is, what do you do when something is detected that's outside the desired specification? The typical response is to quarantine, which is described later in this chapter.

Application Approved List

Applications can be controlled at the OS at start time via verification of the application against a list of approved applications (whitelisting) and a list of blocked or denied applications (blacklisting). *The application approved list* consists of a list of allowed applications. If an application is not on the allowed list, it is blocked. Both whitelisting and blacklisting have advantages and disadvantages. Using a application approved list is easier to employ from the aspect of the identification of applications that are allowed to run, and hash values can be used to ensure the executables are not corrupted. The challenge in this approach is the number of potential applications that are run on a typical machine. For a single-purpose machine, such as a database server, this can be relatively easy to employ. For multipurpose machines, it can be more complicated, as applications can be missed, resulting in errors.

Application Blocklist/Deny List

The use of an *application block or deny list* is essentially noting which applications should not be allowed to run on the machine. This is basically a permanent "ignore" or "call block" type of capability. Also historically called blacklisting, it is difficult, if not impossible, to use against dynamic threats, as the identification of a specific application can easily be avoided through minor changes.

EXAM TIP Whitelisting, or the use of an application allow list, is the use of a list of approved applications. If an app is not on the whitelist, access is denied and the app won't install or run. Blacklisting, or the use of an application blocklist/deny list, is a list of apps that are deemed undesirable. If an app is blacklisted, it won't be installed or allowed to run.

Quarantine

When a system detects a condition that meets a specific set of rules and determines that an action is required, one of the important decisions is the finality of that action. In the case of a firewall, blocking a connection is final; the result cannot be undone. But in the case of a suspicious file, file change, or configuration change, there is the chance of error in the decision, and having a virtual "undo" capability may be desired. This is where the concept of *quarantine* enters the equation. Quarantining an item is to render it disabled but not permanently removed from the system. There are a variety of mechanisms to do this, but the end result is the same: a quarantine option gives the user the opportunity to undo the disablement. If the item had been permanently deleted, this option would not be available. Security tools that offer quarantine options have mechanisms to disable an item, and to re-enable it if instructed by the user.

Configuration Changes

Configurations are the lifeblood of a system. Protecting a system from *configuration changes* is essential to secure the system in the specific configuration that the implementation intended. Alterations to configurations can add functionality, remove functionality, even completely change system functionality by altering elements of a program to include outside code. Protecting a system from unauthorized configuration changes is important for security.

Firewall Rules

Firewalls operate by enforcing a set of rules on the traffic attempting to pass. This set of *firewall rules*, also called the firewall ruleset, is a mirror of the policy constraints at a particular point in the network. Thus, the ruleset will vary from firewall to firewall, as it is the operational implementation of the desired traffic constraints at each point. Firewall rules state whether the firewall should allow particular traffic to pass through or block it. The structure of a firewall rule can range from simple to very complex, depending on the type of firewall and the type of traffic. A packet filtering firewall can act on IP addresses and ports, either allowing or blocking based on this information.

Firewall rules have directionality; there are inbound and outbound rules. Inbound rules protect a machine from incoming traffic. Outbound rules can also protect against sending data (including requests) to unauthorized or dangerous places. An example of these rules and the categories of inbound and outbound are illustrated in Figure 29-1.

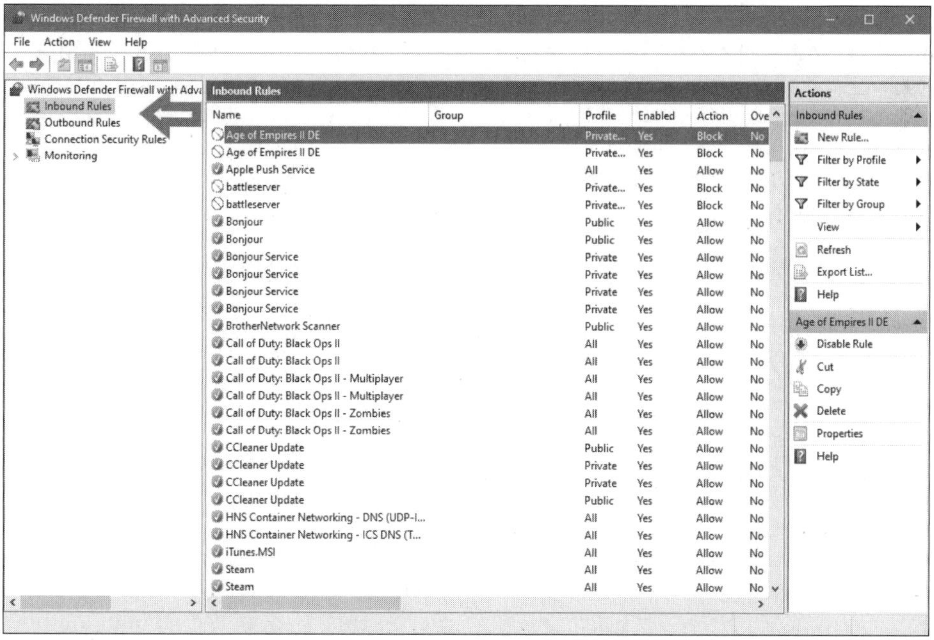

Figure 29-1 Firewall rules in Microsoft Defender, a Windows client solution

EXAM TIP Firewall rules make great performance-based questions—what rules belong on which firewall? Understanding how a rule blocks or allows traffic is essential, but so is seeing how the overall network flow picture is regulated by the rules. Be able to place rules to a network diagram to meet objectives.

MDM

Knowledge of *mobile device management (MDM)* concepts is essential in today's environment of connected devices. MDM began as a marketing term for a collective set of commonly employed protection elements associated with mobile devices. When viewed as a comprehensive set of security options for mobile devices, every corporation should have and enforce an MDM policy. The policy should require the following:

- Device locking with a strong password
- Encryption of data on the device
- Device locking automatically after a certain period of inactivity
- The capability to remotely lock the device if it is lost or stolen
- The capability to wipe the device automatically after a certain number of failed login attempts
- The capability to remotely wipe the device if it is lost or stolen

Password policies should extend to mobile devices, including lockout and, if possible, the automatic wiping of data. Corporate policy for data encryption on mobile devices should be consistent with the policy for data encryption on laptop computers. In other words, if you don't require encryption of portable computers, then should you require it for mobile devices? There isn't a uniform answer to this question because mobile devices are much more mobile in practice than laptops, and more prone to loss. This is ultimately a risk question that management must address: what is the risk and what are the costs of the options employed? This also raises a bigger question: which devices should have encryption as a basic security protection mechanism? Is it by device type or by user based on what data would be exposed to risk? Fortunately, MDM solutions exist, making the choices manageable.

EXAM TIP Mobile device management (MDM) is the term for a collective set of commonly employed protection elements associated with mobile devices.

DLP

Data loss prevention (DLP) refers to technology employed to detect and prevent transfers of data across an enterprise. Employed at key locations, DLP technology can scan packets for specific data patterns. This technology can be tuned to detect account numbers, secrets, specific markers, or files. When specific data elements are detected, the system can block the transfer. The primary challenge in employing DLP technologies is the placement of the sensor. The DLP sensor needs to be able to observe the data, so if the channel is encrypted, DLP technology can be thwarted.

DLP began its life as an enterprise-level device or appliance, but the deployment of this technology has expanded to endpoints, including operating systems and apps such as Microsoft 365. These distributed solutions use DLP policies to detect, monitor, and protect against accidental release or exposure of sensitive information.

EXAM TIP DLP can be classified as a technical control. Its primary goal is to detect breaches and prevent data loss.

Content Filter/URL Filter

Content filters/URL filters are used to limit specific types of content across the Web to users. A common use is to block sites that are not work related, and to limit items such as Google searches and other methods of accessing content determined to be inappropriate. Like all other policy enforcement devices, content filters rely on a set of rules, and rule maintenance is an issue. One of the most common issues with content filters is blocking that is too broad. In a medical environment, blocking the word "breast" will not work, nor will it work in a chicken processing plant. There needs to be a mechanism in place to lift blocks easily and quickly if a user objects and it is easy to determine they should have access.

Update or Revoke Certificates

Certificates are used to pass cryptographic keys as part of a wide variety of processes—from signing data, to authentication services, to setting up cryptographic services between devices. Most of the work with certificates is automated and handled behind the scenes, but it is still reliant on a valid set of certificates and approved certificate chains. For details on how this works, see Chapter 25, "Public Key Infrastructure." A crucial element of certificates is protecting the certificate chain on a machine. Errors in this element can cause certificates to be rejected. Failure to maintain valid certificates is another cause of failures. Many of these failures can go unnoticed, as was demonstrated in automated COVID-19 counts in the state of California. A certificate error with one of the state's laboratory vendors caused a significant undercounting of results, and the cause was an expired certificate.

EXAM TIP Certificates remain valid for a specific duration of time. When a certificate is about to expire, it should be renewed if needed. However, sometimes certificates are revoked because the owner is no longer trusted, the encryption keys have been compromised, or there are changes or other errors with the certificate.

Isolation

Isolation is the use of networking protocols and resultant connectivity to limit access to different parts of a network. This limit can be partial or it can be complete, as offered by an air gap, and this method of separation is used to enforce different trust boundaries. More details about the role of networks is presented in the section "Segmentation," which follows shortly.

Isolation can also be employed as part of an incident response strategy, where affected systems are isolated from the rest of the network. This is done to limit the risk caused by systems that are no longer functioning in a desired manner. In the case of a ransomware infection, this is a key mitigation element if it can be employed early in the incident.

Containment

Containment is a key concept in incident response. *Containment* is the act of performing specific actions that limit the damage potential of an incident, keeping the damage limited, and preventing further damage. Containment can be done using a variety of mechanisms, including network segmentation, quarantining of unauthorized elements, or changing of system configurations. The objective is the same: limit the exposure of the system to the damaging element.

Segmentation

As networks have become more complex, with multiple layers of tiers and interconnections, a problem can arise in connectivity. One of the limitations of the Spanning Tree Protocol (STP) is its inability to manage layer 2 traffic efficiently across highly complex networks. STP was created to prevent loops in layer 2 networks and has been improved in its current version, called Rapid Spanning Tree Protocol (RSTP). RSTP creates a spanning tree within the network of layer 2 switches, disabling links that are not part of the spanning tree. RSTP, IEEE 802.1w, provides a more rapid convergence to a new spanning tree solution after topology changes are detected. The problem with the spanning tree algorithms is that the network traffic is interrupted while the system recalculates and reconfigures. These disruptions can cause problems in network efficiencies and have led to a push for flat network designs, which avoid packet-looping issues through an architecture that does not have tiers.

One name associated with flat network topologies is *network fabric,* a term meant to describe a flat, depthless network. Network fabrics are becoming increasingly popular in data centers and other areas of high-traffic density, as they can offer increased throughput and lower levels of network jitter and other disruptions. While this is good for efficiency of network operations, this "everyone can talk to everyone" idea is problematic with respect to security.

Modern networks, with their increasingly complex connections, result in systems where navigation can become complex between nodes. Just as a DMZ-based architecture allows for differing levels of trust, the isolation of specific pieces of the network using security rules can provide differing trust environments. There are several terms used to describe the resultant architecture, including network *segmentation*, segregation, isolation, and enclaves. *Enclaves* is the most commonly used term to describe sections of a network that are logically isolated by segmentation at the networking protocol. The concept of segregating a network into enclaves can create areas of trust where special protections can be employed and traffic from outside the enclave is limited or properly screened before admission.

Enclaves are not diametrically opposed to the concept of a flat network structure; they are just carved-out areas, like gated neighborhoods, where one needs special credentials to enter. A variety of security mechanisms can be employed to create a secure enclave. Layer 2 addressing (subnetting) can be employed, making direct addressability an issue. Firewalls, routers, and application-level proxies can be employed to screen packets before entry or exit from the enclave. Even the people side of the system can be restricted by dedicating one or more system administrators to manage the systems.

Enclaves are an important tool in modern secure network design. Figure 29-2 shows a network design with a standard two-firewall implementation of a DMZ. On the internal side of the network, multiple firewalls can be seen, carving off individual security enclaves, or zones where the same security rules apply. Common enclaves include those for high-security databases, low-security users (call centers), public-facing kiosks, and the management interfaces to servers and network devices. Having each of these in its own zone provides for more security control. On the management layer, using a nonroutable IP address scheme for all of the interfaces prevents them from being directly accessed from the Internet.

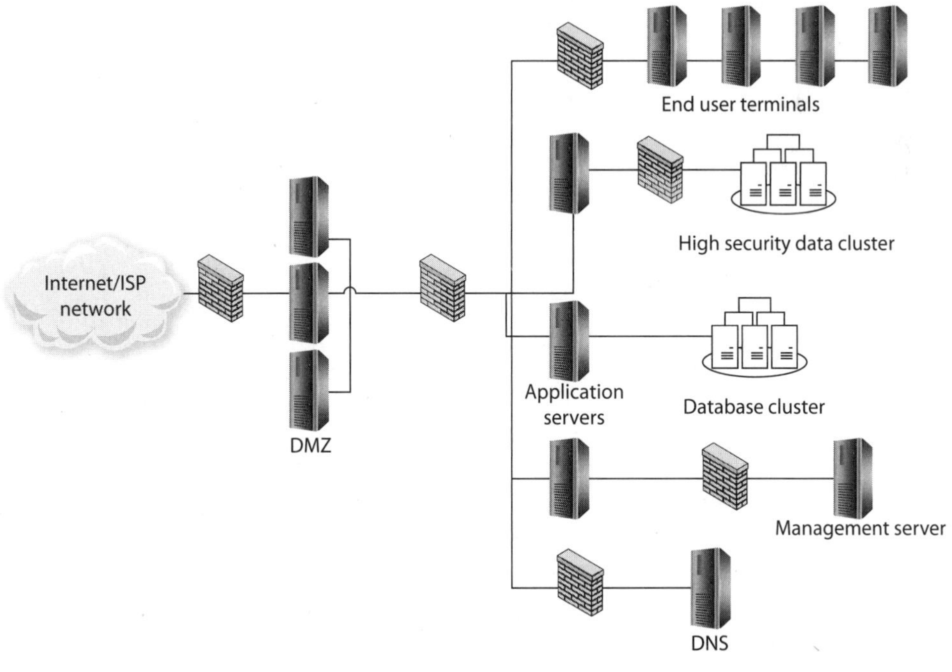

Figure 29-2 Secure enclaves

EXAM TIP Segmentation, as it applies to networking security, is a broad term. VLANs, firewalls, and even storage segmentation and containerization can be used for segmentation purposes.

Secure Orchestration, Automation, and Response (SOAR)

Security operations in an enterprise environment have a lot of moving parts. From a top-level view, you have vulnerability management, threat intelligence, incident response, and automated security operations. All of these operate off of data—data that comes from a myriad of network appliances, intrusion detection systems, firewalls, and other security devices. This data is typically fed into a security information and event management (SIEM) system that can collect, aggregate, and apply pattern matching to the volumes of data. Alerts can then be processed by security personnel. However, this is far from complete integration. *Security orchestration, automation, and response (SOAR)* systems take SIEM data as well as data from other sources and assist in the creation of runbooks and playbooks.

Security administrators can create a series of runbooks and playbooks that can be used in response to a wide range of incident response activities. The details behind runbooks and playbooks are covered next. Combinations of runbooks and playbooks can be used to document different security processes and can provide users with approved procedures for orchestrating even the most complex security workflows. SOAR software integrates all of these elements into manageable solutions for the security operations center personnel, integrating both raw and processed data into actionable steps based on approved procedures.

EXAM TIP SOAR systems are extremely valuable when it comes to incident mitigation of severe threats because they can automate data gathering and initiate threat response.

Runbooks

A *runbook* consists of a series of action-based conditional steps to perform specific actions associated with security automation. These actions might involve data harvesting and enrichment, threat containment, alerts and notifications, and other automatable elements of a security operations process. The primary purpose of a runbook is to accelerate the incident response process by automating a series of approved steps and processes. Runbooks typically are focused on the systems and services and how they are actively managed.

Playbooks

A *playbook* is a set of approved steps and actions required to successfully respond to a specific incident or threat. Playbooks are commonly instantiated as itemized checklists, with all pertinent data prefilled in—systems, team members, actions, and so on. Playbooks provide a simple step-by-step, top-down approach to the orchestration of activities of the security team. They can include a wide range of requirements—technical requirements, personnel requirements, and legal or regulatory requirements—all in a preapproved form that alleviates spur-of-the-moment scrambling when the clock is ticking on an active event.

EXAM TIP A runbook typically focuses on technical aspects of computer systems or networks. A playbook is more comprehensive and has more of a people/general business focus.

Chapter Review

In this chapter, you became acquainted with mitigation techniques and security controls used to secure an environment. The chapter opened with a discussion of configuring endpoint security solutions. Specifically, the topics of application whitelisting, application blacklisting, and quarantine were presented. The next major section covered configuration changes. The subsections in this area included firewall rules, mobile device management, data loss prevention, content filters/URL filters, and update or revoke certificates.

The chapter then covered the topics of isolation, containment, and segmentation. The chapter concluded with the topic of security orchestration, automation, and response (SOAR), along with the subtopics of runbooks and playbooks.

Questions

To help you prepare further for the CompTIA Security+ exam, and to test your level of preparedness, answer the following questions and then check your answers against the correct answers at the end of the chapter.

1. You have been directed by upper management to block employees from accessing Facebook from the corporate machines. Which would be the easiest way to exercise this control?
   A. Application allow list
   B. Application block list
   C. DLP
   D. Content filtering
2. Having an expired certificate is an example of what type of error?
   A. Mobile device management
   B. Configuration
   C. Application whitelisting
   D. Content filter/URL filter

3. A system-focused set of predetermined automation steps is an example of what?
    A. Isolation
    B. Runbook
    C. Playbook
    D. Firewall rules
4. Your business application server sends data to partners using encrypted (signed) messages. You hear from one of the partners that their messages have ceased coming. What should you investigate?
    A. Application whitelist
    B. Application blacklist
    C. The playbook for the system
    D. Configuration settings of the process
5. You have kiosk-based machines in the lobby and scattered through the facility. They do not require a login for guests to access certain items. What is the best way to protect these machines from users introducing trojans?
    A. Application allow list
    B. Application block list
    C. Data loss prevention
    D. Configuration settings of the process
6. To coordinate team activities during an incident response event, what is the best way to communicate approved instructions?
    A. Runbook
    B. MDM solution
    C. Quarantine rule
    D. Playbook
7. Your security system has identified a specific executable as potentially dangerous. What is the best way to handle the specific item that was identified?
    A. Segmentation
    B. Quarantine
    C. Firewall rule
    D. Playbook
8. Your company has merged with another company, and it uses a different release of accounting software than your company does. How could you provision user machines in accounting so they will not inadvertently run the incorrect version?
    A. Application allowlisting
    B. Isolation

C. Configurations associated with the application

D. Application block listing

9. You wish to keep people from using the internal mobile network to play games on their personal phones. What would be the best method of managing this?

A. MDM

B. Application block list

C. Content filter

D. Segmentation

10. What is the primary purpose of a SOAR solution?

A. To collect and aggregate diverse security data

B. To analyze data for anomalies and to create alerts

C. To produce approved, detailed response plans with respect to given incident response scenarios

D. To manage configuration changes on systems

Answers

1. **D.** Facebook is accessed via a browser, so you would need to install content filtering.
2. **B.** A certificate error is typically caused by a configuration error associated with the certificate.
3. **B.** The wording "system-focused" points to a runbook. A playbook is business process focused.
4. **D.** The certificate has likely been revoked or removed from that user's identity and no longer marked valid by the certificate authority. This is a configuration error.
5. **A.** Strict application allow listing will limit what runs on the system to only those applications authorized.
6. **D.** Playbooks focus on communication team responses in the form of business-focused elements as opposed to technical machine elements.
7. **B.** Because the item is an object, quarantine applies. Other methods of isolation belong to networks and systems.
8. **D.** Application block listing the application by version number will prevent specific versions from being executed on selected machines.
9. **A.** Forcing users to install an MDM solution before connecting their phone to the internal network resolves many security issues, including access control issues.
10. **C.** SOARs are known for producing runbooks and playbooks in response to specific conditions.

CHAPTER 30

Digital Forensics

In this chapter, you will

- Learn about the key aspects of digital forensics
- Understand the legal basis behind forensic processes
- Understand the steps of digital forensic processes

Computer forensics is certainly a popular buzzword in computer security. The term *forensics* relates to the application of scientific knowledge to legal problems. Specifically, computer forensics involves the preservation, identification, documentation, and interpretation of computer data. In many cases, digital forensics is the technical side of developing proof as to what happened or didn't happen as part of an incident response effort. Digital forensics specifically uses scientific principles to provide assurance in explaining what digital evidence tells you about what either has or hasn't happened with a computer system.

Certification Objective This chapter covers CompTIA Security+ exam objective 4.5: Explain the key aspects of digital forensics.

Documentation/Evidence

All evidence is not created equal. Some evidence is stronger and better than other, weaker evidence. Several types of evidence can be germane:

- **Direct evidence** Oral testimony that proves a specific fact (such as an eyewitness's statement). The knowledge of the facts is obtained through the five senses of the witness, with no inferences or presumptions.
- **Real evidence** Also known as associative or physical evidence, this includes tangible objects that prove or disprove a fact. Physical evidence links the suspect to the scene of a crime.
- **Documentary evidence** Evidence in the form of business records, printouts, manuals, and the like. Much of the evidence relating to computer crimes is documentary evidence.
- **Demonstrative evidence** Used to aid the jury and can be in the form of a model, experiment, chart, and so on, offered to prove that an event occurred.

A wide range of items can be considered documentation and evidence in an investigation. This chapter examines some of the common types one would run across in a forensics examination and the issues associated with each.

Legal Hold

In the U.S. legal system, legal precedent requires that potentially relevant information be preserved at the instant a party "reasonably anticipates" litigation or another type of formal dispute. Although this sounds technical, it is fairly easy to grasp: once an organization is aware that it needs to preserve evidence for a court case, it must do so. The mechanism is fairly simple as well: once you realize your organization needs to preserve evidence, you must use a *legal hold,* or litigation hold, which is the process by which you properly preserve any and all digital evidence related to a potential case. This event is usually triggered by one organization issuing a litigation hold request to another. Once an organization receives this notice, it is required to maintain a complete set of unaltered data, including metadata, of any and all information related to the issue causing the litigation hold. This means that ordinary data retention policies no longer are sufficient, and that even alterations to metadata can be considered to be a violation of the hold request. If a judge determines that a violation of a hold request may materially affect the ability of a jury to make a decision, the judge can instruct the jury to consider the act as hiding evidence. Major jury awards have been decided based on failure to retain information, as failure to comply can be seen as negligence.

Where does the information subject to a legal hold reside? Everywhere, including e-mail, office documents (electronic and paper), network shares, mobile phones, tablets, databases—everywhere the information is shared, all copies need to be produced unaltered, even if relevant documents were created years ago. Finding and managing all of this information falls under a branch of digital forensics called e-discovery, which deals with the identification, management, and preservation of digital information that is subject to legal hold. The time to prepare for a legal hold situation is before the event occurs because it will take time to create the necessary policies and procedures and make them effective via appropriate awareness training.

EXAM TIP Understanding the consequences of legal hold on record retention is testable, and legal holds supersede any standard corporate policy or procedure.

Video

A convenient method of capturing significant information at the time of collection is video capture. Videos allow high-bandwidth data collection that can show what was connected to what, how things were laid out, desktops, and so forth. A picture can be worth a thousand words, so take the time to document everything with pictures. Pictures of serial numbers and network and USB connections can prove invaluable later in the forensics process. Complete documentation is a must in every forensics process, and photographs can assist greatly in capturing details that would otherwise take a long time and be prone to transcription error.

Another source of video data is in the closed-circuit television (CCTV) cameras that are used for security, both in industry and, in growing numbers, homes. Like all other digital information, CCTV video can be copied and manipulated and needs to be preserved in the same manner as other digital information.

EXAM TIP A digital camera is great for recording a scene and information. Screenshots of active monitor images may be obtained as well. Pictures can detail elements such as serial number plates, machines, drives, cables connections, and more. A photograph is truly worth a thousand words.

Another aspect associated with videos in today's smartphone-dominated world, where millions of videos are captured every day and uploaded to social media sites like Twitter, Facebook, YouTube, and so on, is the legal ramifications of such evidence streams. Add the ability to do AI-generated deep fakes, and the need to validate these "evidence" sources has become a real thing in digital forensics.

Admissibility

For evidence to be credible, especially if it will be used in court proceedings or in corporate disciplinary actions that could be challenged legally, it must meet three standards:

- **Sufficient evidence** The evidence must be convincing or measure up without question.
- **Competent evidence** The evidence must be legally qualified and reliable.
- **Relevant evidence** The evidence must be material to the case or have a bearing on the matter at hand.

For materials to meet these standards for *admissibility*, it is incumbent that proper procedures are followed at all stages during collection, processing, and analysis. An item officially becomes evidence in a legal proceeding when a judge determines that it is admissible. Three rules guide a judge's determination of whether to admit an item into evidence:

- **Best evidence rule** Courts prefer original evidence rather than a copy, to ensure that no alteration of the evidence (whether intentional or unintentional) has occurred. In some instances, an evidence duplicate can be accepted, such as when the original is lost or destroyed by a natural disaster or in the normal course of business. A duplicate is also acceptable when a third party beyond the court's subpoena power possesses the original. Copies of digital records, where proof of integrity is provided, can in many cases be used in court.

NOTE Evidence rules exist at the federal and state levels and vary. Digital evidence is not always considered a "writing" and is not always subject to the best evidence rule.

- **Exclusionary rule** The Fourth Amendment to the U.S. Constitution precludes unreasonable search and seizure. Therefore, any evidence collected in violation of the Fourth Amendment is not admissible as evidence. Additionally, if evidence is collected in violation of the Electronic Communications Privacy Act (ECPA) or other related violations of the U.S. Code, or other statutes, it may not be admissible to a court. For example, if no policy exists regarding the company's intent to monitor network traffic or systems electronically, or if such a policy exists but employees have not been asked to acknowledge it by signing an agreement, sniffing employees' network traffic could be a violation of the ECPA.
- **Hearsay rule** Hearsay is secondhand evidence—evidence offered by the witness that is not based on the personal knowledge of the witness but is being offered to prove the truth of the matter asserted. Hearsay is inadmissible unless it falls under one of the many recognized exceptions (such as those delineated in FRE 803). Typically, computer-generated evidence is considered hearsay evidence, as the maker of the evidence (the computer) cannot be interrogated. Exceptions are being made where items such as logs and headers (computer-generated materials) are being accepted in court. Computer evidence is typically brought into a case by an expert witness who can speak for the data and what it means.

NOTE The laws mentioned here are U.S. laws. Other countries and jurisdictions may have similar laws that would need to be considered in a similar manner.

Chain of Custody

After evidence is collected, it must be properly controlled to prevent tampering. The chain of custody accounts for all persons who handled or had access to the evidence. More specifically, the *chain of custody* shows who obtained the evidence, when and where it was obtained, where it was stored, and who had control or possession of the evidence for the entire time since the evidence was obtained. Any and all access to the evidence is recorded.

The following are the critical steps in a chain of custody:

1. Record each item collected as evidence.
2. Record who collected the evidence along with the date and time it was collected or recorded.
3. Write a description of the evidence in the documentation.
4. Put the evidence in containers and tag the containers with the case number, the name of the person who collected it, and the date and time it was collected or put in the container.
5. Record all message digest (hash) values in the documentation.

6. Securely transport the evidence to a protected storage facility.
7. Obtain a signature from the person who accepts the evidence at this storage facility.
8. Provide controls to prevent access to and compromise of the evidence while it is being stored.
9. Securely transport the evidence to court for proceedings.

EXAM TIP Never analyze the seized evidence directly. The original evidence must be secured and protected with a chain of custody. It should never be subjected to a forensic examination because of the fragile nature of digital evidence. A forensic copy, however, can be examined and, if something goes wrong, discarded, and the copy process can be repeated. A good forensics process will prove that the forensic copy is identical to the original at the start and at the end of the examination. From a practical standpoint, investigators usually make multiple forensic copies and perform their analysis in parallel on the multiple copies.

Timelines of Sequence of Events

Digital forensic investigations begin with a scope, a charge of what is of interest to be investigated. In a modern computer environment, asking for everything that happened is a scope that is impossible to fulfill, for just booting up a machine can result in hundreds of events, in literally seconds. Once a scope is defined, it inevitably includes a time element, typically something in the order of the following: between a beginning date and time and ending date and time, for user XYZ, examine with respect to (insert whatever is of interest here, be it keywords, specific types of actions, and so on). With this information as boundaries, it is common to produce a *timeline of specific events* that fall within the scope and time boundaries. This timeline will have the specifics, including the metadata to document it, demonstrating the sequence of events as recorded by the computer. The sequence can be very important because it provides key clues as to what actually happened, even when there is not a direct artifact. For instance, if the first time a USB drive was attached is after a file was last touched, and metadata is available in the registry, then that file is probably not being transported on the USB. User logins and logoffs also help determine sequencing and operations. If a user is accused of doing transaction X on a network resource at a specific time and date, but their PC shows they were not logged in, then either they used another machine or there is something else happening, such as a hijacked account. Building a timeline of activities from multiple perspectives can provide a lot of useful information as to what did happen, what could have happened, and what makes no sense (more data is needed).

Timestamps

Timestamps are metadata entries associated with artifacts in a computer system. While a log entry may have a timestamp, some items can have multiple timestamps, stored in multiple locations. In NTFS, there are three common file times (Creation, Modification,

Accessed) and one metadata time (MFT Change). These four timestamps are stored in two places: one with the $File_Name attribute and one with $Standard_Info. And if that isn't enough confusion, the two different attributes are updated differently, meaning they may differ. This is important to forensic investigations because timestamps can be changed on systems, and this can lead to erroneous conclusions. Tampering with timestamps is challenging given that most tools do not handle all timestamps in the same way, which can lead to evidence of tampering.

Time is measured differently in Linux and Windows. Linux uses the concept of Epoch time—the number of seconds that have elapsed since January 1, 1970 (midnight UTC/GMT), not counting leap seconds. It is stored as a signed 32-bit number, enabling times before January 1, 1970, as well as after. The system clock has a resolution of a second, although there are timer elements that allow down to nanosecond timing measurements. Microsoft Windows uses a 64-bit value that represents the elapsed time since 12:00 A.M. January 1, 1601 Coordinated Universal Time (UTC), with a resolution of 100-nanosecond intervals. Note that both systems use UTC as a base, and most storage of time elements is done in UTC, with conversions to local time happening upon reading a value.

One of the challenges for all timestamp usage is inconsistency in the OS in keeping values up to date. While Microsoft Windows has a plethora of different timestamps to look at, there is great inconsistency on many of these values being updated by the OS or an application. The primary reason for this revolves around performance, as most timestamps are mere artifacts and are not important in many standard OS functions. Not maintaining the timestamps, or not maintaining all copies of timestamps, can improve performance of some operations.

Time Offset

Record *time offset* is the difference in time between the system clock and the actual time. Computers keep their own internal time, but to minimize record time offset, most computers sync their time over the Internet with an official time source. Files and events logged on a computer will have timestamp markings that are based on the clock time on the machine itself. It is a mistake to assume that this clock is accurate. To allow the correlation of timestamp data from records inside the computer with any external event, it is necessary to know any time offset between the machine clock and the actual time. When collecting forensic data it is vitally important to collect the record time offset so that local variations in time can be corrected.

Another form of time offset is the difference between local time zones and UTC. As discussed earlier, with most time records being in UTC, conversion to local time zones may be necessary to make sense of some records.

NOTE Whenever one is using time, whether timestamps, log times, or comparison to actual calendars, it is important to synchronize all records to the same offset. Many logs use local time. Comparing local time and UTC time will result in errors, except for the GMT time zone, where the local time is UTC. Know what your times are with respect to the zones before use.

EXAM TIP Understanding time elements for forensics is important. Pay attention to time zones and the specific details in the question.

Tags

As previously discussed, a chain-of-custody document records all accesses to evidence from time of collection until destruction. But how does one refer to a specific piece of evidence, especially if it is hardware containing data, such as a USB drive? This is done though tags. Physical serialized *tags* are attached to each item, and the tag number is used to identify a specific item. Frequently the items are then stored in anti-static bags to protect them from damage.

Reports

Reports are the official descriptions of the forensic data. Reports can have a variety of elements—from pure descriptive information, such as machine/device identifiers (make, model and serial number), to information on the data, including size and hash values. Reports can also have specific elements that are derived from this information, such as a timeline, an analysis of keywords, specific artifacts, and present or missing items. An expert can opine on what these elements mean or can mean with respect to the system. For instance, if timestamps are significantly different, the expert may note (opine) that the difference exists. From a professional perspective, it is important for the forensics investigator to stick to just what the information can show and not try to add commentary. For example, if the timestamp data has been tampered with, this is a provable fact. However, opining on who did it is more speculation and may result in the expert being called out on this in court. Experts who stray from the provable can be struck by the judge, and being stricken from a case is a black mark that will call into question one's opinions now and in the future. As such, reports tend to be very sanitized, and the lawyers add the color of the case later.

Event Logs

Ideally, you should minimize the scope of logging so that when you have to search logs, the event you are interested in stands out without being hidden in a sea of irrelevant log items. Before a problem occurs, if as part of the preparation phase the organization limits logging to specific events, such as copying sensitive files, then later, if questions arise as to whether the event happened or not, a log file exists to provide the information. When you have an idea of what information you will want to be able to examine, you can make an active logging plan that ensures the information is logged when it occurs, and if at all possible in a location that prevents alteration. *Active logging* is determined during preparation, and when it comes time for recovery, the advance planning pays off in the production of evidence. Strategic intelligence gathering, covered later in the chapter, can provide the information necessary to build an effective active logging plan.

Interviews

Remember that witness credibility is extremely important. It is easy to imagine how quickly credibility can be damaged if the witness can't answer affirmatively when asked, "Did you lock the file system?" Or, when asked, "When you imaged this disk drive, did you use a new system?", the witness can't answer that the destination disk was new or had been completely formatted using a low-level format before data was copied to it. Witness preparation can be critical in a case, even for technical experts.

As human memory is not as long lasting as computer files, it is important to get witness testimony and collect that data as early as possible. Having them write down what they remember immediately is very helpful in preserving memory.

EXAM TIP The different elements under documentation/evidence work together, not as separate entities. Be sure to understand what the question is specifically asking for when you choose the answer, as several answers may be connected to the correct one, but one will be the principal component.

Acquisition

Acquisition refers to the collection of information that may be evidence in an investigation. Evidence consists of the documents, verbal statements, and material objects admissible in a court of law. Evidence is critical to convincing management, juries, judges, or other authorities that a particular event has occurred. It is vitally important to document all the steps taken in the collection of evidence, as these may be challenged in court and the processes followed as evidenced by the documentation will be all that can be used to demonstrate the veracity of the processes. The steps involved in acquisition are important, as the consequences of the failure to follow proper procedures may not be immediately apparent and may not be repairable after the fact.

The collection, storage, and submission of evidence is challenging, but it is even more challenging when computers are used because the people involved may not be technically educated and thus may not fully understand what has happened. Keep these points in mind as you collect evidence:

- Who collected the evidence?
- How was it collected?
- Where was it collected?
- Who has had possession of it?
- How was it protected and stored?
- When was it removed from storage? Why? Who took possession?

Computer evidence presents yet more challenges, because the data itself cannot be identified with the physical senses—that is, you can see printed characters, but you can't see the bits where that data is stored. Bits of data are merely magnetic pulses on a disk or some other storage technology. Therefore, data must always be evaluated through some kind of "filter" rather than sensed directly. This is often of concern to auditors, because good auditing techniques recommend accessing the original data or a version as close as possible to the original data. What's more, any filtering, if necessary, should not change the meaning of the data.

Order of Volatility

There are many sources of data in a computer system, and if the machine is running, some of these sources are volatile. Items such as the state of the CPU and its registers, RAM, and even storage are always changing, which can make the collection of electronic data a difficult and delicate task. These elements tend to change at different rates, and you should pay attention to the *order of volatility*, or lifetime of the data, so that you can prioritize your collection efforts after a security incident to ensure you don't lose valuable forensic evidence. In some cases, you may have only one chance to collect volatile data, after which it becomes lost forever.

Following is the order of volatility of digital information in a system:

1. CPU, cache, and register contents (collect first)
2. Routing tables, ARP cache, process tables, kernel statistics
3. Live network connections and data flows
4. Memory (RAM)
5. Temporary file system/swap space
6. Data on hard disk
7. Remotely logged data
8. Data stored on archival media/backups (collect last)

EXAM TIP Understanding the order of volatility of digital information in a system is a testable item—commit it to memory.

Failure to pay attention to the order of volatility during data collection will result in data loss, and once lost, the data is gone forever in many of the categories.

EXAM TIP A common data element needed later in the forensics process is an accurate system time with respect to an accurate external time source. A record time offset is calculated by measuring system time with an external clock such as a Network Time Protocol (NTP) server. The offset between system time and true time can be lost if the system is powered down, so it is best to collect it while the system is still running.

Disk

When collecting digital evidence, it is important to use proper techniques and tools. Some of the key elements are the use of write blockers when making forensic copies, hashing and verifying hash matches, documenting handling and storage, and protecting media from environmental change factors. Of particular note is that the data present on a system can be a function of both the file system and the hardware being employed. A physical hard disk drive (HDD) will persist data longer than a solid state drive (SSD). And the newer file systems with journaling and shadow copies can have longer persistence of information than older systems such as File Allocation Table–based (FAT-based) systems. Raw disk blocks can be recovered in some file systems long after data has been rewritten or erased, due to the nature of how the file systems manage the data.

Random-Access Memory (RAM)

Random-access memory (RAM) is the working memory of the computer that handles the current data and programs being processed by the CPU. This memory, once limited to a single megabyte, now commonly consists of 4 GB or more. This memory holds the current state of the system as it is processing and is continuously changing. There are cases of malware that exists only in RAM, and without memory analysis and forensics, you would never see it. But this information is lost forever when the system is powered down.

Swap/Pagefile

The *swap* or *pagefile* is a structure on a system's disk to provide temporary storage for memory needs that exceed a system's RAM capacity. The operating system has provisions to manage the RAM and pagefile, keeping in RAM what is immediately needed and moving excess to the pagefile when RAM is full. This causes a performance hit, and with the reasonable cost of RAM, most systems avoid this by having sufficient RAM. Capturing the pagefile (pagefile.sys stored by default in C:\pagefile.sys) in a forensics investigation is important any time the RAM is captured, as it is an extension of the RAM.

Operating System (OS)

The *OS*, or operating system, is a base computer program that acts as the manager of all activity on a system. The OS is the source of many forensic artifacts, most of which are created to enhance system responsiveness to user requests. The two major OSs, Microsoft Windows and Linux, perform basically the same tasks: they enable applications to perform on a system. How they function, what artifacts are generated, all the technical details relevant to a forensics investigation, are different and thus require separate and specialized treatment with respect to the OS.

Device

One of the most common *device* acquisitions is USB storage devices. These devices are used to transport files between machines and are common in any case where the removal of information is suspected. A number of artifacts can be tied to USB device usage on a system, including when it was connected, link files and prefetch items on the drive, and who was logged in to the machine at the time of use.

Firmware

Firmware is a set of software that is associated with a physical device. Firmware exists for almost every electronic device, not just computers; for example, firmware exists for USB devices. Firmware can be of interest in a forensics investigation when the malfunctioning of a device is an issue, as malware has targeted the firmware. As such, it takes a very specialized set of tools and equipment to analyze the firmware, as it is not readily accessible to outside users.

Snapshot

A *snapshot,* as you can easily guess, is a picture of a particular moment in time. Snapshots are common in virtual machines, providing a point in time to which the machine can be recovered. Operating systems also have adopted this technology for some of their information, using point-in-time recovery to assist in fixing problems from updates or changes to the system. This capturing of points in time can be useful to a forensic investigator because it allows a means of looking at specific content at an earlier point in time. The scope of what is covered by a snapshot can vary between different systems, and this may limit usefulness.

Cache

Caches are temporary storage locations for commonly used items and are designed to speed up processing. Cashes exist all over in computer systems and are performance-enhancing items. Caches exist for files, for memory, for artifacts; they exist for fast retrieval of items that the OS expects. As such, they are inherently relevant to a specific activity that has been done and is likely to be done again and can serve as evidence of specific activities that have been done. An example of this would be an artifact such as a prefetch record of a file, indicating that the user that is logged in has previously opened that file.

Network

An important source of information in an investigation can be the network activity associated with a device. There can be a lot of useful information in the network logs associated with network infrastructure. The level and breadth of this information is determined by the scope of the investigation. While the best data would be from a live network forensic collection process, in most cases this type of data will not be available. There are many other sources of network forensic data, including firewall and IDS logs, network flow data, and event logs on key servers and services.

Artifacts

Artifacts are the key element in modern digital forensics. Most of the items used to demonstrate a specific action as occurring fall into one of two categories: metadata or

OS artifacts. Metadata examples include registry entries, timestamps, and sizes. OS artifacts include prefetch files, jump list artifacts such as most frequently used (MFU) and most recently used (MRU), shell bags, and link files. The metadata artifacts are items that the OS uses to perform its duties, while most of the OS artifacts are related to improving performance. Keeping a cache of links to the most recently used files will speed up activity if the user returns to previous work, which is a common task. Also, deletion of the work (a file) does not delete the associated artifacts. Hence, artifacts can live on after a file is gone, leaving proof that the file existed.

EXAM TIP Artifacts are the principal data element used in forensics. They are connected to how the computer manages data to perform a task. Be sure to choose the correct artifact that's specifically and directly related to the question, not peripherally.

On-premises vs. Cloud

The cloud has become a resource for enterprise IT systems, and as such it is intimately involved in both e-discovery and forensics. Having data that may or may not be directly accessed by the tools of e-discovery and forensics can complicate the needed processes. An additional complication is the legal issues associated with the contracts between the organization and the cloud provider. As both forensics and e-discovery are secondary processes from a business perspective, they may or may not be addressed in a standard cloud agreement. Because these processes can become important—and if they do, it may be too late to contractually address them—it behooves an organization to prepare by addressing them in cloud agreements with third parties.

The issues associated with *on-premises versus cloud* with respect to forensics is one dominated by access. When storage or computing is happening on another party's computing platform, as in the cloud, whether physically at another site or on premises, access is governed by the contracts and agreements covering the relationship.

Right to Audit Clauses

Audits are the mechanism used to verify that systems are performing to their designed levels of purpose, security, and efficiency. The ability to audit involves access to a system and the data. When the information is stored or processed in the cloud, users need the ability to audit the cloud provider. The level and scope of the audit can vary given the dynamic natures of both the cloud and the regulatory environment, but one thing does not vary. The only rights the customer has are detailed in the service level agreements/contracts with the cloud provider. This makes the *Right to Audit clause* a critical requirement of any service level agreement, and its specificity needs to match the operational and regulatory scope of the cloud engagement.

Regulatory/Jurisdiction

Whether on premises or in the cloud, there will be cases where regulatory or law enforcement actions raise jurisdictional issues. If you have your software development data in the cloud, and the servers/storage elements are in a foreign country, whose laws will apply? It is important to consult with the company's legal counsel to understand the ramifications of data location with respect to forensics and subsequent data use.

Data Breach Notification Laws

Data breach notification laws are covered in detail in Chapter 35, "Privacy," but are worthy of mention in our discussion of forensics because the discovery of a breach can occur during a forensic examination. Many forensic investigations are related to the theft of intellectual property, and many times that is also a breach of data protected under privacy laws.

Integrity

Integrity is a very important concept in security because it refers to the veracity of a data element. Has there been an unauthorized change to an element, or can one trust its current value? This works well as a concept, but how is this actually instantiated in a system? It is done through the use of cryptographic hashes, checksums, and data provenance. Managing these elements relies on other system functions, but if one can authenticate where a data element came from (provenance) and that it remains unchanged (hash value), then one can assume its integrity is intact.

Hashing

If files, logs, and other information are going to be captured and used for evidence, you need to ensure that the data isn't modified. In most cases, a tool that implements a hashing algorithm to create message digests is used.

A *hashing algorithm* performs a function similar to the familiar parity bits, checksum, or cyclic redundancy check (CRC). It applies mathematical operations to a data stream (or file) to calculate some number that is unique based on the information contained in the data stream (or file). If a subsequent hash created on the same data stream results in a different hash value, it usually means that the data stream was changed.

The mathematics behind hashing algorithms has been researched extensively, and although it is possible that two different data streams could produce the same message digest, it is very improbable. This is an area of cryptography that has been rigorously reviewed, and the mathematics behind Message Digest 5 (MD5) and Secure Hash Algorithm (SHA) is very sound. In 2005, weaknesses were discovered in the MD5 and SHA algorithms, leading the National Institute of Standards and Technology (NIST) to announce a competition to find a new cryptographic hashing algorithm, which was named SHA-3. SHA-3 has been adopted by NIST in 2015 and has a different internal structure from its predecessors, making it more robust. Although MD5 is still used, best practice would be to use the SHA-2 series, and SHA-3 once it becomes integrated into tools.

The hash tool is applied to each file or log and the message digest value is noted in the investigation documentation. It is a good practice to write the logs to a write-once media such as a CD-ROM. If the case actually goes to trial, the investigator may need to run the tool on the files or logs again to show that they have not been altered in any way.

NOTE The number of files stored on today's hard drives can be very large—literally hundreds of thousands of files. Obviously, this is far too many for the investigator to analyze. However, by matching the message digests for files installed by the most popular software products to the message digests of the files on the drive being analyzed, the investigator can avoid analyzing approximately 90 percent of the files because he can assume they are unmodified. The National Software Reference Library (NSRL) collects software from various sources and incorporates file profiles into a Reference Data Set (RDS) available for download as a service (see www.nsrl.nist.gov).

EXAM TIP Hashing is used throughout digital forensics to measure integrity between copies of data. Checksums do not have the specificity of hashes, so hashes are the primary tool.

Checksums

Checksums are mathematical algorithms that produce a check digit based on an incoming stream. Designed for error testing across small data sets, they have advantages and disadvantages. One advantage is that for error checking, they are fast and can detect a single-bit error. A disadvantage is that they miss larger numbers of errors as a second error can cancel the effect of the first on a checksum. Thus, checksums serve no real purpose in digital forensics. If two checksums are different, the incoming data streams are different. If the checksums are the same, you might still have different data streams.

Provenance

Provenance is a reference to the origin of data. In the case of digital forensics, it is not enough to present a specific data element as "proof"; one must also show where it came from. Provenance is specific, as in where on a file structure and where on a device; in most cases, there will be multiple representations, as in the file structure with respect to where a file resides and with respect to the OS (logical) and its location on a physical drive in sectors (physical). Provenance involves metadata, which can include timestamps, access control information, and a host of other data that can assist in determining which user did which action at what time with respect to the object. In most cases, there is not a single location for this evidence; like the timeline, it must be constructed from several different artifacts.

Preservation

When information or objects are presented to management or admitted to court to support a claim, that information or those objects can be considered as evidence or documentation supporting your investigative efforts. Senior management will always ask a lot of questions—second- and third-order questions that you need to be able to answer quickly. Likewise, in a court, credibility is critical. Therefore, evidence must be properly acquired, identified, protected against tampering, transported, and stored.

One of the key elements in preservation is to ensure nothing changes as a result of data collection. If a machine is off, do not turn it on—the disk drives can be imaged with the machine off. Turning on the machine causes a lot of processes to run and data elements to be changed. When making a forensic copy of a disk, always use a write blocker, as this prevents any changes on the media being imaged. Normal copying leaves traces and changes behind, and a write blocker prevents these alterations.

Digital evidence has one huge, glaring issue: it can change and not leave a record of the change. The fact that the outcome of a case can hinge on information that can be argued as not being static makes the act of preservation a crucial element in determining the veracity of evidence. From the initial step in the forensics process, the most important issue must always be *preservation* of the data. There is no recovery from data that has been changed, so from the beginning of the collection process, safeguards must be in place. There are several key steps that assist the forensic investigator in avoiding data spoilage. First, when data is collected, a solid chain of custody is maintained until the case is completed and the materials are released or destroyed. Second, when a forensic copy of the data is obtained, a hash is collected as well, to allow for the verification of integrity. All analysis is done on forensic copies of the original data collection, not the master copy itself. Also, each copy is verified before and after testing by comparing hash values to the original set to demonstrate integrity.

This process adds a lot of work, and time, to an investigation, but it yields one crucial element—repudiation of any claim that the data was changed, tampered, or damaged in any way. Should a hash value vary, the action is simple: discard the copy, make a new copy, and begin again. This process shows the courts two key things: process rigor to protect the integrity of the data, and traceability via hash values to demonstrate the integrity of the data and the analysis results derived from the data.

EXAM TIP Understanding not only the importance of data preservation but the process of ensuring it uses hash values is a very testable concept.

E-Discovery

Electronic discovery, or *e-discovery,* is the term used for the document and data production requirements as part of legal discovery in civil litigation. When a civil lawsuit is filed, under court approval, a firm can be compelled to turn over specific data from systems pursuant to the legal issue at hand. Electronic information is considered to be the same as paper documents in some respects and completely different in others. The evidentiary value can be identical. The fragility can be substantial—electronic records can be changed without leaving a trace. Electronic documents can also have metadata associated with the documents, such as who edited the document, previous version information, and more.

One of the pressing challenges in today's enterprise record store is the maintenance of the volumes of electronic information. Keeping track of the information stores based on a wide range of search terms is essential to comply with e-discovery requests. It is common for systems to use forensic processes and tools to perform e-discovery searches.

Data Recovery

Recovery in a digital forensics sense is associated with determining the relevant information for the issue at hand—simply stated, recover the evidence associated with an act. But what if the act is not precisely known? For example, suppose a sales manager for a company quits and goes to work with a competitor. Because she is a sales manager, she has had access to sensitive information that would benefit the new employer. But how do you know whether she took sensitive information with her? And even if she did, how do you determine for purposes of recovery which information she took, and where to look for it? Since forensics software has yet to invent a "Find Evidence" button, and there is no field in any computer protocol to tell investigators this is the data they are looking for, the act of recovering the necessary information can be a significant challenge. With today's multiterabyte drives, the volumes of data can be daunting.

Handing a forensic investigator a 1TB drive and saying, "Tell me everything that happened on this machine," is tantamount to giving the investigator a never-ending task. The number of events, files, and processes that occur as a normal part of computing leads to literally thousands of events for every logon–work–logoff cycle. This is not a problem of finding a needle in a haystack; it's a problem of finding a needle in the hay fields of Kansas! There are ways to trim the work: establishing timelines within which the suspected activity occurred; identifying keywords to find strings of information that make a record relevant; and, perhaps the most powerful for building a solid data set, pinpointing specific activities that have associated logs of their occurrence. The latter strategy is associated with the idea of active logging, discussed in the earlier "Event Logs" section.

Nonrepudiation

Nonrepudiation is a characteristic that refers to the inability to deny an action has taken place. This can be a very important issue in transactions via computers that involve money or things of value. Did the transaction occur and did the parties involved actually do it? These are the core questions of nonrepudiation. Using cryptographic elements to establish identity and credentials, along with hash values to establish integrity, the appropriate combinations can yield results that can only happen if the parties are actually involved and the event took place. Designing and creating systems that enable this characteristic are essential elements of trusted systems used in financial and other transactions. Similar details can be achieved via analysis of certain activity on systems combining successful logins and subsequent activity. The only question is whether or not the credentials are still secure. This can be a legitimate question because attackers steal credentials all the time and reuse them.

EXAM TIP Nonrepudiation is an important security concept. In fact, it is listed in two separate exam objectives. Remember, it refers to the inability to deny an action has taken place. Digital signatures, the use of multiple authentication factors, and even audit trails by IP address are examples of nonrepudiation and prove or disprove that something has happened.

Strategic Intelligence/Counterintelligence

Strategic intelligence gathering is the use of all resources to make determinations. This can make a large difference in whether or not a firm is prepared for threats. The same idea fits into digital forensics. Strategic intelligence can provide information that limits the scope of an investigation to a manageable level. If we have an idea of specific acts for which we would like to have demonstrable evidence of either occurrence or nonoccurrence, we can build a strategic intelligence data set on the information. Where it is, what it is, and what is allowed/not allowed are all pieces of information that, when arranged and analyzed, can lead to a data-logging plan to help support forensic event capture. Other events, such as adding data-wiping programs and then removing them, are important to consider. The list of possibilities is long, but just like strategic threat intelligence, it is manageable, and by working in concert with other firms and professionals, and not in isolation, a meaningful plan can emerge.

Counterintelligence gathering is the gathering of information specifically targeting the strategic intelligence effort of another entity. Knowing what people are looking at and what information they are obtaining can provide information into their motives and potential future actions. Making and using a tool so that it does not leave specific traces of where, when, or on what it was used is a form of counterintelligence gathering in action.

Chapter Review

In this chapter, you became acquainted with the principles of digital forensics. The chapter opened with a discussion of documentation and evidence. In this section, the topics of legal hold, video, admissibility, and chain of custody were covered. Timeliness of events, with timestamps and time offsets, were presented as tools used in analysis. This section concluded with tags and reports, followed by event logs and interviews.

The next major section covered the acquisition of data. The first topic, order of volatility, was followed by the memory elements of disks, RAM, and swap/pagefiles. The section continued with a discussion of operating systems, devices, and firmware. The section concluded with snapshots, cache, networks, and artifacts.

An examination of on-premises versus cloud followed, examining the specifics of Right to Audit clauses, regulatory/jurisdiction issues, and data breach notification laws. Next was integrity, with a discussion of the methods of hashing, checksums, and the issue of provenance.

The chapter concluded by covering preservation, e-discovery, data recovery, nonrepudiation, and strategic intelligence/counterintelligence.

Questions

To help you prepare further for the CompTIA Security+ exam, and to test your level of preparedness, answer the following questions and then check your answers against the correct answers at the end of the chapter.

1. Volatile information locations such as the RAM change constantly, and data collection should occur in the order of volatility or lifetime of the data. Order the following list from most volatile (which should be collected first) to least volatile.
   - **A.** Routing tables, ARP cache, process tables, kernel statistics
   - **B.** Memory (RAM)
   - **C.** CPU, cache, and register contents
   - **D.** Temporary file system/swap space
2. A common data element needed later in the forensics process is an accurate system time with respect to an accurate external time source. A record time offset is calculated by measuring system time with an external clock such as a Network Time Protocol (NTP) server. Which of the following must be considered relative to obtaining a record time offset?
   - **A.** The record time offset can be lost if the system is powered down, so it is best collected while the system is still running.
   - **B.** The internal clock may not be recorded to the same level of accuracy, so conversions may be necessary.
   - **C.** External clock times may vary as much as 2 to 3 seconds, so it is best to obtain the time from several NTP servers to gain a more accurate reading.
   - **D.** Recording time to track man-hours is a legal requirement.
3. What is the term used to describe the process that accounts for all persons who handled or had access to a piece of evidence?
   - **A.** Secure e-discovery
   - **B.** Chain of custody
   - **C.** Evidence accountability process
   - **D.** Evidence custodianship

4. Which standard of evidence states the evidence must be convincing or measure up without question?
   - **A.** Direct evidence
   - **B.** Competent evidence
   - **C.** Relevant evidence
   - **D.** Sufficient evidence
5. A judge has issued an order for all e-mail to be preserved and that order is in effect. Which of the following statements is correct?
   - **A.** You can delete old e-mail after the standard retention period.
   - **B.** You should have the legal department determine which records must be saved.
   - **C.** You should continue archiving all e-mail.
   - **D.** You can delete the e-mail after making a copy to save for e-discovery.
6. Which type of evidence is also known as associative or physical evidence and includes tangible objects that prove or disprove a fact?
   - **A.** Direct evidence
   - **B.** Real evidence
   - **C.** Documentary evidence
   - **D.** Demonstrative evidence
7. You have been tasked with assisting in the forensic investigation of an incident relating to employee misconduct. The employee's supervisor believes evidence of this misconduct can be found on the employee's assigned workstation. Which of the following choices *best* describes what should be done?
   - **A.** Create a timeline of events related to the scope.
   - **B.** Copy the user profile to reduce the search space.
   - **C.** Sign in as the user and search through their recent efforts.
   - **D.** Examine log file entries under the user's profile.
8. Which of the following would a capture video *not* be used to collect?
   - **A.** Serial number plates
   - **B.** Cable connections
   - **C.** System image
   - **D.** Physical layout and existence of systems

9. Which of the following performs a function similar to the familiar parity bits, checksum, or cyclic redundancy check?
   A. Record offset
   B. Cryptographic algorithm
   C. Authentication code
   D. Hashing algorithm
10. From the initial step in the forensics process, the most important issue must always be which of the following?
   A. Preservation of the data
   B. Chain of custody
   C. Documenting all actions taken
   D. Witness preparation

Answers

1. **C, A, B,** and **D.** The most volatile elements should be examined and collected first and in this order.
2. **A.** Record time offset will be lost if the system is powered down, so it is best collected while the system is still running.
3. **B.** The chain of custody accounts for all persons who handled or had access to the evidence.
4. **D.** *Sufficient evidence* states the evidence must be convincing or measure up without question. *Direct evidence* is oral testimony that proves a specific fact (such as an eyewitness's statement). The knowledge of the facts is obtained through the five senses of the witness, with no inferences or presumptions. *Competent evidence* states the evidence must be legally qualified and reliable. *Relevant evidence* states the evidence must be material to the case or have a bearing on the matter at hand.
5. **C.** You should continue archiving all e-mail. You must continue to comply with the court order. Letting legal make determinations when the order specifies "all e-mail" is a mistake. Making copies of the e-mail is only legit if you make forensically secure copies, not just backups.
6. **B.** *Real evidence* is also known as associative or physical evidence and includes tangible objects that prove or disprove a fact. Physical evidence links the suspect to the scene of a crime. *Direct evidence* is oral testimony that proves a specific fact (such as an eyewitness's statement). The knowledge of the facts is obtained through the five senses of the witness, with no inferences or presumptions. Evidence in the form of business records, printouts, manuals, and similar objects, which make up much of the evidence relating to computer crimes, is *documentary evidence*. *Demonstrative evidence* is used to aid the jury and can be in the form of a model, experiment, chart, and so on, offered to prove that an event occurred.

7. **A.** The scope defines the boundaries of the investigation, and the timeline shows what a user did within that scope period with respect to items of interest.
8. **C.** A system image is a dump of the physical memory of a computer system and would not be captured in a video. All of the others are static sources of information that a capture video is valuable in recording.
9. **D.** A hashing algorithm performs a function similar to the familiar parity bits, checksum, or cyclic redundancy check (CRC). It applies mathematical operations to a data stream (or file) to calculate some number that is unique based on the information contained in the data stream (or file).
10. **A.** While all of these are important, from the initial step in the forensics process, the most important issue must always be preservation of the data.

PART V

Governance, Risk, and Compliance

CHAPTER 31

Security Controls

In this chapter, you will

- Learn about the three categories of security controls
- Explore different types of security controls

Security controls are the tools used to reduce risk in the enterprise. There are many different types of security controls, and this chapter looks at the different categories and types to provide a means of understanding and classifying controls.

Certification Objective This chapter covers CompTIA Security+ exam objective 5.1: Compare and contrast various types of controls.

Security Controls

Security controls are the mechanisms employed to minimize exposure to risk and mitigate the effects of loss. Using the security attributes of confidentiality, integrity, and availability (CIA) associated with data, it is incumbent upon the security team to determine the appropriate set of controls to achieve the security objectives.

Controls can be of a variety of types, as described in this chapter. The different categories of controls do not act as a taxonomy, as there are overlapping descriptions and some controls' categories are passed down from third-party policies and procedures.

NOTE The National Institute of Standards and Technology (NIST) provides a catalog of controls in its NIST SP 800-53 series. The current revision, revision 5, lists over 600 controls grouped into 18 functional categories. The 18 functional categories are grouped under three major categories: Management, Technical, and Operational. Although the vast majority of these controls are associated with the electronic security of information, many of them extend into the physical world as well.

EXAM TIP The types of security controls are commonly tested on the exam—memorization is recommended.

Categories

Three categories of security controls are specified in a variety of defining documents, and these categories have become the de facto standard for the cybersecurity industry. The use of *categories* separates the controls into separate groups based on what the control uses as its lever: managerial activity, operational activity, or technical control. Each of these is described in the following sections. For some controls, it is possible that they have aspects that span more than one category.

Managerial

Managerial controls are those that are based on overall risk management. These security controls focus on the management of risk or the management of the cybersecurity system. The use of cybersecurity audits is an example of a managerial control. Table 31-1 lists the managerial controls.

NOTE The NIST SP 800 series refers to managerial controls as *management* controls.

Operational

An *operational* control is a policy or procedure used to limit security risk. These security controls are primarily implemented and executed by people, as opposed to systems. Instructions to guards are an example of an operational control. Table 13-2 lists the operational controls.

Technical

A *technical* control uses some form of technology to address a physical security issue. These security controls are primarily implemented and executed by the information system through mechanisms contained in its hardware, software, or firmware components. Biometrics is an example of a technical control. Table 31-3 lists the technical controls.

EXAM TIP The main difference between operational and technical controls is that operational controls are those that people initiate and follow, whereas technical controls are typically automated and involve a machine to execute.

Table 31-1 Managerial Controls

NIST Control Family	Identifier
Risk Assessment	RA
Planning	PL
System and Services Acquisition	SA
Certification, Accreditation, and Security Assessments	CA

Table 31-2 Operational Controls

NIST Control Family	Identifier
Personnel Security	PS
Physical and Environmental Protection	PE
Contingency Planning	CP
Configuration Management	CM
Maintenance	MA
System and Information Integrity	SI
Media Protection	MP
Incident Response	IR
Awareness and Training	AT

Table 31-3 Technical Controls

NIST Control Family	Identifier
Identification and Authentication	IA
Access Control	AC
Audit and Accountability	AU
System and Communications Protection	SC

Control Types

Controls can also be categorized by *control type*. The cybersecurity industry recognizes several different control types, and while these categories can be descriptive, they are not a taxonomy because they are not necessarily exclusive. Controls can fit into multiple types, depending on deployment and use. A door lock is an example of both a physical control and a preventative control.

Preventative

A *preventative control* is one that prevents specific actions from occurring, such as a mantrap prevents tailgating. Preventative controls act before an event, preventing it from advancing. A firewall is an example of a preventative control, as it can block access to a specific resource.

EXAM TIP The key element in passing Exam Objective 5.1 is the ability to compare and contrast various types of controls. How are they alike (compare) and how are they different (contrast)? Understanding the differences can be subtle. For instance, do laws with punishment, if enforced, prevent attacks? Laws may deter attackers, but they do not prevent them from attacking if the deterrent doesn't dissuade them from deciding to attack.

Detective

A *detective control* is one that facilitates the detection of a physical security breach. Detective controls act during an event, alerting operators to specific conditions. Alarms are common examples of detective controls. An IDS is an example of an IT security alarm that detects intrusions.

Corrective

A *corrective control* is used after an event, in an effort to minimize the extent of damage. Load balancers and redundant systems act to reduce the risk from system overloading and are thus corrective controls. Backups are a prime example of a corrective control, as they can facilitate rapid resumption of operations.

Deterrent

A *deterrent control* acts to discourage the attacker by reducing the likelihood of success from the perspective of the attacker. Any control that increases the cost to an attacker is a deterrent control. An example would be laws and regulations that increase punishment, increasing risk and costs for the attacker. Another example would be the use of salts for password hashes to increase the cost of building rainbow tables.

Compensating

A *compensating control* is one that is used to meet a requirement when there is no control available to directly address the threat. Fire suppression systems do not prevent fire damage, but if properly employed, they can mitigate or limit the level of damage from fire.

EXAM TIP The previous five types of controls tend to be exclusive of each other—they describe the point of interaction of the control with the attacker's tools, techniques, and processes.

Physical

A *physical control* is one that prevents specific physical actions from occurring, such as a mantrap prevents tailgating. Physical controls prevent specific human interaction with a system and are primarily designed to prevent accidental operation of something. Physical controls act before an event, preventing it from actually occurring. The use of covers over critical buttons is one example, as is a big red "STOP" button, positioned so it is easily reachable. The former stops inadvertent activation, while the latter facilitates easy activation in an emergency. For further information, Chapter 15, "Physical Security," has a section devoted to physical security controls.

EXAM TIP Physical controls are separate from the previous descriptors and can be used independently of them. It is possible to have a control that is a technical, physical, and preventative control (for example, a door lock).

Chapter Review

In this chapter, you became acquainted with the different categories and types of security controls. Security controls are divided into three categories: managerial, operational, and technical. Security controls can also be categorized by the type of control. The different types of controls covered in the chapter are preventative, detective, corrective, deterrent, compensating, and physical.

EXAM TIP Look for the word *category* or *type* in the question. Categories are managerial, operational, and technical. Types are preventative, detective, corrective, deterrent, compensating, and physical.

Questions

To help you prepare further for the CompTIA Security+ exam, and to test your level of preparedness, answer the following questions and then check your answers against the correct answers at the end of the chapter.

1. Which type of security control is used after the event, in an effort to minimize the extent of damage?
   - **A.** Deterrent
   - **B.** Corrective
   - **C.** Preventative
   - **D.** Detective
2. Which type of security control is used to meet a requirement when the requirement cannot be directly met?
   - **A.** Preventative
   - **B.** Physical
   - **C.** Deterrent
   - **D.** Compensating
3. The use of a penetration test to determine vulnerabilities is an example of what category of control?
   - **A.** Operational
   - **B.** External
   - **C.** Managerial
   - **D.** Technical

4. The use of combination locks as a security control procedure to limit physical security risk is an example of what category of control?
   A. Physical
   B. Technical
   C. Operational
   D. Corrective
5. A mantrap is an example of which type security control? (Choose all that apply.)
   A. Physical
   B. Corrective
   C. Administrative
   D. Preventative
6. Which of the following is *not* a category of security controls?
   A. People
   B. Managerial
   C. Technical
   D. Operational
7. Which category of control is most likely to be automated?
   A. Corrective
   B. Technical
   C. Operational
   D. Compensating
8. There is no direct way to detect and respond to a specific threat. What is the best control type to employ for this case?
   A. Technical
   B. Corrective
   C. Preventative
   D. Compensating
9. An intrusion detection system is an example of what control type?
   A. Detective
   B. Technical
   C. Compensating
   D. Operational

10. Which of the following is the fastest category of control when responding to a known threat?
    A. Operational
    B. Technical
    C. Administrative
    D. Managerial

Answers

1. **B.** Corrective controls are used after the event, in an effort to minimize the extent of damage. A deterrent control acts to influence the attacker by reducing the likelihood of success. A preventative control is one that prevents specific actions from occurring. A detective control is one that facilitates the detection of a security breach.
2. **D.** A compensating control is one that is used to meet a requirement when the requirement cannot be directly met. Fire suppression systems do not prevent fire damage, but if properly employed, they can mitigate or limit the level of damage from fire. A preventative control is one that prevents specific actions from occurring. A physical control is one that prevents specific physical actions from occurring, such as a mantrap prevents tailgating. A deterrent control acts to influence the attacker by reducing the likelihood of success.
3. **C.** A penetration test is a form of risk assessment and thus is a managerial action, as it advises management of the current risk posture associated with a system.
4. **C.** An operational control is a policy or procedure used to limit security risk. The key word in the question is *category.*
5. **A** and **D.** It is possible for a specific security control to fall into more than one type. Because a mantrap is a physical barrier that prevents tailgating, it is both a physical control and a preventative control. Corrective controls are used after the event, in an effort to minimize the extent of damage. An administrative control is simply a distractor.
6. **A.** People is not a defined category of security control. Security controls that function through people's actions are called operational controls.
7. **B.** Technical controls are the most likely to be automated, as they are machine based.
8. **D.** Compensating controls are used when there is no direct way to address a risk.
9. **A.** The key word in the question is *type,* making detective the correct answer. If the question asked for the category, the correct answer would be technical.
10. **B.** Technical controls can be automated and can thus be the fastest to respond to an incident.

CHAPTER 32

Regulations, Standards, and Frameworks

In this chapter, you will

- Examine applicable regulations, standards, and legislation for security
- Explore key frameworks employed in security
- Learn about important security-related benchmarks and secure configuration guides

Developing the correct set of policies, procedures, and operations to achieve a desired level of organizational security is a complex set of tasks with many interdependencies. To assist organizations with developing and deploying these plans are numerous applicable regulations, standards, and frameworks that can impact organizational security posture. This chapter explores these information sources and examines how they can be employed.

Certification Objective This chapter covers CompTIA Security+ exam objective 5.2: Explain the importance of applicable regulations, standards, or frameworks that impact organizational security posture.

Regulations, Standards, and Legislation

Business operations never happen in a vacuum; there are at least some policies and procedures one must follow. But these policies and procedures get their direction from regulations, standards, and legislation. Laws are made by the legislative bodies of government to create a specified set of conditions and penalties. Government agencies develop and issue regulations to implement the laws. Standards are sets of consensus-built specifications for products, services, or systems. A wide range of different bodies create standards, and whether or not one wishes to follow them is a business decision. Laws and regulations must be followed; otherwise, the consequences specified within them can be invoked by the government.

General Data Protection Regulation (GDPR)

The *General Data Protection Regulation (GDPR)*, which was a sweeping rewrite of European privacy regulations, went into effect in May of 2018. The GDPR ushers in a brand-new world with respect to data protection and privacy. With global trade being important to all countries, and the fact that trade rests upon information transfers, including those of personal data, the ability to transfer data, including personal data, between parties becomes important to trade. Enshrined in the Charter of Fundamental Rights of the European Union (EU) is the fundamental right to the protection of personal data, including when such data elements are transferred outside the EU. Recognizing that, the new set of regulations is more expansive and restrictive, making the Safe Harbor provisions obsolete. For all firms that wish to trade with the EU, there is now a set of privacy regulations that will require specific programs to address the requirements.

The GDPR brings many changes—one being the appointment of a Data Protection Officer (DPO). This role may be filled by an employee or a third-party service provider (for example, a consulting or law firm), and it must be a direct report to the highest management level. The DPO should operate with significant independence, and provisions in the GDPR restrict control over the DPO by management.

GDPR

The GDPR requires significant consideration, including the following:

- Assess personal data flows from the EU to the U.S. to define the scale and scope of the cross-border privacy-compliance challenge.
- Assess readiness to meet model clauses, remediate gaps, and organize audit artifacts of compliance with the clauses.
- Update privacy programs to ensure they are capable of passing an EU regulator audit.
- Conduct EU data-breach notification stress tests.
- Monitor changes in EU support for model contracts and binding corporate rules.

The GDPR specifies requirements regarding consent, and they are significantly more robust than previous regulations. Consent requirements are also delineated for specific circumstances:

- Informed/affirmative consent to data processing. Specifically, "a statement or a clear affirmative action" from the data subject must be "freely given, specific, informed and unambiguous."
- Explicit consent to process special categories of data. Explicit consent is required for "special categories" of data, such as genetic data, biometric data, and data concerning sexual orientation.

- Explicit parental consent for children's personal data.
- Consent must be specific to each data-processing operation, and the data subject can withdraw consent at any time.

The GDPR provides protections for new individual rights, and these may force firms to adopt new policies to address these requirements. The rights include the Right to Information, Right to Access, Right to Rectification, Right to Restrict Processing, Right to Object, Right to Erasure, and Right to Data Portability. Each of these rights is clearly defined with technical specifics in the GDPR. The GDPR also recognizes the risks of international data transfer to other parties and has added specific requirements that data protection issues be addressed by means of appropriate safeguards, including Binding Corporate Rules (BCRs), Model Contract Clauses (MCCs), also known as Standard Contractual Clauses (SCCs), and legally binding documents. These instruments must be enforceable between public authorities or bodies, as well as all who handle data.

EXAM TIP Remember that the General Data Protection Regulation (GDPR) specifies requirements for collecting personal information in the European Union (EU).

National, Territory, or State Laws

Laws are the system of rules, or statutes, made by the government of a country, state, or city. Statutes are enacted by a legislative body and then signed by the ranking official (president/governor). With respect to cybersecurity, there are a wide variety of laws from the national and state levels. With the advent of global network connections and the rise of the Internet as a method of connecting computers between homes, businesses, and governments across the globe, a new type of criminal trespass can now be committed. Computer trespass is the unauthorized entry into a computer system via any means, including remote network connections. These crimes have introduced a new area of law that has both national and international consequences. For crimes that are committed within a country's borders, national laws apply. For cross-border crimes, international laws and international treaties are the norm. Computer-based trespass can occur even if countries do not share a physical border.

Computer trespass is treated as a crime in many countries. National laws against computer trespass exist in countries such as Canada, the United States, and the member states of the European Union (EU). These laws vary by country, but they all have similar provisions defining the unauthorized entry into and use of computer resources for criminal activities. Whether called computer mischief, as in Canada, or computer trespass, as in the United States, unauthorized entry and use of computer resources is treated as a crime with significant punishments. With the globalization of the computer network infrastructure, or Internet, issues that cross national boundaries have arisen and will continue to grow in prominence. Some of these issues are dealt with through the application of national laws upon request of another government. In the future, an international treaty may pave the way for closer cooperation.

There are laws that govern conduct such as hacking, making most actions that are unauthorized on networks a criminal act. The Electronic Communications Privacy Act (ECPA) of 1986 addresses a myriad of legal privacy issues that resulted from the increasing use of computers and other technology specific to telecommunications. Sections of this law address e-mail, cellular communications, workplace privacy, and a host of other issues related to communicating electronically. Section I was designed to modify federal wiretap statutes to include electronic communications. Section II, known as the Stored Communications Act (SCA), was designed to establish criminal sanctions for unauthorized access to stored electronic records and communications. Section III covers pen registers and tap and trace issues. Tap and trace information is related to who is communicating with whom, and when. Pen register data is the conversation information.

A major provision of ECPA was the prohibition against an employer's monitoring an employee's computer usage, including e-mail, unless consent is obtained (for example, clicking Yes on a warning banner is considered consent). Other legal provisions protect electronic communications from wiretap and outside eavesdropping, as users are assumed to have a reasonable expectation of privacy and afforded protection under the Fourth Amendment to the Constitution. It is of note that these constitutional protections only apply to searches and seizures by U.S. government agencies and law enforcement (federal, state, or local jurisdiction), but do not apply to private individuals or employers.

The Computer Fraud and Abuse Act (CFAA) of 1986—amended in 1994 and 1996, in 2001 by the USA PATRIOT Act, and in 2008 by the Identity Theft Enforcement and Restitution Act—serves as the current foundation for criminalizing unauthorized access to computer systems. CFAA makes it a crime to knowingly access a computer that is either considered a government computer or used in interstate commerce, or to use a computer in a crime that is interstate in nature, which in today's Internet-connected age can be almost any machine. The act also makes it a crime to knowingly transmit a program, code, or command that results in damage. Trafficking in passwords or similar access information is also criminalized.

In the wake of several high-profile corporate accounting/financial scandals in the United States, the federal government in 2002 passed sweeping legislation, the Sarbanes-Oxley Act (SOX), overhauling the financial accounting standards for publicly traded firms in the United States. These changes were comprehensive, touching most aspects of business in one way or another. With respect to information security, one of the most prominent changes was the provision of Section 404 controls, which specify that all processes associated with the financial reporting of a firm must be controlled and audited on a regular basis. Since the majority of firms use computerized systems, this places internal auditors into the IT shops, verifying that the systems have adequate controls to ensure the integrity and accuracy of financial reporting. These controls have resulted in controversy over the cost of maintaining them versus the risk of not using them.

Section 404 requires firms to establish a control-based framework designed to detect or prevent fraud that would result in misstatement of financials. In simple terms, these controls should detect insider activity that would defraud the firm. This has significant impacts on the internal security controls, because a system administrator with root-level access could perform many if not all tasks associated with fraud and would have the ability to alter logs and cover their tracks. Likewise, certain levels of power users of financial accounting programs would also have significant capability to alter records.

There are a myriad of additional laws covering things such as privacy, digital signatures, medical records, and spam. Additional laws and regulations exist at the state level, and some of the most important are those coming from California. California, home to the U.S. tech industry, is also a progressive state when it comes to legislation. California led the way with respect to privacy laws and event security of Internet of Things (IoT) devices.

California Senate Bill 1386 (SB 1386) was a landmark law concerning information disclosures. It mandates that Californians be notified whenever PII is lost or disclosed. Since the passage of SB 1386, numerous other states have modeled legislation on this bill, and although national legislation has been blocked by political procedural moves, it will eventually be passed. The current list of U.S. states and territories that require disclosure notices is up to 49, with only Alabama, New Mexico, and South Dakota without bills. Each of these disclosure notice laws is different, making the case for a unifying federal statute compelling, but currently it is low on the priority lists of most politicians.

California extended its privacy laws with the California Consumer Privacy Act in 2020. This act requires organizations to obtain consent from individuals to collect and use their data. It also requires them to disclose how the data is used. It grants consumers the right to request that a business disclose the categories and specific pieces of information it collects, the sources of that information, the reasons why the business collects and/or sells that information, and the categories of the third parties that info is shared with. In many ways, this act mirrors the EU's GDPR.

Payment Card Industry Data Security Standard (PCI DSS)

The payment card industry, including the powerhouses of MasterCard and Visa, through its PCI Security Standards Council, designed a private sector initiative to protect payment card information between banks and merchants. The *Payment Card Industry Data Security Standard (PCI DSS)* is a set of contractual rules governing how credit card data is to be protected (see the sidebar "PCI DSS Objectives and Requirements"). The current version is 3.2, which was released in April 2016. The next version, 4.0, was expected in late 2020, but has been delayed due to the worldwide COVID-19 pandemic. PCI DSS is a voluntary, private sector initiative that is proscriptive in its security guidance. Merchants and vendors can choose not to adopt these measures, but the standard has a steep price for noncompliance; the transaction fee for noncompliant vendors can be significantly higher, fines up to $500,000 can be levied, and in extreme cases the ability to process credit cards can be revoked.

PCI DSS Objectives and Requirements

PCI DSS v3 includes six control objectives containing a total of 12 requirements:

1. Build and Maintain a Secure Network

   Requirement 1 Install and maintain a firewall configuration to protect cardholder data.

   Requirement 2 Do not use vendor-supplied defaults for system passwords and other security parameters.

2. Protect Cardholder Data

   Requirement 3 Protect stored cardholder data.

   Requirement 4 Encrypt transmission of cardholder data across open, public networks.

3. Maintain a Vulnerability Management Program

   Requirement 5 Protect all systems against malware and regularly update antivirus software or programs.

   Requirement 6 Develop and maintain secure systems and applications.

4. Implement Strong Access Control Measures

   Requirement 7 Restrict access to cardholder data by business need-to-know.

   Requirement 8 Identify and authenticate access to system components.

   Requirement 9 Restrict physical access to cardholder data.

5. Regularly Monitor and Test Networks

   Requirement 10 Track and monitor all access to network resources and cardholder data.

   Requirement 11 Regularly test security systems and processes.

6. Maintain an Information Security Policy

   Requirement 12 Maintain a policy that addresses information security for all personnel.

PCI DSS has two defined types of information: cardholder data and sensitive authentication data. The protection requirements established for these elements are detailed in Table 32-1.

EXAM TIP The Payment Card Industry Data Security Standard (PCI DSS) protects customer credit card information and is designed to reduce fraud. The contractual standard has a steep financial penalty for noncompliance.

		Data Element	Storage Permitted	Render Stored Data Unreadable
Account Data	**Cardholder Data**	Primary Account Number (PAN)	Yes	Yes
		Cardholder Name	Yes	No
		Service Code	Yes	No
		Expiration Date	Yes	No
	Sensitive Authentication Data	Full Track Data	No	Cannot store per Requirement 3.2
		CAV2 / CVC2 / CVV2 / CID	No	Cannot store per Requirement 3.2
		PIN / PIN Block	No	Cannot store per Requirement 3.2

Table 32-1 PCI DSS Data Retention Guidelines

Key Frameworks

Frameworks provide a means of assessing the path through the maze of regulatory requirements and how they relate to risk management. One of the challenging aspects of cybersecurity operations is determining where one should concentrate efforts, how resources should be deployed, and what balance of emphasis to place between short-term and long-term items to optimize efforts on risk mitigation. Several types of key frameworks can be used as part of this analysis. In the following sections, we will look at frameworks from the Center for Internet Security, the National Institute of Standards and Technology, several ISO standards, SSAE standards, and the Cloud Security Alliance.

Center for Internet Security (CIS)

The *Center for Internet Security (CIS)* is a nonprofit organization that serves the cybersecurity community in a number of ways. It is the guardian of the CIS controls—a set of the top 20 security controls that should be implemented as a baseline of cybersecurity risk management. This set of controls, developed in a consensus manner over the past decade, provides a roadmap of which security controls should be implemented first, second, and so on. These prescriptive items represent the best practices across a wide range of entities, from government to industry, and are implementable by virtually any size entity.

The CIS has also published a set of CIS benchmarks (see www.cisecurity.org/cis-benchmarks/). These benchmarks are consensus-developed, secure configuration guidelines for hardening a wide range of technical items.

National Institute of Standards and Technology (NIST) Risk Management Framework (RMF)/Cybersecurity Framework (CSF)

The National Institute of Standards and Technology (NIST) provides recommended strategies to the U.S. government and others on how to handle a wide range of issues, including risk from cybersecurity issues. The approach taken by NIST is one built around the management of organizational risk through a *risk management framework (RMF)* associated with cybersecurity activities. The NIST RMF is composed of more than 10 publications, spanning virtually every activity associated with cybersecurity.

A second activity published by NIST is the *Cybersecurity Framework (CSF)*. The CSF is designed to assist organizations in the early stages of planning their cybersecurity posture. It breaks down the types of activities into five different functions: identify, protect, detect, respond, and recover. The CSF was mandated by a congressional bill in 2014 that directed NIST to identify "a prioritized, flexible, repeatable, performance based, and cost-effective approach, including information security measures and controls that may be voluntarily adopted by owners and operators of critical infrastructure to help them identify, assess, and manage cyber risks." The latest version of the CSF was published in March of 2020.

The third leg of NIST efforts in cybersecurity documentation is the National Initiative for Cybersecurity Education (NICE) Cybersecurity Workforce Framework. This is an effort to define the ecosystem of cybersecurity education, training, and workforce development needed to create the workforce needed in cybersecurity in government and in industry.

International Organization for Standardization (ISO) 27001/27002/27701/31000

ISO 27001 is the international standard defining an information security management system (ISMS). ISO 27001 is one of many related standards in the 27000 family. ISO 27002 is a document that defines security techniques and a code of practice for information security controls. ISO 27701 is a privacy extension to the 27000 series and adds the requirements to establish and maintain a privacy information management system. The ISO 31000 series is a set of guidelines, principles, framework, and process for managing risk. ISO 31000 addresses all forms of risk and management, not just cybersecurity risk.

SSAE SOC 2 Type I/II

Statement on Standards for Attestation Engagements (SSAE) is a set of auditing standards set by the American Institute of Certified Public Accountants (AICPA) Auditing Standards Board. SOC stands for Service Organization Controls. An SOC 2 report focuses on the internal controls at an organization related to compliance or operations, wrapped around the five trust principles (security, confidentiality, processing integrity, availability, and privacy). Depending on your organization and your business, some or all five of the trust principles would be in scope. The SOC 2 is a separate report that focuses on controls at a service provider relevant to security, availability, processing integrity, confidentiality, and privacy of a system. It ensures that your data is kept private and secure while in storage and in transit and that it is available for you to access at any time. The SOC 1 and SOC 2 reports come in two forms: Type I and Type II. Type I reports evaluate whether proper controls are in place at a specific point in time. Type II reports are done over a period of time to verify operational efficiency and effectiveness of the controls.

EXAM TIP SSAE SOC 2 reports focus on internal controls related to compliance or operations. A SOC Type I report evaluates whether proper controls are in place at a specific point in time. A SOC Type II report is done over a period of time to verify operational efficiency and effectiveness of the controls.

Cloud Security Alliance

Born in 2008 and incorporated in 2009, the Cloud Security Alliance issued the first comprehensive best-practice document for secure cloud computing, "Security Guidance for Critical Areas of Focus for Cloud Computing," and has become the industry body for frameworks, benchmarks, and standards associated with cloud computing worldwide. Some of the key documents developed include the Cloud Controls Matrix (CCM), the user credential Certificate of Cloud Security Knowledge (CCSK), the Certified Cloud Security Professional (CCSP) credential (developed jointly with ISC2), and a security framework for government clouds.

Cloud Controls Matrix

The Cloud Controls Matrix (CCM) is a meta-framework of cloud-specific security controls, mapped to leading standards, best practices, and regulations. This document uses 16 domains to cover 133 security control objectives to address all key aspects of cloud security. The controls listed in this document are mapped to the main industry security standards, including ISO 2700X series, NIST SP 800-53, PCI DSS, ISACA COBIT, and many others.

An example of a CCM control is provided in Table 32-2.

Reference Architecture

The Cloud Security Alliance has an Enterprise Architecture Working Group (EAWG) that has developed the Enterprise Architecture for cloud deployments and services. This framework serves as both a methodology and a set of tools that can be utilized by security

Control Domain	CCM v3.0 Control ID	Control Specification
Encryption & Key Management Sensitive Data Protection	EKM-03	Policies and procedures shall be established, and supporting business processes and technical measures implemented, for the use of encryption protocols for protection of sensitive data in storage (e.g., file servers, databases, and end-user workstations), data in use (memory), and data in transmission (e.g., system interfaces, over public networks, and electronic messaging) as per applicable legal, statutory, and regulatory compliance obligations.

Table 32-2 A Sample Control from CCM v3.0

architects, enterprise architects, and risk management professionals. The objective of the framework is to develop and leverage a common set of solutions that enable the assessment of where internal IT operations and their cloud providers are in terms of security capabilities. The framework can also be used to plan a roadmap to meet the cloud security needs of the enterprise.

EXAM TIP Be prepared to identify Cloud Security Alliance items by their acronyms and understand the difference between them. The Enterprise Architecture (EA) is a broad framework describing all aspects, while the Cloud Controls Matrix (CCM) is a list of security controls for the cloud.

Benchmarks and Secure Configuration Guides

Benchmarks and *secure configuration guides* offer guidance for setting up and operating computer systems to a secure level that is understood and documented. As each organization may differ, the standard for a benchmark is a consensus-based set of knowledge designed to deliver a reasonable set of security across as wide a base as possible. There are numerous sources for these guides, but three main sources exist for a large number of these systems. You can get benchmark guides from manufacturers of the software, from the government, and from an independent organization such as the Center for Internet Security (CIS) and the Cloud Security Alliance (CSA). Not all systems have benchmarks, nor do all sources cover all systems, but searching for and following the correct configuration and setup directives can go a long way in establishing security.

EXAM TIP Organizations often refer to Center for Internet Security (CIS) benchmarks to develop secure configuration postures.

The vendor/manufacturer guidance source is easy—go to the website of the vendor of your product. The government sources are a bit more scattered, but two solid sources are the NIST Computer Security Resource Center's National Vulnerability Database (NVD) and the National Checklist Program (NCP) Repository (https://nvd.nist.gov/ncp/repository). A different source is the U.S. Department of Defense's Defense Information Security Agency (DISA) Security Technical Implementation Guides (STIGs). These are detailed step-by-step implementation guides, a list of which is available at https://public.cyber.mil/stigs/.

Platform/Vendor-Specific Guides

Setting up secure services is important to enterprises, and some of the best guidance comes from the manufacturer in the form of *platform/vendor-specific guides*. These guides include installation and configuration guidance, and in some cases operational guidance as well.

Web Server

Many different web servers are used in enterprises, but the market leaders are Microsoft, Apache, and Nginx. By definition, *web servers* offer a connection between users (clients) and web pages (data being provided), and as such they are prone to attacks. Setting up any external-facing application properly is key to preventing unnecessary risk. Fortunately, for web servers, several authoritative and proscriptive sources of information are available to help administrators properly secure the application. In the case of Microsoft's IIS and SharePoint Server, the company provides solid guidance on the proper configuration of the servers. The Apache Software Foundation provides some information for its web server products as well.

Another good source of information is from the Center for Internet Security, as part of its benchmarking guides. The CIS guides provide authoritative, proscriptive guidance developed as part of a consensus effort among consultants, professionals, and others. This guidance has been subject to significant peer review and has withstood the test of time. CIS guides are available for multiple versions of Apache, Microsoft, and other vendors' products.

OS

The *operating system (OS)* is the interface for the applications that we use to perform tasks and the actual physical computer hardware. As such, the OS is a key component for the secure operation of a system. Comprehensive, proscriptive configuration guides for all major operating systems are available from their respective manufacturers, from the Center for Internet Security and from the DoD DISA STIGs program.

Application Server

Application servers are the part of the enterprise that handles specific tasks we associate with IT systems. Whether it is an e-mail server, a database server, a messaging platform, or any other server, an application server is where the work happens. Proper configuration of an application server depends to a great degree on the server specifics. Standard application servers, such as e-mail and database servers, have guidance from the manufacturer, CIS, and STIGs. The less standard servers—ones with significant customizations, such as a custom set of applications written in-house for your inventory control operations, or order processing, or any other custom middleware—also require proper configuration, but the true vendor in these cases is the in-house builders of the software. Ensuring proper security settings and testing of these servers should be part of the build program so that they can be integrated into the normal security audit process to ensure continued proper configuration.

Network Infrastructure Devices

Network infrastructure devices are the switches, routers, concentrators, firewalls, and other specialty devices that make the network function smoothly. Properly configuring these devices can be challenging but is very important because failures at this level can adversely affect the security of traffic being processed by them. The criticality of these devices makes them targets because, if a firewall fails, in many cases there are no indications until an investigation finds that it failed to do its job. Ensuring these devices are properly configured and maintained is not a job to gloss over, but one that requires professional attention by properly trained personnel and backed by routine configuration audits to ensure they stay properly configured. With respect to most of these devices, the greatest risk lies in the user configuration of the device via rulesets, and these are specific to each user and cannot be mandated by a manufacturer's installation guide. Proper configuration and verification are site specific and, many times, individual device specific. Without a solid set of policies and procedures to ensure this work is properly performed, these devices, while they may work, will not perform in a secure manner.

Chapter Review

In this chapter, you first became acquainted with the applicable regulations, standards, and frameworks that can impact organizational security posture. The chapter opened with an examination of regulations, standards, and legislation. Under this category, the EU's General Data Protection Regulation (GDPR) was covered as well as several national, state, and territorial laws. The first section concluded with the Payment Card Industry Data Security Standard (PCI DSS).

The next major section covered key frameworks that are employed in the enterprise. The frameworks discussed were from the Center for Internet Security (CIS), the National Institute of Standards and Technology Risk Management Framework (RMF)/Cybersecurity Framework (CSF), the International Organization for Standardization (ISO 27001/27002/27701/31000), SSAE SOC Type I/II, and the Cloud Security Alliance (cloud controls matrix and reference architecture).

The chapter wrapped up with an examination of the different types of benchmarks and secure configuration guides. In this section, platform- and vendor-specific guides were presented, including those for web servers, operating systems, application servers, and network infrastructure devices.

Questions

To help you prepare further for the CompTIA Security+ exam, and to test your level of preparedness, answer the following questions and then check your answers against the correct answers at the end of the chapter.

1. Industry-standard frameworks are primarily useful for which of the following purposes?
   A. Aligning with an audit-based standard
   B. Aligning IT and security with the enterprise's business strategy
   C. Providing high-level organization over processes
   D. Creating diagrams to document system architectures

2. Which of the following terms is a privacy regulation?
   A. CFAA
   B. SOX
   C. GDPR
   D. PCI DSS
3. Which of the following are security control lists that can be employed in an enterprise? (Choose all that apply.)
   A. ISO 27001
   B. CSA CCM
   C. CIS top 20 list
   D. NIST RMF
4. Which reports are done over a period of time to verify operational efficiency and effectiveness of controls?
   A. SOC Type I
   B. PCI DSS audit report
   C. CSA CCM
   D. SOC Type II
5. Which of the following is *not* a PCI DSS control objective?
   A. Build and maintain a secure network
   B. Maintain a vulnerability management program
   C. Establish a CSO position
   D. Implement strong access control measures
6. Which ISO standard covers risk management activities?
   A. ISO 27001
   B. ISO 27701
   C. ISO 27002
   D. ISO 31000
7. Guidance for setting up and operating computer systems to a secure level that is understood and documented can be obtained from which of the following? (Choose all that apply.)
   A. ISO
   B. CIS
   C. Government sources
   D. Vendors/manufacturers

8. Which of the following are *not* U.S. laws associated with cybersecurity? (Choose all that apply.)
    A. CFAA
    B. PCI DSS
    C. GDPR
    D. Sarbanes Oxley (SOX)
9. Where would one look for consensus-developed, secure configuration guidelines for hardening a wide range of technical items?
    A. CIS
    B. ISO
    C. Vendors/manufacturers
    D. Peers
10. Comprehensive, proscriptive configuration guides for all major operating systems are available from which of the following? (Choose all that apply.)
    A. Vendors/manufacturers
    B. NIST
    C. CIS
    D. ISO

Answers

1. **B.** Industry-standard frameworks provide a method to align IT and security with the enterprise's business strategy.
2. **C.** GDPR is the EU privacy directive with far-reaching consequences across industries and even country boundaries.
3. **B** and **C.** The Cloud Security Alliance Cloud Controls Matrix is a list of security controls associated with cloud deployments. The CIS top 20 list is an ordered set of security controls for the enterprise. Both ISO 27001 and NIST RMF are procedural documents, not listings of controls.
4. **D.** SOC Type II reports are done over a period of time to verify operational efficiency and effectiveness of controls. SOC Type I reports, on the other hand, evaluate whether proper controls are in place at a specific point in time.
5. **C.** PCI DSS control objectives include:
    1. Build and maintain a secure network
    2. Protect cardholder data
    3. Maintain a vulnerability management program
    4. Implement strong access control measures

5. Regularly monitor and test networks
6. Maintain an information security policy

Nowhere does it mandate specific corporate positions.

6. **D.** ISO 31000 covers risk management processes and procedures.
7. **B, C,** and **D.** Benchmarks and secure configuration guides offer guidance for setting up and operating computer systems to a secure level that is understood and documented. There are numerous sources for these guides, but three main sources exist for a large number of these systems. You can get benchmark guides from manufacturers of the software, from the government, and from an independent organization such as the Center for Internet Security (CIS) or the Cloud Security Alliance (CSA). ISO is a standards organization and does not deal with specific implementation details.
8. **B** and **C.** PCI DSS is a voluntary, contractual-based standard, and GDPR is an EU directive, not a U.S. law.
9. **A.** The key word is *consensus.* CIS has developed a consensus-based set of secure configuration guidelines for hardening a wide range of technical items.
10. **A** and **C.** Vendors/manufacturers and the Center for Internet Security both offer comprehensive configuration guides for operating systems. Another source is the Department of Defense STIG program. NIST and ISO develop guidance for policies and processes, but not specific configurations for operating systems.

CHAPTER 33

Organizational Policies

In this chapter, you will

- Explore policies used to manage organizational security
- Examine processes used in risk management of third parties

Policies and procedures govern the operation of the organization and represent a set of requirements developed from both internal and external sources. External requirements may come from laws and regulations, contractual terms, or customer specifications. There are regulatory situations where specific business actions are required by law or regulation. In many cases, the laws or regulations specify that specific policies are in place to govern compliance. Understanding the specific requirements of the business environment may require assistance from supporting business functions, guidance from industry groups, or help from other sources. Determining the relevant security policies and procedures that apply to third-party relationships is a key endeavor in ensuring that all elements of them are met during business operations. The bottom line is simple: in some business situations, policies and procedures may be mandated by outside regulation, and assistance may be required in ensuring compliance.

Certification Objective This chapter covers CompTIA Security+ exam objective 5.3: Explain the importance of policies to organizational security.

Personnel

A significant portion of human-created security problems results from poor security practices. These poor practices may be those of an individual user who is not following established security policies or processes, or they may be caused by a lack of security policies, procedures, or training within the user's organization. Through the establishment, enforcement, and monitoring of personnel-related policies—*personnel management*—an organization can create a framework that empowers its workers to achieve business objects yet keeps them constrained within recommended security practices. This section covers a dozen security topics related to the management of personnel.

Acceptable Use Policy

An *acceptable use policy (AUP)* outlines what the organization considers to be the appropriate use of its resources, such as computer systems, e-mail, Internet, and networks. Organizations should be concerned about any personal use of organizational assets that does not benefit the company.

The goal of the policy is to ensure employee productivity while limiting potential organizational liability resulting from inappropriate use of the organization's assets. The policy should clearly delineate what activities are not allowed. The AUP should address issues such as the use of resources to conduct personal business, installation of hardware or software, remote access to systems and networks, the copying of company-owned software, and the responsibility of users to protect company assets, including data, software, and hardware. Statements regarding possible penalties for ignoring any of the policies (such as termination) should also be included.

Related to appropriate use of the organization's computer systems and networks by employees is the appropriate use by the organization. The most important of such issues is whether the organization will consider it appropriate to monitor the employees' use of the systems and network. If monitoring is considered appropriate, the organization should include a statement to this effect in the banner that appears at login. This repeatedly warns employees, and possible intruders, that their actions are subject to monitoring and that any misuse of the system will not be tolerated. Should the organization need to use in either a civil or criminal case any information gathered during monitoring, the issue of whether the employee had an expectation of privacy, or whether it was even legal for the organization to be monitoring, is simplified if the organization can point to its repeatedly displayed statement that use of the system constitutes consent to monitoring. Before any monitoring is conducted, or the actual wording on the warning message is created, the organization's legal counsel should be consulted to determine the appropriate way to address this issue.

AUPs are important enough that they are typically presented to employees during onboarding, with refreshers on an annual basis. AUPs are the basis for employee behavior with systems, and the details need to be refreshed for people to be able to adhere to them.

EXAM TIP Make sure you understand that an acceptable use policy outlines what is considered acceptable behavior for a computer system's users. This policy often goes hand-in-hand with an organization's Internet usage policy.

Job Rotation

Another policy that provides multiple benefits is *job rotation*. Rotating through jobs provides individuals with a better perspective of how the various parts of the organization can enhance (or hinder) the business. Since security is often of secondary concern to people in their jobs, rotating individuals through security positions can result in a much wider understanding of the organization's security problems. A secondary benefit is that it also eliminates the need to rely on one individual for security expertise. If all security tasks are the domain of one employee, security will suffer if that individual leaves the organization. In addition, if only one individual understands the security domain, should that person become disgruntled and decide to harm the organization, recovering from their attack could be very difficult.

EXAM TIP Rotating users between roles helps to ensure that fraudulent activity cannot be sustained and improves security awareness across various roles in an organization

Mandatory Vacation

Organizations have been providing vacation time for their employees for many years. Until recently, however, few organizations forced employees to take this time if they didn't want to. Some employees are given the choice to either "use or lose" their vacation time, and if they do not take all of their time, they'll lose at least a portion of it. Many arguments can be made as to the benefit of taking time off, but more importantly, from a security standpoint, an employee who never takes time off is a potential indicator of nefarious activity. Employees who never take any vacation time could be involved in activity such as fraud or embezzlement and might be afraid that if they leave on vacation, the organization would discover their illicit activities. As a result, requiring employees to use their vacation time through a policy of *mandatory vacation* can be a security protection mechanism. Using mandatory vacation as a tool to detect fraud will require that somebody else also be trained in the functions of the employee who is on vacation. Having a second person familiar with security procedures is also a good policy in case something happens to the primary person.

Separation of Duties

Separation of duties is a principle employed in many organizations to ensure that no single individual has the ability to conduct transactions alone. This means that the level of trust in any one individual is lessened, and the ability for any individual to cause catastrophic damage to the organization is also lessened. An example might be an organization in which one person has the ability to order equipment, but another individual makes the payment. An individual who wants to make an unauthorized purchase for their own personal gain would have to convince another person to go along with the transaction.

Separating duties as a security tool is a good practice, but it is possible to go overboard and break up transactions into too many pieces or require too much oversight. This results in inefficiency and can actually be less secure, since individuals may not scrutinize transactions as thoroughly because they know others will also be reviewing them. The temptation is to hurry something along and assume that somebody else will examine it or has examined it.

EXAM TIP Another aspect of the separation of duties principle is that it spreads responsibilities out over an organization so no single individual becomes the indispensable individual with all of the "keys to the kingdom" or unique knowledge about how to make everything work. If enough tasks have been distributed, assigning a primary and a backup person for each task will ensure that the loss of any one individual will not have a disastrous impact on the organization.

Least Privilege

One of the most fundamental principles in security is *least privilege,* which means that an object (which may be a user, application, or process) should have only the rights and privileges necessary to perform its task, with no additional permissions. Limiting privileges limits the amount of harm the object can cause, thus limiting the organization's exposure to damage. Users should only have access to the information and systems necessary to perform their job duties. Enforcing the principle of least privilege helps an organization protect its most sensitive resources and helps ensure that whoever is interacting with these resources has a valid reason to do so.

EXAM TIP The principle of least privilege states that users should only have a level of access permissions required to perform their job.

Clean Desk Space

Preventing access to information is also important in the work area. Firms with sensitive information should have a *clean desk* policy specifying that sensitive information must not be left unsecured in the work area when the worker is not present to act as custodian. Even leaving the desk area and going to the bathroom can leave information exposed and subject to compromise. The clean desk policy should identify and prohibit things that are not obvious upon first glance, such as passwords on sticky notes under keyboards and mouse pads or in unsecured desk drawers.

Background Checks

Personnel are key to security in the enterprise. Hiring good personnel has always been a challenge in the technical field, but it is equally important to hire trustworthy people, especially in key roles that have greater system access. Performing routine *background checks* provides the HR team the necessary information needed to make the correct decisions. Background checks can validate previous employment, criminal backgrounds, financial background, and even social media behavior. Depending on the industry, firm, and position, different elements from these areas may be included.

NOTE It is commonly heard that hiring a talented security hacker requires accepting someone with a shady past. The veracity of that comment aside, the real question to ask is not "Would I hire this person?" but rather "Would I be afraid of firing them?"

Nondisclosure Agreement (NDA)

Nondisclosure agreements (NDAs) are standard corporate documents used to explain the boundaries of company secret material, information over which control should be exercised to prevent disclosure to unauthorized parties. NDAs are frequently used to delineate the level and type of information, and with whom it can be shared. NDAs can be executed between any two parties where one party wishes that the material being shared is not further shared, enforcing confidentiality via contract.

EXAM TIP Nondisclosure agreements are legally binding documents. Signed NDAs are often required by employers during the onboarding process to ensure employees are aware of privacy and confidentiality concerning company data.

Social Media Analysis

The rise of *social media networks and applications* has changed many aspects of business. Whether used for marketing, communications, customer relations, or some other purpose, social media networks can be considered a form of third party. One of the challenges in working with social media networks and/or applications is their terms of use. While a relationship with a typical third party involves a negotiated set of agreements with respect to requirements, there is no negotiation with social media networks. The only option is to adopt their terms of service, so it is important to understand the implications of these terms with respect to the business use of the social network.

The use of social media sites by employees at work brings in additional risks, in the form of viruses, worms, and spear phishing data collection. In years past, employers worried about employees using the machines at work to shop on eBay or surf the Web rather than work. Today, the risks are increased beyond just lost time to now include malware introduction to work machines. It is common for firms to use AUPs to restrict employee personal use of things like social media, peer-to-peer (P2P) networking, BitTorrent, and other non-work-related applications.

Onboarding

A key element when *onboarding* personnel is to ensure that the personnel are aware of and understand their responsibilities with respect to securing company information and assets. Agreements with business partners tend to be fairly specific with respect to terms associated with mutual expectations associated with the process of the business.

Ensuring the correct security elements are covered during onboarding is essential to setting proper employee expectations. These considerations need to be made prior to the establishment of the relationship, not added at the time that it is coming to an end.

EXAM TIP Onboarding policy should include provisions for the handling of data, the disposal of data, acceptable use, and any sanctions that may occur as a result of misuse.

Offboarding

Offboarding refers to the processes and procedures used when an employee leaves an organization. From a security perspective, the offboarding process for personnel is very important. Employee termination needs to be modified to include termination or disablement of all accounts, including those enabled on mobile devices. It's not uncommon to find terminated employees with accounts or even company devices still connecting to the corporate network months after being terminated. E-mail accounts should be removed promptly as part of the employee termination policy and process. Mobile devices supplied by the company should be collected upon termination. Bring-your-own-device (BYOD) equipment should have its access to corporate resources terminated as part of the offboarding process. Regular audits for old or unterminated accounts should be performed to ensure prompt deletion or disablement of accounts for terminated employees. Exit interviews can be powerful tools for gathering information when people leave an organization.

EXAM TIP Onboarding and offboarding business procedures should be well documented to ensure compliance with legal requirements.

User Training

User training is important to ensure that users are aware of and are following appropriate policies and procedures as part of their workplace activities. As in all personnel-related training, two elements need attention. First, retraining over time is necessary to ensure that personnel keep proper levels of knowledge. Second, as people change jobs, a reassessment of the required training basis is needed, and additional training may be required. Maintaining accurate training records of personnel is the only way this can be managed in any significant enterprise.

Gamification

Gamification is the use of games to facilitate user training. This methodology has several interesting advantages. First, it makes rote learning of training material less boring. Second, it enables a more comprehensive situation-based approach to training, with consequences of bad decisions being shared with those taking the training. Third, it allows for group training by using people's job functions in a manner that facilitates both learning and auditing of the policies and procedures in a non-threatening environment.

Capture the Flag

A *capture-the-flag* event is hands-on computer skill training where a user is tested to see if they can perform specific actions. Should they perform the actions correctly, they will uncover a flag that shows they have completed the test successfully. Many hacking competitions are variations of capture-the-flag events.

Phishing Campaigns

Phishing campaigns are a series of connected phishing attacks against an organization. Since phishing is an operational method of social engineering, the greater the level of institutional, organizational, and personal knowledge one possesses about their target, the greater the chance of success. Phishing campaigns use this common knowledge to increase their odds, rather than just randomly attacking targets. This is why internal communications concerning phishing attempts are important, to alert other users that the system may be under attack and that a heightened sense of awareness towards this form of attack is warranted.

Phishing Simulations

To help users learn and identify phishing attacks, there are methods of running *phishing simulations* against users. A phishing attempt is sent to a user, and should they fall prey to it, the system notifies the user that this was only a drill and that they should be more cautious. This also creates a teachable moment where the user can receive training detailing exactly why they should have spotted the phishing attempt.

Computer-Based Training (CBT)

Computer-based training (CBT) is the use of a computer program to manage training of users. Self-paced modules can facilitate skill development across a wide range of skills, and the flexibility of CBT is very attractive. Not all learners learn well under these circumstances, but for those who do, CBT provides a very affordable, scalable training methodology.

Role-Based Training

For training to be effective, it needs to be targeted to the user with regard to their role in the subject of the training. While all employees may need general security awareness training, they also need specific *role-based awareness training* in areas where they have individual responsibilities. Role-based training with regard to information security responsibilities is an important part of information security training.

If a person has job responsibilities that may impact information security, then role-specific training is needed to ensure that the individual understands the responsibilities as they relate to information security. Some roles, such as system administrator or developer, have clearly defined information security responsibilities. The roles of others, such as project manager or purchasing manager, have information security impacts that are less obvious, but these roles require training as well. In fact, the less-obvious but wider-impact roles of middle management can have a large effect on the information security culture, and thus if a specific outcome is desired, it requires training.

EXAM TIP Be sure you are familiar with the various user training methods and how they play a role in organizational security.

Diversity of Training Techniques

Not all learners learn in the same fashion; some people learn by seeing, some people learn better by hearing. Almost everyone learns better by doing, but in some areas, doing a task is not practical or feasible. The bottom line is that there is a wide range of methods of training, and for the best results it is important to match the training methods to the material for the best outcome. In the previous section, several different training methods were covered, including gamification, capture-the-flag exercises, and simulations. There are even more methods to round out a wide diversity of training solutions, including in-person lectures, online content, and practice-based skill development. The key is to match the material to the method and to the learners, and then test outcomes to ensure successful training has been achieved.

Third-Party Risk Management

Every business will have third parties associated with their business operations. Whether these third parties are vendors, suppliers, or business partners, they bring the opportunity for both risk and reward. *Third-party risk management* is a fairly straightforward process. The first step is to recognize that risks are present. You need to inventory and assess these risks and then develop the mitigations necessary to keep them in an acceptable range. The important concept is that risk does not magically vanish because a third party is involved; it still needs to be managed like all other business risks.

Vendors

Vendors are firms or individuals that supply materials or services to a business. These items are purchased as part of a business process and represent some form of a value proposition for the firm purchasing them. But with the value can also come risk. For instance, if an item has embedded code to make it operate, what if the embedded code has vulnerabilities? What if an item that is purchased for a specific purpose fails to meet its specifications? There's a wide range of risks that can be introduced by vendors, and these need to be examined and handled in accordance with standard risk management processes.

Supply Chain

A *supply chain* is a set of firms that operate together to manage the movement of goods and services between firms. If you order a part from a foreign supplier that will become part of your product being manufactured in another country, how do all the parts get to the right place for assembly, at the right time? Supply chains handle the details that make all of this happen. From transportation, to customs and other regulations, to managing schedules, these are all details that are necessary for items to go from one place to another.

If a firm only has a single supplier, then this process is fairly simple. However, having multiple suppliers of multiple parts at different stages of your value chain that must work together is where supply chains matter. The pandemic of 2020 illustrated this clearly, as countries closed borders, firms had difficulty operating, factories closed due to sick workers and stay-at-home orders—and none of this was uniform or occurred during the same time period. Global supply chain disruptions caused follow-on effects, where expected parts were delayed because unrelated parts elsewhere were delayed, thus interrupting different supply chains. The need to understand and manage the risks of supply chain functions and their true costs became very evident. It became clear that with extensive supply chain management, lower costs could be achieved, but at the risk of failure when the supply chain had issues.

Business Partners

Business partners are entities that share a relationship with a firm in their business pursuits. Business partners can be enrolled in a business effort for multiple reasons: to share risk, share liability, share costs, leverage specialty expertise, and more. The key to understanding and navigating business partners with respect to cybersecurity and risk is to ensure that the risks and responsibilities on both partners are understood and agreed to before the risk event occurs. With every partnership comes risk and reward; the key is in understanding the level of each and making business decisions with a clear understanding of these elements.

Service Level Agreement (SLA)

A *service level agreement (SLA)* is a negotiated agreement between parties detailing the expectations between a customer and a service provider. SLAs essentially set the requisite level of performance of a given contractual service. SLAs are typically included as part of a service contract and set the level of technical expectations. An SLA can define specific services, the performance level associated with a service, issue management and resolution, and so on. SLAs are negotiated between customer and supplier and represent the agreed-upon terms. Specific security requirements can be specified in an SLA and enforced once both parties agree. Once entered into, the SLA becomes a legally binding document.

Memorandum of Understanding (MOU)

A *memorandum of understanding (MOU)* and memorandum of agreement (MOA) are legal documents used to describe a bilateral agreement between parties. They are written agreements that express a set of intended actions between the parties with respect to some common pursuit or goal. Typically, an MOU has higher-level descriptions, whereas an MOA is more specific; however, the boundary between these two legal terms is blurry and they are often used interchangeably. Both are more formal and detailed than a simple handshake, but they generally lack the binding powers of a contract. MOUs/MOAs are also commonly used between different units within an organization to detail expectations associated with the common business interest, including security requirements.

Measurement Systems Analysis (MSA)

Many security risk management processes rely on measuring things or events. Measurements and measurement systems have to be calibrated to ensure they are evaluating the actual object of interest. *Measurement systems analysis (MSA)* is a field of study that examines measurement systems for accuracy and precision. Before an enterprise relies on measurement systems, it is important to understand whether the chosen measurement system is acceptable for its intended use, to understand the different sources of variation present in it and to identify and understand sources of bias, errors, and factors associated with repeatability and reproducibility. Performing a measurement systems analysis on the measurement systems employed in a security system is the structured process to get to that information and have confidence in the measures developed and used from the system.

Business Partnership Agreement (BPA)

A *business partnership agreement (BPA)* is a legal agreement between partners that establishes the terms, conditions, and expectations of the relationship between the partners. These details can cover a wide range of issues, including typical items such as the sharing of profits and losses, the responsibilities of each partner, the addition or removal of partners, and any other issues. The Uniform Partnership Act (UPA), established by state law and convention, lays out a uniform set of rules associated with partnerships to resolve any partnership terms. The terms in a UPA are designed as "one size fits all" and are not typically in the best interest of any specific partnership. To avoid undesired outcomes that may result from UPA terms, it is best for partnerships to spell out specifics in a BPA.

EXAM TIP Be sure you understand the differences between the interoperability agreements SLA, BPA, and MOU/MOA for the CompTIA Security+ exam. All of them can be used to communicate security requirements between parties, but each is specific as to when it should be used. Look at usage for hints as to which would apply.

End of Life (EOL)

End of Life (EOL) or end of support is when the manufacturer quits selling an item. In most cases, the manufacturer no longer provides maintenance services or updates. In some cases, this date is announced to be a future date, after which support ends. When something enters the EOL phase, it is at the end of its lifecycle and upgrade/replacement needs to be planned and executed. When a product enters EOL phase, security patches may or may not be still produced and distributed.

End of Service Life (EOSL)

End of service life (EOSL) is the term used to denote that something has reached the end of its "useful life." When EOSL occurs, the provider of the item or service will typically no longer sell or update it. Sometimes the end of updates will be a specified date in the future. EOSL typically occurs because newer models have been released, replacing the older model. During the EOSL phase, some manufacturers may still offer maintenance options, but usually at a premium price. Old versions of software have had this issue, where critical systems cannot easily be upgraded and instead have contracts with the original vendor to maintain the system past its normal EOSL.

EXAM TIP Do not be confused! End of Life (EOL) is the term used to denote that something has reached the end of its "useful life." End of service life (EOSL) or end of support is when the manufacturer quits selling an item. In most cases, the manufacturer no longer provides maintenance services or updates.

NDA

Nondisclosure agreements were covered previously in this chapter, and they work in the same fashion with respect to third parties. Whenever information is shared with a party, inside or outside the company, if the sharing entity wishes to have contractual terms to limit sharing or disclosure, an NDA is used.

Data

System integration with internal and third parties frequently involves the sharing of data. Data can be shared for the purpose of processing or storage. Control over data is a significant issue in third-party relationships. Numerous questions need to be addressed. For example, the question of who owns the data—both the data shared with third parties and subsequent data developed as part of the relationship—is an issue that needs to be established.

Classification

A key component of IT security is the protection of the information processed and stored on the computer systems and network. Organizations deal with many different types of information, and they need to recognize that not all information is of equal importance or sensitivity. This requires classification of information into various categories, each with its own requirements for its handling. Factors that affect the classification of specific information include its value to the organization (what will be the impact to the organization if this information is lost?), its age, and laws or regulations that govern its protection. Data classification is covered in detail in Chapter 35, "Privacy."

Governance

Data *governance* is the process of managing the availability, usability, integrity, and security of the data in enterprise systems. This must be done by policy, as it involves a large number of data owners and users. Data governance should have established data standards and policies that control data usage, security, and retention. Effective governance ensures that data usage is consistent with policies, that data elements are trustworthy, and the data doesn't get misused. The roles and responsibilities of those involved in data governance are covered in Chapter 35, "Privacy."

Retention

Data *retention* is the management of the data lifecycle with an emphasis on when data reaches its end of useful life for an organization. Maintaining old, excess data that no longer serves a business purpose only represents system risk, and thus should be removed from the system and properly destroyed. Having a coordinated data retention policy is more than just labeling how long different types of data should be stored. Some types of data, financial records, tax records, and so on have specific regulatory requirements as to how long they must be maintained. The retention policy must also take into account things like litigation holds on specific data elements, suspending the destruction of those elements, and other regulatory concerns. Developing a data retention policy is relatively easy, but implementing it in an efficient and effective manner can be significantly more challenging given the diverse nature of data across the enterprise and the challenge presented by item-specific litigation holds.

EXAM TIP A litigation hold is a court directive to keep all records associated with a subject of a legal proceeding, and this order takes precedence over normal data retention policies.

Credential Policies

Credential policies refer to the processes, services, and software used to store, manage, and log the use of user credentials. User-based credential management solutions are typically aimed at assisting end users in managing their growing set of passwords. There are credential management products that provide a secure means of storing user credentials and making them available across a wide range of platforms, from local stores to cloud storage locations. System credential management solutions offer the same advantages to system owners, providing a means to manage who is given access to differing resources across the enterprise.

The key method used to control access to most systems is still one based on passwords. In conjunction with a strongly enforced account policy that prohibits sharing of passwords and credentials, use of passwords forms the foundation to support the concept that each user ID should be traceable to a single person's activity. Passwords need to be managed to provide appropriate levels of protection. They need to be strong enough to resist attack, and yet not too difficult for users to remember. An account policy can act to ensure that the necessary steps are taken to enact a secure password solution, both by users and by the password infrastructure system.

Personnel

Users, or *personnel,* require credentials to access specific system resources as part of their job duties. Management of who gets what credentials is part of the access and authorization management system and should be managed via a credential policy. The details behind credentials and policies for access control are covered in Chapter 24, "Implement Authentication and Authorization."

Third Party

Just as users inside a firm require credentials to access systems, there are situations where third parties also require credentials. Whether credentials for a system or physical access, *third-party* credentials should be managed by policies to ensure they are issued when needed to the correct parties, and when access is no longer needed, they are revoked appropriately.

Devices

Devices are physical items that require access to a network or enterprise system. To have this access, they require credentials just like human users. Unlike human users, devices do not have the ability to change their password, so they are typically enabled with very long passwords to prevent hacking and have longer-than-normal password expiration periods. This makes device accounts natural targets for attackers; while their long passwords may not be crackable, they can be stolen. Device accounts should be controlled by policy and monitored as to scope of use.

Service Accounts

Service accounts are special accounts that are used to provision permissions for service, or non-human-initiated system activity. Many computer systems have automated services that function as either part of, in addition to, the operating system to enable certain functionalities. These special programs require permissions like all programs that operate, and service accounts are the mechanism used to enable these items to run. Service accounts require auditing and oversight because they run in the background and frequently have significant capabilities. The enterprise needs a policy to determine who can enable and operate these accounts as well as their audit functions.

EXAM TIP Because device and service accounts do not have human operators using them, their passwords have special properties, including very long expiration periods. This makes them more susceptible to abuse, so their scope and usage should be monitored.

Administrator/Root Accounts

Administrator and *root accounts* have elevated privileges and require closer scrutiny as to who is issued these credentials and how they are used and monitored. Detailed information concerning the additional safeguards needed for these accounts is detailed in Chapter 24, "Implement Authentication and Authorization."

Organizational Policies

The important parts of any organization's approach to implementing security include the policies, procedures, standards, and guidelines that are established to detail what users and administrators should be doing to maintain the security of the systems and network. Collectively, these documents provide the guidance needed to determine how security will be implemented in the organization. Given this guidance, the specific technology and security mechanisms required can be planned for.

Policies are high-level, broad statements of what the organization wants to accomplish. They are made by management when laying out the organization's position on some issue. Procedures are the step-by-step instructions on how to implement policies in the organization. They describe exactly how employees are expected to act in a given situation or to accomplish a specific task. Standards are mandatory elements regarding the implementation of a policy. They are accepted specifications that provide specific details on how a policy is to be enforced. Some standards are externally driven. Regulations for banking and financial institutions, for example, require certain security measures be taken by law. Other standards may be set by the organization to meet its own security goals. Guidelines are recommendations relating to a policy. The key term in this case is *recommendations*—guidelines are not mandatory steps.

Change Management

The purpose of *change management* is to ensure proper procedures are followed when modifications to the IT infrastructure are made. These modifications can be prompted by a number of different events, including new legislation, updated versions of software or hardware, implementation of new software or hardware, and improvements to the infrastructure. The term *management* implies that this process should be controlled in some systematic way, and that is indeed the purpose. Changes to the infrastructure might have a detrimental impact on operations. New versions of operating systems or application software might be incompatible with other software or hardware the organization is using. Without a process to manage the change, an organization might suddenly find itself unable to conduct business. A change management process should include various stages, including a method to request a change to the infrastructure, a review and approval process for the request, an examination of the consequences of the change, resolution (or mitigation) of any detrimental effects the change might incur, implementation of the change, and documentation of the process as it related to the change.

Change Control

Change control is the process of how changes to anything are sourced, analyzed, and managed. Change control is a subset of change management, focused on the details of a change and how it is documented.

EXAM TIP Change management is about the process of applying change. Change control is about the details of the change itself.

Asset Management

Asset management is the policies and processes used to manage the elements of the system, including hardware, software, and the data that is contained within them. In order to secure a system, one must have some form of control over these assets, and asset management involves the processes employed to keep the enterprise in positive control over these valuable items. Failure to control hardware can result in rogue network devices or computers accessing systems. Failure to control software can result in system-level vulnerabilities granting attackers free reign over a system and its data. Failure to control the data assets can result in many forms of failure. This makes asset management one of the most important aspects of security, and it is ranked at the top of virtually every standard list of controls.

Chapter Review

In this chapter, you became acquainted with the importance of policies to organizational security. The chapter opened with a discussion of personnel policies. These policies include the acceptable use, job rotation, and mandatory vacation policies. Next was a discussion of separation of duties and least privilege. Other policies discussed in this section include clean desk policy, the use of background checks, nondisclosure agreements, and social media analysis. Onboarding and offboarding policies were also presented. This section on user training included the topics of gamification, capture-the-flag events, phishing campaigns and simulations, computer-based training, and role-based training. This was followed by an examination of the diversity of training techniques.

The chapter then examined third-party risk management policies, including those for vendors, the supply chain, and business partners. The legal documents of service level agreements, memorandum of understanding, measurement systems analysis, and business partnership agreements were presented. A discussion of end-of-life and end-of-service considerations was presented. The section finished with an examination of NDA policies related to third parties.

Data policies covering data classification, governance, and retention were presented. Next, an examination of credentialing policies to cover personnel, third parties, devices, and service accounts was presented.

The chapter wrapped up with an examination of organizational policies covering change management, change control, and asset management.

Questions

To help you prepare further for the CompTIA Security+ exam, and to test your level of preparedness, answer the following questions and then check your answers against the correct answers at the end of the chapter.

1. Which of the following is a description of a business partnership agreement (BPA)?
   - **A.** A negotiated agreement between parties detailing the expectations between a customer and a service provider
   - **B.** A legal agreement between entities establishing the terms, conditions, and expectations of the relationship between the entities
   - **C.** A specialized agreement between organizations that have interconnected IT systems, the purpose of which is to document the security requirements associated with the interconnection
   - **D.** A written agreement expressing a set of intended actions between the parties with respect to some common pursuit or goal

2. Which of the following is used to essentially set the requisite level of performance of a given contractual service?
   - A. Memorandum of understanding (MOU)
   - B. Nondisclosure agreement (NDA)
   - C. Memorandum of agreement (MOA)
   - D. Service level agreement (SLA)
3. Which of the following is an issue that must be addressed if an organization enforces a mandatory vacation policy?
   - A. Enforcing a mandatory vacation policy in most cases is a costly policy.
   - B. Using mandatory vacations as a tool to detect fraud will require that somebody else also be trained in the functions of the employee who is on vacation.
   - C. Vacations often occur at the most inopportune time for the organization and can affect its ability to complete projects or deliver services.
   - D. Forcing employees to take a vacation if they don't want to often will result in disgruntled employees, which can introduce another security threat.
4. Which of the following are the best reasons for an organization to have a job rotation policy? (Choose all that apply.)
   - A. Since security is often of secondary concern to people in their jobs, rotating individuals through security positions can result in a much wider understanding of the organization's security problems.
   - B. It helps to maintain a high level of employee morale.
   - C. It ensures all important operations can still be accomplished should budget cuts result in the termination of a number of employees.
   - D. It eliminates the need to rely on one individual for security expertise.
5. Which of the following statements are true when discussing separation of duties? (Choose all that apply.)
   - A. Separation of duties is a principle employed in many organizations to ensure that no single individual has the ability to conduct transactions alone.
   - B. Employing separation of duties means that the level of trust in any one individual is lessened, and the ability for any individual to cause catastrophic damage to the organization is also lessened.
   - C. Separating duties as a security tool is a good practice, but it is possible to go overboard and break up transactions into too many pieces or require too much oversight.
   - D. Separation of duties spreads responsibilities out over an organization so no single individual becomes the indispensable individual with all of the "keys to the kingdom" or unique knowledge about how to make everything work.

6. Which of the following statements are true in regard to a clean desk policy for security? (Choose all that apply.)
   A. While a clean desk policy makes for a pleasant work environment, it actually has very little impact on security.
   B. Sensitive information must not be left unsecured in the work area when the worker is not present to act as custodian.
   C. Even leaving the desk area and going to the bathroom can leave information exposed and subject to compromise.
   D. A clean desk policy should identify and prohibit things that are not obvious upon first glance, such as passwords on sticky notes under keyboards and mouse pads.
7. Which of the following is the term for a document used to explain the boundaries of company secret material, information over which control should be exercised to prevent disclosure to unauthorized parties, and to obtain agreement to follow these limits?
   A. Nondisclosure agreement (NDA)
   B. Data access agreement (DAA)
   C. Data disclosure agreement (DDA)
   D. Data release agreement (DRA)
8. What is the name given to a policy that outlines what an organization considers to be the appropriate use of its resources, such as computer systems, e-mail, Internet, and networks?
   A. Resource usage policy (RUP)
   B. Acceptable use of resources policy (AURP)
   C. Organizational use policy (OUP)
   D. Acceptable use policy (AUP)
9. What is the correct term for tracking issues associated with the upgrading of a component in a subassembly, specifically to a newer software version?
   A. Vendor risk
   B. Change control
   C. Supply chain risk
   D. Change management
10. Which of these accounts represents the greater risk due to outside hacker infiltration?
    A. User accounts
    B. Temporary accounts
    C. Service accounts
    D. Third-party accounts

Answers

1. **B.** A business partnership agreement is a legal agreement between entities establishing the terms, conditions, and expectations of the relationship between the entities.
2. **D.** A service level agreement (SLA) essentially sets the requisite level of performance for a given contractual service.
3. **B.** Using mandatory vacation as a tool to detect fraud will require that somebody else also be trained in the functions of the employee who is on vacation. The organization must therefore ensure that they have a second person who is familiar with the vacationing employee's duties.
4. **A** and **D.** Since security is often of secondary concern to people in their jobs, rotating individuals through security positions can result in a much wider understanding of the organization's security problems. A secondary benefit is that it also eliminates the need to rely on one individual for security expertise. If all security tasks are the domain of one employee, security will suffer if that individual leaves the organization.
5. **A, B, C,** and **D.** All of the statements are true when discussing separation of duties.
6. **B, C,** and **D.** A clean desk policy can actually have a positive impact on security for the reasons listed.
7. **A.** Nondisclosure agreements (NDAs) are standard corporate documents used to explain the boundaries of company secret material, information over which control should be exercised to prevent disclosure to unauthorized parties.
8. **D.** An acceptable use policy (AUP) outlines what the organization considers to be the appropriate use of its resources, such as computer systems, e-mail, Internet, and networks.
9. **B.** Tracking and managing the details of a change is change control. The process is change management.
10. **C.** Unmanned accounts such as devices and service accounts have higher risks of abuse by hackers because of the lack of ability to change passwords.

CHAPTER 34

Risk Management

In this chapter, you will

- Explore risk management concepts
- Examine processes used in risk management

Risk management is a core business function of an enterprise because it is through the risk management process that an enterprise can maximize its return on investments. Understanding the business impact of operations associated with the enterprise is key for business success. This can be accomplished using a business impact analysis. Using the data from the analysis, coupled with a threat analysis and a risk assessment process, the enterprise can come to an understanding of the sources of the risk elements it faces and their level of intensity.

Certification Objective This chapter covers CompTIA Security+ exam objective 5.4: Summarize risk management processes and concepts.

Risk Types

Risks can come from a wide range of sources. One way to organize different risks is to categorize them into a series of types. CompTIA Security+ recognizes the following six *risk types:* external, internal, legacy systems, multiparty, IP theft, and software compliance/licensing. These different types are not exclusive and will be discussed in the following sections.

External

External threats come from outside the organization and, by definition, begin without access to the system. Access is reserved for users who have a business need to know and have authorized accounts on the system. Outsiders must first hijack one of these accounts. This extra step and the reliance on external connections typically make external attackers easier to detect.

Internal

Internal threats include disgruntled employees and well-meaning employees who make mistakes or have an accident. Internal threats tend to be more damaging, as the perpetrator has already been granted some form of access. The risk is related to the level of access and the value of the asset being worked on. For instance, if a system administrator working on the domain controller accidently erases a critical value and crashes the system, it can be just as costly as an unauthorized outsider performing a DoS attack against the enterprise.

Legacy Systems

Legacy systems are older, pre-existing systems. But age really isn't the issue—the true issue behind what makes a system a legacy system is the concept of technical debt. Technical debt is the cost occurred over time as a result of not maintaining a system completely. Cutting corners for cost can be legitimized in the now, but over time those cuts amount to issues. Take system modification as an example. If a system has had custom modifications over time to adapt it to a company's business processes, how do those modifications work when a newer version comes out? A common reason for not updating or upgrading a system is that it will break something or void some warranty in place. Over time, this lack of staying current, or drifting away from the desired state, increases costs. Like all debt, there is interest, and technical debt grows over time to where it can become a major issue in IT projects charged with updating older systems. In a world with constantly evolving threats and risk vectors, the inability to respond is a risk in itself.

Multiparty

In traditional risk management, the driving factor under consideration is risk to one's own enterprise. In a traditional two-party system (an attacker versus a firm), the risk equations are fairly easy to determine and optimize. But when a system has multiple parties, each with its own risk determinations, the management of the overall risk equation gets complicated. If a firm is negotiating to make a major system change, and all the stakeholders are within the firm, then it is still considered a single party, but if the financing for the project is from another firm, and subcontractors are involved, other party determinations of acceptable risk levels become an issue very quickly.

IP Theft

If you ask an IT technician about cybersecurity risk, you might get an answer involving data loss, ransomware, viruses, malware, or fraud. These are mostly technical issues, for this is the world most cybersecurity professionals live in. But ask a CEO the same question, and business items such as *intellectual property (IP) theft* come up right away. IP theft can seriously damage a company's future health. If a firm spends a lot of resources developing a product or a market and then is undercut by other parties that don't have to spend those resources, sales can disappear and future revenue streams can dry up. Unlike physical assets, digital assets can be stolen merely through copying, and this is the pathway attackers use for IP data. The attacker will attempt to gain access and copy the data, all the while trying to leave no trace, making the theft not at all obvious until a competitor uses the information and fields a "stolen" product in the form of a copy.

IP theft is hard to attribute, and once the copy is in the marketplace, the only resort is courts via trade secret and patent protection actions. This is a very significant issue with international state-sponsored attacks, as the legal recourses are challenging to use effectively. Investigation and prosecution of IP theft are major items pursued by the FBI as part of its cybersecurity strategy.

Software Compliance/Licensing

Software is everywhere; it forms the functional backbone of our systems. The source of this software is via licensing and in many cases trust. Copies of many software products can be made and used without licenses, and this creates *software compliance/licensing* risk. This form of risk is best battled using policies and procedures that prohibit the activity, followed by internal audits that verify compliance with the policies.

EXAM TIP Be able to identify the various risk types—external, internal, legacy systems, multiparty, IP theft, and software compliance/licensing. Know which risk management strategies and processes in the coming sections should be applied to each of the given risk types discussed.

Risk Management Strategies

Risk management can best be described as a decision-making process. *Risk management strategies* include elements of threat assessment, risk assessment, and security implementation concepts, all positioned within the concept of business management. In the simplest terms, when you manage risk, you determine what could happen to your business, you assess the impact if it were to happen, and you decide what you could do to control that impact as much as you or your management team deems necessary. You then decide to act or not to act, and, finally, you evaluate the results of your decision. The process may be iterative, as industry best practices clearly indicate that an important aspect of effectively managing risk is to consider it an ongoing process.

Risks are absolutes—they cannot be removed or eliminated. You can take actions to change the effects that a risk poses to a system, but the risk itself doesn't really change, no matter what actions you take to mitigate that risk. A high risk will always be a high risk. However, you can take actions to reduce the impact of that risk if it occurs. A limited number of strategies can be used to manage risk. The risk can be avoided, transferred, mitigated, or accepted.

Understand that risk cannot be completely eliminated. A risk that remains after implementing controls is termed a *residual risk*. You have to further evaluate residual risks to identify where additional controls are required to reduce risk even more. This reinforces the statement earlier in the chapter that the risk management process is iterative.

EXAM TIP You can do four things to respond to risk: accept it, transfer it, avoid it, and mitigate it. Understand the differences, as these will all be presented as possible answer choices for a question, and the scenario details will apply to one better than the others.

Acceptance

When you're analyzing a specific risk, after weighing the cost to avoid, transfer, or mitigate a risk against the probability of its occurrence and its potential impact, the best response is to *accept* the risk. For example, a manager may choose to allow a programmer to make "emergency" changes to a production system (in violation of good separation of duties) because the system cannot go down during a given period of time. The manager accepts that the risk that the programmer could possibly make unauthorized changes is outweighed by the high-availability requirement of that system. However, there should always be some additional controls, such as a management review or a standardized approval process, to ensure the assumed risk is adequately managed.

Avoidance

Avoiding the risk can be accomplished in many ways. Although you can't remove threats from the environment, you can alter the system's exposure to the threats. Not deploying a module that increases risk is one manner of risk avoidance.

Transference

Transference of risk is when the risk in a situation is covered by another entity. As mentioned previously in this book surrounding issues such as cloud computing, contracts and legal agreements will denote which parties are assuming which risks. This is defining who has responsibilities and who holds the risk—defining the specific transference up front. The mistake many make is assuming the risk transfers. The only risk transference that occurs across these legal agreements is that defined in the contract.

Another common example of risk transfer is the protection against fraud that consumers have on their credit cards. The risk is transferred to another party, so people can use their cards in confidence. As in the previous discussion, this transference is in the fine print of the credit card agreement.

Cybersecurity Insurance

A common method of transferring risk is to purchase *cybersecurity insurance*. Insurance allows risk to be transferred to a third party that manages specific types of risk for multiple parties, thus reducing the individual cost.

Mitigation

Risk can also be *mitigated* through the application of controls that reduce the impact of an attack. Controls can alert operators so that the level of exposure is reduced through process intervention. When an action occurs that is outside the accepted risk profile, a second set of rules can be applied, such as calling the customer for verification before committing a transaction. Controls such as these can act to reduce the risk associated with potential high-risk operations.

Risk Analysis

To effectively manage anything, there must be appropriate measurements to guide the course of actions. In the case of risk, this is also true. To manage risk, there needs to be a measurement of loss, and potential loss, and much of this information comes by way of *risk analysis*. Risk analysis is performed via a series of specific exercises that reveal presence and level of risk across an enterprise. Then, through further analysis, the information can be refined to a workable plan to manage the risk to an acceptable level.

Risk Register

A *risk register* is a list of the risks associated with a system. It also can contain additional information associated with the risk element, such as categories to group like risks, probability of occurrence, impact to the organization, mitigation factors, and other data. There is no standardized form. The Project Management Institute has one format, other sources have different formats. The reference document *ISO Guide 73:2009 Risk Management—Vocabulary* defines a risk register to be a "record of information about identified risks."

Risk Matrix/Heat Map

A *risk matrix* or *heat map* is used to visually display the results of a qualitative risk analysis. This method allows expert judgment and experience to assume a prominent role in the risk assessment process and is easier than trying to exactly define a number for each element of risk. To assess risk qualitatively, you first determine the likelihood of a threat occurring and also the consequence should it occur. You then take the value of each and multiply them together to get the risk value. For a 5-by-5 risk matrix/heat map, as shown in Figure 34-1, you simply use the numbers 1 to 5 for each of the axes, and this yields risk values from 1 to 25. These values can then be classified as minor, moderate, major, or critical.

Likelihood						
Likelihood	Almost Certain (5)	Moderate 5	Major 10	Major 15	Critical 20	Critical 25
Likelihood	Likely (4)	Minor 4	Moderate 8	Major 12	Major 16	Critical 20
Likelihood	Possible (3)	Minor 3	Moderate 6	Moderate 9	Major 12	Major 15
Likelihood	Unlikely (2)	Minor 2	Minor 4	Moderate 6	Moderate 8	Major 10
Likelihood	Rare (1)	Minor 1	Minor 2	Minor 3	Minor 4	Moderate 5
		Inconsequential (1)	Minor (2)	Moderate (3)	Major (4)	Critical (5)
		Consequence				

Figure 34-1 Risk matrix/heat map

Risk Control Assessment

A *risk control assessment* is a tool used by the Financial Industry Regulatory Authority (FINRA) to assess a series of risks associated with their member institutions. Questions are asked about a wide range of topics, including cybersecurity. Answers to these questions paint a fairly detailed picture of the potential risk exposures a firm has, given its policies and practices.

Risk Control Self-Assessment

Risk control self-assessment is a technique that employs management and staff of all levels to identify and evaluate risks and associated controls. This information is collected and analyzed to produce a more comprehensive map of risks and the controls in place to address it. Engaging multiple viewpoints in the collection of information, identifying risk exposures and determining corrective actions, provides different perspectives and can uncover unnoticed vulnerabilities.

Risk Awareness

Risk awareness is knowledge of risk and consequences. Risk awareness is essential for wide ranges of personnel, with the content tailored to their contributions to the enterprise. For some workers, understanding the risks and defenses against social engineering is important. For others, such as designers of systems, more detailed understanding of risk and the vulnerabilities that cause it are needed. For management and executives, an understanding of the whole risk ecosystem is necessary because they must balance the risk and reward through major system initiatives. Just as the beginning of the famous twelve-step program is acknowledging the problem, becoming aware of risk is important if one is to manage it.

Inherent Risk

Inherent risk is defined as the amount of risk that exists in the absence of controls. This can be confusing, as the definition of "no controls" could include no access controls, no door locks, no personnel background checks—in essence an environment that would equate to everything becoming high risk. A better explanation would be that inherent risk is the current risk level given the existing set of controls rather than the hypothetical notion of an absence of any controls. An example might help. Your car has a lot of controls to enable self-driving, yet there is still risk involved. This is the inherent risk; it is associated with the operation of the system within the environment. And as the environment changes, so can the inherent risk—what is considered safe in terms of speed and environment is different between a sunny day with no traffic, a evening with busy traffic and lots of rain, and nighttime with medium traffic. Each of these situations has different inherent risk and may need specific controls to reduce risk to an acceptable level.

Residual Risk

The presence of risks in a system is an absolute—they cannot be removed or eliminated. As mentioned previously in this chapter, four actions can be taken to respond to risk: accept, transfer, avoid, and mitigate. Whatever risk is not transferred, mitigated, or avoided is referred to as *residual risk* and, by definition, is accepted. You cannot eliminate residual risk, but you can manage risk to drive residual risk to an acceptable level.

Control Risk

Control risk is a term used to specify risk associated with the chance of a material misstatement in a company's financial statements. This risk can be manifested in a couple ways: either there isn't an appropriate set of internal controls to mitigate a particular risk or the internal controls set in place malfunctioned. Business systems that rely on IT systems have an inherent risk associated with cybersecurity risks. What makes these risks become control risks is when they impact the business function in a manner that results in financial misstatements or errors. In the case of an organization that doesn't have adequate internal controls in place to prevent and detect fraud or errors, it has a specific issue of control risk as opposed to inherent risk.

EXAM TIP Inherent risk is the amount of risk that exists in the absence of controls. Residual risk is the amount of risk that remains after controls are accounted for. Control risk is when the risk specifically affects the financial reporting.

Risk Appetite

Different firms in different businesses and environments have different risk exposures, but they also have different tolerances for risk. *Risk appetite* is the term used to describe a firm's tolerance for risk. Even within a sector, with companies of the same size, operating in roughly the same areas, there can be differences in the level of risk each feels comfortable in accepting. This risk appetite is related to other business elements such as reward and loss. Each company's executive structure needs to determine the appropriate risk appetite for that firm, and that becomes the upper limit on acceptable risk in the company's operations.

Regulations That Affect Risk Posture

Regulations can have a dramatic effect on risk exposure. Sometimes that effect is a direct action of a regulation, such as financial firms being forced by regulators to have certain levels of encryption to protect certain types of processes. Other times it is less direct, as in specific monitoring required for reporting, and firms change operations to avoid having to report. The breadth of regulations is wide, but some of the common ones associated with cybersecurity include Sarbanes-Oxley, various financial regulations on protecting data, and Payment Card Industry Data Security Standard (PCI-DSS) for credit card data.

Regulations drive corporate responses because failing to follow regulations can result in penalties, which represent a loss. Therefore, regulations can be viewed as risks with almost certainty of incurring the loss.

EXAM TIP It's important to remember that regulations apply to many areas of cybersecurity. Know that the Sarbanes-Oxley Act of 2002 protects investors from corporate fraud and bad financial reporting, and the Payment Card Industry Data Security Standard (PCI-DSS) is a set of security standards and policies for companies to follow in order to optimize security for consumer payment cards and associated private data.

Risk Assessment Types

A *risk assessment* is a method to analyze potential risk based on statistical and mathematical models. You can use any one of a variety of models to calculate potential risk assessment values. A common method is the calculation of the annual loss expectancy (ALE). Calculating the ALE creates a monetary value of the impact. This calculation begins by calculating a single-loss expectancy (SLE), which is presented in detail later in the chapter.

Qualitative

Qualitative risk assessment is the process of subjectively determining the impact of an event that affects a project, program, or business. Qualitative risk assessment usually involves the use of expert judgment and models to complete the assessment. This type of risk assessment is highly dependent on expert judgment and experience and can also suffer from biases. The risk matrix/heat map presented earlier is an example of a qualitative risk model.

Quantitative

Quantitative risk assessment is the process of objectively determining the impact of an event that affects a project, program, or business. Quantitative risk assessment usually involves the use of metrics and models to complete the assessment. Quantitative risk assessment applies historical information and trends to attempt to predict future performance. This type of risk assessment is highly dependent on historical data and gathering such data can be difficult. Quantitative risk assessment can also rely heavily on models that provide decision-making information in the form of quantitative metrics, which attempt to measure risk levels across a common scale. The models of single-loss expectancy, annual loss expectancy, and annualized rate of occurrence, discussed later in this chapter, are examples of quantitative risk analysis.

EXAM TIP Understand the difference between quantitative and qualitative risk assessments. Quantitative means you can actually count something, whereas qualitative is more subjective, with values such as high, medium, and low.

Likelihood of Occurrence

The *likelihood of occurrence* is the chance that a particular risk will occur. This measure can be qualitative or quantitative, as just discussed. For qualitative measures, the likelihood of occurrence is typically defined on an annual basis so that it can be compared to other annualized measures. If defined quantitatively, it is used to create rank-order outcomes.

Impact

The *impact* of an event is a measure of the actual loss when a threat exploits a vulnerability. Federal Information Processing Standard (FIPS) 199 defines three levels of impact using the terms high, moderate, and low. The impact needs to be defined in terms of the context of each organization, as what is high for some firms may be low for much larger firms. The common method is to define the impact levels in terms of important business criteria. Impacts can be in terms of cost (dollars), performance (service level agreement [SLA] or other requirements), schedule (deliverables), or any other important item. Impact can also be categorized in terms of the information security attribute that is relevant to the problem: confidentiality, integrity, and availability.

Risk is the chance of something not working as planned and causing an adverse impact. Impact is the cost associated with a realized risk. Impact can be in many forms—from human life, as in injury or death, to property loss, to loss of safety, financial loss, or loss of reputation. Losses are seldom absolute and can come in all sizes and combinations. Different levels of risk can result in different levels of impact. Sometimes external events can have an effect on the impact. If everyone in the industry has been experiencing a specific type of loss, and your firm had time and warning to mitigate it, but didn't, the environment defined by these outside factors may well indeed increase the impact to your firm from this type of event. For instance, failing to patch a system can have serious impacts to an organization, as recent data breaches have shown. But failure to patch a system, when you know it will be used against you, is even worse, as it almost invites further attacks.

Life

Many IT systems are involved in healthcare, and failures of some of these systems can and have resulted in injury and death to patients. IT systems are also frequently integral to the operation of machines in industrial settings, and their failure can have similar impacts. Injury and loss of *life* are outcomes that backups cannot address and can result in consequences beyond others. As part of a business impact analysis (BIA), you would identify these systems and ensure that they are highly redundant, to avoid impact to life.

Property

Property damage can be the result of unmitigated risk. Property damage to company-owned property, property damage to property of others, and even environmental damage from toxic releases in industrial settings are all examples of damage that can be caused by IT security failures. This can be especially true in companies that have manufacturing plants and other cyber physical processes. If you think property damage can't happen to your organization because it only has office computers, consider the Shamoon malware that destroyed the computing resources of Saudi Aramco to the point that the company had to buy replacement equipment, as reimaging to a clean state was not a guaranteed, or timely, solution.

Safety

Safety is the condition of being protected from or unlikely to cause danger, risk, or injury. Safety makes sense from both a business risk perspective and when you consider the level of concern one places for the well-being of people. In a manufacturing environment, with moving equipment and machines that can present a danger to workers, government regulations drive specific actions to mitigate risk and make the workplace as safe as possible. Computers are increasingly becoming involved in all aspects of businesses, and they can impact safety. Failures that lead to safety issues will cause work stoppages and increase losses that could otherwise have been avoided. Unsafe conditions that are the result of computer issues will face the same regulatory wrath that unsafe plants have caused in manufacturing—fines and criminal complaints.

Finance

Finance is in many ways the final arbiter of all activities because it is how we keep score. We can measure the gains through sales and profit, and we can measure the losses through unmitigated risks. We can take most events, put a dollar value on them, and settle the books. Where this becomes an issue is when the impacts exceed the expected costs associated with the planned residual risks because then the costs directly impact profit. Impacts to a business ultimately become a financial impact. What starts as a missed patch allows ransomware to infiltrate a system. This results in a business impact that eventually adds costs, which should have been avoided.

Reputation

Corporate *reputation* is important in marketing. Would you deal with a bank with a shoddy record of accounting or losing personal information? How about online retailing? Would the customer base think twice before entering their credit card information after a data breach? These are not purely hypothetical questions; these events have occurred, and corporate reputations have been damaged as a result, thus costing the firms in customer base and revenue.

EXAM TIP Risk is instantiated as impact. Impacts can have effects on life, property, safety, reputation, and finances. Typically, multiple impacts occur from an incident, and finance always pays the bill. Be prepared to parse a question to determine whether its focus is risk, impact, or a specific consequence.

Asset Value

The *asset value (AV)* is the amount of money it would take to replace an asset. This term is used with the exposure factor (EF), a measure of how much of an asset is at risk, to determine the single-loss expectancy (SLE).

EXAM TIP Understand the terms SLE, ALE, and ARO and how they are used to calculate a potential loss. You may be given a scenario, asked to calculate the SLE, ALE, or ARO, and presented answer choices that include values that would result from incorrect calculations.

Single-Loss Expectancy (SLE)

The *single-loss expectancy (SLE)* is the value of a loss expected from a single event. It is calculated using the following formula:

$$\text{SLE} = \text{asset value (AV)} \times \text{exposure factor (EF)}$$

Exposure factor (EF) is a measure of the magnitude of loss of an asset.

For example, to calculate the exposure factor, assume the asset value of a small office building and its contents is $2 million. Also assume that this building houses the call center for a business, and the complete loss of the center would take away about half of the capability of the company. Therefore, the exposure factor is 50 percent, and the SLE is calculated as follows:

$$\$2 \text{ million} \times 0.5 = \$1 \text{ million}$$

Annualized Loss Expectancy (ALE)

After the SLE has been calculated, the *annual loss expectancy (ALE)* is then calculated simply by multiplying the SLE by the likelihood or number of times the event is expected to occur in a year, which is called the annualized rate of occurrence (ARO):

$$\text{ALE} = \text{SLE} \times \text{ARO}$$

This represents the expected losses over the course of a year based on the ALE. If multiple events are considered, the arithmetic sum of all of the SLEs and AROs can be calculated to provide a summation amount.

Annualized Rate of Occurrence (ARO)

The *annualized rate of occurrence (ARO)* is a representation of the frequency of the event, measured in a standard year. If the event is expected to occur once in 20 years, then the ARO is 1/20. Typically, the ARO is defined by historical data, either from a company's own experience or from industry surveys. Continuing our example, assume that a fire at this business's location is expected to occur about once in 20 years. Given this information, the ALE is

$$\$1 \text{ million} \times 1/20 = \$50{,}000$$

The ALE determines a threshold for evaluating the cost/benefit ratio of a given countermeasure. Therefore, a countermeasure to protect this business adequately should cost no more than the calculated ALE of $50,000 per year.

NOTE Numerous resources are available to help in calculating ALE. There are databases that contain information to help businesses (member institutions) manage exposure to loss from natural disasters such as hurricanes, earthquakes, and so forth. These databases include information on property perils such as fire, lightning, vandalism, windstorm, hail, and so forth, and even include granular information to help evaluate, for example, the effectiveness of your building's sprinkler systems.

Disasters

Disasters are major events that cause disruptions. The timescale of the disruption can vary, as can the level of disruption, but the commonality is that the external event that caused the disruption is one that cannot be prevented. Foreseen, yes, but prevented, not necessarily. Common disasters include weather-related events and events that everyone knows will happen eventually, just not where or when. Person-made disasters can be as simple as a misconfiguration that results in the loss of a significant amount of data. By definition, "person-made" indicates the disaster is the result of the action of some person. Foreseeable, yes; preventable, to a degree yes, but even accidents can happen. Having risk management and mitigation strategies in place for disasters is important.

At the time this book was written, the world was gripped by the COVID-19 pandemic. Worldwide, offices, businesses, schools, churches, and various gathering locations went into a lockdown for months. Employees worked from home, if they could, via the Internet. The outcome is still ongoing as of the summer of 2020, but the effect is plain to see—a global pandemic will be one of the largest disasters ever experienced by the current generation and is changing many businesses and business processes.

NOTE Per FEMA, roughly 40 to 60 percent of small businesses never reopen their doors following a disaster. Following a disaster, 90 percent of smaller companies fail within a year unless they can resume operations within five days.

Environmental

One of the largest sources of threats is from the environment. *Environmental* changes can come from a wide variety of sources—weather, lightning, storms, and even solar flares—and these can cause changes to the system in a manner that disrupts normal operations. These changes can increase risk. While IT security measures cannot change the environmental factors that can impact operations, they can have an effect on the risk associated with the environmental issue. Making systems resilient can reduce impacts and mitigate these sources of risk to the enterprise. And there are times when these effects can be felt at a distance; for instance, how can you back up to a remote site if the remote site is down due to power outage as a result of a fallen branch from a storm?

Person-made

Person-made threats are those that are attributable to the actions of a person. But these threats aren't limited to hostile actions by an attacker; they include accidents by users and system administrators. Users can represent one of the greatest risks in an IT system. More files are lost by accidental user deletion than by hackers deleting files, and to the team trying to restore the lost files, the attribution has no bearing on the restoration effort. User actions, such as poor cyber hygiene and password reuse, have been shown to be the starting point for many major cybersecurity events over the past several years. A system administrator that improperly configures a backup, the error being discovered when the backup was needed and there is no data on the backup to recover, can easily be a disaster.

It is not a result of hostile activity, but destructive nonetheless. Proper controls to manage the risk to a system must include controls against both accidental and purposeful acts.

Internal vs. External

As mentioned previously in the chapter, threats can come from internal and external sources. Internal threats have their origin within an organization, whereas external risks come from the outside. When disasters are examined, they can be seen to have originated either within the company or outside the company. While it is easy to always blame an outside force, in many cases, internal policies and procedures increase a firm's risk profile for easily understood external risks. If supply chain decisions are made to go with a single overseas vendor for a minor price advantage, with no backup, and then a disaster strikes the country of the supplier, is this an internal or external risk? It can be viewed as both, but an internal policy decision drives the risk of going with a single vendor.

EXAM TIP When performing a threat assessment, be sure to consider environmental, person-made, and internal threats. On the exam, carefully read the scenario preceding the question to differentiate which of these threat sources is the best answer, as multiple sources are common, but one is usually the higher risk.

Business Impact Analysis

Business impact analysis (BIA) is the process used to determine the sources and relative impact values of risk elements in a process. It is also the name often used to describe a document created by addressing the questions associated with sources of risk and the steps taken to mitigate them in the enterprise. The BIA also outlines how the loss of any of your critical functions will impact the organization. This section explores the range of terms and concepts related to conducting a BIA.

Recovery Time Objective (RTO)

The term *recovery time objective (RTO)* is used to describe the target time that is set for the resumption of operations after an incident. This is a period of time that is defined by the business, based on the needs of the business. A shorter RTO results in higher costs because it requires greater coordination and resources. This term is commonly used in business continuity and disaster recovery operations.

Recovery Point Objective (RPO)

Recovery point objective (RPO), a totally different concept from RTO, is the time period representing the maximum period of acceptable data loss. The RPO defines the frequency of backup operations necessary to prevent unacceptable levels of data loss. A simple example of establishing RPO is to answer the following questions: How much data can you afford to lose? How much rework is tolerable?

NOTE RTO and RPO are seemingly related but in actuality measure different things entirely. The RTO serves the purpose of defining the requirements for business continuity, while the RPO deals with backup frequency. It is possible to have an RTO of 1 day and an RPO of 1 hour, or an RTO of 1 hour and an RPO of 1 day. The determining factors are the needs of the business.

EXAM TIP Know the difference between RTO and RPO. The RTO serves the purpose of defining the requirements for business continuity, while the RPO deals with backup frequency.

Mean Time to Repair (MTTR)

Mean time to repair (MTTR) is a common measure of how long it takes to repair a given failure. This is the average time, and it may or may not include the time needed to obtain parts. The CompTIA Security+ Acronyms list indicates *mean time to recover* as an alternative meaning for MTTR. In either case, MTTR is calculated as follows:

$$\text{MTTR} = (\text{total downtime}) / (\text{number of breakdowns})$$

Availability is a measure of the amount of time a system performs its intended function. Reliability is a measure of the frequency of system failures. Availability is related to, but different than, reliability and is typically expressed as a percentage of time the system is in its operational state. To calculate availability, both the MTBF and the MTTR are needed:

$$\text{Availability} = \text{MTBF} / (\text{MTBF} + \text{MTTR})$$

Assuming a system has an MTBF of 6 months and the repair takes 30 minutes, the availability would be the following:

$$\text{Availability} = 6 \text{ months} / (6 \text{ months} + 30 \text{ minutes}) = 99.9884\%$$

Mean Time Between Failures (MTBF)

Mean time between failures (MTBF) is a common measure of reliability of a system and is an expression of the average time between system failures. The time between failures is measured from the time a system returns to service until the next failure. The MTBF is an arithmetic mean of a set of system failures:

$$\text{MTBF} = \sum (\text{start of downtime} - \text{start of uptime}) / \text{number of failures}$$

Mean time to failure (MTTF) is a variation of MTBF, one that is commonly used instead of MTBF when the system is replaced in lieu of being repaired. Other than the semantic difference, the calculations are the same, and the meaning is essentially the same.

EXAM TIP Although MTBF and MTTR may seem similar, they measure different things. Exam questions may ask you to perform simple calculations. Incorrect answer choices will reflect simple mistakes in the ratios, so calculate carefully.

Functional Recovery Plans

Accidents, disasters, and interruptions to business processes happen. This is why we have business continuity plans (BCPs). But what comes next? *Functional recovery plans* represent the next step—the transition from operations under business continuity back to normal operations. Just as the transition to business continuity operations needs to be planned, so too does the functional recovery plan. While the transition to disaster operations is fast, and planning is based on prioritized assessment of the level of critical importance with respect to continuing operations, the basis for the functional recovery plan is different. The functional recovery plan can be much more organized and staged over time, working to drive consistent efficiencies as opposed to speed. This can be done function by function and is driven by the function needs.

Single Point of Failure

A key principle of security is defense in depth. This layered approach to security is designed to eliminate any specific single point of failure (SPOF). A *single point of failure* is any system component whose failure or malfunctioning could result in the failure of the entire system. An example of a single point of failure would be a single connection to the Internet—fine for a small business, but not so for a large enterprise with servers providing content to customers. Redundancies have costs, but if the alternative cost is failure, then implementing levels of redundancy is acceptable. For mission-essential systems, single points of failure are items that need to be called to management's attention, with full explanation of the risk and costs associated with them. In some scenarios, avoiding a single point of failure may not be possible or practical, in which case everyone in the organization with responsibility for risk management should understand the nature of the situation and the resultant risk profile.

Disaster Recovery Plan (DRP)

A *disaster recovery plan (DRP)* is the plan a firm creates to manage the business impact of a disaster and to recover from its impacts. The details for disaster recovery plans are covered in Chapter 27, "Incident Response Policies and Procedures."

Mission-Essential Functions

When examining risk and impacts to a business, it is important to identify mission-essential functions from other business functions. In most businesses, the vast majority of daily functions, although important, are not mission essential. *Mission-essential functions* are those that, should they not occur or be performed properly, will directly affect the mission of the organization. In other terms, mission-essential functions are those that must be restored first after a business impact to enable the organization to restore its operations. The reason that identification of these functions is vital for risk management is simple: you should spend the majority of your effort protecting the functions that are essential. Other functions may need protection, but their impairment will not cause the immediate impact that impairment of a mission-essential function would.

Identification of Critical Systems

A part of identifying mission-essential functions is identifying the systems and data that support the functions. *Identification of critical systems* enables the security team to properly prioritize defenses to protect the systems and data in a manner commensurate with the associated risk. It also enables the proper sequencing of restoring operations to ensure proper restoration of services.

Site Risk Assessment

Risk assessments can have specific characteristics associated with different sites. This is the basis for a *site risk assessment,* which is simply a risk assessment tailored for a specific site. In organizations with multiple locations, with differing systems and operations, having tailored risk assessments that are specific to the risks associated with each site provides information for the firm. There may be some elements that overall are specific to the firm, but the development and inclusion of the risks associated with each site provide an actionable document that can be used effectively.

Chapter Review

In this chapter, you became acquainted with examining risk from a business impact analysis (BIA) point of view. The chapter opened with an examination of risk types, including external, internal, legacy systems, multiparty, IP theft, and software compliance/licensing. The next section discussed risk management strategies, where acceptance, avoidance, transference (including cybersecurity insurance), and mitigation were covered.

The subject of risk analysis formed the bulk of the chapter, where the topics were risk registers, risk matrix/heat map, risk control assessment, risk control self-assessment, and risk awareness. The next topics presented were inherent risk, residual risk, control risk, and risk appetite. These were followed by regulations that affect risk posture and risk assessment types, including qualitative and quantitative. The section then moved on to the quantitative calculation of risk using likelihood of occurrence, impact, asset value, single-loss expectancy (SLE), annual loss expectancy (ALE), and annualized rate of occurrence (ARO).

Disasters were covered next, including environmental and person-made, and internal versus external risks were examined.

The chapter wrapped up with an examination of business impact analysis. In this section, the technical topics covered were recovery time objective (RTO), recovery point objective (RPO), mean time to repair (MTTR), and mean time between failures (MTBF). The next items discussed were functional recovery plans, single points of failure, disaster recovery plans (DRPs), mission-essential functions, identification of critical systems, and site risk assessments.

Questions

To help you prepare further for the CompTIA Security+ exam, and to test your level of preparedness, answer the following questions and then check your answers against the correct answers at the end of the chapter.

1. Which of the following is the name often used to describe the process of addressing the questions associated with sources of risk, their impacts, and the steps taken to mitigate them in the enterprise?
   A. Risk assessment
   B. Business impact analysis
   C. Threat assessment
   D. Penetration test
2. Which of the following terms is used to describe the target time that is set for the resumption of operations after an incident?
   A. RPO
   B. MTBF
   C. RTO
   D. MTTR
3. Which of the following is a common measure of how long it takes to fix a given failure?
   A. MTTR
   B. RTO
   C. RPO
   D. MTBF
4. Which of the following is a system component whose failure or malfunctioning could result in the failure of the entire system?
   A. Mean time between failures
   B. Single point of failure
   C. Single-loss expectancy
   D. Likelihood of occurrence

5. Which of the following is the process of subjectively determining the impact of an event that affects a project, program, or business?
   A. Likelihood of occurrence
   B. Functional recovery plan
   C. Qualitative risk assessment
   D. Quantitative risk assessment
6. Which of the following describe mission-essential functions? (Choose all that apply.)
   A. Functions that, if they do not occur, would directly affect the mission of the organization
   B. Functions that, if they are not accomplished properly, would directly affect the mission of the organization
   C. Functions that are considered essential to the organization
   D. The routine business functions
7. Which of the following is the best description of risk?
   A. The cost associated with a realized risk
   B. The chance of something not working as planned
   C. Damage that is the result of unmitigated risk
   D. The level of concern one places on the well-being of people
8. Which of the following impacts is in many ways the final arbiter of all activities because it is how we "keep score"?
   A. Reputation
   B. Safety
   C. Finance
   D. Life
9. Which of the following is a representation of the frequency of an event, measured in a standard year?
   A. Annual loss expectancy (ALE)
   B. Annualized rate of occurrence (ARO)
   C. Single-loss expectancy (SLE)
   D. Annualized expectancy of occurrence (AEO)
10. Which of the following represents a method of transferring risk to a third party?
    A. Applying controls that reduce risk impact
    B. Creating a record of information about identified risks
    C. Developing and forwarding the results of a risk matrix/heat map
    D. Purchasing cybersecurity insurance

Answers

1. **B.** Business impact analysis (BIA) is the name often used to describe a document created by addressing the questions associated with sources of risk and the steps taken to mitigate them in the enterprise. A risk assessment is a method to analyze potential risk based on statistical and mathematical models. A common method is the calculation of the annual loss expectancy (ALE). A threat assessment is a structured analysis of the threats that confront an enterprise. Penetration tests are used by organizations that want a real-world test of their security.

2. **C.** The term *recovery time objective (RTO)* is used to describe the target time that is set for the resumption of operations after an incident. Recovery point objective (RPO) represents the maximum time period of acceptable data loss. Mean time between failures (MTBF) is a common measure of reliability of a system and is an expression of the average time between system failures. Mean time to repair (MTTR) is a common measure of how long it takes to repair a given failure.

3. **A.** Mean time to repair (MTTR) is a common measure of how long it takes to repair a given failure. Recovery time objective (RTO) describes the target time that is set for the resumption of operations after an incident. Recovery point objective (RPO) represents the maximum time period of acceptable data loss. Mean time between failures (MTBF) is a common measure of reliability of a system and is an expression of the average time between system failures.

4. **B.** A single point of failure is any aspect of a system that, if triggered, could result in the failure of the entire system. Mean time between failures (MTBF) is a common measure of reliability of a system and is an expression of the average time between system failures. Single loss expectancy (SLE) is the expected loss from the occurrence of a risk on an asset. The likelihood of occurrence is the chance that a particular risk will occur.

5. **C.** Qualitative risk assessment is the process of subjectively determining the impact of an event that affects a project, program, or business. The likelihood of occurrence is the chance that a particular risk will occur. Functional recovery plans represent the transition from operations under business continuity back to normal operations. Quantitative risk assessment is the process of objectively determining the impact of an event that affects a project, program, or business.

6. **A, B,** and **C.** Mission-essential functions are those that, should they not occur or be performed properly, will directly affect the mission of the organization. This is where you spend the majority of your effort—protecting the functions that are essential. It is important to separate mission-essential functions from other business functions.

7. **B.** Risk is the chance of something not working as planned and causing an adverse impact. Impact is the cost associated with a realized risk. Property damage can be the result of unmitigated risk. Safety is when you consider the level of concern one places on the well-being of people.

8. **C.** Finance is in many ways the final arbiter of all activities because it is how we keep score. The others are important but are not considered the final arbiter.
9. **B.** The annualized rate of occurrence (ARO) is a representation of the frequency of the event, measured in a standard year. The annual loss expectancy (ALE) is calculated by multiplying the single-loss expectancy (SLE) by the likelihood or number of times the event is expected to occur in a year. The SLE is calculated by multiplying the asset value times the exposure factor. Annualized expectancy of occurrence (AEO) is not a term used in the cybersecurity industry.
10. **D.** A common method of transferring risk is to purchase cybersecurity insurance. Insurance allows risk to be transferred to a third party that manages specific types of risk for multiple parties, thus reducing the individual costs. Applying controls that reduce risk impact describes risk mitigation. A risk register is "a record of information about identified risks," as defined by the reference document *ISO Guide 73:2009 Risk Management—Vocabulary.* A risk matrix/heat map is used to visually display the results of a qualitative risk analysis.

CHAPTER 35

Privacy

In this chapter, you will

- Explore privacy and sensitive data concepts
- Relate privacy efforts to security efforts

Data security and privacy practices are interrelated because of the basic premise that to have privacy, you must have security. Privacy is defined as the control you exert over your data, and security is a key element of control. Data privacy in an organization is the prevention of unauthorized use of data held by the organization. One method of ensuring privacy is the through the use of privacy-enhancing techniques. Elements that enable data privacy efforts include properly labeling and handling sensitive data, assigning responsibility for protecting data, and securely storing retained data, all of which are covered in this chapter.

Certification Objective This chapter covers CompTIA Security+ exam objective 5.5: Explain privacy and sensitive data concepts in relation to security.

Organizational Consequences of Privacy Breaches

When a company loses data that it has stored on its network, the term used is *data breach.* Data breaches have become an almost daily news item, and the result is that people are becoming desensitized to their occurrence. Data breaches act as a means of notification that security efforts have failed.

Verizon publishes an annual data breach report that examines the types and causes of data breaches over the previous calendar year. These results are presented in multiple forms, by attribution to attack type, attacker type, industry, geographic region, company size, and more, providing a significant level of detailed analysis into the incidents. This report is a framework of what actually happened to real companies with real security programs, or in spite of their security programs. It is an extremely valuable collection of data that can provide guidance with respect to current threat environments and results of actual attacks and errors.

Reputation Damage

Reputation damage is a form of damage against a firm's brand. Customers exert a choice when they engage in a commerce transaction, and businesses spend a lot of time and resources on building brands that facilitate the purchase decision towards their firm. Having to notify all customers of a breach/disclosure event is truly damaging to a firm's brands. An online computer vendor, Egghead, suffered a breach/disclosure event near the holiday shopping season, and it saw sales dry up in that critical period, resulting in bankruptcy shortly thereafter.

Target Corporation continues to be the example of record for costly breaches, with a breach in 2013 that cost hundreds of millions in dollars and cost multiple senior executives their jobs. Facebook joined this club with their Cambridge Analytica scandal of 2018, where they failed to protect the personal information of their users, and have faced legal and regulatory oversight inquiries, as well as triggering EU data protection directive responses.

Identity Theft

Identity theft occurs when a criminal, using stolen information, assumes the identity of another individual to obtain and use credit in the victim's name. If the data disclosure results in loss of customer personal information, regulations may hold a firm responsible for sharing in the risk of identity theft for the victims. The usual response on the part of a company is to purchase an identity theft protection service policy for the affected individuals of a breach. This can cost over $50 per person affected, making a breach of a million records a costly issue.

Fines

Regulatory agencies, such as the Federal Trade Commission (FTC), have the ability to levy fines when regulations are not followed. These fines are not minor. In the EU, General Data Protection Regulation (GDPR) fines can be 4% of a firm's revenue, and fines in the hundreds of millions of euros have been levied. In the U.S., Equifax was fined nearly $700 million to be paid in restitution to users affected by their data breach.

IP Theft

One of the primary targets of an attacker on a system is intellectual property. *IP theft* is a major organizational consequence when it occurs, because when it occurs, the damage may not become evident until the material is used by a competitor. In organizations with significant levels of IP, it is one of the most important items to be protected against loss. Years of investment, and more years of potential sales and profits, can vanish quickly if IP is stolen and used actively against a firm.

EXAM TIP Be aware that organizational consequences of data privacy breaches can result in reputational damage, identify theft, fines, or IP theft.

Notifications of Breaches

In an ideal world, there would never be any data breaches, so there would never be a need for processes in the event of data breaches. But it is not an ideal world, and breaches do happen. And even if one hasn't happened to your firm yet, virtually every government jurisdiction has enacted a series of laws and regulations covering a firm's responsibilities in the event of a breach. Understanding and being prepared to issue *notifications of breaches* in accordance with these laws and directives is important, because once a breach occurs, the timelines to do the correct things are short and the penalties can be significant.

Breach notification laws and regulations typically have specific definitions of what comprises a breach, what entities are covered, what the specific notification requirements are, and key elements such as delays at the request of law enforcement agencies. Because there are so many differing rules and regulations, the best practice is typically to follow the most stringent regulations, such as California privacy regulations in the U.S. and the GDPR in the EU, to ensure complete coverage.

Escalation

When a data breach occurs in the enterprise, it is important to have a process for *escalating* the incident up through your organization. Most data breaches are discovered as part of some incident response process, and the breach needs to have its own response separate from the initiating incident. Establishing a breach escalation policy, with the accompanying procedures, will ensure proper levels of management attention to this critical process. Failure to escalate a breach to the appropriate authorities can result in outside legal and financial risk, and thus management needs to be made aware of the incident and the progress towards the firm's responsibilities.

Public Notifications and Disclosures

Many laws and regulations covering information breaches require public disclosure of computer security breaches in which unencrypted confidential information of any resident may have been compromised. These laws apply to any person or entity that does business in the regulated jurisdiction, even if located out of state, and that owns or licenses computerized data that includes personal information. This was a requirement of California SB 1386, which was the model law used by many other government entities. While there are no universal laws or regulations in this area, most have some form of public disclosure requirement.

Data Types

Data exists in many forms and is stored in systems that are used as part of business processes. Data management is a complex set of tasks that serve the purpose of protecting the data from a wide range of risks, including loss. Managing the large diversity of data types, elements, and their own particular needs from a security perspective is easier to perform if data is grouped into a series of *data types*. These types can cover basic protection needs, or the sources of the data, and thus are not a taxonomy but rather a set of management labels used to alert users of specific requirements associated with the data. Two different sets of data types will be discussed in the following sections: a set of labels identifying processing concerns/restrictions and a labeling of elements as to whether they can be traced to specific individuals. Each of these labels assists the business in the proper protection and processing of data in its lifecycle.

Classifications

Effective data *classification* programs include measures to ensure data sensitivity labeling and handling so that personnel know whether data is sensitive and understand the levels of protection required. When the data is inside an information-processing system, the protections should be designed into the system. But when the data leaves this cocoon of protection, whether by printing, downloading, or copying, it becomes necessary to ensure continued protection by other means. This is where data sensitivity labeling assists users in fulfilling their responsibilities. Training to ensure that labeling occurs and that it is used and followed is important for users whose roles can be impacted by this material.

Training plays an important role in ensuring proper data handling and disposal. Personnel are intimately involved in several specific tasks associated with data handling and data destruction/disposal and, if properly trained, can act as a security control. Untrained or inadequately trained personnel will not be a productive security control and, in fact, can be a source of potential compromise.

A key component of IT security is the protection of the information processed and stored on the computer systems and network. Organizations deal with many different types of information, and they need to recognize that not all information is of equal importance or sensitivity. This requires classification of information into various categories, each with its own requirements for its handling. Factors that affect the classification of specific information include its value to the organization (what will be the impact to the organization if it loses this information?), its age, and laws or regulations that govern its protection. The most widely known system of classification of information is that implemented by the U.S. government (including the military), which classifies information into categories such as Confidential, Secret, and Top Secret. Businesses have similar desires to protect information and often use categories such as Confidential, Private, Public, Proprietary, PII, and PHI. Each policy for the classification of information should describe how it should be protected, who may have access to it, who has the authority to release it and how, and how it should be destroyed. All employees of the organization should be trained in the procedures for handling the information that they are authorized to access.

Public

Public data is data that can be seen by the public and has no needed protections with respect to confidentiality. It is important to protect the integrity of public data, lest one communicate incorrect data as being true. Public-facing web pages, press releases, corporate statements—these are examples of public data that still needs protection, but specifically with respect to integrity.

Private

Data is labeled *private* if its disclosure to an unauthorized party would potentially cause harm or disruption to the organization. Passwords could be considered private. The term *private data* is usually associated with personal data belonging to a person and less often with corporate entities. The level of damage typically associated with private data is lower than confidential but still significant to the organization.

Sensitive

Sensitive data is a generalized term that typically represents data classified as restricted from general or public release. This term is often used interchangeably with confidential data.

Confidential

Data is labeled *confidential* if its disclosure to an unauthorized party would potentially cause serious harm to the organization. This data should be defined by policy, and that policy should include details regarding who has the authority to release the data. Common examples of confidential data include pricing and cost data, customer data, internal business plans, and so on, as the release of these could result in significant loss to the firm.

Critical

Data is labeled *critical* if its disclosure to an unauthorized party would potentially cause extreme harm to the organization. This data should be defined by policy, and that policy should include details regarding who has the authority to release the data. Common examples of critical data include trade secrets, proprietary software code, and new product designs, as the release of these could result in significant loss to the firm. The level of damage from a critical data release would be extreme, material to the business, and could result in the highest levels of loss.

EXAM TIP The difference between critical and confidential data lies in the level of potential damage should the information be released.

Proprietary

Proprietary data is data that is restricted to a company because of potential competitive use. If a company has data that could be used by a competitor for any particular reason (say, internal costs and pricing data), then it needs to be labeled and handled in a manner to protect it from release to competitors. Proprietary data may be shared with a third party that is not a competitor, but in labeling the data "proprietary," you alert the party you have shared the data with that it is not to be shared further.

EXAM TIP Learn the differences between the data sensitivity labels so you can compare and contrast the terms *confidential, private, public,* and *proprietary.* The differences are subtle but will be important to determine the correct answer.

Personally Identifiable Information (PII)

When information is about a person, failure to protect it can have specific consequences. Business secrets are protected through trade secret laws, government information is protected through laws concerning national security, and privacy laws protect information associated with people. A set of elements that can lead to the specific identity of a person is referred to as *personally identifiable information (PII)*. By definition, PII can be used to identify a specific individual, even if an entire set is not disclosed.

CAUTION As little information as the ZIP code, gender, and date of birth can resolve to a single person.

PII is an essential element of many online transactions, but it can also be misused if disclosed to unauthorized parties. For this reason, it should be protected at all times, by all parties that possess it. And when PII is no longer needed, it should be destroyed in accordance with the firm's data destruction policy in a complete, nonreversible manner.

EXAM TIP PII refers to information that can be used to distinguish or trace an individual's identity, either alone or when combined with other personal or identifying information that is linked or linkable to a specific individual.

Health Information

The Health Insurance Portability and Accountability Act (HIPAA) regulations define *protected health information (PHI)* as "any information, whether oral or recorded in any form or medium" that

> *"[i]s created or received by a health care provider, health plan, public health authority, employer, life insurer, school or university, or health care clearinghouse"* and

> *"[r]elates to the past, present, or future physical or mental health or condition of an individual; the provision of health care to an individual; or the past, present, or future payment for the provision of health care to an individual."*

HIPAA's language is built upon the concepts of PHI and Notice of Privacy Practices (NPP). HIPAA describes "covered entities," including medical facilities, billing facilities, and insurance (third-party payer) facilities. Patients are to have access to their PHI and should have an expectation of appropriate privacy and security associated with medical records. HIPAA mandates a series of administrative, technical, and physical security safeguards for information, including elements such as staff training and awareness as well as specific levels of safeguards for PHI when in use, stored, or in transit between facilities.

EXAM TIP Know the difference between PII and PHI, and don't jump to the wrong one on the exam.

Financial Information

Financial information is a major source of PII. Items such as bank accounts, loans, and payment amounts can all be leveraged against knowledge-based authentication systems to achieve access to even more information, such as credit reports. Financial information is one of the most sought-after types of PII because it is the easiest type of information to monetize.

Government Data

The U.S. government as well as governments worldwide collect information as part of their operations. Government regulations concerning the collection, storage, and use of government data exist to assist the government agencies in the proper management of data during its lifecycle in government systems. *Government data* can include PII about people, and this information needs protection in accordance with current rules and regulations.

Customer Data

Customer data is the primary source of PII in an enterprise's systems. This information was collected in response to a specific business need, and it requires appropriate levels of protection to prevent disclosure or release.

Privacy-Enhancing Technologies

One principal connection between information security and privacy is that without information security, you cannot have privacy. If privacy is defined as the ability to control information about oneself, then the aspects of confidentiality, integrity, and availability from information security become critical elements of privacy. Just as technology has enabled many privacy-impacting issues, technology also offers the means in many cases to protect privacy. An application or tool that assists in such protection is called a privacy-enhancing technology (PET).

Encryption is at the top of the list of PETs for protecting privacy and anonymity. One of the driving factors behind Phil Zimmerman's invention of PGP was the desire to enable people living in repressive cultures to communicate safely and freely. Encryption can keep secrets secret and is a prime choice for protecting information at any stage in its lifecycle. The development of Tor routing to permit anonymous communications, coupled with high-assurance, low-cost cryptography, has made many web interactions securable and safe from eavesdropping.

Other PETs include small application programs called cookie cutters that are designed to prevent the transfer of cookies between browsers and web servers. Some cookie cutters block all cookies, while others can be configured to selectively block certain cookies. Some cookie cutters also block the sending of HTTP headers that might reveal personal information but might not be necessary to access a website, as well as block banner ads, pop-up windows, animated graphics, or other unwanted web elements. Some related PET tools are designed specifically to look for invisible images that set cookies (called web beacons or web bugs). Other PETs are available to PC users, including encryption programs that allow users to encrypt and protect their own data, even on USB keys.

Data Minimization

Data minimization is one of the most powerful privacy-enhancing technologies. In a nutshell, it involves not keeping what you don't need. Limiting the collection of personal information to that which is directly relevant and necessary to accomplish a specified purpose still allows the transactions to be accomplished, but it also reduces risk from future breaches and disclosures by not keeping "excess" data. In the EU, privacy rules are built around the idea that individuals own the rights to the reuse of their data, and unless they grant it to a company, the right to store and reuse the data beyond the immediate transaction is prohibited. This serves several purposes, but one important outcome is that when a breach/disclosure event occurs, the reach of the PII loss is limited.

While you may need to have a reasonable amount of PII to process and ship an order, once that process is concluded, do you need the data? There may be a need for a reasonable period for returns, warranty claims, and so on, but once that period has passed, destroying unneeded PII removes it from the chance of disclosure.

Data Masking

Data masking involves the hiding of data by substituting altered values. A mirror version of a database is created, and data modification techniques such as character shuffling, encryption, and word or character substitution are applied to change the data. Another form is to physically redact elements by substituting a symbol such as "*" or "x". This is seen on credit card receipts where the majority of the digits are removed in this fashion. Data masking makes reverse engineering or detection impossible.

EXAM TIP Data masking hides personal or sensitive data but does not render it unusable.

Tokenization

Tokenization is the use of a random value to take the place of a data element that has traceable meaning. A good example of this is when you have a credit card approval, you do not need to keep a record of the card number, the cardholder's name, or any of the sensitive data concerning the card verification code (CVC) because the transaction agent returns an approval code, which is a unique token to that transaction. You can store this approval code, the token, in your system, and if there comes a time you need to reference the original transaction, this token provides you with complete traceability to it and yet, if disclosed to an outside party, reveals nothing.

Tokens are used all the time in data transmission systems involving commerce because they protect the sensitive information from being reused or shared, yet they maintain the desired nonrepudiation characteristics of the event. Tokenization is not an encryption step because encrypted data can be decrypted. By substituting a nonrelated random value, tokenization breaks the ability for any outside entity to "reverse" the action because there is no connection.

EXAM TIP Tokenization assigns a random value that can be reversed or traced back to the original data.

Anonymization

Data anonymization is the process of protecting private or sensitive information by removing identifiers that connect the stored data to an individual. Separating the PII elements such as names, Social Security numbers, and addresses from the remaining data through a data anonymization process retains the usefulness of the data but keeps the connection to the source anonymous. Data anonymization is easier said than done, because data exists in many places in many forms. This permits data aggregators to collect multiple instances and then, through algorithms and pattern matching, de-anonymize the data through multiple cross-references against multiple sources.

Pseudo-Anonymization

Pseudo-anonymization is a de-identification method that replaces private identifiers with fake identifiers or pseudonyms (for example, replacing the value of the name identifier "Mark Sands" with "John Doe"). Not all uniquely identifying fields are changed because some, such as date of birth, may need to be preserved to maintain statistical accuracy. Noise can be added to some fields to remove direct connections, but maintaining the approximate value; for example, randomly adding or subtracting three days to/from the actual date of birth preserves the age but de-identifies to the original record. Pseudonymization preserves statistical accuracy and data integrity, allowing the modified data to be used for training, development, testing, and analytics while protecting data privacy.

EXAM TIP Be sure you can identify the various privacy-enhancing technologies. Know what they do and how they are implemented.

Roles and Responsibilities

Multiple personnel in an organization are associated with the control and administration of data. These *data roles* include data owners, data controllers, data processors, data custodian/stewards, and users. Each of these roles has responsibilities in the protection and control of the data. The leadership of this effort is under the auspices of the data privacy officer.

Data Owners

All data elements in an organization should have defined requirements for security, privacy, retention, and other business functions. It is the responsibility of the designated *data owner* to define these requirements.

Data Controller

The *data controller* is the person responsible for managing how and why data is going to be used by the organization. In the era of GDPR and other privacy laws and regulations, this is a critical position because, under GDPR and other privacy laws, the data controller is the position responsible for protecting the privacy and rights of the data's subject, such as the user of a website. Whether the data is primary data or data from a third party, the data controller remains the point of responsibility for specifying how data is going to be used and processed either internally or externally. There can be multiple data controllers in an organization, with responsibilities over different sets of data.

EXAM TIP In the European Union (EU), General Data Protection Regulation (GDPR) classifies the data controller as the data manager. In other words, the data controller manages the data.

With respect to data with privacy implications, under most privacy regulations and GDPR, the data controller is responsible for deciding the following:

- What data is collected
- Where and how it is used
- With whom and how data is shared
- How long the data is kept and how it is disposed at end of life (EOL)

Data Processor

The *data processor* is the entity that processes data given to it by the data controller. Data processors do not own the data, nor do they control it. Their role is the manipulation of the data as part of business processes. Data processors can be personnel or systems; an example of a system is the use of Google Analytics to manipulate certain elements of data, making them useful for business analysts.

With respect to data with privacy implications, under most privacy regulations and GDPR, data processors are responsible for the following:

- Developing and implementing IT processes and systems that manage personal data
- Implementing security measures that would safeguard personal data
- Using tools and strategies to properly handle personal data

Data Custodian/Steward

A *data custodian* or *data steward* is the role responsible for the day-to-day caretaking of data. The data owner sets the relevant policies, and the steward or custodian ensures they are followed.

Data Privacy Officer (DPO)

The *data privacy officer (DPO)* is the C-level executive who is responsible for establishing and enforcing data privacy policy and addressing legal and compliance issues. Data minimization initiatives are also the responsibility of the data privacy officer. Storing data that does not have any real business value only increases the odds of disclosure. The data privacy officer is responsible for determining the gap between a company's privacy practices and the required actions to close the gap to an approved level. This is called a privacy impact analysis.

The data privacy officer also plays an important role if information on European customers is involved because the EU has strict data protection (privacy) rules. The privacy officer who is accountable for the protection of consumer data from the EU must ensure compliance with EU regulations.

EXAM TIP The data privacy officer is responsible for ensuring legal compliance with data privacy regulations.

Information Lifecycle

Information has a lifecycle—a beginning, a middle, and, at some point, an end. Understanding the lifecycle of information assets—from the point of collection, use, and storage as well as how the assets are shared, protected, and ultimately destroyed—is important if one is to properly handle the information. Not all information has the same time periods, or even steps, associated with it, so lifecycles are unique to different information sources and elements. The lifecycle forms a foundation upon which information management resides.

Impact Assessment

A *privacy impact assessment* (PIA) is a structured approach to determining the gap between desired privacy performance and actual privacy performance. A PIA is an analysis of how PII is handled through business processes and an assessment of risks to the PII during storage, use, and communication. A PIA provides a means to assess the effectiveness of a process relative to compliance requirements and to identify issues that need to be addressed. A PIA is structured with a series of defined steps to ensure a comprehensive review of privacy provisions.

EXAM TIP Organizations that collect, use, store, or process personal information are required to conduct a privacy impact assessment.

The following steps comprise a high-level methodology and approach for conducting a PIA:

1. *Establish PIA scope.* Determine the departments involved and the appropriate representatives. Determine which applications and business processes need to be assessed. Determine applicable laws and regulations associated with the business and privacy concerns.
2. *Identify key stakeholders.* Identify all business units that use PII. Examine staff functions such as HR, Legal, IT, Purchasing, and Quality Control.
3. *Document all contact with PII:*
    - PII collection, access, use, sharing, and disposal
    - Processes and procedures, policies, safeguards, data-flow diagrams, and any other risk assessment data
    - Website policies, contracts, HR, and administrative for other PII
4. *Review legal and regulatory requirements, including any upstream contracts.* The sources are many, but some commonly overlooked issues are agreements with suppliers and customers over information-sharing rights.
5. *Document gaps and potential issues between requirements and practices.* All gaps and issues should be mapped against where the issue was discovered and the basis (requirement or regulation) that the gap maps to.
6. *Review findings with key stakeholders to determine accuracy and clarify any issues.* Before the final report is written, any issues or possible miscommunications should be clarified with the appropriate stakeholders to ensure a fair and accurate report.
7. *Create a final report for management.*

Terms of Agreement

The legal description of *terms of agreement* (commonly known as *terms and conditions*) is a set of items that both parties agree upon before some joint activity. This is used all the time with any external-facing interface, where you have the responding party agree to a published terms of agreement document before granting them access or processing their data elements. A typical terms of agreement document includes the terms, the rules, the guidelines of acceptable behavior, and other useful sections to which users must agree in order to use or access an IT resource, such as website, a mobile app, an order placement page, and so on. Important items in the terms of agreement document include legal terms, governing law, agreement to operating rules, what services are offered and under what business conditions, liabilities, remedies for disagreements (for example, arbitration), and business terms such as the right to cancel, refunds, service level agreements, and so on. This becomes a license that binds the parties to the terms the business wishes to enforce.

Privacy Notice

A *privacy notice* is an exterior-facing statement that describes how the organization collects, uses, retains, and discloses personal information. Privacy notices are also referred to as a privacy statement or a fair processing statement. Special privacy notices are also mandated by specific privacy laws, and a common example of those is the cookies disclosure statement seen on websites that use cookies. The common elements of a privacy notice include the following:

- When you collect personal information
- Why you collect personal information
- What information is collected
- How the information will be protected
- When the information can or will be shared
- Who to contact and where questions should be directed concerning the notice
- How to opt out or opt in
- An effective date of the document

An example of a web cookie notice would be, "We use cookies to deliver our online services. Details of the cookies and other tracking technologies we use and instructions on how to disable them are set out in our Cookies Policy. By using this website, you consent to our use of cookies."

EXAM TIP The key concept to note is that a privacy policy is internally focused, telling employees what they may do with personal information, whereas a privacy notice is externally facing, telling customers, regulators, and other stakeholders what the organization does with personal information.

Chapter Review

This chapter began by explaining privacy and sensitive data concepts in relation to security. The first section opened with an examination of the organizational consequences of privacy breaches, including reputational damage, identity theft, fines, and intellectual property theft. This was followed by a discussion of the notification requirements surrounding breaches, including escalation. This section finished with the topics of public notification and disclosure requirements.

The next major topic discussed was data types, which was divided into two subsections: classifications and personally identifiable information (PII). Under data classifications, the topics of public, private, sensitive, confidential, critical, and proprietary were presented. Under PII, the subjects of health information, financial information, government data, and customer data were presented.

Privacy-enhancing technologies were presented, including data minimization, data masking, tokenization, anonymization, and pseudo-anonymization. The chapter then moved to the roles and responsibilities of data privacy efforts. In this section, the duties of data owners, data controllers, data processors, data custodians/stewards, and data privacy officers were defined and explained.

The chapter wrapped up with an examination of the topics of information lifecycles, impact assessments, terms of agreement, and privacy notices.

Questions

To help you prepare further for the CompTIA Security+ exam, and to test your level of preparedness, answer the following questions and then check your answers against the correct answers at the end of the chapter.

1. Which of the following is not PII?
   - **A.** Customer name
   - **B.** Customer ID number
   - **C.** Customer Social Security number or taxpayer identification number
   - **D.** Customer birth date
2. What does a privacy impact assessment do?
   - **A.** It determines the gap between a company's privacy practices and required actions.
   - **B.** It determines the damage caused by a breach of privacy.
   - **C.** It determines what companies hold information on a specific person.
   - **D.** It's a corporate procedure to safeguard PII.
3. What is privacy?
   - **A.** One's ability to control information about oneself
   - **B.** Being able to keep one's information secret
   - **C.** Making data-sharing illegal without consumer consent
   - **D.** Something that is outmoded in the Internet age
4. Who is responsible for determining what data is needed by the enterprise?
   - **A.** Data steward
   - **B.** Data privacy officer
   - **C.** Data custodian
   - **D.** Data owner

5. Data that is labeled "private" typically pertains to what category?
   A. Proprietary data
   B. Confidential information
   C. Legal data
   D. Personal information
6. Data that is labeled "proprietary" typically pertains to what category?
   A. Information under legal hold
   B. Information to be safeguarded by business partners because it contains business secrets
   C. Personal data
   D. PHI and PII together
7. Information that could disclose the identity of a customer is referred to as what?
   A. Customer identity information (CII)
   B. Personally identifiable information (PII)
   C. Privacy protected information (PPI)
   D. Sensitive customer information (SCI)
8. Which of the following is not a privacy-enhancing technology?
   A. Data minimization
   B. Data masking
   C. Data disclosure
   D. Tokenization
9. What is the term for notifying customers of your privacy policy and its effect on their information?
   A. Impact assessment
   B. Public notification of disclosure
   C. Privacy notice
   D. Terms of agreement
10. Which of the following is important to ensure privacy release concerns are properly handled when discovered by an incident response team?
   A. Escalation
   B. Privacy impact analysis
   C. Privacy-enhancing technologies
   D. Public disclosure and notification

Answers

1. **B.** A customer ID number generated by a firm to track customer records is meaningful only inside the firm and is generally not considered to be personally identifiable information (PII). Note that it is important not to use Social Security numbers for this, for obvious reasons.
2. **A.** A privacy impact assessment (PIA) determines the gap between what a company is doing with PII and what its policies, rules, and regulations state it should be doing.
3. **A.** Although all the possible answers have elements of truth to them, privacy is about controlling one's information, not just hoarding it.
4. **D.** The data owner determines the business need. The privacy officer ensures that laws and regulations are followed, and the custodian/steward maintains the data.
5. **D.** Private data frequently refers to personal data.
6. **B.** Proprietary data may be shared with a third party that is not a competitor, but in labeling the data "proprietary," you alert the party you have shared with that the data is not to be shared further.
7. **B.** Any information that can be used to determine identity is referred to collectively as personally identifiable information (PII).
8. **C.** Data disclosures are not privacy-enhancing technologies; they are the resultant effect of an attacker getting access to sensitive data on a system.
9. **C.** The privacy notice is the vehicle used to notify customers of the effects of a firm's privacy policy on their (the customers') data.
10. **A.** Escalation is important to ensure that the correct teams respond to a privacy-related incident.

PART VI

Appendixes and Glossary

APPENDIX A

OSI Model and Internet Protocols

In this appendix, you will

- Learn about the OSI model
- Review the network protocols associated with the Internet

Networks are interconnected groups of computers and specialty hardware designed to facilitate the transmission of data from one device to another. The basic function of the network is to allow machines and devices to communicate with each other in an orderly fashion.

Networking Frameworks and Protocols

Today's networks consist of a wide variety of types and sizes of equipment from multiple vendors. To ensure an effective and efficient transfer of information between devices, agreements as to how the transfer should proceed between vendors are required.

The term *protocol* refers to a standard set of rules developed to facilitate a specific level of functionality. In networking, a wide range of protocols has been developed—some proprietary and some public—to facilitate communication between machines. Just as speakers need a common language to communicate, or at least must understand each other's language, computers and networks must agree on a common protocol.

Communication requires that all parties have a common understanding of the object under discussion. If the object is intangible or not present, each party needs some method of referencing items in such a way that the other party understands. A *model* is a tool used as a framework to give people common points of reference when discussing items. Mathematical models are common in science, because they give people the ability to compare answers and results. In much the same way, models are used in many disciplines to facilitate communication. Network models have been developed by many companies as ways to communicate among engineers what specific functionality is occurring when and where in a network.

As the Internet took shape, a series of protocols was needed to ensure interoperability across this universal network structure. The Transmission Control Protocol (TCP), User Datagram Protocol (UDP), and Internet Protocol (IP) are three of the commonly used protocols that enable data movement across the Internet. As these protocols work in concert with one another, you typically see TCP/IP or UDP/IP as pairs in use. A basic understanding of the terms and of the usage of protocols and models is essential to discuss networking functionality because it provides the necessary points of reference to understand what is happening where and when in the complex stream of operations involved in networking.

OSI Model

To facilitate cross-vendor and multicompany communication, in 1984, the International Organization for Standardization (ISO) created the Open Systems Interconnection (OSI) model for networking. The OSI model is probably the most referenced and widely discussed model in networking. Although it never fully caught on in North America, portions of it have been adopted as reference points, even to the extent of being incorporated into company names. Layer 2, layer 3, network layer, level 3—these are all references to portions of the OSI model. These references allow people to communicate in a clear and unambiguous fashion when speaking of abstract and out-of-context issues. These references provide context to detail in the complex arena of networking. The terms *level* and *layer* have been used interchangeably to describe the sections of the OSI model, although layer is the more common term.

The OSI model is composed of seven layers stacked in a linear fashion. These layers are, from top to bottom, application, presentation, session, transport, network, data link, and physical. You can use a mnemonic to remember them: All People Seem To Need Data Processing. Each layer has defined functionality and separation designed to allow multiple protocols to work together in a coordinated fashion.

Although the OSI model is probably the most referenced, standardized network model, a more common model, the Internet model, has risen to dominate the Internet. The OSI model enjoys the status of being a formal, defined international standard, while the Internet model has never been formally defined. The Internet model is basically the same as the OSI model, with the top three OSI layers combined into a single application layer, leaving a total of five layers in the Internet model. Both models are shown in Figure A-1.

One aspect of these models is that they allow specific levels of functionality to be broken apart and performed in sequence. This delineation also determines which layers can communicate with others. At each layer, specific data forms and protocols can exist, which makes them compatible with similar protocols and data forms on other machines at the same layer. This makes it seem as if each layer is communicating with its counterpart on the same layer in another computer, although this is just a virtual connection. The only real connection between boxes is at the physical layer of these models. All other connections are virtual—although they appear real to a user, they do not actually exist in reality.

The true communication between layers occurs vertically, up and down—each layer can communicate only with its immediate neighbor above and below. In Figure A-2, the direct communication path is shown as a bold line between the two physical layers. All data between the boxes traverses this line. The dotted lines between higher layers represent virtual connections, and the associated activities and protocols are also listed for

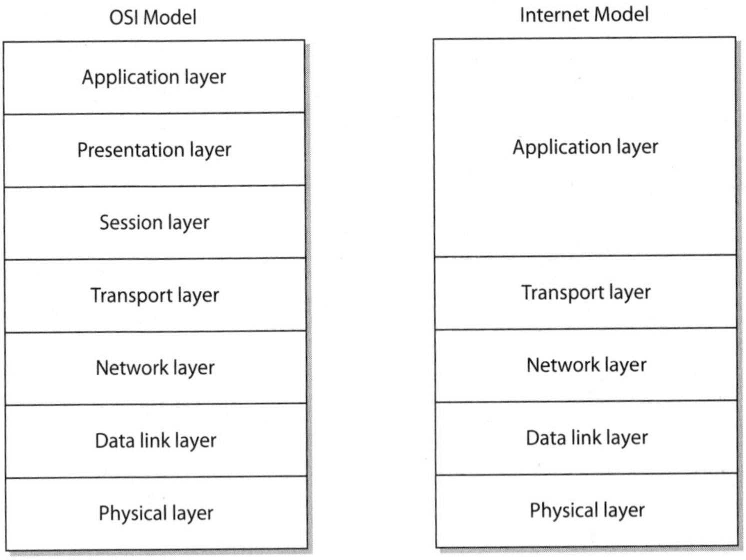

Figure A-1 OSI and Internet network models

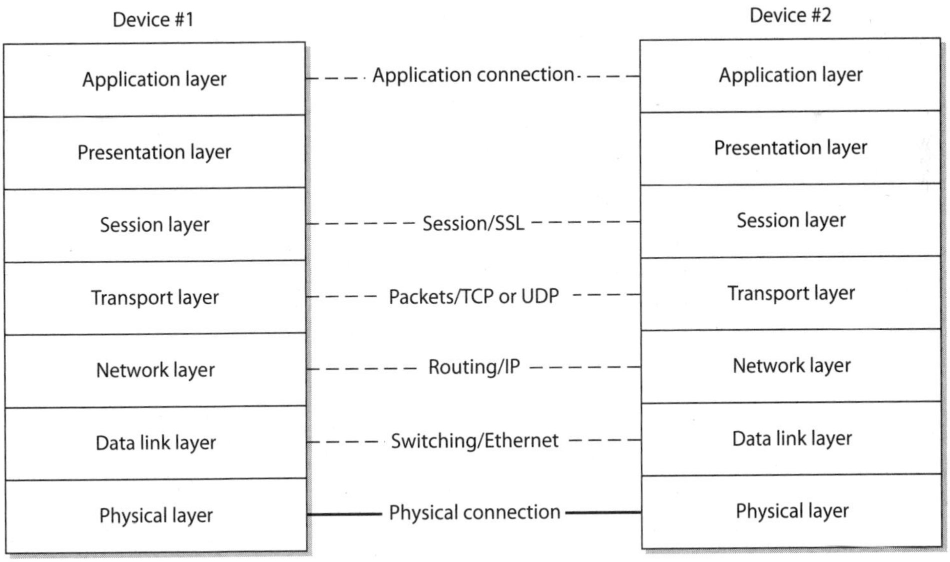

Figure A-2 Network model communication paths

Layer	Commonly Used Protocols
Application	HTTP(S), SNMP, SMTP, FTP(S), Telnet, SSH, DNS
Presentation	XDR, SSL, TLS, IMAP, SSH
Session	NetBIOS, RTP, PPTP
Transport	TCP, UDP, SCTP
Network	IP, IPSec, ICMP, IGMP, RIP, OSPF
Data link	IEEE 802.3 (Ethernet), IEEE 802.5 (Token Ring), ARP, RARP, PPP, SLIP
Physical	IEEE 802.3 (Ethernet) hardware, IEEE 802.5 (Token Ring) hardware, USB, Bluetooth, IEEE 802.11

Table A-1 Common Protocols by OSI Layer

most layers (the protocols are also listed in Table A-1). These dotted lines are virtual—data does not actually cross them, although it appears as though it does. The true path of data is down to the physical layer and back up to the same layer on another machine.

Application Layer

The application layer is the typical interface to the actual application being used. This is the layer of the communication stack that is typically responsible for initiating the request for communication. For example, browsers are application programs that operate in the application layer using HTTP to move data between systems. This layer represents the user's access to the system and the network. While it appears that the application is communicating directly with an application on another machine, this is actually a *virtual* connection. The application layer is also sometimes referred to as layer 7 in the OSI model. Several protocols are commonly found in the application layer, including Hypertext Transfer Protocol (HTTPS), Simple Mail Transfer Protocol (SMTP), and Simple Network Management Protocol (SNMP).

In the OSI model, the application layer actually communicates with the presentation layer only on its own machine. In the Internet model, the immediate level below the application layer is the transport layer, and this is the only layer directly called by the application layer in this model. As a result of the "missing" presentation and session layers in the Internet model, the functionality of these OSI layers is performed by the application layer.

The session layer functionality present in the Internet model's application layer includes the initiation, maintenance, and termination of logical sessions between endpoints in the network communication. The session layer functionality also includes session-level accounting and encryption services. The presentation layer functionality of the OSI model is also included in the Internet model's application layer, specifically functionality to format the display parameters of the data being received. Any other functions not specifically included in the lower layers of the Internet model are specifically included in the application layer.

Presentation Layer

The presentation layer gets its name from its primary function: preparing for the presentation of data. It is responsible for preparing the data for different interfaces on different types of terminals or displays so the application does not have to deal with this task. Data compression, character set translation, and encryption are found in this layer.

The presentation layer communicates with only two layers—the application layer above it and the session layer below it. The presentation layer is also known as layer 6 of the OSI model.

Session Layer

The primary responsibility of the session layer is the managing of communication sessions between machines. The management functions include initiating, maintaining, and terminating sessions. Managing a session can be compared to making an ordinary phone call. When you dial, you initiate a session. The session must be maintained in an open state during the call. At the completion of the call, you hang up and the circuit must be terminated. As each session can have its own parameters, the session layer is responsible for setting them up, including security, encryption, and billing or accounting functions.

The session layer communicates exclusively with the presentation layer above it and the transport layer below it. The session layer is also known as layer 5 of the OSI model.

Transport Layer

The transport layer is responsible for dealing with the end-to-end transport of data across the network connection. To perform this task, the transport layer handles data entering and leaving the network through logical connections. It can add and use address-specific information, such as ports, to accomplish this task. A *port* is an address-specific extension that enables multiple simultaneous communications between machines. Should the data transmission be too large for a single-packet transport, the transport layer manages breaking up the data stream into chunks and reassembling it. It ensures that all packets are transmitted and received, and it can request lost packets and eliminate duplicate packets. Error checking can also be performed at this level, although this function is usually performed at the data link layer.

Protocols can be either connection oriented or connectionless. If the protocol is connection oriented, the transport layer manages the connection information. In the case of TCP, the transport layer manages missing packet retransmission requests via the sliding window algorithm.

The transport layer communicates exclusively with the session layer above it and the network layer below it. The transport layer is also known as layer 4 of the OSI model.

Network Layer

The network layer is responsible for routing packets across the network. Routing functions determine the next best destination for a packet and will determine the full address of the target computer if necessary. Common protocols at this level include IP and Internet Control Message Protocol (ICMP).

The network layer communicates exclusively with the transport layer above it and the data link layer below it. The network layer is also known as layer 3 of the OSI model.

Data Link Layer

The data link layer is responsible for the delivery and receipt of data from the hardware in layer 1, the physical layer. Layer 1 only manipulates a stream of bits, so the data link layer must convert the packets from the network layer into bit streams in a form that can be understood by the physical layer. To ensure accurate transmission, the data link layer adds end-of-message markers onto each packet and also manages error detection, correction, and retransmission functions. This layer also performs the media-access function, determining when to send and receive data based on network traffic. At this layer, the data packets are technically known as *frames,* although many practitioners use *packet* in a generic sense.

The data link layer communicates exclusively with the network layer above it and the physical layer below it. The data link layer is also known as layer 2 of the OSI model, and it is where LAN switching based on machine-address functionality occurs.

Physical Layer

The physical layer is the realm of communication hardware and software, where 1s and 0s become waves of light, voltage levels, phase shifts, and other physical entities as defined by the particular transmission standard. This layer defines the physical method of signal transmission between machines in terms of electrical and optical characteristics. The physical layer is the point of connection to the outside world via standard connectors, again determined by signal type and protocol.

The physical layer communicates with the physical layer on other machines via wire, fiber-optics, or radio waves. The physical layer also communicates with the data link layer above it. The physical layer is also referred to as OSI layer 1.

Internet Protocols

To facilitate cross-vendor product communication, protocols have been adopted to standardize methods. The Internet brought several new protocols into existence, a few of which are commonly used in the routing of information. Two protocols used at the transport layer are TCP and UDP, whereas IP is used at the network layer. In each session, one transport layer protocol and one network layer protocol is used, making the pairs TCP/IP and UDP/IP.

TCP

Transmission Control Protocol (TCP) is the primary transport protocol used on the Internet today, accounting for more than 80 percent of packets on the Internet.

TCP begins by establishing a virtual connection through a mechanism known as the TCP *handshake*. This handshake involves three signals: a SYN signal sent to the target, a SYN/ACK returned in response, and then an ACK sent back to the target to complete the circuit. This establishes a virtual connection between machines over which the data will be transported, and that is why TCP is referred to as being *connection oriented*.

TCP is classified as a reliable protocol and will ensure that packets are sent, received, and ordered using sequence numbers. Some overhead is associated with the sequencing of packets and maintaining this order, but for many communications, this is essential, such as in e-mail transmissions, HTTP, and the like.

TCP has facilities to perform all the required functions of the transport layer. TCP has congestion- and flow-control mechanisms to report congestion and other traffic-related information back to the sender to assist in traffic-level management. Multiple TCP connections can be established between machines through a mechanism known as *ports*. TCP ports are numbered from 0 to 65,535, although ports below 1024 are typically reserved for specific functions. TCP ports are separate entities from UDP ports and can be used at the same time.

UDP

User Datagram Protocol (UDP) is a simpler form of transport protocol than TCP. UDP performs all of the required functionality of the transport layer, but it does not perform the maintenance and checking functions of TCP. UDP does not establish a connection and does not use sequence numbers. UDP packets are sent via the "best effort" method, often referred to as "fire and forget," because the packets either reach their destination or they are lost forever. It offers no retransmission mechanism, which is why UDP is called an unreliable protocol.

UDP does not have traffic-management or flow-control functions as TCP does. This results in much lower overhead and makes UDP ideal for streaming data sources, such as audio and video traffic, where latency between packets can be an issue. Essential services such as Dynamic Host Configuration Protocol (DHCP) and Domain Name Service (DNS) use UDP, primarily because of the low overhead. When packets do get lost, which is rare in modern networks, they can be resent.

Multiple UDP connections can be established between machines via ports. UDP ports are numbered from 0 to 65,535, although ports below 1024 are typically reserved for specific functionality. UDP ports are separate entities from TCP ports and can be used at the same time.

IP

Internet Protocol (IP) is a connectionless protocol used for routing messages across the Internet. Its primary purpose is to address packets with IP addresses, both destination and source, and to use these addresses to determine the next hop to which the packet will be transmitted. As IP is *connectionless,* IP packets can take different routes at different times between the same hosts, depending on traffic conditions. IP also maintains some traffic-management information, such as time-to-live (a function to give packets a limited lifetime) and fragmentation control (a mechanism to split packets en route if necessary).

The current version of IP is version 4, referred to as IPv4, and it uses a 32-bit address space. The newer IPv6 protocol adds significant levels of functionality, such as security, expanded address space to 128 bits, and a whole host of sophisticated traffic-management options. IPv4 addresses are written as four sets of numbers in the form v.x.y.z, with each of these values ranging from 0 to 255. Since this would be difficult to remember, a naming system for hosts was developed around domains, and DNS servers convert the host names, such as www.ietf.org, to IP addresses, such as 4.17.168.6.

Message Encapsulation

As a message traverses a network from one application on one host, down through the OSI model, out through the physical layer, and up another machine's OSI model, the data is encapsulated at each layer. This can be viewed as an envelope-inside-an-envelope scheme. Since only specific envelopes are handled at each layer, only the necessary information for that layer is presented on the envelope. At each layer, the information inside the envelope is not relevant, and previous envelopes have been discarded—only the information on the current envelope is used. This offers efficient separation of functionality between layers. This concept is illustrated in Figure A-3.

As a message traverses the OSI model from the application layer to the physical layer, envelopes are placed inside bigger envelopes. This increases the packet size, but this increase is known and taken into account by the higher-level protocols. At each level, a header is added to the front end, and it acts to encapsulate the previous layer as data.

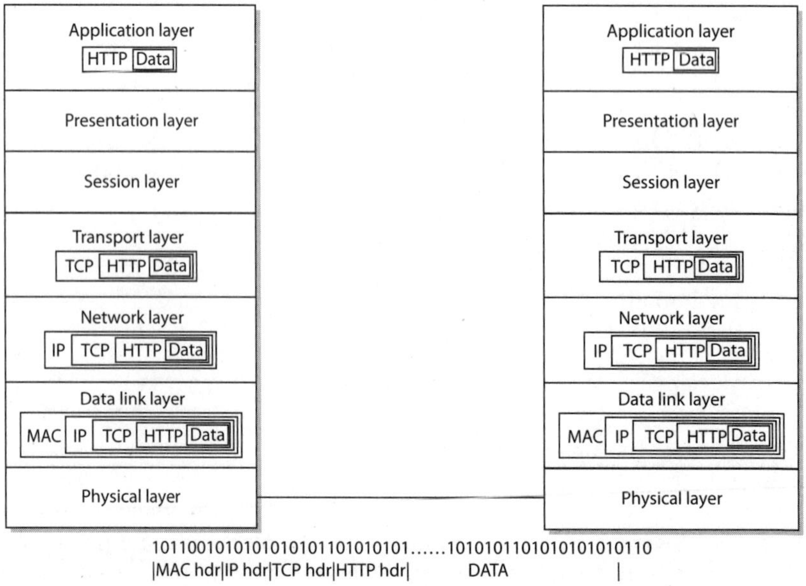

Figure A-3 OSI message encapsulation

At the physical level, the bits are turned into the physical signal and are transmitted to the next station.

At the receiving station, the bits are turned into one large packet, which represents the original envelope-within-an-envelope concept. Then each envelope is handled at the appropriate level. This encapsulation exists at the transport layer and lower, as this is the domain of a packet within a session.

Common Port Assignments

There is a set of common TCP and UDP port assignments (see Table A-2) that should be committed to memory for the exam. Several of these ports serve multiple services; for instance, all SSH secured protocols go over TCP port 22. SSL/TLS secured protocols use

TCP Port Number	UDP Port Number	Keyword	Protocol
20		FTP-Data	File Transfer (Default Data)
21		FTP	File Transfer Control
22		SSH	Secure Shell Login
22		SCP	SCP uses SSH
22		SFTP	SFTP uses SSH
23		TELNET	Telnet
25		SMTP	Simple Mail Transfer
53	53	DNS	Domain Name Server
80		HTTP	Web
110		POP3	E-mail
139		NetBIOS	NetBIOS
143		IMAP	E-mail
161		SNMP	SNMP
162		SNMP	SNMP
443		HTTPS	HTTPS
465		Encrypted SMTP	SMTP over SSL/TLS
636		LDAPS	LDAPS
989		FTPS	FTPS
990		FTPS	FTPS
993		Secure IMAP	Secure IMAP over SSL/TLS
995		Secure POP3	Secure POP3 over SSL/TLS
3269		LDAPS	LDAPS
3389	3389	RDP	Remote Desktop Protocol

Table A-2 Common TCP/UDP Port Assignments

PART VI

a wide variety of TCP ports, which are different for each associated protocol. Note that all secured protocols use TCP, as the handshake and packet sequencing are essential for encrypted protocols.

Review

To help variable systems understand the functions performed in network communication, a common framework is necessary. This framework is provided by the OSI and Internet network models, which specify which functions occur, and in what order, in the transmission of data from one application to another across a network.

An understanding of the OSI model and thus the state in which the data exists as it transits a network enables a deeper understanding of issues related to security. Understanding that SSL occurs before TCP and IP allows you to understand how SSL protects TCP and IP from outside sniffing. Understanding the different protocols and what happens with data loss gives you a better understanding of how certain types of attacks are performed.

The essence of a framework is to allow enhanced understanding of relationships, and these network models perform this function for network professionals.

APPENDIX B

About the Online Content

This book comes complete with TotalTester Online customizable practice exam software with 250 practice exam questions.

System Requirements

The current and previous major versions of the following desktop browsers are recommended and supported: Chrome, Microsoft Edge, Firefox, and Safari. These browsers update frequently, and sometimes an update may cause compatibility issues with the TotalTester Online or other content hosted on the Training Hub. If you run into a problem using one of these browsers, please try using another until the problem is resolved.

Your Total Seminars Training Hub Account

To get access to the online content you will need to create an account on the Total Seminars Training Hub. Registration is free, and you will be able to track all your online content using your account. You may also opt in if you wish to receive marketing information from McGraw Hill or Total Seminars, but this is not required for you to gain access to the online content.

Privacy Notice

McGraw Hill values your privacy. Please be sure to read the Privacy Notice available during registration to see how the information you have provided will be used. You may view our Corporate Customer Privacy Policy by visiting the McGraw Hill Privacy Center. Visit the **mheducation.com** site and click **Privacy** at the bottom of the page.

Single User License Terms and Conditions

Online access to the digital content included with this book is governed by the McGraw Hill License Agreement outlined next. By using this digital content you agree to the terms of that license.

Access To register and activate your Total Seminars Training Hub account, simply follow these easy steps.

1. Go to this URL: **hub.totalsem.com/mheclaim**
2. To register and create a new Training Hub account, enter your e-mail address, name, and password on the **Register** tab. No further personal information (such as credit card number) is required to create an account.

   If you already have a Total Seminars Training Hub account, enter your e-mail address and password on the **Log in** tab.
3. Enter your Product Key: **`pkf0-0b2x-747g`**
4. Click to accept the user license terms.
5. For new users, click the **Register and Claim** button to create your account. For existing users, click the **Log in and Claim** button.

   You will be taken to the Training Hub and have access to the content for this book.

Duration of License Access to your online content through the Total Seminars Training Hub will expire one year from the date the publisher declares the book out of print.

Your purchase of this McGraw Hill product, including its access code, through a retail store is subject to the refund policy of that store.

Restrictions on Transfer The user is receiving only a limited right to use the Content for the user's own internal and personal use, dependent on purchase and continued ownership of this book. The user may not reproduce, forward, modify, create derivative works based upon, transmit, distribute, disseminate, sell, publish, or sublicense the Content or in any way commingle the Content with other third-party content without McGraw Hill's consent.

Limited Warranty The McGraw Hill Content is provided on an "as is" basis. Neither McGraw Hill nor its licensors make any guarantees or warranties of any kind, either express or implied, including, but not limited to, implied warranties of merchantability or fitness for a particular purpose or use as to any McGraw Hill Content or the information therein or any warranties as to the accuracy, completeness, correctness, or results to be obtained from, accessing or using the McGraw Hill Content, or any material referenced in such Content or any information entered into licensee's product by users or other persons and/or any material available on or that can be accessed through the licensee's product (including via any hyperlink or otherwise) or as to non-infringement of third-party rights. Any warranties of any kind, whether express or implied, are disclaimed. Any material or data obtained through use of the McGraw Hill Content is at your own discretion and risk and user understands that it will be solely responsible for any resulting damage to its computer system or loss of data.

Neither McGraw Hill nor its licensors shall be liable to any subscriber or to any user or anyone else for any inaccuracy, delay, interruption in service, error or omission, regardless of cause, or for any damage resulting therefrom.

In no event will McGraw Hill or its licensors be liable for any indirect, special or consequential damages, including but not limited to, lost time, lost money, lost profits or good will, whether in contract, tort, strict liability or otherwise, and whether or not such damages are foreseen or unforeseen with respect to any use of the McGraw Hill Content.

TotalTester Online

TotalTester Online provides you with a simulation of the CompTIA Security+ exam. Exams can be taken in Practice Mode or Exam Mode. Practice Mode provides an assistance window with hints, references to the book, explanations of the correct and incorrect answers, and the option to check your answer as you take the test. Exam Mode provides a simulation of the actual exam. The number of questions, the types of questions, and the time allowed are intended to be an accurate representation of the exam environment. The option to customize your quiz allows you to create custom exams from selected domains or chapters, and you can further customize the number of questions and time allowed.

To take a test, follow the instructions provided in the previous section to register and activate your Total Seminars Training Hub account. When you register you will be taken to the Total Seminars Training Hub. From the Training Hub Home page, select **CompTIA Security+ All-in-One Exam Guide, 6e (SY0-601)** from the Study drop-down menu at the top of the page, or from the list of Your Topics on the Home page. You can then select the option to customize your quiz and begin testing yourself in Practice Mode or Exam Mode. All exams provide an overall grade and a grade broken down by domain.

Technical Support

For questions regarding the TotalTester or operation of the Training Hub, visit **www.totalsem.com** or e-mail **support@totalsem.com**.

For questions regarding book content, visit **www.mheducation.com/customerservice**.

3DES Triple DES encryption—three rounds of DES encryption used to improve security.

802.11 A family of standards that describe network protocols for wireless devices.

802.1X An IEEE standard for performing authentication over networks.

AAA *See* authentication, authorization, and accounting.

ABAC *See* attribute-based access control.

acceptable use policy (AUP) A policy that communicates to users what specific uses of computer resources are permitted.

access A subject's ability to perform specific operations on an object such as a file. Typical access levels include read, write, execute, and delete.

access controls Mechanisms or methods used to determine what access permissions subjects (such as users) have for specific objects (such as files).

access control list (ACL) A list associated with an object (such as a file) that identifies what level of access each subject (such as a user) has as well as what they can do to the object (such as read, write, or execute).

access point (AP) Shorthand for wireless access point, the device that allows devices to connect to a wireless network.

Active Directory (AD) The directory service portion of the Windows operating system that stores information about network-based entities (such as applications, files, printers, and people) and provides a structured, consistent way to name, describe, locate, access, and manage these resources.

Active Server Pages (ASP) An older server-side scripting framework for web servers introduced by Microsoft. Replaced by ASP.NET in 2002.

ActiveX A deprecated Microsoft technology that facilitates rich Internet applications and thus extends and enhances the functionality of Microsoft Internet Explorer. Like Java, ActiveX enables the development of interactive content. When an ActiveX-aware browser encounters a web page that includes an unsupported feature, it can automatically install the appropriate application so the feature can be used.

AD *See* Active Directory.

Address Resolution Protocol (ARP) A protocol in the TCP/IP suite specification used to map an IP address to a Media Access Control (MAC) address.

Address Space Layout Randomization (ASLR) A memory-protection process employed by operating systems where the memory space is block randomized to guard against targeted injections from buffer-overflow attacks.

Advanced Encryption Standard (AES) The current U.S. government standard for symmetric encryption, widely used in all sectors.

Advanced Encryption Standard 256-bit An implementation of AES using a 256-bit key.

advanced persistent threat (APT) A threat vector whose main objective is to remain on the system stealthily, with data exfiltration as a secondary task.

Adversarial Tactics, Techniques, and Common Knowledge (ATT&CK) A framework developed by MITRE for describing the methods used by attackers.

adware Advertising-supported software that automatically plays, displays, or downloads advertisements after the software is installed or while the application is being used.

AEAD *See* Authenticated Encryption with Associated Data.

AES *See* Advanced Encryption Standard.

AES256 *See* Advanced Encryption Standard 256-bit.

AH *See* Authentication Header.

AI Acronym for artificial intelligence.

air gap The forced separation of networks, resulting in a "gap" between systems. Communications across an air gap require a manual effort to move data from one network to another, as no network connection exists between the two networks.

AIS *See* Automated Indicator Sharing.

algorithm A step-by-step procedure—typically an established computation for solving a problem within a set number of steps.

amplification An act of leveraging technology to increase the volume of an attack, such as pinging a network address to get all attached devices to respond.

annualized loss expectancy (ALE) How much an event is expected to cost the business per year, given the dollar cost of the loss and how often it is likely to occur. ALE = single loss expectancy × annualized rate of occurrence.

annualized rate of occurrence (ARO) The frequency with which an event is expected to occur on an annualized basis.

anomaly Something that does not fit into an expected pattern.

antivirus (AV) A software program designed to detect, mitigate, or remove malware and viruses from a system or network.

Anything as a Service (XaaS) A term to describe the wide array of services that can be delivered to users from the cloud.

AP *See* access point.

application A program or group of programs designed to provide specific user functions, such as a word processor or web server.

application programming interface (API) A set of instructions as to how to interface with a computer program so that developers can access defined interfaces in a program.

application service provider (ASP) A company that offers entities access over the Internet to applications and services.

APT *See* advanced persistent threat.

ARP *See* Address Resolution Protocol.

ARP poisoning An attack on the ARP table where values are changed to result in misdirected traffic.

ASLR *See* Address Space Layout Randomization.

ASN.1 Abstract Syntax Notation number one is a formal notation used to describe data transmission in telecommunication protocols.

asset A resource or information that an organization needs to conduct its business.

asset value (AV) The value of an asset that is at risk.

asymmetric encryption Also called public key cryptography, a data encryption system that uses two mathematically derived keys to encrypt and decrypt a message—a public key, available to everyone, and a private key, available only to the owner of the key.

ATT&CK *See* Adversarial Tactics, Techniques, and Common Knowledge.

attribute-based access control (ABAC) An access control mechanism that grants access based on attributes of a user.

audit trail A set of records or events, generally organized chronologically, that records what activity has occurred on a system. These records (often computer files) are often used in an attempt to re-create what took place when a security incident occurred, and they can also be used to detect possible intruders.

auditing Actions or processes used to verify the assigned privileges and rights of a user, or any capabilities used to create and maintain a record showing who accessed a particular system and what actions they performed.

Authenticated Encryption with Associated Data (AEAD) A method of encryption that allows a recipient to check the integrity of both the encrypted and unencrypted information in a message.

authentication The process by which a subject's (such as a user's) identity is verified.

authentication, authorization, and accounting (AAA) Three common functions performed upon system login. Authentication and authorization almost always occur, with accounting being somewhat less common. Authentication and authorization are parts of the access control system.

Authentication Header (AH) A portion of the IPSec security protocol that provides authentication services and replay-detection ability. AH can be used either by itself or with Encapsulating Security Payload (ESP). Refer to RFC 2402.

Automated Indicator Sharing (AIS) The use of STIX and TAXII to share threat information between systems.

AV *See* antivirus or asset value.

availability Part of the "CIA" of security. Applies to hardware, software, and data, specifically meaning that each of these should be present and accessible when the subject (the user) wants to access or use them.

backdoor A hidden method used to gain access to a computer system, network, or application. Often used by software developers to ensure unrestricted access to the systems they create. Synonymous with *trapdoor*.

backup Refers to copying and storing data in a secondary location, separate from the original, to preserve the data in the event that the original is lost, corrupted, or destroyed.

baseline A system or software as it is built and functioning at a specific point in time. Serves as a foundation for comparison or measurement, providing the necessary visibility to control change.

BASH *See* Bourne Again Shell.

Basic Input/Output System (BIOS) A firmware element of a computer system that provides the interface between hardware and system software with respect to devices and peripherals. BIOS has been replaced by Unified Extensible Firmware Interface (UEFI), a more complex and capable system.

Basic Service Set Identifier (BSSID) ID of an access point (AP) in a WLAN, typically the AP's MAC address.

BCP *See* business continuity plan.

BGP *See* Border Gateway Protocol.

BIA *See* business impact analysis.

biometrics Used to verify an individual's identity to the system or network using something unique about the individual, such as a fingerprint, for the verification process. Examples include fingerprints, retinal scans, hand and facial geometry, and voice analysis.

BIOS *See* Basic Input/Output System.

birthday attack An attack methodology based on combinations rather than linear probability. In a room of 30 people, for example, one doesn't have to match a specific birthday but rather have any two birthdays in the room match, making the problem a combinatorial match, which is much more likely.

Blowfish A free implementation of a symmetric block cipher, developed by Bruce Schneier as a drop-in replacement for DES and IDEA. It has a variable-bit-length scheme from 32 to 448 bits, resulting in varying levels of security.

bluebugging The use of a Bluetooth-enabled device to eavesdrop on another person's conversation using that person's Bluetooth phone as a transmitter. The bluebug application silently causes a Bluetooth device to make a phone call to another device, causing the phone to act as a transmitter and allowing the listener to eavesdrop on the victim's conversation in real life.

bluejacking The sending of unsolicited messages over Bluetooth to Bluetooth-enabled devices such as mobile phones, tablets, or laptop computers.

bluesnarfing The unauthorized access of information from a Bluetooth-enabled device through a Bluetooth connection, often between mobile phones, desktops, laptops, and tablets.

Border Gateway Protocol (BGP) The interdomain routing protocol implemented in Internet Protocol (IP) networks to enable routing between autonomous systems.

botnet A collection of software robots, or *bots*, that run autonomously and automatically and, commonly, invisibly in the background. The term is most often associated with malicious software, but it can also refer to the network of computers using distributed computing software.

Bourne Again Shell (BASH) A command language for Linux systems.

bridge protocol data unit (BPDU) A BPDU is a type of data message exchanged across switches within an extended LAN that uses a Spanning Tree Protocol (STP) topology.

bring your own device (BYOD) A term used to describe an environment where users bring their personally owned devices into the enterprise and integrate them into business systems.

buffer overflow A specific type of software coding error that enables user input to overflow the allocated storage area and corrupt a running program.

business availability center (BAC) A software platform that allows the enterprise to optimize the availability, performance, and effectiveness of business services and applications.

business continuity plan (BCP) The plan a business develops to continue critical operations in the event of a major disruption.

business impact analysis (BIA) An analysis of the impact to the business of a specific event.

business partnership agreement (BPA) A written agreement defining the terms and conditions of a business partnership.

BYOD *See* bring your own device.

CA *See* certificate authority.

cache The temporary storage of information before use, typically used to speed up systems. In an Internet context, cache refers to the storage of commonly accessed web pages, graphic files, and other content locally on a user's PC or a web server. The cache helps to minimize download time and preserve bandwidth for frequently accessed websites, and it helps reduce the load on a web server.

Capability Maturity Model (CMM) A structured methodology helping organizations improve the maturity of their software processes by providing an evolutionary path from ad hoc processes to disciplined software management processes. Developed at Carnegie Mellon University's Software Engineering Institute.

CAPTCHA Completely Automated Public Turing Test to Tell Computers and Humans Apart. Software designed to pose tests that require human ability to resolve, preventing robots from filling in and submitting web pages.

CASB *See* Cloud Access Security Broker.

CBC *See* Cipher Block Chaining.

centralized management A type of privilege management that brings the authority and responsibility for managing and maintaining rights and privileges into a single group, location, or area.

CERT *See* Computer Emergency Response Team.

certificate A cryptographically signed object that contains an identity and a public key associated with this identity. The certificate can be used to establish identity, analogous to a notarized written document.

certificate authority (CA) An entity responsible for issuing and revoking certificates. CAs are typically not associated with the company requiring the certificate, although they exist for internal company use as well (such as Microsoft). This term is also applied to server software that provides these services. The term *certificate authority* is used interchangeably with *certification authority*.

Certificate Enrollment Protocol (CEP) Originally developed by VeriSign for Cisco Systems to support certificate issuance, distribution, and revocation using existing technologies.

certificate revocation list (CRL) A digitally signed object that lists all of the current but revoked certificates issued by a given certification authority. This allows users to verify whether a certificate is currently valid even if it has not expired. A CRL is analogous to a list of stolen charge card numbers that allows stores to reject bad credit cards.

certificate signing request (CSR) A message sent from an applicant to a certificate authority in order to apply for a digital identity certificate.

chain of custody Rules for documenting, handling, and safeguarding evidence to ensure no unanticipated changes are made to the evidence.

Challenge Handshake Authentication Protocol (CHAP) Used to provide authentication across point-to-point links using the Point-to-Point Protocol (PPP).

change (configuration) management A standard methodology for performing and recording changes during software development and operation.

change control board (CCB) A body that oversees the change management process and enables management to oversee and coordinate projects.

channel service unit (CSU) A device used to link local area networks (LANs) into a wide area network (WAN) using telecommunications carrier services.

CHAP *See* Challenge Handshake Authentication Protocol.

chief security officer (CSO) The person appointed to oversee security functions in an enterprise.

chief technology officer (CTO) The person appointed to oversee scientific technology functions in an enterprise.

choose your own device (CYOD) A mobile device deployment methodology where each person chooses their own device type.

CIA of security Refers to confidentiality, integrity, and availability—the basic functions of any security system.

cipher A cryptographic system that accepts plaintext input and then outputs ciphertext according to its internal algorithm and key.

Cipher Block Chaining (CBC) A method of adding randomization to blocks, where each block of plaintext is XORed with the previous ciphertext block before being encrypted.

cipher feedback (CFB) A method to make a block cipher into a self-synchronizing stream cipher.

ciphertext The output of an encryption algorithm—the encrypted data.

CIRT *See* Computer Emergency Response Team.

clickjacking An attack against a user interface where the user clicks on something without knowing it, e.g. a hidden or invisible item, triggering a browser action unbeknownst to the user at the time.

closed circuit television (CCTV) A private television system usually hardwired in security applications to record visual information.

Cloud Access Security Broker (CASB) A security policy enforcement mechanism between cloud users and providers.

cloud computing The automatic provisioning of computational resources on demand across a network.

cloud service provider (CSP) A company that offers cloud-based network services, infrastructure, or business applications.

CMS *See* content management system.

CN *See* Common Name.

codecs A system that provides coding and decoding services, used in multimedia streaming.

cold site An inexpensive form of backup site that does not include a current set of data at all times. A cold site takes longer to get the operational system back up, but it is considerably less expensive than a warm or hot site.

collision Used in the analysis of hashing cryptography, a collision is the outcome situation that occurs when a hash algorithm will produce the same hash value from two different sets of data.

Common Access Card (CAC) A smart card used to access U.S. federal computer systems and also acts as an ID card.

Common Name (CN) A characteristic field within a Distinguished Name (DN).

Common Vulnerabilities and Exposures (CVE) An enumeration of known vulnerabilities.

Common Vulnerability Scoring System (CVSS) A framework for scoring the severity of a vulnerability.

Computer Emergency Response Team (CERT) The group responsible for investigating and responding to security breaches, viruses, and other potentially catastrophic incidents. Also known as a Computer Incident Response Team (CIRT).

computer security In general terms, the methods, techniques, and tools used to ensure that a computer system is secure.

computer software configuration item *See* configuration item.

confidentiality Part of the CIA of security, confidentiality refers to the security principle that states that information should not be disclosed to unauthorized individuals.

configuration auditing The process of verifying that configuration items are built and maintained according to requirements, standards, or contractual agreements.

configuration control The process of controlling changes to items that have been baselined.

configuration identification The process of identifying which assets need to be managed and controlled.

configuration item Data and software (or other assets) that are identified and managed as part of the software change management process. Also known as *computer software configuration item.*

configuration status accounting Procedures for tracking and maintaining data relative to each configuration item in the baseline.

content management system (CMS) A management system to manage the content for a specific system, such as a website.

contingency planning (CP) The act of creating processes and procedures that are used under special conditions (contingencies).

continuity of operations planning (COOP) The creation of plans related to continuing essential business operations after any major disruption.

controller area network (CAN) A bus standard for use in vehicles to connect microcontrollers.

cookie Information stored on a user's computer by a web server to maintain the state of the connection to the web server. Used primarily so preferences or previously used information can be recalled on future requests to the server.

COOP *See* continuity of operations planning.

corporate owned, personally enabled (COPE) A form of mobile device ownership/management where the company provides employees with mobile devices and allows them to use the devices as if they owned them.

corrective action report (CAR) A report used to document the corrective actions taken on a system.

Counter Mode (CTM) Turns a block cipher into a stream cipher.

Counter Mode with Cipher Block Chaining–Message Authentication Code Protocol (CCMP) An enhanced data cryptographic encapsulation mechanism based on the Counter Mode with CBC-MAC from AES, designed for use over wireless LANs.

countermeasure *See* security controls.

cracking A term used by some to refer to malicious hacking, in which an individual attempts to gain unauthorized access to computer systems or networks. *See also* hacking.

CRC *See* cyclic redundancy check.

CRL *See* certificate revocation list.

cross-site request forgery (CSRF or XSRF) A method of attacking a system by sending malicious input to the system and relying on the parsers and execution elements to perform the requested actions, thus instantiating the attack. XSRF exploits the trust a site has in the user's browser.

cross-site scripting (XSS) A method of attacking a system by sending script commands to the system input and relying on the parsers and execution elements to perform the requested scripted actions, thus instantiating the attack. XSS exploits the trust a user has for the site.

cryptanalysis The process of attempting to break a cryptographic system.

cryptography The art of secret writing that enables an individual to hide the contents of a message or file from all but the intended recipient.

crypto-malware Malware that uses cryptography to encrypt files for ransom.

CSO *See* chief security officer.

CTR *See* Counter Mode (CTM)—an alternative abbreviation.

CVE *See* Common Vulnerabilities and Exposures.

CVSS *See* Common Vulnerability Scoring System.

cyclic redundancy check (CRC) An error detection technique that uses a series of two 8-bit block check characters to represent an entire block of data. These block check characters are incorporated into the transmission frame and then checked at the receiving end.

DAC *See* discretionary access control.

data encryption key (DEK) An encryption key whose function it is to encrypt and decrypt data.

Data Encryption Standard (DES) A private key encryption algorithm adopted by the U.S. government as a standard for the protection of sensitive but unclassified information. Commonly used in 3DES, where three rounds are applied to provide greater security.

data execution prevention (DEP) A security feature of an OS that can be driven by software, hardware, or both, designed to prevent the execution of code from blocks of data in memory.

data loss prevention (DLP) Technology, processes, and procedures designed to detect when unauthorized removal of data from a system occurs. DLP is typically active, preventing the loss either by blocking the transfer or dropping the connection.

data protection officer The person in charge of privacy/data protection in the EU under GDPR.

data service unit *See* channel service unit.

datagram A packet of data that can be transmitted over a packet-switched system in a connectionless mode.

decision tree A data structure in which each element is attached to one or more structures directly beneath it.

demilitarized zone (DMZ) A network segment that exists in a semi-protected zone between the Internet and the inner, secure trusted network.

denial-of-service (DoS) attack An attack in which actions are taken to deprive authorized individuals from accessing a system, its resources, the data it stores or processes, or the network to which it is connected.

Destination Network Address Translation (DNAT) A one-to-one static translation from a public destination address to a private address.

DES *See* Data Encryption Standard.

DHCP *See* Dynamic Host Configuration Protocol.

Diffie-Hellman A cryptographic method of establishing a shared key over an insecure medium in a secure fashion.

Diffie-Hellman Ephemeral (DHE) A cryptographic method of establishing a shared key over an insecure medium in a secure fashion using a temporary key to enable perfect forward secrecy.

digital forensics and investigation response (DFIR) Another name for the incident response process.

digital signature A cryptography-based artifact that is a key component of a public key infrastructure (PKI) implementation. A digital signature can be used to prove identity because it is created with the private key portion of a public/private key pair. A recipient can decrypt the signature and, by doing so, receive the assurance that the data must have come from the sender and that the data has not changed.

Digital Signature Algorithm (DSA) A U.S. government standard for implementing digital signatures.

direct-sequence spread spectrum (DSSS) A method of distributing a communication over multiple frequencies to avoid interference and detection.

disassociation An attack on a wireless network whereby the attacker sends a de-authentication frame in a wireless connection, to break an existing connection.

disaster recovery plan (DRP) A written plan developed to address how an organization will react to a natural or manmade disaster in order to ensure business continuity. Related to the concept of a business continuity plan (BCP).

discretionary access control (DAC) An access control mechanism in which the owner of an object (such as a file) can decide which other subjects (such as other users) may have access to the object as well as what access (read, write, execute) these subjects can have.

Distinguished Encoding Rules (DER) A method of providing exactly one way to represent any ASN.1 value as an octet string.

Distinguished Name (DN) The name that distinguishes an entry in a naming system.

distributed denial-of-service (DDoS) attack A special type of DoS attack in which the attacker elicits the generally unwilling support of other systems to launch a many-against-one attack.

diversity of defense The approach of creating dissimilar security layers so that an intruder who is able to breach one layer will be faced with an entirely different set of defenses at the next layer.

DLL injection An attack that uses the injection of a DLL onto a system, altering the processing of a program by in essence recoding it.

DNS *See* Domain Name Service/Server.

DNS poisoning The changing of data in a DNS table to cause misaddressing of packets.

DNSSEC *See* Domain Name System Security Extensions.

domain hijacking The act of changing the registration of a domain name without the permission of its original registrant.

Domain Message Authentication Reporting and Conformance (DMARC) An e-mail authentication, policy, and reporting protocol.

Domain Name Service/Server (DNS) The service that translates an Internet domain name (such as www.mhprofessional.com) into an IP address.

Domain Name Service System Security Extensions (DNSSEC) The extension of DNS using cryptographically signed requests and answers.

DRP *See* disaster recovery plan.

DSSS *See* direct-sequence spread spectrum.

dumpster diving The practice of searching through trash to discover material that has been thrown away that is sensitive, yet not destroyed or shredded.

Dynamic Host Configuration Protocol (DHCP) An Internet Engineering Task Force (IETF) Internet Protocol (IP) specification for automatically allocating IP addresses and other configuration information based on network adapter addresses. It enables address pooling and allocation and simplifies TCP/IP installation and administration.

dynamic link library (DLL) A shared library function used in the Microsoft Windows environment.

EAP *See* Extensible Authentication Protocol.

electromagnetic interference (EMI) The disruption or interference of electronics due to an electromagnetic field.

electromagnetic pulse (EMP) The disruption or interference of electronics due to a sudden, intense electromagnetic field in the form of a spike or pulse.

Electronic Code Book (ECB) A block cipher mode where the message is divided into blocks, and each block is encrypted separately.

electronic serial number (ESN) A unique identification number embedded by manufacturers on a microchip in wireless phones.

elliptic curve cryptography (ECC) A method of public key cryptography based on the algebraic structure of elliptic curves over finite fields.

Elliptic Curve Diffie-Hellman Ephemeral (ECDHE) A cryptographic method using ECC to establish a shared key over an insecure medium in a secure fashion using a temporary key to enable perfect forward secrecy.

Elliptic Curve Digital Signature Algorithm (ECDSA) A cryptographic method using ECC to create a digital signature.

Encapsulating Security Payload (ESP) A portion of the IPSec implementation that provides for data confidentiality with optional authentication and replay-detection services. ESP completely encapsulates user data in the datagram and can be used either by itself or in conjunction with Authentication Headers for varying degrees of IPSec services.

Encrypted File System (EFS) A security feature of Windows, from Windows 2000 onward, that enables the transparent encryption/decryption of files on the system.

end of life (EOL) A term used to denote that something has reached the end of its "useful life."

end of service life (EOSL) A term used to denote when the manufacturer quits selling an item. In most cases, the manufacturer no longer provides maintenance services or updates.

escalation auditing The process of looking for an increase in privileges, such as when an ordinary user obtains administrator-level privileges.

ESSID *See* Extended Service Set Identifier.

evidence The documents, verbal statements, and material objects admissible in a court of law.

evil twin An attack involving an attacker-owned router in a wireless system, configured to match a legitimate router.

exposure factor (EF) A measure of the magnitude of loss of an asset. Used in the calculation of single loss expectancy (SLE).

Extended Service Set Identifier (ESSID) The collection of all the BSSIDs on a WLAN; practically the same as the SSID.

Extensible Authentication Protocol (EAP) A universal authentication framework used in wireless networks and point-to-point connections. It is defined in RFC 3748 and has been updated by RFC 5247.

Extensible Markup Language (XML) A text-based, human-readable data markup language.

false acceptance rate (FAR) The rate of false positives acceptable to the system.

false positive Term used when a security system makes an error and incorrectly reports the existence of a searched-for object. Examples include an intrusion detection system that misidentifies benign traffic as hostile, an antivirus program that reports the existence of a virus in software that actually is not infected, and a biometric system that allows system access to an unauthorized individual.

false rejection rate (FRR) The acceptable level of legitimate users rejected by the system.

FDE *See* full disk encryption.

FHSS *See* frequency-hopping spread spectrum.

field programmable gate array (FPGA) A programmable logic circuit instantiation in hardware.

file system access control list (FACL) The implementation of access controls as part of a file system.

File Transfer Protocol (FTP) An application layer protocol used to transfer files over a network connection.

File Transfer Protocol Secure (FTPS) An application layer protocol used to transfer files over a network connection, which uses FTP over an SSL or TLS connection.

firewall A network device used to segregate traffic based on rules.

flood guard A network device that blocks flooding-type DoS/DDoS attacks, frequently part of an IDS/IPS.

forensics (or computer forensics) The preservation, identification, documentation, and interpretation of computer data for use in legal proceedings.

FPGA *See* field programmable gate array.

free space Sectors on a storage medium that are available for the operating system to use.

frequency-hopping spread spectrum (FHSS) A method of distributing a communication over multiple frequencies over time to avoid interference and detection.

full disk encryption (FDE) The application of encryption to an entire disk, protecting all of the contents in one container.

Galois Counter Mode (GCM) A mode of operation for symmetric key cryptographic block ciphers that has been widely adopted because it can be parallelized to increase efficiency and performance.

General Data Protection Regulation (GDPR) European Union (EU) rules on data privacy.

Generic Routing Encapsulation (GRE) A tunneling protocol designed to encapsulate a wide variety of network layer packets inside IP tunneling packets.

Global Positioning System (GPS) A satellite-based form of location services and time standardization.

Gnu Privacy Guard (GPG) An application program that follows the OpenPGP standard for encryption.

GPG *See* Gnu Privacy Guard.

GPO *See* Group Policy object.

graphic processing unit (GPU) A chip designed to manage graphics functions in a system.

Group Policy object (GPO) A method used by Windows for the application of OS settings enterprise-wide.

hacking The term used by the media to refer to the process of gaining unauthorized access to computer systems and networks. The term has also been used to refer to the process of delving deep into the code and protocols used in computer systems and networks. *See also* cracking.

hard disk drive (HDD) A mechanical device used for the storing of digital data in magnetic form.

hardware security module (HSM) A physical device used to protect but still allow the use of cryptographic keys. It is separate from the host machine.

hash A form of encryption that creates a digest of the data put into the algorithm. These algorithms are referred to as one-way algorithms because there is no feasible way to decrypt what has been encrypted.

hash value *See* message digest.

hashed message authentication code (HMAC) The use of a cryptographic hash function and a message authentication code to ensure the integrity and authenticity of a message.

HDD *See* hard disk drive.

heating, ventilation, air conditioning (HVAC) The systems used to heat and cool air in a building or structure.

HIDS *See* host-based intrusion detection system.

high availability (HA) A system design to provide assured availability.

HIPS *See* host-based intrusion prevention system.

HMAC-based one-time password (HOTP) A method of producing one-time passwords using HMAC functions.

homomorphic cryptography A form of cryptosystem where operations can be performed directly on encrypted data.

honeypot A computer system or portion of a network that has been set up to attract potential intruders, in the hope that they will leave the other systems alone. Since there are no legitimate users of this system, any attempt to access it is an indication of unauthorized activity and provides an easy mechanism to spot attacks.

host-based intrusion detection system (HIDS) A system that looks for computer intrusions by monitoring activity on one or more individual PCs or servers.

host-based intrusion prevention system (HIPS) A system that automatically responds to computer intrusions by monitoring activity on one or more individual PCs or servers and responding based on a rule set.

hot site A backup site that is fully configured with equipment and data and is ready to immediately accept transfer of operational processing in the event of failure on the operational system.

HSM *See* hardware security module.

Hypertext Markup Language (HTML) A protocol used to mark up text for use across HTTP.

Hypertext Transfer Protocol (HTTP) A protocol for transfer of material across the Internet that contains links to additional material.

Hypertext Transfer Protocol over SSL/TLS (HTTPS) A protocol for the transfer of material across the Internet that contains links to additional material carried over a secure tunnel via SSL or TLS.

IaaS *See* Infrastructure as a Service.

IAM *See* Identity and Access Management.

ICMP *See* Internet Control Message Protocol.

ICS *See* industrial control system.

identification (ID) The first step in the authentication process where the user establishes a secret with the authentication system and is bound to a user ID.

Identity and Access Management (IAM) The policies and procedures used to manage access control.

identity provider (IdP) A system that creates, maintains, and manages identity information, including authentication services.

IEEE *See* Institute of Electrical and Electronics Engineers.

IETF *See* Internet Engineering Task Force.

impact The result of a vulnerability being exploited by a threat, resulting in a loss.

impersonation A social engineering technique that can occur in person, over a phone, or online, where the attacker assumes a role that is recognized by the person being attacked, and in assuming that role, the attacker uses the potential victim's biases against their better judgment to follow procedures.

incident response The process of responding to, containing, analyzing, and recovering from a computer-related incident.

incident response plan (IRP) The plan used in responding to, containing, analyzing, and recovering from a computer-related incident.

indicators of compromise (IOCs) A set of values that, if found in memory or file storage, indicate a specific compromise event.

industrial control system (ICS) Term used to describe the hardware and software that controls cyber-physical systems.

information security Often used synonymously with computer security, but places the emphasis on the protection of the information that the system processes and stores, instead of on the hardware and software that constitute the system.

infrared (IR) A set of wavelengths past the red end of the visible spectrum used as a communication medium.

Infrastructure as a Service (IaaS) The automatic, on-demand provisioning of infrastructure elements, operating as a service; a common element of cloud computing.

initialization vector (IV) A data value used to seed a cryptographic algorithm, providing for a measure of randomness.

instant messaging (IM) A text-based method of communicating over the Internet.

Institute of Electrical and Electronics Engineers (IEEE) A nonprofit, technical, professional institute associated with computer research, standards, and conferences.

intangible asset An asset for which a monetary equivalent is difficult or impossible to determine. Examples are brand recognition and goodwill.

integrity Part of the CIA of security; the security principle that requires that information is not modified except by individuals authorized to do so.

interconnection security agreement (ISA) An agreement between parties to establish procedures for mutual cooperation and coordination between them with respect to security requirements associated with their joint project.

intermediate distribution frame (IDF) The free-standing or wall-mounted rack for managing and interconnecting the telecommunications cable between end-user devices and the main distribution frame (MDF).

internal segmentation firewall (ISFW) A firewall positioned in the network to provide segmentation of sections of a network.

International Data Encryption Algorithm (IDEA) A symmetric encryption algorithm used in a variety of systems for bulk encryption services.

Internet Assigned Numbers Authority (IANA) The central coordinator for the assignment of unique parameter values for Internet protocols. The IANA is chartered by the Internet Society (ISOC) to act as the clearinghouse to assign and coordinate the use of numerous Internet protocol parameters.

Internet Control Message Protocol (ICMP) One of the core protocols of the TCP/IP protocol suite, used for error reporting and status messages.

Internet Engineering Task Force (IETF) A large international community of network designers, operators, vendors, and researchers, open to any interested individual concerned with the evolution of Internet architecture and the smooth operation of the Internet. The actual technical work of the IETF is done in its working groups, which are organized by topic into several areas (such as routing, transport, and security). Much of the work is handled via mailing lists, with meetings held three times per year.

Internet Key Exchange (IKE) A standard key exchange protocol used on the Internet; an implementation of the Diffie-Hellmann algorithm.

Internet Message Access Protocol version 4 (IMAP4) One of two common Internet standard protocols for e-mail retrieval (the other being POP3).

Internet of Things (IoT) The networking of large numbers of devices via the Internet to achieve a business purpose.

Internet Protocol (IP) The network layer protocol used by the Internet for routing packets across a network.

Internet Protocol Security (IPSec) A protocol used to secure IP packets during transmission across a network. IPSec offers authentication, integrity, and confidentiality services and uses Authentication Headers (AH) and Encapsulating Security Payload (ESP) to accomplish this functionality.

Internet Relay Chat (IRC) An application layer protocol that facilitates communication in the form of text across the Internet.

Internet Security Association and Key Management Protocol (ISAKMP) A protocol framework that defines the mechanics of implementing a key exchange protocol and negotiation of a security policy.

Internet service provider (ISP) A telecommunications firm that provides access to the Internet.

intrusion detection system (IDS) A system to identify suspicious, malicious, or undesirable activity that indicates a breach in computer security.

IOCs *See* indicators of compromise.

IPSec *See* Internet Protocol Security.

ISA *See* interconnection security agreement.

IT contingency plan (ITCP) The plan used to manage contingency operations in an IT environment.

Kerberos A network authentication protocol designed by MIT for use in client/server environments.

key In cryptography, a sequence of characters or bits used by an algorithm to encrypt or decrypt a message.

key distribution center (KDC) A component of the Kerberos system for authentication that manages the secure distribution of keys.

key encrypting key (KEK) An encryption key whose function it is to encrypt and decrypt the data encryption key (DEK).

keyspace The entire set of all possible keys for a specific encryption algorithm.

Layer 2 Tunneling Protocol (L2TP) A Cisco switching protocol that operates at the data link layer.

LDAP *See* Lightweight Directory Access Protocol.

least privilege A security principle in which a user is provided with the minimum set of rights and privileges needed to perform their required functions. The goal is to limit the potential damage that any user can cause.

lightweight cryptography Cryptosystems designed for use in low-power, low-computation systems.

Lightweight Directory Access Protocol (LDAP) An application protocol used to access directory services across a TCP/IP network.

Lightweight Extensible Authentication Protocol (LEAP) A version of EAP developed by Cisco prior to 802.11i to push 802.1X and WEP adoption.

load balancer A network device that distributes computing across multiple computers.

local area network (LAN) A grouping of computers in a network structure confined to a limited area and using specific protocols, such as Ethernet for OSI Layer 2 traffic addressing.

Local Security Authority Subsystem Service (LSASS) The process in Microsoft Windows operating systems that is responsible for enforcing the security policy on the system.

logic bomb A form of malicious code or software that is triggered by a specific event or condition. *See also* time bomb.

loop protection The requirement to prevent bridge loops at the Layer 2 level, which is typically resolved using the Spanning Tree algorithm on switch devices.

LSASS *See* Local Security Authority Subsystem Service.

MAC *See* mandatory access control, Media Access Control, *or* message authentication code.

machine learning (ML) A form of artificial intelligence where machine algorithms learn by examining test cases and solutions.

main distribution frame (MDF) Telephony equipment that connects customer equipment to subscriber carrier equipment.

man-in-the-browser attack (MITB) A man-in-the-middle attack involving browser helper objects and browsers to conduct the attack.

man-in-the-middle attack (MITM) Any attack that attempts to use a network node as the intermediary between two other nodes. Each of the endpoint nodes thinks it is talking directly to the other, but each is actually talking to the intermediary.

managed security service provider (MSSP) A third party that manages the security aspects of a system under some form of service agreement.

managed service provider (MSP) A third party that manages aspects of a system under some form of service agreement.

mandatory access control (MAC) An access control mechanism in which the security mechanism controls access to all objects (files), and individual subjects (processes or users) cannot change that access.

master boot record (MBR) A strip of data on a hard drive in Windows systems meant to result in specific initial functions or identification.

maximum transmission unit (MTU) A measure of the largest payload that a particular protocol can carry in a single packet in a specific instance.

MD5 Message Digest 5, a hashing algorithm and a specific method of producing a message digest.

mean time between failures (MTBF) The statistically determined period of time between failures of the system.

mean time to failure (MTTF) The statistically determined time to the next failure.

mean time to repair/recover (MTTR) A common measure of how long it takes to repair a given failure. This is the average time, and may or may not include the time needed to obtain parts.

Media Access Control (MAC) A protocol used in the data link layer for local network addressing.

memorandum of agreement (MOA) A document executed between two parties that defines some form of agreement.

memorandum of understanding (MOU) A document executed between two parties that defines some form of agreement.

message authentication code (MAC) A short piece of data used to authenticate a message. *See* hashed message authentication code.

message digest The result of applying a hash function to data. Sometimes also called a hash value. *See* hash.

Measurement Systems Analysis (MSA) An assessment of the measurement process to determine sensitivities and error sources.

metropolitan area network (MAN) A collection of networks interconnected in a metropolitan area and usually connected to the Internet.

Microsoft Challenge Handshake Authentication Protocol (MS-CHAP) A Microsoft-developed variant of the Challenge Handshake Authentication Protocol (CHAP).

mitigation Action taken to reduce the likelihood of a threat occurring.

mobile device management (MDM) An application designed to bring enterprise-level functionality onto a mobile device, including security functionality and data segregation.

Monitoring as a Service (MaaS) The use of a third party to provide security monitoring services.

MS-CHAP *See* Microsoft Challenge Handshake Authentication Protocol.

MTBF *See* mean time between failures.

MTTF *See* mean time to failure.

MTTR *See* mean time to repair/recover.

multifactor authentication (MFA) The use of more than one different factor for authenticating a user to a system.

multifunction device (MFD) A device, such as a printer, with multiple functions, such as printing and scanning.

Multimedia Message Service (MMS) A standard way to send multimedia messages to and from mobile phones over a cellular network.

Multiprotocol Label Switching (MPLS) A deterministic routing methodology that is carrier supplied to more efficiently handle different traffic types across the WAN.

NAC *See* network access control.

NAP *See* Network Access Protection.

NAT *See* Network Address Translation.

National Institute of Standards and Technology (NIST) A U.S. government agency responsible for standards and technology.

NDA *See* nondisclosure agreement.

near field communication (NFC) A set of standards and protocols for establishing a communication link over very short distances. Used in mobile devices.

network access control (NAC) An approach to endpoint security that involves monitoring and remediating endpoint security issues before allowing an object to connect to a network.

Network Access Protection (NAP) A Microsoft approach to network access control.

Network Address Translation (NAT) A method of readdressing packets in a network at a gateway point to enable the use of local, nonroutable IP addresses over a public network such as the Internet.

network-based intrusion detection system (NIDS) A system for examining network traffic to identify suspicious, malicious, or undesirable behavior.

network-based intrusion prevention system (NIPS) A system that examines network traffic and automatically responds to computer intrusions.

Network Basic Input/Output System (NetBIOS) A system that provides communication services across a local area network.

network function virtualization (NFV) The use of virtualization technologies to virtualize network infrastructure.

network operating system (NOS) An operating system that includes additional functions and capabilities to assist in connecting computers and devices, such as printers, to a local area network.

Network Time Protocol (NTP) A protocol for the transmission of time synchronization packets over a network.

New Technology File System (NTFS) A proprietary file system developed by Microsoft, introduced in 1993, that supports a wide variety of file operations on servers, PCs, and media.

New Technology LANMAN (NTLM) A deprecated security suite from Microsoft that provides authentication, integrity, and confidentiality for users. Because it does not support current cryptographic methods, it is no longer recommended for use.

next-generation access control (NGAC) One of the primary methods of implementing attribute-based access control (ABAC). The other method is XACML.

next-generation firewall (NGFW) A firewall programmed to use higher levels of a message than just addresses and ports to make the decision.

next-generation secure web gateway (NG-SWG) A solution designed to filter unwanted web traffic from a user-initiated session to enforce policy compliance.

NFC *See* near field communication.

NFV *See* network function virtualization.

NIST *See* National Institute of Standards and Technology.

nondisclosure agreement (NDA) A legal contract between parties detailing the restrictions and requirements borne by each party with respect to confidentiality issues pertaining to information to be shared.

nonrepudiation The ability to verify that an operation has been performed by a particular person or account. This is a system property that prevents the parties to a transaction from subsequently denying involvement in the transaction.

Oakley protocol A key exchange protocol that defines how to acquire authenticated keying material based on the Diffie-Hellman key exchange algorithm.

object identifier (OID) A standardized identifier mechanism for naming any object.

object reuse Assignment of a previously used medium to a subject. The security implication is that before it is provided to the subject, any data present from a previous user must be cleared.

On-the-Go (OTG) *See* Universal Serial Bus (USB) On-The-Go (OTG).

one-time pad (OTP) An unbreakable encryption scheme in which a series of nonrepeating, random bits is used once as a key to encrypt a message. Since each pad is used only once, no pattern can be established and traditional cryptanalysis techniques are not effective.

Online Certificate Status Protocol (OCSP) A protocol used to request the revocation status of a digital certificate. This is an alternative to certificate revocation lists.

Open Authorization (OAUTH) An open standard for token-based authentication and authorization on the Internet.

open source intelligence (OSINT) Security information derived from sources available to the public.

Open Vulnerability and Assessment Language (OVAL) An XML-based standard for the communication of security information between tools and services.

Open Web Application Security Project (OWASP) A non-profit foundation dedicated to improving security in web applications.

operating system (OS) The basic software that handles input, output, display, memory management, and all the other highly detailed tasks required to support the user environment and associated applications.

operational technology (OT) The name for an IT system used in an industrial setting to control physical processes.

OVAL *See* Open Vulnerability and Assessment Language.

over the air (OTA) Refers to performing an action wirelessly.

P12 *See* PKCS #12.

PAC *See* Proxy Auto-Configuration.

Packet Capture (PCAP) The methods and files associated with the capture of network traffic in the form of text files.

Padding Oracle on Downgraded Legacy Encryption (POODLE) A vulnerability in SSL 3.0 that can be exploited.

PAM *See* Pluggable Authentication Modules.

pan-tilt-zoom (PTZ) A term used to describe a video camera that supports remote directional and zoom control.

pass-the-hash attack An attack where the credentials are passed in hashed form to convince an object that permission has been granted.

password A string of characters used to prove an individual's identity to a system or object. Used in conjunction with a user ID, it is the most common method of authentication. The password should be kept secret by the individual who owns it.

Password Authentication Protocol (PAP) A simple protocol used to authenticate a user to a network access server.

Password-Based Key Derivation Function 2 (PBKDF2) A key derivation function that is part of the RSA Laboratories Public Key Cryptography Standards, published as IETF RFC 2898.

patch A replacement set of code designed to correct problems or vulnerabilities in existing software.

Payment Card Industry Data Security Standard (PCI DSS) A contractual data security standard initiated by the credit card industry to cover cardholder data.

PBX *See* private branch exchange.

peer-to-peer (P2P) A network connection methodology involving direct connection from peer to peer.

penetration testing A security test in which an attempt is made to circumvent security controls in order to discover vulnerabilities and weaknesses. Also called a pen test.

perfect forward security (PFS) A property of a cryptographic system whereby the loss of one key does not compromise material encrypted before or after its use.

permissions Authorized actions a subject can perform on an object. *See also* access controls.

personal electronic device (PED) A term used to describe an electronic device, owned by the user and brought into the enterprise, that uses enterprise data. This includes laptops, tablets, and mobile phones, to name a few.

personal health information (PHI) Information related to a person's medical records, including financial, identification, and medical data.

personal identification number (PIN) A number that is secret, known only to the user to establish identity.

Personal Identity Verification (PIV) Policies, procedures, hardware, and software used to securely identify federal workers.

personally identifiable information (PII) Information that can be used to identify a single person.

personal information exchange format (PFX) A file format used when exporting certificates. Also called PKCS #12.

phreaking Used in the media to refer to the hacking of computer systems and networks associated with the phone company. *See also* cracking.

PKCS #12 A commonly used member of the family of standards called Public-Key Cryptography Standards (PKCS), published by RSA Laboratories.

plain old telephone service (POTS) The term used to describe the old analog phone service and later the "land-line" digital phone service.

plaintext In cryptography, a piece of data that is not encrypted. It can also mean the data input into an encryption algorithm that would output ciphertext.

Platform as a Service (PaaS) A third-party offering that allows customers to build, operate, and manage applications without having to manage the underlying infrastructure.

Pluggable Authentication Modules (PAM) A mechanism used in Linux systems to integrate low-level authentication methods into an API.

Point-to-Point Protocol (PPP) The Internet standard for transmission of IP packets over a serial line, as in a dial-up connection to an ISP.

Point-to-Point Protocol Extensible Authentication Protocol (PPP EAP) A PPP extension that provides support for additional authentication methods within PPP.

Point-to-Point Protocol Password Authentication Protocol (PPP PAP) A PPP extension that provides support for password authentication methods over PPP.

Point-to-Point Tunneling Protocol (PPTP) The use of generic routing encapsulation over PPP to create a methodology used for virtual private networking.

Port Address Translation (PAT) The manipulation of port information in an IP datagram at a point in the network to map ports in a fashion similar to Network Address Translation's change of network address.

Post Office Protocol (POP) A standardized format for the exchange of e-mail.

potentially unwanted program (PUP) A software program you likely didn't want installed on your computer. PUPs are common in bundled systems.

power distribution unit (PDU) A system to manage power distribution to multiple components, like in a rack mount system.

pre-shared key (PSK) A shared secret that has been previously shared between parties and is used to establish a secure channel.

Pretty Good Privacy (PGP) A popular encryption program that has the ability to encrypt and digitally sign e-mail and files.

preventative intrusion detection A system that detects hostile actions or network activities and prevents them from impacting information systems.

privacy Protecting an individual's personal information from those not authorized to see it.

Privacy-enhanced Electronic Mail (PEM) Internet standard that provides for secure exchange of e-mail using cryptographic functions.

private branch exchange (PBX) A telephone exchange that serves a specific business or entity.

privilege auditing The process of checking the rights and privileges assigned to a specific account or group of accounts.

privilege escalation The step in an attack where an attacker increases their privilege, preferably to administrator or root level.

privilege management The process of restricting a user's ability to interact with the computer system.

Protected Extensible Authentication Protocol (PEAP) A protected version of EAP developed by Cisco, Microsoft, and RSA Security that functions by encapsulating the EAP frames in a TLS tunnel.

Proxy Auto-Configuration (PAC) A method of automating the connection of web browsers to appropriate proxy services to retrieve a specific URL.

PSK *See* pre-shared key.

PTZ *See* pan-tilt-zoom.

public key cryptography *See* asymmetric encryption.

Public Key Cryptography Standards (PKCS) A series of standards covering aspects of the implementation of public key cryptography.

public key infrastructure (PKI) Infrastructure for binding a public key to a known user through a trusted intermediary, typically a certificate authority.

PUP *See* potentially unwanted program.

qualitative risk assessment The process of subjectively determining the impact of an event that affects a project, program, or business. It involves the use of expert judgment, experience, or group consensus to complete the assessment.

Quality of Service (QoS) The use of technology to manage data traffic, reduce packet loss, and control latency and jitter on a network.

quantitative risk assessment The process of objectively determining the impact of an event that affects a project, program, or business. It usually involves the use of metrics and models to complete the assessment.

RADIUS Remote Authentication Dial-In User Service. A standard protocol for providing authentication services that is commonly used in dial-up, wireless, and PPP environments.

RAID *See* Redundant Array of Inexpensive Disks.

rainbow tables A precomputed set of hash tables for matching passwords by searching rather than computing each on the fly.

rapid application development (RAD) A software development methodology that favors the use of rapid prototypes and changes as opposed to extensive advanced planning.

RAS *See* Remote-Access Service/Server.

RAT *See* Remote-Access Trojan.

RBAC *See* rule-based access control *or* role-based access control.

RC4 A stream cipher used in TLS and WEP.

real-time operating system (RTOS) An operating system designed to work in a real-time environment.

Real-time Transport Protocol (RTP) A protocol for a standardized packet format used to carry audio and video traffic over IP networks.

Recovery Agent (RA) In Microsoft Windows environments, the entity authorized by the system to use a public key recovery certificate to decrypt other users' files using a special private key function associated with the Encrypted File System (EFS).

recovery point objective (RPO) The amount of data a business is willing to place at risk. It is determined by the amount of time a business has to restore a process before an unacceptable amount of data loss results from a disruption.

recovery time objective (RTO) The amount of time a business has to restore a process before unacceptable outcomes result from a disruption.

Redundant Array of Inexpensive Disks (RAID) The use of an array of disks arranged in a single unit of storage for increasing storage capacity, redundancy, and performance characteristics.

refactoring The process of restructuring existing computer code without changing its external behavior to improve nonfunctional attributes of the software, such as improving code readability and/or reducing complexity.

registration authority (RA) Part of the PKI system responsible for establishing registration parameters during the creation of a certificate.

Remote-Access Service/Server (RAS) A combination of hardware and software used to enable remote access to a network.

Remote-Access Trojan (RAT) A set of malware designed to exploit a system providing remote access.

remotely triggered black hole (RTBH) A popular and effective filtering technique for the mitigation of denial-of-service attacks.

replay attack The reusing of data during an attack to cause a system to respond based on previous acts.

repudiation The act of denying that a message was either sent or received.

residual risk Risks remaining after an iteration of risk management.

return on investment (ROI) A measure of the effectiveness of the use of capital.

RFID Radio frequency identification. A technology used for remote identification via radio waves.

RIPEMD A hash function developed in Belgium. The acronym expands to RACE Integrity Primitives Evaluation Message Digest, but this name is rarely used. The current version is RIPEMD-160.

risk The possibility of suffering a loss.

risk assessment or risk analysis The process of analyzing an environment to identify the threats, vulnerabilities, and mitigating actions to determine (either quantitatively or qualitatively) the impact of an event affecting a project, program, or business.

risk management Overall decision-making process of identifying threats and vulnerabilities and their potential impacts, determining the costs to mitigate such events, and deciding what cost-effective actions can be taken to control these risks.

Rivest, Shamir, Adleman (RSA) The names of the three men who developed a public key cryptographic system and the company they founded to commercialize the system.

role-based access control (RBAC) An access control mechanism in which, instead of the users being assigned specific access permissions for the objects associated with the computer system or network, a set of roles the user may perform is assigned to each user.

RTP *See* Real-time Transport Protocol.

rule-based access control (RBAC) An access control mechanism based on rules.

S/MIME *See* Secure/Multipurpose Internet Mail Extensions.

SaaS *See* Software as a Service.

safeguard *See* security controls.

SAML *See* Security Assertion Markup Language.

SAN *See* storage area network.

SCADA *See* supervisory control and data acquisition.

SCEP *See* Simple Certificate Enrollment Protocol.

SDK *See* software development kit.

SDLC *See* software development lifecycle.

SDLM *See* software development lifecycle methodology.

SDN *See* software-defined networking.

SDP *See* Service Delivery Platform.

SDV *See* Software-Defined Visibility.

Secure Copy Protocol (SCP) A network protocol that supports secure file transfers.

Secure FTP A method of secure file transfer that involves the tunneling of FTP through an SSH connection. This is different from SFTP, which is the Secure Shell File Transfer Protocol.

Secure Hash Algorithm (SHA) A hash algorithm used to hash block data. The first version is SHA-1, with subsequent versions detailing the hash digest length: SHA-256, SHA-384, and SHA-512.

Secure Hypertext Transfer Protocol (SHTTP) An alternative to HTTPS in which only the transmitted pages and POST fields are encrypted. Rendered moot, by and large, by widespread adoption of HTTPS.

Secure/Multipurpose Internet Mail Extensions (S/MIME) An encrypted implementation of the MIME protocol specification.

Secure Real-time Transport Protocol (SRTP) A secure version of the standard protocol for a standardized packet format used to carry audio and video traffic over IP networks.

Secure Shell (SSH) A set of protocols for establishing a secure remote connection to a computer. This protocol requires a client on each end of the connection and can use a variety of encryption protocols.

Secure Shell File Transfer Protocol (SFTP) A secure file transfer subsystem associated with Secure Shell (SSH).

Secure Sockets Layer (SSL) An encrypting layer between the session and transport layers of the OSI model designed to encrypt above the transport layer, enabling secure sessions between hosts. SSL has been replaced by TLS.

secure web gateway (SWG) *See* next-generation secure web gateway.

Security Assertion Markup Language (SAML) An XML-based standard for exchanging authentication and authorization data.

security association (SA) An instance of security policy and keying material applied to a specific data flow. Both IKE and IPSec use SAs, although these SAs are independent of one another. IPSec SAs are unidirectional and are unique in each security protocol, whereas IKE SAs are bidirectional. A set of SAs is needed for a protected data pipe, one per direction per protocol. SAs are uniquely identified by destination (IPSec endpoint) address, security protocol (AH or ESP), and security parameter index (SPI).

security baseline The end result of the process of establishing an information system's security state. It is a known-good configuration resistant to attacks and information theft.

Security Content Automation Protocol (SCAP) A method of using specific protocols and data exchanges to automate the determination of vulnerability management, measurement, and policy compliance across a system or set of systems.

security controls A group of technical, management, or operational policies and procedures designed to implement specific security functionality. Access controls are an example of a security control.

security information and event management (SIEM) The name used for a broad range of technological solutions to the collection and analysis of security-related information across the enterprise.

security operations center (SOC) The grouping of security operations in an enterprise.

security orchestration, automation, response (SOAR) A system designed to facilitate responses in incident response situations.

segregation or separation of duties A basic control that prevents or detects errors and irregularities by assigning job responsibilities for increased risk tasks to different individuals so that no single individual can commit fraudulent or malicious actions.

self-encrypting drive (SED) A data drive that has built-in encryption capability on the drive control itself.

Sender Policy Framework (SPF) An e-mail validation system designed to detect e-mail spoofing by verifying that incoming mail comes from a host authorized by that domain's administrators.

Server Message Block (SMB) The Internet standard protocol used by Microsoft Windows to share files, printers, and serial ports.

Service Delivery Platform (SDP) A set of components that provides a service delivery architecture (service creation, session control, and protocols) for a service delivered to a customer or other system.

service level agreement (SLA) An agreement between parties concerning the expected or contracted uptime associated with a system.

Service Set Identifier (SSID) Identifies a specific 802.11 wireless network. It transmits information about the access point to which the wireless client is connecting.

session hijacking An attack against a communication session by injecting packets into the middle of the communication session.

shielded twisted pair (STP) A physical network connection consisting of two wires twisted and covered with a shield to prevent interference.

shimming The process of putting a layer of code between the driver and the OS to allow flexibility and portability.

Short Message Service (SMS) A form of text messaging over phone and mobile phone circuits that allows up to 160-character messages to be carried over signaling channels.

shoulder surfing Stealing of credentials by looking over someone's shoulder while they type them into a system.

signature database A collection of activity patterns that have already been identified and categorized and that typically indicate suspicious or malicious activity.

SIM *See* Subscriber Identity Module.

Simple Certificate Enrollment Protocol (SCEP) A protocol used in PKI for enrollment and other services.

Simple Mail Transfer Protocol (SMTP) The standard Internet protocol used to transfer e-mail between hosts.

Simple Mail Transfer Protocol Secure (SMTPS) The secure version of the standard Internet protocol used to transfer e-mail between hosts.

Simple Network Management Protocol (SNMP) A standard protocol used to remotely manage network devices across a network.

Simple Object Access Protocol (SOAP) An XML-based specification for exchanging information associated with web services.

single loss expectancy (SLE) Monetary loss or impact of each occurrence of a threat. SLE = asset value × exposure factor.

single point of failure (SPoF) A single system component whose failure can result in system failure.

single sign-on (SSO) An authentication process by which the user can enter a single user ID and password and then move from application to application or resource to resource without having to supply further authentication information.

slack space Unused space on a disk drive created when a file is smaller than the allocated unit of storage (such as a sector).

Small Computer System Interface (SCSI) A protocol for data transfer to and from a machine.

SMB *See* Server Message Block.

SMS *See* Short Message Service.

sniffer A software or hardware device used to observe network traffic as it passes through a network on a shared broadcast media.

SOAR *See* security orchestration, automation, and response.

SOC *See* security operations center.

SoC *See* system on a chip.

social engineering The art of deceiving another person so that he or she reveals confidential information. This is often accomplished by posing as an individual who should be entitled to have access to the information.

Software as a Service (SaaS) The provisioning of software as a service, commonly known as on-demand software.

software-defined networking (SDN) The use of software to act as a control layer separate from the data layer in a network to manage traffic.

Software-Defined Visibility (SDV) A framework that enables visibility into network operations and functions.

software development kit (SDK) A set of tools and processes used to interface with a larger system element when programming changes to an environment.

software development lifecycle (SDLC) The processes and procedures employed to develop software.

software development lifecycle methodology (SDLM) The processes and procedures employed to develop software. Sometimes also called *secure development lifecycle model* when security is part of the development process.

solid-state drive (SSD) A mass storage device, such as a hard drive, that is composed of electronic memory as opposed to a physical device of spinning platters.

SONET *See* Synchronous Optical Network Technologies.

spam E-mail that is not requested by the recipient and is typically of a commercial nature. Also known as unsolicited commercial e-mail (UCE).

spam filter A security appliance designed to remove spam at the network layer before it enters e-mail servers.

spear phishing A phishing attack aimed at a specific individual.

spim Spam sent over an instant messaging channel.

spoofing Making data appear to have originated from another source so as to hide the true origin from the recipient.

SSD *See* solid-state drive.

SSID *See* Service Set Identifier.

SSL *See* Secure Sockets Layer.

SSO *See* single sign-on.

storage area network (SAN) A dedicated network that provides access to data storage.

STP *See* shielded twisted pair.

Structured Exception Handler (SEH) The process used to handle exceptions in the Windows OS core functions.

Structured Query Language (SQL) A language used in relational database queries.

Structured Query Language Inject (SQLi) An attack against an interface using SQL.

Structured Threat Information eXpression (STIX) A framework for passing threat information across automated interfaces.

Subject Alternative Name (SAN) A field on a certificate that identifies alternative names for the entity to which the certificate applies.

Subscriber Identity Module (SIM) An integrated circuit or hardware element that securely stores the International Mobile Subscriber Identity (IMSI) and the related key used to identify and authenticate subscribers on mobile telephones.

supervisory control and data acquisition (SCADA) A generic term used to describe the industrial control system networks that interconnect infrastructure elements (such as manufacturing plants, oil and gas pipelines, power generation and distribution systems, and so on) and computer systems.

symmetric encryption Encryption that needs all parties to have a copy of the key, sometimes called a shared secret. The single key is used for both encryption and decryption.

Synchronous Optical Network Technologies (SONET) A set of standards used for data transfers over optical networks.

system on a chip (SoC) The integration of complete system functions on a single chip in order to simplify construction of devices.

tailgating The act of following an authorized person through a doorway without using one's own credentials.

TACACS+ *See* Terminal Access Controller Access Control System Plus.

tactics, techniques, and procedures (TTPs) The methods used by an adversary, organized in a fashion to assist in identification and defense.

tangible asset An asset for which a monetary equivalent can be determined. Examples are inventory, buildings, cash, hardware, software, and so on.

TAXII *See* Trusted Automated eXchange of Intelligence Information.

Telnet An insecure network protocol used to provide cleartext bidirectional communication over TCP. Replaced most often by Secure Shell (SSH).

Temporal Key Integrity Protocol (TKIP) A security protocol used in 802.11 wireless networks.

Terminal Access Controller Access Control System Plus (TACACS+) A remote authentication system that uses the TACACS+ protocol, defined in RFC 1492, and TCP port 49.

threat Any circumstance or event with the potential to cause harm to an asset.

ticket-granting ticket (TGT) A part of the Kerberos authentication system that is used to prove identity when requesting service tickets.

time-based one-time password (TOTP) A password that is used once and is only valid during a specific time period.

time bomb A form of logic bomb in which the triggering event is a date or specific time. *See also* logic bomb.

TKIP *See* Temporal Key Integrity Protocol.

token A hardware device that can be used in a challenge-response authentication process.

Transaction Signature (TSIG) A protocol used as a means of authenticating dynamic DNS records during DNS updates.

Transmission Control Protocol/Internet Protocol (TCP/IP) A connection-oriented protocol for communication over IP networks.

Transport Layer Security (TLS) A replacement for SSL that is currently being used to secure communications between servers and browsers.

trapdoor *See* backdoor.

Trivial File Transfer Protocol (TFTP) A simplified version of FTP used for low-overhead file transfers using UDP port 69.

Trojan horse A form of malicious code that appears to provide one service (and may indeed provide that service) but that also hides another purpose. This hidden purpose often has a malicious intent. This code may also be simply referred to as a *Trojan*.

Trusted Automated eXchange of Intelligence Information (TAXII) A transport framework for STIX data communication.

Trusted Platform Module (TPM) A hardware chip to enable trusted computing platform operations.

TTPs *See* tactics, techniques, and procedures.

typo squatting An attack form that involves capitalizing upon common typographical errors at the URL level, hoping the browser user will not notice they end up on a different site.

unified endpoint management (UEM) The aggregation of multiple products into a single system on an endpoint for efficiency purposes.

Unified Extensible Firmware Interface (UEFI) A specification that defines the interface between an OS and the hardware firmware. This is a replacement to BIOS.

unified threat management (UTM) The aggregation of multiple network security products into a single appliance for efficiency purposes.

Uniform Resource Identifier (URI) A set of characters used to identify the name of a resource in a computer system. A URL is a form of URI.

uninterruptible power supply (UPS) A source of power (generally a battery) designed to provide uninterrupted power to a computer system in the event of a temporary loss of power.

Universal Resource Locator (URL) A specific character string used to point to a specific item across the Internet.

Universal Serial Bus (USB) An industry-standard protocol for communication over a cable to peripherals via a standard set of connectors.

Universal Serial Bus On-the-Go (USB OTG) A standardized specification that allows a device to read data from a USB device without requiring a PC.

unmanned aerial vehicle (UAV) A remotely piloted flying vehicle.

unshielded twisted pair (UTP) A physical connection consisting of a pair of twisted wires forming a circuit.

usage auditing The process of recording who did what and when on an information system.

user acceptance testing (UAT) The application of acceptance-testing criteria to determine fitness for use according to end-user requirements.

User and Entity Behavioral Analytics (UEBA) A security process that uses user behavior patterns to determine anomalies.

User Datagram Protocol (UDP) A protocol in the TCP/IP protocol suite for the transport layer that does not sequence packets—it is "fire and forget" in nature.

user ID A unique alphanumeric identifier that specifies individuals who are logging in or accessing a system.

vampire tap A tap that connects to a network line without cutting the connection.

Variable Length Subnet Masking (VLSM) The process of using variable-length subnets to create subnets within subnets.

video teleconferencing (VTC) A business process of using video signals to carry audio and visual signals between separate locations, thus allowing participants to meet via a virtual meeting instead of traveling to a physical location. Modern videoconferencing equipment can provide very realistic connectivity when lighting and backgrounds are controlled.

virtual desktop environment (VDE) The use of virtualization technology to host desktop systems on a centralized server.

virtual desktop infrastructure (VDI) The use of servers to host virtual desktops by moving the processing to the server and using the desktop machine as merely a display terminal. VDI offers operating efficiencies as well as cost and security benefits.

virtual local area network (VLAN) A broadcast domain inside a switched system.

virtual machine (VM) A form of a containerized operating system that allows a system to be run on top of another OS.

virtual private cloud (VPC) A cloud instance that is virtually isolated by the provider.

virtual private network (VPN) An encrypted network connection across another network, offering a private communication channel across a public medium.

virus A form of malicious code or software that attaches itself to other pieces of code in order to replicate. Viruses may contain a payload, which is a portion of the code that is designed to execute when a certain condition is met (such as on a certain date). This payload is often malicious in nature.

vishing A form of social engineering attack over voice lines (VoIP).

Visual Basic for Applications (VBA) A Microsoft specification for using Visual Basic in applications such as the Office Suite. Microsoft declared this a legacy methodology in 2006.

Voice over IP (VoIP) The packetized transmission of voice signals (telephony) over Internet Protocol.

vulnerability A weakness in an asset that can be exploited by a threat to cause harm.

war dialing An attacker's attempt to gain unauthorized access to a computer system or network by discovering unprotected connections to the system through the telephone system and modems.

war driving The attempt by an attacker to discover unprotected wireless networks by wandering (or driving) around with a wireless device, looking for available wireless access points.

watering hole attack The infecting of a specific target website—one that users trust and go to on a regular basis—with malware.

whaling A phishing attack targeted against a high-value target like a corporate officer or system administrator.

web application firewall (WAF) A firewall that operates at the application level, specifically designed to protect web applications by examining requests at the application stack level.

WEP *See* Wired Equivalent Privacy.

wide area network (WAN) A network that spans a large geographic region.

Wi-Fi Protected Access/Wi-Fi Protected Access 2 (WPA/WPA2) A protocol to secure wireless communications using a subset of the 802.11i standard.

Wi-Fi Protected Access 3 (WPA3) The latest Wi-Fi security standard that tackles the shortcomings of WPA2.

Wi-Fi Protected Setup (WPS) A network security standard that allows easy setup of a wireless home network.

Wired Equivalent Privacy (WEP) The encryption scheme used to attempt to provide confidentiality and data integrity on 802.11 networks.

wireless access point (WAP) A network access device that facilitates the connection of wireless devices to a network.

Wireless Application Protocol (WAP) A protocol for transmitting data to small handheld devices such as cellular phones.

wireless intrusion detection system (WIDS) An intrusion detection system established to cover a wireless network.

wireless intrusion prevention system (WIPS) An intrusion prevention system established to cover a wireless network.

Wireless Transport Layer Security (WTLS) The encryption protocol used on WAP networks.

worm An independent piece of malicious code or software that self-replicates. Unlike a virus, it does not need to be attached to another piece of code. A worm replicates by breaking into another system and making a copy of itself on this new system. A worm can contain a destructive payload but does not have to.

write once read many (WORM) A data storage technology where things are written once (permanent) and then can be read many times, as in optical disks.

X.509 The standard format for digital certificates.

XaaS An abbreviation for Anything as a Service.

XML *See* Extensible Markup Language.

XOR Bitwise exclusive OR, an operation commonly used in cryptography.

XSRF *See* cross-site request forgery.

XSS *See* cross-site scripting.

zero day A vulnerability for which there is no previous knowledge.

INDEX

A

B

C

D

E

F

G

H

I

J

K

L

M

O

Q

R

S

U

V

W

X

Y

Z